Frommer's®

Walt Disney World & Orlando

Here's what the critics say about Frommer's:

"Amazingly easy to use. Very portable, very complete."
—*Booklist*

♦

"The only mainstream guide to list specific prices. The Walter Cronkite of guidebooks—with all that implies."
—*Travel & Leisure*

♦

"Complete, concise, and filled with useful information."
—*New York Daily News*

♦

"Hotel information is close to encyclopedic."
—*Des Moines Sunday Register*

♦

"I use a lot of travel guides when preparing my trips, but I have learned to especially trust Frommer's when it comes to picking lodgings."
—*The Orange County Register*

Other Great Guides for Your Trip:

Frommer's® 2000

Walt Disney World & Orlando

by Mary Meehan

with Online Directory by Michael Shapiro

MACMILLAN • USA

About the Author

From opening day at Universal Studios to the first plunge down the Tower of Terror, **Mary Meehan** has been on hand as travel options have exploded in central Florida. As an Orlando-based writer, whose award-winning work appears in regional and national publications, Meehan has an insider's view of the best things to see and do in central Florida—and the things to avoid.

MACMILLAN TRAVEL

Macmillan General Reference USA, Inc.
1633 Broadway
New York, NY 10019

Find us online at **www.frommers.com**

ISBN 0-02-863022-X
ISSN 1082-2615

Editor: Naomi P. Kraus
Production Editor: Christina Van Camp
Photo Editor: Richard Fox
Design by Michele Laseau
Staff Cartographers: John Decamillis, Roberta Stockwell
Page Creation: Sean Monkhouse, Natalie Evans
Front cover photo: © PhotoDisc, Inc.

SPECIAL SALES

Bulk purchases (10+ copies) of Frommer's and selected Macmillan travel guides are available to corporations, organizations, mail-order catalogs, institutions, and charities at special discounts, and can be customized to suit individual needs. For more information write to Special Sales, Macmillan General Reference, 1633 Broadway, New York, NY 10019.

Manufactured in the United States of America

5 4 3 2 1

Contents

6 Dining 96

7 On Your Mark, Get Set, Go! What to See & Do In & Around Walt Disney World 131

8 What to See & Do Beyond Disney: Universal Studios Escape, Sea World & Other Orlando Attractions 191

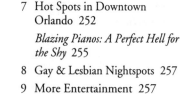

List of Maps

An Invitation to the Reader

In researching this book, we discovered many wonderful places—hotels, restaurants, shops, and more. We're sure you'll find others. Please tell us about them, so we can share the information with your fellow travelers in upcoming editions. If you were disappointed with a recommendation, we'd love to know that, too. Please write to:

Frommer's Walt Disney World & Orlando 2000
Macmillan Travel
1633 Broadway
New York, NY 10019

An Additional Note

Please be advised that travel information is subject to change at any time—and this is especially true of prices. We therefore suggest that you write or call ahead for confirmation when making your travel plans. The authors, editors, and publisher cannot be held responsible for the experiences of readers while traveling. Your safety is important to us, however, so we encourage you to stay alert and be aware of your surroundings. Keep a close eye on cameras, purses, and wallets, all favorite targets of thieves and pickpockets.

What the Symbols Mean
✪ Frommer's Favorites

Our favorite places and experiences—outstanding for quality, value, or both.

The following abbreviations are used for credit cards:

AE	American Express	EURO	Eurocard
CB	Carte Blanche	JCB	Japan Credit Bank
DC	Diners Club	MC	MasterCard
DISC	Discover	V	Visa
ER	enRoute		

Find Frommer's Online

Arthur Frommer's Budget Travel Online (www.frommers.com) offers more than 6,000 pages of up-to-the-minute travel information—including the latest bargains and candid, personal articles updated daily by Arthur Frommer himself. No other Web site offers such comprehensive and timely coverage of the world of travel.

The Best of Walt Disney World & Orlando

When visiting Orlando, the urge to do everything in The World, and then some, can be overwhelming. But, to borrow a phrase from my New York in-laws—fuggedaboudit. As your guide, I can promise you that even a two-week stay isn't long enough to hit all of the theme parks and attractions.

With seven full-blown theme parks, four nighttime entertainment districts, a thriving downtown, a lively local cultural community, hundreds of smaller attractions, and thousands of restaurants, your focus should be on quality, not quantity. But don't panic. I've done it all so you won't have to. I've inspected every inch of every park, every restaurant, and every hotel. (Okay, my husband checked out those theme park men's rooms, and he assures me they are fine.) I provide an insider's view of how to make the most of your time in Orlando. It is, I am proud to say, the place I call home.

Yes, there are enough options here to make your head spin like one of those famous Disney teacups. With this book, though, you will have the necessary tools to plan ahead, and you will have enough information about your choices to be flexible. My goal? To help you make the decisions that will make your trip easy and enjoyable. If I've done my job, you'll actually be able to relax before you return to yours.

Your vacation will also be affordable. For those of you who feel that price is an object, I've included some of the best deals available, and some ways to keep expenses to a minimum while still having the maximum amount of fun.

Of course, such a mind-numbing array of opportunities couldn't have been imagined 30 years ago. In the mid-1960s when Walt Disney started looking for a new home, who knew that Orlando would evolve into such a tourist mecca? Now there are so many theme restaurants that there's actually one with an airline food motif. Seriously: airline seats, tray tables, and meals served in those lovely plastic trays. YIKES!

And as we enter a new millennium, each year seems to bring another full-scale theme park; visitors have never had more to choose from.

Asia, the last region of Disney's exotic zoological theme park Animal Kingdom, opened in 1999. The 500-acre park combines thrill rides, exotic landscapes, and close encounters with wild animals. Another addition to the Disney landscape, DisneyQuest, offers

Disney, which calls its employees "cast members," has continued to create its own lexicon with the opening of its school in the new Disney-designed town of Celebration. Although this is a public school, Disney has imposed a private language. Students are known as "learners," teachers are "specialists," and the principal is called the "director." So Celebration doesn't have a traditional school but "a community of learners."

100,000 square feet of high-tech virtual reality games and interactive activities. And to top it off, Cirque du Soleil, the world-renowned troupe of acrobatic performers, opened a permanent, 1,671-seat theater in Downtown Disney in early 1999.

Another newcomer in 1999 was the latest Disney budget property, the All-Star Movie Resort, whose decor benefits from whimsical touches culled from Disney celluloid classics. And if you feel the need to escape land for a while, Disney Cruise Lines offers park vacations in conjunction with Caribbean cruises on two luxurious vessels.

Universal Studios Florida, which opened in 1990, continues ambitious expansion plans designed to give Disney some true competition. A nighttime entertainment complex called CityWalk—a direct assault on Pleasure Island and Downtown Disney—opened in late 1998. A 750-room Loews resort, Portofino Bay, opened in 1999 and will be joined in 2000 by a Hard Rock Hotel. A second theme park, Islands of Adventure, joined the party in 1999. It targets the young adult and teen audience—okay, all thrill seekers of all ages—with stomach-churning thrill rides that are baby boomer faves, such as Dr. Seuss and Spiderman. Collectively, all the Universal properties are now known as Universal Studios Escape.

Sea World is also growing, adding on a second theme park after years of sprucing up the older attractions, and adding a slew of new ones. If you haven't seen Sea World in five years, you are in for a treat.

For visitors, all this building means more money-saving, multi-day ticket options at Sea World and Universal and, for annual visitors, something to round out their Disney experience.

And, if you have some energy left after touring all of the artificial attractions, there is still an Orlando that most tourists never see, far away from the fairy castles and the splashy whale shows. That Orlando is colored by its deeply Southern pioneer roots.

Of course, Disney is still the premiere vacation spot for kids and families, but if you look closely—and standing in those lines you will have plenty of time—you'll notice a lot of singles and seniors. Obviously, Disney and Universal were keeping these markets in mind when they added themed nightclub districts. Grown-ups are coming in increasing numbers and are finding plenty of PG-rated adult entertainment.

That's not to say that Orlando isn't a kid-friendly place. Many hotels, some with whimsical themes, have video-game arcades and other child-pleasing features, and just about every restaurant in town has a low-priced children's menu.

In this city, visitors—big or small—are the real VIPs. The major players are vying for your business, as they engage in an ongoing, high-stakes game of one-upmanship.

Over 15.6 million people visited the Magic Kingdom in 1998; 10.59 million went to Epcot; 9.47 million went to Disney-MGM Studios; and 6 million visited the newest park, Animal Kingdom.

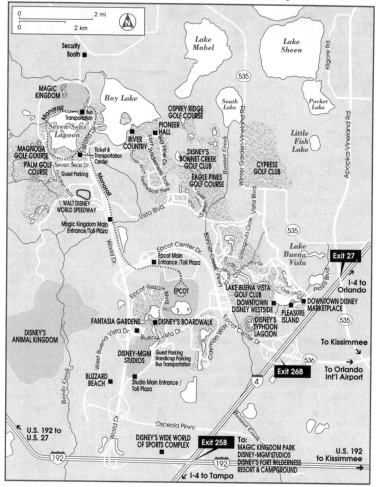

The innovative Disney–MGM Studios theme park, with its movie-magic motif, was countered a year after it opened by Universal Studios Escape, which brought in Steven Spielberg as a creative consultant. Church Street Station, a single-price–admission entertainment complex was followed closely by Disney's Pleasure Island, and now CityWalk at Universal. What's Wet 'n' Wild in town? Disney has three water parks of its own and provides free transportation to them for its vast numbers of resort guests. Busch Gardens in nearby Tampa has an animal park. Well, by gosh, Disney has an entire Animal Kingdom.

Make no mistake—in this war you are the prize, and the stakes and the roller coasters will continue to rise. For the next few years, after Universal has opened its Jurassic Park attraction, the big question will be: Will Disney create real dinosaurs from DNA found in amber?

In the Words of Walt Disney

I only hope we never lose sight of one thing . . . that it was all started by a mouse.

1 Frommer's Favorite Orlando Experiences

From Cinderella's Castle to Space Mountain, everybody loves the Magic Kingdom, but here are some other great things to try, both at Disney and in the greater Orlando area.

- **A Day at Epcot.** You can travel around the world in an afternoon at the World Showcase pavilions and then have a truly hands-on experience at Innoventions, where rides and a variety of interactive games awaits you.

- **Visit Disney–MGM Studios.** More grown-up than the Magic Kingdom, but still has lots of great activities for the kids. Don't miss The Tower of Terror and the latest nighttime show, Fantasmic, an innovative mix of live-action, water-works, and fireworks.

- **Check Out Disney's Wide World of Sports.** From top tennis stars to an NFL "experience," this huge sports complex is worth checking out. There are also numerous other sporting options for the whole family in Orlando—great golfing, tennis, boating, fishing, water-skiing, cycling . . . you name it.

- **Experience the Movies at Universal Studios Florida.** Universal combines cutting-edge, high-tech effects with great creativity. Adults will find Universal—A Day in the Park with Barney notwithstanding—a hip and sophisticated park, not afraid to poke fun at itself, or the Mouse down the road. Not-to-be-missed attractions: Back to the Future, Jaws, Terminator 2: 3-D Battle Across Time, Twister...Ride it Out, and Earthquake—The Big One.

- **Stroll Around Cypress Gardens.** Two hundred acres of gorgeous botanical gardens punctuated by lakes and lagoons, waterfalls, and sculpture. A very laid-back attraction that is popular with seniors.

- **An Evening at Church Street Station.** Dance halls, old-fashioned saloons, dining rooms, and shopping make this the prime non-Disney attraction in Orlando. Top-flight musicians provide entertainment in this renovated down-town train depot spanning real cobblestone streets. Just a few blocks away is the heart of downtown Orlando, and dozens of restaurants and bars.

- **Eco-entertainment at Sea World.** With the opening of a major thrill ride, Journey to Atlantis, Sea World has added a little thrill, but it's better to enjoy what this park does best—hands-on encounters with dolphins and stingrays, and up-close views of sea animals, from polar bears to killer whales.

2 The Best Hotel Bets

- **Best for Families:** All the Disney properties cater to families, with special menus for kids, character meals, video-game arcades, free transportation to the parks, and many, many recreational facilities. Camping at woodsy **Fort Wilderness** (☎ **407/W-DISNEY** [934-7639] or 407/824-2900) makes for a special family experience. Bunk beds and a geyser going off in the lobby? What more could kids ask for? Find out at the **Wilderness Lodge** (☎ **407/W-DISNEY** [934-7639] or 407/824-3200).

Fun Fact

Star Tours, the Star Wars ride that has been a part of the park when it opened in 1989, has updated its video with a new film from George Lucas. The film will reflect the first "prequel" to the popular trilogy.

Chills & Thrills

If you are a speed freak who lives for the ups and downs of a good thrill ride, here are the top seven stomach turners in Orlando:

- **Bomb Bay** (Wet 'n' Wild). Here you shoot through a tube down a 76-foot, nearly vertical, slide with only the water between you and the slide. Need I say more?

- **Back to the Future** (Universal Studios Florida). Great special effects combine with a dipping, twisting ride through an alternative universe. You'll want to go again.

- **The Incredible Hulk Coaster** (Islands of Adventure). You'll blast from 0 to 40 in 2 seconds, spin upside down 100 feet from the ground, and execute seven rollovers and two deep drops on this glow-in-the-dark roller coaster.

- **Space Mountain** (Magic Kingdom). An oldie but a goodie. Comets soaring overhead contribute to the spectacular preshow atmosphere. For a really great ride, get in the first car; you'll feel like you're blasting through space.

- **Terminator 2, 3-D** (Universal Studios Florida). He's back, and this combination of amazingly crisp video technology and good old-fashioned fear makes this ride one of the top tickets in town.

- **Tower of Terror** (Disney–MGM Studios). This free-fall experience is more than thrilling; it is truly scary. Once your legs stop shaking, you'll want to ride again.

- **Twister...Ride it Out** (Universal Studios Florida). This unusual ride envelops you in pelting rain and gusting wind to sweep you up in the drama of life in the heart of Tornado Alley.

- **Best Moderately Priced Hotels:** Both Disney's **Dixie Landings** (☎ 407/ W-DISNEY [934-7639] or 407/934-6000) and **Port Orleans Resort** (☎ 407/ W-DISNEY [934-7639] or 407/934-5000) offer magnificently landscaped grounds and extensive facilities; they could easily charge more for a stay here.

- **Best Inexpensive Hotels:** That's easy: Disney's **All-Star Music Resort** (☎ 407/ W-DISNEY [934-7639] or 407/939-6000) and **All-Star Sports Resort** (☎ 407/W-DISNEY [934-7639] or 407/939-5000). You can't beat 'em with a stick. The Best Western **Mount Vernon Inn** in Winter Park offers old-fashioned Southern hospitality—without the airs—at a low price (☎ 407/647-1166), but is some distance from the Disney theme parks.

- **Best Budget Motel:** The rooms are clean, it's centrally located, and there is a restaurant right next door. All these things make the **Ramada Inn**, 4559 W. Bronson Memorial Hwy. (☎ 800/544-5712 or 407/396-1212), a great budget choice. Rates here range from $29.95 to $59.95, and microwaves and refrigerators are available upon request.

Millennium Alert

Forget about partying like it's 1999 at Disney on New Year's Eve. All the rooms on Disney property—yes *all* the rooms—have supposedly been booked for years. One determined, and hopeful, man has reportedly faxed the reservations office for several years reminding them to give him a call if anything opens up for New Year's Eve.

- **Best for Business Travelers:** Marriott's **Orlando World Center** (☎ 800/621-0638 or 407/239-4200) offers full concierge service, 24-hour room service, fine restaurants, spacious lounges, and an extensive array of business services, not to mention golf, tennis, and other recreational facilities should you find time to relax.

- **Best for a Romantic Getaway:** The 1,500-acre grounds of the **Hyatt Regency Grand Cypress Resort** (☎ 800/233-1234 or 407/239-1234) are a veritable botanical garden surrounding a swan-inhabited lake. Couples enjoy stunning accommodations, great service, first-rate restaurants, and every imaginable facility. You should also consider the luxurious lodgings—with fireplaces and whirlpool tubs—at the adjoining Villas of Grand Cypress (☎ 800/835-7377 or 407/239-4700).

- **Best Location: Disney's Grand Floridian Beach Resort** (☎ 407/W-DISNEY [934-7639] or 407/824-3000), **Polynesian Resort** (☎ 407/W-DISNEY [934-7639] or 407/824-2000), or **Contemporary Resort** (☎ 407/W-DISNEY [934-7639] or 407/824-1000)—all are right on the monorail that will whisk you straight to the parks for an early opening.

- **Best Service:** The elegant **Peabody Orlando** (☎ 800/PEABODY or 407/352-4000) offers 24-hour concierge and room service, nightly bed turndown, and other attentive pampering.

- **Best Pools:** All of the Walt Disney World resorts have terrific swimming pools—generally Olympic-sized, and often based on themes. The pool at the **Caribbean Beach Resort** (☎ 407/W-DISNEY [934-7639] or 407/934-3400), for instance, replicates a Caribbean fort with stone walls and cannons; it also has a water slide. Outside the Disney complex, the **Grand Cypress Resort** (☎ 800/233-1234 or 407/239-1234) also has a notable pool: A half-acre lagoonlike affair, it flows through rock grottoes, is spanned by a rope bridge, and has 12 waterfalls and two steep water slides.

- **Best Health Club:** The **Walt Disney World Dolphin** (☎ 800/227-1500 or 407/934-4000) has a fully equipped Body By Jake club, complete with a weight room overlooking a lake. It contains a full complement of Polaris, Lifestep, Lifecycle, and Liferower equipment; offers aerobics classes throughout the day, plus personal training, massage, and body wraps; and has saunas and a large whirlpool.

3 The Best Dining Bets

- **Best for Kids:** Kids adore the meals with Disney characters offered at almost **all Walt Disney World resorts** and elsewhere in the Walt Disney World (WDW) complex (details follow). Don't forget the jungle-theme **Rainforest Cafe** (☎ 407/827-8500) at two locations—Downtown Disney Marketplace and Animal Kingdom—where monkey business is encouraged.

- **Best Spot for a Romantic Dinner:** The elegant candlelit **Dux** at the Peabody Orlando (☎ 407/345-4550) combines a warmly inviting ambience with great food.

- **Best Spot for a Business Lunch:** Generally, **Hemingway's,** an upscale, Key West–style restaurant at the Grand Cypress Resort (☎ 407/239-1234), is kid-free, and its intimate dining areas are perfect for business lunches.

- **Best Decor:** **Victoria & Albert's** takes the prize, with its plush Louis XIII–style furnishings, brocaded walls, and central dome (☎ 407/WDW-DINE [939-3463]).

- **Best View: Artist Point** (☎ 407/WDW-DINE [939-3463]). This carefully crafted resort restaurant offers the illusion of dining in a rustically elegant, turn-of-the-century national-park lodge. Large windows overlook a lake and a waterfall. Weather permitting, there's also terrace seating.
- **Best Wine List:** "Sip" for yourself why **Maison et Jardin** (☎ 407/862-4410) in Altamonte Springs was recently honored by *Wine Spectator* magazine for its outstanding wine cellar.
- **Best Value:** At **Romano's Macaroni Grill** (☎ 407/239-6676), the ambience and the northern Italian cuisine are first rate, and prices are low, low, low.
- **Best American Cuisine:** Meat loaf and mashed potatoes that would make Mama proud are served at **B-Line Diner,** in the Peabody Orlando hotel (☎ 407/345-4460).
- **Best Chinese Cuisine: Ming Court** (☎ 407/351-9988) features delicacies from all regions of China.
- **Best California Cuisine:** Waterfalls and animal sounds can't drown out the flood of flavorful dishes at the **Rainforest Cafe** (☎ 407/827-8500).
- **Best Barbecue:** You can follow your nose to **Bubbaloo's Bodacious BBQ** (☎ 407/295-1212) after catching a whiff of tangy hickory smoke. It tastes as good as it smells.
- **Best Italian Cuisine:** I'd pick the northern Italian fare at the charming **Capriccio** in the Peabody Orlando (☎ 407/352-4000), or the sedate and elegant **Tuscany** at Marriott's Orlando World Center (☎ 407/239-4200).
- **Best Seafood:** The 19th-century-style clambake buffet at the **Cape May Café** at Disney's Beach Club Resort (☎ 407/WDW-DINE [939-3463]) is a feast—seafood stews, clams, mussels, lobster, and more cooked in a rockweed steamer pit.
- **Best Tapas: Cafe Tu Tu Tango** (☎ 407/248-2222) takes the tapas concept international, with items ranging from Cajun egg rolls to Thai salad.
- **Best Steak House:** At the **Yachtsman Steakhouse** at Disney's Yacht Club Resort (☎ 407/WDW-DINE [939-3463]), aged prime steaks, chops, and seafood are grilled over oak and hickory.
- **Best Late-Night Dining:** The trendy **B-Line Diner** (☎ 407/345-4460) at the Peabody Orlando is open around the clock for eclectic fare, ranging from filet mignon to a falafel sandwich.
- **Best Spot for a Celebration: Emeril's** at Universal CityWalk (☎ 407/224-2424) is a good place for romantic celebrations, and for the pure party factor, you can't beat **Jimmy Buffet's Margaritaville** (☎ 407/224-2155), also at Universal City-Walk.
- **Best Character Breakfast:** At the revolving **Garden Grill** (☎ 407/WDW-DINE [939-3463]), in the Land Pavilion at Epcot, diners enjoy hearty family-style fare, a just-folks country-style theme, and interesting changes of scenery as the restaurant circles through environments, ranging from a prairie to a rain forest; all this and Minnie and Mickey, too.
- **Best Outdoor Dining:** The terrace at **Artist Point** (☎ 407/WDW-DINE [939-3463]), the premier restaurant at Disney's Wilderness Lodge, overlooks a lake, waterfall, and scenery evocative of America's national parks.
- **Best People-Watching:** The upstairs patio at **Bongo's Cuban Cafe,** Downtown Disney West Side, (☎ 407/828-0999) is where it's at.
- **Best Afternoon Tea: The Peabody Orlando** (☎ 407/345-4550) hosts afternoon teas on weekdays from 3 to 4:30pm in its gorgeous skylit atrium lobby. The

Peabody's resident ducks frolicking in a nearby fountain will entertain you as you sip your Earl Grey. The cost is $8.95 per person.

- **Best Brunch: Capriccio** at the Peabody Orlando (☎ **407/352-4000**) offers a lavish buffet of first-rate fare with free-flowing champagne.
- **Best Special Brunch: The House of Blues** (☎ **407/934-2583**) in Disney's West Side has a down-home gospel brunch, $28 for adults and $15 for kids 4 to 12, featuring foot-stomping music and an awe-inspiring array of Southern fare such as cheese grits and sausage. Foreign visitors may especially enjoy this cultural immersion. Make reservations early since it regularly sells out.

Planning a Trip to Walt Disney World & Orlando

Orlando is so packed with attractions that advance planning is crucial. In this chapter, I've compiled everything you need to know before you go. In addition to the information below, you'll find tips in chapters 5 (Accommodations), 7 (Walt Disney World), and 8 (Other Attractions in the Orlando Area).

1 Visitor Information You Can Get Before Your Trip

As soon as you know you're going to Orlando, write or call the **Orlando/Orange County Convention & Visitors Bureau,** 8723 International Dr., Suite 101, Orlando, FL 32819 (☎ **407/ 363-5871**). The bureau can answer all your questions and will be happy to send you maps and brochures (including the informative *Official Visitors Guide,* the *African-American Visitors Guide,* the *Area Guide* to local restaurants, and the *Official Accommodations Guide*). The packet, which should arrive in about 3 weeks, includes the "Magicard," good for discounts of 10 to 50% on accommodations, attractions, car rentals, and more.

For general information about **Walt Disney World**—and for a copy of the informative *Walt Disney World Vacations* brochure—write or call the Walt Disney World Co., Box 10000, Lake Buena Vista, FL 32830-1000 (☎ **407/934-7639**).

For information about **Universal Studios Florida, CityWalk,** and **Islands of Adventure,** call ☎ **800/837-2273** or 407/ 363-8000. You can also write to **Universal Studios Escape,** 1000 Universal Studios Dr., Orlando, FL 32816.

You may also contact the **Kissimmee–St. Cloud Convention & Visitors Bureau,** 1925 E. Irlo Bronson Memorial Hwy. (U.S. 192), Kissimmee, FL 34744, or P.O. Box 422007, Kissimmee, FL 34742-2007 (☎ **800/327-9159** or 407/847-5000). They'll send maps, brochures, discount coupon books, and the *Kissimmee–St. Cloud Vacation Guide,* which details the area's accommodations and attractions.

For information about the entire state—including Orlando and Kissimmee—write or call the Florida Department of Commerce, **Division of Tourism,** Visitor Inquiry, 126 Van Buren St., Tallahassee, FL 32399-2000. You can also call the **Florida Tourism Industry Marketing Corp.** (☎ **888/735-2872**) for information

---

Fun Fact

For the first time, Disney is allowing us regular folks—not just travel agents—to book reservations online. The service, which became available in 1999, began by allowing resort and package reservations, and it will be expanded to include air reservations. It can be found at **www.disney.com**.

---

about the state. Or you can write to **Visit Florida,** P.O. Box 1100, Tallahassee, FL 32391-1100. They also offer a seasonal visitor's guide that includes information on special events and discounts.

For information about the **Winter Park** area, contact the Winter Park Chamber of Commerce, 150 New York Ave., P.O. Box 280, Winter Park, FL 32790 (☎ **407/ 644-8281**).

ONLINE INFORMATION

If you have Internet access, you can visit Walt Disney World's own Web site at **www.disneyworld.com**. It has extensive, entertaining, and regularly updated information, including a live-action look from video cameras perched throughout the various parks. (These are mostly long-distance shots of tourists walking about, but it is still a chance to see those blue Orlando skies, and dream ahead to vacation time.)

Information about Universal Studios Escape is available at **www.universal studiosescape.com,** and you'll find Sea World information at **www.seaworld. com.** Both sites offer maps and a basic description of rides, shows, and ticket information.

The city newspaper, the *Orlando Sentinel,* also produces *Orlando Sentinel Online* at **www.orlandosentinel.com.** Once there, click on "Theme Park Central" for a variety of information and updates on happenings at local attractions. If you are connected to the Internet through AOL, type **Go2Orlando** as a keyword and you will land on a site, produced by Orlando Sentinel Interactive, that is full of regularly updated information on a variety of attractions. Also try **www.insidecentral florida.com** for information on theme parks and special events.

The Orlando/Orange County Convention and Visitors Bureau has a Web site at **www.goflorida.com/orlando.** The state has a Web site at **www.flausa.com.**

2 Money

Disney parks, resorts, shops, and restaurants (but not most fast-food outlets) accept the three major credit cards—American Express, MasterCard, and Visa. Disney offers some of its resort guests a debit card that can be used in park shops and restaurants. This is sometimes referred to as a Disney credit card, but it isn't a true credit card since you've got to settle the bill when you leave.

You can also purchase **Disney dollars** (currency bearing the images of Mickey, Goofy, and Minnie), available in $1, $5, and $10 denominations. They're good at shops, restaurants, and resorts throughout the Disney realm, as well as in Disney stores everywhere. I don't recommend buying these Disney dollars, because you'll have to cash in any leftover bills for real currency upon leaving Walt Disney World, which means another line on your last day.

You can get cash advances on your MasterCard and Visa, cash traveler's checks, cash personal checks of $25 or less (drawn on U.S. banks, upon presentation of a valid driver's license and a major credit card), and exchange foreign currency at

What Things Cost in Orlando	U.S.$	U.K.£
As of this writing,	1.60	1
Taxi from airport to WDW area	41.00	25.60
Bus from airport to WDW area (adult fare)	25.00	15.60
Double room at Disney's Grand Floridian Beach Resort (very expensive)	294.00–545.00	183.75–340.60
Double room at Marriott's Orlando World Center (expensive)	152.00–259.00	95.00–161.90
Double room at Disney's Port Orleans Resort (moderate)	119.00–154.00	74.40–96.25
Double room at Disney's All-Star Music Resort (inexpensive)	74.00–89.00	46.25–55.65
Double room at Days Inn, Kissimmee (inexpensive)	39.00–59.00	24.40–36.90
Seven-course fixed-price dinner for one at Victoria & Albert's, not including tip or wine (very expensive)	80.00–160.00	50.00–100.00
All-you-can-eat buffet dinner at Akershus in Epcot, not including tip or wine (inexpensive)	18.50	11.55
Bottle of beer (restaurant)	2.50	1.55
Coca-Cola (restaurant)	1.25	.80
Cup of coffee	1.25	.80
Roll of ASA 100 Kodacolor film, 36 exposures, purchased at Walt Disney World	9.35	5.85
Adult 4-Day Value Pass admission to Walt Disney World	150.00	93.75
Child 4-Day Value Pass admission to Walt Disney World	120.00	75.00
Adult 1-day admission to Sea World	42.00	26.25
Child 1-day admission to Sea World	34.00	21.25
Adult 1-day admission to Universal Studios Escape	42.00	26.25
Child 1-day admission to Universal Studios Escape	34.00	21.25

branches of the **SunTrust** on Main Street in the Magic Kingdom, open daily from 9am to 4pm (☎ **407/828-6102**) and at 1675 Buena Vista Dr., across from the Disney Village Marketplace, open weekdays from 9am to 4pm, until 6pm on Thursday (☎ **407/828-6106**).

ATM machines are conveniently located on Main Street and in Tomorrowland in the Magic Kingdom; at the entrances to Disney–MGM Studios and Epcot; at Pleasure Island; at Disney Village Marketplace; at the All-Star Sports Resort; and at the Crossroads Shopping Center.

There are also ATM machines near the entrance to Sea World, and at Universal Studios, where they are located in the **First Union National Bank** inside the main entrance, near Guest Services.

It may come as a surprise to foreign visitors just how prevalent ATM machines are in central Florida. Most malls have at least one ATM, and they can even be found in many convenience stores, namely 7-11s and Circle Ks. They are also increasingly showing up in grocery stores and drugstores. But there is often an extra charge for using these nonbank machines. Depending on your institution, charges usually range from $1 to $1.50 per transaction. The fee may be higher in areas with heavy tourist traffic.

Be sure to exercise caution when accessing ATM machines, especially at night, and in areas that are not well-lit and are not heavily traveled. Don't let the land of Mickey lull you into a false sense of security. Orlando is a major city, and its crime rate is the same as any other urban location. When entering your ATM Personal Identification Number (PIN), be sure to shield the keyboard from anyone who may be in line, or observing from a distance. Also, keep all doors locked when accessing a drive-through ATM. The common ATM networks are Cirrus, Honor, Master-Card, Plus, and Van.

3 When to Go

Orlando is essentially a theme-park destination, and its busiest seasons are when-ever kids are out of school—summer (early June to about August 20), holiday week-ends, Christmas season (mid-December to mid-January), and Easter/spring break. Obviously, the whole experience is more enjoyable when the crowds are thinnest, and the weather is the most temperate. Hotel rooms are also priced lower off-season, but the off-season doesn't follow the traditional winter/summer pattern of most areas.

Peak season rates can be put into effect during large conventions and special events. Even something as remote as Bike Week in Daytona Beach can raise prices, even in the off-season. These kinds of events especially impact moderately-priced properties outside of Walt Disney World. **Best times:** The week after Labor Day until the day before Thanksgiving, the week after Thanksgiving until mid-December, and the 6 weeks before and after school spring vacations. **Worst times:** during the Christmas holidays and summer, when many locals haul their families to the parks, and many visitors take advantage of breaks from school. Packed parking lots are also the norm during the week before and after Christmas. In summer, it's a double whammy: Crowds are very large, and weather is oppressively hot and humid. I probably shouldn't say this, but I would pull the kids out of school for a few days around an off-season weekend to avoid long lines. Keep in mind, however, that the large number of international visitors guarantees substantial crowds year-round.

If you're taking advantage of one of the increasing numbers of available land/cruise packages, make sure that you take into account the hurricane season, which runs from the end of summer through the first week in November. Although generally not much of a problem inland, there's nothing like 20-foot swells to ruin a trek at sea.

Fun Fact

Money really can't buy you love. Denver Bronco's coach Mike Shanahan made news before the 1998 Super Bowl by declining a $30,000 offer to utter the catchphrase "I'm going to Disney World." Shanahan, apparently a Universal man, said "I don't care how much they pay me."

Central Florida Average Temperatures

	Jan	Feb	Mar	Apr	May	June	July	Aug	Sept	Oct	Nov	Dec
High °F	71.7	72.9	78.3	83.6	88.3	90.6	91.7	91.6	89.7	84.4	78.2	73.1
°C	22.0	22.7	25.7	28.7	31.3	32.5	33.2	33.1	32.0	29.1	25.7	22.8
Low °F	49.3	50.0	55.3	60.3	66.2	71.2	73.0	73.4	72.5	65.4	56.8	50.9
°C	9.6	10.0	12.5	15.7	19.0	21.8	22.7	23.0	22.5	18.6	13.8	10.5

Orlando Area Calendar of Events

January

- ✪ **CompUSA Florida Citrus Bowl.** January kicks off with this football event, located in downtown Orlando and featuring two of the year's top college teams. Tickets ($55) go on sale in late October or early November. Call ☎ 407/423-2476 for information or TicketMaster at 407/839-3900 for tickets. A downtown parade is held a few days before the game and features dozens of marching bands, parade units, and a few floats. Sidewalk viewing along the parade route is free.

- ✪ **Walt Disney World Marathon.** About 90% of the runners finish this 26.2-mile marathon winding through the resort and theme-park areas. The race is open to all, including runners with disabilities. Some Disney resort packages include the $65 entry fee in the room price. The registration deadline is usually in early December, and preregistration is required. Call ☎ **407/ 939-7810.**

- • **The Atlanta Braves.** The Braves have been holding spring training at Disney's Wide World of Sports Complex since 1998, and play is ensured there through at least 2001. There are about 18 games during the 1-month season. Tickets are $10.50 and $15.50. Season tickets run about $250. The season's schedule generally is not announced until mid-December. For general information, call ☎ **407/828-3267.** To purchase tickets call TicketMaster ☎ **407/839-3900.** You can also get information online at **www.majorleaguebaseball.com/spring-training/atl.sml.**

- ✪ **The Zora Neale Hurston Festival.** This 4-day celebration in Eatonville, the first incorporated African-American town in America, highlights the life and works of author Zora Neale Hurston and is usually held the last weekend in January. Eatonville is about 25 miles north of the theme parks. Admission is under $3. Additional fees are charged for special lectures or seminars. Call ☎ **800/352-3865** or 407/647-3307 for details.

February

- ✪ **The Silver Spurs Rodeo.** Featuring real cowboys in contests of calf roping, bull and bronco riding, barrel racing, and more, the rodeo is a celebration of the area's rural, pre-Disney roots. It's held at the Silver Spurs Arena, 1875 E. Irlo Bronson Memorial Hwy. (U.S. 192) in Kissimmee, on the third weekend in February. Call ☎ **407/847-5000** for details. Tickets are $15.

- • **Mardi Gras at Universal Studios Escape.** Authentic parade floats from New Orleans, stilt walkers, and traditional doubloons and beads thrown to the crowd add to the fun of this event, and all is included in the regular park admission during this time. Special entertainment also adds to the festivities. Held in mid-February. For information call ☎ **(800) 837-2273** or 407/363-8000, or online at **www.usf.com.**

- • **Bike Week.** More than 500,000 motorcyclists from across the United States—and increasingly from foreign countries—descend on Daytona Beach each year in late February and early March. People-watching and some street events are free. Prices vary for other special events, including motorcycle races at Daytona Speedway. Since Daytona is only 50 miles northeast of Orlando, many bikers base themselves in Orlando and roar down the highway daily to Bike Week. For information, call ☎ **800/854-1234** or surf on over to **www.officialbikeweek.com.**

March

- **Kissimmee Bluegrass Festival.** Major bluegrass and gospel entertainers, from all over the country, perform at this 4-day event, beginning the first weekend of March at the Silver Spurs Arena, 1875 E. Irlo Bronson Memorial Hwy. Tickets are $12 to $20; multiday packages are available. Call ☎ **800/473-7773** for details.

- ✪ **Bay Hill Invitational.** Hosted by Arnold Palmer and featuring some Orlando-based golfers like Tiger Woods, this PGA Tour event is held in mid-March at the Bay Hill Club, 9000 Bay Hill Blvd. One-day admission on Tuesday and Wednesday costs $28; week-long tickets are $50 for grounds-only access; $70 for clubhouse access. Call ☎ **407/876-2888** for details.

- **The Spring Flower Festival.** From March to May at Cypress Gardens, the festival features more than 30,000 brightly colored bedding plants and flowers, creating beautiful topiaries shaped as butterflies, birds, and animals. You have to pay admission to the park to get into the festival: adults $32.80, seniors $27.90, children 6–17 one admission free with paying adult or senior; additional children $22.20. Call ☎ **941/324-2111** for details, or visit **www.cypressgardens.com.**

- **The Sidewalk Art Festival.** Held in Winter Park's Central Park, this exhibition draws artists from all over North America during the third full weekend in March. The festival is consistently named one of the best in the nation by the national magazine *Sunshine Artist.* Call ☎ **407/672-6390** or 407/644-8281 for details. Admission is free, although you may have to pay for parking.

April

- ✪ **Orlando International Fringe Festival.** Over 100 diverse acts from around the world participate in this eclectic event, held for 10 days at various stages in downtown Orlando. Entertainers perform drama, comedy, political satire, and experimental theater. Everything performed on outdoor stages, from sword swallowing to a 7-minute version of Hamlet, is available to Fringegoers free after they purchase a festival button for under $5. Ticket prices vary, but individual performances are generally under $12. Call ☎ **407/648-0077** for details.

- **Orlando Rays Baseball Season.** The Chicago Cubs farm team plays at Walt Disney Wide World of Sports. Admission is $3 to $7. Season tickets, for all 70 or so games, range from $199 to $299. For general information, call ☎ **407/828-3267.** To purchase tickets, call TicketMaster ☎ **407/839-3900.**

- **Easter Sunrise Service.** An interdenominational service, with music, is presented at the Atlantis Theatre at Sea World, 7007 Sea World Dr. It is hosted by a well-known person each year, most recently Elizabeth Dole. Admission is free. Call ☎ **407/351-3600,** or head over to **www.seaworld.com,** for details.

- **Easter Sunday** is celebrated in Walt Disney World (☎ **407/824-4321;** www.disneyworld.com) with an old-fashioned Easter Parade, and early opening/late closing hours throughout the holiday period.

May

- **Epcot International Flower and Garden Festival.** A month-long event with theme gardens, topiary characters, special floral displays, speakers, and seminars. The festival is free with regular park admission. For more information, visit **www.disneyworld.com.**

June

⊙ **Gay Weekend.** The first weekend in June has become known for attracting tens of thousands of gay and lesbian travelers to central Florida. This has all grown out of "Gay Day," which has been held unofficially at Walt Disney World since the early 1990s, drawing upward of 40,000 folks. Special events at other attractions, including Universal and Sea World, also cater to gay and lesbian travelers. You can get online information, including discounts and packages, at **www.gayday.com.**

• **Walt Disney World Wine Festival.** More than 60 wineries from all over the United States participate. Events include wine tastings, seminars, food, and celebrity-chef cooking demonstrations. Call ☎ **407/827-7200** or 407/824-4321 for details.

• **Walt Disney World All-American College Orchestra and College Band.** The best collegiate musical talent in the country performs at Epcot and the Magic Kingdom throughout the summer. Call ☎ **407/824-4321** for details.

July

• **Independence Day.** Walt Disney World's Star-Spangled Spectacular brings bands, singers, dancers, and unbelievable fireworks displays to all the Disney parks, which stay open late. Call ☎ **407/824-4321** for details. Sea World also features a dazzling laser/fireworks spectacular; call ☎ **407/351-3600** for details. There is also a free fireworks display in downtown Orlando at Lake Eola Park. For information call ☎ **407/246-2827.** Other local fireworks events are listed in the local paper, the *Orlando Sentinel.*

September

• **Night of Joy.** One weekend in September, the Magic Kingdom hosts a festival of contemporary Christian music featuring top artists. This is a very popular event; obtain tickets early. Each year performers make a personal appearance at Long's Christian Bookstore in nearby College Park, about 20 minutes north of Disney. Admission to the concert is about $25 to $30 per night. Exclusive use of Magic Kingdom attractions is included. Call ☎ **407/824-4321** for concert details; for information about the free appearance at Long's, call ☎ **407/422-0293.**

October

⊙ **Orlando Magic Basketball.** Penny Hardaway and his teammates continue to perform magic long after Shaquille O'Neal's departure to Hollywood and the Los Angeles Lakers. In a nonlockout season, the Magic does battle against visiting teams between October and April at the Orlando Arena, 600 W. Amelia St. Ticket prices range from about $13 to $50. A few tickets, usually single seats, are often available the day before games involving lesser-known NBA challengers. Call ☎ **407/896-2442** for details, **407/839-3900** for tickets.

⊙ **Halloween Horror Nights.** Universal Studios Escape (☎ **800/ 837-2273** or 407/363-8000; www.usf.com) transforms its studios and attractions for several weeks before, and after, Halloween, with haunted attractions, live bands, a psychopath's maze, special shows, and hundreds of ghouls and goblins roaming the studio streets. The studio essentially closes at dusk, reopening in a new macabre form a few hours later. Special admission is charged for this event, geared to grown-ups, where the liquor flows freely.

⊙ **National Car Rental Golf Classic at Walt Disney World Resort.** Top PGA tour players compete at WDW golf courses in October's major golf event. Many tour professionals, including Tiger Woods, call Orlando home, so there is usually plenty of first-rate talent on display. Daily ticket prices range from $10 to $20. Tickets for the entire 3-day event run about $35. Tickets may be purchased by writing to Walt Disney World Golf Sales, P.O. Box 10000, Lake Buena Vista, FL 32830. For 1-day tickets call TicketMaster ☎ **407/839-3900.**

- **Biketoberfest** Held at the end of October, this event is not as large—yet—as it's spring-time sister. It is, however, another celebration of all things bright and powerful, with concerts and special events and thousands and thousands of leather-clad types on display along with their machines. For information, contact the Daytona Beach Area Convention & Visitors Bureau at ☎ **904/ 255-0415** or go online to **www.biketoberfest.com.**

- **Walt Disney World Village Boat Show.** Central Florida's largest in-the-water boat show, featuring the best new watercraft. It's held at the Village Marketplace over a 3-day weekend early in the month. Call ☎ **407/824-4321** for details.

November

- **Mum Festival.** November's month-long flower festival at Cypress Gardens (☎ 941/324-2111; www.cypressgardens.com) features millions of mums, their colorful flowers displayed in beds, "blooming" gazebos, poodle baskets, and bonsai.

- ✪ **The Walt Disney World Festival of the Masters.** One of the largest art shows in the South takes place at Disney's Village Marketplace for 3 days, including the second weekend in November. The exhibition features top artists, photographers, and craftspeople—winners of juried shows throughout the country. Free admission. Call ☎ **407/824-4321** for details, or visit **www.disneyworld.com.**

- **Walt Disney World Doll and Teddy Bear Convention.** The top doll and teddy-bear designers from around the world travel to WDW for this major November event. Call ☎ **407/824-4321** for details, or view them online at **www.disneyworld.com.**

- ✪ **Jolly Holidays Dinner Shows.** From late November to mid-December, these all-you-can-eat events are offered at the Contemporary Resort's Fantasia Ballroom. More than 100 Disney characters, singers, and dancers perform in an old-fashioned Christmas extravaganza. Call ☎ **407/W-DISNEY** (934-7639) for details and ticket prices; online, go to **www.disneyworld.com.**

- **Poinsettia Festival.** A spectacular floral showcase of more than 40,000 red, white, and pink poinsettia blooms (including topiary reindeer) highlights this flower festival from late November to mid-January at Cypress Gardens (☎ **941/ 324-2111;** www.cypressgardens.com). This is actually one of the best ways to view the park.

- **Super Soap Weekend.** Disney takes advantage of its corporate connection with ABC by bringing in stars from all of that network's major soaps for a fan-fest featuring special contests and events. It's free with admission to Disney-MGM Studios. Call ☎ **407/W-DISNEY** (934-7639) for details; online, go to **www. disneyworld.com.**

December

- **Burger King Classic Half-Marathon** and **Hooter's 5K Run.** This annual race, early in December, takes place in downtown Orlando, beginning at Church Street Market, 200 S. Orange Ave. It starts at 8am, and anyone can participate. An entry fee is charged. The event kicks off the Citrus Bowl season. Call ☎ **407/ 423-2476** for information.

- ✪ **Christmas at Walt Disney World.** During the Walt Disney World Christmas festivities, Main Street is lavishly decked out with lights and holly, and visitors are greeted by carolers. An 80-foot tree is illuminated by thousands of colored lights. Epcot and MGM Studios also offer special embellishments and entertainment throughout the holiday season, as do all Disney resorts. Some holiday highlights include **Mickey's Very Merry Christmas Party,** an after-dark ticketed event. This takes place weekends at the Magic Kingdom and offers a traditional

---

Disney Fun Fact

It's a story even Disney couldn't make up. The Osbornes of Arkansas apparently took to heart the old hymn that says, "You can't be a beacon if your light don't shine." Their Christmas-light collection of 2-million-plus blinkers, twinklers, and strands shone so brightly that neighbors complained. There were rumors that even air traffic was disrupted, and the flow of the faithful in cars, caused mile-long backups in a mostly rural area where a couple of pickups in front of the feed store is considered a major delay. The neighbors, finally seeing the light, went to court in what became a nationally known battle. Disney came to the rescue and, in 1995, moved the whole thing to Orlando, adding a million or so bulbs. The display is now known as the Osborne Family Christmas Lights. No complaints, yet.

Christmas parade and a breath-taking fireworks display. The admission price, usually under $35, includes free cookies and cocoa, and a souvenir photo. The best part? The short lines for the rides. The **Candlelight Procession** at Epcot features hundreds of candle-holding carolers, a celebrity narrator telling the Christmas story, and a 450-voice choir. Call ☎ **407/824-4321** for details on all of the above; ☎ **407/W-DISNEY** (934-7639) to inquire about hotel/events packages. **The Osborne Family Christmas Lights** came to Disney–MGM Studios in 1995 when the Arkansas family ran into trouble with local authorities over their multimillion-light display. In a twinkle, Disney moved the whole thing to central Florida. For online information on all the Christmas activities, go to **www.disneyworld.com.**

- **Christmas at Sea World.** Sea World features a special Shamu show and a luau show called "Christmas in Hawaii." The 400-foot sky tower is lit like a Christmas tree nightly. Call ☎ **407/351-3600** for details. Online go to **www. seaworld. com.**
- **Walt Disney World New Year's Eve Celebration.** For one night a year, the Magic Kingdom is open until 2am for a massive fireworks exhibition. Other New Year's festivities in the WDW parks include a big bash at Pleasure Island featuring music headliners, a special Hoop-Dee-Doo Musical Revue show, and guest performances by well-known musical groups at Disney–MGM Studios and Epcot. Call ☎ **407/824-4321** for details, or visit **www.disneyworld.com.**
- **Church Street Station** (☎ **407/422-2434**) in downtown Orlando also offers a New Year's celebration, complete with miniature dropping ball.
- ✪ **The Citrus Bowl Parade.** On an annually selected date in late December, the parade features lavish floats and high-school bands for a nationally televised parade. Reserved seats in the bleachers are $12, but you can watch along the route in downtown Orlando for free. Call ☎ **407/423-2476** for details.
- **CompUSA Florida Citrus Bowl New Year's.** The official New Year's Eve celebration of the CompUSA Florida Citrus Bowl takes place at Sea World. Events include headliner concerts, a laser and fireworks spectacular, a countdown to midnight, and special shows throughout the park. Admission is charged. Call ☎ **407/423-2476** for details.

4 Tips for Travelers with Special Needs

FOR TRAVELERS WITH DISABILITIES   There is no reason why those with disabilities can't fully enjoy all the theme parks have to offer, if they engage in a little advance planning.

Visitor Information   Call the **Florida Governor's Alliance,** 345 S. Magnolia Dr., Suite D-11, Tallahassee, FL 32301 (☎ **904/487-2223,** or 904/487-2222 for Telecommunications Devices for the Deaf [TDD]), for a free copy of *The Florida Planning Companion for People with Disabilities.* It offers valuable information on accessibility at tourist facilities throughout the state.

Accommodations   Every hotel and motel is required by law to have a special room or rooms equipped for wheelchairs. A few, including **Best Western Buena Vista Suites** (☎ **407/239-8588**), **Embassy Suites** (☎ **407/239-1144**), and **Sleep Inn** (☎ **407/396-1600**), have wheel-in showers. Walt Disney World's **Coronado Springs Resort** (☎ **407/W-DISNEY** (934-7639), 407/934-6632, or 407/824-1000), which opened in 1997, has 99 rooms designed to accommodate guests with disabilities. Make your special needs known when making reservations. For other information about special rooms, call ☎ **407/939-7807.**

Transportation   All public buses in Orlando have a hydraulic lift and restraining belts for wheelchairs, and they serve Universal Studios, Sea World, the shopping areas, and downtown Orlando. When staying at Disney, you can catch a shuttle bus from your hotel that will accommodate wheelchairs.

If you need to rent a special wheelchair van in Orlando, call **Wheelers Inc.** (☎ **407/826-0616**) or **Vantage Mini Vans** (☎ **407/521-8002**).

Amtrak (☎ **800/872-7245**) provides redcap service, wheelchair assistance, and special seats, if you give them 72-hours notice. Travelers with disabilities are also entitled to a discount of 15% off the lowest available adult coach fare. Children ages 2 to 15 with disabilities can get a 50% discount on already discounted one-way fares for adults with disabilities. Documentation from a doctor or an ID card proving your disability is required. Amtrak also provides wheelchair-accessible sleeping accommodations on long-distance trains. Service dogs are permitted aboard and travel free of charge. For a free booklet called *Amtrak's America,* which has a chapter detailing services for passengers with disabilities, call ☎ **800/872-7245** or write to Amtrak Distribution Center, P.O. Box 7717, Itasca, IL 60143.

Greyhound (☎ **800/752-4841**) allows a passenger with disabilities to travel with a companion for a single fare, and if you call 48 hours in advance, they will arrange help along the way.

Theme Parks   Most attractions at the various theme parks, especially the newer ones, are designed to be accessible to a wide variety of people. People with wheelchairs, and their parties, are often given preferential treatment so they can avoid long lines.

The available assistance is outlined by each major park in a brochure, and all the parks offer some parking as close as possible to the park entrance for those with disabilities. Let the booth attendant know your needs, so you will be directed to the appropriate spot. Wheelchair rentals are available at most major attractions, but you will probably be most comfortable in your chair from home. Keep in mind, however, that wheelchairs wider than 24.5 inches may be difficult to navigate through some attractions.

At Walt Disney World: Disney does everything possible to assist guests with disabilities. Its many services are detailed in the *Guidebook for Guests with Disabilities.*

Phone Tip

If you are making a local call in Orlando's 407 area code region, you must now dial the area code followed by the number you wish to call, for a total of 10 digits.

To obtain a copy prior to your visit, write Guest Letters, P.O. Box 10040, Lake Buena Vista, FL 32830-0040, ☎ **407/824-4321.** Also call that number for answers to any questions regarding special needs. Some examples of Disney services:

- Almost all Disney resorts have rooms for those with disabilities.
- Braille directories are located inside the Magic Kingdom in front of the Main Street train station, and in a gazebo in front of the Crystal Palace restaurant, and complimentary guided-tour audiocassette tapes and recorders are available at Guest Services to assist visually impaired guests.
- All parks have special parking lots.
- Personal translator units are available to amplify the audio at selected Epcot attractions (inquire at Earth Station).
- Wheelchairs can be rented at all of the Disney parks.
- Downtown Disney, with its crowded shops and bars, may be hard to navigate in a wheelchair. The movie theater is, however, wheelchair-accessible.
- For information about Telecommunications Devices for the Deaf (TDDs) at Disney World, call ☎ **407/827-5141.**

At Universal Studios Escape: Guests with disabilities should go to Guest Services, located just inside the main entrance, for a *Disabled Guest Guidebook,* a Telecommunications Device for the Deaf (TDD), or other special assistance. Wheelchair rentals are available; look for wheelchair rentals in the concourse area of the parking garage. Universal also provides audio descriptions on cassette for visually impaired guests, and has sign-language guides and scripts for all its shows (advance notice is required; ☎ **407/363-8000** for details).

At Sea World: The park has a guide for guests with disabilities, although most of its attractions are easily accessible to those in wheelchairs. Sea World also provides a Braille guide for the visually impaired, and a very brief synopsis of its shows for the hearing impaired. For information call ☎ **407/351-3600.**

Nationwide Resources   Mobility International USA, P.O. Box 10767, Eugene, OR 97440 (☎ **541/343-1284**), offers accessibility information and has many interesting travel programs for those with disabilities. Membership ($30 a year) includes a quarterly newsletter called *Over the Rainbow.*

Help (accessibility information and more) is also available from the **Society for the Advancement of Travel for the Handicapped** (SATH), 347 Fifth Ave., Suite 610, New York, NY 10016 (☎ **212/447-7284;** www.trav.org/sath/). It charges $5 to send requested information.

Accessible Journeys (☎ **800/846-4537** or 610/521-0339; www.disabilitytravel.com) and **Flying Wheels Travel** (☎ **800/535-6790** or 507/451-5005) offer tours for people with physical disabilities. Accessible Journeys can also provide nurse/companions for travelers. **Guided Tour Inc.** (☎ **215/782-1370**) has tours for people with physical or mental disabilities and seniors.

Recommended Books   Twin Peaks Press, Box 129, Vancouver, WA 98666 (☎ **360/694-2462**), specializes in books for people with disabilities. Order their *Disability Bookshop Catalog* for $5.

FOR SENIORS   Always carry some form of photo ID so that you can take advantage of discounts wherever they're offered. Age limits vary from 50 on up so it never hurts to ask.

If you haven't already done so, consider joining the **American Association of Retired Persons** (AARP) (☎ **202/434-2277**). Annual membership costs $8 per person, or per couple. You must be at least 50 to join. Membership entitles you to many discounts. Write to Purchase Privilege Program, AARP Fulfillment, 601 E St.

NW, Washington, DC 20049, to receive a free list of hotels, motels, and car-rental firms nationwide that offer discounts to AARP members.

Elderhostel is a national organization that offers low-priced educational programs for people over 55 (your spouse can be any age; a companion must be at least 50). Programs are generally a week long, and prices average about $335 per person, including room, board, and classes. For information on programs in Florida, call or write Elderhostel Headquarters, 75 Federal St., Boston, MA 02110-1941 (☎ 617/ 426-7788) and ask for a free U.S. catalog. Or call the Florida office at ☎ 813/ 864-8312.

Amtrak (☎ 800/872-7245) offers a 15% discount off the lowest available coach fare (with certain travel restrictions) to people 62 and over.

Greyhound also offers discounted fares for senior citizens. Call your local Greyhound office for details.

FOR FAMILIES   No city in the world is more geared to family travel than Orlando. In addition to its theme parks, Orlando's recreational facilities provide abundant opportunities for family fun. Every restaurant in town has a low-priced children's menu, and many hotels maintain children's activity centers (see chapter 5 for details). Keep an eye out for coupons that offer discounts on meals and attractions. The Calendar section in Friday's edition of the local newspaper, *The Orlando Sentinel,* often contains coupons and special deals. Many local restaurants, especially those in tourist areas, offer great discounts that are yours for the clipping. Check the information you receive from the Convention & Visitors Bureau. *Central Florida Family* magazine and *Black Family Today* both highlight family-friendly—often free—festivals and other events in the Orlando area.

Disney–MGM Studios and **Universal Studios Escape** offer parent-swap programs in which parents with children can switch off watching the young ones while the other parent rides. In both parks, ask attendants at the specific attraction what you need to do in order to swap.

Here are a few general suggestions for making traveling with kids easier:

Are Your Kids Old Enough?   I know everybody does it, but you should think long and hard before bringing infants or toddlers to the overcrowded, often overheated world of the theme parks. How well will very young children enjoy, or for that matter remember, a trip that will cost you a considerable amount of money? When pondering this question, temper your vision of that adorable photo with Mickey, with the sweaty image of hours standing in packed lines while waiting to get on rides, into rest rooms, food lines, monorails, etc.

Planning Ahead   Make reservations for "character breakfasts" at Disney when you make your hotel reservations. Also, in any park, check the daily schedule for character appearances, and make sure the kids know when they are going to get to meet their heroes. (This is often a kiddy highlight.) This advance preparation will help you avoid running after every character you see. All the parks—including Universal and Sea World—post designated areas and times for meet and greet opportunities with characters. Some of these times are listed on the park map; others are listed on boards near the entrance. The "in" thing is getting character autographs, so you may want to purchase an autograph book at home instead of buying a more expensive one in the park.

Packing   Although your home may be toddler-proof, hotel accommodations are not. Bring blank plugs to cover outlets, and whatever else is necessary to prevent an accident from occurring in your room. Locals can spot tourists by their bright red, just-toasted glow; both parents and children should heed this reminder: *Don't*

Kid-Friendly Tours

Sea World earns its reputation as a park that makes education fun with a variety of tours. One of the most interesting is the **Polar Expedition Guided Tour.** This hour-long tour provides kids with a chance to visit with Sea World's new sea lion stars, Klondike and Snow. It also offers a behind-the-scenes look at penguins. Another kid-friendly tour is Sharks! This hour-long tour provides a backstage view of sharks at "Terrors of the Deep," and a better understanding of how Sea World aquarists care for sharks and stingrays. Both tours are generally suitable for kids of all ages, although smaller children may be a little leery of an up-close encounter with a shark. Both tours are booked on a first-come, first-serve basis, so make reservations at the Guided Tour Information desk when you enter the park. The cost is $6.95 for adults and $5.95 for children, plus park admission. Tours are scheduled throughout the day. For more information call ☎ **407/ 363-2380.**

Camp Sea World: During June, July, and August, Sea World's Education department also offers more than 200 summer camp classes, including sleepover programs and courses for families. For information, or reservations, call ☎ **407/ 363-2380.**

At Walt Disney World, half-day **Disney Day Camp** excursions are divided into two groups, one for children ages 7 to 10, and the other group of programs is for children 11 to 15. From exploring special effects at Disney–MGM Studios, to experiencing the wonders of China at Epcot, these tours provide a good opportunity for kids to interact with their peers, while providing parents with a little time alone. Disney offers two programs each day, the first from 8am to noon, the second from 1:30 to 5pm. A half-day program costs $59, and a whole day— which includes two programs—costs $89. A box lunch is provided for an additional charge. Theme park admission is not required to take part in a program.

The only tour available at Animal Kingdom is the **Backstage Safari** for ages 16 and older. This 3½-hour tour, costing $60, provides an up-close look at the care and feeding of Disney's wildlife. Tours focus on the animal pens, the nursery, and the feeding areas. The tours are held Monday, Wednesday, and Friday, and advanced registration is required. For information call ☎ **407/939-8687.** Tours are also included in some of Disney's comprehensive vacation packages.

forget the sunscreen. If you forget to bring sunscreen with you, it is available at convenience stores and drugstores. Some shops at most of the theme parks also carry sunscreen; ask at the visitor's information desk where it can be purchased. Young children should be slathered, even if they're in a stroller, and be sure to pack a hat for infants and toddlers. Adults and children should also drink plenty of water to avoid dehydration.

Accommodations   Children under 12, and in many cases even older, stay free in their parents' rooms in most hotels. Look for establishments that have pools and other recreational facilities. If you don't want to rent a car and aren't staying at Disney, then International Drive is the place to be. Public buses run here frequently, hotels often offer family discounts, and some provide free shuttle service to the homes of the Mouse, the Whale, and King Kong.

Ground Rules   Set up ground rules before leaving home about issues such as bedtime and spending money on souvenirs. Turn the bottom drawer of a dresser into the place to keep toys from home and newly acquired treasures. This keeps the mess down and lets the kids have easy access to their stuff without having to bother you.

At the Parks   All park maps explain the height restrictions for certain attractions or identify rides that may unsettle young children. Do yourself and your kids a favor by knowing these restrictions before you get in line. These rules are not bent, no matter how much your child may cry. Also heed those "too intense for children" warnings. One bad trip down a darkened tunnel can make your toddler apprehensive and cranky all day, even on rides that should be fun. Read over our suggestions on that front; some parks underestimate the impact dark, scary rides can have on children.

Take a Break   The Disney parks, Universal Studios, and Sea World all have stylized play areas offering parents and kids a rest. Schedule time to take advantage of these facilities. Since most of these kid zones include toys involving water, and all the parks have major water-related attractions, you'd be smart to pack a change of clothes for the whole family. Rent a locker and store the spare duds until you need them. During the summer months, the Florida humidity can keep you feeling soggy all day, so you'll appreciate the fresh clothing.

Show Time   Schedule an inside, air-conditioned show for mid-afternoon. You may even get your littlest tikes to nap in the darkened theater. For all shows, arrive at least 20 minutes early, but not so early that the kids go nuts waiting. Most of the big shows have arena-style seating and huge stages, so there are no bad seats in the house.

Snack Times   When dreaming of your vacation, you probably don't envision hours spent standing in lines and waiting, and waiting. It helps to store some lightweight snacks in an easy-to-carry backpack, especially when traveling with small children. This may save you some headaches, and will certainly save you some money.

Bring Your Own?   Unless you are unusually attached to your stroller, or it is specially designed for triplets, it's better to use one provided by the park. That way you avoid hauling yours to and from the car, and on and off the trams, trains, or monorails. A portable "umbrella" stroller could be an option. For small children, you may want to bring a snugly, sling, or backpack-type carrier for use in traveling to and from the parking lots, and while you're in line for attractions.

FOR PEOPLE IN RECOVERY   Those friends of Bill W. and members of other 12-step programs can call the **Central Florida Intergroup of Alcoholics Anonymous** (☎ **407/521-0012**). This is the local AA hot line, and it's manned by volunteers 24 hours a day. Please be considerate, however, and don't call at 3am in the morning just for tourist information. They can provide information, including directions, to meetings in Orange and Seminole counties, as well as those in tourist areas. Disney does not allow meetings on the property, so you will need a car, or lots of cash for cab fare, to get to a meeting. Hot-line workers can also provide numbers for other local 12-step programs, such as Narcotics Anonymous, Al-Anon, and Overeaters Anonymous, groups that also have information hot lines, but generally don't operate 24 hours.

Those looking to party away from the sometimes alcohol-drenched tourist areas can have an alcohol-free night at **Club Soda,** 6341 N. Orange Blossom Trail, about 35 miles from the heart of tourist central, near the intersection of Clarcona–Ocoee Road and Orange Blossom Trail. For information call ☎ **407/523-1556.** There is sometimes live entertainment or theme nights, such as karaoke.

FOR GAY & LESBIAN TRAVELERS   The popularity of Orlando with gay and lesbian travelers is evidenced by the expansion of the traditional June 6 "Gay Day" celebration at Disney World into a "Gay Weekend," including events at Universal Studios and Sea World. In 1998, the ever-growing event attracted attention of a different kind when dozens of conservative Christian protesters descended on the area. (The promised confrontation with gays and lesbians in Magic Kingdom fizzled when four would-be crusaders entered Magic Kingdom, only to be ignored by the overwhelmingly gay crowd.)

Gay Day has evolved into a "Gay Weekend" with Universal Studios, Sea World, and Church Street Station hosting special events. ("Gay Day," unofficially held at Walt Disney World since the early 1990s, has drawn as many as 40,000 folks. Parkgoers are supposed to wear red on Gay Day to signify their support of the gay and lesbian community.) You can get information on the event online by accessing **www.gayday.com.**

For information about events for that weekend, or throughout the year, contact **Gay, Lesbian & Bisexual Community Services of Central Florida** by writing 714 E. Colonial Dr., Orlando, FL 32804; ☎ **407/425-4527.** Ask for a welcome packet. This will include the latest issue of the *Triangle,* a monthly newspaper dedicated to gay and lesbian issues, and a calendar of events pertaining to the gay and lesbian community. This is not a tourist-specific packet, but it does contain valuable information. Check out the advertisement for nightclubs catering to a gay and lesbian crowd. For information on the *Triangle* specifically—for example, where it can be picked up in tourist areas—call ☎ **407/849-0099.** *Watermark* is another gay-friendly publication, and it can be found in many bookstores.

Orlando is a Southern town, but the entertainment industry and the theme parks have helped in the building of a strong gay and lesbian community. Same-sex dancing is acceptable at most of the clubs at WDW's Pleasure Island, especially the large, crowded Mannequins. (Really, who can tell who is dancing with whom most of the time?) Many of Universal's CityWalk establishments are similarly gender blind. The tenor of crowds can change, depending on what tour is in town, so respect your own intuition.

Same-sex dancing is not expressly forbidden at Church Street Station, but the biggest dance hall is a country honky-tonk frequented by some real, local cowboys, and this *is* Dixieland. I've never heard of anyone being asked to leave for dancing, but the crowd probably won't make for your most comfortable two-step. (There's lots of line dancing, though.)

There are a few exclusively gay or lesbian bars and clubs in Orlando, and they're described in chapter 10.

5 Getting There

BY PLANE

THE MAJOR AIRLINES   There are about 40 scheduled airlines, and 38 charter services, serving more than 22 million passengers a year. **Delta** (☎ 800/221-1212) has the most flights—over 25%—into Orlando International Airport. It offers service from 200 cities, and has a Fantastic Flyer program for kids. **Delta Express** offers direct service from 14 cities and also has the Fantastic Flyer program for kids.

Other carriers include **Air Jamaica** (☎ 800/523-5585), **America West** (☎ 800/235-9292), **American** (☎ 800/433-7300), **American Trans Air** (☎ 800/293-6194), **Canadian Airlines** (☎ 800/426-3838), **Continental** (☎ 800/231-0856), **Midway** (☎ 800/446-4392), **Northwest** (☎ 800/225-2525), **SunJet**

(☎ 800/4SUNJET), **TWA** (☎ 800/221-2000), **United** (☎ 800/241-6522), and **US Airways** (☎ 800/428-4322).

Several so-called no-frills airlines—low fares but no meals or other amenities—fly to Florida. The biggest is ○ **Southwest Airlines** (☎ 800/435-9792; www.iflyswa.com), which has flights from many U.S. cities to Fort Lauderdale, Jacksonville, Orlando, and Tampa. Other discount airlines flying to Florida include **Kiwi International** (☎ 800/538-5494) and **Tower Air** (☎ 800/348-6937).

FINDING THE BEST AIRFARE There's no shortage of **discounted and promotional fares** to Florida. November, December, and January often see fare wars that can result in savings of 50% or more. Watch for advertisements in your local newspaper and on TV, call the airlines, or check out their Web sites. (See Appendix B for Web addresses and phone numbers.) Here are some tips for discovering the lowest airfares:

- Ask the airlines for their lowest fares, and ask if it's cheaper to book in advance, fly in midweek, or stay over a Saturday night. Don't stop at the 7-day advance purchase; ask how much the 14- and 30-day plans cost. These fares can be as much as 75% lower than fares booked at the last minute. Decide when you want to go before you call, since many of the best deals are nonrefundable.

- The more flexible you can be about your travel dates and length of stay, the more money you are likely to save. Flying at off times (for instance, at night) when planes are less likely to be full will usually save you money.

- Visit a large travel agency to investigate all options. Sometimes a good agent knows about fares you won't find on your own. Major Internet providers, such as AOL, offer travel sections that can provide pricing comparisons. You can book tickets for some airlines via the Internet, but a travel agent may still be a better bet.

- No-frills airlines have reduced their price advantage, but some **charter flights** still go to Florida, especially during the winter season and particularly from Canada, such as **Air Transat** (☎ 800/470-1011) and **Canada 3000** (☎ 800/993-4378). They often cost less than regularly scheduled flights, but they are very complicated. It's best to go to a good travel agent and ask him or her to find one for you and to explain the disadvantages as well as the advantages.

- Also known as bucket shops, **consolidators** are a good place to find low fares. Consolidators buy seats in bulk from the airlines and then sell them back to the public at prices below even the airlines' discounted rates. Their small, boxed ads usually run in the Sunday travel sections of major newspapers at the bottom of the page. Before you pay, however, ask for a confirmation number from the consolidator and then call the airline itself to confirm your seat. Be prepared to book your ticket with a different consolidator—there are many to choose from—if the airline can't confirm your reservation. Also be aware that bucket shop tickets are usually non-refundable or rigged with stiff cancellation penalties, often as high as 50% to 75% of the ticket price.

Among the consolidators, **Council Travel** (☎ 800/226-8624; www.counciltravel.com) and **STA Travel** (☎ 800/781-4040; www.sta.travel.com) cater especially to young travelers, but their bargain basement prices are available

Travel Tip

A great Web site, **www.vacationpackager.com,** allows you to shop for, and to compare, dozens of vacation packages at once. It could save you time and money.

to people of all ages. **Travel Bargains** (☎ **800/AIR-FARE;** www.1800airfare. com) was formerly owned by TWA but now offers the deepest discounts on many other airlines, with a 4-day advance purchase. Other reliable consolidators include **1-800-FLY-CHEAP** (www.1800flycheap.com); **TFI Tours International** (☎ **800-745-8000** or 212/736-1140), which serves as a clearinghouse for unused seats; or "rebators" such as **Travel Avenue** (☎ **800/333-3335** or 312/876-1116) and the **Smart Traveller** (☎ **800/448-3338** in the U.S. or 305/448-3338), which rebate part of their commissions to you.

- Try joining a travel club such as **Moment's Notice** (☎ **718/234-6295**) or **Sears Discount Travel Club** (☎ **800/433-9383**, or 800/255-1487 to join); they supply unsold tickets at discounted prices. You pay an annual membership fee to get the club's hot line number. Of course, you're limited to what's available, so you have to be flexible. You may not even have to join these clubs to get the deals, however, because some airlines now unload unsold seats directly through their Web sites.

- It's possible to get some great deals not only on airfare, but on hotels and car rentals as well, via the **Internet.** Among the leading travel sites are: **Arthur Frommer's Budget Travel Online** (www.frommers.com); **Microsoft Expedia** (www.expedia.com); **Travelocity** (www.travelocity.com); **The Trip** (www.thetrip. com); and **Smarter Living** (www.smarterliving.com), which offers a newsletter service that will send you a weekly customized e-mail summarizing the discount fares available from your departure city.

For more information on finding travel bargains on the Web see "Frommer's Online Directory" in the back of this book.

ORLANDO'S AIRPORT **Orlando International Airport** (☎ **407/825-2001**) offers direct or nonstop service from 70 U.S. cities and about two dozen international destinations, serving over 26 million passengers each year. It's a thoroughly modern and user-friendly facility with restaurants, shops, a 450-room on-premises Hyatt Regency Hotel, and centrally located information kiosks. All major car-rental companies are located at or near the airport; see "Getting Around" in chapter 4 for more information on car rentals.

Airport Transportation The airport is 25 miles from Walt Disney World, and 20 minutes from downtown. **Mears Transportation Group** (☎ **407/423-5566**) has shuttle vans that ply the route from the airport (you board outside the baggage claim area) to all Disney resorts and official hotels, as well as most other area properties. Their comfortable, air-conditioned vehicles operate around the clock, departing every 15 to 25 minutes in either direction. Rates vary with your destination. Round-trip cost for adults is $21 between the airport and downtown Orlando or International Drive, $25 for Walt Disney World/Lake Buena Vista or Kissimmee/Hwy. 192. Children ages 4 to 11 pay $14 to downtown and $17 to WDW. Children 3 and under ride free.

Driving to Walt Disney World To get from the airport to the attractions area, take the **North** exit out of the airport to **528 West.** Follow signs to **I-4;** it will take about 20 minutes to get to Walt Disney World if the traffic isn't too heavy. When you get to I-4, head **west** toward the attractions.

Note: It's always a good idea when you make your reservations to ask about transportation options between the airport and your hotel. Also be sure to ask how far you have to travel to pick up and drop off your car. Some lots are located miles from the airport and, when you add up the time spent waiting in line and catching shuttles, returning your car can turn into a half-day trip.

Delta, Walt Disney World's official airline, has stopped allowing families with children to board first on its Orlando flights. It's fairer to the other passengers, and better for the kids, who won't be cooped up as long.

BY CAR

Orlando is 436 miles from Atlanta; 1,312 miles from Boston; 1,120 miles from Chicago; 1,009 miles from Cleveland; 1,170 miles from Dallas; 1,114 miles from Detroit; 1,088 miles from New York City, and 1,282 miles from Toronto.

From Atlanta, take I-75 south to the Florida Turnpike to I-4 west.

From points northeast, take I-95 south to I-4 west.

From Chicago, take I-65 south to Nashville and then I-24 south to I-75 south to the Florida Turnpike to I-4 west.

From Cleveland, take I-77 south to Columbia, South Carolina, and then I-26 east to I-95 south to I-4 west.

From Dallas, take I-20 east to I-49 south to I-10 east to I-75 south to the Florida Turnpike to I-4 west.

From Detroit, take I-75 south to the Florida Turnpike to I-4 west.

From Toronto, take Canadian Route 401 south to Queen Elizabeth Way south to I-90 (New York State Thruway) east to I-87 (New York State Thruway) south to I-95 over the George Washington Bridge, and continue south on I-95 to I-4 west.

AAA (☎ 800/222-4357) members and some other automobile-club members can call local offices for maps and optimum driving directions.

BY TRAIN

Amtrak trains (☎ 800/872-7245) pull into stations at 1400 Sligh Blvd., between Columbia and Miller streets in downtown Orlando (about 23 miles from Walt Disney World), and 111 Dakin Ave., at Thurman Street in Kissimmee (about 15 miles from Walt Disney World). There are also stops in Winter Park, about 10 miles north of downtown Orlando, at 150 W. Morse Blvd., and in Sanford, about 23 miles northeast of downtown Orlando. The Sanford Station, located at 600 Persimmon Ave., is also the end terminal for the Auto Train.

FARES   As with airline fares, you can sometimes get discounts if you book far in advance. There may be some restrictions on travel dates for discounted fares, mostly around very busy holiday times. Traveling into Orlando instead of Winter Park, just about 10 miles away, will save you some money. Amtrak also offers money-saving packages—including hotel accommodations (some at WDW resorts), car rentals, tours, and more—with your train fare (☎ 800/321-8684). Zoned fares, available for 45 days to U.S. residents, range from about $400 during peak season (from Jan to May and from July to mid-Sept) to about $320 during off-peak season (June and from mid-Sept to Dec).

AMTRAK'S AUTO TRAIN   Amtrak's Auto Train offers you the convenience of bringing your car to Florida without having to drive it there. The Auto Train begins in Lorton, Virginia—about a 4-hour drive from New York, 2 hours from Philadelphia—and terminates at Sanford, Florida, about 23 miles northeast of Orlando. Once again, reserve early for the lowest fares. The Auto Train departs Lorton and Sanford daily at 4:30pm, arriving at its destination the next morning at 9am. *Note:* You have to arrive 1 or 2 hours before the departure time, so your car can be boarded. Call ☎ 800/872-7245 for details.

BY BUS

Greyhound buses connect the entire country with Orlando. They pull into a terminal at 555 N. Magruder Blvd. (John Young Parkway), between West Colonial Drive and Winter Garden Road, a few miles west of downtown Orlando (☎ **407/292-3422**), or in Kissimmee, they stop at 16 N. Orlando Ave., between Emmett and Mabbette streets, about 14 miles from Walt Disney World (☎ **407/847-3911**). There is van transport from the Kissimmee terminal to most area hotels and motels. From Orlando, you can call for a **Mears shuttle** van (☎ **407/423-5566**), which will cost $13 to $14 one-way to a Walt Disney World–area hotel, $10 for children ages 4 to 11, free for those under 3 (round-trip fares are less). For the return trip, call Mears from your hotel 24 hours in advance. A taxi to Walt Disney World–area hotels will cost about $40. Greyhound's fare structure tends to be complex, but the good news is that when you call to make a reservation, the agent will always give you the lowest-fare options. Once again, advance-purchase fares booked 3 to 21 days prior to travel represent vast savings. Check your phone book for a local Greyhound listing or call ☎ **800/231-2222**.

6 Money-Saving Packages

Frankly, the number, and the diversity, of package tours to Orlando is staggering. But significant savings are available for those willing to do the research. Best bet: Stop at a sizable travel agency and pick up brochures from several companies. Pore over them at home and compare the offerings to find the optimum package for your trip. Also, obtain the *Walt Disney World Vacations* brochure (see details at the beginning of this chapter), which lists the company's own packages. Try to find a package that meets, rather than exceeds, your needs; there's no sense in paying for elements you won't use. Also, read the advantages given to Disney resort guests in chapter 5 carefully; some packages list as selling points services that are automatically available to every Walt Disney World guest.

Although not on the same scale as Disney's options, Universal offers its own travel packages that can include resort stays, VIP access to the park, and discounts to other non-Disney parks. They also offer "fun and sun" packages that include beach trips to Tampa. Some packages do include travel and transportation. The packages are expanding with the ever-growing Universal property, so check out what is available.

You can contact **Universal Studio Vacations** at ☎ **888/322-5537** or 407/224-7000, or check their packages online at **www.usevacations.com.**

Sea World also offers 3-night packages that include hotel accommodations at a handful of Orlando hotels, car rental, and tickets to Sea World and, in some cases, other parks. You can get information at ☎ **800/423-8368,** or online at **www.seaworld.com/vacation/orlando.**

Examples of airline-run packages are the **Delta Dream Vacations,** in several price ranges. These packages may include round-trip air transport, accommodations (including state and hotel-room tax, and baggage gratuities), an air-conditioned rental car with unlimited mileage or round-trip airport transfer, a "Magic Passport" that provides unlimited admission to all Walt Disney World parks for the length of your stay, and a choice of nine items from Disney's Flex Feature list. Those who stay off Disney property on a Delta package can also gain early entrance into certain parks on certain days. In packages utilizing Walt Disney World Resorts, you get all the advantages given to guests at these properties (see chapter 5 for details). There are three price options available—standard, ultimate, and preferred. The prices vary widely depending on the property you choose, your departure destination, and the time of year. To ascertain the availability and cost of a Delta Disney package, go to **www.deltavacations.com/disney.**

Delta also has Orlando packages for which WDW tickets and resorts are optional. For details, call ☎ **800/872-7786.**

American Express Vacations (☎ **800/241-1700;** www.americanexpress.com) is the "official card of Walt Disney World." Card members can book reservations at a Disney resort, and receive a variety of perks, including discounts on merchandise, dinner shows, and certain Disney-related tours.

Continental Airlines Vacations (☎ **800/525-0280** for general information; for Spanish-speaking operators 800/537-9277; for international numbers 800/231-0856) offers a variety of packages, including airfare, car rental, and hotel stays at numerous central Florida hotels, and five moderately priced properties at Walt Disney World. The airlines frequent-flyer program can be applied to some packages, and you can make reservations with or without air service. To book online, head to **www.coolvacations.com.**

Kingdom Vacations (☎ **800/626-8747**), the national preferred tour operator of AAA, offers numerous deals and packages to Orlando.

Marriott Villas Vacations (☎ **888/255-5338;** www.marriottvillas.com) features packages that include round-trip air reservations on Delta or Continental, accommodations, and a rental car. The hotels are more upscale, condo-type accommodations. You can also use the service to make reservations without airfare.

SunStyle (☎ **888-786-7895**) is a wholesale tour operator that offers a variety of packages targeting not only Disney and Disney properties, but also Universal Studios Escape and Sea World, and the hotels located near those parks. You can also book airfare and car rental through this agency.

Touraine Travel (☎ **800/967-5583**) also offers a wide variety of tour packages to Disney and Disney properties, Universal Studios Escape, and Sea World.

Additional sources for airfare-inclusive packages are **US Airways Vacations** (☎ **800/455-0123;** www.usairwaysvacations.com), and **American Airlines Vacations** (☎ **800/321-2121;** www.americanair.com).

7 Weddings at Walt Disney World

Want to fly down the aisle on Aladdin's magic carpet? Be pulled in a glass coach by six white horses? Have Mickey and Minnie greet guests at the reception? Take the plunge, literally and figuratively, on the Twilight Zone Tower of Terror?

If you've always dreamed of meeting Prince Charming and then having a fairy-tale wedding, the folks at Disney are happy to oblige—for a price. Recognizing Disney World's popularity as a honeymoon destination, Disney, in 1995, cut out the middleman, and officially went into the wedding business.

Disney's first move was building a multimillion-dollar nondenominational chapel in the middle of the Seven Seas Lagoon. Its next step was letting the world know the Disney wedding chapel was open for business. The first nuptials were televised live on Lifetime television. (Construction was still in progress at the chapel, so the bride and groom wore white hard hats.) About 1,700 couples were married that first year, and now thousands of couples mix matrimony with Disney magic at the pavilion, which resembles a Victorian summerhouse.

An intimate gathering for two runs about $2,000. The average Disney wedding costs $19,000 and is attended by 100 people (Prince Charming not included). People from as far away as the Netherlands have traveled to Orlando for sometimes unusual celebrations to recognize their lifetime commitment to one another. One couple had every guest wear Mickey Mouse ears to the ceremony. Another exchanged Donald and Daisy caps instead of wedding rings. A third walked out of the church to "Zip-a-dee-doo-dah," and one blushing bride topped her veil with Mickey's famous ears. Those are just the examples Disney is willing to promote.

Certainly with the only limits on the festivities being imagination and money, there have been wackier weddings. From rented coachmen to topiaries in the shape of Pluto, Disney serves up whichever Disney reference or character the couple desires, even if it is "Goofy." For further details on **Disney weddings** (and honeymoons, of course), call ☎ **407/828-3400.**

8 Disney (& Other) Cruise Packages

Construction delays pushed back the inaugural voyage of the *Disney Magic,* the Walt Disney company's first venture onto the high seas.

The ship, constructed in Italy, has been lauded for its attention-to-design details, and for providing a complete Disney experience. Construction problems also delayed the launch of the *Magic*'s sister ship, the *Disney Wonder,* until the fall of 1999.

Both ships offer a wide variety of items that will occupy guests' time, including dining, nightlife, shows, and activity packages designed specifically for adults, kids, or teens. There are numerous restaurants and clubs aboard, and many areas on the ship are devoted to children and teenagers. There is even a stop at a company-owned island, Castaway Cay, a 1,000-acre playground for cruise guests.

Seven-day cruise packages include 3 or 4 days afloat, with the rest of the week divided among the landlocked properties and the theme parks. Prices range from $1,295 to $4,225 per adult, depending on the level of accommodations. Some of the land/sea packages include round-trip air transportation, unlimited admission to the Disney parks, Pleasure Island, the water parks, and Disney's Wide World of Sports. Cruise-only options range from $799 to $2,789 for a 3-day cruise, and $909 to $2,999 for a 4-day cruise.

Cruises depart from Port Canaveral, about an hour by car from Orlando. Book well in advance. Each ship holds up to 1,760 passengers, but the cruises are proving popular with the legions of true fans looking for something new. For information call ☎ **407/566-3500,** or look at the cruise line's Web site at **www.disneycruise.com.**

Premier Cruise Lines (the "Big Red Boat"), previously the official Disney cruise line, continues to offer 3- and 4-night luxury ocean cruises to the Bahamas (Nassau and Port Lucaya) in conjunction with 3- or 4-day Orlando theme-park vacations. Cruises depart from, and return to, Port Canaveral, located about an hour from Walt Disney World. You can add the island segment before or after your stay in Orlando. Since Disney began making its own splash, Premier is focusing on other Orlando-area attractions, and you'll probably find better deals here if you're interested in visiting Universal, Sea World, and other non-Disney area attractions. Looney Tunes characters (Bugs Bunny, Tweety, Daffy Duck) are your on-board hosts. Package prices include all meals on board ship, an Alamo rental car with unlimited mileage for 7 days, round-trip bus transportation to/from Orlando, and admission to various attractions. Rates depend on your stateroom and hotel category, and the season during which you're traveling. At this writing, packages range from $899 to $1,899 per person. For information, call ☎ **800/990-7770.**

Fun Fact

Over 950 feet in length the *Disney Magic* is longer than the Eiffel Tower and its smokestacks play that Disney favorite, "When You Wish Upon a Star."

All ships are equipped with swimming pools, Jacuzzis, health clubs, jogging tracks, movie theaters, beauty salons, casinos, bars/lounges, video-game arcades, shops, and nightclubs.

Tip: Nothing spoils a cruise vacation quite like a tropical storm and 20-foot swells. You might want to avoid the height of hurricane season, from September through mid-November. Take it from someone who spent 36 hours of her honeymoon in bed—seasick—the lower hurricane season rates are not worth the upheavals. If you do go during hurricane season, be sure to pack some anti-motion sickness medicine, or check out the seasick remedies, such as a shot or skin patch, available on board.

Other cruise options include:

Cape Canaveral Cruise Line   Specializes in short, inexpensive cruises geared toward first-time cruisers. It offers several theme park/cruise vacation packages. Cruise-only prices range from $199 to $369 for a 2-night cruise, and from $369 to $669 for a 4-night cruise. Land/sea packages range from $289 to $609 for a 2-night cruise, and $459 to $919 for a 4-night cruise. For information call ☎ **800/910-SHIP** or 407/783-4052.

Carnival Cruise Line   Specializes in 3- and 4-day cruises to the Bahamas. Prices for a 3-day cruise range from $609 to $1039 per person. Prices for a 4-day cruise run from $699 to $1279 per person. For more information call ☎ **800/227-6482.**

For Foreign Visitors 3

This chapter will provide some specifics about getting to Orlando as economically as possible from overseas, plus some helpful information about how things are done in the United States—from mailing a postcard to making a phone call.

1 Preparing for Your Trip

VISITOR INFORMATION IN THE UNITED KINGDOM

There is an **Orlando Tourism Office** in London. For information from that office, write to 18–24 Westbourne Grove, London, England, W25RH (☎ **44/171-243-8072;** fax 44/171-243-8487). You can also e-mail that office at **06211.1754@compuserve.com.**

ENTRY REQUIREMENTS

Immigration laws are a hot political issue in the United States these days, and the following requirements may have changed somewhat by the time you plan your trip. Check at any U.S. embassy or consulate for current information and requirements. You can also plug into the **U.S. State Department's** Web site at **http://state.gov.**

VISAS Canadian citizens may enter the United States without visas; they need only proof of residence.

The U.S. State Department has a **Visa Waiver Pilot Program** allowing citizens of certain countries to enter the United States without a visa for leisure or business stays of up to 90 days. At press time, these included Andorra, Argentina, Australia, Austria, Belgium, Brunei, Denmark, Finland, France, Germany, Iceland, Ireland, Italy, Japan, Liechtenstein, Luxembourg, Monaco, the Netherlands, New Zealand, Norway, San Marino, Slovenia, Spain, Sweden, Switzerland, and the United Kingdom. Citizens of these countries need only a valid passport and a round-trip air or cruise ticket in their possession upon arrival.

Citizens of these visa-exempt countries who first enter the United States may then visit Mexico, Canada, Bermuda, and/or the Caribbean Islands and then re-enter the States, by any mode of transportation, without needing a visa. Further information is available from any U.S. embassy or consulate. See "Fast Facts: For the Foreign Traveler," later in this chapter.

Walt Disney World Services for International Visitors

Walt Disney World, which welcomes thousands of foreign visitors each year, has numerous services designed to meet their needs. Unless otherwise indicated, call ☎ **407/W-DISNEY** (934-7639) for details. Services include:

- A special phone number (☎ **407/824-7900**) to speak with someone in French or Spanish (other languages are sometimes available as well).
- Personal translator units (in French, German, and Spanish) to translate narration at some shows and attractions.
- Detailed guidebooks to the three major parks in Spanish, French, German, Portuguese, and Japanese (available at any guest relations location).
- Currency exchange (see "Money" section below).
- World Key Terminals at Epcot offer basic park information and assistance with dining reservations in Spanish.
- Resort phones equipped with software that expedites international calls by allowing guests to dial direct to foreign destinations.

Citizens of countries other than those listed above, including citizens of Australia, must have two documents: a valid **passport,** with an expiration date at least 6 months later than the scheduled end of the visit to the United States; and a **tourist visa,** available without charge from the nearest U.S. consulate.

Obtaining a Visa   To obtain a visa, a traveler must submit a completed application form (either in person or by mail) with a 1½-inch-square photo and demonstrate binding ties to a residence abroad.

You can usually obtain a visa immediately or within 24 hours, but it may take longer during the summer rush from June to August. If you cannot go in person, contact the nearest U.S. embassy or consulate for directions on applying by mail. Your travel agent or airline office may also be able to provide you with visa applications and instructions. The U.S. consulate or embassy that issues your visa will determine whether you will be issued a multiple- or single-entry visa and any restrictions regarding the length of your stay.

Immigration Questions   Telephone operators will answer your inquiries regarding U.S. immigration policies or laws at the **Immigration and Naturalization Service's Customer Information Center** (☎ **800/375-5283**). Representatives are available from 9am to 3pm, Monday through Friday. The INS also runs a 24-hour automated information service, for commonly asked questions, at ☎ **800/755-0777.**

Medical Requirements   No inoculations are needed to enter the United States unless you are coming from, or have stopped over in, areas known to be suffering from epidemics, particularly cholera or yellow fever.

If you have a disease requiring treatment with medications containing narcotics, or with drugs requiring a syringe, carry a valid signed prescription from your physician to allay any suspicions that you are smuggling drugs.

For **HIV-positive visitors,** requirements for entering the United States are somewhat vague and change frequently. INS may stop you because you look sick or because you are carrying AIDS/HIV medicine.

If INS suspects you are HIV positive, it will deny you a visa unless you ask for a special waiver for visitors. This waiver is for people visiting the United States for a short time, to attend a conference, for instance, to visit close relatives, or to receive medical treatment. It can be a confusing situation, so for up-to-the-minute information concerning HIV-positive travelers, contact the Centers for Disease Control's **National Center for HIV** (☎ 404/332-4559; www.hivatis.org) or the **Gay Men's Health Crisis** (☎ 212/367-1000; **www.gmhc.org**).

PASSPORTS   All visitors to the United States must have a valid passport. See below for details on how to obtain one. Safeguard your passport in an inconspicuous, inaccessible place like a money belt. If you lose it, visit your country's nearest consulate as soon as possible for a replacement.

Canadian residents can pick up a passport application at one of 28 regional passport offices or most travel agencies. The passport is valid for 5 years and costs $60. Children under 16 may be included on a parent's passport, but need their own to travel unaccompanied by the parent. Applications, which must be accompanied by two identical passport-sized photographs and proof of Canadian citizenship, are available at travel agencies throughout Canada or from the central **Passport Office, Department of Foreign Affairs and International Trade,** Ottawa, Ont. K1A 0G3 (☎ **800/567-6868; www.dfait-maeci.gc.ca/passport**). Processing takes 5 to 10 days if you apply in person, or about 3 weeks by mail.

Residents of the **United Kingdom** can pick up an application for a regular 10-year passport (the Visitor's Passport has been abolished) at the nearest passport office, major post office, or travel agency. You can also contact the London Passport Office at ☎ **0171/271-3000** or search its Web site at **www.open.gov.uk/ukpass/ukpass.htm.** Passports are £21 for adults and £11 for children under 16.

Irish citizens can apply for a 10-year passport, costing IR£45, at the Passport Office, Setanta Centre, Molesworth Street, Dublin 2 (☎ **01/671-1633; www.irlgov.ie/iveagh/foreignaffairs/services**). Those under age 18 and over 65 must apply for a IR£10, 3-year passport. You can also apply at 1A South Mall, Cork (☎ **021/272-525**), or over the counter at most main post offices.

Australian residents can apply at their local post office or passport office or search the government Web site at **www.dfat.gov.au/passports/.** Passports for adults are A$126 and for those under 18 A$63.

CUSTOMS REQUIREMENTS   Every visitor over 21 years of age may bring in free of duty: 1 liter of wine or hard liquor; 200 cigarettes or 100 cigars (but no cigars from Cuba) or 3 pounds of smoking tobacco; and $100 worth of gifts. These exemptions are offered to travelers who spend at least 72 hours in the United States and who have not claimed them within the preceding 6 months. It is altogether forbidden to bring into the country foodstuffs (particularly cheese, fruit, cooked meats, and canned goods) and plants (vegetables, seeds, tropical plants, and so on). Foreign tourists may bring in or take out up to $10,000 in U.S. or foreign currency with no formalities; larger sums must be declared to Customs upon entering or leaving.

Travel Tip

Never take an opened bottle of perfume or nail polish remover onto an airplane with you. The cabin pressure—especially during a long flight—will cause the liquid to evaporate, and may damage your luggage. The smell won't make you popular with your fellow travelers either.

INSURANCE

There is no national health-care system in the United States. Because the cost of medical care is extremely high, we strongly advise every traveler to secure health coverage before setting out.

You may want to take out a comprehensive travel policy that covers (for a relatively low premium) sickness or injury costs (medical, surgical, and hospital); loss or theft of your baggage; trip-cancellation costs; bail guarantee in case you are arrested; and costs of accident, repatriation, or death. Such packages (for example, "Europ Assistance" in Europe) are sold by automobile clubs and travel agencies at attractive rates. **Worldwide Assistance Services, Inc. (☎ 800/821-2828)** is the agent for Europ Assistance in the United States.

Walk-in medical clinics are available in Orlando, with a visit usually costing under $50, not including prescriptions. **Centra-Care,** operated by a locally run Florida hospital, is a reputable medical facility with more than a dozen locations throughout the Orlando area. For information and the nearest location, call **☎ 407/660-8118.** Be wary of other "doc in a box" facilities. There have been problems with disreputable companies in the last few years operating in tourist areas. Prescriptions can be filled at pharmacies such as **Eckerd** or **Walgreens;** many discount department stores, such as **Kmart** or **Target,** also have pharmacies. And don't worry about being left on a street corner to die in an emergency; the American way is to fix now, and bill the living daylights out of you later.

Insurance for British Travelers   Think carefully before buying insurance from your travel agent in conjunction with your holiday. **Britain's Consumers' Association** recommends that you insist on seeing the policy and reading the fine print before buying travel insurance. **The Association of British Insurers (☎ 0171/600-3333)** gives advice by phone and publishes the free *Holiday Insurance*, a guide to policy provisions and prices. You might also shop around for better deals: Try **Columbus Travel Insurance Ltd. (☎ 0171/375-0011)** or, for students, **Campus Travel (☎ 0171/730-2101).**

Insurance for Canadian Travelers   Canadians should check with their provincial health plan offices or call **HealthCanada (☎ 613/957-2991)** to find out the extent of their coverage and what documentation and receipts they must take home in case they are treated in the United States.

MONEY

CURRENCY & EXCHANGE   The U.S. monetary system is painfully simple: The most common bills (all ugly, all green) are the $1 (colloquially, a "buck"), $5, $10, and $20 denominations. There are also $2 bills (seldom encountered), $50 bills, and $100 bills (the last two are usually not welcome as payment for small purchases). Note that a newly redesigned $100 and $50 bill were introduced in 1996, and a redesigned $20 bill in 1998. Expect to see redesigned $10 and $5 notes in the year 2000. Despite rumors to the contrary, the old-style bills are still legal tender.

There are six denominations of coins: 1¢ (1 cent or "a penny"), 5¢ (5 cents or "a nickel"), 10¢ (10 cents or "a dime"), 25¢ (25 cents or "a quarter"), 50¢ (50 cents or "a half dollar"), and prized, by collectors, the rare $1 piece (the older, large silver dollar and the newer, small Susan B. Anthony coin). A new gold $1 piece will be introduced by the year 2000.

The exchange bureaus so common in Europe are rare even at airports in the United States, and are nonexistent outside major cities. Try to avoid changing foreign money (or traveler's checks that are not denominated in U.S. dollars) at a small-town bank, or even at a branch in a big city.

If you must, you can exchange foreign currency at **Guest Services** windows in all three Disney parks, or at **City Hall** in the Magic Kingdom and **Earth Station** at Epcot. Currency can also be exchanged at Walt Disney World resorts and at the **Sun Bank** across from the Village Marketplace. There are also exchange services at the Orlando International Airport.

TRAVELER'S CHECKS Traveler's checks denominated in U.S. dollars are readily accepted at most hotels, motels, restaurants, and large stores, though they're much less convenient than using cash or a credit card. The best place to change traveler's checks is at a bank; do not bring traveler's checks denominated in foreign currency or you'll lose big.

The three traveler's checks that are most widely recognized—and least likely to be denied—are **Visa, American Express,** and **Thomas Cook.** Be sure to record the numbers of the checks, and keep that information separately in case they get lost or stolen. You should have no trouble using traveler's checks in the theme parks or in areas frequented by tourists, such as International Drive. Remember: You'll need identification, such as a driver's license or passport, to change a traveler's check.

CREDIT CARDS & ATMs Credit cards are the most widely used form of payment in the United States: Visa (BarclayCard in Britain), MasterCard (EuroCard in Europe, Access in Britain, Chargex in Canada), American Express, Diners Club, Discover, and Carte Blanche. You must have a credit card to rent a car. It can also be used as proof of identity (often carrying more weight than a passport), or as a "cash card," enabling you to draw money from banks that accept them. Most establishments will post a list of the credit cards they accept near the cash register. There are a handful of shops that won't take them, so check in advance.

You can save yourself trouble by using plastic rather than cash or traveler's checks in most hotels, motels, restaurants, and retail stores. American Express, MasterCard, and Visa are accepted for admission to the Disney Parks and all restaurants therein. They are also accepted at the other major parks, Sea World, and Universal.

Some automated teller machines will allow you to draw U.S. currency against your bank and credit cards. Check with your bank before leaving home, and remember that you will need your personal identification number (PIN) to do so. Most accept Visa, MasterCard, and American Express, as well as ATM cards from other U.S. banks. Expect to be charged up to $3 per transaction, however, if you're not using your own bank's ATM. (See "Money" in chapter 2 for ATM locations in Orlando.)

SAFETY

While the Walt Disney World/Orlando area in general—and the theme parks in particular—are extremely safe, there are some general precautions you can take to minimize your chances of being the victim of a crime.

GENERAL SAFETY U.S. urban areas tend to be less safe than those in Europe or Japan. Visitors should always stay alert. In spite of some recently publicized carjackings in central Florida, Orlando is not an especially high-crime area; but as with all U.S. cities, visitors should exercise caution. Improved street signage in downtown Orlando has helped to steer visitors away from less-desirable neighborhoods. It is wise to ask the local tourist office, or your car rental agency, if you're in doubt about which neighborhoods are safe. Avoid deserted areas, especially at night. Don't go into any city park at night unless there is an event that attracts crowds. Avoid carrying valuables with you on the street, and don't display expensive cameras or electronic equipment.

Booooommmmm, Booooommmmm

Tourists may find themselves occasionally awakened by window-rattling double booms. Don't worry; it's not part of the rumored American crime culture. It's the space shuttle landing. The twin sonic booms are produced as the shuttle reenters the atmosphere. The loud, thunderous sound can be heard from Cape Canaveral on the coast throughout Orange, Seminole, and Osceola counties, including the tourist areas. When skies are clear, the night launches of the shuttles and larger rockets can be seen throughout central Florida.

Remember also that hotels are open to the public, and in a large hotel, security may not be able to screen everyone entering. Even if you are staying at a resort on Disney property, always lock your room door, even if you are simply going to retrieve ice from the machine; take your key or key card. Don't assume that once inside your hotel you are automatically safe and no longer need to be aware of your surroundings. Confirm the identity of the person knocking before answering the door, even if it is hotel staff. If you have not requested assistance from the front desk, call to confirm that someone associated with the hotel has indeed been sent to your room.

Always park in well-lighted areas and be on the look out for suspicious characters hanging out in the parking lots or hallways. If you have concerns about someone lurking in the parking lot, head toward the hotel lobby or a public area, such as a restaurant or bar, before going to your room. Immediately report the person to a member of the hotel staff.

DRIVING

DRIVER'S LICENSES   Most foreign driver's licenses are recognized in the U.S., although you may want to get an international driver's license if your home license is not written in English.

ASSISTANCE   There is a toll-free number that can help Orlando visitors by providing general directions. Operators speaking over 100 languages are available. The number is sponsored by the **Florida Tourism Industry Marketing Corporation,** the state tourism promotions board (☎ **800/647-9284**).

SPEED LIMITS   Obey all posted speed limits. On city highways, it is usually 55 or 65 miles per hour. In some rural areas, it goes up to 70 miles per hour. In residential areas, 35 miles per hour is generally safe. The corridor between the attractions and downtown Orlando is rumored to be one of the most heavily ticketed stretches of road in the United States. Traffic fines are *doubled* in construction areas, which, because of the building boom in Orlando, are plentiful.

SEAT BELTS   Seat belts for all passengers—children and adults—are required by Florida law. Children under 3 must ride strapped in a car seat, and police will issue tickets to parents who do not put their children in restraints while driving. Rental-car agencies will provide car seats, some for free.

AIR BAG SAFETY   Children, in or out of car seats, should ride only in the back seats of cars that are equipped with air bags. Air bags have been linked to several deaths involving children in the United States. Air bags are a standard feature on most new model cars.

DRINKING & DRIVING   Law enforcement frowns on drunk drivers, and in Florida the rules are strict, and strictly enforced. If you are planning to drink alcohol, especially after an exhausting day in the parks, designate a sober driver or find an alternative means of transportation. Some nightclubs provide free soft drinks to designated drivers. It doesn't hurt to ask.

DEFENSIVE DRIVING   Drive with extra care in tourist-heavy areas. It's not uncommon for cars to make sudden turns or to slow down unexpectedly when reading road signs. People often come to near stops on the highway while attempting to decipher the Disney signs, and they frequently veer across lanes unexpectedly. The tourist areas in Orlando pack a double traffic punch: Workers in a hurry to get to a major employment center, and tourists on vacation. Assume that all other drivers have no idea where they are going—which is often close to the truth—and you should do fine.

One of the best things you can do is to keep a safe distance between you and the car ahead of you. The bench mark is generally a 3-second break. And, while this may sound like common sense, don't read your map while driving. Use this book to determine your exit, or call ahead to your destination to find out which highway exit you should take. Stay in the far right lane, the slow lane, when you are nearing your exit.

DRIVING IN THE RAIN   Watch for a hazardous condition called "black ice," where oil on the road creates slick patches when the road is wet. Rainstorms in Florida are intense and frequent; they are almost a daily occurrence in summer. Exercise extreme caution and drive in the slow lane—the far right lane—if you are driving significantly slower than the speed limit. Do not pull off onto the shoulder of the road. If visibility is especially poor, pull off at the first exit and wait out the storm, which seldom lasts more than an hour. Florida law requires that drivers turn on their lights during rainstorms.

IF YOU GET LOST   You may have to be content to simply turn around and reenter the highway by accessing the on-ramp near where you just got off. Downtown Orlando is the exception to this rule, but signage has been improved to help direct tourists and visitors from the suburbs. Avoid pulling over to ask directions from people on the street. Instead, stop at a convenience store or gas station and ask the clerk, who should be able to help with basic directions.

SAFETY WHILE DRIVING   Question your rental agency about personal safety, or ask for a brochure of traveler safety tips when you pick up your car. Obtain written directions from the agency, or a map with the route marked in red, showing how to get to your destination. And, if possible, arrive and depart during daylight hours.

Recently, more and more crime has involved cars and drivers. If you drive off a highway into a doubtful neighborhood, leave the area as quickly as possible. If you have an accident, even on the highway, stay in your car with the doors locked until you assess the situation or until the police arrive. If you are bumped from behind on the street or are involved in a minor accident with no injuries and the situation appears to be suspicious, motion to the other driver to follow you. Never get out of your car in such situations. Go directly to the nearest police precinct, well-lighted service station, or all-night store.

If you see someone on the road who indicates a need for help, do not stop. Take note of the location, drive on to a well-lighted area, and telephone the police by dialing ☎ **911.**

Park in well-lighted, well-traveled areas if possible. Always keep your car doors locked, whether attended or unattended. Look around before you get out of your car, and never leave any packages or valuables in sight. Although theme park lots are patrolled, it is best to secure valuables at all times. For extra caution, lock any electronic equipment in the lockers available near all park entrances. If someone attempts to rob you or steal your car, do not try to resist the thief/car-jacker. Report the incident to the police department immediately.

2 Getting To & Around the U.S.

BY PLANE   Travelers from overseas can take advantage of the **APEX** (Advance Purchase Excursion) fares offered by all the major U.S. and European carriers.

British Airways (☎ 0345/222-111 from within the U.K.) offers direct flights from London to Miami and Orlando, as does **Virgin Atlantic** (☎ 0129/374-774 from within the U.K.). You can also try **Continental** (☎ 0293/776-446).

Canadian readers may book flights with **Air Canada** (☎ 800/361-8620), which offers service from Toronto and Montréal to Miami and Tampa. Other airlines that fly to Florida from Canada include **US Airways** (☎ 800/428-4322); **Delta** (☎ 800/361-6770); **TWA** (☎ 800/892-4141); **American** (☎ 800/624-6262); and **Northwest** (☎ 800/225-2525).

Some large American airlines (for example, TWA, American Airlines, Northwest, United, and Delta) offer travelers on their transatlantic or transpacific flights special discount tickets under the name **Visit USA,** allowing travel between U.S. destinations at minimum rates. They are not on sale in the United States and must therefore be purchased before you leave your foreign point of departure. This system is the best, easiest, and fastest way to see the United States at low cost. You should obtain information well in advance from your travel agent or the office of the airline concerned, since the conditions attached to these discount tickets can be changed without advance notice.

The visitor arriving by air, no matter what the port of entry, should cultivate patience and resignation before setting foot on U.S. soil. Getting through Immigration Control may take as long as 2 hours on some days. Add in the time it takes to clear Customs, and you'll see that you should make very generous allowances for delays in planning connections between international and domestic flights—an average of 2 to 3 hours, at least.

In contrast, travelers arriving by car or by rail from Canada will find border-crossing formalities streamlined to the vanishing point. And air travelers from Canada, Bermuda, and some places in the Caribbean can sometimes go through Customs and immigration at the point of departure, which is much quicker and less painful.

BY CAR   Though I give some tips on train and bus passes below, you're going to need a car to get around Orlando unless you are committed to staying at Disney. Motor homes and motorcycles are available if you want something a little different to roam the city in. Relying on public transportation in the United States is only possible in those few urban areas having comprehensive mass transit systems—Orlando is not one of them.

To rent a car, you need a major credit card and a valid driver's license (sometimes a hefty cash deposit can be used instead of a credit card). You also must be at least 25 years old. Some companies do rent to younger people, but add a daily surcharge. Be sure to return your car with the same amount of gas (petrol) you started out

Travel Tip

Airplane cabins are notoriously dry; if you wear contact lenses, either remove them, or bring plenty of eye drops with you on the plane.

with; rental companies charge excessive prices for gasoline. All the major car-rental companies are represented in Florida (see "Getting Around" in chapter 4 for a list).

If you wish, you can rent a motor home in Orlando. The following companies rent mobile homes, and all have outlets in Orlando: **Cruise America,** 613 E. Colonial Dr., Orlando, FL 32804 (☎ **800/327-7799** or 407/273-5020); **Florida RV World,** 4260 U.S. 92 E., Plant City, FL 33566 (☎ **800/330-6171**); **Giant Recreation World,** 13906 W. Colonial Dr., Winter Garden, FL 34787 (☎ **407/ 656-6444**).

The increasing popularity of Bike Week, and a growing number of weekend road warriors, has sparked an increase in places specializing in motorcycle rental. The Harley Davidson, in all shapes and sizes, is the most popular. Nearly all the rental agencies are located closer to downtown Orlando or Kissimmee than to the attractions. You must be at least 21 years of age, have a motorcycle license, and have a major credit card. The average rental fee varies from around $800 to $1,200 for 1 week and includes helmets, locks, and a brief orientation. You can rent bikes at **Cruise America Motorcycle Rentals,** 2915 N. Orange Blossom Trail, Kissimmee, FL 34744 (☎ **407/931-1409**); and at **Eaglerider Motorcycle Rental,** 527 W. Miller St., Orlando, FL 32804 (☎ **407/316-1409**). The supply is small, so call ahead. Plan months in advance if visiting during Bike Week, late February and early March, or Biketober Fest in mid-October. (Both events are in Daytona Beach.)

BY TRAIN   International visitors can buy a **USA Railpass,** good for 15 or 30 days of unlimited travel on **Amtrak** trains (☎ **800/872-7245**). The pass is available through many foreign travel agents. You can buy passes for a specific region, for example the Southwest or Southeast, or for the entire United States. Prices in 1999 for a pass to travel the entire country were as follows: a 15-day pass costs $285 off-peak (Jan–May), $425 peak (June–Dec); a 30-day pass costs $375 off-peak, $535 peak.

With a foreign passport, you can also buy passes at some Amtrak offices in the United States, including locations in San Francisco, Los Angeles, Chicago, New York, Miami, Boston, and Washington, D.C. Reservations are usually required, and should be made for each part of your trip as early as possible.

Visitors should be aware of the limitations of long-distance rail travel in the United States. With a few notable exceptions (for instance, the Northeast Corridor line between Boston and Washington, D.C.), service is rarely up to European standards: Delays are common, routes are limited and often infrequently served, and fares are rarely significantly lower than discount airfares. Thus, cross-country train travel should be approached with caution.

BY BUS   Bus travel in the United States can be both slow and uncomfortable, so this option is not for everyone. Although the bus is often the most economical form of public transit for short hops between cities, at this writing bus passes are priced slightly higher than similar train passes. **Greyhound** (☎ **800/231-2222;** www.greyhound.com), the sole nationwide bus line, offers an **International Ameripass** for unlimited travel that must be purchased before entering the United States. It is available through many foreign travel agents. The 1999 rates were 7 days ($179), 15 days ($269), 30 days ($369), or 60 days ($539).

For further information about travel to Florida, see "Getting There," in chapter 2.

Fast Facts: For the Foreign Traveler

Automobile Organizations   Auto clubs will supply maps, suggested routes, guidebooks, accident and bail-bond insurance, and emergency road service. The major auto club in the United States, with 983 offices nationwide, is the **American Automobile Association (AAA).** Members of some foreign auto clubs have reciprocal arrangements with AAA and enjoy its services at no charge. If you belong to an auto club, inquire about AAA reciprocity before you leave. AAA can provide you with an International Driving Permit validating your foreign license. You may be able to join AAA even if you are not a member of a reciprocal club. (This membership may entitle you to travel-related discounts.) To inquire, call ☎ **800/222-4357.** AAA has a nationwide emergency road service telephone number (☎ **800/AAA-HELP**).

Business Hours   Bank lobby hours are open weekdays from 9am to 5pm. Drive through hours extend until about 6pm on Friday. There is usually 24-hour access to the automatic teller machines (ATMs) at most banks and other outlets. Some branch offices in Florida are open until noon on Saturday. Generally, business offices are open weekdays from 9am to 5pm. Stores are open 6 days a week, with many open on Sunday, too; department stores usually stay open until 9pm from Monday through Saturday, and until about 6pm on Sunday.

Climate   See "When to Go," in chapter 2.

Currency & Exchange   See "Money" in the section "Preparing for Your Trip," earlier in this chapter.

Drinking Laws   The legal age for purchase and consumption of alcoholic beverages is 21; proof of age is required and often requested at bars, nightclubs, and restaurants, so it's always a good idea to bring ID when you go out. Beer and wine can often be purchased in supermarkets, but liquor laws vary from state to state.

Do not carry open containers of alcohol in your car or any public area that isn't zoned for alcohol consumption. The police can, and probably will, fine you on the spot. And nothing will ruin your trip faster than getting a citation for DWI ("driving while intoxicated"), so don't even think about driving while under the influence. Also see "Liquor Laws" under "Fast Facts" in chapter 4.

Electricity   Like Canada, the United States uses 110 to 120 volts, 60 cycles, compared to 220 to 240 volts, 50 cycles, as in most of Europe and Australia. In addition to a 100-volt converter (difficult to find in the U.S., so bring one with you), small appliances of non-American manufacture, such as hair dryers or shavers, will require a plug adapter having two flat, parallel pins.

Embassies & Consulates   All embassies are located in Washington, D.C. Some consulates are located in major cities, and most nations have a mission to the United Nations in New York City. Foreign visitors can obtain telephone numbers for their embassies and consulates by calling "Information" in Washington, D.C. (☎ **202/555-1212**).

The **Canadian consulate** closest to Orlando is at 200 S. Biscayne Blvd., Suite 1600, Miami, FL 33131 (☎ 305/579-1600). The **British consulate** is located at 1001 S. Bayshore Dr., Miami, FL 33131 (☎ 305/374-1522); the Orlando office for the British consulate is open Monday through Friday, from 9am to 5pm in the downtown **Orlando SunTrust building,** 200 S. Orange Ave., Orlando, FL 32801 (☎ 407/426-7855). Other consulate offices in Orlando are: **Cusulado de Argentino de Orlando,** 400 S. Orange Ave., Orlando, FL 32801 (☎ 407/481-2602); **Consulate of Mexico,** 823 E. Colonial Dr., Orlando, FL 32803 (☎ 407/894-0514); **Consulate of France** (☎ 407/294-5844); **Consulate of the Netherlands,** 400 S. Orange Ave., Orlando, FL 32801 (☎ 407/425-8000). All of these consulates operate with small staffs and many keep abbreviated business hours. Don't be surprised if you get an answering machine.

Emergencies   Call ☎ **911** to report a fire, contact the police, or get an ambulance. This call is free from all public telephones and should be the first call made in case of any serious medical emergency or accident.

Another number (☎ **800/647-9284**) is available to help visitors. The number is sponsored by the Florida Tourism Industry Marketing Corporation, the state tourism promotions board. With operators speaking over 100 languages, it can provide general directions and can help with lost travel papers and credit cards, medical emergencies, accidents, money transfer, airline confirmation, and much more.

Gasoline (Petrol)   Petrol is known as gasoline (or "gas") in the U.S. and is sold at gas or service stations. One U.S. gallon equals 3.75 liters, and 1.2 U.S. gallons equal 1 Imperial gallon. There are several grades (and price levels) of gasoline available at most gas stations, and you'll notice that their names change from company to company. The unleaded ones with the highest octane are the most expensive. Most rental cars take the least expensive, "regular" unleaded gas. Gas costs about $1 a gallon, and will be a few cents cheaper per gallon outside of the main tourist areas and away from the theme parks.

Holidays   Banks, government offices, post offices, and many stores, restaurants, and museums are closed on legal national holidays: January 1 (New Year's Day); third Monday in January (Martin Luther King, Jr., Day); third Monday in February (Presidents' Day, Washington's Birthday); last Monday in May (Memorial Day); July 4 (Independence Day); first Monday in September (Labor Day); second Monday in October (Columbus Day); November 11 (Veterans' Day/Armistice Day); fourth Thursday in November (Thanksgiving Day); and December 25 (Christmas). The Tuesday following the first Monday in November is Election Day and is a legal holiday in 2000 due to the presidential election.

Languages   Major hotels may have multilingual employees. Unless your language is very obscure, they can usually supply a translator on request. Especially in southern Florida and, increasingly, in central Florida, many people are fluent in Spanish. Establishments catering to tourists make a special effort to have bilingual speakers on staff.

Legal Aid   As a foreign tourist, you will probably never become involved with the American legal system. If you are stopped for a minor infraction, such as speeding or some other traffic violation, never attempt to pay the fine directly to a police officer; you may be arrested on the much more serious charge of attempted bribery. Pay fines by mail, or directly into the hands of the clerk of the court. If you are accused of a more serious offense, it's wise to say and do nothing before consulting a lawyer. Under U.S. law, an arrested person is allowed one telephone call to a party of his or her choice. Call your embassy or consulate.

Mail   If you want to receive mail on your vacation and you aren't sure of your address, your mail can be sent to you, in your name, ℅ General Delivery at the main post office of the city or region where you expect to be. Orlando's main post office (☎ **407/850-6288**) is located at 1040 Post Office Blvd. Lake Buena Vista's main post office (☎ **407/850-6288**) is located at 12133 S. Apopka-Vineland Rd. You must pick up your mail in person and produce proof of identity (driver's license, credit card, passport, and so on).

Often found at intersections, mailboxes are blue with a red-and-white stripe and carry the inscription U.S. MAIL. Make sure you see this inscription; overnight delivery companies also often have drop-off boxes along the road. Don't forget to add the five-figure postal code, or ZIP code, after the two-letter abbreviation of the state to which the mail is addressed (FL for Florida, NY for New York, and so on).

Within the United States, it costs 20¢ to mail a standard-size postcard and 33¢ to send letters weighing up to 1 ounce (that's about five pages, 8-by-11-inch paper), plus 23¢ for each additional ounce. A standard postcard to Mexico costs 30¢, a half-ounce letter 35¢; a postcard to Canada costs 30¢, a 1-ounce letter 40¢. A postcard to Europe, Australia, New Zealand, the Far East, South America, or elsewhere costs 40¢, and a letter is 60¢ for each half-ounce.

Measurements   The United States does not operate on the metric system. For a full explanation of the American system of measurements, please see "Metric Conversions" on the inside back cover.

Newspapers & Magazines   National newspapers include the *New York Times, USA Today,* and the *Wall Street Journal.* National news weeklies include *Newsweek, Time,* and *U.S. News & World Report.* All over Florida, you'll be able to purchase the *Miami Herald,* one of the most respected dailies in the country. The local newspaper is the *Orlando Sentinel.*

Many Walgreens and Eckerd drugstores in areas catering to tourists also carry newspapers from the United Kingdom. Since 1997 the *London Daily Mail* is printed in Orlando for distribution along the East Coast. Because of the time difference, British travelers can actually pick up a paper at the airport and read the next day's newspaper on the way home.

Radio & Television   There are five coast-to-coast broadcast networks—ABC, CBS, NBC, Fox, PBS (the Public Broadcasting System)—in America. These, plus two newer, smaller networks (UPN and WB) are available in Orlando. Options on your hotel TV set may be limited, though.

You'll also find a wide choice of local radio stations, each broadcasting particular kinds of talk shows and/or music, punctuated by news broadcasts and frequent commercials. Most central Florida cable networks also carry at least two Spanish-language stations, and there are numerous Spanish-language radio stations, mostly on the AM dial.

Taxes   In the United States, there is no VAT (Value-Added Tax) or other indirect tax at a national level. Every state, city, and county, has the right to levy its own local tax on all purchases, including hotel and restaurant checks, airline tickets, and so on. In Florida, sales tax is 6%. Hotel tax in Orlando and Kissimmee (which includes sales tax) is 11%.

Telephone, Telegraph & Fax   Pay phones can be found in most restaurants, hotels, gas stations, and stores. Local calls in the United States usually cost 35¢. Pay phones do not accept pennies, and few will take anything larger than a

---

Fun Fact

Orlando, especially Disney World, is a popular destination for rich Saudi Arabian princes, who routinely rent entire hotel floors, and drop tens of thousands of dollars at local shops. But why do Disney hotels carry Arab TV on their cable network? Well, it seems a Saudi prince, who heavily invested in Disneyland Paris, also owns the network. It is, I think, what Michael Eisner calls "synergy."

quarter. *Note: If you are making a local call in Orlando's 407 area code region, you must now dial the area code followed by the number you wish to call, for a total of 10 digits.*

Most long-distance and international calls can be dialed directly from any phone. For direct overseas calls, dial 011 first, then the country code (Australia, 61; Republic of Ireland, 353; New Zealand, 64; United Kingdom, 44) followed by the city code, and then the number you wish to call. To place a call to Canada, the Caribbean, or another U.S. state, dial 1 followed by the area code and the seven-digit number.

For "collect" (reversed-charge) calls and for "person-to-person" calls, dial 0 (zero, not the letter "O") followed by the area code and number you want. An operator will then come on the line, and you should specify that you are calling collect, or person-to-person, or both. If your operator-assisted call is international, ask for the overseas operator.

Because the telephone system in the U.S. is privately operated, long-distance rates can vary widely. Generally, hotel surcharges on long-distance and local calls are astronomical. You are usually better off using a public pay telephone. Hotels sometimes even charge a fee if you use your own telephone credit card or call a toll-free number (with an 800, 877, or 888 area code), so ask about surcharges before you dial.

Prepaid calling cards, which generally provide a fair per-minute rate—probably lower than that charged by your hotel—are becoming increasingly popular. Calling cards are sold in many convenience stores and drugstores and can generally be purchased in $5 or $10 increments. Make sure to check for an expiration date before purchasing the card.

For local directory assistance ("Information"), dial ☎ **411;** for long-distance information in Canada or the United States, dial 1, then the appropriate area code and ☎ **555-1212.** There are two kinds of directories in the U.S. The White Pages lists private household numbers and business subscribers in alphabetical order. It also includes government numbers, usually printed on blue paper. The inside cover of the directory lists emergency numbers for the police, and so on. The Yellow Pages lists all local services and businesses; it often includes maps listing zip codes and public transportation routes.

Most telegraph and telex services in the U.S. are provided by Western Union. You can bring your telegram into the nearest Western Union office (there are hundreds across the country) or dictate it over the phone (a toll-free call, ☎ **800/325-6000**). You can also telegraph money, or have it telegraphed to you, very quickly over the Western Union system.

It's also easy to send a fax. Most hotels have fax service. If yours doesn't, small copy shops found in most neighborhoods provide fax service. Kinko's is a prominent local printing chain that also provides fax service. There is a Kinko's (☎ **407/363-2831**) at 9800 International Dr., Orlando, FL 32819; other branches are listed in the White Pages of the telephone directory. Faxes are sent for a small fee—usually around $2 per page. If you make arrangements, some places will also receive faxes for you and call you when anything arrives.

Time   The United States is divided into four time zones (six, if Alaska and Hawaii are included). From east to west, these are: eastern standard time (EST), central standard time (CST), mountain standard time (MST), Pacific standard time (PST), Alaska standard time (AST), and Hawaii standard time (HST). Orlando, like most of Florida, is on eastern standard time, which is 8 hours behind Greenwich Mean Time. When it is noon in Orlando, it's 11am in New

Orleans (CST), 10am in Salt Lake City (MST), 9am in Los Angeles (PST), 8am in Anchorage (AST), and 7am in Honolulu (HST).

Daylight saving time is in effect from the first Sunday in April through 2am on the last Sunday in October, except in Arizona, Hawaii, part of Indiana, and Puerto Rico. Daylight saving time moves the clock 1 hour ahead of standard time.

Tipping Tipping is so ingrained in the American way of life that the annual income tax of tip-earning service personnel is based on how much they should have received in light of their employers' gross revenues. Accordingly, they may have to pay tax on a tip you didn't actually give them.

Service in the United States tends to be good, but it is rarely included in the price of anything. The amount you should tip does depend on the service you have received. Good service warrants the following tips: Bartenders (do tip them here), 15%; cab drivers, 15%; checkroom attendants, $1 per garment (unless there is a charge, then no tip); hairdressers, 15% to 20%; parking valets, $1; red-caps (in airports), at least $1 per piece; restaurants and nightclubs, 15%. Many restaurants in tourist areas of central Florida will automatically add the gratuity to checks for parties of six or more. In hotels, tip bellhops at least $1 per bag ($2 to $3 if you have a lot of luggage) and tip the chamber staff $1 to $2 per day (more if you've left a disaster area for her to clean up, or if you are traveling with kids and/or pets).

Toilets Foreign visitors often complain that public toilets or "rest rooms" are hard to find in most U.S. cities. True, there are none on the streets, but you can usually find one in a bar, restaurant, hotel, museum, department store, convenience store, or service station—and it will probably be clean. In particular, Mobil service stations have made, and kept, a public pledge to provide spic-and-span bathrooms, most decorated with homey touches. Note, however, that restaurants and bars in resorts or heavily visited areas may reserve their rest rooms for the use of their patrons. Some establishments display a notice that toilets are for the use of patrons only. You can ignore this sign or, better yet, avoid arguments by paying for a cup of coffee or a soft drink, which will qualify you as a patron. Within the theme parks, rest rooms will be clearly marked on the park maps. Don't panic if you can't find a handle to flush. Many new toilets are installed with lasers that trigger the flush automatically when you leave the stall.

Getting to Know Walt Disney World & Orlando

It's true that 30 years ago there wasn't a whole lot to see outside Walt Disney World except palmetto fronds and orange groves. Orlando was a typical, slow-lane Southern town before Disney World moved here in 1971. The fancy stores of downtown were giving way to peep shows and tattoo parlors as commerce relocated to the landscaped acres of suburban malls.

Oh, but how success breeds competition. Disney World has expanded to include four major parks and two nighttime entertainment districts. Over the years, Disney has added everything from water parks to miniature golf to try to keep those tourist dollars from migrating off the very large Disney lot.

No one pretends that Disney isn't King Mouse. The Magic Kingdom is what, at least initially, beckons the masses. But all that unrelenting cheerfulness, days of $3 sodas, and the just-roasted aroma of sweaty, sunburned crowds can make it a small world, after all. You're cheating yourself if you don't plan to spend some time away from Walt Disney's world, visiting Universal Studios Escape, with its new CityWalk nighttime entertainment district, and its new theme park, Islands of Adventure, which is packed with thrill rides and funky scenery. Also plan to spend at least one night away from the theme parks altogether, going into downtown Orlando to dine and to enjoy a little real nightlife, not the kind imagined by Disney. Visitors, especially those from other countries, don't really come all this way just to see the theme park version of America. (Heck, for that they could go to Disneyland Paris.)

Because of major renovations, even places you've seen before, such as Sea World, or downtown Orlando, are worth another look. Sea World has added a major attraction nearly every year, and is working on a second theme park; downtown Orlando sports an increasing number of fine restaurants and funky clubs where real people mix and mingle. If you do travel, many area hotels offer transportation to the airport and city attractions.

1 Orientation

VISITOR INFORMATION

Once you're in Orlando, stop by the **Orlando/Orange County Convention & Visitors Bureau,** 8723 International Dr., Suite 101, Orlando, FL 32819 (☎ **407/363-5871**). They can answer all your questions and give you maps, brochures, and discount coupons if you haven't sent away for these already. Discount tickets to attractions other than Disney parks are sold on the premises, and the multilingual staff can also make dining reservations and hotel referrals. The bureau is open daily, except Christmas, from 8am to 8pm.

If you're driving, you can stop at the **Disney/AAA Travel Center** in Ocala, Florida, at the intersection of I-75 (exit 68) and Fla. 200, about 90 miles north of Orlando (☎ **904/854-0770**). Here you can purchase tickets and Mickey ears, get help planning your park itinerary, and make hotel reservations. Hours are 9am to 6pm; until 7pm June through August.

The **Kissimmee–St. Cloud Convention & Visitors Bureau** is located at 1925 E. Irlo Bronson Memorial Hwy. (P.O. Box 422007), Kissimmee, FL 34742-2007 (☎ **800/327-9159** or 407/847-5000). They have maps, brochures, and discount coupon books.

If you're looking for state of Florida tourism information, there are five **Florida welcome centers** in the state, located 4 miles north of Jennings on I-75 South; 3 miles north of Campelton on Hwy. 231; 7 miles north of Yulee on I-95; 16 miles west of Pensacola on I-10 East; and another at the capitol in Tallahassee.

Finally, nearly all hotel lobbies have a rack containing brochures for various area attractions. If this guidebook doesn't convince you of which places to hit, these pamphlets might help you make up your mind. The brochures also often include discount coupons.

INFORMATION AT THE AIRPORTS

At the Orlando International Airport, arriving passengers can stroll over to one of two Disney shops, **The Magic of Disney** (☎ **407/825-2301**) or **Disney's Flight of Fantastic.** They are located in both A and B terminals. This facility sells WDW multiday park tickets, makes dinner show and hotel reservations at Disney hostelries, and provides brochures and assistance. It's open daily from 6am to 9pm.

Also in the airport, you'll find the **Universal Studios Store** (☎ **407/825-2473**), which is open daily from 6:30am to 10pm, and sells park tickets, and sometimes features special offers such as "Second Day Free." The **Sea World** stores, also located in the A and B terminals are open daily from 6:30am to 10pm. They sell tickets and will be advertising any current discounts or offers.

CITY LAYOUT

Orlando's major artery is Interstate 4 or, as the locals call it, **I-4,** which runs diagonally across the state from Tampa to Daytona Beach. Exits from I-4 take you to all Walt Disney World properties, Sea World, International Drive, U.S. 192, Kissimmee, Lake Buena Vista, Church Street Station, downtown Orlando, and Winter Park. Most of the exits are well marked, but construction is common in this growing region, and exit numbers can change. Keep this in mind when you are traveling along I-4, so you don't end up lost and confused.

The **Florida Turnpike** crosses I-4 and links up with I-75 to the north. **U.S. 192,** a major east-west artery, stretches from Kissimmee (along a major motel strip) to U.S. 27, crossing I-4 near the Walt Disney World entrance road. Farther north, a toll road called the **Bee Line Expressway** (Fla. 528) goes east from I-4 past Orlando International Airport to Cape Canaveral. The **East-West Expressway** (also known as Fla. 408) is a toll road that might be helpful in bypassing surface traffic outside of the main tourist areas.

Walt Disney World is bounded roughly by I-4 and Fla. 535 to the east (the latter also north), World Drive (the entrance road) to the west, and U.S. 192 to the south.

Orlando Neighborhoods

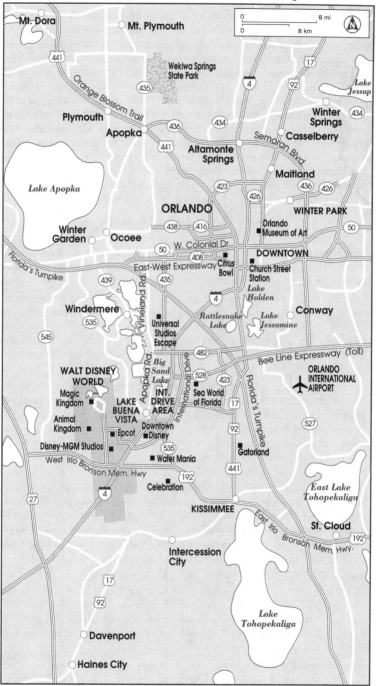

Epcot Center Drive (Hwy. 536/the south end of International Drive) and Buena Vista Drive cut across the complex in a more or less east-west direction; the two roads cross at Bonnet Creek Parkway. Despite an excellent highway system and explicit signage, it is relatively easy to get lost here. Again, pay close attention and drive carefully, because chances are that everyone else is lost, too. Don't panic or pull across multiple lanes of traffic to make your specific exit once on Disney property. All roads lead to Disney, and you will soon find another sign directing you to the same place on Disney property. It may take a little longer, but think how a crash would ruin your day. Clever landscaping hides the fact that many sections of the Disney parks are actually very close together. (Actually the way some of the roads twist and turn, it makes me wonder if Disney didn't make it purposely convoluted so visitors would drive past other attractions to whet their appetite.) *Note:* Disney parks are actually much closer to Kissimmee than Orlando.

Orlando Neighborhoods in Brief

Walt Disney World   A city unto itself, WDW sprawls over more than 26,000 acres, containing theme parks, resorts, hotels, shops, restaurants, and recreational facilities galore. Read on for copious details.

Lake Buena Vista   This area centers on a hotel village/marketplace owned and operated by Walt Disney World on the eastern edge of Disney property. Although Disney owns all the real estate here, many of the hotels and some shops and restaurants are independently owned. Lake Buena Vista is a charming area of manicured lawns and verdant thoroughfares with traffic islands shaded by towering oak trees.

Celebration   Imagine living in a Disney world? Disney tries to re-create its squeaky-clean, completely controlled magic in this town, the first residential area ever to receive the special Disney touch. Located on 4,900 acres in northwest Osceola County, Celebration will eventually have thousands of residents living in Disney-designed homes, and attending a Disney-run school. The homes start at about $193,000. Celebration's downtown is, however, designed for the tourist trade, being architecturally interesting, and offering some first-rate shops and restaurants.

Downtown Disney   This is more a Disney creation than an actual neighborhood, but with the ever-present signs it is worth explaining. Simply put, Downtown Disney is what WDW has taken to calling its two nighttime entertainment districts, Pleasure Island and Disney's West Side, and the shopping complex, Disney's Village Marketplace. Just so you understand, we consider this area a part of Lake Buena Vista, so you'll find establishments here under that heading.

Kissimmee   South of the Disney parks, Kissimmee centers on U.S. 192/Irlo Bronson Memorial Highway—a somewhat tacky strip, as archetypal of American cities as Main Street. U.S. 192 is lined with budget motels, lesser attractions—like Gatorland—and every fast-food restaurant you can name. Kissimmee is still, in many ways, true to its cowboy roots, and there are still some wide, open spaces to explore if you are in the mood for a ride in the country.

International Drive Area (Fla. 536)   Can you say tourist mecca? This area extends 7 to 10 miles north of the Disney parks between Fla. 535 and the Florida Turnpike. From bungee jumping to ice skating and dozens of theme restaurants and T-shirt shops, this is the tourist strip in central Florida. It contains numerous hotels, restaurants, shopping centers, the Orange County Convention Center, and it also offers easy access to Sea World and Universal Studios. The place is already packed, but, somehow, developers manage year after year to find space for just one more attraction. *Note:* Locally, this road is always referred to as **I-Drive.**

Downtown Orlando   No, not Downtown Disney, which is not *really* downtown. To get to the real thing you have to travel on I-4 East, before reaching a burgeoning Sunbelt metropolis 17 miles northeast of Walt Disney World. It includes the entertainment/shopping complex Church Street Station and the Orlando Science Center, a recently completed multimillion-dollar complex, which is the largest in the Southeast. Hundreds of clubs, shops, and restaurants are located in the heart of the city, one of the fastest-growing in the country. Dozens of antique shops line "Antique Row" on Orange Avenue near Lake Ivanhoe.

Winter Park   Just north of downtown Orlando, Winter Park is the place many of central Florida's old-money families call home. As the name implies, it began as a haven for Yankees traveling away from the cold. Today, it's home to Park Avenue, a collection of upscale shops and restaurants along an original cobblestone street that is frequented by local ladies who lunch. With the main attractions being shopping, dining, and several small museums, Winter Park is definitely a grown-up diversion.

2 Getting Around

In a city that thrives on its visitor attractions, you won't find it difficult to get around—especially if you have a car. Don't count on the city bus system to get you where you want to go. (Okay, it may be able to get you there, but not very quickly.) If you are traveling outside of the tourist areas, avoid traveling during peak rush-hour times—7 to 9am and 4 to 6pm—so you don't get caught in the daily traffic jams. (Not everyone is on vacation, and thousands of people are coming home from work about the same time you're hankering to go to dinner.) International Drive, which has become a prime cruising spot for teens, can get very congested during spring break, and on weekends. You may get there just as fast by parking and walking along the sidewalks.

Another travel option is the **I-Ride Trolley,** which is a group of shuttle cars that run from one end of I-Drive to the other with stops about every two blocks. The trolley runs from 7am–midnight, and costs about 75¢ for adults and 25¢ for seniors. Children under 12 ride free when accompanied by adults. Due to I-Drive's large volume of traffic, this may be the best way to get around the area if you are staying at a hotel on the strip. It will certainly cut down on the hurry-up-and-wait frustration of bumper-to-bumper traffic.

Signage problems in the downtown area have been corrected using brightly colored signs that display a definite Disney influence. The best way to avoid dangerous action on the road is to follow the directions we supply for the various attractions and hotels. Another good way to avoid problems is to call the numbers we provide for explicit driving directions before heading to a new destination. Most attractions offer directions as a voice mail option when you call a main number, but you can also be connected to an operator for further clarification. The automated directions should take into account any changes due to ongoing construction.

Nearly all but the very inexpensive hotels offer transport to and from the theme parks and other tourist destinations; however, most of them will charge you for this service. It's not difficult getting around town, but it can be expensive.

BY THE DISNEY TRANSPORTATION SYSTEM

If you plan to stay at a Disney resort and will spend a majority of your time visiting Disney parks and attractions, there's a thorough, free transportation network that runs throughout the Disney complex.

Disney resorts and official hotels offer unlimited complimentary transportation via bus, monorail, ferry, and water taxi to all of Disney's major parks from 2 hours prior to opening until 2 hours after closing. There is also service to Downtown Disney, Typhoon Lagoon, River Country, Blizzard Beach, Pleasure Island, Fort Wilderness, and other Disney resorts. Disney properties offer transportation to other area attractions as well, but you'll have to pay extra.

There are advantages to using the on-property transportation system: It's free, providing big savings on car rental, insurance, and gas; you don't have to pay for parking ($5 per day in Walt Disney World); you will avoid a long wait to enter the parking lots, and if your party wants to split up, you can easily board transport to different areas.

The disadvantages? You are at the mercy of Disney's schedule, and you often have to take a ferry to catch a bus to get the monorail to go to the hotel. Consider this when making your hotel reservations, especially if you are not planning to rent a car. The system makes a complete route, but not necessarily an easy or quick one. You will have to wait as each bus makes multiple stops, loading and unloading a large number of passengers. You may also have to endure long waits while waiting to make connections when traveling to some of the parks and resorts.

It can easily take an afternoon to get somewhere that looks like it's right across the lagoon on the map. Never fear, though, you will eventually get to your destination, since the transportation network goes everywhere on the Disney property. The best rule when traveling on the network? Ask the bus driver or someone at your hotel's information desk to make sure you are heading the right way and getting on the right bus. Keep asking questions along the way. Unlike missing a highway exit, missing a stop on the bus route means you will be riding for a while.

BY CAR

To rent or not to rent that is the question? First, you must clearly envision your vacation plans. If you will stay happily immersed in everything Disney, or if you are staying on International Drive, you'll probably do just as well without your own wheels. If you're staying at a Disney property, the question to ask when deciding whether to rent a car is how, exactly, will you get to the major parks? If the Magic Kingdom is accessible only by taking a bus, switching to the monorail, and then catching a ferry, you may want to opt for a car. The least expensive properties, the All-Star resorts, are the farthest from the parks. Wait times between buses can be considerable.

During peak hours in the busiest seasons, you may have trouble getting a seat on the bus, so keep that in mind if you are traveling with seniors or with travelers with disabilities. Also, if you are hauling children and strollers, consider the frustration factor of loading and unloading strollers and kiddie paraphernalia on and off buses, ferries, and trams. (Although, as in earlier chapters, we suggest you rent strollers at the park.)

A car may drastically cut the commute time between the parks and hotels not directly on the monorail routes, so decide how much your time is worth before making the decision to rent.

In general, if you will spend all your time at Disney and you're laid-back enough to go with the flow of traffic within the transportation network, there's no sense renting a car that will sit in the parking lot between trips to the airport.

But if you're on an extended stay—more than a week—you will probably want to rent a car for at least a day or two to venture beyond the tourist areas. (Yes, there is something beyond the tourist areas.) Discover downtown Orlando, visit museums, the Space Coast, or just hang out at the beach; it will be good for your soul. The tourist areas of Orlando are kind of like Las Vegas: You can't spend too much time in a world of bright lights and make-believe without needing a good dose of reality.

Once you have decided to rent a car, you should, if possible, contract with an agency that operates at, or near, your hotel. This will help you save time—and a few headaches. Dropping a car off at an airport-based rental service often means riding a shuttle to an off-site lot, which means that turning in the car will eat up much of your final vacation day. This is especially true during holidays and the peak season when lots of other folks will be doing the same thing. *Somebody* is renting the miles upon miles of rental cars stored in the lots visible from the freeway.

All major rental companies are represented in Orlando and maintain desks at the airport. Many major car-rental agencies provide discount coupons in publications targeted at tourists. When planning your trip and poring over all those brochures, keep an eye out for discounts on car rentals. You may also want to ask your travel agent if he or she has a recommendation, or whether a discount is included in any available packages. Also, it never hurts to ask if there is a special available.

Value Rent-A-Car (☎ 800/GO-VALUE) offers excellent service and 24-hour pickup and return. Some other handy phone numbers: **Alamo** (☎ 800/327-9633), **Avis** (☎ 800/331-1212), **Budget** (☎ 800/527-0700), **Dollar** (☎ 800/800-4000), **Enterprise** (☎ 800/325-8007), **Hertz** (☎ 800/654-3131), **National Car Rental** (☎ 800/227-7368), and **Thrifty** (☎ 800/367-2277). If you are looking for something a little more upscale, say a Jaguar or a Porsche, try **Exotic Car Rentals** (☎ 407/855-6325).

BY BUS

Mears Transportation Group (☎ **407/423-5566**) operates buses to all major attractions, including Cypress Gardens, Kennedy Space Center, Universal Studios, Sea World, Busch Gardens (in Tampa), and Church Street Station, among others. Call for details.

BY MOTORCYCLE

The increasing popularity of Bike Week (see "Orlando Area Calendar of Events," in chapter 2) has resulted in a growing number of weekend road warriors roaring through central Florida. If you have a motorcycle license, you can join them. The Harley Davidson, in all shapes and sizes, is the most popular bike rental. Most motorcycle rental agencies are located closer to downtown Orlando than to the attractions. You must be at least 21 years old, have a valid motorcycle license, and have a major credit card. The average rental price varies from around $800 to $1,200 for 1 week, and includes helmets, locks, and a brief orientation.

You can rent bikes at **Cruise America Motorcycle Rentals** (☎ **407/931-1409**), **Eaglerider Motorcycle Rental** (☎ **407/316-1409**), or **Saddle Sore Inc.** (☎ **407/ 872-3115**). The supply of bikes is small, so call ahead. Plan months in advance if you are visiting during **Bike Week**—late February and early March—or **Biketober Fest** in mid-October. (Both events are held in Daytona Beach.)

BY TAXI

Taxis line up in front of major hotels, and at smaller properties, the front desk will be happy to call you a cab. You can also call **Yellow Cab** (☎ **407/699-9999**). The charge is $2.75 for the first mile, $1.50 per mile thereafter.

Fast Facts: Walt Disney World & Orlando

Ambulances   See "Emergencies," below.

American Express   There is an American Express Travel Service Office at Epcot's main gate, and in the lobby of Disney's Contemporary Resort.

Baby-sitters   Most Orlando hotels offer baby-sitting services. Several Disney properties and several major hotels have marvelous child-care facilities with counselor-supervised activity programs on the premises. Disney properties have used KinderCare sitters since 1980 (☎ **407/827-5444**), so you can be sure they've been very carefully checked out, including a criminal background check. If you're not staying at a Disney accommodation, you can call them on your own. You can even have them take your kids to the park or to any of the services at your resort, except swimming. Rates for in-room service are: $11 per hour for one child, $12 per hour for two children, $13 per hour for three children, and $14 per hour for four or more children. There is a 4-hour minimum, the first half hour of which is travel time for the sitter. Advance notice of 24 hours is required.

Business Hours   Theme park hours vary, depending on the time of year. Most open at 9am or 10am and close around 10pm or 11pm during the peak season, and 6pm or 7pm during the off-season. Office hours for central Florida businesses are generally Monday through Friday from 9am to 5pm. Bars are usually open until 2am or 3am. There are a few "rave" and after-hours clubs that stay open until the wee hours. These after-hours clubs do not serve alcohol.

Car Rentals   See section 2, "Getting Around," in this chapter.

Climate   See "When to Go," in chapter 2.

Convention Center   The Orange County Convention/Civic Center is located at 9800 International Dr. in downtown Orlando (☎ **407/345-9800**).

Crime   See "Safety," below.

Doctors and Dentists   There are basic first-aid centers in all the major parks. Unfortunately, tourists have encountered ill-trained doctors making housecalls to the hotels. You can get a reputable referral from **Ask-A-Nurse.** They will ask whether you have insurance, but that is for information purposes only, so they can track who uses the system. It is a free service open to everyone. In Kissimmee call ☎ 407/ 870-1700; in Orlando call ☎ 407/ 897-1700. Disney also offers an in-room medical service available 24 hours a day by calling ☎407/238-2000.

Walk-in medical clinics are also available, with a visit usually costing under $50. Prescriptions are extra. Centra-Care, operated by a locally run Florida Hospital, is a reputable medical facility with more than a dozen locations throughout the Orlando area. Several walk-in clinics have popped up in recent years, and not all are created equal, so we suggest that you opt for Centra-Care. For information, and the nearest location, call ☎ 407/660-8118.

To find a dentist, call Dental Referral Service (☎ 800/917-6453). They can tell you the nearest dentist who meets your needs. Phones are manned daily from 5:30am to 6pm. Check the Yellow Pages for 24-hour emergency services.

Emergencies   Dial ☎ 911 to contact the police or fire department, or to call an ambulance. Always call 911 in case of a serious medical emergency or accident. For less urgent requests, call ☎ 800/647-9284, a number sponsored by the Florida Tourism Industry Marketing Corporation, the state tourism promotions board. With operators speaking over 100 languages, it can provide general directions and help with lost travel papers and credit cards, medical emergencies, accidents, money transfers, airline confirmation, and much more.

Florist   Floral and fruit arrangements can be delivered anywhere on Walt Disney World Resort property by calling ☎ 407/827-3505 between 8am and 8pm. Elsewhere in central Florida, try ☎ 1-800-FLOWERS (800/356-9377) or Flower Star at ☎ 800/311-0404.

Hospitals   Sand Lake Hospital, 9400 Turkey Lake Rd. (☎ 407/351-8550), is about 2 miles south of Sand Lake Road. From the WDW area, take I-4 east to Exit 29, turn left at the exit onto Sand Lake Road, and make a left on Turkey Lake Road. The hospital is 2 miles up on your right. Celebration Health, (☎407/764-4000) located in the Disney-owned town of Celebration, is at 400 Celebration Pl. From I-4, take Exit 25a. At the first traffic light, turn right onto Celebration Avenue. At the first stop sign, take another right.

Kennels   All of the major theme parks offer animal-boarding facilities at reasonable fees. At Walt Disney World, there are kennels at Fort Wilderness, Epcot, the Magic Kingdom, Animal Kingdom, and Disney–MGM Studios. Resort guests can board their pets overnight for $9; others pay $11. Sea World and Universal also offer kennels where you can leave your animals during the day. If you're traveling with a pet, don't leave it in the car—even with a window cracked—while you enjoy the park. Many pets have perished this way in the hot Florida sun, and you may be charged with animal cruelty.

Kosher Food   It can be arranged at restaurants at Disney parks and resorts with 24-hour advance notice. Call ☎ 407/WDW-DINE (939-3463).

Liquor Laws   Minimum drinking age is 21. No liquor is served in the Magic Kingdom at Walt Disney World. However, drinks are available at the other parks, and are quite evident at Universal's Mardi Gras celebration and its Halloween Horror Nights.

Lockers   You can rent lockers at all of the Disney parks, and at Universal Studios and Sea World. Many other attractions, such as miniature golf courses or water parks, also offer this service. The cost is usually around $1 to $2 for the day. Inquire at a Guest Relations desk. For safety purposes, it is better to keep valuables, such as camera equipment, in a locker rather than in your car.

Lost Children   Every theme park has a designated spot for parents to meet up with lost children (or lost spouses). Find out where it is when you enter any park and instruct your children to ask park personnel to take them there if they are lost. Point out what park personnel look like. Young children should have name tags that include their parents' names, the name of the hotel where they are staying, and a contact number back home in the very rare case that parents can't be located.

Newspapers and Magazines   The *Orlando Sentinel* is the major local newspaper, but you can also purchase the Sunday editions of major city papers (most notably, the *New York Times*) in most hotel gift shops. Don't count on finding daily editions of west coast papers, such as the *Los Angeles Times* without making special arrangements. The Friday edition of the *Sentinel* includes extensive entertainment and dining listings. The *Orlando Weekly* is a free, alternative paper that has significant entertainment and art listings, most of them focused on events outside of the tourist areas.

Pharmacies   Walgreens drugstore, 1003 W. Vine St. (Hwy. 192), just east of Bermuda Avenue (☎ **407/847-5252**), operates a 24-hour pharmacy. They will deliver to hotels for a charge ($10 from 7am to 5pm, $15 at all other times). There is an Eckerd drugstore at 7324 International Dr. (☎ **407/345-0491**), open 24 hours a day. There is also a 24-hour Eckerd's store at 1306 Bermuda Ave. (☎ **407/847-5174**).

Photography   Two-hour film processing is available at all major parks. Look for the Photo Express sign. You can also buy film, and rent or buy 35mm, disc, and video cameras in all four parks. Many convenience and discount stores, such as Walgreens, Eckerd, Kmart, and Target, also offer next-day photo processing. These discount stores often provide coupons for half-off photo processing, which could save you a significant amount of money.

Post Office   The main post office in Lake Buena Vista is at 12541 Fla. 535, near T.G.I. Friday's in the Crossroads Shopping Center (☎ **407/828-2606**). It's open Monday through Friday from 9am to 4pm, Saturday from 9am to noon. You can buy stamps and mail letters at most hotels.

Safety   Don't let the aura of Mickey Mouse allow you to relax your guard here; Orlando has a crime rate that is comparable to that of other major U.S. cities. Stay alert, and remain aware of your immediate surroundings. It's a good idea to keep your valuables in a safe-deposit box (inquire at the front desk), although nowadays, some hotels are equipped with in-room safes. Do keep a close eye on your valuables when you're in a public place—restaurant, theater, even an airport terminal. Renting a locker is always preferable to leaving your valuables in the trunk of your car, even in the theme park parking lots. Be cautious, even in the theme parks, and avoid carrying large amounts of cash in a backpack, or fanny pack, which could be easily accessed while you are standing in line for a ride or show.

If you are renting a car, carefully read the safety instructions that the rental company provides. Never stop for any reason in an unpopulated area, and remember that children should never ride in the front seat of a car equipped with air bags.

Taxes   Hotel tax in Orlando and Kissimmee is 11%, which includes a state sales tax (6%) that is charged on all goods, except most grocery store items and medicines.

Telephone   Because of its growth spurt, Orlando has recently instituted a change in its local calling procedures. If you are making a **local** call in Orlando's 407 area code region, **you must now dial the area code followed by the number you wish to call,** for a total of 10 digits.

Time   Orlando is in the eastern standard time zone, which is 1 hour later than Chicago and 3 hours later than Los Angeles. Call ☎ **407/646-3131** for the correct time and temperature.

Tourist Information   See section 1, "Orientation," in this chapter.

Weather   Call ☎ **407/851-7510** for a weather recording. Also look for "The Weather Channel" on Time Warner Cable, the local cable provider. Most hotels carry basic cable. The *Orlando Sentinel* also includes a daily forecast. A local 24-hour news station, channel 13, offers weather forecasts several times an hour.

5 Accommodations

There are more than 88,000 hotel rooms in the Orlando region for vacationers to choose from, with dozens of properties located near the biggest tourist draws—Walt Disney World, Universal Studios Escape, and Sea World. Beautifully landscaped resorts are the rule when you're talking about Disney properties and those in the vicinity of Lake Buena Vista. Throughout the area, however, you are sure to find something to fit your taste and budget. If you are looking for inexpensive and moderately priced hotels check out the available options in Kissimmee, and those along International Drive. I've even listed a couple of bed & breakfasts.

For all accommodations, you should reserve as far in advance as possible—ideally, the minute you've decided on the dates of your trip. This is always important at the busy WDW properties, but planning ahead is especially crucial in this year of the new millennium. Advanced reservations are also a good idea for the properties around Universal Studios Escape, as it continues to draw big crowds to its new theme park, Islands of Adventure.

HOW TO CHOOSE A HOTEL & SAVE MONEY

All of the rates cited below are "rack rates," which means they are the typical prices listed in hotel brochures. You will almost always be able to negotiate a better rate, either through a package deal or some sort of organizational discount. This is where your membership in the Elks, or some other organization, may really come in handy. Many organizations, including the biggies—AARP and AAA—offer discount hotel reservations to their members. Discount rates at chain hotels are often included among the perks offered by many credit cards. Ask about available discounts when making your reservations.

Many people assume that motels outside the Disney realm cost less than staying on WDW premises, but that isn't always the case. The **average hotel rate** for the Orlando metro area, is about $81, of course that rate climbs about 10% a year. The lowest room rates at WDW are $74 to $104 (rooms in the three All-Star Resorts). Of course, these properties tend to fill up quickly.

Overall room rates are **lowest** in July, August, and September; they are **highest** in January, February, and March.

If you don't have a car, be sure to note the price of **hotel shuttle buses** to and from the theme parks. Compute these charges—

which can be as high as $14 per person per day—in determining a hotel's price value. Or, if you drive your own car, don't forget to count parking fees, usually $5 a day at WDW and $6 at Universal Studios Escape. All Disney-owned properties and Disney "official" hotels offer complimentary transportation to and from WDW parks (for more details on this, and the other advantages of staying at Disney properties, see "The Perks of Staying with Mickey" below). However, the least expensive WDW properties are some distance from the parks, so you have to weigh the value of your time.

In or out of Walt Disney World, if you book your hotel as part of a **package** (see "Money-Saving Packages" in chapter 2 for details), you'll likely enjoy big savings.

Many people don't know that you can bargain with the reservations clerk when booking a hotel. The reason: An unoccupied room nets a hotel zero dollars, and any reasonable offer is better than getting nothing. Of course, this works only if you book upon arrival, preferably late in the afternoon when the desk knows there will be empty rooms. It will also work better outside of Walt Disney World; you probably won't have a lot of success doing this at WDW hotels.

Another money-saving tip: Reserving via **toll-free numbers** at chain hotels sometimes puts you in the running for lower rates than reserving at individual properties. Ask about special discounts for students, government employees, senior citizens, military, AAA, and/or corporate clients. Special discounts and packages may also be featured on hotel Web sites, especially those of larger chains. If you do not have a computer, it may be worth it to ask for help from a computer savvy friend, or to visit a public library with Internet access to do a little research.

Also, Disney does not have an 800 number, so you're better off reviewing your choices **online** if you have Internet access or can get online at your local library. At the very least, obtain literature and **review your options** before going through the involved reservation process.

In the descriptions of accommodations, under "Amenities," I mention **concierge levels** whenever they are available. In these "hotels within a hotel," guests enjoy a luxurious private lounge (usually with spectacular views) that is the setting for complimentary continental breakfasts, hot and cold hors d'oeuvres served at a cocktail hour, and late-night cordials and pastries. Rooms are usually on high floors and the room decor is upgraded. Guests are pampered with special services (private registration and checkout, a personal concierge, nightly bed turndown) and amenities (upgraded toiletries, bathroom scales, terry robes, hair dryers). Ask for specifics when you reserve your room. Concierge levels are especially attractive to businesspeople traveling on their own.

You'll also find counselor-supervised **child-care** or **activity centers** in some of the hotels "Amenities" listings. Very popular in Orlando, these are marvelous, creatively run facilities where kids enjoy movies, video games, arts and crafts, storytelling, puppet shows, indoor and outdoor activities, and much more. Some centers provide meals and/or have beds where a child can go to sleep while you're out on the town. Check individual hotel listings for these facilities, and call the hotels to find out exactly what is offered.

RESERVATION SERVICES

Many of the Kissimmee hotels listed under "Best Hotel Bets" in chapter 1 can be booked by calling the **Kissimmee–St. Cloud Convention & Visitors Bureau** at ☎ **800/333-KISS** (5477).

You should also consider using the services of an Orlando-based organization called **Check-In** (☎ **800/237-1033** or 941/756-4880; fax 941/739-2703). A central booking agency, it has listings for hundreds of condos, resorts, hotels, villas, and luxurious private homes in all price ranges. A minimum stay of 3 nights is required. Check-In doesn't accept credit cards, but it does take personal checks. There's no fee for the service.

You can get Internet information on Disney hotels at **www.disneyworld.com.** To cruise through the information, click on "Resorts & Spas." To make reservations, click on "Resort Reservations." Disney recently offered the general public the ability to make reservations themselves, a perk that had previously been limited to travel agents. The reservations icon looks like a computer screen and invites you to reserve your hotel room online.

HOW TO USE THIS CHAPTER

The hotels listed below are first divided by location, and then by price category alphabetically within a given district. All of the properties I've selected offer easy access to the Disney parks and other nearby major attractions. As you might expect, most of the inexpensive properties tend to be farthest from the action.

Hotels listed in the **inexpensive** category are those charging $80 or less for a double room (don't blame me, I didn't invent inflation). Properties offering $80 to $150 rooms make up the **moderate** category, $150 to $200 rooms are listed as **expensive,** and anything above that ranks as **very expensive.** Any extras included in the rates (for example, breakfast or other meals) are listed for each property. Categories are variable because hotel rates change, depending on whether you visit during peak or off-seasons.

Keep in mind that Orlando doesn't operate on a traditional winter/summer pattern of off-season and peak season. Overall room rates are **lowest** in July, August, and September; they are **highest** in January, February, and March. Peak season rates can, however, be put into effect during large conventions and special events. Even something as remote as Bike Week in Daytona Beach can raise prices in the off-season. These kinds of events especially impact moderately-priced properties outside of Walt Disney World.

1 The Perks of Staying with Mickey

Described in the next section are the 18 Disney-owned properties (hotels, resorts, villas, wilderness homes, and campsites), and the 9 privately-owned properties designated as "official" hotels. All are within the Walt Disney World complex, either in the formal "park" areas or in nearby Lake Buena Vista.

In addition to location (they all offer close proximity to the parks), there are other distinct advantages to staying at a Disney property or official hotel, especially the former. The following are included at all Disney resorts and official hotels:

- Unlimited complimentary transportation via bus, monorail, ferry, and water taxi to and from all four Disney parks, from 2 hours prior to opening until 2 hours after closing. Unlimited complimentary transport is also provided to and from Disney Village Marketplace/Downtown Disney, Typhoon Lagoon, River Country, Blizzard Beach, Downtown Disney, Fort Wilderness, and the other Disney resorts. Three properties—the Polynesian, Contemporary, and Grand Floridian—are stops on the monorail. This free transport can save a lot of the money you'd otherwise have to spend on a rental car or expensive hotel shuttle buses. It also means you're guaranteed admission to all parks, even during peak times when parking lots sometimes fill up.
- "Surprise Mornings" where selected rides at different parks are opened early to resort guests on certain days.

- Free parking at WDW parking lots (other visitors pay $5 a day).
- Reduced-price children's menus in almost all restaurants.
- Character breakfasts and/or dinners at many restaurants.
- TVs equipped with the Disney channel and Walt Disney World information stations.
- A guest-services desk where you can purchase tickets to all WDW theme parks and attractions and obtain general information.
- Use of—and in some cases, complimentary transport to—the Disney-owned golf courses and preferred tee times (these can be booked up to 30 days in advance).
- Access to most of the Disney Resorts' recreational facilities.
- Mears airport shuttle service.

Additional perks at Disney-owned hotels, resorts, villas, and campgrounds—as well as at the Walt Disney World Swan and Dolphin, but not at the other official hotels—include the following:

- Charge privileges at restaurants and shops throughout Walt Disney World.
- On-premises National Car Rental desk.

WALT DISNEY WORLD CENTRAL RESERVATIONS OFFICE

To reserve a room at Disney hotels, resorts, and villas; official hotels; or Fort Wilderness homes and campsites, contact **Central Reservations Operations (CRO),** P.O. Box 10000, Lake Buena Vista, FL 32830-1000 (☎ **407/W-DISNEY** [934-7639]), open Monday through Friday from 8am to 10pm, Saturday and Sunday from 9am to 6pm. Have your dates and credit card ready when you call. Remember, this is not a toll-free call, so it's best to be prepared.

CRO can recommend accommodations that will suit your specific needs as to price, location (perhaps you wish to be closest to Epcot or the Magic Kingdom, etc.), and facilities such as counselor-supervised child-care centers, a pool large enough for lap swimming, a state-of-the-art health club, on-premises golf or tennis (or other recreational facilities), a kitchen, and so on.

Be sure to inquire about Disney's numerous package plans, which include meals, tickets, recreation, and other features. The right package plan can save you money and time (more of your vacation is planned in advance), and a comprehensive plan is helpful in computing the cost of your vacation in advance.

CRO can also give you information about various park ticket options, and make dinner-show reservations for you at the Hoop-Dee-Doo Musical Revue or the Polynesian Luau Dinner Show when you book your room.

OTHER SOURCES FOR PACKAGES

In addition to the CRO, there are other sources for packages utilizing Disney resorts. These include Delta Dream Vacations (☎ 800/872-7786), US Airways Vacations (☎ 800/455-0123), American Airlines Fly Away Vacations (☎ 800/ 321-2121), American Express Vacations (☎ **800/241-1700**), Travel Impressions (☎ **800/941-2639**), and Kingdom Tours (☎ 800/872-8857). Best bet: Stop at a sizable travel agency and pick up brochures from all of the above (and others). Pore over them at home, comparing the offerings to find the optimum package for your trip.

On a slightly smaller scale, Universal Studios Escape offers travel packages that can include resort stays, VIP access to the park, and discounts to other Orlando-area attractions. They also offer "fun and sun" packages that include beach trips to Tampa. Some Universal packages also include air travel and transportation.

You can book a package through Universal Studio Vacations at ☎ **888/322-5537** or ☎ 407/224-7000, or you can go online to **www.usevactions.com.**

COMING SOON

There is still talk of a new resort adjacent to Animal Kingdom, tentatively called The **Safari Lodge.** Keep an eye out for details on this African-themed hotel, designed to complement Disney's newest park.

Universal Studios also has ambitious expansion plans. The 750-room Portofino Bay opened in 1999. The 650-room Hard Rock Hotel is expected to open late in 2000. A yet-to-be named resort with a South Seas theme and 1,000 rooms is expected to open at Universal in 2001. All in all, Universal plans to open five properties, containing approximately 5,000 rooms, over the next few years so it can go head-to-head with Disney for on-site accommodations.

2 Places to Stay in Walt Disney World

The resorts in this section are all either Disney-owned hotels or "official" hotels (affiliated with, but not owned by, Disney). More importantly, all the hotels in this section are on the Disney transportation system, which means you may not need to rent a car if you stay at one of these choices.

When you begin planning your trip, call to get the Disney World Vacations brochure, which lists Disney's hotel options. Once you have narrowed your choices, it's best to call the first number listed with each property. This is the central reservation number. (There is no 800 number.) The other number listed in the brochure is for the front desk of the hotel. If you call this number they will refer you back to the central reservations operator. Also, if you have access to the Internet, complete information on all WDW properties can be found at **www.disneyworld.com;** click on "Resorts & Spas." There you can review packages and even make your own reservations.

Once you're on Disney property, large colorful signs along all the major roads will direct you to all the WDW hotels. You'll find all these hotels listed on the map "Walt Disney World & Lake Buena Vista Accommodations" in this section.

All the prices listed below reflect the range of prices available at each resort. Prices vary depending on the season and room location, but the numbers should allow you to determine how individual properties will fit into your budget.

VERY EXPENSIVE

✪ **Disney's Beach Club Resort.** 1800 Epcot Resorts Blvd. (off Buena Vista Dr.; P.O. Box 10000), Lake Buena Vista, FL 32830-0100. ☎ **407/W-DISNEY** (934-7639) or 407/934-8000. Fax 407/934-3850. 597 units. A/C MINIBAR TV TEL. $264–$535 double; $425–$1,110 suites. Prices depend on view and season. AE, MC, V. Free self- and valet parking.

The Beach Club resembles a luxurious Victorian Cape Cod resort, and its location—within walking distance of Epcot Center—is just one of many attractive features. A big draw here—especially for families—is Stormalong Bay, a vast free-form swimming pool/water park that sprawls over 3 acres between the Beach Club and the Yacht Club, and flows into a lake; it includes a 150-foot serpentine water slide. So posh is the Beach Club—and so extensive are its sports facilities—that it would make an excellent upscale resort destination, even without the draw of the Disney parks nearby. The charming rooms, some with balconies, can comfortably accommodate five people, and are furnished in bleached woods and pastels. Rooms are equipped with ceiling fans, extra phones in the bathroom, and safes. The Beach Club is slightly less formal than its sister properties, the Yacht Club and the Grand Floridian.

Dining: Ideal for family dining is the Cape May Café, serving character breakfasts and authentic New England clambake buffet dinners. At the adjoining property, the

Yacht Club, The Yachtsman Steakhouse, open only for dinner, specializes in hearty meals such as porterhouse steak, Chateaubriand, and prime rib. Other facilities here serve drinks, wine by the glass, light fare, and ice cream.

Amenities: Room service (24 hours), baby-sitting, guest-services desk, complimentary daily newspaper, boat transport to MGM theme park, large outdoor swimming pool, whirlpool, quarter-mile sand beach, boat rental, fishing, two tennis courts, state-of-the-art health club, volleyball, croquet, bocci ball courts, 2-mile jogging trail, coin-op washers/dryers, unisex hair salon, shops, business center, video-game arcade, and the Sandcastle Club, a counselor-supervised children's activity center.

☼ Disney's BoardWalk. 2101 N. Epcot Resorts Blvd. (off Buena Vista Dr.; P.O. Box 10000), Lake Buena Vista, FL 32830-1000. ☎ **407/W-DISNEY** (934-7639) or 407/939-5100 (407/939-6200 for villas). Fax 407/934-5150. 378 units, 532 villas. A/C TV TEL. $254–$580 double; $590–$1,540 for villas. Rates depend on view and season. Children 17 and under stay free in parents' room. AE, MC, V. Free self- and valet parking.

Night owls will appreciate a stay at the BoardWalk, a plush 1920s-style "seaside" resort occupying 45 acres along the shores of Lake Crescent. A large deck with rocking chairs overlooks a village green and the lake beyond, and the stunning 70-foot lobby has a working fireplace. The property connects to a quarter-mile boardwalk that offers shops, restaurants, and street performers. It is also within walking distance of Epcot, and the Yacht and Beach Clubs. There's plenty to do here once the sun goes down, making it a good choice for singles and couples without children. Guests can choose between inn-style rooms or villas. The B&B-style accommodations are large and beautifully decorated; they may include two brass queen beds, or a four-poster bed. All have safes, irons and ironing boards, and hair dryers; refrigerators are available. The villas, though pricey, may be a good choice for large families or groups; they can sleep up to 12, offer kitchenettes or full kitchens, washer/dryers, and some contain whirlpool tubs.

Dining/Diversions: Situated along the boardwalk promenade to provide scenic water views, the dining facilities here include the upscale Flying Fish Café for steak and seafood; Spoodle's, a casual spot serving Mediterranean fare; the Big River Grille and Brewing Works (featuring hand-crafted beers and ales); ESPN Club, a sports bar; a bakery; and a coffee bar. A 10-piece orchestra plays music from the 1940s through today's Top 40s at Atlantic Dance, a 1920s-style dance hall. Jellyrolls, a sing-along bar, features dueling pianos. There are also several cocktail lounges and a carousel-themed pool bar.

Amenities: Concierge, room service (24 hours), baby-sitting, boat transport (to MGM, Epcot, and the Epcot resorts), guest-services desk, complimentary daily newspaper, large outdoor swimming pool with water slide, two additional secluded pools, kiddie pool, whirlpool, two tennis courts, croquet, bike rental, 2-mile jogging path, playground, convention center, full business center, shops, extensively equipped health club, two video-game arcades, Community Hall (for games, crafts, recreational equipment rentals, videotapes, and books), and the Harbour Club, a counselor-supervised child-care activity center.

☼ Disney's Contemporary Resort. 4600 N. World Dr. (P.O. Box 10000), Lake Buena Vista, FL 32830-1000. ☎ **407/W-DISNEY** (934-7639) or 407/824-1000. Fax 407/824-3535. 1,121 units. A/C TV TEL. $214–$460 double; $680–$1,365 suites. AE, MC, V. Free self- and valet parking.

If location is a priority, the Contemporary is a good bet; since it is literally on the monorail system, you can zip right to the parks. Centering on a sleek, 15-story A-frame tower, the resort comprises 26 acres bounded by a natural lake and the

Walt Disney World & Lake Buena Vista Accommodations

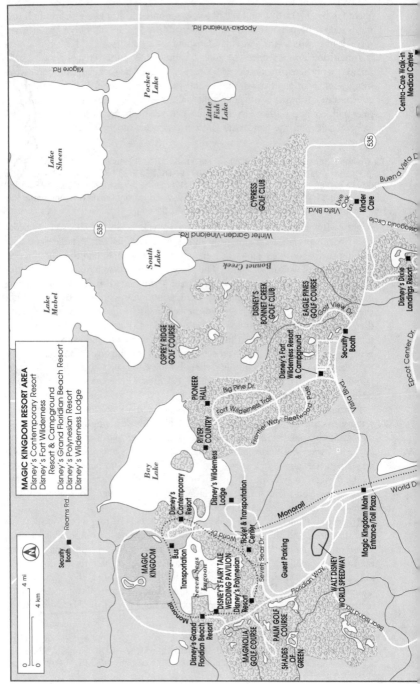

MAGIC KINGDOM RESORT AREA
Disney's Contemporary Resort
Disney's Fort Wilderness
  Resort & Campground
Disney's Grand Floridian Beach Resort
Disney's Polynesian Resort
Disney's Wilderness Lodge

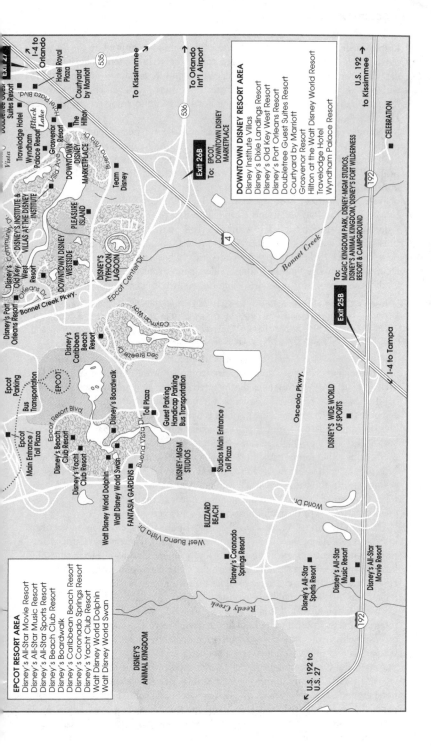

EPCOT RESORT AREA

Disney's All-Star Movie Resort
Disney's All-Star Music Resort
Disney's All-Star Sports Resort
Disney's Beach Club Resort
Disney's Boardwalk
Disney's Caribbean Beach Resort
Disney's Coronado Springs Resort
Disney's Yacht Club Resort
Walt Disney World Dolphin
Walt Disney World Swan

DOWNTOWN DISNEY RESORT AREA

Disney Institute Villas
Disney's Dixie Landings Resort
Disney's Old Key West Resort
Disney's Port Orleans Resort
Doubletree Guest Suites Resort
Courtyard by Marriott
Grosvenor Resort
Hilton at the Walt Disney World Resort
Travelodge Hotel
Wyndham Palace Resort

Exit 26B
To: EPCOT, DOWNTOWN DISNEY MARKETPLACE

Exit 25B
To: MAGIC KINGDOM PARK, DISNEY-MGM STUDIOS, DISNEY'S ANIMAL KINGDOM, DISNEY'S FORT WILDERNESS RESORT & CAMPGROUND

Disney-made Seven Seas Lagoon. A major renovation has spruced up the 29-year-old hotel's decor, so that it no longer appears so retro-modern. The neutrally-decorated rooms are among Disney's biggest—a plus for families— and most come with two queen beds, a daybed, and breathtaking views. Kids will be thrilled when the monorail whizzes right through the hotel; they'll also enjoy the on-premises character meals.

Dining: The magnificent 15th-floor California Grill (see chapter 6) provides panoramic vistas of the Magic Kingdom. Other options here are the Concourse Steakhouse, the garden-themed Chef Mickey's Buffet (for character breakfasts and prime rib buffet dinners), and several other spots offering drinks and light fare.

Amenities: Room service (24 hours), guest-services desk, daily newspaper delivery, baby-sitting, boat transport (to Fort Wilderness and River Country), monorail to the Polynesian and Grand Floridian resorts. Two swimming pools, kiddie pool, white-sand beach with volleyball court, shuffleboard, boat rental, unisex hair salon, six tennis courts (lessons available), shops, American Express desk, car-rental desk, coin-op washers/dryers, full business center, extensive health club, sauna/massage/tanning rooms, video-game arcade, and the Mouseketeer Clubhouse, a counselor-supervised child-care/activity center.

✪ Disney's Grand Floridian Beach Resort. 4401 Floridian Way (P.O. Box 10000), Lake Buena Vista, FL 32830-1000. ☎ **407/W-DISNEY** [934-7639] or 407/824-3000. Fax 407/824-3186. 933 units. A/C MINIBAR TV TEL. $299–$645 double, depending on view and season; $754–$1,875 suites. AE, MC, V. Free self- and valet parking.

The world-renowned Grand Floridian is magnificent from the moment you step into its opulent, five-story domed lobby (complete with a Chinese Chippendale aviary). Here a pianist entertains during afternoon tea, and an orchestra plays big-band music every evening. The hotel is a romantic choice for couples—even honeymooners (the Disney wedding pavilion is here, by the way, if you'd like to tie the knot during your stay). And if you're into fitness, you'll appreciate the first-rate health club and spa. The large sunny rooms—with private balconies or verandahs overlooking either formal gardens, the pool, or a 200-acre lagoon—have two-poster beds dressed with lovely floral-chintz spreads. In-room amenities include safes and ceiling fans; in the bathroom you'll find an extra phone, a hair dryer, and a terry robe. The resort's location—on the monorail line, and off the Seven Seas Lagoon— offers quick access to the parks, boating, and water activities.

Dining/Diversions: Victoria & Albert's, Orlando's finest restaurant, is described in "Places to Dine in Walt Disney World" in chapter 6. There is also Citricos, featuring light, flavorful French cuisine. The lovely Grand Floridian Café, overlooking formal gardens, features Southern specialties. The exposition-themed 1900 Park Fare is the setting for character breakfasts and dinners. Flagler's offers northern Italian fare. At the gazebolike Narcoossee's, grilled meats and seafood are prepared in an exhibition kitchen. Intimate and very Victorian, Mizner's Lounge features an international selection of ports, brandies, and appetizers. The Garden View Lounge, off the lobby, is the setting for elegant afternoon teas. Other options include the Gasparilla Grill (open 24 hours) and a pool bar.

Amenities: On-premises monorail, boat transport to Magic Kingdom, room service (24 hours), nightly turndown, baby-sitting, free trolley transport around the hotel grounds, shoe shine, massage, guest-services desk, complimentary daily newspaper. Large outside swimming pool with poolside changing area, kiddie pool, whirlpool, two tennis courts, boat rental, water-skiing, croquet, volleyball, playground, jogging trails, fishing excursions, white-sand beach, unisex hair salon, coin-op washers/dryers, shops, car-rental desk, state-of-the-art spa, video-game arcade, organized children's activities in summer and peak seasons, and the Mouseketeer Clubhouse, a counselor-supervised child-care activity center.

Disney's Old Key West Resort. 1510 N. Cove Rd. (off Community Dr.; P.O. Box 10000), Lake Buena Vista, FL 32830-1000. ☎ **407/W-DISNEY** (934-7639) or 407/827-7700. Fax 407/827-7710. 709 units. A/C TV TEL. $195–$215 deluxe; $229–$1,050 villa. Range reflects high and low seasons and 1-, 2-, and 3-bedroom villas. AE, MC, V. Free self-parking.

An understated theme (at least by Disney standards) makes the Old Key West a good choice for those seeking a quieter environment. Architecturally mirroring Key West at the turn of the century, this is a "vacation ownership" (time-share) property that rents accommodations when they're not in use by the owners. The 156-acre complex is beautifully landscaped: Tree-lined, brick walkways are edged by white picket fences, and the air is scented with honeysuckle. Most of the villas are gorgeous homes away from home, with living rooms (equipped with large-screen TVs and VCRs, smaller sets and extra phones in the bedroom), fully equipped kitchens, furnished patios (offering water, woodland, or fairway views; the property overlooks the Buena Vista Golf Course), and laundry rooms. The accommodations range from standard rooms to two-bedroom villas. Many units contain whirlpool tubs in the master suite, and the Grand Villas have stereo systems.

Dining: The Key West–themed Olivia's Cafe, overlooking a canal, serves all meals. There are a few other spots for drinks and light fare.

Amenities: Guest-services desk, ferry service to Disney Village Marketplace and Downtown Disney, free bus transport around the grounds, food shopping; two tennis courts, basketball court, white-sand play area, four swimming pools, whirlpool, kiddie pool, bicycle rental, boat rental, playground, extensive health club, sauna, shuffleboard, horseshoes, volleyball, complimentary use of washers/dryers, general store, video-game arcade, video library. The Community Hall, a recreation center, shows Disney movies nightly and offers various activities.

✪ **Disney's Polynesian Resort.** 1600 Seven Seas Dr. (P.O. Box 10000), Lake Buena Vista, FL 32830-1000. ☎ **407/W-DISNEY** (934-7639) or 407/824-2000. Fax 407/824-3174. 853 units. A/C TV TEL. $275–$580 double, depending on view and season; $595–$1,425 suites. AE, MC, V. Free self- and valet parking.

Just below the Magic Kingdom, the 25-acre Polynesian Resort is fronted by lush tropical foliage, waterfalls, and koi ponds. Inside, its skylit lobby is a virtual rain forest of tropical plants—gorgeous by day, but rather depressingly lit at night. A private white-sand beach—dotted with canvas cabanas, hammocks, and large swings—overlooks a 200-acre lagoon. Waterfalls, grottoes, and a water slide enhance an immense swimming pool. The large, beautiful rooms—most with balconies or patios—have canopied beds, bamboo and rattan furnishings, and walls hung with Gauguin prints. This is a great choice for families traveling with kids, who will enjoy the Polynesian theme and child-pleasing restaurants. The resort also boasts a good location; it's right on the monorail system.

Dining/Diversions: 'Ohana (see section 2, "Places to Dine in Walt Disney World" in chapter 6) is the setting for character breakfasts and all-you-can-eat island dinners featuring open-pit rock-grilled specialties. Luau Cove hosts Mickey's Tropical Luau and the Polynesian Luau Dinner Show. Kona Cafe specializes in gourmet coffee, along with Pacific-influenced New American cuisine.

There are several other restaurants and bars, including a 24-hour ice-cream parlor.

Amenities: Room service, baby-sitting, on-premises monorail, boat transport (to the Magic Kingdom and the Grand Floridian Beach Resort), guest-services desk, complimentary daily newspaper, two swimming pools, kiddie pool, boat rental,

The Disney Institute: The Mouse Grows Up

The Disney Institute is a concept designed strictly for adults and older children (10 and up). Resembling a small town with a village green, and architecture evocative of barns, mills, and country houses, it sprawls over 265 acres of lakes, streams, and woodlands.

The Institute enables guests to custom-design Walt Disney World vacations that focus on interactive programs in dozens of diverse areas. This is a great 1-day adventure for couples, seniors, or adult children traveling with older parents, and it provides a pleasant alternative to trekking through the theme parks. Since classes are small, participants spend real face-to-face time with their instructors. My mom and I enjoyed a morning program on Asian cooking, and spent an afternoon taking an introduction course in animation. We left with the recipes from the cooking class and a tape of our first (and probably last) short film. We even got to eat our (culinary) creations for lunch. The classes tend to be relatively fast-paced because professionals have just a few hours to provide a broad overview, but most are designed with the novice in mind and offer step-by-step instructions.

Gourmets will be especially interested in the programs offered in conjunction with the International Wine Festival in June. During that time, you can learn the culinary secrets of prominent chefs. All classes are taught by professionals, and many are enhanced by noted guest artists and speakers. Marshall Brickman, Chris Columbus, Randy Newman, and Morton Gould are among the dozens of well-known directors, critics, singers, and composers that Disney has tapped to participate in its Entertainment Arts programs. The arts programs are augmented by evening concerts and other related activities. The Institute hasn't caught on with individuals as much as Disney had originally planned, so participants are increasingly part of a group. That narrows your choices a bit, but programs are

water-skiing, volleyball, playground, 1½-mile jogging trail, fishing excursions, coin-op washers/dryers, shops, video-game arcade, and the Neverland Club, a counselor-supervised evening activity center for children.

✪ **Disney's Yacht Club Resort.** 1700 Epcot Resorts Blvd. (off Buena Vista Dr.; P.O. Box 10000), Lake Buena Vista, FL 32830-1000. ☎ **407/W-DISNEY** (934-7639) or 407/934-7000. Fax 407/924-3450. 642 units. A/C MINIBAR TV TEL. $264–$540 double, depending on view and season; $445–$1,285 concierge-level double. AE, MC, V. Free self- and valet parking.

Though first-time visitors to Orlando—who generally spend all their time in the parks—rarely make use of a resort's recreational facilities, return visitors will appreciate the extensive sports and entertainment options here. This stunning resort—its main five-story, oyster-gray clapboard building evoking a turn-of-the-century New England yacht club—shares a 25-acre lake, facilities, and gorgeous landscaping with the adjacent Beach Club (described earlier). The nautical theme carries over to the very inviting rooms, decorated in snappy blue and white, with brass sconces, ship lights, and vintage maps on the walls. The rooms sleep up to five, and have French doors that open onto porches or balconies. Amenities include ceiling fans, extra phones in the bathroom, and safes. Business travelers will especially appreciate the concierge-level rooms on the fifth floor.

Dining/Diversions: The plush Yachtsman Steakhouse grills select cuts of steak, chops, and fresh seafood over oak and hickory. The Yacht Club Galley, a comfortable family restaurant, serves American regional fare. The Crew's Cup Lounge airs still available in areas such as Sports and Fitness, Lifestyles, Story Arts, Culinary Arts, Design, the Environment, and Architecture—options are almost limitless. You might opt for a golf or tennis clinic, indulge in an array of luxurious spa treatments, learn topiary gardening, canoe on local waterways, or try rock climbing.

The Institute's resort-style public areas and accommodations (bungalows and one- and two-bedroom town houses) are gorgeous. The cuisine at the elegant on-premises restaurant, Seasons, changes nightly. There are extensive sporting facilities, an 18-hole/par-72 championship golf course, tennis courts, and swimming pools.

Nightly performances and recitals take place in a 1,150-seat open-air amphitheater and a 250-seat performance center. Films are screened weeknights in a state-of-the-art movie theater. A counselor-supervised youth center, comfortably appointed with couches, videos, and games, offers a full roster of daytime programs and activities for children ages 10 to 12, and teens, as well as evening activities for teens.

The Institute is adjacent to the Disney Village Marketplace at 1960 N. Magnolia Way. Package rates range from 3-night stays for around $600 to 7-night stays for about $2,000. A good bet for the budget-minded is a single-day admission, costing around $100, that includes programs and classes, but not accommodations. Single-day visitors should allow plenty of time to find the bungalow classrooms. The signs can be confusing, and we were misdirected several times by employees during our visit. But once you find what you're looking for, you'll be glad you made the effort. For further information on programs and rates, call ☎ **800/4-WONDER** (496-6337) or 407/827-4800.

sporting events and features international beers. And the cozy Ale and Compass Lounge, a lobby bar with a working fireplace, offers specialty coffees and cocktails.

Amenities: Room service (24 hours), baby-sitting, guest-services desk, complimentary daily newspaper, boat transport to the MGM theme park, tram and boat transport to Epcot. Yacht Club facilities are identical to those of the Beach Club (described earlier).

✪ **Walt Disney World Dolphin.** 1500 Epcot Resorts Blvd. (off Buena Vista Dr.; P.O. Box 22653), Lake Buena Vista, FL 32830-2653. ☎ **800/227-1500** or 407/934-4000. Fax 407/934-4884. www.swandolphin.com. 1,509 units. A/C MINIBAR TV TEL. $275–$430 double, depending on view and season; $395–$2,990 suites. Up to 2 children under 18 stay free in parents' room. Inquire about packages. AE, CB, DC, DISC, JCB, MC, V. Free self-parking; valet parking $6. Take I-4 east to 25B. This is the exit to Epcot/Magic Kingdom. Follow purple and red signs to the resort areas.

Though distinctive architecture is its keynote, sports enthusiasts will also relish this Sheraton resort's health club, pools, boat rentals, and tennis facilities. Designed by whimsical architect Michael Graves, the property centers on a 27-story pyramid with two 11-story wings crowned by 56-foot twin dolphin sculptures. Graves dubs his more-Disneyesque-than-Disney creations "entertainment architecture." A free-form rock-sculpted grotto pool—with waterfalls, a water slide, rope bridge, and three secluded whirlpools—sprawls over 2 acres between the Dolphin and the adjoining Swan. Both properties also share a white sandy beach on Crescent Lake.

Art enthusiasts could spend hours studying the thousands of works of art that adorn the public areas. In the rooms, walls are hung with art prints (Picasso, Matisse, and more), and painted wood furnishings are stenciled with palm trees and pineapples. The fairly large rooms contain two queen beds, and some feature a balcony. Amenities include pay movies, desk and bedside phones, safes, coffeemakers, hair dryers, and irons/ironing boards. The Dolphin Towers comprise a 77-room concierge level.

Dining/Diversions: The elegant Sum Chows serves haute-cuisine pan-Asian dinners. Juan and Only's Bar & Jail offers moderately priced Tex-Mex fare. Harry's Safari Bar & Grille, highlighting steak and seafood, is open for dinner nightly and Sunday character-brunch buffets. Other venues are the delightful fish-themed Coral Cafe for American fare, an ice-cream/malt shop, a 24-hour cafeteria, Copa Banana (with a DJ spinning tunes for nightly dancing plus karaoke), a lobby lounge, and a poolside bar.

Amenities: Water-launch transport to Epcot and MGM, concierge, 24-hour room service, guest-services desk (sells tickets and arranges transport to all nearby attractions), baby-sitting, Japanese tour desk, water volleyball, boat rentals, four hard-surface night-lit tennis courts, tennis pro shop, fully equipped Body by Jake health club, two beach volleyball courts, miniature golf, 3-mile jogging trail, coin-op washers/dryers, unisex hair salon, shops, full business center, Delta Airlines desk, large video-game arcade, and Camp Dolphin, a counselor-supervised children's activity center, open daily.

Walt Disney World Swan. 1200 Epcot Resorts Blvd. (off Buena Vista Dr.; P.O. Box 22786), Lake Buena Vista, FL 32830-2786. ☎ **800/248-SWAN** (7926), 800/228-3000, or 407/934-3000. www.swandolphin.com. (*Note:* You may get a lower rate by reserving through the second toll-free number for Westin Hotels.) Fax 407/934-4499. 758 units. A/C MINIBAR TV TEL. $275–$430 double, depending on view and season; $330–$2,990 suites. Children under 18 stay free in parents' room. Inquire about packages. AE, CB, DC, DISC, JCB, MC, V. Free self-parking; valet parking $8.

Operated by Westin Hotels & Resorts, this 12-story hotel—its rooftop flanked by 45-foot swan statues and seashell fountains—is adjacent to the aforementioned Dolphin, and offers you another opportunity to stay on WDW property without being bombarded by things Disney. It shares its white-sand lakeside beach and facilities with the Dolphin, and the hotels are connected by a canopied walkway. Here, Michael Graves has created a festive interior replete with swan fountains, sea horse–motif chandeliers, hallway walls painted with beach scenes, and striped room doors evocative of cabanas. The luxurious accommodations, decorated in cheerful pastels, are similar to the Dolphin's, but the Swan's rooms are a bit smaller, and some offer king beds. In-room amenities include pay movies, desk and bedside phones, and safes. King-bedded rooms have pullout sleeper sofas. The 11th and 12th floors comprise the Royal Beach Club, a concierge level.

Dining/Diversions: Serving dinner only, the casually elegant Italian-modern Palio has large windows overlooking scenic canals. Strolling musicians entertain while you dine. The delightful Garden Grove Café serves steaks and prime rib, and, in the morning, a traditional Japanese breakfast is offered. Another venue is Kimono's, which serves a wide selection of sushi, and becomes a karaoke bar after 8:30pm.

Amenities: Water launch to Epcot and MGM, concierge, 24-hour room service, guest-services desk, complimentary daily newspaper, nightly turndown on request, baby-sitting, Olympic-size lap pool, children's wading pool, fully equipped health club, full business center, children's playground, shops, video-game arcade. See also the earlier description of facilities at the Dolphin.

EXPENSIVE

✪ **Disney's Wilderness Lodge.** 901 West Timberline Dr. (on the southwest shore of Bay Lake just east of the Magic Kingdom; P.O. Box 10000), Lake Buena Vista, FL 32830-1000. ☎ **407/W-DISNEY** (934-7639) or 407/824-3200. Fax 407/824-3232. 728 units. A/C TV TEL. $180–$390 double, depending on view and season; $575–$825 suites. AE, MC, V. Free self- and valet parking.

The geyser out back, the mammoth stone hearth in the lobby, and bunk beds for the kids, are just a few reasons this is one of my favorite WDW resorts. The main dining room, with its sweeping view of 340-acre Bay Lake, may even inspire some romance. Reminiscent of a rustic turn-of-the-century national park lodge, this 56-acre resort is surrounded by towering oak and pine forests. Wilderness Lodge has the advantage of feeling removed from the rest of WDW but, unfortunately, is one of the more difficult places to access via the WDW transportation system. Five-minute geyser shows take place in the meadow periodically throughout the day, and nightly electric water pageants can be viewed from the shores of Bay Lake. A lakefront sand beach and an immense serpentine swimming pool, seemingly excavated out of the rocks, make up for the modest-sized rooms.

The guest rooms—with patios or balconies overlooking the lake, woodlands, or meadow scenery—are furnished in Mission style and adorned with tribal friezes and landscape paintings of the Northwest. Most have two queen beds, but there are several that contain a single queen and bunk beds—ideal for families. In-room safes are a plus. To get the lower rooms rates, ask for a "standard view."

Dining: The stunning lodgelike Artist Point, overlooking Bay Lake, is adorned with murals based on the works of Rocky Mountain School painters such as Albert Bierstadt; the menu highlights steak, seafood, and game specialties.

Amenities: Immense swimming pool (see above), kiddie pool with water slide, lakefront sand beach, spa pools, boat rental, bicycle rental, 2-mile jogging/bike trail, video-game arcade, gift shop, Cub's Den (a counselor-supervised activity center for children 4 to 12), room service; guest-services desk; baby-sitting; boat transport to the Magic Kingdom and Contemporary Resort; bus transport to MGM, Epcot, and other park areas.

MODERATE

✪ **Disney's Caribbean Beach Resort.** 900 Cayman Way (off Buena Vista Dr.; P.O. Box 10000), Lake Buena Vista, FL 32830-1000. ☎ **407/W-DISNEY** (934-7639) or 407/934-3400. Fax 407/934-3288. 2,112 units. A/C MINIBAR TV TEL. $119–$184 double. Children 16 and under stay free in parents' room. AE, MC, V. Free parking.

Though the facilities here aren't as extensive as those at some other Disney resorts, the Caribbean Beach offers especially good value for families. It occupies 200 lush, palm-fringed tropical acres, with accommodations grouped into five distinct Caribbean "villages" around a large, duck-filled lake. The main swimming pool here replicates a Spanish-style Caribbean fort, complete with water slide, kiddie pool, and whirlpool. There are other pools as well as lakefront white-sand beaches in each village. A 1.4-mile promenade—popular for jogging—circles the lake. An arched wooden bridge leads to Parrot Cay Island where there's a short nature trail, an aviary of tropical birds, and a picnic area. The rooms are charming, with oak furnishings and two double beds covered in chintz bedspreads. In-room amenities include coffeemakers and ceiling fans; refrigerators are available at $5 per night. The food service here is woefully limited for a resort of this size, so a rental car may be in order if you decide to eat off-premises a lot.

Dining: Facilities include a festive food court, the nautical-themed Captain's Tavern for American fare, and a pool bar.

Amenities: Room service (pizza only), guest-services desk, baby-sitting, complimentary shuttle around the grounds, seven swimming pools, video-game arcade, shops, boat rental, bicycle rental, coin-op washers/dryers, playgrounds.

Disney's Coronado Springs Resort. 1000 Buena Vista Dr., near All-Star Resorts and Blizzard Beach, Lake Buena Vista, FL 32830. ☎ **407/W-DISNEY** (934-7639), 407/934-6632, or 407/939-1000. Fax 407/939-1001. 1,967 units. A/C MINIBAR TV TEL. $119–$184 double, depending on view and season; $238–$655 suites. Children under 17 stay free in parents' room. AE, MC, V. Free parking.

Explore the American Southwest at this resort, decorated with lots of muted pastels, sculptured wolves, and cacti. Its four- and five-story haciendalike buildings have terra-cotta tile roofs and palm-shaded courtyards. The property also houses a major 95,000-square-foot convention center, and the largest ballroom in the Southeast. Swimmers will enjoy a dip in the Mayan temple-inspired main pool. Rooms feature two double beds, and caffeine addicts will delight in the in-room coffeemakers. There are 99 rooms specially designed to accommodate travelers with disabilities, and nearly three-fourths of the rooms are nonsmoking. Since the hotel is new, this means the rooms have always been smoke free. Because this is a convention-oriented hotel, the food here is a bit pricier and there tends to be less families here than at the other moderate resorts.

Dining/Diversions: There is a 420-seat food court, called the Pepper Market, to satisfy the munchies with a variety of fast food. Francisco's is a sit-down, 200-seat Mexican restaurant with the feeling of an outdoor cafe. You won't find a triple-decker burrito here, but rather superbly prepared native dishes such as corn tamales in a spicy green sauce. Siestas offers snacks and light fare.

Amenities: Room service from 6am to 11pm, nightly turndown, lounge, transportation to all WDW parks, white-sand beach, beach volleyball, boat rentals, four large outdoor swimming pools, kiddie pool, arcade, complimentary parking, boutiques, shops, access to golf course, voice-mail system, spa, coin-op laundry.

○ Disney's Dixie Landings Resort. 1251 Dixie Dr. (off Bonnet Creek Pkwy.; P.O. Box 10000), Lake Buena Vista, FL 32830-1000. ☎ **407/W-DISNEY** (934-7639) or 407/934-6000. Fax 407/934-7777. 2,048 units. A/C TV TEL. $119–$184 room for up to 4. AE, MC, V. Free parking.

Low rates, extensive child-oriented facilities, and a food court make the Dixie Landings popular with families, even though the rooms are mid-sized, and the bathrooms rather small. Adults traveling alone may prefer a more sedate setting. Nestled on the banks of the "mighty Sassagoula River," and dotted with bayous, it shares its 325-acre site with the Port Orleans Resort (see below). It includes Ol' Man Island, a woodsy 3½-acre recreation area containing an immense swimming pool with waterfalls cascading from a broken bridge and a water slide, a playground, a children's wading pool, a whirlpool, and a fishin' hole (you can rent bait and poles and angle for catfish and bass). The accommodations areas, modeled on the Louisiana countryside, are divided into "parishes." Most rooms have double beds, and all are housed in stately colonnaded plantation homes, or rural Cajun-style dwellings fronted by brick courtyards.

Dining/Diversions: Boatwright's Dining Hall, housed in a replica of an 1800s boat-building factory, serves American/Cajun fare at breakfast and dinner. The Cotton Co-op lounge airs Monday Night Football and offers entertainment (singers and comedians) Tuesday to Saturday nights. A food court and pool bar round out the facilities.

Amenities: Six large swimming pools (one with a water slide), 1.7-mile riverfront jogging/biking path, Fulton's General Store, room service (pizza only), guest-services desk, baby-sitting, boat transport (to Port Orleans, Village Market-place, and Downtown Disney), coin-op washers/dryers, video-game arcade, car-rental desk, bicycle and boat rental.

✪ **Disney's Port Orleans Resort.** 2201 Orleans Dr. (off Bonnet Creek Pkwy.; P.O. Box 10000), Lake Buena Vista, FL 32830-1000. ☎ **407/W-DISNEY** (934-7639) or 407/934-5000. Fax 407/934-5353. 1,008 units. A/C TV TEL. $119–$184 room for up to 4. AE, MC, V. Free parking.

This beautiful resort, resembling turn-of-the-century New Orleans, shares a site on the banks of the Sassagoula with Dixie Landings, described above. Its identical room rates and comparable facilities make it, too, a good bet for families. The mid-sized rooms, equipped with small bathrooms and two double beds, are housed in pastel buildings with shuttered windows and lacy wrought-iron balconies; they're fronted by lovely flower gardens opening onto fountained courtyards. Cherrywood furnishings, swagged draperies, and walls hung with botanical prints and family photographs make for pretty room interiors. Gardeners will especially appreciate the property's landscaping, which features stately oaks, formal boxwood hedges, azaleas, and fragrant jasmine.

Dining/Diversions: Bonfamille's Café is open for breakfast and dinner, the latter featuring Creole specialties. Scat Cat's Club, a cocktail lounge off the lobby, airs Monday Night Football and features family-oriented live entertainment. A food court and pool bar round out the facilities.

Amenities: Room service (pizza only), guest-services desk, baby-sitting, boat transport (to Dixie Landings, Village Marketplace, and Downtown Disney). The larger-than-Olympic-size Doubloon Lagoon swimming pool has an enormous water slide. Whirlpool, kiddie pool, coin-op washers/dryers, video-game arcade, bicycle rental, car-rental service, boat rental, 1.7-mile riverfront jogging path, shops.

INEXPENSIVE

✪ **Disney's All-Star Movie Resort.** 1991 W. Buena Vista Dr., Lake Buena Vista, FL 32830-1000. ☎ **407/W-DISNEY** (934-7639) or 407/939-7000. Fax 407/939-7111. 1,900 units. A/C TV TEL. $74–$104 double. Children 17 and under stay free in parents' room. AE, MC, V. Free parking.

This is the latest Disney budget property, and from the giant Dalmatians leaping from the balconies to the bigger-than-life-sized versions of a host of other Disney characters, this property continues the grand Disney tradition of theme accommodations. Like the other All-Star resorts, the small rooms here are the tradeoff for the lowest price in the World. But, with Blizzard Beach right next door, you won't be spending too much time in your room anyway. There is a food court, movie-themed of course, that serves pizza, pasta, sandwiches, and family dinner platters. There is also a full-sized pool. Baby-sitting and activities for children are also available. Visitors looking for quiet should look elsewhere.

✪ **Disney's All-Star Music Resort.** 1801 W. Buena Vista Dr. (at World Dr. and Osceola Pkwy.; P.O. Box 10000), Lake Buena Vista, FL 32830-1000. ☎ **407/W-DISNEY** (934-7639) or 407/939-6000. Fax 407/939-7222. 1,920 units. A/C TV TEL. $74–$104 double. Children 17 and under stay free in parents' room. AE, MC, V. Free parking.

Though the unbeatable combination of rock-bottom rates and extensive facilities at Disney's All-Star Music and Sports resorts may be very attractive to families, there is one caveat: The rooms are small (a mere 260 square feet). They're okay for single adults or couples traveling with one child; larger families had best be into together-ness. Set amid pristine pine forests, this Disney hostelry is part of a 246-acre complex that also includes the adjacent All-Star Sports Resort (see below) and All-Star Movie Resort (see above). Its 10 buildings are musically themed around country, jazz, rock, calypso, and Broadway show tunes. The calypso building, for instance, has balconies adorned with tropical birds and musical notes, while a convoy of 18-wheelers travels around the country building, which is decorated with fiddles and banjos. Oversized icons in the public areas—such as three-story cowboy boots or a walk-through jukebox—are lit by neon and fiber optics at night. The attractive rooms have two double beds, and musically themed bedspreads, paintings, and wallpaper borders. The tiny bathrooms may have you singing the blues. In-room safes are a plus. There's a cheerful food court with an adjoining bar. Room service (pizza only), baby-sitting, guest-services desk. Two vast swimming pools, kiddie pool, playground, coin-op washers/dryers, large retail shop, car-rental desk, video-game arcade.

✪ **Disney's All-Star Sports Resort.** 1701 W. Buena Vista Dr. (at World Dr. and Osceola Pkwy.; P.O. Box 10000), Lake Buena Vista, FL 32830-1000. ☎ **407/W-DISNEY** (934-7639) or 407/939-5000. Fax 407/939-7333. 1,920 units. A/C TV TEL. $74–$104 double. Children 17 and under stay free in parents' room. AE, MC, V. Free parking.

Adjacent to the All-Star Music Resort (described above), this 82-acre hostelry will delight sports fans. The rooms are housed in buildings designed around football, baseball, basketball, tennis, and surfing motifs. For instance, the turquoise surf buildings have waves along their roofs, surfboards mounted on the exterior walls, and pink fish swimming along the balcony railings. The immense public-area icons include tennis ball–can stairways and four-story football helmets and whistles. The cheerful rooms feature double beds and sports-action-motif bedspreads, paintings, and wallpaper borders; in-room safes are among the amenities. As noted above, however, the rooms here are small, and since the All-Star Resorts tend to attract families, it can be noisy.

There's a brightly decorated food court with an adjoining bar. Room service (pizza only), baby-sitting, guest-services desk. Two vast outdoor swimming pools (one surfing themed with two 38-foot shark fins, the other shaped like a baseball diamond with an "outfield" sundeck), kiddie pool, playground, coin-op washers/dryers, shops, car-rental service, video-game arcade.

A DISNEY CAMPGROUND

✪ **Disney's Fort Wilderness Resort and Campground.** 3520 N. Fort Wilderness Trail (P.O. Box 10000), Lake Buena Vista, FL 32830-1000. ☎ **407/W-DISNEY** (934-7639) or 407/824-2900. Fax 407/824-3508. 784 campsites, 408 wilderness cabins. A/C TV TEL (homes only). $35–$54 campsite (depending on season, location, number of people, size, and extent of hookup); $180–$235 wilderness cabins. AE, MC, V. Free self-parking.

This woodsy 780-acre camping resort—shaded by towering pines and cypress trees, and crossed by fish-filled streams, lakes, and canals—is ideal for family vacations. Though it's a tad less central than other Disney hostelries, its abundance of on-premises facilities more than compensates. Secluded campsites offer 110/220-volt outlets, barbecue grills, picnic tables, and children's play areas. There are also wilderness cabins—rustic, one-bedroom cabins with piney interiors that accommodate up to six people (although space will be tight). These have cozy living rooms with Murphy beds, fully equipped eat-in kitchens, picnic tables, and barbecue grills. Guests here enjoy extensive recreational facilities ranging from a riding stable to a nightly campfire program hosted by Chip 'n' Dale.

Dining: The rustic log-beamed Trails End offers buffet meals, and the cozy Crockett's Tavern features Texan fare. During summer, guests enjoy a dazzling electrical water pageant from the beach, nightly at 9:45pm. And the rambunctious *Hoop-Dee-Doo Musical Revue* takes place in Pioneer Hall nightly (details in chapter 10).

Amenities: Guest-services desk, baby-sitting, boat transport (to Downtown Disney, the Magic Kingdom, and the Contemporary Resort), comfort station in each campground area (with rest rooms, private showers, ice machines, phones, and laundry rooms), two large swimming pools, white-sand beach, horseback riding (trail rides), petting farm, pony rides, fishing, three sand volleyball courts, ball fields, tetherball, shuffleboard, bike rentals, boat rental, 1½-mile nature trail, 2.3-mile jogging path, two tennis courts, two 18-hole championship golf courses, shops, kennel, two video-game arcades.

3 "Official Hotels" in Lake Buena Vista

These properties, designated "official" Walt Disney World hotels, are located on and around Hotel Plaza Boulevard. Guests at these hotels enjoy many privileges (see section 2, "The Perks of Staying with Mickey" earlier in this chapter), including complimentary transportation to the Disney parks. However, these hotels are not on the Disney Transportation System. Nevertheless, the location is excellent—close to the Disney parks, and within walking distance of Disney Village Marketplace and Crossroads shops and restaurants, as well as Downtown Disney's nightlife.

One difference between "official" hotels and actual Disney resorts is that the former (with the exception of the Swan and Dolphin) generally have less relentless Disneyesque themes; decide for yourself if that's a plus or a minus.

You can make reservations for all of the below-listed properties through Central Reservations Operations ☎ **407/W-DISNEY** (934-7639); see the description of this service earlier in the chapter. However, you should call each hotel, or its parent chain, to see if there are any specials available.

You'll find all these hotels located on the map "Walt Disney World & Lake Buena Vista Accommodations" earlier in this chapter.

EXPENSIVE

Doubletree Guest Suites. 2305 Hotel Plaza Blvd. (just west of Apopka–Vineland Rd./ Fla. 535), Lake Buena Vista, FL 32830. ☎ **800/222-8733** or 407/934-1000. Fax 407/ 934-1011. 229 units. A/C TV TEL. $169–$239 1-bdrm suites for up to 6; $375–$1,015 2-bdrm suites. Rates depend on view and season. Children 17 and under stay free in parents' room. AE, CB, DC, DISC, JCB, MC, V. Free parking. From I-4, Exit 27, to Disney Village Marketplace. Left on Hotel Plaza Blvd.

Entered via a cheerful, skylit atrium lobby featuring an aviary of tropical birds and theme-park murals, this seven-story all-suite hotel is a great choice for families. Children have their own check-in desk where they receive a free gift. The large one-bedroom suites—which can sleep up to six—are delightfully decorated and include full living rooms, dining areas, and separate bedrooms. Among your in-room amenities are a wet bar, refrigerator, coffeemaker, microwave oven, TVs with pay-movie options in the living room and bedroom, a smaller black-and-white TV in the bathroom, two phones, and a hair dryer.

Dining/Diversions: The festive Streamers serves buffet and a la carte breakfasts and dinners featuring American fare with Southwestern specialties. A bar/lounge adjoins, as does a theater where kids can watch Disney movies while Mom and Dad linger over coffee. Another bar serves the pool.

Amenities: Free shuttles to WDW parks. Room service, baby-sitting, guest-services desk (sells tickets and arranges transport to all nearby attractions), large swimming pool, whirlpool, kiddie pool with fountain, two tennis courts, jogging path, volleyball, playground, car-rental desk, exercise room, shops (including a grocery), coin-op washers/dryers, video-game arcade, and boat rental at the nearby Disney Village Marina.

The Wyndham Palace Resort. 1900 Buena Vista Dr. (just north of Hotel Plaza Blvd.; P.O. Box 22206), Lake Buena Vista, FL 32830. ☎ **800/327-2990** or 407/827-2727. Fax 407/827-6034. 1,014 units. A/C MINIBAR TV TEL. $209–$278 double; $229–$529 1- and 2-bdrm suites; range reflects view and season. Children 17 and under stay free in parents' room. AE, CB, DC, DISC, MC, V. Free self-parking; valet parking $7. From I-4 west, take Exit 27; at end of ramp, turn left. At first light, turn left into Walt Disney World Village. At first stop light, turn right onto Buena Vista Dr. First hotel on the right.

This luxurious 27-acre resort, formerly known as the Buena Vista Palace, underwent a complete overhaul in 1997. A European-style spa, added in 1996, is just one perk, along with extensive boating and recreational facilities. The spacious accommodations—most with lake-view balconies or patios—are appealingly decorated and equipped with Spectravision, safes, bedroom and bathroom phones, and ceiling fans. There are also luxurious one- and two-bedroom suites with living and dining rooms and a 10th-floor concierge level. For those with sensitive systems, or a Howard Hughes bent for cleanliness, there are 65 eco-friendly rooms featuring nonallergenic pillows and blankets; dye-free tissues, towels, and linens; filtered water; and extra air-cleaning systems.

Dining/Diversions: Arthur's 27 (perched on the 27th floor) offers haute cuisine and panoramic park views, as well as live jazz, piano-bar entertainment, and dancing in an adjoining lounge. In the Outback Restaurant, complete with a three-story indoor waterfall, an Australian storyteller entertains during dinner; steak and seafood are featured. Character breakfasts take place in the Watercress Cafe. Other venues include pool and snack bars, a pastry shop, and the Laughing Kookaburra Good Time Bar, which offers a selection of 99 beers, and hosts nightly happy-hour buffets and live bands for dancing.

Amenities: Free shuttle service to WDW, two large swimming pools, whirlpool, kiddie pool, three tennis courts, boat rental, 2- and 3-mile jogging paths, sand volleyball court, bike rental, playground, car-rental desk, room service (24 hours), baby-sitting, guest-services desk, complimentary newspaper for crown-level guests, full business center, shops, coin-op washers/dryers, video-game arcade, counselor-supervised child-care program. The spa offers massage, herbal wraps, and a fully equipped health club.

MODERATE

Courtyard by Marriott. 1805 Hotel Plaza Blvd. (between Lake Buena Vista Dr. and Apopka–Vineland Rd./Fla. 535), Lake Buena Vista, FL 32830. ☎ **800/223-9930** or 407/828-8888. Fax 407/827-4623. www.marriott.com. 323 units. A/C TV TEL. $89–$169 double, depending on view and season. AE, CB, DC, DISC, JCB, MC, V. Free parking. From I-4, Exit 27 to Downtown Disney, Walt Disney World Village. Turn left on Hotel Plaza Blvd. On left.

The Courtyard is a moderately-priced link in the Marriott chain, with the lower prices achieved through limited services. But don't envision a spartan, no-frills atmosphere. This property was recently renovated to the tune of $4.5 million, and it's looking great. The attractive, standard-sized rooms—most with balconies—have in-room safes, coffeemakers, pay-movie options, and refrigerators available on request. Kids will love the in-room Nintendo.

Dining/Diversions: A full-service restaurant serves American fare at all meals and provides room service. There's also a lobby cocktail lounge, a poolside bar (in season), and an on-premises deli featuring pizza and frozen yogurt.

Amenities: Free transportation to WDW parks and attractions. The guest-services desk sells tickets and arranges transport to all nearby attractions. Two out-door swimming pools, whirlpool, kiddie pool, boat rental at nearby Disney Village Marina, playground, car-rental desk, exercise room, shops, coin-op washers/dryers, and video-game arcade.

Grosvenor Resort. 1850 Hotel Plaza Blvd. (just east of Buena Vista Dr.), Lake Buena Vista, FL 32830. ☎ **800/624-4109** or 407/828-4444. Fax 407/828-8192. www.grosvenorresort. com. 626 units. A/C TV TEL. $99–$175 room for up to 4 people, depending on view and season. AE, CB, DC, DISC, JCB, MC, V. Free self-parking; valet parking $6. From I-4, take Exit 27 to Walt Disney World Resort. Turn left.

In the moderately priced category, this is a comfortable choice with a British colonial theme, and a few unique entertainment options. Occupying 13 lushly-landscaped lakeside acres, it centers on a 19-story peach stucco building fronted by towering palms. The rooms are nicely decorated in an attractive resort motif, and are equipped with VCRs (tapes can be rented), coffeemakers, safes, and minibars (stocked on request); refrigerators can be rented.

Dining/Diversions: Baskervilles Restaurant—with a Sherlock Holmes museum on the premises—hosts Saturday-night mystery dinner-theater, and offers buffet breakfasts and dinners, some with Disney characters. Also here: a 24-hour food court, a pool bar, and a lounge where sporting events are aired on a large-screen TV.

Amenities: Free shuttle to WDW parks and attractions, guest-services desk (sells tickets and arranges transport to all nearby attractions), doctor on call, limited room service, baby-sitting for a fee, free daily newspaper, two swimming pools, whirlpool, kiddie pool, exercise room, two tennis courts, boat rental, playground, lawn games, car-rental desk, coin-op washers/dryers, shops, video-game arcade, video rentals.

Hotel Royal Plaza. 1905 Hotel Plaza Blvd. (between Buena Vista Dr. and Apopka–Vineland Rd./Fla. 535), Lake Buena Vista, FL 32830. ☎ **800/248-7890** or 407/828-2828. Fax 407/827-6338. www.royalplaza.com. 394 units. A/C MINIBAR TV TEL. $109–$229 double, depending on view and season. AE, CB, DC, DISC, JCB, MC, V. Free self-parking; valet parking $7 a day. From I-4, take Exit 27. Turn into Walt Disney World Village. It's the tall, pink-hued building.

The Royal Plaza recently completed a $24-million renovation and upgrade, including the refurbishment of all accommodations and public areas. Spiffy new rooms—decorated in soft resort hues with bleached oak furnishings—are equipped with VCRs (movies can be rented), safes, coffeemakers, and hair dryers. Pool-view rooms have patios or balconies. Both executive kings and concierge-level rooms, which are among the more expensive choices, contain Jacuzzis (the former also offer full living rooms). These rooms all have a patio or balcony.

Dining/Diversions: The Verandah, a full-service restaurant, specializes in foods with a hint of the islands. Plaza Diner is a full-service family restaurant featuring American foods such as burgers, meat loaf, and daily specials. Intermission, a sports bar with a handful of big-screen televisions, offers a chance to catch that big game—whether hockey, basketball, baseball, or football. A pool bar is set up during the busy season.

Amenities: Free shuttle service to Disney parks, room service, guest-services desk (sells tickets and arranges transport to all nearby attractions), baby-sitting, foreign-currency exchange, extensive meeting facilities, large L-shaped swimming pool, whirlpool, four tennis courts, boat rental, sauna, coin-op washers/dryers, shops, video-game arcade.

Travelodge Hotel. 2000 Hotel Plaza Blvd. (between Buena Vista Dr. and Apopka–Vineland Rd./Fla. 535), Lake Buena Vista, FL 32830. ☎ **800/348-3765** or 407/828-2424. Fax

407/828-8933. www.travelodge.com. 325 units. A/C MINIBAR TV TEL. $103–$179 room for up to 4 people, depending on room size and season. Inquire about packages. AE, CB, DC, DISC, JCB, MC, V. Free parking. From I-4, take Exit 27. Go to Downtown Disney. Turn left onto Hotel Plaza Blvd. Across from the Doubletree Hotel.

This 12-acre lakefront hotel is well-kept and immaculate, with more upscale rooms and public areas than you would expect at a Travelodge. The rates are also higher than the Travelodge norm, but represent good value for your money. The reason: This is the company's flagship hotel. Designed to resemble a Barbados plantation manor house, it has a Caribbean-resort ambiance, enhanced by tropical foliage and bright floral-print fabrics. The rooms are particularly inviting, with light bleached-wood furnishings, and lovely framed botanical prints and floral friezes. Furnished balconies overlook Lake Buena Vista. In-room perks include Spectravision movies, Nintendo, coffeemakers, safes, hair dryers, and free local phone calls.

Dining/Diversions: Traders, with a wall of windows overlooking a wooded area, is open for breakfast, and steak and seafood dinners. On the 18th floor, Toppers offers magnificent views of Lake Buena Vista, as well as dancing, music videos, pool tables, and dart boards; it's a great vantage point for watching Disney's nightly laser shows and fireworks. There's also a cocktail bar and a casual self-service eatery.

Amenities: Free shuttle to the Disney parks, room service, baby-sitting, guest-services desk (sells tickets and arranges transport to all nearby attractions), free weekday newspaper, large swimming pool, kiddie pool, boat rental, playground, car-rental desk, coin-op washers/dryers, shops, video-game arcade.

4 Other Lake Buena Vista–Area Hotels

All of the hotels listed below are within a few minutes drive of WDW parks, and in the midst of the "official" hotels. They offer the location, but not the privileges, of staying at an official hotel.

VERY EXPENSIVE

✪ **Hyatt Regency Grand Cypress Resort.** One Grand Cypress Blvd. (off State Rd. 535), Orlando, FL 32836. ☎ **800/233-1234** or 407/239-1234; 800/835-7377 or 407/239-4700 for villas. Fax 407/239-3800, or 407/239-7219 for villas. 750 units, 146 villas. A/C MINIBAR TV TEL. $205–$265 double; $1,400 deluxe villa. AE, CB, DC, DISC, JCB, MC, V. Free self-parking; valet parking $9. I-4 to Exit 27, right on County Rd. 535, left at second traffic light onto S.R. 535. Two lights on right.

Although only a mile from WDW, this 1,500-acre retreat, ablaze with bougainvillea and hibiscus, is a world away (see the map "Walt Disney World & Lake Buena Vista Accommodations," earlier in this chapter). An award-winning golf course, a top-notch equestrian center, and a major renovation in 1997 put this romantic getaway in a class by itself. Spacious rooms are a welcome respite from the crowded parks—that's if you really find a need to leave. Topping the list of the outstanding facilities here is a half-acre swimming pool spanned by a rope bridge that flows through rock grottoes (with 12 waterfalls and 2 steep water slides). Relax on the white-sand beach, play a few sets on 12 tennis courts, or take a swing on a Jack Nicklaus–designed golf course.

Deluxe accommodations with wicker furnishings evoke the Southern luxury of a bygone era. The Regency Club, a concierge level, comprises two floors. Especially lavish are the Mediterranean-style Villas of Grand Cypress, all possessing patios, kitchens, living rooms, and dining rooms; some equipped with working fireplaces and whirlpool baths.

Dining/Diversions: Casual yet elegant, Hemingway's serves Florida seafood at lunch and dinner. The lodgelike Black Swan, overlooking the golf course, features haute American/continental dinners. Similar fare is offered at the plush La Coquina, where a harpist entertains at dinner, and the Sunday brunches are exquisite. Other venues include the White Horse Saloon, for prime rib dinners and country music; Trellises, a bar/lounge where a jazz ensemble entertains evenings; the lovely lake-view Cascade, serving American fare at all meals, plus Japanese breakfasts; and several poolside and snack bars.

Amenities: Free transportation around grounds and to all major attractions except for WDW, hourly shuttle to all WDW parks (round-trip fare $6 per day), concierge (sells tickets to WDW parks and other nearby attractions), room service (24 hours), baby-sitting, Mears airport shuttle. Golf and tennis instruction and pro shops (the golf school here has been called one of the finest in the country), 45-acre Audubon nature walk, 4.7-mile jogging path, racquetball, volleyball, shuffleboard courts, playground, car-rental desk, unisex beauty salon, full business center, state-of-the-art health club, shops, helicopter landing pad, video-game arcade, and a counselor-supervised child-care center/Camp Hyatt activity center.

💧 **Marriott's Orlando World Center.** 8701 World Center Dr. (on Fla. 536 between I-4 and Fla. 535), Orlando, FL 32821. ☎ **800/621-0638** or 407/239-4200. Fax 407/238-8777. www.marriott.com. 1,599 units. A/C MINIBAR TV TEL. $224–$269 room for up to 5 people, range reflects season; $265–$2,400 suites. AE, CB, DC, DISC, JCB, MC, V. Free self-parking; valet parking $8.

Providing the only viable competition for the Grand Cypress Resort (described above), this sprawling 230-acre resort, just 2 miles from the WDW parks, is a top convention venue that also offers recreational facilities for the tourist. These include three swimming pools (one larger than Olympic size, with slides and waterfalls), eight tennis courts, and an 18-hole/par-71 Joe Lee–designed championship golf course. A grand palm-lined driveway, flanked by rolling golf greens, leads to the main building—a massive 27-story tower fronted by flower beds and fountains.

Spacious guest rooms are cheerfully decorated in pastel hues with bamboo and rattan furnishings. All have patios or balconies, extensive pay-movie options, irons and ironing boards, safes, and hair dryers. Step outside the tower and you'll find magnificently landscaped grounds, punctuated by rock gardens, shaded groves of pines and magnolias, and cascading waterfalls; swans and ducks inhabit over a dozen lakes and lagoons spanned by arched bridges.

Dining/Diversions: The luxurious Tuscany, Marriott's premier restaurant, offers northern Italian haute cuisine dinners. The Mikado Japanese Steak House is a serene setting for classic teppanyaki dinners. JW's Steakhouse serves breakfasts and lunches on a screened balcony, and cozy dinners in a rustic pine interior. Allie's American Grille is an elegant family restaurant. Among several smaller restaurants and bars are the plush Pagoda Lounge for nightly piano-bar entertainment and Champion's, a first-rate sports bar.

Amenities: Mears transportation/sightseeing desk (sells tickets to all nearby attractions, including WDW parks; also provides transport, by reservation, to WDW, other attractions, and the airport; the round-trip fare to WDW parks is $5 per day, free for children 11 and under), concierge, room service (24 hours), baby-sitting, shoe shine, complimentary newspaper weekdays, 1-hour film developing. Golf and tennis pro shops and instruction, 18-hole miniature golf course, two volleyball courts, four whirlpools, large kiddie pool, car-rental desk, unisex beauty salon, extensive business center, state-of-the-art health club, coin-op washers/dryers, shops, video-game arcade, and the Lollipop Lounge, a counselor-supervised child-care/activities center. Inquire as well about organized children's activities—games, movies, nature walks, and more.

Summerfield Suites Lake Buena Vista. 8751 Suiteside Dr. (off Apopka–Vineland Rd./Fla. 535), Lake Buena Vista, FL 32836. ☎ **800/830-4964** or 407/238-0777. Fax 407/238-0778. www.summerfield-orlando.com. 150 units. A/C TV TEL. $119–$249 1-bdrm suites for up to 4; $159–$319 2-bdrm suites for up to 8. Range reflects season. Rates include continental breakfast. AE, CB, DC, DISC, MC, V. Free parking.

This all-suite property, offering free transport to and from the nearby Disney parks, is an excellent choice for families (see the map "International Drive Area Accommodations & Dining," later in this chapter). It's notable for its friendliness and immaculate accommodations—in 1998, the suites underwent a complete redecoration, adding brighter, livelier colors. The spacious suites—in buildings surrounding a palm-fringed brick courtyard with umbrella tables, fountains, and gazebos—have fully equipped eat-in kitchens, comfortable living rooms, and a bathroom for each bedroom. In-room amenities include bedroom and kitchen phones (with two lines), TVs in each bedroom and in the living room (with pay-movie options), VCRs (movies can be rented), and irons and ironing boards. There are also coffeemakers and unstocked refrigerators in all rooms.

Dining: Guests enjoy continental breakfast in the pleasant dining room, or at umbrella tables in the courtyard; omelets and waffles may be purchased. An on-premises lobby deli (which sells light fare and liquor) also serves the pool area. Many local restaurants deliver to the hotel.

Amenities: Free shuttle to the Disney parks, a $35 per person round-trip shuttle to the airport and other attractions, guest-services desk (sells tickets to WDW parks and other nearby attractions, many of them discounted), free daily newspaper, complimentary grocery shopping, baby-sitting, large swimming pool, whirlpool, kiddie pool, car-rental desk, full business services, exercise room, coin-op washers/dryers, shops, video-game arcade.

MODERATE

✪ **Holiday Inn Sunspree Resort Lake Buena Vista.** 13351 Fla. 535 (between Fla. 536 and I-4), Lake Buena Vista, FL 32821. ☎ **800/FON-MAXX** or 407/239-4500. Fax 407/239-7713. www.kidsuites.com. email: max@kidsuites.com. 507 units. A/C TV TEL. $89–$159 kid-suites available for up to 4 people, depending on season. AE, CB, DC, DISC, JCB, MC, V. Free parking.

About a mile from the Disney parks, this Holiday Inn offers the chain's "no surprises" dependability, while catering to children in a big way (see the map "Orlando Area Accommodations & Dining," in chapter 6). Kids "check in" at their own pint-size desk; receive a free fun bag containing a video-game token coupon, a lollipop, and a small gift; and get a personal welcome from animated raccoon mascots, Max and Maxine. There are more than 200 of these "kidsuites" available. Camp Holiday activities—magic shows, clowns, sing-alongs, arts and crafts, and much more—are available at a minimal charge for kids ages 2 to 12. Parents can arrange (by reservation) for Max to come tuck a child into bed. The pretty rooms have kitchenettes with refrigerators, microwave ovens, and coffeemakers. And if you're renting a second room for the children, "kidsuites" here—designed as igloos, space capsules, Noah's Ark, and others—sleep up to three. Amenities include VCRs (tapes can be rented), hair dryers, safes, coffeemakers, and unstocked refrigerators in all rooms. Ask about special offers for grandparents traveling with grandchildren.

Dining: Maxine's serves all meals, including steak and seafood dinners. Max's Funtime Parlor offers nightly bingo and karaoke; it also airs sporting events on a

🛈 Family-Friendly Hotels

Days Inns at 4104 and 4125 W. Irlo Bronson Memorial Hwy. *(see p.82)* Good basic service and a central location make these hotels good bets for families. There is a swimming pool on the property, but, more importantly, there are restaurants, shops, and movie theaters within walking distance.

Disney-Owned Resorts & Official Hotels *(see pp. 60–72)* These offer many advantages for kids, including proximity to Walt Disney World parks, complimentary transportation between the hotel and the parks, reduced-price children's menus, and Disney character appearances in hotel restaurants. Facilities may include lakefront beaches, boating, water-skiing, bike rentals, playgrounds, video-game arcades, swimming pools with waterfalls and slides, and/or organized children's activities.

Disney's Fort Wilderness Resort and Campground *(see p. 72)* All of the above perks and more are offered here, including nightly campfire programs with Chip 'n' Dale, trail rides, pony rides, and a petting farm, plus you get to go camping.

Holiday Inn Sunspree Resort Lake Buena Vista *(see p. 78)* This Holiday Inn has a special check-in desk for kids, and on-premises mascots to welcome them. Rooms are equipped with kitchenettes, and themed "kidsuites" are available. Kids under 12 eat free in their own restaurant, where movies and cartoons are shown. Numerous organized children's activities are free.

Residence Inns *(see pp. 79 and 90)* They not only have swimming pools, children's playgrounds, and other recreational facilities, but also have accommodations with fully equipped kitchens—a potential money-saver for families. And the rates include breakfast.

large-screen TV. Kids 12 and under eat all meals free, either in a hotel restaurant with parents or in Kid's Kottage, a cheerful facility where movies and cartoons are shown, and dinner includes a make-your-own sundae bar.

Amenities: Guest-services desk (sells tickets to all nearby attractions, including WDW parks), free scheduled transport to WDW parks (there's a charge for transport to other nearby attractions), large swimming pool, two whirlpools, kiddie pool, playground, fitness center, coin-op washers/dryers, shops, car rental, video arcade, Camp Holiday (a counselor-supervised child-care/activity center for ages 2 to 12), and room service.

✪ **Residence Inn by Marriott.** 8800 Meadow Creek Dr. (just off Fla. 535 between Fla. 536 and I-4), Orlando, FL 32821. ☎ **800/331-3131** or 407/239-7700. Fax 407/239-7605. 688 units. A/C TV TEL. $85–$135 suites; range reflects season. Rates include full breakfast. AE, CB, DC, DISC, JCB, MC, V. Free parking.

This delightful all-suite property occupies 50 acres, alternating wooded grounds with neatly manicured lawns, duck-inhabited ponds, fountains, and flower beds (see the map "International Drive Area Accommodations & Dining," later in this chapter). Guests, up to four in a single suite and up to six in a double, enjoy a serene environment offering the seclusion and safety of a private community. They can also avail themselves of the extensive facilities at the adjoining Marriott Orlando World Center (see above) with room-charge privileges. The tastefully decorated accommodations—with fully equipped eat-in kitchens, private balconies or patios, and large living rooms—are equipped with Spectravision, VCRs (tapes can be rented), two phones (kitchen and bedroom), ceiling fans, and safes. The two-bedroom units have two bathrooms.

Dining: A full breakfast is available in the gatehouse each morning, a Pizza Hut is on the premises, and local restaurants deliver food.

Amenities: Guest-services desk (sells tickets and provides transport to all nearby theme parks and attractions; round-trip to WDW parks is $8), baby-sitting, complimentary daily newspaper, next-day film developing, free food-shopping service, Mears airport shuttle, three large swimming pools, two whirlpools, sports court (basketball, badminton, volleyball, paddle tennis, shuffleboard), tennis court, playground, coin-op washers/dryers, shops, two video-game arcades.

Riu Orlando Hotel. 8688 Palm Pkwy. (between Fla. 535 and I-4), Lake Buena Vista, FL 32830. ☎ **407/239-8500.** Fax 407/239-8591. www.riuhotels.com. 167 units. A/C TV TEL. $80–$175 double, depending on season. Children 17 and under stay free in parents' room. AE, CB, DC, DISC, MC, V. Free self-parking.

This six-story property is located on a pleasant, tree-lined street and overlooks a lake out back—a big plus. The Crossroads Shopping Center and Walt Disney World Village Marketplace/Downtown Disney put dozens of shops, services, and restaurants within easy walking distance. There are free shuttles to all the major attractions, and the in-room coffeemakers are a plus for families. The rooms have cable, Nintendo, hair dryers, irons and ironing boards.

Dining: The Garden Café, serving American fare at breakfast and dinner, has an outdoor poolside seating area and an adjoining bar/lounge.

Amenities: Room service, baby-sitting, and a complimentary daily newspaper are available. The guest-services desk sells tickets (many of them discounted) and arranges transport to all nearby attractions. On the premises are a nice-size swimming pool and whirlpool, coin-op washers/dryers, an exercise room, a business center, and a small video-game arcade.

INEXPENSIVE

Days Inn Lake Buena Vista Village. 12490 Apopka Vineland Rd., Lake Buena Vista , FL 32703. ☎ **800/521-3297** or 407/239-4646. Fax 407/239-8469. A/C TV TEL. $39–$119. AE, DC, DISC, MC, V. From I-4, take Exit 27. At the bottom of the ramp turn left. Property is ½ mile on the left.

Although not far from Disney, this property is probably better suited for those planning to spend most of their time at Universal and Sea World.

This hotel is another good option for families; you can request connecting rooms and cribs, and microwaves and refrigerators are available for an additional fee. A coin-operated laundry, a "kids-eat-free" program and a kiddie pool round out the perks for tikes. For the grown-ups, there is an outdoor pool, free transportation to Disney parks, and pets are accepted.

Hampton Inn, Orlando Disney Maingate. 3000 Maingate Lane, Kissimmee, FL 34747. ☎ **800/426-7866** or 407/396-6300. Fax 407/396-8989. www.hamptoninn.com. 118 units. A/C TV TEL. $59–$99 double. AE, DISC, MC, V. From I-4 take Exit 25B to U.S. 192 west for about 2 miles. Turn right on Maingate Lane.

Since this is one of the newer budget hotels in the Disney World area, rooms show none of the wear of some older properties. The property is clean and nicely, if simply, landscaped. Although the rooms are only average in size, there are connecting rooms and cribs available. Those, along with a coin-operated laundry, make this a good location for a large family or several families traveling together. Other pluses are the free continental breakfast buffet, a pool, and a car-rental desk.

5 Places to Stay in the U.S. 192/Kissimmee Area

This very American stretch of highway, dotted with fast-food eateries, isn't what you'd call scenic, but it does contain many inexpensive hotels and motels within 1 to 8 miles of Walt Disney World parks. Almost all provide, or can arrange, for shuttle service to WDW and other attractions. The cost usually runs from $10 to $14 per person. New to this stretch of highway are markers, about 20 feet tall, along the side of the road. Aptly tagged with the word "Marker" and a number, they are an attempt to help tourists find their way along this stretch of U.S. 192.

You'll find all the places described here on the map "Kissimmee Area Accommodations" in this section.

MODERATE

Comfort Inn Maingate. 7571 W. Irlo Bronson Memorial Hwy. (U.S. 192; between Reedy Creek Blvd. and Sherbeth Rd., markers 15 and 16), Kissimmee, FL 34747. ☎ **800/221-2222** or 407/396-7500. 225 units. A/C TV TEL. $69–$199 double. AE, DC, DISC MC, V. Free self-parking. Just 6 miles from the WDW parks, and 7 miles from Universal Studios.

The guest room interiors were recently refurbished, and include refrigerators, microwaves, and sleep sofas. The rooms are a little small, but large enough for a family to be comfortable.

Courtyard Marriott Maingate. 7675 Irlo Bronson Memorial Hwy., Kissimmee, FL 34747. ☎ **800/568-3352** or 407/396-4000. Fax 407/396-0714. 198 units. A/C TV TEL. $69–$135. AE, DC, DISC, MC, V. Free parking. From I-4 take Exit 25B. Go west on U.S. 192 about 2 miles. Near marker 5.

The plain, brown five-story brick building belies a pleasant, tropical theme executed in the lobby and rooms. All rooms have two double or one king-sized bed, and a small table and chair. In-room extras include a full-length mirror, mini coffeemaker, safe, and hair dryer. Kids and adults will enjoy the plain, but serviceable, outside recreation area that's adorned with a few palm trees, and includes a pool, kiddie pool, small whirlpool, and an outdoor bar.

Dining: The breakfast-only Courtyard Café serves a full buffet each morning, and for each paying adult, one child (9 years old and younger) eats free.

Amenities: Free shuttle service to WDW parks, transportation to other area attractions for a fee; gym; handicapped accessible; kiddie pool; and video-game room.

Holiday Inn Nikki Bird Resort. 7300 Irlo Bronson Memorial Hwy., Kissimmee, FL 34747. ☎800/206-2747 or 407/396-7300. Fax 407/396-7555. 529 units. A/C TV TEL. $79.95–$129. AE, DC, DISC, MC, V. Free parking. Take I-4 to Exit 25B. It's 1.5 miles past the Disney entrance on the left, between markers 5 and 6.

How many hotels have their own roaming mascot? Yes, Nikki Bird, who strolls the grounds giving hugs, is just one of the family-friendly perks at this property. There is a large game arcade in the lobby, and connecting rooms and roll-away beds are available. All rooms are equipped with a refrigerator, microwave, safe, and hair dryer. Children under 12 eat free at the full-breakfast buffet next door at Angel's Diner; nightly entertainment includes songs, puppet shows, and games. Free transportation is provided to WDW parks.

INEXPENSIVE

In addition to the accommodations described here, there are scores of other inexpensive, but perfectly serviceable, motels within a few miles of the WDW parks. All have swimming pools and arrange transportation to the Disney parks for a fee.

Orlando Bed & Breakfasts

Although most of the properties in Orlando are mega-resorts or standard chains, there are a few bed-and-breakfast options. These properties offer a nice respite from the crowded, commercial world of the theme parks, and are ideal for couples traveling without children and looking for a little quiet time.

The Perrihouse, in Lake Buena Vista, is an eight bedroom, gray brick house nestled among 6 acres of flowers and trees. Opened in 1990, it initially operated as a rooming house for Disney employees, but soon switched to a B&B. An onsite bird sanctuary will draw raves from nature lovers. Each room has a private bathroom, and an expanded continental breakfast is offered each morning. For more information, call ☎ 407/876-4830 or go online to www.perrihouse.com. Room rates range from $99–$129.

The Unicorn Inn, in Kissimmee, offers an authentic English experience in the midst of this still-rural American town. Opened in 1995, the Unicorn Inn is housed in a blue-shingled house originally built in 1901. The eight rooms offer basic accommodations that are clean and cozy. For more information, call ☎ 407/846-1200. The price is $75 a night, including a full breakfast.

Many sell tickets to attractions, but there have been problems with the tickets' low prices truly being too good to be true. Tourists have ended up at the gates of attractions without valid tickets. Stick to ordering tickets through the parks themselves.

Days Inn. 4104 and 4125 W. Irlo Bronson Memorial Hwy. (U.S. 192; at Hoagland Blvd. N., markers 15 and 16), Kissimmee, FL 34741. ☎ **800/647-0010,** 800/DAYS-INN, or 407/846-4714. Fax 407/932-2699. 220 units. A/C TV TEL. $39–$99.95 room for up to 4, depending on season; $37–$63 efficiency; $55–$75 Jacuzzi room (for 1 or 2 people). Rates include continental breakfast. Rates may be higher during major events. AE, CB, DC, DISC, MC, V. Free parking.

Offering good value for your hotel dollar, these two Days Inns—on either side of U.S. 192—share facilities, including two swimming pools, coin-op washers and dryers, and a video-game arcade. Several restaurants (which deliver food), a large shopping mall with a 12-theater movie house, and a supermarket are within close walking distance.

The rooms at both locations are clean and attractive standard motel units. The best bets are the efficiency units with fully equipped kitchenettes at no. 4104. The Jacuzzi rooms are at no. 4125, and come with a refrigerator and a microwave oven. All accommodations offer pay-movie options and in-room safes, and both locations serve free coffee, juice, and doughnuts in their lobbies each morning. The guest-services desk at no. 4104 sells tickets (many of them discounted) and arranges transport to all nearby attractions, including the WDW parks. A big plus: Round-trip transport to WDW parks is free. Airport transfers can be arranged.

Econo Lodge Maingate East. 4311 W. Irlo Bronson Memorial Hwy. (U.S. 192), Kissimmee, FL 34756. ☎ **800/ENJOY-FL** or 407/396-7100. www.enjoyfloridahotels.com. A/C TV TEL. $49.95–$109.95. AE, DC, DISC, MC, V. Free parking. From I-4, take Exit 25A; the motel is across the street from Medieval Times, at marker 15.

This property, a good bargain, is set well back from the highway to prevent disturbance from traffic noise (although you should ask for a room away from the balconies). A new lobby has been added, but the same standard of service and cleanliness continues. There are free shuttles to WDW parks, and transportation is available to other attractions. There is also a heated swimming pool.

Kissimmee Area Accommodations

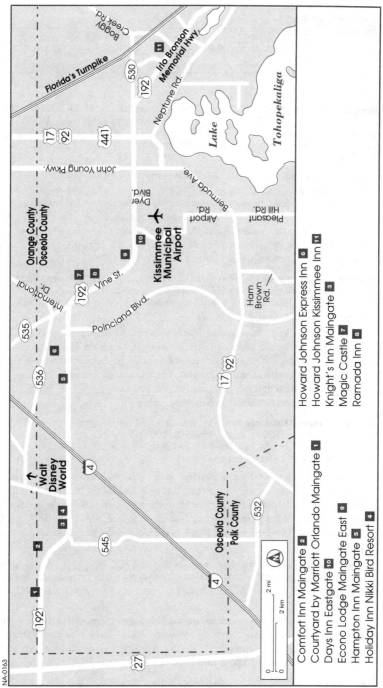

Comfort Inn Maingate **2**
Courtyard by Marriott Orlando Maingate **1**
Days Inn Eastgate **10**
Econo Lodge Maingate East **9**
Hampton Inn Maingate **5**
Holiday Inn Nikki Bird Resort **4**

Howard Johnson Express Inn **6**
Howard Johnson Kissimmee Inn **11**
Knight's Inn Maingate **3**
Magic Castle **7**
Ramada Inn **8**

NA-0163

Driving Tip

U.S. 192 is also known as W. Irlo Bronson Memorial Highway and eventually turns into Vine Street.

Hampton Inn Maingate. 3104 Parkway Blvd., Kissimmee, Fl. 34747. ☎ **800/426-7866** or 407/396-8484. Fax 407/396-7644. www.hamptoninn.com. 164 units. A/C TV TEL. $59–$95 double. Rates include continental breakfast. AE, DC, DISC, MC, V. Free parking. Take I-4 to Exit 25A. At the first traffic light turn left, between markers 8 and 9. (Across the street from Celebration.)

Sitting just ¼-mile off the road, this wooded property has a laid-back, secluded feel. The rooms here, as you might expect, are nothing fancy, but they are well-maintained and clean. You can choose from two double beds or one king-sized bed, and there is a small safe in the closet. Recreational activities are limited to a small rectangular pool, and basketball and shuffleboard courts. There is no room service, but a pretty good complimentary breakfast is served in a small dining area off the lobby. A host of restaurants are located nearby on U.S. 192.

Howard Johnson Express Inn. 4836 W. Irlo Bronson Hwy. (U.S. 192), Kissimmee, FL 34746. ☎ **800/952-5464** or 407/396-4762. Fax 407/396-4866. 131 units. A/C TV TEL. $39.95–$66 double. AE, DC, DISC, MC, V. Free parking. Take I-4 to Exit 25A, 3½ miles on right, between markers 11 and 12.

As a lakefront property, this is one of the more scenic Kissimmee offerings. You can have picnics by the lake or rent jet skis for about $60 an hour. The pink-and-blue buildings contain clean, comfortable rooms; some of the suites contain an in-room Jacuzzi, microwave oven, and refrigerator. There is a large, heated swimming pool and a video-game room. Another plus is a free shuttle to the WDW parks. Transportation to other attractions can be arranged for a fee.

Howard Johnson Kissimmee Inn. 2323 U.S. Hwy. 192 East, Kissimmee, 34744. ☎ **800 521-4656** or 407/846-4900. Fax 407/846-9700. 200 units. A/C TV TEL. $35–$94 double. AE, DC, DISC, MC, V. Free parking. Take I-4 to Exit 25A, go east on U.S. Hwy. 192 for 12 miles. The property is located pass the turnpike entrance.

This property is a bit off the beaten track, which makes this a nice budget selection for those looking to get away from the congestion and tourist bustle. In this price range, clean, basic rooms are what you are shooting for, and this property delivers. Pet owners will be happy to know they won't have to leave Fido at home—pets are accepted here. There is a pool and a small game room. Refrigerators are available for a fee.

Knights Inn Maingate. 7475 W. Irlo Bronson Memorial Hwy. (U.S. 192), Kissimmee, FL. 34746. ☎ **800/944-0062** or 407/396-4200. Fax 407/396-8838. 121 units. A/C TV TEL. $32–$64 double. AE, DISC, MC, V. Free self-parking. From I-4 take Exit 25B. 1 mile past Disney World entrance at marker 6.

The rooms here are standard, inexpensive hotel fare, although good housekeeping puts them a notch above some other budget inns. Location—just a mile from Disney—and price are what makes this property special. The first-floor rooms have been renovated within the last few years, so make sure you ask for one of them when booking.

Magic Castle. 5055 W. Irlo Bronson Memorial Hwy. (U.S. 192), Kissimmee, FL 34746. ☎ **800/446-5669** or 407/396-2212. Fax 407/396-0253. 107 units. A/C TV TEL. $35.95–$61.95 room for up to 4, depending on season. Rates include continental breakfast. AE, DC, DISC, MC, V. Free self-parking. From I-4, take Exit 25A, near marker 11; the motel is about 3½ miles on the left, next to the Olive Garden.

The owner of this property has discontinued his affiliation with Ramada, but this three-story stucco building continues to provide adequate accommodations at a good price. The standard-sized rooms are equipped with cable TV (with Disney Channel and HBO movies), safes, and refrigerators. Facilities include an outdoor swimming pool and coin-op washers/dryers. Continental breakfast is served in the lobby each morning. Shuttle service to WDW parks is available for $9 per person, round-trip. Service to other parks will cost around $12–$14. Pets are accepted for an additional $6 per night.

✪ **Ramada Inn.** 4559 W. Irlo Bronson Memorial Hwy. (U.S. 192), Kissimmee, FL 34746. ☎ **800/544-5712** or 407/396-1212. Fax 407/396-7926. 114 units. A/C TV TEL. $39.95–$59.95 for up to 4; range reflects season. AE, DC, DISC, MC, V. Free self-parking. From I-4, between markers 13 and 14, take Exit 25A; the motel is about 5 miles on left, across from Jungleland.

This Ramada offers standard motel rooms, which are a little on the small side, with cable TV and safes; refrigerators and microwaves are available on request for $8 a night. Facilities include coin-op washers/dryers, a swimming pool, a children's playground, and picnic tables. The 1950s-style Hollywood Diner, which has an adjoining bar/lounge, serves American fare at all meals. Shuttle service to WDW parks is available for $10 per person, round-trip. Pets are accepted ($6 per night). Children stay and eat free.

6 Places to Stay in the International Drive Area

The hotels and resorts listed here are 7 to 10 miles north of the Walt Disney World parks (a quick freeway trip), and close to Universal Studios Escape and Sea World. Though you won't get away from rambunctious kids anywhere in this town, International Drive hotels do tend to be more adult-oriented. You'll find all of these places located on the map "International Drive Area Accommodations & Dining" in this section.

VERY EXPENSIVE

✪ **Peabody Orlando.** 9801 International Dr. (between the Bee Line Expwy. and Sand Lake Rd.), Orlando, FL 32819. ☎ **800/PEABODY** (732-3639) or 407/352-4000. www. peabodyorlando.com. Fax 407/351-0073. 891 units. A/C MINIBAR TV TEL. $300–$360 for up to 3 people; $495–$1,450 suites. Children 17 and under stay free in parents' room. Inquire about packages and holiday/summer discounts, and senior rates for those over 50. AE, CB, DC, DISC, JCB, MC, V. Free self-parking; valet parking $7.

Okay, let's get the pun out of the way: This property's amenities are just ducky, especially the famous avian ambassadors who make their daily march of the mallards through the lobby to John Philip Sousa. Its location across from the Orange County Convention Center makes it especially popular with business travelers and entertainers. There may be a little disarray here through 2000, since a second 700-room tower is under construction, but that may translate into better deals. The Peabody's hallmark ambiance of sophistication, which extends to its top-rated restaurants, is not found anywhere else in Orlando and will surely survive the jackhammers.

The existing, already luxurious rooms, underwent a renovation and redecoration in 1999, but still contain two phones, Spectravision, and laser-disc movie setups (there's a vast video library). The bathrooms have cosmetic lights, fine European toiletries, a hair dryer, and small TV. The concierge-level Peabody Club occupies the top three floors. Seniors should take advantage of the over-50 prices—compensation for wrinkles indeed.

Dining/Diversions: Dux, the Peabody's signature restaurant, and the casual 24-hour B-Line Diner are detailed in chapter 6. Capriccio, for sophisticated Italian fare, is open for dinner, and for champagne Sunday brunches. Combos play jazz, blues, and show tunes in the atrium Lobby Bar nightly. The lobby is the setting for exquisite afternoon English teas on weekdays. Sporting events are aired in the cozy Mallards Lounge, and alfresco jazz concerts take place on the fourth-floor recreation level in the spring and fall.

Amenities: Concierge (7am to 11pm), room service (24 hours), baby-sitting, nightly bed turndown on request, free daily newspaper, transport between the hotel and all WDW parks throughout the day (unlimited daily round-trips cost $6), Mears transportation/sightseeing desk (sells tickets to all nearby attractions, including WDW parks and dinner shows; also provides transport, by reservation, to attractions and the airport), Olympic-length swimming pool, outdoor whirlpool, kiddie pool, four tennis courts, 7-mile jogging path, car-rental desk, Delta Airlines desk, full-service unisex salon, business center, state-of-the-art health club, shops, video-game arcade, and golf privileges at four nearby courses.

EXPENSIVE

Summerfield Suites. 8480 International Dr. (between the Bee Line Expwy. and Sand Lake Rd.), Orlando, FL 32819. ☎ **800/833-4353** or 407/352-2400. Fax 407/238-0778. 146 units. A/C TV TEL. $119–$219 1-bdrm suites for up to 4; $159–$319 2-bdrm suites for up to 8. Range reflects room size and season. Rates include continental breakfast. AE, CB, DC, DISC, MC, V. Free parking. From I-4, take Exit 29 (Sand Lake Rd.) to International Dr. Turn right on International Dr. Hotel is ½ mile on right.

This delightful hotel—with potted palms on open-air balconies that create a welcoming resort ambiance—is built around a nicely landscaped central courtyard. Like its sibling property in Lake Buena Vista, it's notably friendly and well run. The spacious, neat-as-a-pin suites are attractively decorated, and contain fully equipped eat-in kitchens, comfortable living rooms, and large dressing areas. All offer irons and ironing boards, phones in each bedroom and kitchen, and satellite TVs (with pay-movie options) in each bedroom and living room (the latter with a VCR; rent movies downstairs).

Dining: An extensive continental breakfast buffet is served in a charming dining room (waffles and omelets can be purchased), and the cozy lobby bar is a popular gathering place in the evenings. Local restaurants deliver food to the premises.

Amenities: Concierge/tour desk (sells tickets to WDW parks and other nearby attractions), daily newspaper delivery, transport between the hotel and all WDW parks (round-trip fare is $7), shuttle available to the airport and nearby attractions, complimentary grocery shopping, nice-size swimming pool, whirlpool, kiddie pool, car-rental desk, business services, exercise room, coin-op washers/dryers, 24-hour shop, and a video-game arcade.

MODERATE

Country Hearth Inn. 9861 International Dr. (between Bee Line Expwy. and Sand Lake Rd.), Orlando, FL 32819. ☎ **800/447-1890** or 407/352-0008. Fax 407/352-5449. 150 units. A/C TV TEL. $69–$109 double, depending on view and season. Extra person $10. Children under 18 stay free in parents' room. Rates include continental breakfast. AE, CB, DC, DISC, MC, V. Free self-parking.

Though it doesn't offer much in the way of resort facilities, the Country Hearth Inn's low rates, great location, pretty rooms, and restaurant—not to mention the wine-and-cheese receptions held for guests several times a week—make this an appealing choice. Watch the world go by from a wicker rocking chair on the Inn's balcony, or take a dip in the free-form swimming pool. Charming guest rooms, furnished in handsome maple or mahogany pieces, are adorned with floral friezes

International Drive Area Accommodations & Dining

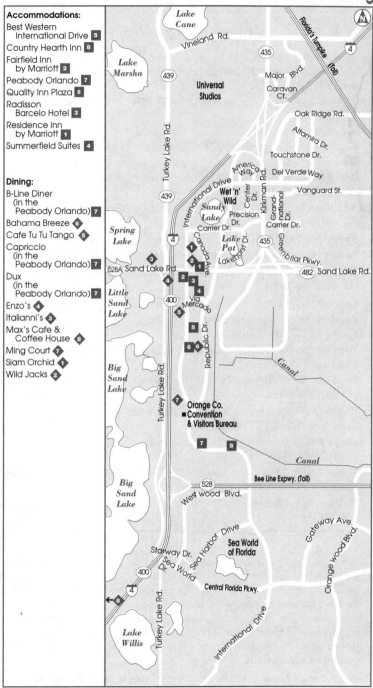

Accommodations:

Best Western
   International Drive **5**
Country Hearth Inn **8**
Fairfield Inn
   by Marriott **2**
Peabody Orlando **7**
Quality Inn Plaza **6**
Radisson
   Barcelo Hotel **3**
Residence Inn
   by Marriott **1**
Summerfield Suites **4**

Dining:

B-Line Diner
   (in the
   Peabody Orlando) **7**
Bahama Breeze **6**
Cafe Tu Tu Tango **5**
Capriccio
   (in the
   Peabody Orlando) **7**
Dux
   (in the
   Peabody Orlando) **7**
Enzo's **4**
Italianni's **3**
Max's Cafe &
   Coffee House **8**
Ming Court **7**
Siam Orchid **1**
Wild Jacks **2**

So I Didn't Book a Room . . .

If you're looking for a basic room, you can try these chain hotels and motels. They are all moderate or inexpensive in price, and located in the budget motel corridors of Kissimmee/U.S. 192 or International Drive; all relatively convenient to the attractions. While we can't vouch for them personally, their brand names generally mean reliability:

In Kissimmee

Best Western Eastgate, 5565 W. Irlo Bronson Memorial Hwy., Kissimmee (☎ 407/396-0707).

Best Western Kissimmee, 2261 E. Irlo Bronson Memorial Hwy., Kissimmee (☎ 407/846-2221).

Best Western Maingate, 8600 W. Irlo Bronson Memorial Hwy., Kissimmee (☎ 407/396-0100).

Budget Inn East, 307 E. Vine St., Kissimmee (☎ 407/847-8010).

Budget Inn West, 4686 W. Vine St., Kissimmee (☎ 407/846-1547).

Comfort Inn Maingate, 7571 W. Irlo Bronson Memorial Hwy., Kissimmee (☎ 407/396-7500).

Comfort Suites Hotel, 4018 W. Vine St., Kissimmee (☎ 407/870-2000).

Comfort Suites Maingate Hotel, 7888 W. Irlo Bronson Memorial Hwy., Kissimmee (☎ 407/390-9888).

Days Inn East of the Magic Kingdom, 5840 W. Irlo Bronson Memorial Hwy., Kissimmee (☎ 407/396-7969).

Days Inn West-Maingate, 7980 W. Irlo Bronson Memorial Hwy., Kissimmee (☎ 407/396-1000).

Doubletree Guest Suites Resort, 4787 W. Irlo Bronson Memorial Hwy., Kissimmee (☎ 407/397-0555).

Econo Lodge Hawaiian, 7514 W. Irlo Bronson Memorial Hwy., Kissimmee (☎ 407/396-2000).

Econo Lodge Maingate Central, 4985 W. Irlo Bronson Memorial Hwy., Kissimmee (☎ 407/396-4343).

Holiday Inn Kissimmee, 2009 W. U.S. Hwy. 192, Kissimmee (☎ 407/826-2713).

and 19th-century folk art. French doors open onto patios, balconies, or courtyards, and bathrooms have art-nouveau lighting fixtures. In-room amenities include cable TVs (with HBO and Spectravision movie options), coffeemakers, phones with modem jacks, wood-bladed chandelier ceiling fans, safes, and small refrigerators. The larger deluxe rooms offer sleeper sofas, microwave ovens, and hair dryers. The Country Parlor restaurant serves American fare at all meals, and there is also a lounge. Transportation is available to the theme parks and the airport for an additional fee.

Radisson Barcelo Hotel. 8444 International Dr., Orlando, FL 32819. ☎ **800/333-3333** or 407/345-0505. Fax 407/352-5894. 299 units. A/C TV TEL. $99–$119. AE, DC, DISC, MC, V.

Hotel & Suites Main Gate East, 5678 Irlo Bronson Memorial Hwy., Kissimmee (☎ **800/366-5437** or 407/396-4488).

Howard Johnson, 4643 W. Irlo Bronson Memorial Hwy., Kissimmee (☎ **407/396-1340**).

Motel 6, 7455 W. Irlo Bronson Memorial Hwy., Kissimmee (☎ **407/ 396-6422**).

Motel 6, 5731 W. Irlo Bronson Memorial Hwy., Kissimmee (☎ **407/ 396-6333**).

Quality Inn on Lake Cecile, 4944 W. Irlo Bronson Memorial Hwy., Kissimmee (☎ **407/396-4455**).

Quality Suites Maingate East, 5876 W. Irlo Bronson Memorial Hwy., Kissimmee (☎ **407/396-4455**).

Ramada Limited, 5055 W. Irlo Bronson Memorial Hwy. (☎ **407/396-2212**).

Ramada Plaza Hotel Gateway, 7370 W. Hwy. 192, Kissimmee (☎ **407/ 396-4400**).

In the International Drive Area:

Days Inn, 9990 International Dr., Orlando (☎ **407/352-8700**).

Days Inn, 7200 International Dr., Orlando (☎ **407/351-1200**).

Days Inn/East of Universal Studios, 5827 Caravan Ct., Orlando (☎ **407/351-3800**).

Econo Lodge International Dr., 5859 American Way, Orlando (☎ **407/345-8880**).

Holiday Inn Express International Dr., 6323 International Dr., Orlando (☎ **407/351-4430**).

Holiday Inn International Drive Resort, 6515 International Dr., Orlando (☎ **407/351-3500**).

Ramada Hotel Resort Florida Center, 7400 International Dr., Orlando (☎ **407/351-8400**).

Roadway Inn International, 6327 International Dr., Orlando (☎ **407/ 351-4444**).

Free parking. From I-4, take Exit 29 (Sand Lake Rd.). Turn right on International Dr. Turn right on the *second* entrance to Jamaican Ct. The hotel is on the left.

The hotel's location—just a few minutes from Universal Studios and Sea World, and about 20 minutes from Walt Disney World—puts you in the heart of Orlando's action. You'll also reap the benefits of a 1997 room renovation. All rooms have bright, tropical decor, two queen beds, two phones, Nintendo-equipped televisions, and refrigerators. Fitness buffs can work out in the adjacent YMCA Aquatic Center, which houses two Olympic-size pools, 23 Nautilus machines, and racquetball courts. (The hotel also has its own outdoor heated pool.) Since it's located in the heart of the I-Drive tourist hub, there are dozens of restaurants and shops nearby. The hotel's restaurant serves a full breakfast buffet, which is included in some room rates. There is also a "kids-eat-free" program.

Residence Inn by Marriott. 7975 Canada Ave. (just off Sand Lake Rd., a block east of International Dr.), Orlando, FL 32819. ☎ **800/227-3978** or 407/345-0117. Fax 407/352-2689. www.marriott.com. 176 units. A/C TV TEL. $85–$135. Rates include extended continental breakfast. AE, DC, DISC, MC, V. Free parking.

Marriott's Residence Inns were designed to offer home-away-from-home comfort for traveling businesspeople, but the concept also works well for families. The accommodations buildings are surrounded by well-tended lawns, shrubs, and beds of geraniums, and the handsomely decorated suites offer full eat-in kitchens and comfortable living-room areas. All but studio doubles have wood-burning fireplaces, and two-bedroom penthouses (great for families) have full bathrooms upstairs and down. In-room amenities include iron, ironing board, and safe. There is also a large swimming pool, a whirlpool, and a basketball court. Continental breakfast is served daily, and local restaurants will deliver to the hotel. Transportation is available to all the theme parks, and to the airport.

INEXPENSIVE

Best Western Plaza International. 8738 International Dr., Orlando, FL 32819. ☎ **800/654-7160** or 407/345-8195. Fax 407/352-8196. 672 units. A/C TV TEL. $80–$95. AE, DC, DISC, MC, V. Free parking. From I-4 take Exit 29 (Sand Lake Rd.) The first traffic light is International Dr., the hotel is 1 mile on the right.

Although it offers free transportation to WDW parks, this hotel, located less than 3 miles from Sea World is a good bet for those planning to spend most of their time at that park, or at Universal Studios Escape. All the standard features such as a coin-operated laundry, and connecting rooms and cribs, are here. Fitness-conscious guests have access to a nearby, and quite large, YMCA. There is a kiddie pool and outdoor pool on the property, plus a small game room.

Fairfield Inn by Marriott. 8342 Jamaican Ct. (off International Dr. between the Bee Line Expwy. and Sand Lake Rd.), Orlando, FL 32819. ☎ **800/228-2800** or 407/363-1944. Fax 407/363-1944. www.marriott.com. 134 units. A/C TV TEL. $69–$79 room for up to 4; range reflects season. Rates include continental breakfast. AE, CB, DC, DISC, JCB, MC, V. Free parking. From I-4 take Exit 29 (Sand Lake Rd.), go east 1 block, turn right on International Dr. Turn right on Jamaican Ct. The hotel is on the right.

I love this inn's quiet and safe location in a secluded area off International Drive. It's nestled in Jamaican Court, a neatly landscaped complex of hotels and restaurants (that means a number of places are within walking distance). The spiffy-looking rooms offer cable TV with HBO, and the phones are equipped with 25-foot cords and modem jacks. Daily newspapers and local calls are free, as is the continental breakfast served in the lobby each morning. A small outdoor swimming pool and video-game arcade are on the premises, and the lobby has a microwave oven for guest use. The guest-services desk sells tickets (most of them discounted) and can arrange transport to all nearby theme parks and attractions and the airport; round-trip to WDW parks is $10.

Quality Inn Plaza. 9000 International Dr., Orlando, FL 32819. ☎ **800/999-8585** or 407/345-8585. Fax 407/996-6839. 1,020 units. A/C TV TEL. $39.95–$79.95. AE, DISC, MC, V. Free parking. From I-4, take Exit 29 (Sand Lake Rd.). Turn right at the bottom of ramp. Turn at the first right, International Dr. The property is 1 mile on the right, next to the Amazing Animals attraction.

The rooms at this property are spread throughout five-, six-, and seven-story buildings, with rooms featuring two double beds. Built in 1983, the property is clean, but its furnishings are the bare necessities. Cribs are available, there are in-room safes, and an outdoor pool. The hotel's proximity to the nightlife, restaurants, and shops along International Drive is a plus. The lobby includes a restaurant, bar, game room, and a shop that sells snacks and premade sandwiches. Kids under 11 eat free in the hotel restaurant with a paying adult. Pets are accepted.

7 At the Airport

Hyatt Regency Orlando International Airport. 9300 Airport Blvd., Orlando, FL 32827. ☎ **800/233-1234** or 407/825-1234. Fax 407/856-1672. 469 units. A/C TV TEL. $205 double; $225–$450 suites. Children under 18 stay free in parents' room. AE, CB, DC, DISC, JCB, MC, V. Self-parking $8; valet parking $11.

If you have to catch an early-morning flight out of Orlando, treat yourself to a night at this beautiful hotel, right in the airport's main terminal. Large, resort-style rooms—off balconies bordered by planters of bougainvillea or philodendrons—are attractively decorated and equipped with large desks, three phones (desk, bedside, and bathroom), cable TVs (with channels for Spectravision movie, tourism information, and flight arrival/departure), full-size ironing boards/irons, and hair dryers. The rooms are soundproof, so you won't hear planes taking off and landing.

Dining/Diversions: The elegant Hemisphere Restaurant serves sophisticated American fare at lunch, and northern Italian specialties at dinner; a pianist entertains weekend nights. McCoy's Bar & Grill features a display kitchen with an oak-burning pizza oven. You can also try the airport eating establishments, including a food court.

Amenities: 24-hour concierge/room service, shoe shine, car rental, baby-sitting, full business center, currency exchange. Airport shopping mall, airline desks, unisex hair salon, swimming pool, sundeck, fully equipped health club, travel agency, game rooms, and shopping arcade.

8 Places to Stay Elsewhere in Orlando

There are two good reasons to stay away from all the hustle and hassle of the attractions: crowds and money.

If you are traveling in the middle of peak season—during the summer or around Christmas—you will find yourself elbow to elbow with the sweating masses almost everywhere you go. Those theme park crowds spill over into the shops, the restaurants, even the bathrooms, making it difficult to get a few moments of quiet when you are not in your room. (If you are traveling with kids, not even then.) The world can feel pretty small after several days of very close encounters. And, the nearer to the attractions, the higher the cost of just about everything from rooms to soda. The difference may be a nickel here and 50¢ there, but those pennies can add up to serious dollars if you are traveling with your family.

The disadvantages? Well, you will have to travel along I-4 to get back and forth from the parks. But if you travel before 7am or after 10am in the morning, and after 6pm in the evening, you will encounter minimal traffic congestion, and your trip will take 20 minutes. If you have a family, though, it will be harder to escape back to your hotel's pool for an afternoon swim, or to your room for a nap.

The biggest determining factor when choosing a hotel location should be the type of vacation you have planned. If you're the kind of person who will explore the Disney parks all day, and then spend the night dancing at Pleasure Island, it makes more sense to stay on Disney property, or at least close by. If you would like to get away from it all, take a quite stroll along a city sidewalk, see a museum, or

Hotel Boom

The war is on. In addition to competing with Disney for theme park visitors, Universal Studios Escape is now battling for resort guests.

Portofino Bay Hotel is the first of five planned properties built by Universal Studios Escape, after it decided to go head-to-head with Disney by offering on-property resorts adjacent to its theme parks. Opened in late 1999, the 750-room Portofino Bay features eight restaurants/lounges, a spa and fitness center, and a playground. The Loews hotel resembles a Mediterranean seaside village, and is set into a harbor. Portofino Bay's facilities, from bocci ball courts to its two swimming pools, carry through this old-world theme.

Just as at Disney, there are perks for staying at a Universal hotel. These include:

- Free water-taxi transportation to Universal Studios, Islands of Adventure, and CityWalk.
- Early theme park admission, 1 hour before the general public.
- Front-of-the-line access to specific attractions within the theme parks during the first hour the park is open to the general public.
- Resort ID card that can be used to purchase food, merchandise, and other items at Universal Studios, Islands of Adventure, and CityWalk.
- Priority seating at restaurants.
- Length-of-stay tickets that provide park access for the duration of a visit.

For information about Portofino Bay, write 5601 Universal Blvd., Orlando, FL 32819 or call ☎ **407/503-1000.** Packages can be booked through Universal Studio Vacations at ☎ 888/322-5537 or 407/224-7000. Online, go to **www. usevacations.com.**

experience life in a real American city, try staying in downtown Orlando or Winter Park.

You'll find all the places described here on the map "Orlando Area Accommodations & Dining" in chapter 6.

IN ORLANDO

All of the following fall within the "Moderate" price category.

The Courtyard at Lake Lucerne. 211 N. Lucerne Circle E., Orlando, FL 32801. ☎ **800/ 444-5289** or 407/648-5188. Fax 407/246-1368. 24 units. A/C TV TEL. $125–$199 suites. Rates include continental breakfast. AE, DC, MC, V. Free self-parking. Take Orange Ave. south, immediately following City Hall (domed building with fountains and glass sculpture), turn left onto Anderson. After 2 lights, at Delaney Ave., turn right. Take first right onto Lucerne Circle N. Be aware of one-way streets. Follow the brown "historic inn" signs.

Orlando literally grew around this B&B, which stands incongruously amid a tangle of interstate ramps. A different artist or decorator designed each unit in the three distinct buildings that make up the property. Suites at the I. W. Phillips House, built in 1916, are the quietest. The solitude isn't as complete in the front rooms of Norment–Perry; traffic sounds there are minimal, but audible. Since opening in 1986, the Courtyard has served mostly business VIPs and locals on weekend getaways. With few amenities, it's a place for simple, private pleasures. Suites are basic, and most have claw-foot tubs and sunrooms. Suites in the Wellborn include mini-kitchens with refrigerators, microwaves, and coffeemakers. Downtown's most famous entertainment district, Church Street Station, is less than 6 blocks north.

Walk or take a cab to begin the night, but for safety reasons, you should ride home. The Courtyard is undergoing an expansion as this book goes to press; more rooms should be available in the future.

Hampton Inn at Universal Studios. 5621 Windhover Dr., Orlando, FL 32819. ☎ 800/231-8395. Fax 407/363-1711. 120 units. A/C TV TEL. $59–$89. Rates include complimentary breakfast buffet. AE, DISC, DC, MC, V. Take I-4 to Exit 30B. Go through 2 traffic lights; turn right at Shoney's Restaurant. It's a 5-story white building.

There is nothing fancy about this simple hotel, but its location is ideal if you plan to spend most of your stay at Universal Studios Escape, Sea World, or the rest of Orlando (it's just 2 blocks from Universal Studios). There are no permanent shuttles to the Disney parks, and although they can be arranged, the cost ($35 one way) would make it cheaper to rent a car. The rooms themselves are average-sized, and each has an in-room coffeemaker. Microwaves and refrigerators are available in some units. There is a small game room, in-room cable, an outdoor heated pool, and valet laundry service. Restaurants are within walking distance.

The Harley of Orlando. 151 E. Washington St., Orlando, FL 32801. ☎ 800/321-2323 or 407/841-3220. Fax 407/849-1839. 264 units. A/C TV TEL. $99–$109 double. AE, MC, V. Free parking. Take I-4 to the Anderson St. exit. Turn left on Rosalind. The hotel entrance is located on the left, directly across from the entrance to Lake Eola Park.

Just 15 minutes from Orlando International Airport, and about 25 minutes from the attractions, the Harley of Orlando is an urban alternative to the Disney resorts. Request a balcony room overlooking Lake Eola Park, one of the most beautiful spots in the city. The carpet in this five-story structure is a little threadbare in places, but the small rooms, done in dark colors, are comfortable and clean. Allergy-sufferers can request a nonsmoking room. There is a small pool and sundeck. Room service is available, or you can eat in the hotel's restaurant; there's also a lounge. Church Street Station is just a short walk away, or you can catch the free city bus, Lymmo, just up the block from the hotel.

Radisson Place Hotel Orlando. 60 S. Ivanhoe Blvd., Orlando, FL 32804. ☎ 800/333-3333 or 407/425-4455. Fax 407/425-7440. 367 units. A/C TV TEL. $104–$129. AE, DISC, MC, V. Take I-4 to Princeton St. (Exit 43). Turn right at the bottom of the ramp. Turn left on Orange Ave. Go through the light, bearing to the right around the landscaping and the miniature Statue of Liberty; the hotel is on the left.

The 15-story Radisson Place Hotel, built in 1985, is definitely geared more toward the business traveler than the family-leisure crowd. Nevertheless, its location right off I-4—just blocks from downtown, and 15 minutes from the airport—makes it a good bet for families, too. The rooms are tastefully appointed with solid-colored bedspreads and carpets. Most rooms have minibars, and some of them are designed to accommodate travelers with disabilities. The views of downtown Orlando from the upper floors are impressive, and the suites are a cut above those you will find for the same price elsewhere. Fitness fanatics can use the swimming pool, Jacuzzi, tennis courts, and health club. The hotel's restaurants offer solid, if not spectacular, dining, and room service is available. Visit the Greater Orlando Chamber of Commerce next door for brochures and information on attractions.

Radisson Twin Towers Hotel. 5780 Major Blvd., Orlando, FL 32819. ☎ 800/327-2110 or 407/351-1000. Fax 407/363-0106. 761 units. A/C TV TEL. $89–$179 double, depending on the season. AE, DC, DISC, MC, V. Located directly across from the main gate of Universal Studios.

Built originally as a convention hotel, the property underwent a makeover when families began flocking to Universal Studios, located right across the street. The hotel offers an International Drive address without the usual congestion, and you'll be minutes from WDW, while avoiding that area's higher prices. The hotel still attracts a lot of convention business, but the meeting facilities are separate from the guest towers, so aside from the occasional human Elk encounter in the elevator, you'll hardly notice. Rooms contain one king or two queen beds, and some offer a sofa bed as well. Extras include in-room coffeemakers and hair dryers. There's a restaurant and lounge on premises, and several good restaurants, such as the Hard Rock Café, are within walking distance. Amenities include room service, a pool, sauna, playground, and children's program. On a side note: That red building on the property that looks like an old-fashioned schoolhouse is just that—the Little Red School House, a public school run in cooperation with the local school district for the children of Twin Towers employees.

Ramada Inn & Suites by Sea World. 6800 Villa D Costa Dr., Orlando, FL 32821. ☎ **800/ 272-6232** or 407/239-0707. Fax 407/239-8243. www.marriott.com. A/C TV TEL. 158 units. $129–$209. AE, DISC, DC, MC, V. From the Walt Disney World area, take I-4 east to Exit 27A. At the first traffic light, turn right.

This all-suite resort offers a roomy alternative: double suites including two bedrooms and two bathrooms that are ideal for a larger family, or two couples traveling together. Each suite has a complete kitchen, and all rooms have coffeemakers. The recreational facilities aren't as extensive as those found elsewhere, but the hotel is clean and comfortable, and has facilities for nonsmokers and those with disabilities. Parents will appreciate the availability of a baby-sitting service and the on-site convenient store. RV-enthusiasts will find parking available for their vehicles.

Renaissance Orlando Hotel. 6677 Sea Harbour Dr., Orlando, FL 32821 (across from Sea World). ☎ **407/351-5555.** Fax 407/351-9991. 780 units. A/C TV TEL. $139–$259, depending on location and season. AE, DISC, DC, MC, V. From I-4 follow signs to Sea World.

This is a quality hotel, with good-sized rooms, fine service, and luxurious surroundings. However, its most valuable feature is its location; it is ideal for visitors who will be going to Disney, but who also want to explore the other attractions and Orlando proper. The rooms are huge, as are the marble bathrooms. There's a health club, swimming pool, and a small playground. Baby-sitting service is available, and so is day care. The hotel has five restaurants and three lounges to choose from, or you can order room service. Located across the street from Sea World, the hotel offers special packages that include Sea World tickets. It is only about 10 minutes— in light traffic—from Walt Disney World. Nonsmoking rooms and rooms for travelers with disabilities are available.

IN WINTER PARK

○ **Best Western Mount Vernon Inn.** 110 S. Orlando Ave., Winter Park, FL 32789 ☎ **407/647-1166.** Fax 407/647-8011. 147 units. A/C TV TEL. $78–$88 double. AE, MC, V. Free self-parking. The Inn is located on U.S. Rte. 17–92, between Fairbanks Ave. and Lee Rd., across from Houston's Steakhouse.

This is one of the best bargains in town; a place where old-money families know their guests will get comfortable accommodations at a reasonable price. Look for lots of late-model Caddies in the parking lot. There are some rooms that have nice views overlooking the pool; across the street, about a block away, is a city park the kids will love. But overall, there is nothing too fancy about the Mount Vernon. It is, however, centrally located between the beaches and the theme parks, and very close to downtown Winter Park and downtown Orlando. A dining room serves a decent breakfast and lunch, and there are many fine restaurants nearby.

✪ **Langford Resort.** 300 E. New England Ave. (at Interlachen Ave.), Winter Park, FL 32789. ☎ **407/644-3400.** Fax 407/628-1952. 220 units. A/C TV TEL. $75–$115 double; $200 suites. Children 17 and under stay free in parents' room. Rooms with kitchenettes $10 extra. AE, DC, MC, V. Free self-parking. I-4 West through downtown Orlando to Winter Park. Take Fairbanks Exit 69. Go east 2 miles to Park Ave. Turn left, go 2 blocks, and turn right on New England. 2 blocks on right.

In pre-Disney days, Winter Park was one of central Florida's most-visited resorts, and the Langford was the place to stay. The guest roster proudly listed Eleanor Roosevelt, Mamie Eisenhower, Lillian Gish, and Vincent Price; Ronald and Nancy Reagan celebrated their 25th wedding anniversary here. Stars and plain-folk alike, came to gawk at the hotel's garishly decorated rooms, as well as the poolside bathrooms with their wacky paintings of mermaids and mermen. Today, the resort is kitschy, but no longer glamorous; nevertheless, it offers extensive facilities at very reasonable rates. The mid-sized rooms show some wear and tear, but the lobby and hallways have recently been renovated. Room decor varies and is notably eclectic. Many rooms have balconies and/or fully equipped kitchenettes with two-burner stoves and small refrigerators. An on-site spa offers a full range of treatments: sauna, steam, massage (shiatsu, Swedish, and deep athletic), body wraps, seaweed wraps, salt glows, facials, manicures, pedicures, and day-of-beauty packages. The little ones will love the kiddie pool and the small video-game arcade.

6 Dining

Orlando has fast become the theme-restaurant capital of the Planet (Hollywood, anyone?). From souped-up cars to supermodels to superheroes, every category is represented. But there are still some restaurants where the focus is not only on the decor, but on the delicacies.

Since most visitors spend the majority of their time in the Walt Disney World area, I've focused on the best dining choices there. Also listed are some worthwhile restaurants beyond Mickey's realm. These "local" establishments often benefit from the high concentration of culinary talent brought to central Florida by the attractions. In the past few years, several high-quality restaurants have opened in downtown Orlando, providing visitors to Church Street Station with more dining options.

Parents will be pleased to note that most mid-priced restaurants offer a children's menu. Many offer kiddie distractions like coloring books or mazes to complete.

If you go to a place catering to children, expect the noise level to be high. Kids don't take a vacation from screaming, howling, and throwing tantrums. That's the bad news. The good news is, the higher the average cost of an entree, the less likely you are to find little people. If you're looking for a quiet meal, head for the fancier restaurants farther from the Disney parks, on International Drive, or in Orlando proper. Or patronize the more expensive park offerings. If those howling youngsters belong to you, take advantage of the many in-hotel baby-sitting services for one night, while you go out alone.

If kids really get your goat, then by all means steer clear of any dining establishment that features "characters." (See the listings for dinner shows in chapter 10.)

Listings are divided by the following price categories: **very expensive** (the average main course at dinner is more than $25), **expensive** ($20 to $25), **moderate** ($10 to $20), and **inexpensive** (under $10). Keep in mind that these categories refer to dinner prices, and lunch prices are often cheaper—especially at WDW restaurants. Also, keep in mind that your complete meal could cost more than twice the main course, especially if you order several courses and wine. Note, however, that some very expensive restaurants offer affordable lunches and/or cheaper early bird dinners. Also, I'm operating on the assumption that you're not stinting when you order.

Some restaurants, for instance, have main courses ranging from $12 to $20. In most cases, you can dine for less if you order carefully. Especially noteworthy restaurants and those that offer especially good value are marked with a star ✪.

American Express produces a handy, pocket-sized guide that lists basic information about dining and recreational opportunities within WDW. It also lists discounts, which can run about 10%, at selected Disney restaurants. The book is available to American Express cardholders only.

You can get a copy if you book a "White Glove" package through American Express, or if you call ☎ **800/528-4802.** (It takes about a month to get the information sent through the mail.) Cardholders can also get a copy at the American Express office at the entrance to Epcot, and in the Contemporary Resort's lobby.

For additional online information about area restaurants, use the keyword **Orlando** on **America Online** to visit **Digital City Orlando.** From there, click on "Entertainment," and you'll find a complete listing of, among other things, Orlando restaurants, A to Z.

PRIORITY SEATING AT WDW RESTAURANTS

Priority seating is similar to a reservation, but it's less rigid. It means that you get the next table available *after* you arrive at a restaurant, but a table is not kept empty pending your arrival. Therefore, you may end up waiting a bit, even if you arrive at the time you scheduled your priority seating. You can arrange priority seating up to 60 days in advance at almost all full-service restaurants in the Magic Kingdom, Epcot, Disney–MGM Studios, Animal Kingdom, Disney resorts, and Downtown Disney. Priority seating can also be arranged for character meals and shows throughout the World. To make any of these arrangements, call ☎ **407/WDW-DINE** (939-3463). Nighttime shows can actually be booked as far in advance as you wish.

Note: Since this priority-seating phone number was instituted in 1994, it has become much more difficult to obtain a table as a walk-in. I strongly advise you to avoid disappointment by calling ahead.

However, if you don't reserve in advance, you can take your chances by making reservations once you have arrived in the parks themselves:

- **At Epcot:** Make reservations at the Worldkey interactive terminals at Guest Relations in Innoventions East, at Worldkey Information Service Satellites located on the main concourse to World Showcase and at Germany in World Showcase, or at the restaurants themselves.
- **At the Magic Kingdom:** Reserve at the restaurants themselves.
- **At Disney–MGM Studios:** Make reservations at the Hollywood Junction Station on Sunset Boulevard or at the restaurants themselves.
- **At Animal Kingdom:** Make reservations by visiting the guest-services desk near the entrance. And good news: You can get priority seating at the Rainforest Cafe at Animal Kingdom. You can make that request up to 30 days in advance, and, since this is a very popular place, the sooner you make the call the better.

You may also want to keep these restaurant facts in mind:

- All park restaurants have nonsmoking interiors; you can smoke on patios and terraces.
- Magic Kingdom restaurants serve no alcoholic beverages, but liquor is available at Animal Kingdom, Epcot, and Disney–MGM Studios restaurants and elsewhere in the WDW complex.
- All sit-down restaurants in Walt Disney World take American Express, MasterCard, Visa, and the Disney Card.

- Guests at Disney resorts and official properties can make restaurant reservations through guest-services or concierge desks.
- All WDW restaurants offer low-priced children's menus.

1   Restaurants by Cuisine

AMERICAN

B-Line Diner (International Drive Area, *M*)

Cinderella's Royal Table (Magic Kingdom, *E*)

Crystal Palace (Magic Kingdom, *M*)

Dexter's at Thorton Park (Orlando, *M*)

50's Prime Time Cafe (Disney–MGM Studios, *M*)

Garden Grill (Epcot, *M*)

Hollywood Brown Derby (Disney–MGM Studios, *E*)

Liberty Tree Tavern (Magic Kingdom, *M*)

Max's Cafe & Coffee House (Celebration, *IE*)

McDonald's Fun House (Disney's West Side, *IE*)

Planet Hollywood (Pleasure Island, *M*)

The Plaza Restaurant (Magic Kingdom, *IE*)

Sci-Fi Dine-In Theater Restaurant (Disney–MGM Studios, *M*)

White Wolf Cafe (Downtown Orlando, *M*)

AMERICAN/CONTINENTAL

Black Swan (Lake Buena Vista, *VE*)

BARBECUE

Bubbaloo's Bodacious BBQ (Winter Park, *IE*)

Wild Jacks (International Drive, *M*)

BRITISH

Rose & Crown Pub & Dining Room (Epcot, *M*)

CALIFORNIA

California Grill (Magic Kingdom Resort Area, *E*)

Pebbles (Lake Buena Vista, *M*)

Rainforest Cafe (Downtown Disney Marketplace & Animal Kingdom, *M*)

Wolfgang Puck Cafe (Disney's West Side, Disney, *M*)

CANADIAN

Le Cellier (Epcot, *M*)

CARIBBEAN

Bahama Breeze (International Drive, *M*)

CHARACTER BREAKFASTS & DINNERS

Artist Point (Disney's Wilderness Lodge, *E*)

Cape May Café (Disney's Beach Club Resort, *E*)

Chef Mickey's (Disney's Contemporary Resort; Breakfast *E*, Dinner *M*)

Cinderella's Royal Table (Cinderella Castle, *E*)

Liberty Tree Tavern (Liberty Square, *M*)

Mickey's Tropical Luau (Disney's Polynesian Resort, *M*)

Minnie's Menehune (Disney's Polynesian Resort, *E*)

1900 Park Fare (Disney's Grand Floridian Beach Resort; Breakfast *E*)

Watercress Café (Wyndham Resort, *M*)

CHINESE

Lotus Blossom Café (Epcot, *IE*)

Ming Court (International Drive, *M*)

Nine Dragons (Epcot, *M*)

CUBAN

Bongo's Cuban Cafe (Disney's West Side, *M*)

Rolando's (Casselberry, *IE*)

IE = Inexpensive; *M* = Moderate; *E* = Expensive *VE* = Very Expensive

FOOD COURT

Sunshine Season Food Fair (Epcot, *IE*)

FRENCH

Les Chefs de France (Epcot, *E*)

Le Provence (Downtown Orlando, *E*)

Maison et Jardin (Altamonte Springs, *E*)

GERMAN

Biergarten (Epcot, *M*)

Sommerfest (Epcot, *M, IE*)

INTERNATIONAL

Dux (International Drive, *VE*)

Victoria & Albert's (Magic Kingdom Resort Area, *VE*)

ITALIAN

Capriccio (International Drive, *M*)

Enzo's (International Drive, *IE*)

Italianni's (International Drive, *M*)

L'Originale Alfredo di Roma (Epcot, *E*)

N.Y.P.D. (Downtown Orlando, *IE*)

Portobello Yacht Club (Pleasure Island, *M*)

Romano's Macaroni Grill (Lake Buena Vista, *IE*)

Sergio's (Downtown Orlando, *E*)

Tony's Town Square Restaurant (Magic Kingdom, *E*)

Toy Story Pizza Planet (Disney–MGM Studios, *IE*)

Tuscany (Lake Buena Vista, *E*)

JAPANESE

Mikado Japanese Steak House (Lake Buena Vista, *E*)

Tempura Kiku Restaurant (Epcot, *E*)

Yakitori House (Epcot, *IE*)

MEXICAN

Cantina de San Angel (Epcot, *IE*)

San Angel Inn (Epcot, *M*)

MISSISSIPPI DELTA

House of Blues (Disney's West Side, *M*)

MOROCCAN

Marrakesh (Epcot, *M*)

NEW ORLEANS

Boatwright's Dining Hall (Lake Buena Vista, *IE*)

Bonfamille's Cafe (Lake Buena Vista, *IE*)

Copeland's of New Orleans (International Drive, *M*)

NORWEGIAN

Akershus (Epcot, *M*)

Kringla Bakeri og Kafe (Epcot, *IE*)

PACIFIC RIM

'Ohana (Magic Kingdom Resort Area, *M*)

SEAFOOD/STEAKS/CHOPS

Artist Point (Magic Kingdom Resort Area, *M*)

Cape May Café (Lake Buena Vista, *IE*)

Coral Reef (Epcot, *M*)

Fulton's Crab House (Pleasure Island, *E*)

Hemingway's (Lake Buena Vista, *E*)

Yachtsman Steakhouse (Epcot Resort Area, *E*)

TAPAS

Cafe Tu Tu Tango (International Drive, *M*)

Spoodles (Epcot Resort Area, *E*)

THAI

Siam Orchid (International Drive, *M*)

VIETNAMESE

Little Saigon (Orlando, *IE*)

---

2 Places to Dine in Walt Disney World

The following listings encompass restaurants in the Disney theme parks (Epcot, Magic Kingdom, Disney–MGM Studios, and Animal Kingdom), the Disney-owned resorts, and the official hotels. Restaurants in the entertainment and shopping areas

(Pleasure Island, Downtown Disney's West Side, and Downtown Disney Marketplace) are listed in the Lake Buena Vista section.

IN EPCOT

Though an ethnic meal at one of the World Showcase pavilions is a traditional part of the Epcot experience, many of the following establishments are just a tad pricey for the value received. Unless money is no object, you may want to consider the numerous lower-priced walk-in places located throughout the park that don't require reservations (for details, check the Epcot Guidemap that you'll receive upon entering the park). You can also eat at the sit-down restaurants at lunchtime, when entree prices are lower. Almost all of the establishments listed here serve lunch and dinner daily (hours vary with park hours), and, unless otherwise noted, they offer children's meals for under $5. These restaurants are located on the map "Epcot Dining" in this section.

Note: Since the clientele at even the fanciest Epcot World Showcase restaurants come directly from the park, you don't have to dress up for dinner. **Priority seating,** which reserves you a place, but not a specific table, is available at all WDW sit-down restaurants, and is strongly recommended. The chances of getting a table without a long wait are pretty slim. Call ☎ **407/WDW-DINE** (939-3463).

EXPENSIVE

Les Chefs de France Restaurant. France Pavilion, World Showcase. ☎ **407/WDW-DINE** (939-3463). Priority seating. Main courses $9.95–$15.95 at lunch; $17.95–$26.25 at dinner. AE, MC, V. Daily noon until 1 hr. before park closes. FRENCH.

Three of France's best chefs supervise the menus of this restaurant, whose artnouveau/fin-de-siècle interior is agleam with mirrors and brass candelabra chandeliers. Etched-glass and brass dividers create intimate dining areas, and tables are elegantly appointed. Start your gastronomic journey with the seafood cream soup with crab dumplings. Main courses at dinner include a superb broiled salmon in sorrel cream sauce (served with ratatouille and new potatoes), braised beef burgundy, and sautéed beef tenderloin with raisins and brandy sauce. The dessert of choice is a sumptuous soufflé Grand-Marnier. There is a substantial wine list, and you may purchase wines on the list at Au Palais du Vin, a wine shop in the pavilion.

L'Originale Alfredo di Roma Ristorante. Italy Pavilion, World Showcase. ☎ **407/WDW-DINE** (939-3463). Priority seating. Main courses $9.25–$18 at lunch; $11–$27 at dinner. AE, MC, V. Daily noon–park closing. ITALIAN.

Patterned after Alfredo De Lelio's celebrated establishment in Rome, L'Originale Alfredo di Roma Ristorante evokes a seaside Roman palazzo with the beautiful Veronese-inspired frescoes on its walls. The theatricality of its exhibition kitchen, the charming Italian waiters, and the exuberant strolling musicians create a festive ambiance. The noise level in the dining room can be high; for a quieter setting, ask for a seat on the verandah. Pasta is the way to go in this restaurant. De Lelio invented fettuccine Alfredo, and it is the premiere dish here. Other recommendations include a garlicky linguine al pesto and the veal scaloppine served with roasted potatoes and vegetables. Indulge in a sublime tiramisu for dessert if you have room—you may not, since the food here tends to be heavy. A special vegetarian menu (with excellent grilled veggies, among other items) is available, and the list of Italian wines is extensive. The three-course early-bird dinner here is a great deal.

Tempura Kiku. Japan Pavilion, World Showcase. ☎ **407/WDW-DINE** (939-3463). Priority seating for teppanyaki; reservations not accepted at the tempura counter. Teppanyaki main courses $10–$20 at lunch, $15–$30 at dinner; fixed-price menu $39.50 for 2 at lunch, $59.90

Epcot Dining

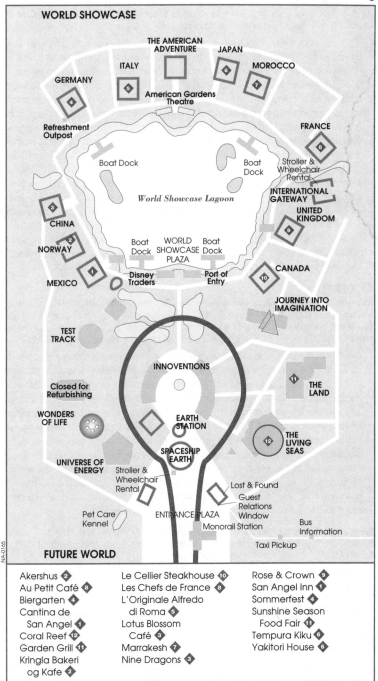

WORLD SHOWCASE

THE AMERICAN ADVENTURE

JAPAN

ITALY

MOROCCO

GERMANY

American Gardens Theatre

FRANCE

Refreshment Outpost

Boat Dock

Boat Dock

Stroller & Wheelchair Rental

World Showcase Lagoon

INTERNATIONAL GATEWAY

CHINA

UNITED KINGDOM

NORWAY

Boat Dock

WORLD SHOWCASE PLAZA

Boat Dock

CANADA

MEXICO

Disney Traders

Port of Entry

JOURNEY INTO IMAGINATION

TEST TRACK

INNOVENTIONS

THE LAND

Closed for Refurbishing

WONDERS OF LIFE

EARTH STATION

THE LIVING SEAS

UNIVERSE OF ENERGY

SPACESHIP EARTH

Stroller & Wheelchair Rental

Lost & Found

Guest Relations Window

Pet Care Kennel

ENTRANCE PLAZA

Monorail Station

Bus Information

Taxi Pickup

FUTURE WORLD

NA-0165

Akershus ❷
Au Petit Café ❽
Biergarten ❹
Cantina de San Angel ❶
Coral Reef ⑫
Garden Grill ⑪
Kringla Bakeri og Kafe ❷

Le Cellier Steakhouse ➓
Les Chefs de France ❽
L'Originale Alfredo di Roma ❺
Lotus Blossom Café ❸
Marrakesh ❼
Nine Dragons ❸

Rose & Crown ❾
San Angel Inn ❶
Sommerfest ❹
Sunshine Season Food Fair ⑪
Tempura Kiku ❻
Yakitori House ❻

101

for 2 at dinner; tempura $9.25–$11.95 at lunch, $14.75–$22.75 at dinner. AE, MC, V. Daily 11am until 1 hr before park closes. JAPANESE.

The Tempura Kiku centers on a teppanyaki steak house where diners sit at grill tables, and white-hatted chefs rapidly dice, slice, stir-fry, and propel cooked food onto your plate with amazing dexterity. Kids especially enjoy watching the chef wield his cleaver and utensils. Several parties are seated together at the teppanyaki tables, which makes for a convivial dining experience, especially for single travelers looking for some conversation. An elaborate dinner for two (an abbreviated version is available at lunch) includes a shrimp appetizer, salad with ginger dressing, soup (ask for the *misroshiru*–soybean soup with tofu and mushrooms), grilled fresh vegetables with *udon* noodles, succulent morsels of grilled beef tenderloin and lobster, steamed rice, choice of dessert (perhaps chestnut cake), and green tea. Portions are plentiful, and even a la carte entrees include plenty of extras. Kirin beer, plum wine, and sake are among your beverage options, along with specialty drinks, such as tachibana (light rum, orange curaçao, and mandarin orange juice) and nonalcoholic ones for kids.

Adjoining the teppanyaki rooms is a U-shaped tempura counter where you can eat shrimp, scallops, chicken, and fresh vegetables that have been lightly battered and deep-fried. Some sushi and sashimi items are served here as well.

MODERATE

Akershus. Norway Pavilion, World Showcase. ☎ **407/WDW-DINE** (939-3463). Priority seating. Lunch buffet $11.95 for adults, $5.25 for children 4–9, free for children 3 and under; dinner buffet $18.95 for adults, $7.95 for children. There are also nonsmorgasbord children's meals for $4.75. AE, MC, V. Daily noon–3:30pm and 4:30pm–park closing. NORWEGIAN.

Akershus is housed in the re-creation of a 14th-century castle fortress that stands in Oslo's harbor, and offers diners the chance to sample quality Scandinavian cuisine at a decent price. Its pristine white-stone interior, with lofty beamed ceilings and leaded glass windows, features intimate dining niches divided by Gothic archways. The 40-item buffet offered here is an immense smorgasbord of traditional *smavarmt* (hot) and *koldtbord* (cold) dishes—smoked pork with honey mustard, strips of venison in cream sauce, gravlax in mustard sauce, smoked mackerel, Norwegian tomato herring, an array of Norwegian breads and cheeses, potato salad, red cabbage, boiled red potatoes, and much more. Norwegian beer and aquavit complement a list of French and California wines. And do consider the Lillehammer brandy for an after-dinner drink. Desserts, such as a "veiled maiden"—an applesauce and whipped cream concoction—can be ordered a la carte.

Biergarten. Germany Pavilion, World Showcase. ☎ **407/WDW-DINE** (939-3463). Priority seating. Lunch buffet $10.95 for adults, $5.50 for children 3–11; dinner buffet $15.75 and $6.99. AE, MC, V. Daily noon–3pm and 4pm–park closing. GERMAN.

Lit by street lamps, the Biergarten simulates a Bavarian village courtyard at Oktoberfest with autumnal trees, a working waterwheel, and geranium-filled flower boxes adorning the surrounding Tudor-style houses. The food here is acceptable, but it's the festive atmosphere that delights most diners. Entertainment might be an

Fun Fact

Plenty of shiny coins are dropped into Disney fountains as visitors pick a scenic location and make a wish. To literally squeeze every dime out of its operations, Disney has devised an elaborate mechanized system to retrieve that change from the fountains and put it into the tills of its restaurants and stores—dried, sorted, and rolled—sometimes before the end of the day.

oompah band, or a strolling accordionist, and guests are encouraged to dance or sing along. All-you-can-eat buffet meals featuring traditional Bavarian fare (sauerbraten, spaetzle with gravy, sauerkraut with salads) are offered at lunch and dinner. Beverages and desserts are extra. Wash it all down with a stein of Beck's, or a glass of Kirschwasser.

Coral Reef. Living Seas Pavilion, Future World. ☎ **407/WDW-DINE** (939-3463). Priority seating. Main courses $13–$21 at lunch; $13–$25 at dinner—more for lobster or a clambake combination. AE, MC, V. Daily 11:30am–2:45pm and 4pm–park closing. SEAFOOD.

Dine under the sea at the enchanting Coral Reef, where tables ring a 5.6-million-gallon aquarium inhabited by more than 4,000 denizens of the deep. Debussy's "La Mer" and Handel's "Water Music" play softly in the background to further enhance the subdued aquatic tone. This is the most notable restaurant—and the busiest—in Epcot's Future World, and a favorite of Disney cast members. Tiered seating—much of it in semicircular booths—ensures everyone a good view, and diners are given "fish-identifier" sheets with labeled pictures, so they can put names to the species swimming by. The menu features (what else?) seafood—creamy lobster bisque, sautéed mahimahi in lemon-caper butter, and shrimp satay served atop red-pepper pasta. There are also some steak and chicken dishes, but you're better off sticking to fish. For dessert, choose frangelico-laced white-chocolate mousse cake served on crème anglaise, and crowned with dark chocolate Mickey ears. Coral Reef features premium wines by the glass and matches nightly entrees with selected labels.

Le Cellier Steakhouse. Canadian Pavilion, World Showcase. ☎ **407/WDW-DINE** (939-3463). Priority seating. Main courses $8.50–$14.50 at lunch; $11.50–$19.25 at dinner. AE, MC, V. Daily noon–park closing. CANADIAN.

This a la carte family steak house, the only one in Epcot, is a good choice for families. Located in the Victorian Hotel du Canada, Le Cellier, with its French Gothic facade and steeply pitched copper roofs, has a castlelike ambiance. The dining room resembles a wine cellar, and you'll sit in tapestry-upholstered chairs under vaulted stone arches, with amber light emanating from black, wrought-iron sconces. All of the red-meat dishes here are good, from the steaks to the burgers. Regional dishes include cheddar-cheese soup, carved pemeal bacon (a pork loin with a light cornmeal crust), a French-Canadian pork-and-potato-filled pie called *tourtière*, chicken and meatball stew, and maple-syrup pie. Wash down your meal with a vintage Canadian wine, or choose from a selection of Canadian beers.

✪ Marrakesh. Morocco Pavilion, World Showcase. ☎ **407/WDW-DINE** (939-3463). Priority seating. Main courses $9.95–$14.95 at lunch; $14.95–$24.95 at dinner. AE, MC, V. Daily noon–park closing. MOROCCAN.

For a romantic dining experience with a truly authentic flavor, head for Marrakesh. The palatial restaurant—with its hand-set mosaic tile work, latticed teak shutters, and a ceiling painted with elaborate Moorish motifs—represents 12 centuries of Arabic design. Exquisitely carved faux-ivory archways frame the central dining area, where belly dancers perform to Middle-Eastern music. Of all Epcot restaurants, this exotic venue best typifies the international spirit of the park. The excellent Moroccan *diffa* (traditional feast) that lets you sample a variety of tasty dishes is recommended. At dinner it includes a hearty saffron-seasoned *harira* soup flavored with onions, tomatoes, lentils, and lamb; beef *brewats* (minced beef seasoned with coriander, ginger, cinnamon, and saffron, rolled in thin pastry layers, and fried); roast lamb served with almond- and raisin-studded rice; braised *tagine* of chicken with green olives and preserved lemon; couscous with seasonal vegetables;

Moroccan pastries; and mint tea. Combination appetizer plates are another way to experience the culinary diversity. French and Moroccan wines are available to complement your meal.

✪ **Nine Dragons.** China Pavilion, World Showcase. ☎ **407/WDW-DINE** (939-3463). Priority seating. Main courses $8.50–$18.50 at lunch (most are under $15); $10.50–$23.75 at dinner. AE, MC, V. Daily 11:30am–park closing. CHINESE.

One of the most attractive World Showcase restaurants, Nine Dragons, with windows overlooking the lagoon, has intricately carved rosewood paneling and furnishings, and a beautiful dragon-motif ceiling. Start your meal off with a selection of dim sum, such as honey-glazed spareribs, delicious shrimp toast, pan-fried dumplings (pot stickers) stuffed with pork and vegetables, and ginger-nuanced steamed dumplings stuffed with pork, shrimp, and water chestnuts. Main dishes highlight the cuisine of four regions of China—**Mandarin, Shanghai, Cantonese, and Szechuan.** The regional specialties are Great Wall duck shredded with green and red peppers and served with pancakes; a saucy stir-fried boneless chicken with onions, carrots, and green peas; tender sliced sirloin and broccoli stir-fried in oyster sauce; and deep-fried shrimp ambrosia in a Mao Tai liqueur-spiked fruit sauce respectively. You can order Chinese or California wines with your meal, but the fresh melon juice is wonderful, either alone, or mixed with rum or vodka. For dessert, there's red-bean ice cream with fried banana, or Chinese pastries.

Rose & Crown Pub & Dining Room. United Kingdom Pavilion, World Showcase. ☎ **407/WDW-DINE** (939-3463). Priority seating for the Dining Room; reservations not accepted for the pub. Main courses $9–$15 at lunch; $10–$30 at dinner. Traditional afternoon tea is served daily at 3:30pm for $9.95. AE, MC, V. Daily 11am until 1 hr before park closes. BRITISH.

You'll dine in merry old England at The Rose & Crown, a restaurant/pub with dark oak wainscoting, beamed Tudor ceilings, English folk music, and saucy servers. If you opt for a late dinner seating, ask to be seated at one of the outdoor tables overlooking the lagoon—you'll have a fantastic view of IllumiNations. Dine on traditional English fare here, including fish and chips (which comes wrapped in newspaper, just like it is in London), and prime rib with Yorkshire pudding. For dessert, try the sherry trifle. Another option is bar fare (sausage rolls, Cornish pasties, a Stilton cheese and fruit plate), all under $10. Wash your food down with a pint of Irish lager, Bass ale, or Guinness stout. Priority seating isn't necessary to stop in at the bar section of the Rose & Crown, a popular drinking spot.

San Angel Inn. Mexico Pavilion, World Showcase. ☎ **407/WDW-DINE** (939-3463). Priority seating. Main courses $8.95–$14.95 at lunch; $12.50–$23.25 at dinner. AE, MC, V. Daily 11am–park closing. MEXICAN.

It's always nighttime at the San Angel Inn, and you'll dine at one of several romantic candlelit tables located in a hacienda courtyard surrounded by dense jungle foliage. The shadow of a crumbling Yucatán pyramid looms in the distance, and you'll hear the sound of faraway birds. The ambiance of this restaurant, located inside the Mexico Pavilion, is exotic, and the fare here is authentic and prepared from scratch. Order an appetizer of *queso fundido* (melted cheese with Mexican pork sausage, served with homemade corn or flour tortillas). Entree specialties include *mole poblano* (chicken simmered with more than 20 spices and a hint of chocolate) and *filete ranchero* (grilled tenderloin of beef served over corn tortillas with sauce ranchero, poblano pepper strips, Monterey Jack cheese, onions, and refried beans). Combination platters are available at both meals. There's chocolate Kahlúa mousse pie for dessert, and your drinking options include Dos Equis beer and margaritas. A special vegetarian menu is also available.

⑪ Family-Friendly Restaurants

Keep in mind that almost all Walt Disney World restaurants offer inexpensive kids' meals (usually $4), as do most restaurants in this very child-oriented town. Themes that appeal to youngsters and placemats with puzzles and pictures to color are also the norm. Of course, all the character meals described in this chapter will delight the kids. Some other notables:

Sci-Fi Dine-In Theater Restaurant *(see p. 111)*   A drive-in movie theater at Disney–MGM Studios where you dine in actual convertible cars, eyes glued to a movie screen.

50's Prime Time Cafe *(see p. 110)*   Also at Disney–MGM Studios, this restaurant re-creates the world of 1950s sitcoms. TV sets that air old shows are visible from every table, and "Mom" urges you to clean your plate. The era's homey food, such as meat loaf and mashed potatoes, is served.

Mickey's Tropical Luau *(see p. 130)*   Not just a meal, but a Polynesian floor show featuring Minnie, Mickey, Pluto, and Goofy along with a cast of South Sea islanders at Disney's Polynesian Resort in Luau Cove. Character breakfasts take place here, too.

Cape May Café Clambake Buffet *(see p. 115)*   This old-fashioned nightly clambake at Disney's Beach Club Resort is fun for the whole family.

'Ohana *(see p. 114)*   Centering on an 18-foot fire-pit grill, 'Ohana, at Disney's Polynesian Resort, is a sumptuous island feast enhanced by storytellers, hula-hoop contests, and lots of audience participation.

Hoop-Dee-Doo Musical Revue *(see p. 245)*   I've never met anyone who didn't have a great time at this whoopin' and hollerin' country-music dinner show in Fort Wilderness's Pioneer Hall. A less expensive variation on the same theme is the **Diamond Horseshoe Saloon Revue** in the Magic Kingdom's Frontierland.

Rainforest Cafe *(see p. 117)*   Monkeys screech in the background, waterfalls drop near your table, you sit atop zebra or rhinoceros legs. Perfect for kids.

Planet Hollywood *(see p. 116)*   Kids love all the action and excitement—a fiber-optic ceiling, video walls, hundreds of movie costumes and props on display, and the elusive possibility that they'll actually see someone famous. Long waits in line to get in, however.

INEXPENSIVE

Cantina de San Angel. Mexico Pavilion, World Showcase. ☎ **407/827-8570.** Reservations not accepted. Entrees start at $6.50. Children's meal under $5. AE, MC, V. Daily 11am until 1 hr. before park closes. MEXICAN.

Cantina de San Angel, a cafeteria with outdoor seating at umbrella tables overlooking the lagoon, offers affordable tacos, burritos, and combination plates, along with frozen margaritas.

Kringla Bakeri og Kafe. Norway Pavilion, World Showcase. ☎ **407/560-5179.** Reservations not accepted. Most entree prices around $6.50. AE, MC, V. Daily 11am until 1 hr. before park closes. NORWEGIAN.

An informal cafe in the Norway pavilion, Kringla Bakeri og Kafe offers covered outdoor seating and inexpensive light fare. The menu includes open-faced sandwiches (such as smoked salmon stuffed with hard-boiled egg), cheese and fruit platters, waffles sprinkled with powdered sugar, and fresh-baked Norwegian pastries.

Lotus Blossom Café. China Pavilion, World Showcase. ☎ **407/827-5678.** Reservations not accepted. Most entrees around $6; children's meal under $5. AE, MC, V. Daily 11am until 1 hr before park closes. CHINESE.

Try the open-air Lotus Blossom Café, a pleasant (and inexpensive) self-service outlet for light fare—egg rolls, pork fried rice, and entrees such as stir-fried chicken and vegetables served over noodles. Cooking demonstrations take place near the entrance several times a day.

Sommerfest. Germany Pavilion, World Showcase. ☎ **407/WDW-DINE** (939-3463). Reservations not accepted. All items under $7. AE, MC, V. Hours vary with park hours. GERMAN.

At Sommerfest—a cafeteria with indoor seating backed by a mural of German castles and countryside, and courtyard tables overlooking a fountain—you can purchase bratwurst sandwiches with sauerkraut, goulash soup, and apple strudel.

Sunshine Season Food Fair. Land Pavilion, Future World. ☎ **407/WDW-DINE** (939-3463). Reservations not accepted. Prices start at $6.95. AE, MC, V. Hours vary with park hours. FOOD COURT.

Located on the lower level of the Land Pavilion, the Sunshine Season Food Fair is a good choice for family dining. Vendors offer an array of low-priced items—barbecued chicken and ribs, homemade soups and fresh salads, immense cinnamon rolls, fresh fruit, pastas, stuffed baked potatoes, sandwiches, oven-fresh cakes and pastries, ice cream, and more. Colorful umbrella tables under a skylit tent-top ring a splashing fountain, and hot-air balloons add to the festive decor. It can get very crowded, however, during prime meal times.

Yakitori House. Japan Pavilion, World Showcase. ☎ **407/WDW-DINE** (939-3463). Reservations not accepted. All items under $8; children's meal under $5. AE, MC, V. Hours vary with park hours. JAPANESE.

Housed in a replica of the 16th-century Katsura Imperial Villa in Kyoto is Yakitori House, a bamboo-roofed cafeteria serving shrimp tempura over noodles, chicken yakitori, and other Japanese snack fare. Umbrella tables on a terrace overlooking a rock waterfall are a plus.

IN THE MAGIC KINGDOM

In addition to the five places mentioned below, there are plenty of fast-food outlets located throughout the park. You may find, however, that a quiet sit-down meal is an essential respite from theme-park hullabaloo. These restaurants are located on the "Walt Disney World & Lake Buena Vista Dining" map in this section and (more specifically) "The Magic Kingdom" in chapter 7.

EXPENSIVE

Cinderella's Royal Table. Cinderella's Castle, Fantasyland. ☎ **407/WDW-DINE** (939-3463). Priority seating. Main courses $11–$16 per person at lunch; $19–$26 at dinner. AE, MC, V. Daily 11:30am–3pm and 4pm–park closing. AMERICAN.

Cinderella's Royal Table has a Gothic interior with leaded-glass windows and heraldic banners suspended from a vaulted ceiling. The only anachronistic note: Background music is from Disney movies. The menu features hearty cuts of beef such as prime rib and grilled sirloin served with fresh sautéed vegetables and soup. Less caloric entrees include grilled swordfish, and a vegetarian plate. There's berry and apple cobbler topped with vanilla ice cream for dessert. Although it's the fanciest of the Magic Kingdom's restaurants, its location inside Cinderella's Castle,

Dining Tip

Disney offers a meal plan called "Dining Disney Style" to those who book Disney vacation packages. If you plan on eating all of your meals on Disney property—and you have a big appetite—it may work for you. Call ☎ **407/934-7639** for details.

and Cinderella's frequent appearances in the entrance hall, make the restaurant very popular with families. *Note:* Cinderella's Royal Table also hosts a daily character breakfast; see details later in this chapter.

Tony's Town Square Restaurant. Main St. ☎ **407/WDW-DINE** (939-3463). Priority seating. Breakfast items under $10; main courses $10–$20 at lunch, $20–$30 at dinner. AE, MC, V. Daily 8:30–10:45am, noon–3pm, and 3:45pm–park closing. ITALIAN.

Inspired by *Lady and the Tramp,* Tony's Town Square Restaurant is Victorian plush, with rich cherrywood beams and paneling, a central fountain, cut-glass mirrors, and globe lighting fixtures. The original movie cels on the walls may inspire some couples to re-enact the film's famous spaghetti smooch. There's additional seating in a sunny, plant-filled solarium. Tony's opens early for breakfast, and you can eat here while waiting for the other lands to open. Breakfast menu items range from Lady and the Tramp–shaped waffles to French toast tossed in cinnamon sugar and served with warm maple or fruit syrup. The rest of the day, the fare is Italian, featuring appetizers such as a five-cheese vegetable pizza and fried calamari with marinara sauce. The lunch menu lists a variety of pastas, calzones, subs, and salads. For dinner, try the 12-ounce strip steak/sautéed lobster combination, served with linguine in garlic cream sauce.

MODERATE

Crystal Palace. Main St., USA. ☎ **407/WDW-DINE** (939-3463). Priority seating. Breakfast buffet $13.95 adults, $7.95 children 3–11; lunch $14.95 adults, $7.95 children 3–11; dinner $19.95 adults, $9.95 children 3–11. AE, MC, V. Daily 8–10:30am, 11:30am–3:15pm, and 4pm–park closing. AMERICAN.

This all-buffet restaurant offers a changing menu of such home-cooked standards as fried chicken, macaroni and cheese, and a variety of vegetables and desserts. The food is filling, if not exactly overwhelming. The real treats here are the characters, Winnie the Pooh and pals, who are on location throughout the day. The characters are kid-magnets, and this family restaurant is not exactly the place for a romantic getaway. Also, because of the popularity of the characters, priority seating is essential.

Liberty Tree Tavern. Liberty Sq. ☎ **407/WDW-DINE** (939-3463). Priority seating. Main courses $10–$17 at lunch; dinners here are all-you-can-eat character meals (discussed in section 6 of this chapter). AE, MC, V. Daily 11:30am–3pm and 4pm–park closing. AMERICAN.

The Liberty Tree Tavern replicates an 18th-century pub, with pegged oak-plank floors, displays of pewterware in oak hutches, and a vast brick fireplace hung with copper pots in its entranceway. Background music is appropriate to the period, and even the windows have panes of hand-pressed glass, a detail typical of Disney thoroughness. Start your meal with a bowl of creamy New England clam chowder, or Boston crab cakes. Entrees range from New England pot roast braised in burgundy and served with mashed potatoes and vegetables, to a traditional roast turkey dinner with all the trimmings. There are a few heart-healthy options on the menu. There's apple crisp topped with vanilla ice cream for dessert. The food here is better than at Cinderella's Royal Table, and this restaurant is also more likely to be able to seat large parties.

Walt Disney World & Lake Buena Vista Dining

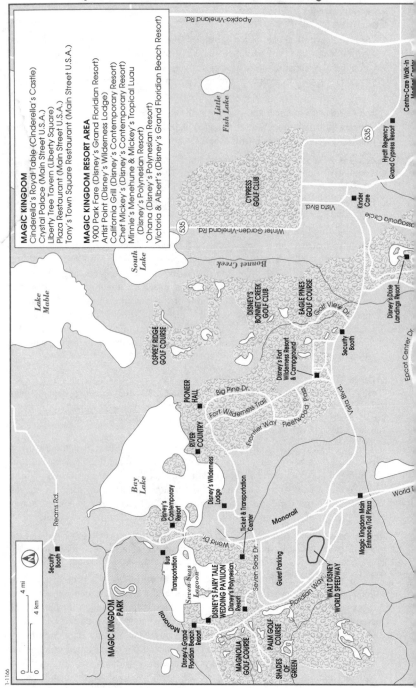

MAGIC KINGDOM
Cinderella's Royal Table (Cinderella's Castle)
Crystal Palace (Main Street U.S.A.)
Liberty Tree Tavern (Liberty Square)
Plaza Restaurant (Main Street U.S.A.)
Tony's Town Square Restaurant (Main Street U.S.A.)

MAGIC KINGDOM RESORT AREA
1900 Park Fare (Disney's Grand Floridian Resort)
Artist Point (Disney's Wilderness Lodge)
California Grill (Disney's Contemporary Resort)
Chef Mickey's (Disney's Contemporary Resort)
Minnie's Menehune & Mickey's Tropical Luau
  (Disney's Polynesian Resort)
'Ohana (Disney's Polynesian Resort)
Victoria & Albert's (Disney's Grand Floridian Beach Resort)

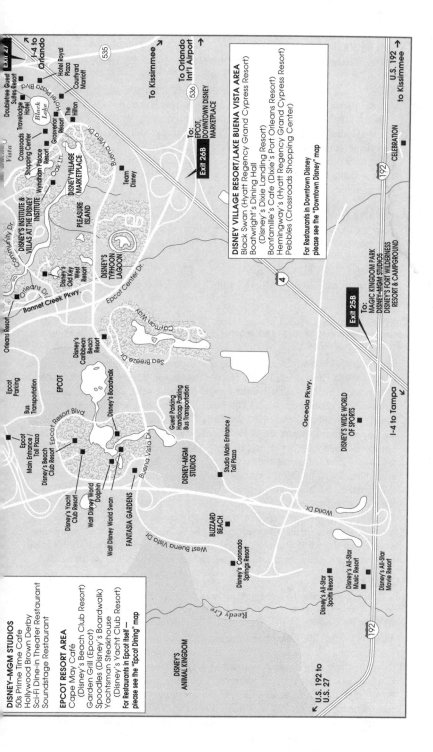

DISNEY-MGM STUDIOS
50s Prime Time Cafe
Hollywood Brown Derby
Sci-Fi Dine-in Theater Restaurant
Soundstage Restaurant

EPCOT RESORT AREA
Cape May Café
  (Disney's Beach Club Resort)
Garden Grill (Epcot)
Spoodles (Disney's Boardwalk)
Yachtsman Steakhouse
  (Disney's Yacht Club Resort)
For Restaurants in Epcot itself —
please see the "Epcot Dining" map

DISNEY VILLAGE RESORT/LAKE BUENA VISTA AREA
Black Swan (Hyatt Regency Grand Cypress Resort)
Boatwright's Dining Hall
  (Disney's Dixie Landing Resort)
Bonfamille's Cafe (Dixie's Port Orleans Resort)
Hemingway's (Hyatt Regency Grand Cypress Resort)
Pebbles (Crossroads Shopping Center)

For Restaurants in Downtown Disney
please see the "Downtown Disney" map

109

INEXPENSIVE

The Plaza Restaurant. Main St. ☎ **407/WDW-DINE** (939-3463). Priority seating. Sandwiches, burgers, and salads $7.75–$10.75. AE, MC, V. Daily 11am–park closing. AMERICAN.

If you scream for ice cream, head for the pretty Plaza Restaurant, located in a Victorian-style building near the end of Main Street. The art nouveau dining room is a beautiful place to eat, or you can dine outside on a verandah with a view of Cinderella's Castle. Waitresses dressed in Victorian costume serve burgers, salads, and sandwiches (tuna and Swiss on whole wheat, a Reuben, hot roast-beef double-deckers) that you can wash down with a vanilla, chocolate, or strawberry shake. Or skip the shake and leave room for a hot-fudge sundae—the World's best. There's waiter service.

AT DISNEY–MGM STUDIOS

There are more than a dozen places to eat in this Hollywood theme park, and they have movie-lot monikers such as the Studio Commissary and Starring Rolls Bakery. The three listed below are the best of the bunch. These restaurants are located on two maps, "Walt Disney World & Lake Buena Vista Dining" (in this chapter) and, more specifically, "Disney–MGM Studios Theme Parks" (in chapter 7).

EXPENSIVE

Hollywood Brown Derby. Hollywood Blvd. ☎ **407/WDW-DINE** (939-3463). Priority seating. Main courses $9.95–$17.50 at lunch; $17.50–$25 at dinner. AE, MC, V. Hours vary with park hours. AMERICAN.

The Hollywood Brown Derby, modeled after the famed Los Angeles celebrity haunt where Louella Parsons and Hedda Hopper held court, has interior palm trees and roomy, semicircular leather booths lighted by derby-shaded sconces. Mahogany wainscoted walls are hung with 1,600 caricatures of major stars who patronized the California restaurant—everyone from Bette Davis to Sammy Davis. Brown Derby legends abound: It was at the Brown Derby that Clark Gable proposed to Carole Lombard; Wallace Beery poured ketchup over his sponge cake; and Lucille Ball and Jack Haley chucked dinner rolls at each other across the tables! A pianist entertains while you dine. The Derby's signature dish is the Cobb salad, invented by owner Bob Cobb in the 1930s. Dinner entrees come with a choice of soup or salad (select the champagne-nuanced oyster brie, available a la carte at lunch). Go on to an entree of baked grouper meunière, served atop pasta in a light, lemony white-wine cream sauce. Grapefruit cake with cream-cheese frosting is the Derby's signature dessert, but the white-chocolate cheesecake may be a better choice. There's a full bar, a good selection of California wines, and after-dinner drinks are a specialty.

MODERATE

50's Prime Time Cafe. Near the Indiana Jones Stunt Spectacular. ☎ **407/WDW-DINE** (939-3463). Priority seating. Main courses $10–$18 at lunch; $13–$22 at dinner. AE, MC, V. Daily 11am–park closing. AMERICAN.

The 50's Prime Time Cafe places diners in a 1950s time warp/sitcom psychodrama. Eating areas look like homey 1950s kitchens, wherein black-and-white TV sets show clips from classics like *My Little Margie* and *Topper*. The wait staff greets diners like family ("Hi Sis, I'll go tell Mom you're home."), and may threaten to withhold dessert if you don't eat your veggies, or tell on you for resting your elbows on the table. The food—meat loaf with mashed potatoes, Granny's pot roast, Dad's chili, and such—isn't all that great, but the place is so much fun, you'll love it anyway. Desserts include banana splits and S'mores. The adjacent Tune-In Lounge serves inexpensive light fare.

Sci-Fi Dine-In Theater Restaurant. Across from the Monster Sound Show. ☎ **407/WDW-DINE** (939-3463). Priority seating. Main courses $8–$13.50 at lunch; $10–$25 at dinner. AE, MC, V. Daily 10:30am–park closing. AMERICAN.

The Sci-Fi Dine-In Theater Restaurant replicates a 1950s Los Angeles drive-in movie emporium. Diners are ensconced in flashy, chrome-trimmed convertible cars (complete with fins and whitewalls) under a twinkling, starlit sky with the Hollywood hills as a backdrop. Friendly carhops bring your food order and complimentary popcorn. While you eat, you can watch the movie screen, where a mix of zany newsreels (for example, "News of the Future") is interspersed with cartoons, and "B" horror-movie clips (*Frankenstein Meets the Space Monster*). The food could be better, but the creative theming is ample compensation. Menu items have names like the Towering Terror (barbecued pork ribs with veggies and fries) and Plucked from Deepest Space (a grilled-chicken sandwich with Cajun remoulade sauce and fries). Finish up with the Cheesecake That Ate New York. Though the restaurant basically appeals to kids (whose menu items are all under $4), beverages include wine and beer (there's a full bar), as well as milk shakes. Your bill is presented as a speeding ticket.

INEXPENSIVE

Toy Story Pizza Planet. In the Muppet's Courtyard. ☎ **407/WDW-DINE** (939-3463). No reservations accepted. All main courses under $10. AE, MC, V. Open 10:30am–park closing. PIZZA.

This restaurant offers what the name implies, along with salads, espresso, and cappuccino. The food is not exactly gourmet, but meals are reasonably priced. This is part arcade/part restaurant, and kids of all ages will love the many games and diversions. This boisterous, family pizzeria, however, is not a quiet place to get away.

IN THE ANIMAL KINGDOM

The Rainforest Cafe here, just like the one in Downtown Disney Marketplace, is a big draw for sit-down dining. Other options include **Tuskers House** in Africa, which serves rotisserie, grilled, and fried chicken and salads. The **Restaurantorsaurus**—yup, you guessed it, this one is in DinoLand U.S.A.—serves hamburgers, hot dogs, and authentic McDonald's French fries and Chicken McNuggets.

IN THE WALT DISNEY WORLD RESORTS

These restaurants are located on the map "Walt Disney World & Lake Buena Vista Dining" in this chapter.

VERY EXPENSIVE

✪ **Victoria & Albert's.** In Disney's Grand Floridian Beach Resort, 4401 Floridian Way. ☎ **407/WDW-DINE** (939-3463). Reservations required. Jackets required for men. Not recommended for children. Fixed-price meal $80 per person, $30 additional for Royal Wine Pairing; $115–$160 Chef's Table. AE, MC, V. 2 dinner seatings daily, 5:45–6:30pm and 9–9:45pm. Free self- and validated valet parking. INTERNATIONAL.

It's not often that I'd describe a dining experience as flawless, but Victoria & Albert's, the World's most elite restaurant (Walt Disney World's, that is), managed to win that adjective from me. Its intimate dining room is plush; diners sink into leather-upholstered Louis XIII–style chairs at exquisitely appointed tables lit by silver-shaded Victorian lamps. A maid and butler (always named Victoria and Albert) provide deft and gracious service, and a harpist plays softly while you dine.

Dinner, a seven-course affair, is described in a personalized menu sealed with a gold wax insignia. The fare changes nightly. You might begin with an hors d'oeuvre of Florida lobster tail with aïoli. A more formal appetizer is the vermouth-poached

The Chef's Table: The Best Seat in the World

There's a special dining option at **Victoria & Albert's.** Reserve the Chef's Table here, and dine in a charming alcove hung with copper pots and dried flower wreaths at an elegantly appointed candlelit table . . . right in the heart of the kitchen! You'll sip champagne with chef Scott Hunnell while discussing your food preferences for the seven- to nine-course menu he'll be creating especially for you. There's a cooking seminar element to this experience: Diners get to tour the kitchen and observe the artistry of highly skilled chefs at work. The Chef's Table can accommodate up to six people a night. It's a leisurely affair, lasting 3 or 4 hours. The price is $115 without wine, $160 per person including five wines (I strongly recommend the latter). Let me further whet your appetite: There's a surprise during dinner, but I can't tell you what it is or it won't be one. The Chef's Table is immensely popular. Reserve months in advance by calling **407/WDW-DINE** (939-3463) or 407/824-1089.

jumbo sea scallops served in a crisp rice-noodle basket on shallot-chive sauce with garnishes of caviar and Chinese tat soi leaves. A shot of peppered vodka adds piquancy to a velvety plum-tomato bisque sprinkled with smoked bacon and lightly topped with a pesto cream sauce. For an entree, you could select a fan of pink, juicy sautéed Peking duck breast slices with wild rice and crabapple chutney. A salad of exotic greens in an orange sherry vinaigrette clears the palate for the next course— English Stilton served with pine-nut bread, port wine, and a pear poached in burgundy, cognac, and cinnamon sugar. The conclusion: I would suggest a sumptuous hazelnut-and-Frangelico soufflé, followed by coffee and chocolate truffles. There is, of course, an extensive recherché wine list. I suggest you opt for the Royal Wine Pairing, which provides an appropriate wine with each course and lets you sample a variety of selections from the restaurant's distinguished cellars.

EXPENSIVE

✪ **California Grill.** At Disney's Contemporary Resort, 4600 N. World Dr. ☎ **407/WDW-DINE** (939-3463) or 407/824-1576. Reservations recommended. Main courses $14.75–$27.50. AE, MC, V. Daily 5:30–10pm. Lounge daily noon–midnight. CALIFORNIA.

You may glimpse Disney CEO Michael Eisner dining here with fellow corporate honchos; it's one of his favorite WDW dining rooms. High above the Magic Kingdom (on the Contemporary Resort's 15th floor), this stunning California-style restaurant offers scenic views of the park and lagoon below. A Wolfgang Puckish interior incorporates art deco elements (a cove ceiling, curved pear-wood walls, vivid splashes of color, polished black granite surfaces), but the central focus is a dramatic exhibition kitchen with a hearthlike wood-burning oven and rotisserie. Gorgeous flower arrangements and cornucopialike displays of fruits and vegetables are further embellishments.

Chef Clifford Pleau's menus change seasonally. A sushi sampler makes a good beginning here, as does ravioli filled with goat cheese, shiitake mushrooms, and sun-dried tomatoes. And whole-wheat-crust pizzas may comprise a light entree. Heartier choices include braised lamb shank (with wild chanterelle risotto and orange-nuanced bread topping) or grilled pork tenderloin served atop polenta with crimini mushrooms and a garnish of crispy fried sage. For dessert, it's hard to surpass the butterscotch crème brûlée with almond biscotti. If you like a close-up view of chefs at work, ask to sit at the kitchen counter. There's a good selection of

California wines to complement your meal. Light fare (sushi, quesadillas, spring rolls) is available at the plush adjoining bar lounge.

Spoodles. On the Disney Boardwalk, Lake Buena Vista. ☎ **407/939-3463.** Priority seating. Main courses $10–$22. AE, MC. V. Daily 7–11am, noon–2pm, and 5–10pm. TAPAS/MEDITER-RANEAN.

Follow the trail of soft, pale-colored buildings along Disney's Boardwalk to Spoodles, one of Disney's newer, and most acclaimed, restaurants. The food at Spoodles, however, is not for those with a pastel palette. It serves true Mediterranean cuisine, and was recognized in 1997 as one of the nation's top 20 restaurants by *Wine Trader* magazine.

Chef David Reynoso has added spice to traditional Spanish tapas. The barbecued Moroccan beef skewers with raisins, toasted almonds, and couscous are drenched in a hot, tangy sauce. The artichoke ravioli with garlic, cherry tomatoes, and arugula is a vegetarian delight. Those with heartier appetites—or those not inclined to share—can try the "Tapas Grande," such as potato-crusted salmon simmered with wild mushrooms in a veal broth with truffle oil. Disney has gone to great lengths to provide an impressive wine menu, so be sure to indulge. Tableside sangria presentations, where the fruit-laced libation is sliced and spiked before your eyes, will add something special to the evening. There is a kid's menu featuring a "you make it, we bake it" pizza combination. During the height of the summer tourist season, Spoodles can get crowded, and the wait can be long, even with priority seating, so this may not be the best option for famished families coming straight from the parks. It is, however, a nice, relaxed option for adults.

✪ **Yachtsman Steakhouse.** In Disney's Yacht Club Resort, 1700 Epcot Resorts Blvd. ☎ **407/WDW-DINE** (939-3463). Main courses $20–$29. AE, MC, V. Daily 5:30–10pm. Free self- and valet parking. SEAFOOD/STEAK/CHOPS.

The Yacht Club, a magnificent resort inspired by New England's grand turn-of-the-century summer mansions, houses a fittingly elegant signature restaurant. Lacquered knotty-pine beams, paneling, and plank flooring create a warm, woody feel that is enhanced by burgundy leather-upholstered oak chairs. USDA grain-fed beef—hand-selected to ensure top marbling for natural juices and tenderness—is aged, cured, cut, and ground on the premises. You can see these prime cuts on display in a glass-enclosed beef-aging room, and an exhibition kitchen provides a tantalizing glimpse of sizzling steaks, chops, and seafood being grilled over oak and hickory.

You might begin your meal with an appetizer of garlicky escargots marinated in dry vermouth and served en croûte with rich burgundy sauce. Beef entrees—such as succulent filet mignon, prime rib of beef au jus, or an 18-ounce Kansas City strip steak served on the bone (it's a cattle-drive tradition)—are served with baked potato, a board of fresh-baked bread, and a choice of béarnaise or bordelaise sauce. Side dishes, such as a skillet of fresh mushrooms sautéed in cognac and creamed spinach, are noteworthy. Other dishes run the gamut from lamb chops with apple mint butter and rosemary gin sauce to crisp-grilled chicken in apricot brandy sauce. And for the truly intrepid, there's a brownie fudge sundae for dessert. An extensive wine list is available, and a children's menu offers full meals for $5 to $10.

MODERATE

✪ **Artist Point.** In Disney's Wilderness Lodge, 901 W. Timberline Dr. ☎ **407/WDW-DINE** (939-3463). Main courses $17–$26. AE, MC, V. Daily 5:30–10pm. Free self- and valet parking. SEAFOOD/STEAK/GAME SPECIALTIES.

This stunning resort restaurant centers on western-theme murals inspired by Rocky Mountain School artists Albert Bierstadt and Thomas Moran (the theme does deviate a bit however—look for the hidden Mickeys). The illusion that you're dining in a rustic turn-of-the-century national park lodge is enhanced by the large windows overlooking a lake and waterfall. Weather permitting, there's also terrace seating.

The menu changes seasonally. On a recent visit, I enjoyed a Northwest salmon sampler appetizer (smoked pepperlachs, cured gravlax, and pan-seared salmon served with onion/pepper/caper relish). Entrees ranged from a 16-ounce grilled porterhouse steak (served with red-skin potatoes, fire-roasted onions, garlic, and mushrooms) to grilled, maple-glazed king salmon (served with roasted vegetables, roasted apples, and couscous studded with morsels of sun-dried cherries, pignoli nuts, and smoked onion). Game specials and Pacific Northwestern wines are featured. Desserts—such as chocolate-silk bread pudding topped with vanilla ice cream and chocolate sauce—are immense (consider sharing) and delicious.

'Ohana. At Disney's Polynesian Resort, 1600 Seven Seas Dr. ☎ **407/WDW-DINE** (939-3463). Family-feast $20.95 for adults, $9.95 for children 3–11 (see also "Dining with Disney Characters," later in this chapter). AE, MC, V. Daily 7:30–11am and 5–10pm. Free self- and valet parking. PACIFIC RIM.

You'll be welcomed here with warm island hospitality by a server who addresses you as "cousin." 'Ohana means "family" in Hawaiian, and you will enjoy a convivial meal with the extended clan. The setting is South Seas exotic, with thatched roofing and tapa-cloth tenting overhead, carved Polynesian columns, and an open kitchen centering on a wood-burning, 18-foot fire-pit grill. There's lots going on at all times. The blowing of a conch shell summons a storyteller, coconut races take place down the central aisle, couples get up and dance to island music, and people celebrating birthdays participate in hula hoop contests as everyone sings "Happy Birthday" to them in Hawaiian. Kids especially love all the hoopla, but if you're looking for an intimate venue, this isn't it.

Soon after you're seated, a lazy Susan arrives, laden with steamed dumplings in soy/sesame oil, Napa cabbage slaw with honey mustard, black-bean and corn relish, and several tangy sauces. Courses will succeed each other in rapid succession (ask your waiter to slow the pace if it's too fast). The feast includes salad, fresh-baked herbed focaccia bread, grilled chicken, smoky pork sausage, marinated turkey breast, mesquite-seasoned beef, teriyaki ribs, jumbo shrimp, stir-fried noodles and vegetables, fresh pineapple with caramel sauce, soft drinks, and coffee. Passion-fruit crème brûlée is extra, but worth it. A full bar offers tropical drinks, including non-alcoholic ones for kids, and there is a limited selection of wines.

INEXPENSIVE

Boatwright's Dining Hall. In Disney's Dixie Landings Resort, 1251 Dixie Dr. (off Bonnet Creek Pkwy.). ☎ **407/WDW-DINE** (939-3463). Breakfast items $6.25–$9; sandwiches $7.95; main courses $11–$19. AE, MC, V. Daily 7:30–11:30am and 5–10pm. Free self-parking. NEW ORLEANS.

Boatwright's is designed to look like an 1800s boat-building factory, complete with the wooden hull of a Louisiana fishing boat suspended from its lofty beamed ceiling. An uncommonly pretty factory, it has oak-plank floors and two large working brick fireplaces. Kids will enjoy the wooden toolboxes on every table; each contains a salt shaker that doubles as a level, a wood-clamp sugar dispenser, a pepper-grinder-cum-ruler, a jar of unmatched utensils, shop rags (to be used as napkins), and a little metal pail of crayons.

Cajun breakfasts offer intriguing possibilities. French toast here is made from a sourdough–sweet potato baguette tossed in rich egg custard, deep-fried, and coated with cinnamon sugar. Another option: a pan of sautéed crawfish, mushrooms, green onions, and tomatoes in mustard cream sauce (served with home-style potatoes topped with two eggs, and an oven-fresh buttermilk biscuit). Start with deep-fried bacon-wrapped oysters and scallops, then follow with an entree of rich bouillabaisse redolent of oaken cognac, or a medley of blackened seafood served over brown-buttered pasta in creamy garlic sauce. For dessert, there's homemade fruit cobbler topped with vanilla ice cream and smothered in whipped cream.

Bonfamille's Cafe. In Disney's Port Orleans Resort, 2201 Orleans Dr. (off Bonnet Creek Pkwy.). ☎ **407/WDW-DINE** (939-3463). Breakfast items $4.25–$6.95; salads and po'boy sandwiches $6.95; main courses $8.25–$14.95. AE, MC, V. Daily 7:30–11:30am and 5–10pm. Free self-parking. NEW ORLEANS.

Named for a character in *The Aristocats,* the charming Bonfamille's is patterned after a French Quarter courtyard with fountains. Exposed-brick walls are hung with paintings of New Orleans, big baskets of flowering plants are suspended from beams overhead, and Dixieland jazz plays softly in the background. During breakfast it's light and sunny; in the evening, candle lamps provide soft lighting.

Louisiana-style breakfasts range from fresh, hot beignets and café au lait, to a skillet of crawfish and andouille sausage topped with zesty Creole sauce and melted sharp cheddar. The latter is served with home-style fried potatoes topped with eggs, and a hot buttermilk biscuit. A typical dinner here: an appetizer of chicken wings tossed in spicy Louisiana hot sauce served with celery and blue-cheese dip, followed by grilled Atlantic salmon (served with spicy pecan butter, rice, and sautéed vegetables), and a dessert of Bourbon Street pudding with strawberry and caramel bourbon sauces. After dinner, families can head over to the hotel's Scat Cats Lounge, where entertainment—sing-alongs and live music with lots of audience participation—is featured most nights.

✪ **Cape May Café.** At Disney's Beach Club Resort, 1800 Epcot Resorts Blvd. ☎ **407/WDW-DINE** (939-3463). Priority seating. Character breakfast $14.95 adults, $8.50 children; dinner $19.95 for adults, $9.50 for children 3–11; AE, MC, V. Daily 5:30–9:30pm. Free valet and self-parking. CLAMBAKE BUFFET.

A hearty 19th-century-style New England clambake is featured here nightly. Sand sculptures and furled striped beach umbrellas create the ambiance of an upscale seaside resort. Aromatic New England chowder, steamed clams and mussels, corn on the cob, chicken, and red-skin potatoes are cooked up in a crackling rockweed steamer pit that serves as the restaurant's centerpiece. And these traditional clambake offerings are supplemented by dozens of salads, hot dishes (barbecued pork ribs, smoked sausage, pastas), and a wide array of oven-fresh breads and desserts. There's a full bar.

3 Places to Dine in Lake Buena Vista

In this section are restaurants located in Downtown Disney and in the Lake Buena Vista area.

Located about 2½ miles from Epcot off Buena Vista Drive, Downtown Disney encompasses the Downtown Disney Marketplace, a very pleasant complex of cedar-shingled shops and restaurants overlooking a scenic lagoon; the adjoining Pleasure Island, a nighttime entertainment center; and Downtown Disney's West Side, a slightly more upscale collection of shops, restaurants, and a movie theater.

Note: You don't have to pay the entrance fee to Pleasure Island to dine at any of its restaurants.

AT PLEASURE ISLAND
EXPENSIVE

Fulton's Crab House. Aboard the riverboat docked at Pleasure Island. ☎ **407/934-BOAT** (2628). Priority seating recommended, especially during peak season. Main courses $8.95–$15.95 at lunch; $4.95–$50 at dinner. AE, MC, V. Daily 4pm–midnight. SEAFOOD/STEAKS.

Fulton's operates aboard a replica of a 19th-century Mississippi riverboat that is permanently moored on the shores of Lake Buena Vista. An interior decorated with nautical artifacts reflects the seafood menu. There is a deck for outdoor dining. The casual Stone Crab Lounge (open 11:30am–2am) serves light fare. Start with the Florida Stone Crab claws with mustard sauce and lime, or sample the oyster bar. For your main course, try tuna filet mignon, grilled and served with lemongrass dipping sauce. A hearty eater may want to try the steak and lobster dinner, served with asparagus and a tangy house steak sauce. For a tart taste of Florida, try the Key lime cheesecake for dessert. Fulton's has one of the area's better wine lists. A character breakfast, 8:30am and 10am daily, is $12.95 for adults, $7.95 for children and features Mickey, Minnie, Pluto, and Goofy. A children's menu is available at lunch and dinner.

MODERATE

Planet Hollywood. Pleasure Island; look for the large, globe-shaped restaurant. ☎ **407/827-7827.** Reservations not accepted. Lines can get long during special events and peak season. Main courses $7.50–$18.95 (most under $13). AE, DC, MC, V. Daily 11am–2am. AMERICAN.

Planet Hollywood was born in 1994 with a lavish opening-night party hosted by Arnold, Sly, Bruce, and Demi. The excitement they generated has started to dim, and the once hours-long lines have thinned. A fiber-optic ceiling creates a planetarium effect, and a veritable show-business museum displays more than 300 items ranging from Peter O'Toole's *Lawrence of Arabia* costume to the front end of the bus from *Speed* (it's suspended from the ceiling). Previews of soon-to-be-released movies and video montages from films and TV are aired while you dine.

The big surprise amid all the special effects is that the food is pretty good. You can opt to nosh on appetizers—hickory-smoked buffalo wings, pot stickers, or nachos. There are also large burgers, sandwiches, salads, pizzas, pastas, and platters of grilled steak, ribs, or pork chops. The desserts are definitely worth saving room for.

Portobello Yacht Club. Pleasure Island. ☎ **407/934-8888.** Reservations strongly recommended. Main courses $7.95–$8.95 at lunch; $14.95–$29.95 at dinner; pizzas $6.95–$8.95. AE, MC, V. Daily 11:30am–midnight (dinner served from 4pm). Free self-parking; valet parking $5. REGIONAL ITALIAN.

Occupying a gabled Bermuda-style house, Yacht Club, which recently underwent extensive renovations, is casual, with an interior suggesting a luxury cruise ship. From the lively mahogany-paneled bar, you can watch pizzas being prepared over an oak fire in an exhibition kitchen. Multipaned windows overlook Lake Buena Vista, as do the tables on the awning-covered patios. The pizzas, with thin crisp crusts and toppings such as *quattro formaggi* (mozzarella and provolone) with sundried tomatoes, are a tasty deal for lunch or dinner. For the evening meal, try *Costoletta Di MaiAle,* marinated roasted pork loin with fennel, carrots, and roasted garlic whipped potatoes. You should also try the spaghettini alla portobello with

Alaskan crab and other seafood in a light sauce of olive oil, wine, and herbs. A dessert of *crema bruccioto* (white-chocolate custard with a caramelized sugar glaze) is recommended. There's an extensive wine list.

AT DOWNTOWN DISNEY MARKETPLACE

✪ **Rainforest Cafe.** Downtown Disney Marketplace; look for the smoking volcano. ☎ **407/827-8500.** Reservations accepted on-site; expect long waits. Main courses $5.50–$17.95. AE, DISC, MC, V. Sun–Thurs 10:30am–11pm; Fri–Sat 10:30am–midnight. CALIFORNIA.

Don't arrive starving. Waits of 4 hours aren't unheard of here, so plan to make reservations and then spend some time exploring the rest of Downtown Disney. (The Rainforest Cafe near Animal Kingdom uses priority seating, making the wait time there much shorter.) With its lush, dark interiors, calls of the wild, and unique animal-style bar stools, you feel far removed from the rush of the parks. Kids especially love the junglelike setting. This is, after all, one place where monkey business is encouraged. The food is pretty good, too. Try unusual delicacies like Rasta Pasta, bowtie noodles mixed with spinach, roasted red peppers, broccoli, and Parmesan cheese—the whole dish smothered in a garlic-pesto cream sauce. There is an extensive menu, including a reduced-price menu for children. Top off your meal with coconut bread pudding with dried apricots; the lavish garnish of whipped cream, toasted coconut, and chocolate shavings is almost as good as the dessert itself. There is a good selection of beers and wines. The tables here are very close together, so those with physical disabilities may find it difficult to maneuver.

DISNEY'S WEST SIDE

✪ **Bongo's Cuban Cafe.** Disney's West Side. ☎ **407/828-0999.** No reservations. Priority seating for parties of 7 or more. Main courses $8.95–$24.95. AE, DISC, DC, V, MC. Daily 11am–2am. CUBAN.

Created by Cuban-American songstress Gloria Estefan and husband, Emilio, this cafe is Disney's version of old Havana. The chairs are leopard-spotted, and the mosaic bar stools are shaped like bongo drums. A Desi Arnaz look-alike might even show up to sing a few tunes. The upbeat salsa music makes this a noisy location, so seek out the patio or the upstairs lounge for some privacy and quiet. A Cuban sandwich—thinly toasted bread with ham and cheese—is done right here (kids may like it). Start with the thick, slightly spicy, black bean soup and try a dinner of *arroz con pollo* (chicken with rice). Coffee-lovers should sample the thick, dark Cuban coffee.

✪ **House of Blues.** Disney's West Side, under the old-fashioned water tower. ☎ **407/934-2583.** Reservations not accepted (except for Gospel Brunch). Main courses $13.95–$18.95. AE, DISC, MC, V. Daily 11am–2pm; the club and concert hall is open 7pm–2am. MISSISSIPPI DELTA.

Hearty portions of down-home food served in an atmosphere literally shaking with rock 'n' roll. Exceedingly crowded on days of big concerts, the music in the nightclub next door is as much of a draw as the food. Funky, colorful folk art covers the rustic walls from floor to ceiling. (Take a walk through the small courtyard.) The back patio has seating and a nice view of the bay. Let's not forget the food. The spicy jambalaya and gumbo are good bets. The baby back ribs with garlic mashed potatoes and turnip greens are literally finger-lickin' good. Try the bread pudding for dessert. A children's menu, with staples like grilled cheese and hamburgers, is available. The Sunday Gospel Brunch ($28 for adults and $15 for children 4–12) features foot-stomping music, and an awe-inspiring array of Southern fare such as cheese grits and sausage. Foreign visitors will especially enjoy this cultural immersion. Make reservations early since it regularly sells out.

McDonald's Fun House. Disney's West Side. ☎ **407/WDW-DINE** (939-3463). No reservations. Daily 11am–midnight. Sandwiches and meals $4.95–$9.95. HAMBURGERS.

With over 10,000 square feet, this is one mammoth Mickey D's. This restaurant is equal parts eatery and playground, and has such diversions as Grimace's Game Room, decorated in his signature purple, with wall-mounted toys, tubes, balls, and buzzers. You gotta love the French Fry Organ and the soda cup chandeliers, but bear in mind that this is a very kid-intensive place except for late in the evening.

Wolfgang Puck Café. Disney's West Side. ☎ **407/WDW-DINE** (939-3463). Reservations recommended. Main courses $8.95–$18.95. AE, V, MC. Daily 11am–midnight. CALIFORNIA.

Avant-garde chef Wolfgang Puck brings his West Coast creations to the heart of Florida. You can eat gourmet pizza, with a thin, crisp crust and exotic toppings, either on an outdoor patio or inside. An appetizer of vegetable spring rolls, or a sampling from the sushi bar, should be followed by the fresh grilled chicken or the Chinois chicken salad. The restaurant is busy, and often noisy, so conversation may be difficult.

ELSEWHERE IN LAKE BUENA VISTA
VERY EXPENSIVE

Black Swan. In the Hyatt Regency Grand Cypress Resort, 1 Grand Cypress Blvd. (off Fla 535). ☎ **407/239-1999.** Reservations recommended. Main courses $25–$34. AE, CB, DC, DISC, JCB, MC, V. Daily 6–10pm. Free self-parking. AMERICAN/CONTINENTAL.

Overlooking the magnificent emerald fairways of this posh resort's golf course, the Black Swan has a lodgelike, split-level interior with a big working fireplace and a cross-beamed knotty-pine cathedral ceiling. Large, pine-framed windows overlook the 9th hole, and inside, you'll find lovely floral arrangements and planters of greenery. Golfers make up the majority of the clientele. It's not unusual here to see someone rise up excitedly from a table and demonstrate how he eagled the 17th and birdied the 18th hole to win a match. Barring those mini-dramas, dinner entertainment consists of a pianist at a white baby grand.

A meal here could begin with an appetizer of grilled marinated portobello mushrooms nestled on a bed of wilted arugula, and topped with wild mushrooms and Asiago cheese gratinée. A main dish of roast rack of lamb (thick, juicy slices grilled in an herbed honey-Dijon crust) comes with mashed potatoes and rosemary jus. Another choice, corn-tortilla-crusted breast of chicken, is served with black beans and roasted corn relish and cilantro chili fettuccine. A warm, crisp apple tart on caramel sauce topped with honey-vanilla ice cream and whipped cream will provide a fitting finale. The Black Swan has an extensive wine list with many after-dinner libations (cognacs, ports, and more).

EXPENSIVE

✪ **Hemingway's.** In the Hyatt Regency Grand Cypress Resort, 1 Grand Cypress Blvd. (off Fla. 535). ☎ **407/239-1234.** Reservations recommended. Main courses $7.50–$19.75 at lunch; $20–$28 at dinner. AE, CB, DC, DISC, JCB, MC, V. Tues–Sat 11:30am–2:30pm; daily 6–10:30pm. Free self- and validated valet parking. SEAFOOD.

Fronted by a waterfall that cascades into stone-lined streams, Hemingway's evokes Key West, and honors its most famous denizen; walls are hung with sepia photographs of "Papa" and his fishing and hunting trophies. This casually elegant (and generally child-free) restaurant is a good choice for romantic dinners. In a warren of intimate dining areas set under a high, weathered-pine ceiling, elegantly appointed tables are lit by gleaming brass hurricane lamps. Weather permitting, you can sit on a screened wooden deck near the waterfall.

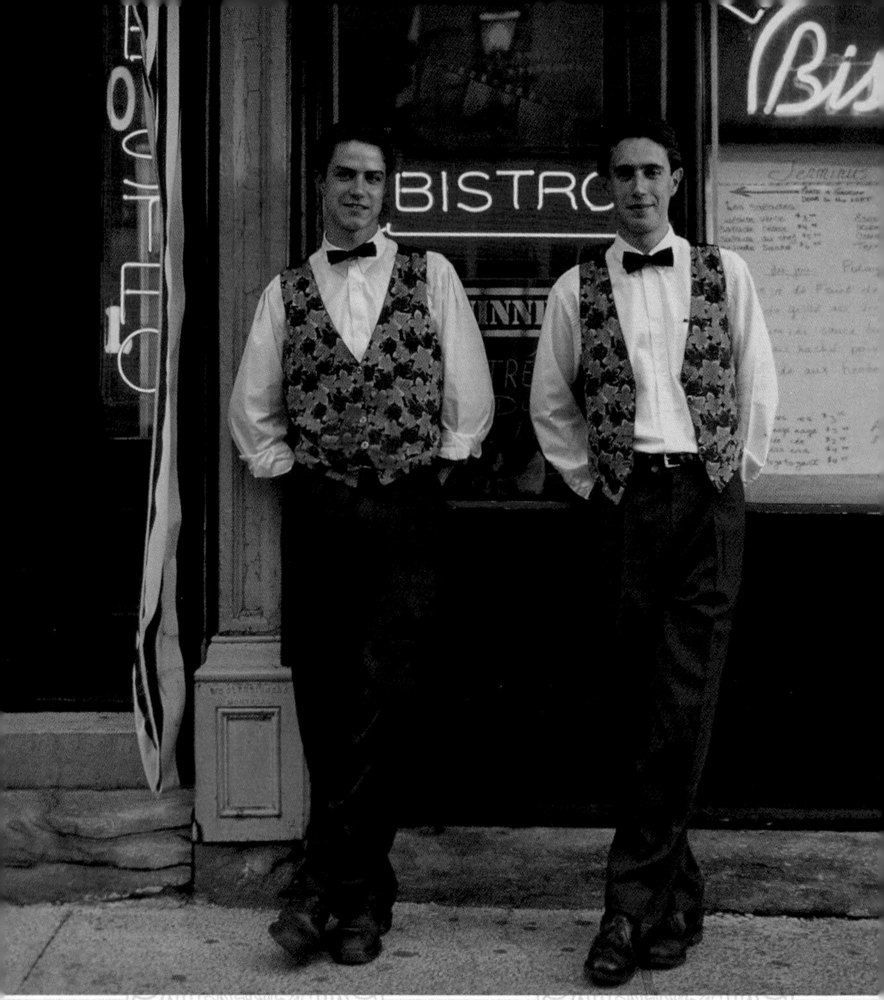

In case you're running low.

We're here to help with more than 190,000 Express Cash locations around the world. In order to enroll, just call American Express at 1 800 CASH-NOW before you start your vacation.

do more

Express Cash

And in case you'd rather be safe than sorry.

We're here with American Express® Travelers Cheques. They're the safe way to carry money on your vacation, because if they're ever lost or stolen you can get a refund, practically anywhere or anytime. To find the nearest place to buy Travelers Cheques, call 1 800 495-1153. Another way we help you do more.

do more   AMERICAN EXPRESS

Travelers Cheques

Ask not for whom the bell tolls, but rather for an appetizer of deep-fried baby squid and grilled eggplant in garlicky herb-seasoned tomato coulis. Follow up with an entree of golden brown beer-battered coconut shrimp; it's served with roasted potatoes, a colorful array of al dente vegetables, and orange marmalade–horseradish sauce. Also recommended are the deliciously light, moist, and fluffy crab cakes; try the Cajun tartar sauce with them. For dessert, Key lime pie appropriately reaches its apogee here. The lunch menu offers similar fare, along with paella, sandwiches, and salads. In the adjoining Hurricane Lounge—a most congenial setting with a beautiful oak bar—specialties include a variety of island rums and the Papa Doble, a potent tropical rum and fruit libation invented by Hemingway himself (legend has it he once drank 16 of them at one sitting!).

The restaurants below can be located on the map, "Orlando Area Accommodations & Dining," later in this chapter.

Mikado Japanese Steak House. In Marriott's Orlando World Center, 8701 World Center Dr. (off Fla. 536). ☎ **407/238-8664.** Reservations recommended. Main courses $12.95–$28.95. AE, CB, DC, DISC, JCB, MC, V. Daily 6–10pm. Free self- and validated valet parking. JAPANESE.

This gorgeous, 230-acre resort houses a beautiful teppanyaki restaurant. Its serene interior, with intimate seating areas created by shoji screens, has windows overlooking rock gardens, reflecting pools, and a palm-fringed pond. Japanese music helps set the tone. Plan to arrive early, and enjoy a cocktail at sunset on the wooden deck overlooking the swimming pool.

Meals here are teppanyaki style—which means you're seated with other patrons at a grill-topped table. For businesspeople dining alone, the socializing that happens naturally here can be a plus. A highly trained chef wheels a cart full of raw food to the table and with dazzling dexterity trims, chops, sautés, and flips it onto your waiting plate. Appetizer selections include softshell crab, smoked salmon, cucumber sushi, and assorted tempura vegetables and shrimp. Entrees—offering various combinations of steak and seafood—come with a complimentary hors d'oeuvre of grilled shrimp or scallops, soup (try the tasty miso), salad, steamed rice (yummy fried rice is available for an additional $2.25), an array of stir-fried vegetables, and green tea. A decanter of warm sake is recommended, and green tea or ginger ice cream makes a refreshing dessert. Low-priced meals are available for children.

✪ Tuscany. In Marriott's Orlando World Center, 8701 World Center Dr. (off Fla. 536). ☎ **407/239-4200.** Reservations recommended. Main courses $15–$27. AE, CB, DC, DISC, JCB, MC, V. Daily 6–10pm. Free self-parking; valet parking available. TUSCAN.

The showplace restaurant of a luxury resort, Tuscany has rich cherry- and mahogany-paneled walls hung with gilt-framed Michelangelo prints. Tables are set with fresh flowers, and diners are comfortably ensconced in roomy tapestry-upholstered armchairs, booths, and Regency chairs. Soft lighting and opera music complete the ambiance.

A pasta appetizer is a good way to begin your meal here—most notably, the gnocchi served with Gorgonzola sauce and a garnish of diced plum tomatoes. Impressive entrees—such as rack of lamb in a light demiglace sauce with roasted eggplant puree, white beans, potato croquette, and *haricots verts*—are aesthetically presented on large white platters. Herbed focaccia bread served with light, garlicky goat cheese accompanies your meal. An extensive European/California wine list includes many by-the-glass selections. Desserts change nightly; but if it's offered, the exquisite, thin-sliced apple tart served atop crème anglaise and garnished with fresh berries is delicious.

MODERATE

Pebbles. 12551 Fla. 535, in the Crossroads Shopping Center, Lake Buena Vista. ☎ **407/827-1111.** Reservations not accepted. Main courses mostly $9.95–$19.95. AE, DC, DISC, MC, V. Sun–Thurs 11am–11pm; Fri–Sat 11am–midnight. Free self-parking. CALIFORNIA.

Pebbles is one of Orlando's most popular restaurants, especially with a young yuppie crowd. The multilevel dining room centers on a sunken bar under a cross-beamed skylit ceiling, and though it's a large space, white wooden shutters and windowed enclosures create a cluster of intimate dining areas. Lush tropical greenery, fountains, and canvas tenting contribute to the garden-party ambiance. During the day, sunshine streams in; at night, flickering hurricane lamps provide romantic lighting.

The same menu is offered throughout the day, supplemented by specials. Start off with a "lite bite" of creamy baked chèvre served atop chunky tomato sauce with hot garlic bread. Pebbles offers the option of a casual meal—perhaps a cheddar burger on toasted brioche, honey-roasted spareribs, or a Caesar salad tossed with grilled chicken. Or you can select a more serious entree, such as tender leg of smoked duck that has been rubbed with fennel, glazed with triple sec, and slow-roasted to sear in flavorful juices. Dessert of choice: the goldbrick sundae—a scoop of vanilla ice cream encased in a candylike chocolate/almond shell and served atop caramel sauce with fresh strawberries. There's a full bar and a recently updated wine list. Pebbles also has locations in downtown Orlando at 17 W. Church St. (☎ **407/839-0892**), and in Winter Park at 2516 Aloma Ave. (☎ **407/678-7001**).

INEXPENSIVE

✪ **Romano's Macaroni Grill.** 12148 Apopka–Vineland Rd. (just north of Country Rd. 535/Palm Pkwy.). ☎ **407/239-6676.** Main courses $4.95–$8.25 at lunch; $6.95–$15.95 at dinner (most under $10). AE, CB, DC, DISC, MC, V. Sun–Thurs 11am–10pm; Fri–Sat 11am–11pm. Free self-parking. NORTHERN ITALIAN.

Though friends had raved about the Macaroni Grill, I hadn't really expected much from a chain restaurant. Upon entering, I was favorably impressed by its cheerful interior, with arched stone walls, shuttered windows, colorful murals of Venice, and lights festively strung overhead. A welcoming glow emanated from the exhibition kitchen, where white-hatted chefs tended an oak-burning pizza oven, and foodstuffs, Chianti, flowers, and desserts were aesthetically arranged on counters.

But the big surprise was the food. Everything is made from the freshest ingredients, and the quality of the cuisine would have been notable at twice the price. The thin-crust pizzas—such as the Mediterranean, topped with fresh tomato sauce, shrimp, and feta and mozzarella cheeses—are scrumptious, as is a dish of bow tie pasta tossed with grilled chicken, pancetta, and red and green onions in Asiago cream sauce. Equally good: an entree of sautéed chicken with mushrooms, artichoke hearts, capers, and pancetta in lemon butter; it comes with spaghettini. There are fresh-baked breads, as well—focaccia and *ciabatta* (a crusty, country loaf) for sopping up sauces, or dipping in extra-virgin olive oil. And desserts—especially an apple custard torte with hazelnut crust and caramel topping—keep to the same lofty standard. There's a full bar, premium wines are sold by the glass, and a children's menu offers an entree and beverage for just $3.25. Bravo Romano!

4 Places to Dine in the International Drive Area

Some of the best area restaurants are along International Drive, within about 10 minutes of Walt Disney World parks by car. These restaurants are located on the map "International Drive Area Accommodations & Dining" in chapter 5.

VERY EXPENSIVE

✪ **Dux.** In the Peabody Orlando, 9801 International Dr. ☎ **407/345-4550.** Reservations recommended. Main courses $19–$45. AE, CB, DC, DISC, JCB, MC, V. Mon–Thurs 6–10pm; Fri–Sat 6–11pm. Free self- and validated valet parking. INTERNATIONAL.

Named for the hotel's signature ducks that parade ceremoniously into the lobby each morning to "Sousa's King Cotton March," Dux is one of central Florida's most highly acclaimed restaurants. Upholstered bamboo chairs and cushioned banquettes provide seating at candlelit tables set with flowers and beautiful ceramic plates. A lavish dessert display table with a floral centerpiece serves as the dining room's visual focus, and the textured gold walls are hung with ornately framed mirrors and watercolors (representing 72 ducks, of course).

The menu varies seasonally. One of the best appetizers is a unique version of pot stickers—stuffed with portobello mushrooms, scallions, and creamed goat cheese, and garnished with Asiago twigs. An entree of Sonoma lamb chops glazed with Hunan barbecue sauce is accompanied by roasted Chinese mushrooms and green onions, with a small "treasure packet" of Pacific rice concealed under the lamb. Another good choice is a grilled Florida black grouper marinated in fearless (read *hot*) West Indian spices and served with a plantain-yam mash and tropical chutney. Desserts include a sublime hazelnut meringue napoleon topped with homemade frangelico ice cream and a dusting of Brazilian cocoa. Dux has an extensive, award-winning wine list.

MODERATE

✪ **B-Line Diner.** In the Peabody Orlando, 9801 International Dr. ☎ **407/345-4460.** Reservations not accepted. Main courses $2.75–$8.50 at breakfast; $6.50–$10.95 at lunch; $5.95–$29 (most under $15) at dinner. AE, CB, DC, DISC, JCB, MC, V. Daily 24 hours. Free self- and validated valet parking. AMERICAN.

This popular local diner is of the nouvelle art deco genre; in other words, it's an idealized version of America's ubiquitous roadside establishments. Its interior gleams with chrome edging that adorns everything from a cove ceiling to peach Formica tables, and the jukebox is stocked with oldies tunes. Gorgeous flower arrangements add upscale panache. Though the B-Line is a sophisticated venue, kids get their own low-priced menu, an (ever-present) duck-themed coloring/activities book, and crayons; they will also enjoy the ice-cream sundaes here.

The seasonally varying menu offers haute versions of diner food such as a superior chicken pot pie, pan-seared pork (with grilled apples, sun-dried cherry stuffing, and brandy honey sauce), or a ham-and-cheese sandwich on a baguette. Other items—such as a falafel sandwich on pita bread with mint yogurt sauce—bear no relation to traditional diner fare. Come with an appetite: Portions are hearty. A glass display case up front is filled with scrumptious fresh-baked desserts: everything from coffee and chocolate eclairs to white-chocolate/Grand Marnier mousse cake. There's a full bar.

✪ **Bahama Breeze.** 8849 International Dr. ☎ **407/248-2499.** Reservations not accepted. Main courses $6.95–$15.95; sandwiches and salads $5.95–$6.95. AE, MC, V. Sun–Thurs 4pm–1am; Fri–Sat 4pm–2am. CARIBBEAN.

Traditional Caribbean foods are used to create unusual items such as the moist and tasty "fish in a bag"—strips of mahimahi in a parchment pillow flavored with carrots, sweet peppers, mushrooms, celery, and spices. Also try the paella, a rice dish brimming with shrimp, fish, mussels, chicken, and chunks of sausage. The coconut curry chicken is a light-tasting treat—sautéed chunks of chicken sprinkled with fresh coconut. For dessert try the piña-colada bread pudding, a cube of custard bread in a sweet coconut sauce, or the tart key lime pie. Created by Orlando-based

Dining at CityWalk

Universal's answer to Pleasure Island and Disney's West Side opened in 1999. This entertainment complex could easily be renamed theme-restaurant heaven. It's not only home to the world's largest **Hard Rock Cafe**—the grande dame of all theme restaurants—but also the **NASCAR Cafe,** the **Motown Cafe,** and **Emeril's,** starring cuisine from the spunky chef Emeril Lagasse, who appears on the Food Channel

Go farther south for a taste of Florida's Key West at **Jimmy Buffet's Margaritaville,** and round out your culinary tour in the islands with Jamaican food at **Bob Marley, A Tribute to Freedom.** For complete descriptions of the clubs and restaurants at CityWalk see chapter 10.

Darden Restaurants, the same folks who brought you Red Lobster and Olive Garden, this Bahama Breeze is essentially a test kitchen for what may soon be a national chain. Unlike Darden's other creations, which serve solid but not necessarily savory offerings, Bahama Breeze is a unique dining experience that challenges the taste buds. You can even watch your entrees being prepared in the open kitchen. The drink menu includes over 50 beers and the expected collection of fruity, pseudo-exotic drinks, such as the Very Berry Daiquiri. Happy-hour prices are featured round-the-clock. Be prepared for a long wait—sometimes up to 2 hours during prime meal hours—since the restaurant doesn't accept reservations.

✪ **Cafe Tu Tu Tango.** 8625 International Dr. (just west of the Mercado). ☎ **407/248-2222.** AE, DISC, MC, V. Tapas (small plates) $3.75–$7.95. AE, DC, DISC, MC, V. Sun–Thurs 11:30am–11pm; Fri and Sat 11:30am–1am. Free self- and valet parking. INTERNATIONAL/TAPAS.

Though one may question the need for yet one more theme experience outside the parks, this zany restaurant is a welcome respite from Orlando's predictable "chain gang." For one thing, an ongoing performance-art experience takes place while you dine. One evening, an elegantly dressed couple may tango past your table. Another time, a belly dancer might perform, or a magician might do a few tricks tableside. In addition, there are always artists in a studio area creating pottery, paintings, and jewelry.

Tu Tu's colorful ambience is a lot of fun, but its food is the real draw. The larger your party, the more dishes you can sample; two of the small plates will satisfy most appetites. My favorites include Cajun egg rolls (filled with blackened chicken, corn, and cheddar and goat cheeses, served with chunky tomato salsa and Creole mustard) and pepper-crusted, seared tuna sashimi with crispy rice noodles and cold spinach in a sesame-soy vinaigrette. International wines can be ordered by the glass or bottle. There are great desserts here too, such as creamy almond/amaretto flan, and rich guava cheesecake with strawberry sauce.

✪ **Capriccio.** In the Peabody Orlando, 9801 International Dr. ☎ **407/352-4000.** Reservations recommended. Main courses mostly $12–$22 (with most pizza and pasta dishes priced below $14); Sun champagne brunch buffet $24.95 for adults, $12.95 for children 4–12, under 4 free. AE, CB, DC, DISC, JCB, MC, V. Tues–Sun 6–11pm; Sun brunch 11am–2:30pm. Free self- and validated valet parking. ITALIAN.

Capriccio's striking Italian moderne interior features a gleaming black-and-white checkerboard marble-tile floor and black Italian marble tables elegantly appointed with Tuscan-looking Villeroy & Boch show plates. An exhibition kitchen occupying an entire wall showcases chefs tending mesquite-burning pizza ovens and grills.

Seasonally changing menus bring verve and imagination to traditional Italian cookery. The appetizer of fried calamari is served with three aïolis (garlicky Basque mayonnaises) flavored, respectively, with sun-dried tomato, basil, and saffron. Also scrumptious: a pasta dish of bucatini tossed with chunks of mesquite-grilled chicken and mushrooms in a slightly garlicky herbed white-wine/pesto sauce and finished with tomato concasse. The entree of pan-seared tuna with braised fennel and radicchio is served with lentil flan and a buttery citrus sauce. The kitchen also turns out fabulous pizzas, and oven-fresh breads are accompanied by herb-infused extra-virgin olive oil—dip and exult. But save room for Capriccio's desserts, which include the definitive zuppa inglese. An extensive, award-winning wine list is available. *Note:* Capriccio also serves a great champagne Sunday brunch.

Copeland's of New Orleans. 8255 International Dr. ☎ **407/354-2220.** Reservations recommended. Main courses $7–$24. AE, DC, DISC, MC, V. Sun–Thurs 11am–11pm; Fri–Sat 11am–11:30pm. Free self-parking. NEW ORLEANS.

Tucked back in a shopping center, this taste of New Orleans is a pleasant surprise. Copeland's is part of a franchise out of New Orleans, but the food is so fresh and spicy, you'd hardly believe it. You can't go wrong with New Orleans staples like jambalaya or gumbo, or try the fresh fish with lacombe sauce. There is a full bar.

Italianni's. 8148 International Dr. ☎ **407/345-8884.** Main courses $7.95–$17.95. AE, DC, DISC, MC, V. Daily 10:30am–11pm. ITALIAN.

This is a chain restaurant from the people who created T.G.I. Friday's. Italianni's shares that restaurant's laid-back atmosphere and friendly service. You can't go wrong with the chicken Italianni or one of the many pasta selections. The cheesecake is worth saving room for.

✪ **Ming Court.** 9188 International Dr. (between Sand Lake Rd. and the Bee Line Expwy). ☎ **407/351-9988.** Reservations recommended. Dim sum mostly $1.95–$2.50; main courses $4.50–$7.95 at lunch, $12.50–$19.95 at dinner. AE, CB, DC, DISC, JCB, MC, V. Daily 11am–2:30pm and 4:30pm–midnight. Free self-parking. CHINESE.

At this Chinese restaurant, the clientele includes more local food cognoscenti than tourists. Ming Court is fronted by a serpentine "cloud wall," crowned by engraved sea-green Chinese tiles (it's a celestial symbol; you dine above the clouds here, like the gods). The newly renovated candlelit interior is stunningly decorated in soft earth tones. Glass-walled terrace rooms overlook lotus ponds, filled with colorful koi, and a plant-filled area under a lofty skylight ceiling. A musician plays classical Chinese music on a zheng (a long zither) at dinner.

The innovative menu offers specialties from diverse regions of China, and often features fresh Florida seafood. Begin with a variety of appetizers such as wok-charred Mandarin pot stickers, crispy wontons stuffed with vegetables and cream cheese, and wok-smoked shiitake mushrooms topped with sautéed scallions. Entrees will open up new culinary vistas to even the most sophisticated diners. Lightly battered, deep-fried chicken breast is served with a delicate lemon-tangerine sauce. Szechuan charcoal-grilled filet mignon is topped with a toasted onion/garlic/chili sauce and served with stir-fried julienne vegetables. At lunch, you can order dim-sum items in addition to other menu offerings. There's an extensive wine list. As a concession to Western palates, Ming Court features sumptuous desserts such as a moist cake layered with Mandarin oranges, Key lime, and fresh whipped cream in an orange-vanilla sauce. Dress is upscale but casual.

Siam Orchid. 7575 Republic Dr. (between Sand Lake Rd. and Carrier Dr.). ☎ **407/351-0821.** Reservations recommended. Main courses $10.25–$16.95. AE, DC, DISC, MC, V. Daily 5–11pm. Free self-parking. THAI.

Patterned after a palace in northern Thailand, Siam Orchid centers on a platform used to display wood carvings of angels and musicians representing figures from the Ramayana, an ancient Hindu epic poem. The split-level dining room, with a lofty knotty-pine cathedral ceiling on either side, seats diners in cushioned booths and banquettes and bamboo chairs; some tables overlook a lake. For intimate dining, request a *khun toke*—a private carved-teak enclosure that is the Thai answer to Japanese tatami rooms.

Owners Tim and Krissnee Martsching grow many necessary ingredients—fresh chilies, mint, cilantro, lemongrass, and wild lime—in their own garden, and their fare is authentic and delicious. Begin with *tom kha gai* (a savory chicken-and-mushroom soup) and continue with shared appetizers such as *satay* (grilled skewers of pork or chicken, marinated in coconut cream and mild curry, served with hot peanut sauce) and *tod man* (crispy fried chicken patties flavored with lemongrass, basil, and wild lime leaf). Not to be missed (share an order) is an entree of pad Thai (soft rice noodles tossed with ground pork, fresh minced garlic, shrimp, crab claws, crabmeat, crushed peanuts, and bean sprouts in a tangy-sweet sauce). Curries—such as the royal Thai, replete with chunks of chicken, potato, and onion in a yellow curry sauce—are also a specialty. There's a full bar, and beverage choices include sake, plum wine, and Thai beers. Homemade coconut ice cream topped with crushed peanuts makes a refreshing dessert.

Wild Jacks. 7364 International Dr. (between Sand Lake Rd. and Carrier Dr.). ☎ **407/ 352-4407.** Reservations not accepted. AE, CB, DC, DISC, JCB, MC, V. Main courses $9.45–$17.95. Daily 4:30–11pm. Free self-parking. STEAKS AND BARBECUE.

This upscale, but exuberantly western, steak-and-barbecue restaurant has a whimsical decor, including neon beer signs, mounted buffalo heads, and a longhorn steer poised to jump from a giant horseshoe above the copper bar. Soft lighting emanates from massive, wrought-iron wagon-wheel chandeliers, as well as from fixtures with antler and steer-head motifs. The exhibition kitchen has an open-pit grill. Diners are seated at tables covered with checkered plastic cloths. And the music is country.

Appetizers here are first rate: skewers of tangy barbecued shrimp served over Texas rice (it's studded with corn kernels and red and green peppers), miniature tacos filled with smoked chicken and cheeses, and spicy potato skins topped with melted cheese, chunks of chicken, pico de gallo, sour cream, and guacamole. The best entree choice is the smoked brisket barbecue, served with salad, warm molasses bread and honey, and your choice of two side dishes—I'd recommend the jalapeño mashed potatoes and grilled corn on the cob. Steaks and prime rib are other options, along with pasta dishes. For dessert, there's peach cobbler topped with vanilla ice cream sprinkled with cinnamon. The bar has an iced-beer well.

INEXPENSIVE

Enzo's. 7600 Dr. Phillips Blvd., Suite 12, in the Marketplace Shopping Center (off Sand Lake Rd., just west of I-4). ☎ **407/351-1187.** Reservations not accepted. Panini $4.75–$5.95; main courses $4.50–$6.95 at lunch, $8.50–$12.75 at dinner. AE, CB, DC, DISC, MC, V. Mon–Thurs 11:30am–10pm; Fri–Sat 11:30am–11pm. Free self-parking. ITALIAN.

Upon entering this charming little restaurant and Italian charcuterie, you'll walk past display cases filled with antipasti, deli meats, pâtés, and cheeses, and shelves stocked with homemade pastas and other fancy foodstuffs. And if that's not enough to whet your appetite, you'll also glimpse chefs tending a pizza oven in an exhibition kitchen. The dining area is cheerful and inviting, with glossy pine-plank floors, peach walls hung with fine-art prints, and tables covered with butcher paper (crayons are provided). Italian music (most of it operatic arias) enhances the atmosphere. Enzo's is a casual kind of place that's a local favorite.

Pretty much the same menu is available throughout the day. Families troop in for pizzas—either the traditional American kind or Napoli pies with more sophisticated toppings and crisp, delicate crusts. Until 4:30pm, you can also opt for panini (sandwiches on crusty Italian bread), with fillings such as Italian sausage, grilled onions, and peppers; they're served with potato salad. A more serious dinner might begin with an appetizer of paper-thin slices of Norwegian salmon and onion served with extra-virgin olive oil, capers, lemon, and red peppers. Homemade pastas include fat bucatini tossed with mushrooms, freshly grated Parmesan, prosciutto, bacon, and peas in a robust sauce. Enzo's most fabulous entree is *pollo alla cecco* (roasted breast of free-range chicken with rosemary potatoes and an Italian version of ratatouille). Beer and wine are available. For dessert try zuccotto (Italian sponge cake soaked in Grand Marnier, layered with fresh fruit and crème anglaise, and topped with chocolate shavings). In busy seasons, arrive off-hours to avoid a wait.

Max's Cafe & Coffee House. 701 Front St., Celebration. ☎ **407/566-1144.** Main courses $6.95–$12.95. AE, DC, DISC, MC, V. Daily 8am–9pm. Free self-parking. AMERICAN.

Located in the Disney-created town of Celebration, this is a modern version of the old greasy spoon. The art deco decor is a re-creation of the real thing, but the food offerings are stick-to-your-rib favorites. You get your money's worth here; the sandwiches and meals come in hearty portions. Try the pot roast or fried chicken. The meat loaf, a large slab best sampled with mashed potatoes, is better than Mom used to make. (No offense, Ma.)

5 Places to Dine Elsewhere in Orlando

Visitors wanting a break from theme restaurants can enjoy some of the local favorites, like great barbecue and authentic Cuban cuisine. There is epicurean life outside of Disney.

For more Orlando restaurants, check out the **Church Street Station** listing in chapter 10. All directions assume you are coming from the WDW/International Drive area.

The restaurants in this section are located on the map "Orlando Area Accommodations & Dining" in this section.

EXPENSIVE

Le Provence. 50 E. Pine St., in downtown Orlando. ☎ **407/843-1320.** Reservations recommended. Main courses $14.95–$26.95. AE, DC, MC, V. Mon–Fri 5:30–9:30pm; Sat 5:30–10:30pm. Closed Sunday. Valet parking available. FRENCH.

This is a local upscale favorite, which features expertly prepared delicacies, including wonderful dishes that star duck and veal. Enjoy a good martini and a cigar at Monaco's, a bar next door, while waiting for your table. Dress is casual, but jeans and sneakers may make you feel a bit conspicuous. There is metered street parking available, but it may be hard to find, so opt for the valet.

✪ **Maison et Jardin.** 430 Wymore Rd., Altamonte Springs, 10 min. north of downtown Orlando. ☎ **407/862-4410.** Main courses $18.50–$28.50. AE, DISC, DC, MC, V. Sun 11am–2pm and 6–9pm; Mon–Sat 6–10pm. Free self-parking. Take I-4 East to Maitland Blvd./East exit. Stay in the far lane, turning right at Lake Destiny Dr. At the next light, turn left onto Wymore Rd. FRENCH.

The succulent beef Wellington served here—a local special-occasion favorite—tastes even better after a diet of theme park burritos. If you're game, try the Elk Medallions sautéed and served with a raspberry sauce. For dessert: the crepes Suzette. You can order from a full bar, but what really makes Maison et Jardin worth the drive is one of the best wine cellars in the world. The restaurant was recently honored by *Wine Spectator* magazine for its outstanding selection. This is the place for lovers of good wine. (And definitely not the place for children.)

Sergio's. 355 N. Orange Ave, in downtown Orlando. ☎ **407/428-6162.** Reservations recommended, especially for dinner. Main courses $9–$26. AE, DC, DISC, MC, V. Mon–Fri 11:30am–10:30pm; Sat–Sun 5:30am–11:30pm. Take I-4 to downtown Orlando. Take Exit 41 (Amelia Ave.). Go 1 block, and turn right. Turn right again on Orange Ave. The restaurant is 20 yards ahead on the left, past Livingston St., next to LaBelle's Fur. ITALIAN.

A 1997 move into the heart of the city made this old Orlando favorite more accessible to visitors. Careful attention to detail, such as individual lighting adjustments for each table, makes this a nice retreat from the typical tourist fare. The menu is created by the same chef who set the tone for Bahama Breeze (see above). That same Florida flavor is apparent, but here true Italian cooking wins out. Start with the antipasti for an appetizer, and don't miss the spinach pasta with Gorgonzola and pine nuts. The daily specials often highlight the freshest fish available. Heartier eaters should try the veal chop. For dessert, try the tiramisu. You'll find a full wine list.

MODERATE

Dexter's of Thorton Park. 808 E. Washington St., near downtown Orlando. ☎ **407/649-2777.** Reservations not accepted. Main courses $5.99–$16.95. AE, DC, DISC, MC, V. Sun 5–10pm; Mon–Sat 11am–midnight. From I-4, take the Anderson St. exit. Travel to Mills Ave., and take a left. Turn left again on Central Blvd., and continue on Central to Hyer St. Turn left on Hyer; the restaurant is at the corner of Hyer and Washington. AMERICAN.

This popular neighborhood bar/restaurant is just a few blocks from Lake Eola in the center of downtown. The fare ranges from basic soups and salads to quiche and more adventurous menu items, such as black-and-white sesame grouper and andouille sausages quesadilla. You'll also find tempting daily specials. There is a limited beer and wine menu, and the desert menu varies. Many of the seats are at high tables, where you sit on bar stools; if you find these seats uncomfortable, you may have a long wait. This is an upbeat, noisy crowd filled with regulars.

White Wolf Cafe. 1829 N. Orange Ave. (about 1 mile from Loch Haven Pk.), Orlando. ☎ **407/895-9911.** Reservations not accepted. Main courses $4.25–$6.75 at lunch; $6.95–$12.95 at dinner. AE, MC, V. Mon 10am–6pm; Tues–Thurs 10am–10pm; Fri–Sat 10am–midnight. Free self-parking. Take I-4 east to Princeton St. (Exit 43). Turn right at Orange Ave. Look for striped awnings on the left. AMERICAN.

Even White Wolf's often clueless, and notoriously slow, servers can't overshadow the first-rate food. No mass-producing theme machine for tourists, this restaurant creates fresh meals from a tiny, deli-style kitchen. With rough-cut marble tables, a furry mascot panting near the door, and an eclectic, handwritten menu, it seems like you're eating in the crowded, funky, and slightly pretentious downtown loft of friends.

For lunch, you could share the meaty Caribbean chicken salad, lightly accented with tangy apricot vinaigrette (just get extra dressing). For an appetizer pick black bean soup kissed with onion. Three-cheese lasagna, firm pasta slathered in a lightly spiced marinara, is a dinner favorite served with a warm hunk of French bread. Avoid the salmon lavosh. Regulars warn that the slow service rules out firm post-dinner plans. Fortunately, peanut-butter-and-brownie ice cream pie, a lush sugar rush dripping with hot fudge, is the perfect reward for your patience.

INEXPENSIVE

✪ **Bubbaloo's Bodacious BBQ.** 1471 Lee Rd., Winter Park (about 5 min. from downtown Orlando). ☎ **407/295-1212.** Reservations not accepted. Main courses $4.95–$7.95. AE, MC, V. Mon–Thurs 10am–9pm; Fri–Sat 10am–10:30pm; Sun 11am–9pm. Free self-parking.

Orlando Area Accommodations & Dining

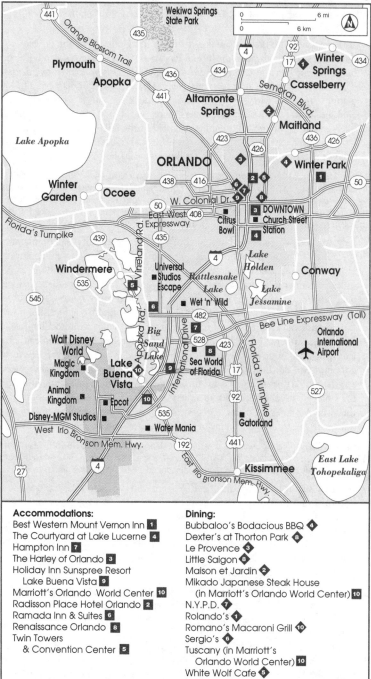

Accommodations:
Best Western Mount Vernon Inn 1
The Courtyard at Lake Lucerne 4
Hampton Inn 7
The Harley of Orlando 3
Holiday Inn Sunspree Resort
   Lake Buena Vista 9
Marriott's Orlando World Center 10
Radisson Place Hotel Orlando 2
Ramada Inn & Suites 6
Renaissance Orlando 8
Twin Towers
   & Convention Center 5

Dining:
Bubbaloo's Bodacious BBQ 4
Dexter's at Thorton Park 8
Le Provence 3
Little Saigon 8
Maison et Jardin 2
Mikado Japanese Steak House
   (in Marriott's Orlando World Center) 10
N.Y.P.D. 7
Rolando's 1
Romano's Macaroni Grill 10
Sergio's 6
Tuscany (in Marriott's
   Orlando World Center) 10
White Wolf Cafe 5

127

Take I-4 east to Lee Rd. (Exit 45). Follow your nose; Bubbaloo's is on the left, next to a dry cleaners. BARBECUE.

You can smell the hickory smoke emerging from this restaurant for blocks, the tangy scent cutting through the humid Florida air. This is, hands down, some of the best barbecue you'll find anywhere. And, if nothing else, you gotta love the name. There are other things on the menu, such as fried clams, but go for the full pork platter that comes with a heaping helping of pork and all the fixin's. The uninitiated should stay away from the "Killer" sauce, which produces a tongue buzz that's likely to last for hours; you might even taste test the mild before moving up to the hot. The beans are the perfect side dish. Only the sometimes-soggy garlic bread brings the meal down, but not too far. Beer is available.

Little Saigon. 1106 E. Colonial Dr. (Colonial is also called Hwy. 50.), near downtown Orlando. ☎ **407/423-8539.** Reservations not accepted. Main courses under $5 at lunch; $4.95–$10.95 at dinner. AE, DISC, MC, V. Daily 10am–9pm. Free self-parking. Take the Colonial Dr. (Hwy. 50) exit; head east. Located between Mills and Thorton aves. Look for the fish mural. Turn right onto Thorton. Lot is immediately to the left. VIETNAMESE.

Few would expect to find a Little Saigon, a bustling enclave of Asian immigrants, in the midst of Orlando. But both the community and the first-class restaurant of the same name make their home near downtown. For an appetizer, don't miss the unfried summer rolls, a soft wrap filled with rice, shrimp, and pork, served with a delicious peanut sauce. At $2.50 for two, you could easily make a meal of these sumptuous rolls. Don't. Go on to sample some of the healthy, light dishes from the dozens of menu selections. Try one of the traditional soups with noodles, rice, vegetables, and either chicken, beef, or seafood. The numbered menu is in badly translated English—"soup serve aside"—so don't be afraid to ask your servers exactly what goes into No. 86. Little Saigon's one drawback is the scarcity of English-speaking servers, so don't hesitate to ask for the manager. As for the restaurant's authenticity, the tables are usually filled with members of the local Vietnamese community, with the owner working the tables, too. Stay away from the weak, slightly bitter iced tea. Stick with hot tea, soda, or some of the limited beer and wine options available.

N.Y.P.D. 373 N. Orange Ave., in downtown Orlando. ☎ **407/481-8680.** Main courses $4.25–$13.95. No credit cards. Mon–Fri 11:30am–9pm; Sat 12:30–8pm. Take I-4 to downtown and take the Robinson exit. Turn right on Livingston; take it to Orange Ave. and turn left. PIZZA.

N.Y.P.D. stands for New York Pizza Delivery, and this restaurant has become well known to downtowners for its bicycle delivery carts. With a husband whose last name is Campagna, I can vouch for the authentic Italian cuisine here. There is a selection of Italian basics such as eggplant parmagiana and lasagna, but the New York–style pies are the real standouts. The white pizza, with a gooey and spicy selection of cheese toppings is especially good. There is also deep-dish Sicilian style pizza. But there is no smoking.

✪ **Rolando's.** 870 E. Fla. 436 (Semoran Blvd., between Red Bug Rd. and U.S. 17/92), in Casselberry. ☎ **407/767-9677.** Reservations not accepted. Main courses $3.25–$4.75 at lunch; $5.75–$11.50 at dinner. AE, DISC, MC, V. Sun 1–8pm; Tues–Sat 11am–10pm. Free self-parking. Take I-4 east to the East-West Expwy., head east, and make a left on Fla. 436. CUBAN.

About 40 minutes from Walt Disney World, this inexpensive Mom-and-Pop place serves up huge portions of authentic Cuban fare. Its two dining rooms are pleasant but plain, with Formica tables, stucco walls hung with photographs of Cuba, and pots of philodendrons suspended from the ceiling. Soft lighting adds a smidge of ambiance.

I recommend ordering up a bunch of appetizers to share: deep-fried ripe plantains, *papas rellenas*—breaded, deep-fried balls of mashed potato stuffed with spicy picadillos (garlicky ground beef cooked with onions, olives, raisins, and green pep-pers in a tomato sauce)—flavorful Cuban tamales topped with picadillos, and slightly sweet batter-fried corn fritters that are light as air. An entree of roast chicken is brushed with crushed garlic, white-wine vinegar, cumin, and oregano, then briefly deep-fried just before serving. Tender, shredded beef is simmered in a richly seasoned, tomato-based sauce with potatoes, olives, peas, pimentos, onions, green peppers, and sweet red peppers. Paella is an option if you call a few hours in advance to order it. Entrees are served with freshly baked hot rolls, house salad, rice, and plantains or yucca (a chewy root plant); take the plantains. For dessert, try the *dulce de tres leche* (a meringue-topped yellow cake mixed with condensed milk, evapo-rated milk, and cream). At lunch, a hearty sandwich of hot Cuban bread stuffed with slices of ham, roast pork, Swiss cheese, and pickles is served with black bean soup. Beer and wine are available.

6 Only in Orlando: Dining with Disney Characters

Especially for the 10-and-under set, it's a thrill to dine in a restaurant where costumed Disney characters show up to greet the customers, sign autographs, pose in family photos, and interact with little kids. Make reservations as far in advance as possible for these very popular meals. It's best to make reservations when you book your hotel.

The prices for all these character meals are pretty much the same, no matter where you are dining. The **breakfast** prices are all around **$15 for adults** and **$8 for children;** at **dinner $20 for adults, $9 for children** 3–11, free for children 2 and under. The prices do vary a bit, though, from location to location, the character luau at the Polynesian Resort being more expensive than the others.

To make **reservations** for any WDW character meal, call ☎ **407/WDW-DINE** (939-3463). American Express, MasterCard, and Visa are accepted at all character meals.

You'll find all the restaurants mentioned in this section on the map "Walt Disney World & Lake Buena Vista Dining" earlier in this chapter.

Artist Point. At Disney's Wilderness Lodge, 901 Timberline Dr. Breakfast with Winnie the Pooh, Tigger, and the other inhabitants of the Hundred Acre Woods. Daily 7:30–11am.

In a rustic lodgelike dining room with a beamed ceiling supported by tree-trunk beams and large windows providing scenic lake views, **Pooh** and **Tigger** host an all-you-can-eat buffet breakfast.

Cape May Café. At Disney's Beach Club Resort, 1800 Epcot Resorts Blvd. Daily 7:30–11am.

The Cape May Café, a delightful New England–themed dining room, serves lavish buffet character breakfasts hosted by Admiral **Goofy** and his crew—**Chip 'n' Dale** and **Pluto** (exact characters may vary).

Chef Mickey's. At Disney's Contemporary Resort, 4600 N. World Dr. Daily 7:30–11:30am and 5–9:30pm.

The whimsical Chef Mickey's is the setting for buffet character breakfasts and dinners. On hand to meet, greet, and mingle with guests are **Mickey** and various pals. Chef Mickey's character prime-rib buffet dinners include a make-your-own-sundae bar.

Cinderella's Royal Table. In Cinderella's Castle in the Magic Kingdom. Daily 8–10am.

This Gothic castle—the focal point of the park—serves up character-breakfast buf-fets daily. Hosts vary, but **Cinderella** always puts in an appearance. This is one of the most popular character meals in the park, so reserve far in advance. It's a great way to start your day in the Magic Kingdom.

✪ **Garden Grill.** In The Land Pavilion at Epcot. Daily 8:30am–8pm.

This revolving restaurant has comfortable, semicircular booths. As you dine, your table travels past desert, prairie, farmland, and rain-forest environments. There's a "Momma's-in-the-kitchen" theme here: You'll be given a straw hat at the entrance, and the just-folks service staff speaks in country lingo. Hearty family-style meals are hosted by **Mickey, Minnie,** and **Chip 'n' Dale.** (Boy that Mickey sure gets around.) American breakfast and lunch choices are extensive. Dinners include several entrees (roast chicken, farm-raised fish, and hickory-smoked steak), mashed potatoes, vegetables, squaw bread and biscuits, salad, beverage, and dessert.

Liberty Tree Tavern. In Liberty Sq. in the Magic Kingdom. Daily 4pm to park closing.

This colonial-styled 18th-century pub offers character dinners hosted by **Mickey, Goofy, Pluto, Chip 'n' Dale,** and **Tigger** (some or all of them). Meals, served family style, consist of salad, roast chicken, marinated flank steak, trail sausages, mashed potatoes, rice pilaf, vegetables, and a dessert of warm apple crisp with vanilla ice cream.

Note: In the Magic Kingdom you can also find Pooh and friends at the Crystal Palace on Main Street all day.

Minnie's Menehune & Mickey's Tropical Luau. At Disney's Polynesian Resort, 1600 Seven Seas Dr. $38 adults, $19.50 children 3–11, free for children 2 and under; taxes and gratuities extra. Daily 6:45 and 9:30pm. Free self- and valet parking. No characters at the regular luau dinner show.

Luau Cove, an exotic open-air facility, is the setting for an island-themed character show called Mickey's Tropical Luau. It's an abbreviated version of the Polynesian Luau Dinner Show described in chapter 10 and features Polynesian dancers along with **Mickey, Minnie, Pluto,** and **Goofy.** Your prix-fixe meal includes honey-roasted chicken, vegetables, glazed cinnamon bread, and an ice-cream sundae. Guests are presented with shell leis on entering.

The Polynesian also hosts Minnie's Menehune Character Breakfast in the Polynesian-themed 'Ohana (described earlier in the section "In the Walt Disney Resorts"). Traditional breakfast foods are prepared on an 18-foot fire pit and served family-style. **Minnie, Goofy,** and **Chip 'n' Dale** appear, and there are children's parades with Polynesian musical instruments.

1900 Park Fare. At Disney's Grand Floridian Beach Resort, 4401 Floridian Way. Daily 7:30–11:30am and 5:30–9pm.

This exquisitely elegant Disney resort hosts character meals in the festive exposition-themed 1900 Park Fare. Big Bertha—a French band organ that plays pipes, drums, bells, cymbals, castanets, and the xylophone—provides music. **Mary Poppins, Winnie the Pooh, Goofy, Pluto, Chip 'n' Dale,** and **Minnie** appear at the elaborate buffet breakfasts. **Mickey and Minnie** appear at nightly buffets featuring prime rib, stuffed pork loin, fresh fish, and more.

Watercress Café. At the Wyndham Resort, 1900 Buena Vista Dr. ☎ **407/827-2727.** Reservations not accepted. Sun 8–10:30am.

This breakfast is not at a Disney-owned property but rather at one of the "official" Disney hotels in the Lake Buena Vista area. Prices are similar. The plant-filled Watercress Café—with large windows overlooking Lake Buena Vista—is the setting for Sunday-morning character breakfasts featuring **Minnie, Goofy,** and **Pluto.** Both a la carte and buffet meals are offered. Since reservations are not accepted, arrive early to avoid a wait.

On Your Mark, Get Set, Go! What to See & Do In & Around Walt Disney World

7

We all know what the big attraction is here—the one that put Orlando on the map. With the exception of conventioneers (and I'm sure many of them sneak off to the parks, as well), most people who come to Orlando have come to meet—or become reacquainted with—the Mouse.

Walt Disney World, attracting more than 13 million visitors annually, is one of the world's most popular travel destinations. All of the Disney parks make the industry's top 10 list for attendance. And why not? They provide a welcome retreat in a star-spangled, all-American fantasyland where wonderment, human progress, and old-fashioned family fun are the major themes. And these themes are presented in spectacular parades and fireworks displays; 3-D, and 360° CircleVision movies; and adventure-filled journeys through time and space. Though it's not inexpensive, you'll seldom hear people complain about not getting their money's worth. Disney delivers!

One reason is that rides and shows are periodically updated and, as with some of the attractions at the latest park Animal Kingdom, if something doesn't quite work Disney is willing to fix it. As part of this process, the company conducts extensive interviews with park-goers to determine how well things are working.

There have been many changes and additions to the Magic Kingdom since it opened in 1971. The oldest section, Tomorrow-land, was actually looking a little dated by the time it underwent a recent upgrade and renovation. Other recent additions to WDW include Disney's West Side, a collection of shops, restaurants, and nightclubs that opened in 1997, joining with Pleasure Island and the Disney Village Marketplace to become what WDW is calling Downtown Disney. In 1998, the fourth major park, Animal Kingdom, dedicated to wildlife, opened four of its five sections. In 1999, the final section was opened and rides and attractions continue to be changed and fine-tuned even at press time. But those are just the latest additions. Smaller changes are taking place throughout Walt's World, which includes Epcot, where guests take exhilarating voyages around the world and into the future, and Disney–MGM Studios, centered on "Hollywood Boulevard" and providing a thrilling behind-the-scenes look at motion-picture and TV studios. Recent additions at MGM include a new nighttime entertainment show, Fantasmic. (A version of this show has been playing at California's Disneyland for some time, but Disney folks promise the Florida version still delivers some surprises.)

Other Disney parks include Pleasure Island, an ongoing street festival in a 6-acre complex of nightclubs and shops (see chapter 10 for details), featuring live concerts nightly as well as Planet Hollywood; Disney Village Marketplace, a charming lakeside enclave of shops and restaurants; Typhoon Lagoon, a 56-acre water park where you can catch the world's largest man-made waves or plummet down steep water flumes; River Country, another water park; Blizzard Beach, even another water park that's meant to be "a ski resort in the tropics." Rounding out the Disney attractions are two miniature golf courses, Fantasia Gardens, and the latest, Winter Summerland, which opened in 1999 and has a winter wonderland theme.

1 Essentials

GETTING INFORMATION IN ADVANCE

Before leaving home, call or write the Walt Disney World Co., Box 10000, Lake Buena Vista, FL 32830-1000 (☎ 407/934-7639), for a copy of the very informative *Walt Disney World Vacations* brochure—an invaluable planning aid. When you call, also ask about special events that will be going on during your stay. Although we list major events in "When to Go," in chapter 2 of this book, there are many other events that may be of interest. This is especially true in 2000 when many millennium-based special events will take place in the parks.

Once you've arrived in town, guest-services and concierge desks in all the area hotels—especially Disney properties and "official" hotels—have up-to-the-minute information about happenings in the parks. Stop by to ask questions and pick up literature, including a schedule of park hours and special events. If you have questions your hotel can't answer, call ☎ 407/824-4321.

A very handy pocket-sized guidebook is produced for American Express cardholders and lists basic recreational and dining opportunities within WDW. It also details discounts available with American Express.

There are also information locations in each park—at City Hall in the Magic Kingdom, at Innoventions East near the WorldKey terminals in Epcot, and at the Guest Services building in Disney–MGM Studios.

If you are hooked up to the Internet, or have access to a library with Internet access, there is a Web site at **www.disneyworld.com,** which has extensive, entertaining, and regularly updated information, including a live-action look from video cameras perched throughout the various parks. (This consists mostly of long-distance shots of tourists walking about, but it's still a chance to see those blue Orlando skies and dream ahead to vacation time.)

The city newspaper, the *Orlando Sentinel,* also produces **Orlando Sentinel Online** at **www.orlandosentinel.com.** Once there, click on "Theme Park Central" for a variety of information and updates on activities at local attractions. During the peak tourist season, the *Orlando Sentinel* also has special tourist information, including park hours and weather, on the front page of the "Local & State" section. If you are on AOL, type **Go2Orlando** as a keyword and you will land on a site, produced by Orlando Sentinel Interactive, that is full of regularly updated information about a variety of attractions. Another site, although less comprehensive, is at **www.insidecentralflorida.com.** This site is geared more to locals, but does have information about attractions, hotels, theme parks, and special events. The Orlando/Orange County Convention and Visitors Bureau has a Web site at **www.goflorida.com/orlando.** The state has a Web site at **www.flausa.com.**

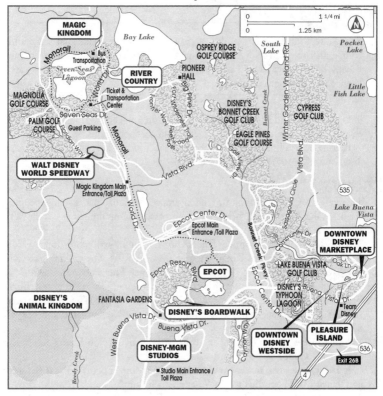

GETTING TO WDW BY CAR

The exits to all the Disney parks are well marked. From Interstate 4, exits 25, 26, and 27 lead to the Disney parks. Once inside, colorful signs will direct you to your destination. If you miss the exit marked for your specific park, *don't panic.* Simply get off at the next one and turn around. It may take a little more time, but it's safer than slashing through five lanes of traffic to make the off-ramp. Drive with extra caution in the attractions area. Disney drivers are divided into two categories: workers (in a hurry to make their shift) and tourists (driving and looking at a map).

Upon entering WDW grounds, you can tune your radio to 1030 AM when you're approaching the Magic Kingdom, or 850 AM when approaching Epcot, for park information. Tune to 1200 AM when departing from the Magic Kingdom, or 910 AM when departing Epcot. TVs in all the Disney resorts and official Disney hotels also have park information stations.

PARKING

All of the WDW lots are tightly controlled; the Disney folks have parking cars down to a science. You park where those nice young people in their yellow-striped shirts tell you to park—or else. Remember, however, to note your parking place. Those nice young people won't be there to direct you to your car when you leave the park, and at the end of the day, you would be surprised at how many cars look alike.

Visitors are also encouraged to ride the trams. Do this if you're parked in the massive Magic Kingdom lot, or at Animal Kingdom. You can skip waiting for the trams

Fun Fact

Single-day admission and multiday pass prices do not include sales tax and, of course, are subject to change. Annual price increases have become the norm, but are usually limited to $1 or $2 on a single-day admission. The pass options can also change slightly from year to year.

in lots at Epcot and MGM Studios and walk on up. The parking lots are not necessarily designed for pedestrians, so watch out for those trams.

Parking generally costs $5. There are special lots at each park for travelers with disabilities (☎ **407/824-4321** for details).

TICKETS

There are several ticket options, ranging from 1- to 7-day passes. Most people get the best value from 4- and 5-day passes. All passes offer unlimited use of the WDW transportation system.

The **4-Day Park Hopper Passes** provide unlimited admission to Magic Kingdom, Epcot, Animal Kingdom, and Disney-MGM. For a 4-day pass, adults pay $167; children, $134. A **5-Day Park Hopper Plus Pass** also includes your choice of two admissions to either Typhoon Lagoon, River Country, Blizzard Beach, Pleasure Island, or Disney's Wide World of Sports. The 5-day pass costs adults $229; children, $183. Passes for 6 and 7 days are available; call (☎ **407/824-4321** for details.

Adult prices are paid by anyone over 10 years of age. **Children's rates** are for ages 3 to 9. **Children 2 and under** are admitted free.

A **1-day, one-park ticket for the Magic Kingdom, Epcot, Animal Kingdom, or Disney-MGM Studios** is $44 for adults, $36 for children.

A **1-day ticket to Typhoon Lagoon or Blizzard Beach** is $26.95 for adults, $21.50 for children.

A **1-day ticket to River Country** is $15.95 for adults, $12.50 for children.

A **1-day ticket to Pleasure Island** is $18.95. Since this is primarily an 18 and over entertainment complex, there is no special pricing for children.

If you're staying at any Walt Disney World resort or "official" hotel (see chapter 5, "Accommodations"), you're also eligible for a money-saving **Unlimited Magic Pass,** which is priced according to the length of your stay. It also offers special perks.

If you plan on visiting Walt Disney World more than one time during the year, inquire about a money-saving **annual pass** ($309 adults, $259 children).

OPERATING HOURS

Hours of operation vary somewhat throughout the year and can be influenced by special events, so it is generally a good idea to call during your visit to check opening/closing times.

The **Magic Kingdom** and **Disney–MGM Studios** are generally open from 9am to 7pm, with extended hours—sometimes as late as midnight—during major holidays and the summer months. **Animal Kingdom** is open from 8am to 6pm, but opens as early as 7am and closes at 7pm during the peak season.

Epcot is generally open from 9am to 9pm, with **Future World** open from 9am to 9pm and **World Showcase** from 11am to 9pm—once again with extended holiday hours.

Typhoon Lagoon and **Blizzard Beach** are open from 10am to 5pm most of the year (with extended hours during some holidays), and 9am to 8pm in summer.

River Country is open from 10am to 5pm most of the year (with extended hours during some holidays), and 10am to 7pm in summer.

Note: Epcot and MGM sometimes open a half hour or more before the posted time. Keep in mind, too, that Disney-resort guests enjoy early admission to all the major parks, except Animal Kingdom, on designated days.

2 Making Your Visit More Enjoyable

HOW WE'VE MADE THIS CHAPTER USEFUL TO PARENTS

Before every listing in the four major parks, you'll note the "Recommended Ages" entry that tells the appropriate ages that will most appreciate each ride. Though most families will want to do everything, you may find this guideline helpful in planning your daily itinerary. In our ride ratings, we've indicated whether a ride will be more enjoyable for children than for adults. Many rides, even those in Magic Kingdom, are simply too intense for young children. One bad experience can spook youngsters for the rest of the day.

BEST TIME OF YEAR TO VISIT

Because of the large number of international visitors, there is really no "off" season for Disney, but during the winter months, usually from January through April, the park crowds are smallest, the weather coolest, and the air least humid. The crowds also thin after September until the week before Thanksgiving. The summer months, when the masses throng to the park, are not only crowded, but hot, hot, hot, sticky, and humid. During the cooler months, you also don't have to worry about the daily summer thunderstorms.

BEST DAYS TO VISIT

The busiest days at the Magic Kingdom, Animal Kingdom, and Epcot are Monday to Wednesday; at Disney–MGM Studios, they're Thursday and Friday. Surprisingly, weekends are the least busy at all parks. Sunday is generally a slow day. The periods surrounding major holidays attract throngs to the parks—the period between Christmas and New Years is especially busy—and wait times can be oppressive. In peak seasons especially, arrange your visits accordingly. Crowds tend to thin out later in the day, so an afternoon excursion may be an easier one.

The big attractions at Animal Kingdom are, obviously, the live animals, and the best time to see them is in the early morning hours, so plan to be there when the gates open.

PLAN YOUR VISIT

How you plan your time at Walt Disney World will depend on a number of factors, including the ages of children in your party, what you've seen on previous visits, your specific interests, and whether you're traveling at a peak time or off-season (when lines are shorter and you can cram more in). Planning, however, is essential. So is choosing age-appropriate activities.

Nothing can spoil a day in the parks more than a child devastated because he or she can't do something promised. Before you get to the park, review this book and the **suggested ages** for children, especially **height restrictions.** The WDW staff will not bend those rules, no matter how loud your little one may wail.

Unless you're staying for considerably more than a week, you can't possibly experience all the rides, shows, and attractions here—not to mention the vast array of recreational facilities. A single ride may last 5 minutes, but the line to get in may stretch for an hour. And you'll only wear yourself to a frazzle trying to hit everything.

It's far better to follow a relaxed itinerary, including leisurely meals and some recreation, than to make a demanding job out of trying to see everything.

Note: Many of these suggestions are also applicable at non-Disney theme parks.

CREATE AN ITINERARY FOR EACH DAY

Read the previously mentioned *Walt Disney World Vacations* brochure and the detailed descriptions in this book, and plan your visit to include all shows and attractions that pique your interest and excitement. Take into consideration your personal loyalties. Winnie the Pooh may not move me in the same way he moves you. Put the ride featuring your favorite character, or your child's favorite character, at the top of the list. It's a good idea to make a daily itinerary, putting your choices in some kind of sensible geographical sequence, so you're not zigzagging all over the place. Familiarize yourself in advance with the layout of each park.

I repeat this advice—schedule sit-down shows, recreational activities (a boat ride or swim late in the afternoon can be wonderfully refreshing), and at least some unhurried meals. It will save you from exhaustion and aggravation. My suggested itineraries below will allow you to see a great deal of the parks while avoiding frazzled nerves at the end of the day.

Suggested Itineraries: A Day in the Magic Kingdom

The key to getting the most out of your theme-park experience is going **against the crowd.** Do arrive with everyone else a little before opening time with your already purchased tickets. When the gates open, don't make a dash for Fantasyland, which is where everyone else will go. Start in one of the lesser realms to avoid the crowds.

While the families are still going loco over the Lion King, hightail to **Frontierland** and ride **Splash Mountain**—another biggie—before long lines form there. There is little shade near this ride, so you definitely don't want to be waiting there in the middle of the day. When you come off, it will still be early enough to beat the lines at another major attraction; head over to **Adventureland** and do **Pirates of the Caribbean.**

Complete whatever else interests you in Adventureland. Or eat a heavy snack, like a turkey leg from one of the vendor carts, and keep riding during lunch to take advantage of shorter lunchtime lines. Have lunch while taking in the early-afternoon shows in the **Diamond Horseshoe Saloon Revue show** (they don't take reservations, so arrive early).

By 2:30pm (earlier in peak seasons), you should start looking for a seat along the **parade** route. Liberty Square is where most people settle, so look at the map and pick a spot farther down the route, which winds through the park.

If you are a ride junkie, skip the parade and hit **Alien Encounters** and other high-volume rides while the rest of the crowd concentrates along the curb.

This is an especially good idea if the **Main Street Electrical Parade** will be put on during your stay. That is the parade to see. After the parade, it should be safe to venture into **Fantasyland,** although there is never a truly good time to visit, since it contains the heart of what most adults remember from their first Disney visit.

If you have little kids (8 and under) in your party, start your day instead by taking the **WDW Railroad** from Main Street to Mickey's Toontown Fair. That should provide a sufficient Mickey fix, so you can work your way through Adventureland and

In the Words of Walt Disney

Family fun is as necessary to modern living as a kitchen refrigerator.

Part of the Disney success is our ability to create a believable world of dreams that appeals to all age groups.

Tomorrowland. Save Fantasyland for after lunch. Take an air-conditioned break at the **Country Bear Jamboree** in Frontierland.

That's a long enough day for most young children, and your best plan is to go back to your hotel for a nap or swim.

If You Can Spend Only 1 Day at Epcot

Epcot really requires at least 2 days, so this is a highlight tour. As suggested for the Magic Kingdom itinerary, arrive early, tickets in hand. If you haven't already made lunch reservations by calling ☎ **407/WDW-DINE** (939-3463) (see chapter 6, "Dining"), make your first stop at the WorldKey terminals in Innoventions East. I suggest a 1pm lunch at the San Angel Inn Restaurant in Mexico. If you don't like Mexican food, move up one pavilion to Norway and reserve for the buffet at Akershus. You can make dinner reservations at the same time. Plan dinner for about 7pm, which will allow you time to eat and find a good viewing spot for **Illumi-Nations** (usually at 9pm, but check your schedule).

Spend no more than an hour exploring **Innoventions East.** Then move on to the **Universe of Energy.** Continue to the **Wonders of Life Pavilion,** where must-sees include **Body Wars, Cranium Command,** and **The Making of Me.**

If time allows—it will depend on line waits at attractions—take in the show at **Test Track** before heading into World Showcase for lunch. Over lunch, check your show schedule and decide which shows to incorporate into your day.

Then walk around the lagoon, visiting highlight attractions such as **Wonders of China, The American Adventure, Impressions de France,** and **O Canada!,** allowing yourself some time for browsing and shopping. After dinner, stay on for IllumiNations.

If You Can Spend 2 Days at Epcot

Ignore the 1-day itinerary just described, but do begin your day by making all necessary restaurant reservations—once again for lunch in Mexico or Norway at about 1pm. Make reservations for Day 2 at the same time.

Skip Innoventions East for now and work your way thoroughly through the **Universe of Energy, Wonders of Life,** and **Test Track** pavilions, keeping your lunch reservation time in mind.

After lunch, walk clockwise around the lagoon, visiting each pavilion and taking in as many shows as you like (consult your show schedule and try to keep pace as well as possible). Leave IllumiNations for your second day's visit.

Begin your **second day** exploring **Innoventions East** and proceed counterclockwise, taking in **Spaceship Earth, Innoventions West, The Living Seas** (its Coral Reef restaurant is a good choice for lunch), and all the other pavilions on the west side of the park. Cap off your Epcot visit with **IllumiNations.**

A DAY AT DISNEY–MGM STUDIOS THEME PARK

Since show times change frequently here, it's impossible to really give you a workable itinerary. Upon entering the park, if you haven't already made dining arrangements, stop at the Hollywood Brown Derby (details in chapter 6) and make reservations for lunch. Or you may want to conserve park-touring time by having a light lunch at a casual fast-food joint, saving the Derby for a relaxing dinner.

Nutritional needs accounted for, make a beeline for the **Twilight Zone Tower of Terror.** While you're waiting in line, plan the rest of your schedule, being sure to include these not-to-be-missed attractions: the **Magic of Disney Animation,** the **Indiana Jones Epic Stunt Spectacular, and Jim Henson's Muppet*Vision 3D.**

If you have girls under 11 in your party, "The Voyage of the Little Mermaid" and "Beauty and the Beast" will probably be major priorities; for the latter shows, get in line 45 minutes prior to show time.

The **afternoon parades** are generally themed to a recent Disney movie release. These parades, the latest focuses on *Mulan,* are nothing to compete with the parades in Magic Kingdom. (Some other Disney production will probably take over by the time of your visit as the parade theme.) If your child is wild about the latest release highlighted in the parade, you may have to go. If so, snag good seats on the parade route 30 minutes ahead of time. Keep in mind that people tend to congregate along the route near the back of the park, so go where everyone else is not. If there is not a special interest in the parade theme, skip it. The nighttime show, Fantasmic, is far more impressive.

Time for more? Do **The Great Movie Ride, Star Tours, Inside the Magic,** and the **Backstage Studio Tour.** To cap off your day, see the new nighttime show that debuted in the fall of 1998; **Fantasmic** is a 25-minute combination of dancing waters, lasers, and a real-life cast of 50.

A DAY AT ANIMAL KINGDOM

If you have 1 day at Animal Kingdom, try to arrive early and be there when the gates open, sometimes as early as 7am, but generally around 8am. (Call Disney information ☎ 407/934-7639 to check the time.) This will give you the best chance of actually seeing animals since they are most active in the cool morning air. If you want to eat at the Rainforest Cafe, make your reservations early. The size of the park (500 acres) means a considerable amount of travel time once you pass through the opening gates. Don't linger in The Oasis area or around the Tree of Life; instead, head directly to the back of the park to be first in line for the **Kilimanjaro Safari.** This will allow you to see more animals before it gets hot, and before the waiting time stretches to a couple of hours. Work your way back through Africa, visiting **Pangani Forest Exploration Trail,** and if you have children, take the **train to Conservation Station.**

If it is late in the morning, grab an early lunch at the **Tusker House Restaurant,** if you want a real sit-down meal. If a cheeseburger and chips will suffice, try **Mr. Kamal's Burger Grill,** a fast food stand located on the path between Asia and Africa.

Once in Asia, check the show schedule for **Flights of Wonder,** and go to **Kali River Rapids** during the show. This will considerably shorten the time you spend in line. While waiting for the right time to shoot the rapids, tour the **Maharajah Jungle Trek.** If it is still relatively early in the afternoon—after you've explored the **Kali River Rapids** and the **Maharajah Jungle Trek**—you can catch **Flights of Wonder.**

If not, go back to the Safari Village to tour the **Tree of Life** and watch "**It's Tough to Be a Bug.**" Take a breather and buy a snack from a cart vendor, while you enjoy some of the street performers or African storytellers. If you have children, head over to **Camp Minnie-Mickey** after lunch to greet some characters, and catch a showing of the **Lion King show.** After that, head to **Dinoland** to play in the

| **Fun Fact** |

Many of Animal Kingdom's restaurants have tables tucked back into the landscape away from the restaurant itself. If you don't find a table, keep walking—there may be additional seating further down the path.

Boneyard and, if the kids are tall enough, ride **Countdown to Extinction.** Adults will want to skip Camp Minnie-Mickey and go straight to Dinoland, and then catch the last Lion King show.

A nice way to end the day is with a leisurely stroll through the animal habitats in The Oasis, where you can also shop for souvenirs. **Disney Outfitters,** across from the **Tree of Life** before you enter **The Oasis,** has a nice selection of Animal Kingdom keepsakes and Disney paraphernalia with an African theme, such as frames in the classic Mickey Mouse silhouettes adorned with zebra stripes or leopard spots. While that store is geared toward adults, **Creature Comforts** has a great selection of merchandise for children. (**Creature Comforts** is next to Pizza-fari, near the entrance to **"It's Tough to Be a Bug."**) If you are having dinner at the Rainforest Cafe, save time to explore The Oasis while you wait for your table to be ready.

SERVICES & FACILITIES IN THE PARKS

ATMs   Money machines are available near the entrances to all parks and usually one other place inside the park. These machines honor cards from banks using the Cirrus, Honor, and Plus systems, and they are marked on the park guide map.

Baby Care   All parks have a Baby Care Center equipped with rocking chairs and selling basic supplies such as disposable diapers. Disposable diapers are also available at Guest Services. All women's rest rooms, and some men's rest rooms, are equipped with changing tables.

Cameras & Film   Film and Kodak disposable cameras are sold at various locations in all parks. Camcorders are available for rent in Epcot and MGM but not in the Magic Kingdom or Animal Kingdom.

First Aid   All parks have manned first-aid stations near the entrances.

Lost Children   Every park has a designated spot for lost children and also keeps written records of those children. In the Magic Kingdom, it's usually City Hall or the Baby Care Center; in Epcot, the Earth Center or the Baby Care Center; in Disney–MGM Studios, Guest Services; in Animal Kingdom, the Safari Village. Children under 7 should wear name tags.

Package Pickup   Clerks at nearly all WDW stores can arrange for large packages to be taken to the front of the park. Allow at least 3 hours for delivery.

Pets   Don't leave your pet in a parked car, even with a window cracked open. The interior of a car becomes incredibly hot baking in the Florida sun. (A dead pet will not enhance your trip.) Only service animals are permitted in the parks, but there are five kennels in the WDW complex. Those at the Transportation and Ticket Center in the Magic Kingdom and near the entrance to Fort Wilderness board animals overnight. Day accommodations are offered at kennels just outside the Entrance Plaza at Epcot and at the entrances to Disney–MGM Studios and Animal Kingdom. For more information on kennels, see "Fast Facts" in chapter 4.

Stroller Rental   Strollers are available for rent near the entrances of all the parks. The cost is $6. Deposits, usually $1 or $2, may vary.

Wheelchair Rental   Both electric and regular wheelchairs are available at all the parks. A regular wheelchair costs about $6. Electric wheelchairs rent for $32 to $35. The deposit, usually only a few dollars, may vary.

FOR TRAVELERS WITH SPECIAL NEEDS

WDW does everything possible to facilitate guests with disabilities. Its many services are detailed in the *Guidebook for Guests with Disabilities.* To obtain a copy prior to your visit, write **Guest Letters,** P.O. Box 10040, Lake Buena Vista, FL 32830-0040, or call ☎ **407/824-4321.** Also call that number for answers to any questions regarding special needs. Some examples of Disney services: Almost all Disney resorts have rooms for those with disabilities; there are Braille directories inside the Magic Kingdom—in front of the Main Street train station and in a gazebo in front of the Crystal Palace restaurant; there are special parking lots at all three parks; complimentary guided-tour audiocassette tapes and recorders are available at Guest Services to assist visually impaired guests; personal translator units are available to amplify the audio at selected Epcot attractions (inquire at Earth Station); and wheelchairs can be rented at all of the Disney parks. For information about Telecommunications Devices for the Deaf (TDDs), call ☎ **407/827-5141.**

3 The Magic Kingdom

Centered around Cinderella's Castle—its Gothic spires are Walt Disney World's most recognizable symbol, after Mickey Mouse—the Magic Kingdom occupies about 100 acres, with numerous attractions, restaurants, and shops in **seven theme sections,** or **"Lands."**

ARRIVING   From the parking lot, you have to take a short monorail or ferry ride to the Magic Kingdom entrance. During peak attendance times, arrive at the Magic Kingdom no later than an hour before opening time to avoid long lines at these conveyances. Sections of the parking lot are named for Disney characters (Goofy, Pluto, Minnie, and so on), and aisles are numbered. Be sure to write down where you parked.

Upon entering the park, consult your *Magic Kingdom Guidemap* to get your bearings. It details every shop, restaurant, and attraction in every Land. Also consult your **entertainment schedule** to see what's on for the day. There are parades, musical extravaganzas featuring Disney characters, fireworks, band concerts, barbershop quartets, Disney-character appearances, and more.

If you have questions, all park employees are very knowledgeable, and City Hall, on your left as you enter, is both an information center and, along with Toontown Fair, a likely place to meet up with costumed characters.

HOURS   Generally 9am to 7pm with extended hours—sometimes as late as midnight—during major holidays and the summer months.

TICKETS & PRICES $44 for adults, $36 for children, children under 4 are free. See "Tickets" earlier in this chapter for information on 4- and 5-day passes.

SERVICES & FACILITIES IN THE MAGIC KINGDOM

ATMs   These machines honor cards from banks using the Cirrus, Honor, and Plus systems and are located at the main entrance, the SunTrust Bank on Main Street, and in Tomorrowland.

Baby Care   Located next to the Crystal Palace at the end of Main Street, the Baby Care Center is furnished with rocking chairs and toddler-size toilets. Disposable diapers, formula, baby food, and pacifiers are for sale. There are changing tables here as well as in all women's rest rooms and some men's rest rooms. Disposable diapers are also sold at Guest Services.

Cameras & Film   Film and Kodak's disposable Fun Saver cameras are available throughout the park. Although once available, 35mm cameras and camcorders are no longer for rent at the Magic Kingdom.

First Aid   The First Aid Center, staffed by registered nurses, is located alongside the Crystal Palace.

Lockers   Lockers can be found in an arcade underneath the Main Street Railroad Station. The cost is $6, including a $2 refundable deposit.

Lost Children   Lost children in the Magic Kingdom are usually taken to City Hall or the Baby Care Center where lost children logbooks are kept. Children under 7 should wear name tags.

Package Pickup   Any large package you purchase can be sent by the shop clerk to Guest Relations in the Entrance Plaza. Allow 3 hours for delivery.

Pet Care   The Transportation and Ticket Center at Magic Kingdom boards animals overnight. There are also four other kennels in the WDW complex. (See "Pets" above.)

Strollers   These can be rented at the Stroller Shop near the entrance to the Magic Kingdom. The cost is $6 a day, including a $1 deposit.

Wheelchair Rental   For wheelchairs, go to the gift shop to the left of the ticket booths at the Transportation and Ticket Center, or to the Stroller and Wheelchair Shop inside the main entrance to your right. Cost is $6 regular and $32 electric, including a $2 deposit.

FROMMER'S RATES THE RIDES

Because there is so much to do, here's a guide to help you decide quickly which options might be best for you. You'll notice most of the grades are *As, Bs,* and *Cs.* All that research and development Disney park designers put into their job hasn't gone to waste. There are few options that rate a *D* for Dud. Here's what the Frommer's ratings mean:

A+ =   Your trip wouldn't be complete without it.
A   =   Put at the top of "to do" list.
B+ =   Make a real effort to see or do.
B   =   Fun but not a "must see."
C+ =   A nice diversion; see if you have time.
C   =   Go if lines are short.
D   =   Dud. Don't waste your time.

MAIN STREET, U.S.A.

Designed to replicate an archetypal turn-of-the-century American street (okay, so it culminates in a 13th-century European castle), this is the gateway to the Kingdom. Don't dawdle on Main Street when you enter the park; leave it for the end of the day when you're heading back to your hotel.

Main Street Cinema

Frommer's Rating: B
Recommended Ages: all ages

A mannequin is in charge of the ticket booth here, so you can sneak right in without paying. Just kidding—there's no charge for admission. Main Street Cinema, which underwent a renovation in 1998, is an air-conditioned hexagonal

The Magic Kingdom

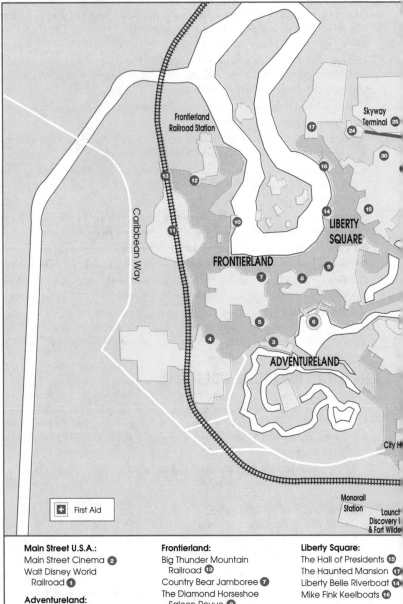

Main Street U.S.A.:
Main Street Cinema ②
Walt Disney World
   Railroad ①

Adventureland:
Jungle Cruise ③
Pirates of the
   Caribbean ④
Swiss Family Treehouse ⑥
Enchanted Tiki Room ⑤

Frontierland:
Big Thunder Mountain
   Railroad ⑬
Country Bear Jamboree ⑦
The Diamond Horseshoe
   Saloon Revue ⑨
Frontierland Shootin'
   Arcade ⑧
Splash Mountain ⑪
Tom Sawyer Island ⑩
Walt Disney World
   Railroad ⑫

Liberty Square:
The Hall of Presidents ⑮
The Haunted Mansion ⑰
Liberty Belle Riverboat ⑭
Mike Fink Keelboats ⑯

Fantasyland:
Ariel's Grotto ㉖
Castle Forecourt Stage ⑱
Cinderella's Castle ⑲
Cinderella's Golden
   Carousel ⑳

142

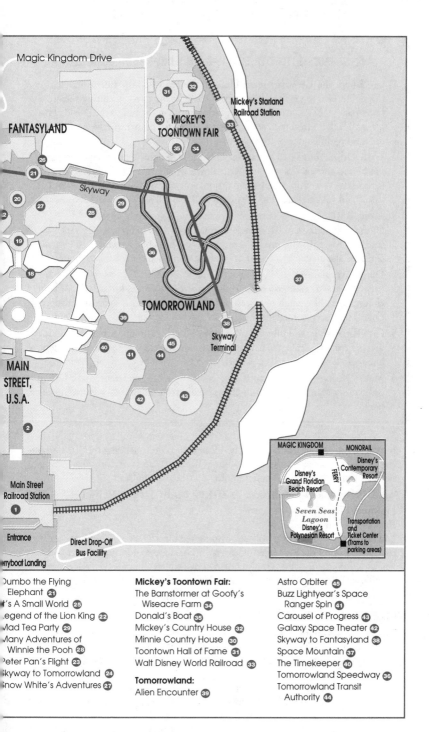

Magic Kingdom Drive

FANTASYLAND

Mickey's Starland
Railroad Station

**MICKEY'S
TOONTOWN FAIR**

Skyway

TOMORROWLAND

Skyway
Terminal

**MAIN
STREET,
U.S.A.**

Main Street
Railroad Station

Entrance

Direct Drop-Off
Bus Facility

Ferryboat Landing

MAGIC KINGDOM · MONORAIL

Disney's
Grand Floridian
Beach Resort

Disney's
Contemporary
Resort

FERRY

*Seven Seas
Lagoon*
Disney's
Polynesian Resort

Transportation
and
Ticket Center
(Trams to
parking areas)

Dumbo the Flying
Elephant 21
It's A Small World 25
Legend of the Lion King 22
Mad Tea Party 29
Many Adventures of
Winnie the Pooh 28
Peter Pan's Flight 23
Skyway to Tomorrowland 24
Snow White's Adventures 27

Mickey's Toontown Fair:
The Barnstormer at Goofy's
Wiseacre Farm 34
Donald's Boat 35
Mickey's Country House 32
Minnie Country House 30
Toontown Hall of Fame 31
Walt Disney World Railroad 33

Tomorrowland:
Alien Encounter 39

Astro Orbiter 45
Buzz Lightyear's Space
Ranger Spin 41
Carousel of Progress 43
Galaxy Space Theater 42
Skyway to Fantasyland 38
Space Mountain 37
The Timekeeper 40
Tomorrowland Speedway 36
Tomorrowland Transit
Authority 44

143

A Dozen Tips So You'll Have Fewer Headaches

1. **Go Where the Crowds Aren't:** Head to the left when the rush is moving to the right. Save the major attractions for late in the day—or during the afternoon parade. Eat a little earlier or a little later than the rest of the crowd. That means 11:30am for lunch and around 5:30pm for dinner. A few minutes can make a big difference in the restaurant line.

2. **Write Down Your Car's Location:** That purple minivan in the next space may not be there when you get out. Write down where your car is, or do what ever is necessary to commit the location to memory. This is especially important at Epcot and MGM where lots are not as well marked as in the Magic Kingdom.

3. **Avoid Rush Hour:** I-4 is woefully over capacity, so avoid traveling the roads during rush hour, from 8 to 9am and from about 4:30 to 6pm. This is especially true if you are driving toward the downtown area. But remember, the theme parks are also staffed by thousands of office workers keeping bankers' hours.

4. **Don't Overplan:** Face it, you aren't going to be able to do everything in any park. Agree as a group to a list of three "must-do" activities for each day. If your children are old enough to be responsible, split and reunite at an agreed-upon time. I have seen some families keep in touch by walkie talkie or cell phone.

5. **Pace Yourself:** It's not unusual to see people literally running across the parking lot to the trams. Relax, the park isn't going anywhere. Once inside, stagger long lines with air-conditioned shows or even breaks on a bench in the shade.

6. **Make Dining Reservations:** If a sit-down dinner is important, make sure to get priority-seating reservations either before your visit or when you enter the park.

theater where vintage black-and-white Disney cartoons (including the 1928 *Steamboat Willie,* in which Mickey and Minnie debuted) are aired continually on two screens. You have to watch these standing up; there are no seats.

Walt Disney World Railroad & Other Main Street Vehicles
Frommer's Rating: C+
Recommended Ages: 2–8
You can board an authentic 1928 steam-powered train here for a 15-minute journey clockwise around the perimeter of the park. There are stations in Frontierland and Mickey's Toontown. There are also horse-drawn trolleys, horseless carriages, jitneys, omnibuses, and fire engines plying the short route along Main Street from Town Square to Cinderella's Castle.

SHOPPING ON MAIN STREET
The vast **Disneyana Collectibles** carries limited-edition movie cels, antique Disney clocks and porcelain figures, and collectible dolls and items such as a 1947 Donald Duck cookie jar that today is worth $2,000! Why did I ever let Mom throw out my old toys?

The Emporium, in Town Square, houses the park's largest selection of Disneyana, everything from Mickey-logo golf balls to Dumbo cookie jars. Note the Animatronic window displays.

Basically an old-fashioned candy store, the **Market House** also has an interesting line of pipes and tobaccos, as well as Disney-theme kitchenware—Mickey cupcake papers, ice-cube molds, and cookie cutters.

7. **Set a Spending Limit:** Kids should know they have a set amount to spend on take-home trinkets. So should Mom and Dad. Set a budget, building in a small contingency fund for emergencies.

8. **Take a Break:** If you are staying at a WDW property, spend the late afternoon napping or unwinding. Return to parks for a few more attractions and the closing shows.

9. **Dress Comfortably:** This may seem like a no-brainer, but judging by the limping, blistered crowds, some people don't understand that they will be walking—a lot. This is not the place to break in those way-cool clogs. Comfortable walking shoes are a must.

10. **Sunscreen, Sunscreen, Sunscreen:** Locals spot tourists by their painful bright-red glow. The Florida sun can bake you, even in the shade and even in the cooler months. A bad first-day burn can ruin your whole trip. Protect yourself and your kids. Bring hats for toddlers and infants, even if they will spend most of their time in a stroller. Also, drink plenty of water in the summer to avoid dehydration. This is especially important for children.

11. **Travel Light:** Don't carry large amounts of cash. The Pirates of the Caribbean aren't the only thieves in WDW. There are ATM machines in all the parks if you start to run short of cash.

12. **Get a Little Goofy:** Relax, put on those Mickey Mouse ears, eat that extra piece of fudge, even sing along at the shows. Don't worry about what the staff thinks; they've seen just about everything. And everyone else is on vacation, too.

Over at the **Harmony Barber Shop,** where nostalgic men's grooming items are sold (mustache wax, spice colognes, shaving mugs), a barbershop quartet called The Dapper Dans performs on the hour all day (except at 3pm).

Autographed sports memorabilia and team clothing—Joe Namath–signed footballs, Pittsburgh Steeler T-shirts, Bulls jerseys, a Babe Ruth–autographed 1936 World Series program, and the like—are available at the **Main Street Athletic Club.**

At **Crystal Arts,** you can watch craftspeople create the intricate animals, cut-glass vases and bowls, and other glittering items sold here. And at the adjoining **Shadow Box,** silhouette artists create cut-out portraits of customers on black paper.

At the end of Main Street, the **Main Street Gallery,** inside Cinderella's Castle, is cluttered with family crests, tapestries, suits of armor, and other medieval wares, as well as miniature carousels. An artisan demonstrates damascening, a form of metal engraving that originated in Damascus circa A.D. 600.

ADVENTURELAND

Cross a bridge to your left and stroll into an exotic jungle of lush tropical foliage, thatch-roofed huts, and carved totems. Amid dense vines and stands of palm and bamboo, drums are beating, and swashbuckling adventures are taking place.

Note: If you're heading toward Adventureland or Frontierland first thing in the morning, wait for the gates to open at the bridge in front of the Crystal Palace, to your left as you enter.

> ### ❷ Did You Know?
>
> - The movie portion of Universal Studios' Back to the Future attraction took 2 years to make and was the most expensive film per minute ever made.
> - Mickey Mouse has more than 80 different outfits, ranging from a scuba suit to a tuxedo. Minnie has only 50.
> - There are enough Mickey Mouse–ear hats sold each year to cover the head of every man, woman, and child in Pittsburgh.
> - In real life, the shaking on the Earthquake ride at Universal Studios Escape would equal 8.3 on the Richter scale.
> - Shamu, the killer whale at Sea World, eats more than 65,000 pounds of fish a year.
> - Every day, an average of 100 pairs of sunglasses are turned in to the Lost and Found at the Magic Kingdom.
> - Since Walt Disney World opened in 1971, the total miles logged by the monorail trains is equal to more than 24 trips to the moon.
> - The volume of air rushing through Twister . . . Ride It Out in one minute is enough to fill more than four full-sized blimps.
> - Both Disneyland and Walt Disney World were built on former citrus groves in counties named Orange.

Jungle Cruise
Frommer's Rating: B+
Recommended Ages: 4–14

What a cruise! In the course of about 10 minutes, your boat sails through an African veldt in the Congo, an Amazon rain forest, the Mekong River in Southeast Asia, and along the Nile. Amidst the lavish scenery, with ropes of hanging vines, cascading waterfalls, and lush tropical and subtropical foliage (most of it real), are dozens of audio-animatronic birds and animals—elephants, zebras, lions, giraffes, crocodiles, tigers, even fluttering butterflies. On the shore, you'll pass a Raiders-like Cambodian temple cave fronted by a Buddha and guarded by snakes, a rhino and jackal chasing terrified African beaters up a tree, and a jungle camp taken over by apes. But the adventures aren't all on shore. Passengers are menaced by everything from water-spouting elephants to fierce warriors who attack with spears. The guide keeps up an amusing patter.

Pirates of the Caribbean
Frommer's Rating: B+
Recommended Ages: 6–adult

Although the Disneyland version of this ride has been adapted to be more politically correct, the pirates still chase the wenches in Florida. You'll proceed through a long grottolike passageway to board a boat into a pitch-black cave. Therein, elaborate scenery and hundreds of audio-animatronic figures (including lifelike dogs, cats, chickens, pigs, and donkeys) depict a rambunctious pirate raid on a Caribbean town. To a background of cheerful "yo-ho-yo-ho" music, the sound of rushing waterfalls, squawking seagulls, and screams of terror, passengers pass through the line of fire in a raging pirate battle and view tableaux of fierce-looking pirates swigging rum, looting, and plundering. This might be scary for kids under 5.

Swiss Family Treehouse
Frommer's Rating: C+
Recommended Ages: 4–12

This attraction, based on the 1960 Disney movie version of Johann Wyss's *Swiss Family Robinson,* was renovated in 1998. But die-hard fans needn't worry. It is still basically still the grown-up sized tree house in the sprawling banyan tree. Visitors traverse a rope-suspended bridge and ascend the 50-foot tree for a close-up look into the rooms. The "tree" itself, designed by Disney "Imagineers," has 330,000 polyethylene leaves sprouting from a 90-foot span of branches; although it isn't real, it is draped with actual Spanish moss. *Note:* People with limited mobility should be aware that this attraction does involve a bit of climbing.

Enchanted Tiki Room
Frommer's Rating: C+
Recommended Ages: 2–10

Formerly the Tropical Serenade, this attraction was given new hosts and a new hipper attitude. New characters include Iago, of Lion King fame. It is still housed in a large hexagonal Polynesian-style dwelling, with a thatched roof, bamboo beams, and tapa-bark murals, and is home to 250 tropical birds, chanting totem poles, and singing flowers who whistle, tweet, and warble. Younger children are most likely to appreciate this attraction.

SHOPPING IN ADVENTURELAND

The exotic **Traders of Timbuktu** carries carved wooden and soapstone animals, masks, and cowhide drums from Kenya, among other ethnic wares.

Plaza del Sol Caribe, a Mexican mercado, has piñatas, baskets, straw hats, stuffed and papier-mâché toucans and parrots, and much more.

For the Indiana Jones look, check out the clothing and accessories at **Elephant Tales.** The little **Tiki Tropic Shop** carries surfer-theme merchandise.

Shell mobiles and hangings, plus a wide selection of straw hats, are sold at the **Zanzibar Shell Shop. Island Supply,** a Disney version of The Nature Company, offers nature-theme books, posters, toys, bird feeders, and more.

And both the **House of Treasure** and the adjoining **Lafitte's Portrait Deck** retail pirate merchandise: hats, Captain Hook T-shirts, ships in bottles, and toy muskets and daggers; the latter has a pirate ship photo setup.

FRONTIERLAND

From Adventureland, step into the wild and woolly past of the American frontier, where Disney employees (they're called "cast members") are clad in denim and calico, sidewalks are wooden, rough-and-tumble architecture runs to log cabins and rustic saloons, and the landscape is Southwestern scrubby with mesquite, saguaro cactus, yucca, and prickly pear. Across the river is Tom Sawyer Island, reachable via log rafts.

Big Thunder Mountain Railroad
Frommer's Rating: A
Recommended Ages: 10–adult

This mining disaster–theme roller coaster—its thrills arising from hairpin turns and descents in the dark, rather than sudden steep drops—is situated in a 200-foot-high red-stone mountain with 2,780 feet of track winding through windswept canyons and bat-filled caves. You enter the ride via the ramshackle headquarters of the Big Thunder Mining Company and board a runaway train that careens through the ribs of a dinosaur, under a thundering waterfall, past spewing geysers and bubbling mud pots, and over a bottomless volcanic pool. Audio-animatronic characters (such as the long john–clad fellow navigating the floodwaters in a bathtub) and animals (goats, chickens, donkeys, possums) enhance the scenic backdrop, along with several-hundred-thousand dollars' worth of authentic antique mining equipment. Riding after dark adds to the thrill. *Note:* You must be 40 inches tall to ride.

Country Bear Jamboree
Frommer's Rating: A (A+ for kids)
Recommended Ages: 4–adult

I've always loved the Country Bear Jamboree, a 15-minute show featuring a troupe of fiddlin', banjo strummin', harmonica playin' audio-animatronic bears belting out rollicking country tunes and crooning plaintive love songs. The chubby Trixie, decked out in a satiny skirt, laments lost love as she sings "Tears Will Be the Chaser for Your Wine." Teddi Barra descends from the ceiling in a swing to perform "Heart We Did All That We Could." Other star performers include a country-western group called the Five Bear Rugs, Liver Lips McGrowl, and the 7-foot-tall master of ceremonies, Henry. In the rousing show finale, the entire cast joins in a foot-stompin' sing-along. Wisecracking commentary comes from a mounted buffalo, moose, and deer on the wall. A special holiday show plays throughout the Christmas season each year.

Diamond Horseshoe Saloon Revue & Medicine Show
Frommer's Rating: B+
Recommended Ages: 6–adult

Sit yourself down in air-conditioned comfort and enjoy a rousing western revue at Dr. Bill U. Later's turn-of-the-century saloon. Marshall John Charles sings and banters with the audience, Jingles the Piano Man plays honky-tonk tunes, there's a magic act, and Miss Lucille L'Amour and her troupe of dance-hall girls do a spirited cancan—all with lots of humor and audience participation. There are seven shows daily; plan on going around lunchtime, so you can eat during the show. The menu features deli or peanut-butter-and-jelly sandwiches served with chips.

Frontierland Shootin' Arcade
Frommer's Rating: C+
Recommended Ages: 8–adult

Combining state-of-the-art electronics with a traditional shooting-gallery format, this vast arcade presents an array of 97 targets (slow-moving ore cars, buzzards, and gravediggers) in a three-dimensional 1850s gold-mining town scenario. Fog creeps across the graveyard, and the setting changes as a calm, starlit night turns stormy with flashes of lightning and claps of thunder. Coyotes howl, bridges creak, and skeletal arms reach out from the grave. If you hit a tombstone, it might spin around and mysteriously change its epitaph. To keep the western ambiance authentic, new-fangled electronic firing mechanisms loaded with infrared bullets are concealed in

> ### Touring Tip
>
> For an extra $10, Disney resort guests holding multiday passports can purchase tickets for the **Magic Kingdom E-Ride Nights,** held several times each month. A selection of attractions—including Splash Mountain and Big Thunder Mountain Railroad—remains open for 3 hours after official closing time. You'll never see shorter lines, and you can ride as many times as you want.

genuine Hawkins 54-caliber buffalo rifles. When you hit a target, elaborate sound and motion gags are set off. Fifty cents buys you 25 shots.

Splash Mountain

Frommer's Rating: A+

Recommended Ages: 10–adult

Based on Walt Disney's 1946 film, *Song of the South,* Splash Mountain takes you on an enchanting journey in a hollowed-out log craft along the canals of a flooded mountain, past 26 brilliantly colored tableaux of backwoods swamps, bayous, spooky caves, and waterfalls. Riders are caught up in the bumbling schemes of Brer Fox and Brer Bear as they pursue the ever-wily Brer Rabbit, who, against the advice of Mr. Bluebird, has left his briar-patch home in search of adventure and the "laughing place." The music from the film forms a delightful audio backdrop. Your log craft twists, turns, and splashes—sometimes plummeting in total darkness—all leading up to a thrilling five-story, 45°-angle splashdown from mountain top to briar-filled pond at 40 miles per hour! And that's not the end. The ride continues, and finally it's a Zip-A-Dee-Doo-Dah kind of day. *Note:* You must be 40 inches tall to ride.

Tom Sawyer Island

Frommer's Rating: C for adults, B+ for antsy children who need a break from lines.

Recommended Ages: 4–14

Board Huck Finn's raft for a 1-minute float across the river to the densely forested Tom Sawyer Island, where kids can explore the narrow passages of Injun Joe's cave (complete with scary sound effects, like whistling wind), a walk-through windmill, a serpentine abandoned mine, or Fort Sam Clemens, where an audio-animatronic drunk is snoring-off a bender. Maintaining one's balance while crossing rickety swing and barrel bridges is part of the fun. Narrow, winding dirt paths lined with oaks, pines, and sycamores create an authentic backwoods island atmosphere. It's easy to get briefly lost and stumble upon some unexpected adventure. You can combine this attraction with lunch at Aunt Polly's restaurant, which serves light fare (fried chicken, sandwiches, and the like), and has outdoor tables on a porch overlooking the river. Adults can rest weary feet over coffee, while the kids explore the island.

SHOPPING IN FRONTIERLAND

Mosey into the **Frontier Trading Post** for western-look leather items, cowboy boots and hats, western shirts, coonskin caps, turquoise jewelry, belts, and toy rifles. **Prairie Outpost & Supply** sells Native American items such as drums, headdresses, and bows and arrows, many of them related to Pocahontas.

Visit the **Briar Patch,** under Splash Mountain, for Uncle Remus and Winnie the Pooh merchandise.

LIBERTY SQUARE

Serving as a transitional area between Frontierland and Fantasyland, Liberty Square evokes 18th-century America with Federal and Georgian architecture, Colonial

Williamsburg–type shops, and neat flower beds bordering manicured lawns. Thirteen lanterns, symbolizing the colonies, are suspended from the Liberty Tree, an immense live oak. You might encounter a fife and drum corps marching along Liberty Square's cobblestone streets. The Liberty Tree Tavern here (details in chapter 6) is my favorite Magic Kingdom restaurant.

Boat Rides

Frommer's Rating: C
Recommended Ages: 6–adult

A steam-powered sternwheeler called the *Liberty Belle* and two Mike Fink Keelboats (the *Bertha Mae* and the *Gullywhumper*) depart (the latter, summers and holidays only) from Liberty Square for scenic cruises along the Rivers of America. The passing landscape evokes the Wild West. Both ply the same route and make a restful interlude for foot-weary parkgoers.

Hall of Presidents

Frommer's Rating: B
Recommended Ages: 10–adult

In this red brick colonial hall with a giant bell suspended in its tower, all American presidents—from George Washington to Bill Clinton (whose actual voice was recorded for this attraction)—are represented by incredibly lifelike audio-animatronic figures; if you look closely enough, you will see them fidget and whisper during the performance. The show begins with a film, projected on a 180°, 70mm screen, about the importance of the Constitution. The curtain then rises on the 42 assembled American leaders, and, as each is spotlighted, he nods or waves with presidential dignity. Lincoln then rises and speaks, occasionally even referring to his notes. In a stunning example of Disney thoroughness, painstaking research was done in creating the figures and scenery, with each president's costume reflecting not only period fashion, but period fabrics and tailoring techniques! Poet and author Maya Angelou narrates.

Haunted Mansion

Frommer's Rating: A+
Recommended Ages: 6–adult

What better way to exhibit Disney special-effects wizardry than a haunted mansion? Macabre attendants harry groups of visitors past a graveyard (make sure to glance at the epitaphs), turning them over to a ghost host who encloses them in a windowless, doorless portrait gallery (are those eyes following you around?) where the floor seems to descend. Its ambiance enhanced by inky darkness, spooky music, eerie howling, and mysterious screams and rappings, this mansion is replete with bizarre scenes and objects: a ghostly banquet and ball, a graveyard band, a suit of armor that comes alive, cobweb-covered chandeliers, luminous spiders, a talking head in a crystal ball, weird flying objects, and much more. At the end of the ride, a ghost joins you in your car. The experience is more amusing than terrifying, so you can take small children inside.

SHOPPING IN LIBERTY SQUARE

The Yankee Trader is a charming country store, its shelves stocked with Lion King and Winnie the Pooh cookie jars, Mickey cookie cutters, and fancy food items.

Over at **Heritage House,** you can purchase parchment copies of famous American documents as well as actual historic framed letters (one signed by President Andrew Johnson in 1864 was priced at $2,350). Old campaign buttons, Civil War

> **Behind the Scenes** ────────────────────────────
>
> Ever wonder why you never catch a glimpse of, say, Mickey relaxing with his head off, or Pluto taking a cigarette break? The people inside the characters at Disney have a very strict code of conduct: Absolutely no talking, and Minnie Mouse must always sign her name in cursive. But, beyond that, the characters and their keepers, along with all the Disney "cast," travel around the park through an intricate system of underground tunnels that are strictly off-limits to the public.

hats, and presidential signatures are here, too. A craftsperson on the premises makes jewelry cut from coins.

FANTASYLAND

The attractions in this happy land—themed after Disney film classics such as *Snow White, Peter Pan,* and *Dumbo*—are especially popular with young visitors. If your kids are 8 and under, you may want to make it (and Mickey's Toontown; details later in this section) your first stop in the Magic Kingdom.

Cinderella's Castle
Frommer's Rating: A
Recommended Ages: 2–10
There's not a lot to see here, but its status as the Magic Kingdom icon makes it a must-see. At the end of Main Street, in the center of the park, you'll come to a fairyland castle, 185 feet high and housing a restaurant (Cinderella's Royal Table) and shops. Mosaic murals inside depict the Cinderella story, and Disney family coats of arms are displayed over a fireplace. Cinderella herself, dressed for the ball, often makes appearances in the lobby area. You'll be able to see shows on the Castle Forecourt Stage.

Cinderella's Golden Carousel
Frommer's Rating: B+
Recommended Ages: all ages
It's a beauty, built by Italian wood-carvers in the Victorian tradition in 1917 and refurbished by Disney artists who added 18 hand-painted scenes from the Cinderella story on the wooden canopy above the horses. The carousel organ plays Disney classics such as "When You Wish Upon a Star."

Dumbo, the Flying Elephant
Frommer's Rating: A for parents with kids, B for others
Recommended Ages: 2–10
This is a very tame kiddie ride in which the cars—large-eared baby elephants (Dumbos)—go around and around in a circle gently rising and dipping. But it's very exciting for wee ones.

It's a Small World
Frommer's Rating: A
Recommended Ages: 2–14
It rates an A because—love it or hate it—it's something that you have to do. You know the song—and if you don't, you will. It plays continually as you sail "around the world" through vast rooms designed to represent different countries. They're inhabited by appropriately costumed audio-animatronic dolls and animals—all singing "It's a small world after all . . ." in tiny, doll-like voices. This cast of

thousands includes Chinese acrobats, Russian kazatski dancers, Indian snake charmers in front of the Taj Mahal, French cancan dancers . . . you get the picture. It's nauseatingly cute, but it just wouldn't be a visit to Disney without it.

Legend of the Lion King
Frommer's Rating: A+
Recommended Ages: 4–12
This stage spectacular based on Disney's blockbuster motion-picture musical combines animation, movie footage, sophisticated puppetry, and high-tech special effects. The show is enhanced by the Academy Award–winning music of Elton John and Tim Rice, and among the actors providing voices are Whoopi Goldberg and Cheech Marin as laughing hyenas.

Mad Tea Party
Frommer's Rating: C
Recommended Ages: 4–16
This is a traditional amusement park ride à la Disney, with an Alice in Wonderland theme. Riders sit in oversized pastel-hued teacups on saucers that careen around a circular platform while tilting and spinning. In the center of the platform is a big teapot, out from which pops a woozy mouse. Believe it or not, this can be a pretty wild ride—or a tame one. It depends on how much you spin, a factor under your control via a wheel in the cup.

The Many Adventures of Winnie the Pooh
Frommer's Rating: B
Recommended Ages: all ages
This replaces Mr. Toad's Wild Ride, which actually drew a small cadre of protesters to witness its demise. This ride, which is similar in concept to Pirate's of the Caribbean, features the cute-and-cuddly fellow—whose resurgence in popularity can be credited to Disney—along with all his pals, Eyeore, Piglet, and the others. You ride through a storybook version of the Hundred Acre Woods in your Honey Pot, keeping an eye out for the Heffalumps and Woozles. To take advantage of Pooh's best-selling status, second only to Mickey, the ride empties into a gift shop.

Peter Pan's Flight
Frommer's Rating: B+ for kids, C+ for others
Recommended Ages: 4–10
Riding in airborne versions of Captain Hook's ship, passengers careen through dark passages while experiencing the story of Peter Pan. The adventure begins in the Darlings' nursery and includes a flight over nighttime London to Never-Never Land, where riders encounter mermaids, Indians, a ticking crocodile, the lost boys, Princess Tiger Lilly, Tinker Bell, Hook, Smee, and the rest—all to the movie music "You Can Fly, You Can Fly, You Can Fly." It's fun.

In the Words of Walt Disney

Fantasy, if it's really convincing, can't become dated, for the simple reason that it represents a flight into a dimension that lies beyond the reach of time . . . nothing corrodes or gets run down. . . . And nobody gets any older.

We have never lost our faith in family entertainment—stories that make people laugh, stories about warm and human things, stories about historic characters and events, and stories about animals.

Skyway
Frommer's Rating: A
Recommended Ages: all ages

This is another one of the experiences that is signature Disney, so it rates a high mark. Its entrance close to Peter Pan's Flight, the Skyway is an aerial tramway to Tomorrowland that makes continuous trips throughout the day. A good chance to let those tired feet rest and catch one of the rare Florida breezes. If you are afraid of heights though, this is one attraction you may want to skip.

Snow White's Scary Adventures
Frommer's Rating: B
Recommended Ages: 4–14

Finally, Disney has changed this ride to actually include Snow White and eliminate the way-too-scary-for-kids encounter with the wicked witch.

This attraction once focused only on the more sinister elements of Grimm's fairy tale—most notably the evil queen and the cackling, toothless witch—leaving small children screaming in terror. It's been toned down now, with Snow White appearing in a number of pleasant scenes—at the castle-courtyard wishing well, in the dwarfs' cottage, and riding off with the prince to live "happily ever after." There are new audio-animatronic dwarfs, and the interior colors have also been brightened up and made less menacing. Even so, this could be scary for kids under 7.

SHOPPING IN FANTASYLAND

It's always the holiday season at Sir **Mickey's,** supply central for a variety of Disney-motif trinkets.

Little girls will adore **Tinker Bell's Treasures,** its wares comprising Peter Pan merchandise, costumes (Tinker Bell, Snow White, Cinderella, Pocahontas, and others), and collector dolls.

MICKEY'S TOONTOWN FAIR

Head off those cries of "Where's Mickey?" by taking the kids to the 2-acre replacement for Mickey's Starland that was unveiled during the 25th Anniversary celebration in 1996. Toontown Fair offers kids a chance to meet their favorite Disney characters including Mickey, Minnie, Donald Duck, and Goofy. Set in a whimsical collection of candy-striped tents harking back to those turn-of-the-century county fairs, highlights include the **Toontown Hall of Fame,** animated shorts hosted by the stars, **Donald's Boat,** and both **Mickey's and Minnie's country houses.** Kids, whose height would keep them off most of Disney's thrill rides, can board **Goofy's Barnstormer,** a kid-sized roller coaster. Everything is brightly colored and kid-friendly in the best Disney tradition. It's fun for all ages, but the under-10 set will enjoy it most. Toontown Fair has its own stop on the WDW Railroad.

TOMORROWLAND

This land focuses on the future—most notably, space travel and exploration. In 1994, the Disney people decided that Tomorrowland (originally designed in the 1970s) was beginning to look like "Yesteryear." (Although something looking suspiciously like some of the old polyester ride uniforms can be found hanging in The Gap.)

It's now been revamped to reflect the future as a galactic, science fiction–inspired community inhabited by humans, aliens, and robots. A vast state-of-the-art video-game arcade has also been added.

Alien Encounter
Frommer's Rating: A+
Recommended Ages: 10–adult
Director George Lucas, of *Star Wars* fame, contributed his space-age vision to this major Tomorrowland attraction. The action begins at the Interplanetary Convention Center where a mysterious corporation called X-S Tech—a company from a distant planet—is marketing a "teletransporter" to Earthlings. The device is capable of beaming living beings between planets light-years apart. After a slick corporate presentation, S.I.R., a rather sinister robot, demonstrates the product on Skippy, a cute and fuzzy alien, though not with total success. Skippy ends up discombobulated and with singed fur! Despite this dubious beginning, X-S technicians try to teleport their sinister corporation head, Chairman Clench, to Earth. But the machine malfunctions, sending Clench instead to a distant planet and, inadvertently, teleporting a fearsome extraterrestrial to Earth. Dark and truly scary, it is not your typical thrill ride. It's no fantasy that your heart is racing as you work your way through lots of high-tech effects—from the alien's breath on your neck to a mist of alien slime. *Note:* You must be 48 inches tall to ride. Too intense for younger children.

Astro Orbiter
Frommer's Rating: C
Recommended Ages: 8 and under
This is a tame, typical amusement-park ride. The "rockets" are on arms attached to "the center of the galaxy," and they move up and down while orbiting spinning planets. The line here tends to move slowly, so unless it's short, you may want to skip this one.

Buzz Lightyear's Space Ranger Spin
Frommer's Rating: B
Recommended Ages: 5 and up
Join Buzz Lightyear as he tries to save the universe. It is cool to pilot your own cruiser with a joy stick through a world you will recognize from the movie *Toy Story.* The kids enjoy using the laser cannons as you spin through a world filled with gigantic toys. If you are a good shot, you can set off sight and sound gags with these light sabers. A display in the car keeps the shooters' score so that means multiple cars for the family if you have more than one child. This is one of the newer additions to Tomorrowland, and one of the few that is truly interactive.

Skyway
Frommer's Rating: A
Recommended Ages: all ages
Located near the Tomorrowland entrance just west of Space Mountain, this aerial tramway to Fantasyland makes continuous round-trips throughout the day.

Space Mountain
Frommer's Rating: A+
Recommended Ages: 10–adult
Space Mountain entertains visitors on its long lines with space-age music and exhibits, as meteorites, shooting stars, and space debris whiz about overhead. These "illusioneering" effects, enhanced by appropriate audio, continue during the ride itself, which is a cosmic roller coaster in the inky, starlit blackness of outer space. Your rocket climbs high into the universe before racing through a serpentine complex of aerial galaxies, making thrilling hairpin turns and rapid plunges. (Though it

---

Touring Tip

Many of the attractions at Walt Disney World offer a Ride-Share program for parents traveling with small children. One parent can ride an attraction while the other stays with the kids, and then the adults can switch places without having to stand in line again. Notify a cast member if you wish to participate when you get in line. Many of the other Orlando theme parks offer this program as well.

---

feels as if you're going at breakneck speed, your car actually never goes faster than 28 miles per hour.) Nab the front seat of the train for the best ride. Now that Alien Encounters has come on line, the queues to Space Mountain, which accommodates 3,000 people an hour, are usually relatively short. *Note:* You must be 40 inches tall to ride.

The Timekeeper
Frommer's Rating: C+
Recommended Ages: 10–adult
This Jules Verne/H. G. Wells–inspired multimedia presentation combines Circle-Vision and IMAX footage with audio-animatronics. It's hosted by Timekeeper, a mad-scientist robot and his assistant, 9-EYE, a flying female camera-headed droid and time machine test pilot. In an unpredictable jet-speed escapade, the audience hears Mozart as a young prodigy playing his music to French royalty, visits medieval battlefields in Scotland, watches Leonardo at work, and floats in a hot-air balloon above Moscow's Red Square. Can you pick out the famous voices of Jeremy Irons, Robin Williams, and Rhea Perlman?

Tomorrowland Speedway
Frommer's Rating: A+ for kids, C for single adults
Recommended Ages: 6–16
This is a great thrill for kids (including teens still waiting to get their driver's licenses) who get to put the pedal to the metal, steer, and vroom down a speedway in an actual gas-powered sports car. Maximum speed on the 4-minute drive around the track is about 7 miles per hour, and kids have to be 52 inches tall to drive alone. Adults will find the ride's choppy steering irksome, and not worth the long wait time.

Tomorrowland Transit Authority
Frommer's Rating: C
Recommended Ages: all ages
A futuristic means of transportation, these small five-car trains have no engines. They work by electromagnets, emit no pollution, and use little power. Narrated by a computer guide named Horack I, TTA offers an overhead look at Tomorrowland, including a pretty good preview of Space Mountain. If you're in the Magic Kingdom for only 1 day, skip this.

Walt Disney's Carousel of Progress
Frommer's Rating: D
Recommended Ages: all ages
Apologies to all the fans of this ride, but this 22-minute show takes up too much time and space, for its limited "wow factor." A revolving theater features an audio-animatronic family in various tableaux demonstrating a century of development (beginning in 1900) in electric gadgetry and contraptions from Victrolas to virtual reality.

SHOPPING IN TOMORROWLAND

Mickey's Star Traders, a large Disneyana shop is your best bet.

PARADES, FIREWORKS & MORE

You'll get an **Entertainment Show Schedule** when you enter the park, which lists all kinds of special goings-on for the day. These include concerts (everything from steel drums to barbershop quartets), encounters with Disney characters, holiday events, and the three major happenings listed next.

During the fireworks and the parades, there are designated viewing spots roped off for those with disabilities and their parties. Consult your park map or a park employee at least an hour before the parade. Like all space along the parade route, the spaces for those with disabilities also fill up quickly.

Fireworks

Frommer's Rating: A+

Recommended Ages: all ages

It's the Fourth of July every night with Fantasy in the Sky Fireworks, probably the most explosive display you have ever seen. Pyrotechnics is a Disney art. Although the water-walking creatures in the Sea World closing show are certainly worth seeing, this is clearly the best way to end your day. It is preceded by Tinker Bell's magical flight from Cinderella's Castle, and takes place nightly in summer, on selected nights during Christmas and Easter vacation times, and during other special celebrations. Consult your *Entertainment Show Schedule* for details. Suggested viewing areas are Liberty Square, Frontierland, and Mickey's Toontown Fair. Many of the Disney hotels close to the park also offer excellent views.

Disney's Magical Moments

Frommer's Rating: C+

Recommended Ages: all ages

With only six major floats, all showcasing Disney movies, your interest in this parade depends on how much time you are willing to take away from seeing attractions. The parade, which includes dozens of dancers and extras, is entertaining. But, with everyone else distracted and camped out on the curb, this is a great chance to hit some of the most crowded rides. If you have the patience for only one parade, see the Main Street Electrical Parade. Disney's Magical Moments is held at 3pm year-round, beginning on Main Street and meandering through Liberty Square and Frontierland. The route is outlined in your *Entertainment Show Schedule.*

The only problem: Even in slow seasons, you have to snag a seat along the curb a good half hour before the parade begins—earlier during peak travel times. That's a long time to sit on a hard curb. You might want to consider bringing along an inflatable pillow. And remember, stay off the grass, or the Disney lawn police will shoo you away from what you thought was a prime viewing spot.

✪ Main Street Electrical Parade

Frommer's Rating: A+

Recommended Ages: all ages

This old Disney favorite, which ran for 20 years from 1971 until 1991, has been brought back. This parade includes the same floats and costumes once used at Disneyland. (The old Disney World show, Spectromagic, has been shipped to Disneyland Paris.) The Electrical Parade features a half million lights on floats depicting characters and scenes from Disney movies, such as Cinderella. If you can see only one parade, see this one. Once again, very early arrival is essential to get a seat on the curb. Consult your *Entertainment Show Schedule* for details.

WHERE TO FIND CHARACTERS

Mickey's Toontown Fair was designed as a place where kids can meet and mingle with their favorite characters all day. This is a sure thing, and it doesn't hurt that it's air-conditioned. Mickey, Minnie, Goofy, and Donald Duck are stars in residence. In **Fantasyland** up to eight Disney characters, including Chip 'n' Dale, are available for autographs in a covered area across from The Many Adventures of Winnie the Pooh. Ariel from *The Little Mermaid* can be found in Ariel's Grotto.

4 Epcot

Although details on all the festivities have yet to be announced—those Disney folks can be *very* tight lipped—Epcot will host the **Walt Disney World Millenium Celebration** from October 1, 1999 to January 1, 2001 as Walt & Co. ring in the new century. More than 35 nations will participate in the festivities, and events will include fireworks, cultural exhibits and new technology exhibits, so ask if there is anything planned when you make your reservations. Or, if you have access to a computer with an Internet connection, go online to **www.disneyworld.com** about a month before you visit to see what is in the works.

This is the place that Disney really celebrates the future. In 1982, Disney opened Epcot (Experimental Prototype Community of Tomorrow) as its second major theme park. Its aims are described in a dedication plaque: "May Epcot entertain, inform and inspire. And, above all . . . instill a new sense of belief and pride in man's ability to shape a world that offers hope to people everywhere." Ever growing and changing, Epcot today occupies 260 acres so stunningly landscaped, they are worth visiting for botanical beauty alone—so stop and smell the roses. There are two major sections, Future World and World Showcase.

Epcot is huge, and walking around it can be exhausting (some people say its acronym stands for "Every Person Comes Out Tired"). Depending on how long you intend to linger at each of the countries in the World Showcase, it can still be enjoyed in one day. One good way to conserve your energy is by taking launches across the lagoon from the edge of Future World to Germany or Morocco. There are also double-decker buses circling the World Showcase Promenade and making stops at Norway, Italy, France, and Canada.

Unlike the Magic Kingdom, Epcot's parking lot is right at the gate. Sections of the parking lot are named for Epcot themes (Harvest, Energy, and so on), and aisles are numbered. You can either catch the tram or walk on up.

Stop by the Guest Relations lobby to the left of Spaceship Earth to pick up an *Epcot Guidemap* and entertainment schedule, and, if you so desire (and haven't already done so by calling ☎ **407/WDW-DINE** [939-3463]), make reservations for lunch or dinner at the WorldKey terminals just outside the lobby. (Many Epcot restaurants are described in chapter 6.) Then check out your show schedule and incorporate the shows you want to see into your itinerary.

HOURS   Generally 9am to 9pm with extended hours—sometimes as late as midnight—during major holidays and the summer months.

TICKET PRICES $44 for adults, $36 for children, free for children under 4. See "Tickets," earlier in this chapter, for 4- and 5-day passes.

SERVICES & FACILITIES IN EPCOT

ATMs   These machines accept cards issued by banks using the Cirrus, Honor, and Plus systems and are located at the front of the park, in Germany, and on the bridge between World Showcase and Future World.

Top 10 Orlando-Area Attractions for Grown-Ups

1. **Innoventions**   Epcot, generally, is more geared to adults than the other Disney parks, but this display of future technologies is especially intriguing, providing a cogent preview of life in the 21st century.

2. **Sea World**   With its lush landscaping and laid-back pace, Sea World is a nice change from the go-go world of the other attractions. Mixing education with entertainment and lots of hands-on animal interaction, this is one of Orlando's most adult attractions, although kids love it, too.

3. **World Showcase Pavilions**   Experience a 'round-the-world journey visiting 11 nations in microcosm—with authentically reproduced architectural highlights, restaurants, shops, and cultural performances.

4. **Universal Studios Florida**   Okay, I'm an adult, but sometimes this really is a great place to play. The thrill rides can't be beat, the shows are fast-paced and funny, and now even the Terminator is back.

5. **Islands of Adventure**   Comic book fans and anyone who knows about *Green Eggs and Ham,* will love the Marvel comics and Dr. Seuss–themed areas. Plus the thrill rides offer some serious scares.

6. **Cypress Gardens**   Stroll 200 acres of gorgeous botanical gardens—roses, bougainvillea, crape myrtle, and magnolias—amid ponds, lagoons, waterfalls, Italian fountains, and manicured lawns.

7. **Kennedy Space Center**   Acquaint yourself with the history, present state, and future of America's space program. The kids will like this, too.

8. **A Day in Winter Park**   This charming town has a recently expanded museum filled with masterpieces by Louis Comfort Tiffany and other noted 19th-century artists, great upscale shopping, and fine restaurants. Stay overnight at the Langford, and arrange a day of beauty at its multifacility spa. Stroll through the shops on Park Avenue and lunch at one of the sidewalk bistros.

9. **A Resort Vacation**   Top-of-the-line accommodations, fine restaurants, magnificent grounds, golf, tennis, swimming, first-rate health clubs, and other elements of a plush resort vacation are available at the Hyatt Regency Grand Cypress, Marriott's Orlando World Center, the Peabody Orlando, and Disney's Grand Floridian.

10. **A Night on the Town**   Visit an Orlando restaurant and enjoy a night on the town, a carriage ride through downtown Orlando, a few hours at a club, or at Church Street Station. This is the other Orlando, the one for grown-ups.

Baby Care   Epcot's Baby Care Center is located near the Odyssey Restaurant in Future World. It is furnished with rocking chairs, and disposable diapers, formula, baby food, and pacifiers are for sale. There are also changing tables in all women's rest rooms, as well as in some of the men's rest rooms. Disposable diapers are available at Guest Services.

Cameras & Film   Kodak's disposable Fun Saver cameras are available throughout the park. Video camcorders are available for rent from the Kodak Camera Center at the Entrance Plaza. You can also rent from the Lagoon's Edge World Traveler, at the end of the promenade between Future World and the World Showcase, and at Cameras and Film at Journey into Imagination. Cost for camcorder rental is $25, plus a $300 deposit.

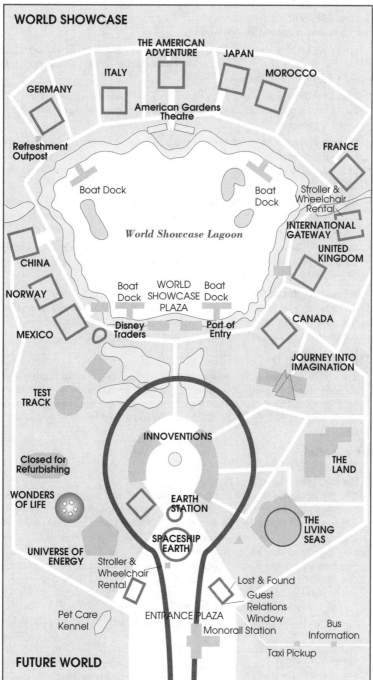

WORLD SHOWCASE

THE AMERICAN ADVENTURE

JAPAN

MOROCCO

ITALY

GERMANY

American Gardens Theatre

Refreshment Outpost

FRANCE

Boat Dock

Boat Dock

Stroller & Wheelchair Rental

INTERNATIONAL GATEWAY

World Showcase Lagoon

UNITED KINGDOM

CHINA

NORWAY

Boat Dock

WORLD SHOWCASE PLAZA

Boat Dock

CANADA

MEXICO

Disney Traders

Port of Entry

JOURNEY INTO IMAGINATION

TEST TRACK

INNOVENTIONS

THE LAND

Closed for Refurbishing

WONDERS OF LIFE

EARTH STATION

THE LIVING SEAS

SPACESHIP EARTH

UNIVERSE OF ENERGY

Stroller & Wheelchair Rental

Lost & Found

Guest Relations Window

Pet Care Kennel

ENTRANCE PLAZA

Monorail Station

Bus Information

Taxi Pickup

FUTURE WORLD

First Aid   The First Aid Center, staffed by registered nurses, is located near the Odyssey Restaurant in Future World.

Lockers   Lockers can be found to the west of Spaceship Earth, outside the Entrance Plaza, and in the Bus Information Center by the bus parking lot. The cost is $3 a day, plus a $2 deposit.

Lost Children   Lost children in Epcot are usually taken to Earth Center or the Baby Care Center where lost children logbooks are kept. Children under 7 should wear name tags.

Package Pickup   Any large package you purchase can be sent by the shop clerk to Guest Relations in the Entrance Plaza. Allow 3 hours for delivery. There is also a package pickup location at the International Gateway entrance in the World Showcase.

Pet Care   Day accommodations are offered at kennels just outside the Entrance Plaza at Epcot for $6. Proof of vaccination is required. There are also four other kennels in the WDW complex. (See "Fast Facts" in chapter 4 for more details.)

Strollers   These can be rented from special stands on the east side of the Entrance Plaza and at World Showcase's International Gateway. The cost is $6, including a $1 refundable deposit.

Wheelchair Rental   Rent wheelchairs inside the Entrance Plaza to your left, to the right of ticket booths at the Gift Shop, and at World Showcase's International Gateway. The cost for regular chairs is $6, including a $1 refundable deposit. Electric chairs cost $32 a day, including a $2 refundable deposit.

FUTURE WORLD

The northern section of Epcot (where you enter the park) comprises Future World, centered on a giant geosphere known as Spaceship Earth. Future World's 10 theme areas, sponsored by major corporations, focus on discovery, scientific achievements, and tomorrow's technologies in areas running the gamut from energy to undersea exploration.

Innoventions

Frommer's Rating: A

Recommended Ages: 8–adult

The pair of crescent-shaped buildings to your right and left just beyond Spaceship Earth house a constantly evolving 100,000-square-foot exhibit that showcases cutting-edge technologies and future products. Leading manufacturers sponsor ever-changing exhibit areas here. Visitors get a chance to preview virtual reality, electric cars, experience interactive television, and try out more than 200 new computer programs and games. Kids will be thrilled to preview new Sega video games. It is a chance to feel, hear, and see the future, hands-on.

The virtual-reality offerings—from swimming with the sharks at the Vivid Group pod or a walking tour of St. Peter's Basilica by ENEL—are the latest high-tech wonders and a chance to experience what you have been reading about in science magazines.

There are several show areas: You can be interviewed by Jay Leno on TV, or let Sky Cyberguy take you on a tour of the future of wireless communication. At the Honeywell's Home Automation at the House of Innoventions Tour, visit the computer-controlled abode of the future. The computer literate will find this a fascinating place to play. The technologically challenged will find it less rewarding.

Behind the Scenes: Special Tours in Walt Disney World

In addition to the greenhouse tour in Epcot's Land pavilion, the Disney parks offer a number of walking tours and learning programs. The times, descriptions, and prices are subject to change. These represent the most recent information available at press time. It is best to call ahead to make reservations.

- **Family Magic Tour** explores the nooks and crannies of the Magic Kingdom in the form of a 2-hour scavenger hunt. You meet and greet characters at the end. Children 3–9, $15; adults, $25. You must also buy admission tickets to the park and you must book in advance. Call ☎ **407/939-8687** for information.

  The following tours are for those 16 and older.

- The 2-hour **Hidden Treasures of World Showcase** and the 5-hour Hidden Treasures of World Showcase both explore the architectural and entertainment offerings of Epcot. The 5-hour tour on Wednesday is only $85 and includes lunch. Park admission is not required if you don't intend to stay in the park after the tour. The 2-hour tour Tuesdays, Wednesdays, and Saturdays is $49 per person, and park admission is required. Call ☎ **407/939-8687** for information.

- **Gardens of the World,** a 3-hour tour of the extraordinary landscaping at Epcot led by a Disney horticulturist ($49 per person (adults only); ☎ **407/ 939-8687** for information).

- The 4-hour **Keys to the Kingdom** provides an orientation to the Magic Kingdom and a glimpse into the high-tech operational systems behind the magic ($45 per person; ☎ **407/WDW-TOUR** [939-8687]).

  There are also learning programs on subjects ranging from animation to international cultures. For details, call ☎ **407/363-6000.**

The two-story **Discovery Center,** located on the right side of Innoventions, includes an information resource area where guests can get answers to all their questions about Epcot attractions, in particular, and Walt Disney World, in general. For instance, if after visiting The Land, you would like to learn more about hydroponics, they can print out an information sheet on it. The Discovery Center also houses a shop called Field Trips, featuring educational products and software.

Journey Into Imagination
Frommer's Rating: B
Recommended Ages: 6–adult

In this terrific pavilion, even the fountains are magical, with arching streams of water that leap into the air like glass rods. The pavilion has been closed for most of 1999 and is scheduled to reopen in 2000, after adding more high-tech gadgets, and sprucing some of the old favorites. At press time, the new rides were supposed to be associated with the *Honey I Shrunk the Audience* film (see below).

Honey I Shrunk the Audience is a 3-D attraction based on the Disney hit *Honey I Shrunk the Kids* film. The audience, after being menaced by hundreds of mice and a 3-D cat, is shrunk and given a good shaking by a gigantic 5-year-old. Dramatic 3-D action is enhanced by vibrating seats and creepy tactile effects. Finally, everyone returns to proper size—everyone but the family dog, which creates the final, not altogether pleasant, special effect (I won't reveal it).

Note: This attraction will remain open while the rest of Journey Into Imagination is closed for renovation.

The Land
Frommer's Rating: B
Recommended Ages: 8–adult
This largest of Future World's pavilions highlights humankind's relation to food and nature.

Living with the Land is a 13-minute boat ride through three ecological environments (a rain forest, an African desert, and the windswept American plains), each populated by appropriate audio-animatronic denizens. New farming methods and experiments—ranging from hydroponics to plants growing in simulated Martian soil!—are showcased in real gardens. If you'd like a more serious overview, take a 45-minute guided walking tour of the growing areas, offered daily. Sign up at the Green Thumb Emporium shop near the entrance to Food Rocks. The cost is $5 for adults, $3 for children 3 to 9, free for children 2 and under. It's not, by the way, really geared to children.

Circle of Life combines spectacular live-action footage with animation in a 15-minute, 70mm motion picture based on *The Lion King*. In this cautionary environmental tale, Timon and Pumbaa are building a monument to the good life called Hakuna Matata Lakeside Village, but their project, as Simba points out, is damaging the savanna for other animals. The message: Everything is connected in the great circle of life. Recommended age group: 6 to 16.

In **Food Rocks,** audio-animatronic mock rock performers deliver an entertaining message about nutrition. Neil Moussaka sings "Don't Take My Squash Away from Me," the Refrigerator Police perform "Every Bite You Take," and the Peach Boys harmonize a rendition of "Good Vibrations" ("Good, good, good, good nutrition . . ."), while Excess, a trio of disheveled, obnoxious hard rockers, counters by extolling the virtues of junk food. Rapper Tone Loc (as Füd Wrapper, the show's host), Chubby Checker, Neil Sedaka, Little Richard, and the Pointer Sisters perform the actual voice-over parodies of their music. Recommended age group: 6 to 14.

The Living Seas
Frommer's Rating: B
Recommended Ages: 12–adult
This United Technologies–sponsored pavilion contains the world's sixth "ocean," a 5.7-million-gallon saltwater aquarium (including a complete coral reef) inhabited by more than 4,000 sea creatures—sharks, barracudas, parrot fish, rays, and dolphins among them. While waiting in line, visitors pass exhibits tracing the history of undersea exploration, including a glass diving barrel used by Alexander the Great in 332 B.C. and Sir Edmund Halley's first diving bell (1697).

A 2½-minute multimedia preshow about today's ocean technology is followed by a 7-minute film demonstrating the formation of the earth and seas as a means to support life.

After the films, visitors enter hydrators for a rapid "descent" to the sunlit ocean floor. Upon arrival, they board Seacabs that wind around a 400-foot-long tunnel to enjoy stunning close-up views (through acrylic windows) of ocean denizens in a natural coral-reef habitat. The ride concludes in the Seabase Concourse, which is the visitor center of **Seabase Alpha,** a prototype ocean-research facility of the future. Here exhibits include a 22½-foot scuba tube used by Seabase Alpha scientists to enter and leave the waters. And seven informational modules contain

---

Touring Tip

Try **Behind the Seeds,** A Special Guided Greenhouse Tour to discover amazing things about plants, hydroponics and biotechnology, and fish farming during this 1-hour walking tour of The Land's greenhouses and labs. Sign up at the podium near the Green Thumb Emporium on the lower level of The Land. $6 adults, $4 children (ages 3 to 9).

---

numerous exhibits focusing on ocean ecosystems, harvestable resources grown in controlled undersea environments, marine mammals (dolphins, sea lions, manatees), earth systems (the relationship between the planet's seas and its land masses), the study of oceanography from space, undersea exploration (featuring an audio-animatronic deep-sea submersible robot), and life in a coral-reef community. Many of these exhibits are hands-on. You can step into a diver's JIM Suit and use controls to complete diving tasks and expand your knowledge of oceanography via interactive computers. *Note:* A program called Epcot DiveQuest, enables certified divers to participate in a program that includes a 30- to 40-minute scuba dive in the Living Seas aquarium; for details, call ☎ **407/WDW-TOUR** (937-8687).

Spaceship Earth
Frommer's Rating: B
Recommended Ages: all ages

This massive, silvery geosphere symbolizes Epcot, so it is a must-do. But long lines can be avoided by saving it until later in the day when you can, more than likely, simply walk on in. The show/ride takes visitors on a 15-minute journey through the history of communications. You board time-machine vehicles to the distant past, where an audio-animatronic Cro-Magnon shaman recounts the story of a hunt while others record it on cave walls. You advance thousands of years to ancient Egypt, where hieroglyphics adorn temple walls and writing is recorded on papyrus scrolls. You'll progress through the Phoenician and Greek alphabets, and the Gutenberg printing press and the Renaissance (trying not to notice that several of these guys look an awful lot like Barbie's dream date Ken). Technologies develop at a rapid pace, through the telegraph, telephone, radio, movies, and TV. It's but a short step to the age of electronic communications. You are catapulted into outer space to see "spaceship earth" from a new perspective, returning for a finale that places the audience amid interactive global networks. High-tech special effects, animated sets, and laser beams create an exciting experience.

At the end of this journey through time, AT&T invites guests to sample an interactive computer-video wonderland that includes a motion-simulator ride through the company's electronic network. This exhibit complements Innoventions, detailed earlier.

Test Track
Frommer's Rating: A
Recommended Ages: 8–adult

Called a mix of General Motors engineering and Disney imagineering, the newest Epcot attraction puts guests in the driver's seat to experience the rigors of automobile testing. During a preshow—essentially a GM commercial—guests will learn how the company works to promote automotive safety, reliability, and performance. Then they'll board full-scale, six-passenger test cars and travel upon what appears to be an actual roadway, accelerating on long straight-aways, hugging hairpin turns, climbing steep hills, and braking abruptly—often on less-than-perfect road conditions. The ride culminates in a terrifying high-speed outdoor run along the track's steeply banked "speed loop," which extends far beyond the pavilion facility. Cars top out at a speed of 65 miles per hour. This was formerly World of Motion.

Universe of Energy
Frommer's Rating: B
Recommended Ages: 8–adult

Sponsored by Exxon, this pavilion—its roof glistening with solar panels—aims to better our understanding of America's energy problems and potential solutions via a 32-minute ride-through attraction. Recently refurbished, it's called **Ellen's Energy Adventure** and features comedian and television sitcom star Ellen DeGeneres as an energy expert tutored by Bill Nye the Science Guy to be a "Jeopardy" contestant. On a massive screen in Theater I, an animated motion picture depicts the Earth's molten beginnings, its cooling process, and the formation of fossil fuels. You move from Theater I to travel back 275 million years into an eerie, storm-wracked landscape of the Mesozoic Era, a time of violent geological activity. Here, you're menaced by giant audio-animatronic dragonflies, pterodactyls, dinosaurs, earthquakes, and streams of molten lava before entering a steam-filled tunnel deep through the bowels of the volcano, finally emerging back in the 20th century in Theater II. In this new setting, which looks like a NASA Mission Control room, a 70mm film projected on a massive 210-foot wraparound screen depicts the challenges of the world's increasing energy demands and the emerging technologies that will help meet them. Your moving seats now return to Theater I, where swirling special effects herald a film about how energy impacts our lives. It ends on a dramatically upbeat note—with a vision of an energy-abundant future, and Ellen as a new "Jeopardy" champion.

Wonders of Life
Frommer's Rating: B
Recommended Ages: 8–adult

Housed in a vast geodesic dome fronted by a 75-foot replica of a DNA strand, this pavilion offers some of Future World's most engaging shows and attractions.

The *Making of Me,* starring Martin Short, is a captivating 15-minute motion picture combining live action with animation and spectacular inutero photography to create the sweetest introduction imaginable to the facts of life. Don't miss it, although the presentation may prompt some questions from young children (recommended for ages 10 and up). Short travels back in time to witness his parents as children, their meeting at a college dance, their wedding, and their decision to have a baby. Along with him, we view his development inside his mother's womb and witness his birth.

You're miniaturized to the size of a single cell for a medical rescue mission inside the immune system of a human body during **Body Wars.** Your objective: to save a miniaturized immunologist who has been accidentally swept into the bloodstream. This motion-simulator ride takes you on a wild journey through gale-force winds (in the lungs) and pounding heart chambers (recommended for ages 6 and up). Although you know they are part of the Disney show, if you've ever seen the movie *Outbreak,* it is a little eerie passing through dermatopic purification stations in order to undergo miniaturization. Leonard Nimoy directed.

In the hilarious, multimedia **Cranium Command,** Buzzy, an audio-animatronic brain-pilot-in-training, is charged with the seemingly impossible task of controlling the brain of a typical 12-year-old boy. The boy's body parts are played by Charles

Grodin, Jon Lovitz, Bob Goldthwait, Kevin Nealon and Dana Carvey (as Hans and Franz), and George Wendt. It's another must-see attraction (recommended for ages 8 and up). The audience is seated inside Bobby's head as Buzzy guides him through a day of typical preadolescent traumas—running for the school bus, meeting a girl, fighting bullies, and a run-in with the school principal.

There are large areas filled with fitness-related shows, exhibits, and participatory activities, including a film called *Goofy About Health,* and **Coach's Corner,** where your tennis, golf, or baseball swing is analyzed by experts, and the **Sensory Funhouse** where you can test your perceptions. Grown-ups and kids will enjoy playing here, in air-conditioned comfort. Try working out on a video-enhanced exercise bike, get a computer-generated evaluation of your health habits, and take a video voyage to investigate the effects of drugs on your heart. There's much, much more. You could easily spend hours here.

WORLD SHOWCASE

Surrounding a 40-acre lagoon at the park's southern end is World Showcase—a permanent community of 11 miniaturized nations, all with authentically indigenous landmark architecture, landscaping, background music, restaurants, and shops. The cultural facets of each nation are explored in art exhibits, dance performances, and innovative rides, films, and attractions. And all of the employees in each pavilion are natives of the country represented.

All pavilions offer some kind of live entertainment throughout the day. Schedules are usually posted near the entrance to that particular "country."

The American Adventure

Frommer's Rating: B+

Recommended Ages: 10–adult

Housed in a vast, Georgian-style structure, **The American Adventure** is a 29-minute dramatization of U.S. history, utilizing a 72-foot rear-projection screen, rousing music, and a large cast of lifelike audio-animatronic figures, including narrators Mark Twain and Ben Franklin. The "adventure" begins with the voyage of the *Mayflower* and encompasses major historic events. You'll view Jefferson writing the Declaration of Independence, the expansion of the frontier, Matthew Brady photographing a family about to be divided by the Civil War, the stock market crash of 1929, Pearl Harbor, and the *Eagle* heading toward the moon. John Muir and Teddy Roosevelt discuss the need for national parks. Susan B. Anthony speaks out on women's rights; Frederick Douglass, on slavery; Chief Joseph, on the situation of Native Americans. While waiting for the show to begin, you'll be entertained by the wonderful **Voices of Liberty** singers performing American folk songs in the Main Hall. Note the quotes from famous Americans on the walls here.

Formal gardens shaded by live oaks, sycamores, elms, and holly complement the pavilion's 18th-century architecture. A shop called Heritage Manor Gifts sells signed presidential photographs, needlepoint samplers, afghans and quilts, pottery, candles, Davy Crockett hats, books on American history, historically costumed dolls, classic political campaign buttons, and vintage newspapers with banner headlines like "Nixon Resigns!" An artisan at the shop makes jewelry out of coins.

In the Words of Walt Disney

In my view, wholesome pleasure, sport, and recreation are as vital to this nation as productive work and should have a large share in the national budget.

Note: International cultural performances take place here in the **America Gardens Theater.**

Canada

Frommer's Rating: A
Recommended Ages: 8–adult

Our neighbors to the north are represented by diverse architecture ranging from a mansard-roofed replica of Ottawa's 19th-century French-style Château Laurier (here called the Hôtel du Canada) to a British-influenced rustic stone building modeled after a famous landmark near Niagara Falls.

An Indian village—complete with rough-hewn log trading post and 30-foot replicas of Ojibwa totem poles—signifies the culture of the Northwest, while the Canadian wilderness is reflected by a steep mountain (a Canadian Rocky), a waterfall cascading into a whitewater stream, and a "forest" of evergreens, stately cedars, maples, and birch trees. Don't miss the stunning floral displays of azaleas, roses, zinnias, chrysanthemums, petunias, and patches of wildflowers inspired by the Butchart Gardens in Victoria, British Columbia.

The pavilion's highlight attraction is **O Canada!**—a dazzling, 18-minute, 360° CircleVision film that reveals Canada's scenic splendor from sophisticated Montréal to the thundering flight of thousands of snow geese departing an autumn stopover near the St. Lawrence River.

Canada pavilion shops carry sandstone and soapstone carvings, fringed leather vests, duck decoys, moccasins, a vast array of Eskimo stuffed animals and Native American dolls, Native American spirit stones, rabbit-skin caps, heavy knitted sweaters, and, of course, maple syrup.

China

Frommer's Rating: B
Recommended Ages: 10–adult

Bounded by a serpentine wall that snakes around its perimeter, the China pavilion is entered via a vast, triple-arched ceremonial gate inspired by the Temple of Heaven in Beijing, a summer retreat for Chinese emperors. Passing through the gate, you'll see a half-size replica of this ornately embellished red-and-gold circular temple, built in 1420 during the Ming dynasty. Gardens simulate those in Suzhou, with miniature waterfalls, fragrant lotus ponds, groves of bamboo, corkscrew willows, and weeping mulberry trees.

The highlight here is **Wonders of China,** a 20-minute, 360° CircleVision film that explores 6,000 years of dynastic and communist rule and the breathtaking diversity of the Chinese landscape. Narrated by 8th-century Tang dynasty poet Li Bai, it includes scenes of the Great Wall (begun 24 centuries ago!), a performance by the Beijing Opera, the Forbidden City in Beijing, rice terraces of Hunan Province, the Gobi Desert, and tropical rain forests of Hainan Island. Adjacent to the theater, an art gallery houses changing exhibits of Chinese art.

A bustling marketplace—the **Yong Feng Shangdian Shopping Gallery**—offers an array of merchandise including silk robes, lacquer and inlaid mother-of-pearl furniture, jade figures, cloisonné vases, tea sets, silk rugs and embroideries, dolls, fans, wind chimes, and Chinese clothing. Artisans here demonstrate calligraphy.

France

Frommer's Rating: C
Recommended Ages: 8–adult

Focusing on La Belle Epoque—a period from 1870 to 1910 in which French art, literature, and architecture flourished—this pavilion is entered via a replica of the beautiful cast-iron Pont des Arts footbridge over the "Seine." It leads to a park with bleached sycamores, Bradford pear trees, flowering crape myrtle, and sculptured parterre flower gardens inspired by Seurat's painting *A Sunday Afternoon on the Island of La Grande Jatte.* A replica (¹⁄₁₀ the size) of the Eiffel Tower constructed from Gustave Eiffel's original blueprints looms above *les grands boulevards,* and period buildings feature copper mansard roofs and casement windows.

The highlight here is **Impressions de France.** Shown in a palatial (mercifully sit-down) theater à la Fontainebleau, this 18-minute film is a breathtakingly scenic journey through diverse French landscapes projected on a vast, 200°-view wrap-around screen and enhanced by the music of French composers.

Emporia in the covered shopping arcade, with art-nouveau Métro facades at either end, have interiors ranging from a turn-of-the-century bibliothèque to a French chateau. Merchandise includes French art prints and original art, cookbooks, cookware, wines (there's a tasting counter), fancy French foodstuffs, Madeline and Babar books and dolls, perfumes, and original letters of famous Frenchmen ranging from Jean Cocteau to Napoleon. Another marketplace/tourism center revives the defunct Les Halles, where Parisians used to sip onion soup in the wee hours. The heavenly aroma of a *boulangerie* (bakery) penetrates the atmosphere, and mimes, jugglers, and strolling *chanteurs* (singers) entertain.

Germany

Frommer's Rating: B
Recommended Ages: 8–adult

Enclosed by castle walls and towers, this festive pavilion is centered on a cobble-stoned *platz* (square) with pots of colorful flowers girding a fountain statue of St. George and the Dragon. An adjacent clock tower is embellished with whimsical glockenspiel figures that herald each hour with quaint melodies. The pavilion's outdoor **Biergarten**—where it's Oktoberfest all year long—was inspired by medieval Rothenberg. And 16th-century building facades replicate a merchant's hall in the Black Forest and the town hall in Frankfurt's Römerberg Square.

Shops here carry Hummel figurines, crystal, glassware, cookware, cuckoo clocks, cowbells, Alpine hats, German wines (there's a tasting counter) and specialty foods, toys (German Disneyana, teddy bears, dolls, and puppets), and books. An artisan demonstrates molding and painting Hummel figures; another paints detailed scenes on eggs. Background music runs from oom-pah bands to Mozart symphonies.

Model train enthusiasts and children will especially enjoy the exquisitely detailed miniature version of a small Bavarian town—complete with working train station—that lies between Germany and Italy.

Italy

Frommer's Rating: C+
Recommended Ages: 10–adult

One of the prettiest World Showcase pavilions, Italy lures visitors over an arched stone footbridge to a replica of Venice's intricately ornamented pink-and-white Doge's Palace. Other architectural highlights include the 83-foot Campanile (bell tower) of St. Mark's Square, Venetian bridges, and a central piazza enclosing a version of Bernini's Neptune Fountain. A garden wall suggests a backdrop of provincial countryside, and Mediterranean citrus, olive trees, cypress, and pine frame a formal garden. Gondolas are moored on the lagoon.

Shops here carry cameo and filigree jewelry, Armani figurines, kitchenware, Italian wines and foods, Murano and other Venetian glass, alabaster figurines, and inlaid wooden music boxes. A troupe of street actors performs a contemporary version of 16th-century *commedia dell'arte* in the piazza.

Great Things to Buy at Epcot

Sure, *you* want to be educated about the cultures of the world but for most of us the two big attractions at the World Showcase are eating and shopping. Dining options are explained in some detail in chapter 6. This list will give you an idea of some of the more unusual items available for purchase.

The prices listed below do not include tax. Prices and availability may vary. If you'd like to check out the amazing scope of Disney merchandise at home—everything from furniture to bath toys—you can order a catalogue by calling ☎ **800/237-5751.**

- The silver jewelry at the Mexico pavilion is truly beautiful. Choose from something really affordable, such as a hairclip adorned with abalone flowers for $8, or go all out purchasing a kidney-shaped stone and silver bracelet for $145.

- There are lots of great sweaters available in the shops of Norway, but I was really taken by the Scandinavian trolls. So ugly, you have to love them; these trolls range in price from $30 to $68.

- Forget about all those knock-off products stamped "Made in China." The goods here are actually among the more expensive to be found in Epcot. A multicolored jade bracelet here runs about $360. Jade teardrop earrings, about $90.

- Porcelain and cuckoo clocks are the things to look at in Germany. I was taken by the Goebel Collectible Winnie the Pooh, which sells for $150. For the true fan, there is the handcrafted Pooh cuckoo clock that sells for $1,500.

- In Italy look for 100% silk scarves in a variety of patterns for about $48, or silk ties for $35.

- Your funky teenager might like the Taquia Knit Cap, a colorful fez-like chapeau, that's available in Morocco for $8. I also like the celestial-patterned pottery, available in vases and platters, which range from $22 to $50.

- Tennis fans may be interested in the Wimbledon shirts, shorts, and skirts available in the United Kingdom for $50 to $65 per piece. There is also a lovely assortment of rose-patterned tea accessories, ranging from $10 for an 8-inch plate to $120 for a teapot.

Japan

Frommer's Rating: A
Recommended Ages: 8–adult

Heralded by a flaming red *torii* (gate of honor) on the banks of the lagoon and the graceful, blue-roofed Goju No To pagoda (inspired by a shrine built at Nara in A.D. 700), this pavilion focuses on Japan's ancient culture. In a traditional Japanese garden, cedars, yew trees, bamboo, "cloud-pruned" evergreens, willows, and flowering shrubs frame a contemplative setting of pebbled footpaths, rustic bridges, waterfalls, exquisite rock landscaping, and a pond of golden koi. The Yakitori House is based on the renowned 16th-century Katsura Imperial Villa in Kyoto, designed as a royal summer residence and considered by many to be the crowning achievement of Japanese architecture. Exhibits ranging from 18th-century Bunraki puppets to samurai armor take place in the moated **White Heron Castle,** a replica of the Shirasagi-Jo, a 17th-century fortress overlooking the city of Himeji.

And the **Mitsukoshi Department Store** (Japan's answer to Macy's) is housed in a replica of the Shishinden (Hall of Ceremonies) of the Gosho Imperial Palace, built in Kyoto in A.D. 794. It sells lacquerware, kimonos, kites, fans, dolls in traditional costumes, origami books, samurai swords, Japanese Disneyana, bonsai trees, Japanese foods, Netsuke carvings, and pottery—even modern electronics. In the courtyard, artisans demonstrate the ancient arts of *anesaiku* (shaping brown rice candy into dragons, unicorns, and dolphins), *sumi-e* (calligraphy), and origami (paper folding).

Be sure to include a performance of traditional Japanese music and dance at this pavilion in your schedule. It's one of the best shows in the World Showcase.

Mexico
Frommer's Rating: A
Recommended Ages: 8–adult
You'll hear the music of marimbas and mariachi bands as you approach the festive showcase of Mexico, fronted by a towering Mayan pyramid modeled on the Aztec temple of Quetzalcoatl (God of Life) and surrounded by dense Yucatán jungle landscaping. Upon entering the pavilion, you'll find yourself in a museum of pre-Colombian art and artifacts.

Down a ramp is a small lagoon, the setting for **El Rio del Tiempo** (River of Time), where visitors board boats for an 8-minute cruise through Mexico's past and present. Passengers get a close-up look at the Mayan pyramid and the erupting Popocatepetl volcano. Dance performances focusing on the cultures of Mayan, Toltec, Aztec, and colonial Mexico are presented in film segments and by an audio-animatronic cast in vignettes ranging from a Day of the Dead skeleton band to children breaking a piñata. Additional film footage focuses on Mexican tourist spots. The show culminates in a Mexico City fiesta with exploding fiber-optic fireworks. *Note:* At press time, it was likely that this ride would be shut down in 1999 for refurbishing, to reopen at some point in 2000.

Shops in and around the **Plaza de Los Amigos** (a "moonlit" Mexican *mercado* with a tiered fountain and street lamps) display an array of leather goods, baskets, sombreros, piñatas, pottery, embroidered dresses and blouses, maracas, jewelry, serapes, paper flowers, colorful papier-màché birds, and blown-glass objects (an artisan gives demonstrations). La Casa de, sponsored by the Mexican Tourist Office, provides travel information.

Morocco
Frommer's Rating: B+
Recommended Ages: 10–adult
This exotic pavilion—its architecture embellished with intricate geometrically patterned tile work, minarets, hand-painted wood ceilings, and brass lighting fixtures—is heralded by a replica of the Koutoubia Minaret, the prayer tower of a 12th-century mosque in Marrakesh. Note the imperfections in each mosaic tile; they were put there on purpose in accordance with the Muslim belief that only Allah is perfect.

The **Medina** (old city), entered via a replica of an arched gateway in Fez, leads to Fez House (a traditional Moroccan home) and the narrow, winding streets of the *souk,* a bustling marketplace where all manner of authentic handcrafted merchandise is on display. Here you can peruse or purchase pottery, brassware, hand-knotted Berber carpets, colorful Rabat carpets, ornate silver and camel-bone boxes, straw baskets, and prayer rugs. There are weaving demonstrations in the souk throughout the day. The Medina's rectangular courtyard centers on a replica of the ornately tiled Najjarine Fountain in Fez, the setting for musical entertainment.

The pavilion's **Royal Gallery** contains an ever-changing exhibit of Moroccan art, and the Center of Tourism offers a continuous three-screen slide show. Morocco's landscaping includes a formal garden, citrus and olive trees, date palms, and banana plants.

Norway

Frommer's Rating: B

Recommended Ages: 10–adult

Centered on a picturesque cobblestone courtyard, this pavilion evokes ancient Norway. A *stavekirke* (stave church), styled after the 13th-century Gol Church of Hallingdal, its eaves embellished with wooden dragon heads, houses changing exhibits. A replica of Oslo's 14th-century **Akershus Castle,** next to a cascading woodland waterfall, is the setting for the pavilion's featured restaurant. Other buildings simulate the red-roofed cottages of Bergen and the timber-sided farm buildings of the Nordic woodlands.

There's a two-part attraction here. **Maelstrom,** a boat ride in a dragon-headed Viking vessel, traverses Norway's fjords and mythical forests to the music of Peer Gynt—an exciting journey during which you'll be menaced by polar bears prowling the shore, and trolls who cast a spell on the boat. The watercraft crashes through a narrow gorge and spins into the North Sea, where a violent storm is in progress. But the storm abates, and passengers disembark safely to a 10th-century Viking village to view the 70mm film *Norway,* which documents a thousand years of history. Featured images include *Oseberg bat* (a 1,000-year-old Viking ship), a small fishing village, festive national-holiday celebrations in Oslo, and soaring jumps at the Holmenkollen ski resort.

Shops feature hand-knit wool hats and sweaters, toys (there's a Lego table where kids can play while you shop), wood carvings, Scandinavian foods, pewterware, and jewelry.

United Kingdom

Frommer's Rating: C+

Recommended Ages: 10–adult

Centered on **Britannia Square**—a formal London-style park, complete with copper-roofed gazebo bandstand, a ubiquitous red phone booth, and a statue of the Bard—the U.K. pavilion evokes Merry Olde England. Four centuries of architecture are represented along quaint cobblestoned streets; troubadours and minstrels entertain in front of a traditional British pub; and a formal garden with low box hedges in geometric patterns, flagstone paths, and a stone fountain replicates the landscaping of 16th- and 17th-century palaces.

Don't miss the **Old Globe Players** who present delightfully wacky performances of Shakespeare in the square. There is a lot of audience participation, and you may be tapped to try your hand at Hamlet.

High Street and Tudor Lane shops display a broad sampling of British merchandise—toy soldiers, Paddington bears, personalized coats of arms, tobaccos and pipes, Scottish clothing (cashmere and Shetland sweaters, golfwear, tams, knits, and tartans), fine English china, Waterford crystal, and pub items (tankards, dartboards, and the like). A tea shop occupies a replica of Anne Hathaway's thatch-roofed 16th-century cottage in Stratford-upon-Avon. Other emporia represent the Georgian, Victorian, Queen Anne, and Tudor periods. Background music ranges from "Greensleeves" to the Beatles.

Illuminations 2000: Reflections of Earth

Recommended Ages: 3–adult

Disney will introduce a new nighttime spectacular in honor of their Millenium Celebration in October 1999. Like its predecessor, Illuminations 2000 will feature a grandiose display of pyrotechnics, lasers, and fountains. A new score was composed specifically for the production, which will also feature the world's first spherical video display system. The show will focus on the future of the planet and humanity's progress. If it's as good as the previous production, it's a should-not-be-missed event. Find a seat around the lagoon about a half-hour before show time.

Tapestry of Nations
Recommended Ages: 3–adult
This new pageant/parade will be trotted out for Disney's Millenium Celebration in October 1999. Presented twice daily, the street festival will march past the World Showcase pavilions to the tune of an original score. More than 120 giant-sized puppets—designed by the same man who created the puppets for Disney's Broadway production of the "Lion King"—will join 16 gigantic percussion units, in a colorful salute to the nations of the world.

OTHER SHOWS

Live shows, especially those in World Showcase, make up an important part of the Epcot experience. Among others, these might include Chinese lion dancers and acrobats, German oom-pah bands, Caledonian bagpipers, Mexican mariachi bands, Moroccan storytellers and belly dancers, Italian "living statues" and stilt walkers, colonial fife and drum groups, and much more. Two especially good shows are the Voices of Liberty singers at the American Adventure pavilion and the traditional music and dance displays in Japan. Check your show schedule when you come in and plan your day to include some of them.

SHOPPING AT EPCOT

The most fascinating shops are found in World Showcase pavilions, which comprise an international bazaar selling everything from Berber rugs to Japanese kimonos. Noshing and shopping are the best reasons to walk around the World Showcase. You'll find descriptions of merchandise available in these pavilions in the World Showcase listings.

5 Disney–MGM Studios

Disney–MGM Studios offers exciting movie- and TV-themed shows and behind-the-scenes "reel-life" adventures. You'll see the eerie Tower of Terror and the Earrfel Tower, a water tower with mouse ears, off in the distance. Once inside, its main streets include Hollywood Boulevard and Sunset Boulevard, with art deco movie sets evoking Hollywood's glamorous golden age. There's also a New York Street lined with Gotham landmarks (the Empire State, Flatiron, and Chrysler buildings), and typical New York characters including peddlers hawking knock-off watches. Here you'll find some of the best street performing in the Disney parks. More importantly, this is a working movie-and-TV studio, where shows are in production even as you tour the premises.

Arrive at the park early, tickets in hand. Unlike the Magic Kingdom, MGM's 110 acres of attractions can pretty much be seen in 1 day. The parking lot is right at the gate, although trams do run. Pay attention to your parking location, which is not as distinctly marked as in the Magic Kingdom.

If you don't get a *Disney–MGM Studios Guidemap* and entertainment schedule when you enter the park, you can pick it up at Guest Services (MGM's information center). The first thing to do is check show times and work out an entertainment schedule based on highlight attractions and geographical proximity. My favorite MGM restaurants are described in chapter 6.

HOURS   Generally 9am to 7pm with extended hours—sometimes as late as midnight—during major holidays and the summer months.

TICKET PRICES   A 1-day park ticket is $44 for adults, $36 for children, free for children under 4.

SERVICES & FACILITIES IN DISNEY–MGM STUDIOS

ATMs   ATM machines accepting cards from banks using the Cirrus, Honor, and Plus systems are located at the main entrance.

Baby Care   MGM has a small Baby Care Center where you'll find facilities for nursing and changing, disposable diapers, formula, baby food, and pacifiers are for sale. Changing tables are also in all women's rest rooms and some men's rest rooms. Disposable diapers are also available at the Guest Services building.

Cameras & Film   Film and Kodak's disposable Fun Saver cameras are available throughout the park. Video camcorders are available for rent at Hollywood Boulevard for $30 a day, plus a $450 deposit.

First Aid   The First Aid Center, staffed by registered nurses, is in the Entrance Plaza adjoining Guest Services.

Lockers   Lockers are located alongside Oscar's Classic Car Souvenirs, to the right of the Entrance Plaza after you pass through the turnstiles. The cost is $3 to $5 a day, depending on the size.

Lost Children   Lost children at Disney–MGM Studios are taken to Guest Services where lost children logbooks are kept. Children under 7 should wear name tags.

Package Pickup   Any large package you purchase can be sent by the shop clerk to Guest Services in the Entrance Plaza. Allow 3 hours for delivery.

Pet Care   Day accommodations are offered at kennels just outside the entrance for $6 a day. There are also four other kennels in the WDW complex. (See "Fast Facts" in chapter 4 for more details.)

Strollers   Strollers can be rented at Oscar's Super Service, inside the main entrance, for $6.

Wheelchair Rental   Wheelchairs are rented at Oscar's Super Service inside the main entrance. The cost for regular chairs is $6 a day. Electric chairs rent for $35.

MAJOR ATTRACTIONS & SHOWS

ABC Sound Studios
Frommer's Rating: B
Recommended Ages: all ages
Scream. Wave your hands. Making a little noise is likely to help get you out of the audience and onto the stage, where you will then help create sound effects to go along with ABC Saturday morning television shows. The real stars are the tourists trying to make it all happen like the professionals. Volunteer. You're on vacation. You'll probably never see these people again. If you can't muster the gumption to go on stage, the postshow, *Soundworks,* provides the opportunity to make a little joyful noise on interactive computers away from the maddening crowd. Don't miss experiencing the "3-D sound effects" in the **Soundstations** booths there.

The main show features some of the 20,000-plus ingenious gadgets created by sound master Jimmy Macdonald during his 45 years with Disney Studios.

The American Film Institute Showcase
Frommer's Rating: C
Recommended Ages: 10–adult
This exhibit brings into focus the efforts of all those folks—editors, cinematographers, producers, and directors—whose names blur by as the credits roll. Created in 1996 in

Disney-MGM Studios Theme Park

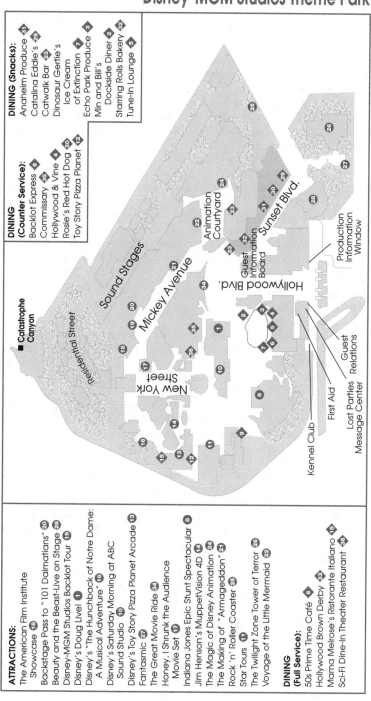

ATTRACTIONS:

The American Film Institute
Showcase 18
Backstage Pass to "101 Dalmatians" 20
Beauty and the Beast–Live on Stage 28
Disney-MGM Studios Backlot Tour 19
Disney's Doug Live! 1
Disney's "The Hunchback of Notre Dame:
A Musical Adventure" 16
Disney's Saturday Morning at ABC
Sound Studio 10
Disney's Toy Story Pizza Planet Arcade 13
Fantasmic! 27
The Great Movie Ride 34
Honey, I Shrunk the Audience
Movie Set 17
Indiana Jones Epic Stunt Spectacular 8
Jim Henson's MuppetVision 4D 14
The Magic of Disney Animation 24
The Making of "Armageddon" 31
Rock 'n' Roller Coaster 25
Star Tours 11
The Twilight Zone Tower of Terror 26
Voyage of the Little Mermaid 22

DINING
(Full Service):

50s Prime Time Café 6
Hollywood Brown Derby 35
Mama Melrose's Ristorante Italiano 45
Sci-Fi Dine-In Theater Restaurant 36

DINING
(Counter Service):

Backlot Express 9
Commissary 42
Hollywood & Vine 4
Rosie's Red Hot Dog 50
Toy Story Pizza Planet 12

DINING (Snacks):

Anaheim Produce 41
Catalina Eddie's 49
Catwalk Bar 43
Dinosaur Gertie's
Ice Cream
of Extinction 7
Echo Park Produce 3
Min and Bill's
Dockside Diner 2
Starring Rolls Bakery 32
Tune-In Lounge 5

Sound Stages

Catastrophe Canyon

Residential Street

Mickey Avenue

New York Street

Animation Courtyard

Sunset Blvd.

Hollywood Blvd.

Guest Information Board

Production Information Window

Guest Relations

First Aid

Lost Parties Message Center

Kennel Club

173

partnership with the Los Angeles–based American Film Institute, this walk-through tour also highlights some of the organization's winners of the Lifetime Achievement Award. They include Bette Davis, Jack Nicholson, and Elizabeth Taylor.

Backstage Pass to 101 Dalmatians

Frommer's Rating: B

Recommended Ages: all ages

Have a De Vil of a good time spotting Cruella and the other stars of Disney's live-action remake of the animated classic. The stark, eerie sets from Cruella's movie are among the top attractions during this short tour. Wizzer, the most fluid of the canine actors, is featured in a film about the life of a four-pawed star. Taking a cue from Universal, where you Ride the Movies, the special-effects show allows one lucky—usually tall and male—spectator to ride in the movies by re-creating Jeff Daniels' runaway-bike scene. Real Dalmatians are also on display. But don't call PETA yet. The pups pull only 2-hour shifts and are treated better, one employee grumbled, than most two-legged "cast members."

Note: The nearby "Making of" exhibits are tied to the latest Disney movie release. At press time, it featured *Armageddon,* but that is likely to change by the time of your visit.

Backstage Studio Tour

Frommer's Rating: B

Recommended Ages: 10–adult

This 30-minute tram tour takes you behind the scenes for a close-up look at the vehicles, props, costumes, sets, and special effects used in your favorite movies and TV shows. You'll see costumers at work in the wardrobe department (Disney has the world's largest costume collection—more than 2 million garments), house facades of *The Golden Girls* and *Empty Nest* on Residential Street, and carpenters building sets. Most of the props are from short-lived series that you've never heard of, but it's still interesting. The real fun begins once the tram ventures into **Catastrophe Canyon,** where an earthquake in the heart of desert oil country causes canyon walls to rumble, and riders are threatened by a raging oil fire, massive explosions, torrents of rain, and flash floods! Then you're taken behind the scenes to see how filmmakers use special effects to create such disasters. Almost as interesting as the ride is the preshow. While waiting in line, you can watch entertaining videos—hosted by Tom Selleck and Carol Burnett—of well-known actors and directors on overhead monitors: Penny Marshall talking about the piano scene in *Big,* Richard Dreyfuss sharing how he landed the role in *Jaws* that launched his movie career, Mel Brooks on why he was "forced" to become a director/producer, and many more. After the tram tour, visit **Studio Showcase,** a changing walk-through display of sets and props from popular and classic movies.

Beauty and the Beast Live on Stage

Frommer's Rating: A

Recommended Ages: 4–adult

This 1,500-seat, covered amphitheater is currently presenting a 25-minute live Broadway-style production, *Beauty and the Beast,* adapted from the movie version. Musical highlights from the show range from the rousing "Be Our Guest" opening number to the poignant title song featured in a romantic waltz-scene finale complete with the release of white doves. A highlight is "The Mob Song" scene in a dark forest, in which villagers led by Gaston (the beast's rival for Belle) and armed with axes, hoes, and pitchforks set out on a rampage to "kill the beast," setting up the emotional climax. Sets and costumes are lavish, production numbers spectacular. Arrive early to get a good seat.

Note: Beauty and the Beast has been enjoying a long run here; a new show, based on a more recent Disney hit, may be in progress by the time you visit.

Disney's Doug Live
Frommer's Rating: B
Recommended Ages: all ages
This show, one of the newest in MGM Studios, combines live performances and animation while telling the story of a 12-year-old and his interaction with the popular television cartoon character. This is a must-see for fans of the show—no matter what their ages. Others may find it less intriguing. Audience members are invited to be part of the show, so go ahead, raise your hand. You'll never see these people again.

Fantasmic!
Frommer's Rating: A+
Recommended Ages: all ages
With more than 50 performers, more than 1 million gallons of water, a 32,000 pound dragon, a 59-foot-tall mountain, and laser lights and pyrotechnics, this is one of the best nighttime shows in Disney's World. The 25-minute show, which debuted late in 1998, has been shown at Disneyland since 1992, but Disney officials promise that those who have seen the California show are still in for some surprises. It mixes special effects with classic movie clips projected on huge water screens, and features Sorcerer Mickey and a host of other Disney favorites from the Little Mermaid to animal puppets from the Lion King. It is held in a 6,500-seat theater behind the Tower of Terror off Sunset Boulevard. There is also room for 2,500 standing guests, but try to arrive at least 30 minutes early to get a seat. (Earlier during peak seasons.) The noise level may be intense for young children. *Tip:* Keep away from those splash zones if you don't want to get wet!

The Great Movie Ride
Frommer's Rating: C+ for kids, B for older adults
Recommended Ages: 10–adult
Film footage and 50 audio-animatronic replicas of movie stars are used to re-create some of the most famous scenes in filmdom on this ride through movie history. You'll relive magic moments from the 1930s through the present: Bergman and Bogart's classic airport farewell in *Casablanca;* Rhett carrying Scarlett up the stairs of Tara for a night of passion; Brando bellowing "Stellllaaaa"; Sigourney Weaver fending off slimy alien foes; Gene Kelly singin' in the rain; Johnny Weissmuller's trademark Tarzan yell and vine-swing across the jungle; and many more. Action is enhanced by dramatic special effects, and your tram is always hijacked en route by outlaws or gangsters. "Fasten your seat belts. It's going to be a bumpy night." The setting for this attraction is a full-scale reproduction of Hollywood's famous Mann's Chinese Theatre, complete with handprints of the stars out front.

Hunchback of Notre Dame: A Musical Adventure
Frommer's Rating: B+
Recommended Ages: all ages
This reprises many of the songs you have heard—over and over and over again—on the video. This rollicking stage shows brings the animated features main characters to life. Arrive a few minutes early to insure a seat, since the theater can fill to capacity.

Find the Hidden Mickeys

Hiding Mickeys in designs began as an inside joke among early Walt Disney World "Imagineers," and became a park tradition. Today, dozens of subtle hidden Mickeys—the world-famous set of ears, profiles, and full figures—are concealed in attractions and resorts throughout Walt Disney World. No one even knows their exact number. See how many HMs (Hidden Mickeys) you can locate during your visit. A few to look for include the following:

In the Magic Kingdom

In the Haunted Mansion banquet scene, check out the arrangement of plate and adjoining saucers on the table.

In the Africa scene of It's a Small World, note the purple flowers on a vine on the elephant's left side.

While riding Splash Mountain, look for Mickey lying on his back in the pink clouds to the right of the steamboat.

Hint: There are four HMs in The Timekeeper and five in the Carousel of Progress.

At Epcot

In Journey into Imagination, check out the little girl's dress in the lobby film of *Honey I Shrunk the Audience,* one of five HMs in this pavilion.

In The Land pavilion, don't miss the small stones in front of the Native American man on a horse, and the baseball cap of the man driving a harvester in the *Circle of Life* film.

As your boat cruises through the Mexico pavilion on the El Rio del Tiempo attraction, notice the arrangement of three clay pots in the marketplace scene.

In Maelstrom, in the Norway pavilion, a Viking wears Mickey ears in the wall mural facing the loading dock.

There are four HMs in Spaceship Earth, one of them in the Renaissance scene, on the page of a book behind the sleeping monk. Try to find the other three.

At Disney–MGM Studios

On the Great Movie Ride, there's an HM on the window above the bank in the gangster scene, and four familiar characters are included in the hieroglyphics wall opposite Indiana Jones.

At Jim Henson's Muppet*Vision 3D, take a good look at the top five reasons for turning in your 3-D glasses sign, and note the balloons in the film's final scene.

In the Twilight Zone Tower of Terror, note the bell for the elevator behind Rod Serling in the film. There are five other HMs in this attraction.

There are also HMs at many Disney resorts. The best place to look for them is at Wilderness Lodge, which has over a dozen that I know about.

Indiana Jones Epic Stunt Spectacular

Frommer's Rating: A+

Recommended Ages: 6–adult

Visitors get a glimpse into the world of movie stunts in this dramatic 30-minute show, which re-creates major scenes from the Indiana Jones series. The show opens on an elaborate Mayan temple backdrop. Indiana Jones crashes dramatically onto the set via a rope, and, as he searches with a torch for the golden idol, he encounters booby traps, fire and steam, and spears popping up from the ground, before being chased by a vast rolling boulder! The set is dismantled to reveal a colorful Cairo marketplace where a sword fight ensues and the action includes virtuoso bull-whip maneuvers, lots of gunfire, and a truck bursting into flame. An explosive finale takes place in a desert scenario. The action is enhanced by movie theme music and entertaining narrative, and, throughout, guests get to see how elaborate stunts are pulled off. (Here it is, another opportunity to be part of the fun. Arrive early and sit near the stage for your shot at short-lived stardom. Go ahead, you're running out of chances—*this time you get to wear a turban.*)

Inside the Magic
Frommer's Rating: B
Recommended Ages: 10–adult
Movie and TV special effects, and production facets, are the focus of this behind-the-scenes walking tour of studio facilities. You'll see how a naval battle—complete with burning ships, torpedoes, and undersea explosions—is created and then view the results on videotape. Two young volunteers from the audience help demonstrate how miniaturization was achieved in *Honey, I Shrunk the Kids.* You'll visit three studio soundstages (on some tours, you'll get to see movies or TV shows being filmed from a soundproof catwalk); view a short comedy called *The Lottery* starring Bette Midler and learn how its special effects were achieved; and head to the Walt Disney Theater where, blessed relief, you'll get to sit down and enjoy a behind-the-scenes look at the company's latest animation feature. To find the entrance to this attraction, follow the big pink footsteps of Roger Rabbit.

Jim Henson's Muppet*Vision 3D
Frommer's Rating: A+
Recommended Ages: 4–adult
They added an additional "D" and some more zany effects to this delightful film starring Kermit and Miss Piggy. The film combines Jim Henson's puppets with Disney audio-animatronics and special-effects wizardry, 70mm film, and cutting-edge 3-D technology. Wow! The coming-right-at-you action includes flying Mup-pets, cream pies, cannonballs, high winds, fiber-optic fireworks, bubble showers, even an actual spray of water. Kermit is the host, Miss Piggy sings "Dream a Little Dream of Me," Statler and Waldorf critique the action (which includes numerous mishaps and disasters) from a mezzanine balcony, and Nicki Napoleon and his Emperor Penguins (a full Muppet orchestra) provide music from the pit. Kids in the first row get to interact with the characters. In the preshow area, guests view an entertaining Muppet video on overhead monitors and see movie props belonging to Muppet superstars. Note the cute Muppet fountain out front and the Muppet ver-sion of a Rousseau painting inside.

The Magic of Disney Animation
Frommer's Rating: A
Recommended Ages: 8–adult
You'll see Disney characters come alive at the stroke of a brush or pencil as you tour actual, glass-walled animation studios and watch artists at work. Walter Cronkite and Robin Williams (guess who plays straight man?) explain what's going on via video monitors, and they also star in a very funny 8-minute Peter Pan–themed film

Fun Fact

Mulan was the first Disney animated feature to be produced completely at the Orlando studios.

about the basics of animation. It's painstaking work: To produce an 80-minute film, the animation team must complete more than a million individual cels (drawings/paintings on clear celluloid sheets) of characters and scenery! Original cels from famous Disney movies, and some of the many Oscars won by Disney artists, are on display here. The tour also includes very entertaining video talks by animators and a grand finale of magical moments from Disney classics such as *Pinocchio, Snow White, Bambi, Beauty and the Beast,* and *The Hunchback of Notre Dame.*

Rock 'n Roller Coaster
Frommer's Rating: A
Recommended Ages: 6 and up
In what some see as an attempt to go head to head with Universal's Islands of Adventure, this is Disney's first inverted roller coaster. The indoor coaster, similar to Space Mountain, is fast and furious and set to rocking music. Your 24-person "limo" speeds from 0 to 60, tearing through three buildings in this must-do for coaster fans. It is not for the faint of heart. *Note:* Check for height restrictions.

Star Tours
Frommer's Rating: B+
Recommended Ages: 8–adult
Cutting edge when it first debuted, this galactic journey based on the original *Star Wars* trilogy (George Lucas collaborated on its conception), can't compete with the latest technology, but is still plenty of fun. The movie was recently replaced to reflect the new Star Wars "prequel" movie that hit the theaters in 1999. The preshow area—where R2-D2 and C-3PO are running an intergalactic travel agency—will be a hit with die-hard fans. As with the old version, passengers board a 40-seat "spacecraft" for an other-worldly journey and suffer sudden drops, violent crashes, and oncoming laser blasts. Check out the *Star Wars* merchandise shop at the end of the ride.

The Twilight Zone Tower of Terror
Frommer's Rating: A+
Recommended Ages: 10–adult
This is a truly stomach-churning ride, and Disney has continued to fine tune it to make it even better. Legend has it that during a violent storm on Halloween night of 1939, lightning struck the Hollywood Tower Hotel, causing an entire wing— along with an elevator full of people—to disappear. And you're about to meet them as you become the star in a special episode of . . . *The Twilight Zone.* En route to this formerly grand hotel, guests walk past overgrown landscaping and faded signs that once directed them to stables and tennis courts; the vines over the entrance trellis are dead, and the hotel itself is a crumbling ruin. Eerie corridors lead to a dimly lit library, where you can hear a storm raging outside. After various spooky adventures, the ride ends in a dramatic climax: a terrifying 13-story fitful, free-fall plunge into *The Twilight Zone!* This is the best thrill ride at Disney, with a "preshow" so authentic that maintenance crews kept fixing leaking pipes designed to drip as part of the ambiance. *Note:* You must be 40 inches tall to ride.

Voyage of the Little Mermaid
Frommer's Rating: A
Recommended Ages: 4–adult
Hazy lighting, creating an underwater effect in a reef-walled theater, helps set the mood for this charming musical spectacular based on the Disney feature film. The show combines live performers with more than 100 puppets, movie clips, and innovative special effects. Sebastian sings the movie's Academy Award–winning

A family picture is one the kids can take their parents to see and not be embarrassed.

song, "Under the Sea"; the ethereal Ariel shares her dream of becoming human in a live performance of "Part of Your World"; and the evil, tentacled Ursula, 12 feet tall and 10 feet wide, belts out "Poor Unfortunate Soul." It all has a happy ending, as most of the young audience knows it will; they've seen the movie. This is a great place to rest your feet on a hot day; the theater feels misted to enhance the sealike atmosphere.

PARADES, SHOWS, FIREWORKS & MORE

A parade celebrating *Mulan,* Disney's 36th full-length animated feature, has replaced the *Hercules* parade in Disney–MGM Studios. The short parade is based on the story of a young, high-spirited girl who saves her father's life by disguising herself as a man and joining the Chinese army in his place. It will be performed daily along Hollywood Boulevard. This parade in no way matches the size and scope of the parades in the Magic Kingdom, so unless you're a big fan of the movie, this might be a good time to drop in on the Tower of Terror while the lines are shorter. The parade takes place daily; check your entertainment schedule for routes and times.

The **Sorcery in the Sky** fireworks show is presented nightly during summer and peak seasons. Check your entertainment schedule to see if it's on.

The **Visiting Celebrity** program features frequent appearances by stars such as Betty White, Burt Reynolds, Joan Collins, Leonard Nimoy, and Billy Dee Williams. They appear at attractions, record their handprints in front of the Chinese Theatre, and appear at question-and-answer sessions with park guests. Check your entertainment schedule to see if it's on. Kids ages 10 and up will enjoy it.

The *Honey, I Shrunk the Kids* **Movie Set,** an 11,000-square-foot playground based on the film, is located near New York Street. Everything in it is larger than life and will appeal to kids ages 2 to 10. A thicket of grass is 30 feet tall, mushroom caps are three stories high, and a friendly "ant" makes a suitable seat. Play areas—enhanced by sounds such as the buzzing of giant crickets and bees—include a massive cream cookie, a 52-foot garden hose (with leaks), cereal loops 9 feet in diameter (cushioned for jumping), a waterfall cascading from a leaf to a dell of fern sprouts (the sprouts form a musical stairway, activated when guests step from sprout to sprout), a root maze with a flower-petal slide, a "filmstrip" slide in a giant Kodak film can, and a huge spider web with 11 levels to climb.

Centering on a gleaming 14½-foot-tall bronze Emmy, the **Academy of Television Arts & Sciences Hall of Fame Plaza (ATAS),** honors TV legends. Bronze statues of television luminaries Carol Burnett, Sid Caesar, James Garner, Andy Griffith, Barbara Walters, Rod Serling, Bill Cosby, Mary Tyler Moore, Red Skelton, Danny Thomas, and Milton Berle are displayed, along with one of Walt Disney. This is really for adults; kids may not know all these names yet. Additional statues will be added each year. ATAS holds its annual Hall of Fame induction ceremonies at the Disney–MGM Studios.

SHOPPING AT DISNEY–MGM STUDIOS

There's some really interesting shopping here. The **Animation Gallery** carries collectible cels, books about animation, arts-and-crafts kits for future animators, and collector figurines.

Heat Alert!

This is one place where you don't want to go for the burn. The scalding Florida sun can get you in many directions. Slather that sunscreen on your back, shoulders, and the backs of your legs.

Sid Cahuenga's One-of-a-Kind sells autographed photos of the stars, original movie posters, and star-touched items, such as a bracelet that once belonged to Joan Rivers.

Over at **Cover Story,** you can have your photograph put on the cover of your favorite magazine, anything from *Forbes* to *Psychology Today* to *Golf Digest.* Costumes are available.

Celebrity 5 & 10, modeled after a 1940s Woolworth's, has movie-related merchandise: *Gone With the Wind* memorabilia, MGM Studio T-shirts, movie posters, Elvis mugs, and more.

The major park attractions all have complementary merchandise outlets selling Indiana Jones adventure clothing, *Little Mermaid* stuffed characters and logo-wear, *Star Wars* souvenirs, and so on. There is a package pick-up system that allows purchases to be delivered to the front of the park so you can pick them up as you leave. Take advantage of this free service.

6 Animal Kingdom

Disney's fourth major park combines animals, elaborate landscapes, and a handful of rides to create yet another reason not to venture outside of the Disney World. The bulk of the park opened in 1998, the final "land" Asia, opened in 1999. Michael Eisner says it's the next best thing to going to Africa, but don't cancel that safari vacation yet. It is definitely a different theme park experience, filled with lush landscapes and exotic wildlife. There are also a few great shows—notably the Lion King. If the animals are cooperative, you can have an up close encounter that you aren't likely to find anywhere else.

This park does grow on you. I have enjoyed it a little more with each visit. However, if this is your first visit to Walt Disney World, and you have children, you'll probably want to target the parks with more thrill rides—Magic Kingdom and Disney MGM—before this one. Animal lovers, and those who like to photograph wildlife, may want to put it at the top of their lists.

Animal Kingdom is divided into five "regions": **Safari Village,** a shopping/entertainment area; **Africa,** the main animal-viewing area, which is dedicated to the wildlife in Africa today; **Dinoland,** focusing on issues of extinction; and **Camp Minnie-Mickey,** the Animal Kingdom equivalent of Mickey's Toontown in the Magic Kingdom. **Asia,** the final section to open, has a water roller coaster called **Kali River Rapids,** and features wildlife exhibits, including Bengal tigers, in the **Maharajah Jungle Trek.**

The park covers more than 500 acres—nearly twice the size of Epcot—and your feet will tell you that you have covered the territory at the end of the day.

Most of the rides are accessible to guests with disabilities, but the hilly terrain, large crowds, narrow passages, and long hikes can make for a strenuous day if there is a wheelchair-bound member of your party. Anyone with heart, neck, or back problems, and pregnant women, will not be able to enjoy the major attraction, **Kilimanjaro Safaris.** Also remember that the animals will be most active early in the morning and late in the afternoon.

Animal Kingdom

The Boneyard Playground **13**
Character Greeting Trails **4**
Countdown to Extinction **16**
Cretaceous Trail **15**
Festival of the Lion King **3**
Flights of Wonder **11**
Fossil Preparation Lab **14**
Harambe Village **7**
It's Tough to Be a Bug **6**
Journey into Jungle Book **12**
Kilimanjaro Safaris **8**
Pangani Forest
   Exploration Trail **9**
Pocahontas & her
   Forest Friends **2**
Rainforest Café **1**
Safari Village Trails **5**
Wildlife Express **10**

AFRICA

Conservation
Station

ASIA

Maharajah
Jungle Trek

Kali River
Rapids

Safari Village

Tree of Life

Dinoland
USA

The
Oasis

Camp
Minnie-
Mickey

Main Entrance

Parking Area

Parking Area

At the heart of the park is a purportedly 14-story **Tree of Life,** which Disney must have measured from the lowest root stock to the tallest leaf. It is an intricately carved free-form representation of animals, handcrafted by a team of artists over the period of a year. It is not nearly as tall or imposing as the silver golf-ball dome, also known as Spaceship Earth, that has come to best symbolize Epcot or Cinderella's Castle. The artwork is impressive, though, with new animals seemingly appearing at every glance. Parents, however, may have some trouble keeping kids from wanting to climb. It is, after all, a tree, and there are lots of handy footholds.

The **Asia** section of the park, which opened in 1999, includes **Kali River Rapids** and **Maharajah Jungle Trek** along with displays of giant fruit bats, and Bengal tigers along with other animals, and an elaborate series of buildings that resemble the ruins of an ancient city.

ARRIVING   Once in the parking lot, you can take a tram to the park. If you park in the Peacock section, you can easily walk. But watch out for the trams, since the parking lots are not designed for pedestrians. Also make certain to mark your location. The parking lot signs are not as prominent as in the Magic Kingdom, and all the rows look alike when you come back out. Upon entering the park, consult your guide map as to any special events or entertainment. If you have questions, ask the park personnel, who are dressed in various, wildly colored "native" costumes.

HOURS   Animal Kingdom is open from 8am to 6pm but hours can be extended to 7am to 7pm.

TICKETS & PRICES $44 for adults, $36 for children, children under 3 are free. See "Tickets" earlier in this chapter for information on 4- and 5-day passes.

SERVICES & FACILITIES IN ANIMAL KINGDOM

ATMs   There is one ATM in Animal Kingdom, located near Garden Gates Gifts just inside the park entrances. It accepts cards from banks using the Cirrus, Honor, and Plus systems.

Baby Care   The Baby Care Center is located near Creature Comforts in Safari Village, but as in the other Disney parks, you'll find changing tables in both men's and women's rest rooms, and you'll be able to buy disposable diapers at Guest Services.

Cameras & Film   You can drop film off for same-day developing at the Kodak Kiosk and in Africa and Garden Gate Gifts near the park entrances. Single-use cameras and film are available in Disney Outfitters in Safari Village; the Kodak Kiosk in Africa, near the entrance to the Kilimanjaro Safari; and Garden Gate Gifts.

First Aid   The First Aid Center, which is staffed by registered nurses, is located near Creature Comforts in Safari Village.

Lockers   Lockers are located in Garden Gate Gifts to your right as you enter the park. They are also located to the left, near Rain Forest Cafe.

Lost Children   A center for lost children is located near Creature Comforts in Safari Village. This is also the site of same-day lost and found.

Package Pickup   Any large packages can be sent to the front of the park at Garden Gate Gifts. You can send packages back to Disney resort rooms or send them home through Federal Express from here as well.

Pet Care   Pet facilities are located just outside the park entrance. There are four other kennels located in the WDW complex. (See "Fast Facts" in Chapter 4 for more information.)

Strollers Stroller rentals are available at the Garden Gates Gifts shop to the right as you enter the park. There are also satellite locations throughout the park. Ask a Disney employee for those locations.

Wheelchair Rentals You can rent wheelchairs at the Garden Gates Gifts shop to the right as you enter the park. There are also satellite locations throughout the park. Ask a Disney employee for those locations.

THE OASIS

With the taped sounds of birds chirping and its garden entrance, this painstakingly designed landscape of streams, grottoes, and waterfalls sets the tone for the rest of the park. A misty fog provides a jungle tone, but makes seeing the animals sometimes difficult. This is one of the key places to see animals such as wallabies, sloths, and several different kinds of birds. Those traveling with children, who will likely be eager to see the rest of the park, will probably have more time to enjoy these exhibits on the way out.

SAFARI VILLAGE

Like Cinderella's Castle in the Magic Kingdom and the silver, golf-ball dome in Epcot, the 14-story **Tree of Life** located here has been designed to be the park's central landmark. It is an intricately carved, free-form representation of animals, the handcrafted work of Disney artists. Teams of artists worked for months creating the various sculptures, and it is worth a leisurely stroll through the roots. The intricate design makes it appear as if a different animal appears from every angle. One of the creators says he expects it to become one of the most photographed works of art in the world. (Watch out Mona Lisa.) There is a wading pond directly in front of the tree that often features flamingos.

It's Tough to Be a Bug!
Frommer's Rating: A
Recommended Ages: 6 and up
Located inside the Tree of Life in a 430-seat theater, this creepy (crawly) special-effects laden tour of a bug's life will keep you on the edge of your seat. The crowd sits on long benches in what looks like a darkened burrow to experience a 3-D film accompanied by some very special effects that address all the senses. Once you put on your "bug eye" glasses along comes a parade of characters from Disney's animated release of the same name. Young children, however, may find the theater dark and the bugs scary; the volume here is high, and there are some creepy surprises making it too intense for little guests.

The Garden Path
Frommer's Rating: C
Recommended Ages: All ages
The Garden Path is a leisurely stroll—are you detecting a theme here?—through the root system of the Tree of Life. This soft landscape is filled with otters, flamingos, tamarinds, lemurs, tortoises, and colorful ducks, storks, cranes, and cockatoos.

Radio Disney River Cruise
Frommer's Rating: C
Recommended Ages: All Ages
If you've already hit the major attractions, this round-trip cruise may be a nice break at the end of the day. Guests listen to a radio broadcast—supposedly emanating

from the top of the Tree of Life—as they take a relaxing tour through the waterway snaking through the park. The "broadcast" consists of songs, special guests, and trivia quizzes, and is hosted by "Just Plain" Mark and Zippy from the Radio Disney broadcast that airs across the nation.

DINOLAND U.S.A.

Enter by passing under "Olden Gate Bridge," a 40-foot-tall Brachiosaurus reassembled from excavated fossils. Preopening publicity said you would find a world filled with a series of wooden cabins and national parklike structures that give the land a nostalgic look from the 1950s and 1960s, but the buildings didn't make much of an impact on me.

The Boneyard
Frommer's Rating: B for children, D for adults
Recommended Ages: all ages
Kids love the chance to slip, slither, slide, and crawl through this giant playground and dig site where they can discover the remains of triceratops, T-rex, and other vanished giants. You can even dig up the bones of a woolly mammoth in the dig site. Contained within a latticework of metal bars and netting, this children's play area reminds me of a prisoner of war camp, but the kids still like it. This area is fun, but isn't nearly as inviting as the *Honey I Shrunk the Kids* play area in Disney–MGM Studios.

Countdown to Extinction
Frommer's Rating: C
Recommended Ages: 8 and up
This ride is reminiscent of Snow White's Adventures in the Magic Kingdom. You hurl through the darkness in "time machines" past an array of snarling dinosaurs. This is far from a smooth ride, and children may find the dinosaurs and darkness frightening. As a thrill ride, well, it's not very thrilling. The snarling dinos are interesting, but you speed by them so quickly there's little time to appreciate them. In a weird glitch in Disney's usually faultless storytelling, the dinosaur that you are supposed to be retrieving by traveling back in time never appears anywhere at the end of the ride. *Note:* You must be 46 inches tall to ride.

Cretaceous Trail
Frommer's Rating: C
Recommended Ages: all ages
Wander leisurely—there's that theme again—back in time as you stroll down a path filled with living plants and animal species that have survived since the age of the dinosaur. You'll encounter a Chinese alligator, a Florida soft-shelled turtle, and red-legged seriema. The animals are interesting, but skip the re-creation of the dig site.

CONSERVATION STATION

This offers a behind-the-scenes look at how Disney cares for animals inside the park. You walk past a series of nurseries and vet stations. The problem is that these facilities have to be staffed in order to be interesting, and that is not always the case. (I did spy a rare *biologist humanus* sitting at his computer.)

Conservation Station includes the **Affection Section,** where you can cuddle with some friendly animals, explore their private habitats, and learn how they are cared

Show Alert!

The show "Journey Into Jungle Book" closed in the summer of 1999. At press time, it was likely that it would be replaced by a Tarzan-themed production.

Fun Fact _____

An early version of the Kilimanjaro Safaris had Disney killing off a mother elephant; there was even a fake carcass visible from the trucks. This plan was, wisely, changed after Imagineers discovered that the dead mother upset young children.

---

for and fed. The coolest thing here, however, is the pair of elephant sculptures that serve as the hand washer and blow dryer.

Check out **Eco Heroes,** interactive videos that connect you to endangered animal information and world-famous biologists and conservationists, and **Song of the Rainforest,** which surrounds you with the sounds of the endangered wildlife in a deep jungle. This lecture/audio adventure is kind of interesting, but skip it if there is a long wait. You can get jungle-sounds CD at the local music store without the annoying whir of a chain saw. Unless you are into doing a little research on your vacation, skip **Eco Web,** a computer link to conservation organizations worldwide.

CAMP MINNIE-MICKEY

Join your favorite Disney characters "on vacation" in Camp Minnie-Mickey, an entire land that re-creates a kid-friendly Adirondack resort.

Character Greeting Pavilions

Frommer's Rating: A for children (C for adults)
Recommended Ages: all ages
This is a must-do for people traveling with children. A variety of Disney characters, from Winnie the Pooh to Timon and Baloo, greet you. Mickey, in recognition of his star status, can be found in his own pavilion.

Festival of the Lion King

Frommer's Rating: A
Recommended Ages: all ages
Arrive early for this popular attraction that regularly draws enough people to fill the 1,000-seat pavilion. Based loosely on the animated movie, this stage show combines the pageantry of a parade with a tribal celebration. In an interesting switch, the audience is seated in the center of the theater as the action moves around them. The show is fast-paced, the music lively, and the acrobatic "monkeys" are a real treat to watch. This is definitely the best show in the park.

Grandma Willow's Cove

Frommer's Rating: C
Recommended Ages: all ages
The hour-plus wait—and that was on a slow day—frankly wasn't worth this disappointing 15-minute show in a 350-seat theater.

Pocahontas and Grandmother Willow, as well as some living forest creatures, perform a heavy-handed skit about the importance of treating nature with respect. If you decide to go, arrive early to get a seat. They do allow standing-room crowds but standing makes the slow-paced show even slower.

AFRICA

Enter through the town of Harambe, a run-down representation of an African coastal village poised on the edge of the 21st century. Costumed employees will greet you with cries of "Jumbo" as you enter the buildings. The whitewashed structures, built of coral stone and thatched with reed by craftspeople brought over from Africa, surround a central marketplace rich with local wares and colors.

Kilimanjaro Safaris
Frommer's Rating: B+
Recommended Ages: all ages
This is one of the few "rides" in Animal Kingdom. Essentially, you board a very big truck for a very bumpy ride through the faux African landscape. The vehicle is open, so open you can get thwacked in the face with foliage, and the animals sometimes wander in very close. But this is hit or miss, depending on how much wildlife you actually get to spot. Once you come within arms-length of a giraffe, however, you forget about all the vacant velt. A story line about chasing a poacher doesn't add much to the whole experience although you will really feel as if you are traveling over the back roads of a reserve. If you have small children, you will need to wrangle a seat on the end so they will be able to look out the sides of the car. The ride gets bumpy, so those with heart, back, and neck problems, as well as pregnant women, should skip it.

Pangani Falls Exploration Trail
Frommer's Rating: C+
Recommended Ages: all ages
You can get a pretty good look at birds and the ever active mole rats, but the gorillas are hard to spy and difficult to track. Small viewing areas give you a glimpse into various parts of the habitat, but because the animals are elusive, lines get three or four people deep when you can actually catch a glimpse. Children—okay, adults too—may find this frustrating. Also the swaying rope bridge you must traverse to reach the compound may be a little tricky for those in wheelchairs and their companions.

ASIA
Disney's Imagineers have outdone themselves in creating this mythical kingdom, **Anadapour.** The intricately painted artwork visible at the main attractions is something not to be missed—it also helps make the lines seem to move a little faster.

Flights of Wonder
Frommer's Rating: B
Recommended Ages: all ages
Mixing live-animal action with a traditional Disney character show, Flights of Wonder, which has undergone several transformations since the park opened, is a low-key break for the family, complete with a few laughs and some aviary feats that will ruffle your feathers.

Kali River Rapids
Frommer's Rating: A
Recommended Ages: 6 and up.
With churning water that mimics real-life rapids, and optical illusions that will have you wondering if you are about to go over the falls, this is a premiere water roller coaster. The ride begins with a peaceful tour of lush foliage, but soon you are dipping—and dripping—as your tiny ship is tossed. You will definitely get wet. The

---

Fun Fact

All the Disney water parks are refurbished annually. That means if you are traveling in the fall or early winter one of the three parks will likely be closed temporarily.

---

lines are long here, but keep your head up—literally—and enjoy some of the marvelous artwork painted overhead and on the beautiful murals. There is a 42-inch height requirement.

Maharajah Jungle Trek

Frommer's Rating: A

Recommended Ages: 6 and up.

Disney keeps its promise to provide up close views of animals with this exhibit. Bengal tigers seem just inches away as you peer through thick glass, watching the graceful cats in their grassy natural surroundings. Nothing but air divides you from the dozens of giant fruit bats hanging in what appears to be an abandoned court-yard, while cocooned in their leathery wings. (Fortunately for those with a bat-phobia, you can bypass the bat habitat.) Helpful guides are on-hand to answer questions, and you can also check a printed guide that lists the various animals you may spot; it's available on your right as you enter the exhibit. Small children may find the proximity to the animals, especially the bats, disturbing.

7 Other WDW Attractions

TYPHOON LAGOON

Ahoy swimmers, floaters, run-aground boaters!
A furious storm once roared 'cross the sea
Catching ships in its path, helpless to flee . . .
Instead of a certain and watery doom
The winds swept them here to TYPHOON LAGOON.

Such is the Disney legend relating to Typhoon Lagoon, which you'll see posted on consecutive signs as you enter the park. Located off Lake Buena Vista Drive, halfway between the Disney Village Marketplace and Disney–MGM Studios, this is the ultimate in water-theme parks. Its fantasy setting is a palm-fringed tropical island village of ramshackle, tin-roofed structures, strewn with cargo, surfboards, and other marine wreckage left by the "great typhoon." A storm-stranded fishing boat dangles precariously atop the 95-foot-high Mount Mayday, the steep setting for several major park attractions. Every half hour the boat's smokestack erupts, shooting a 50-foot geyser of water into the air.

ESSENTIALS

HOURS   The park is open from 10am to 5pm most of the year (with extended hours during some holiday periods), 9am to 8pm in the summer.

ENTRANCE FEES   A 1-day ticket to Typhoon Lagoon is $26.95 for adults, $21.50 for children.

HELPFUL HINTS   In summer, arrive no later than 9am to avoid long lines. The park is often filled to capacity by 10am and then closed to later arrivals. Beach towels and lockers can be obtained for a minimal fee, and all beach accessories can be purchased at **Singapore Sal's.** Light fare is available at two eateries, **Leaning**

Palms and **Typhoon Tillie's Galley and Grog.** A beach bar called **Let's Go Slurpin'** sells beer and soft drinks, and there are also picnic tables (consider bringing picnic fare; you can keep it in your locker until lunchtime). Guests are not permitted to bring their own flotation devices into the park.

ATTRACTIONS IN THE PARK

Castaway Creek

Hop onto a raft or inner tube and meander along this 2,100-foot lazy river. Circling the lagoon, Castaway Creek tumbles through a misty rain forest, past caves and secluded grottoes. It has a theme area called Water Works, where jets of water spew from shipwrecked boats and a Rube Goldberg assemblage of broken bamboo pipes and buckets sprays and dumps water on passersby. Tubes are complimentary.

Ketchakiddie Creek

Many of the other attractions require guests to be at least 4 feet tall. This section of the park is a kiddie area exclusively for those under 4 feet. An innovative water playground, it has bubbling fountains to frolic in, mini–water slides, a pint-size whitewater tubing adventure, spouting whales and squirting seals, rubbery crocodiles to climb on, grottoes to explore, and waterfalls to loll under.

Shark Reef

Guests are given free snorkel equipment (and instruction) for a 15-minute swim through this 362,000-gallon simulated coral-reef tank populated by about 4,000 rainbow parrot fish, queen angelfish, yellowtail damselfish, and other colorful denizens of the deep. Underwater scenery includes shipwrecked boats, and there's a rock waterfall at one end. If you don't want to get in the water, you can observe the fish via portholes in a walk-through area.

Typhoon Lagoon

This large and lovely lagoon, the size of two football fields and surrounded by a white sandy beach (complete with volleyball setup), is the park's main swimming area. The chlorinated water's turquoise hue evokes the Caribbean. Large waves for surfing and bobbing crash against the shore every 90 seconds. A foghorn sounds to warn you when a wave is coming. Young children can wade in the lagoon's more peaceful tidal pools—Blustery Bay or Whitecap Cove.

Water Slides

Humunga Kowabunga consists of two 214-foot Mount Mayday water slides that drop you down the mountain before rushing into a cave and out again at 30 miles per hour. Three longer (about 300 feet each) but less steep slides—Jib Jammer, Rudder Buster, and Stern Burner—take you on a serpentine route through waterfalls and bat caves, past nautical wreckage at about 20 miles per hour before depositing you in a bubbling catch pool; each offers slightly different views and thrills. There's seating for nonparticipatory parents whose kids have commissioned them to "watch me." Women should wear a one-piece on the slides if they don't want to put on a different sort of show for the viewing bleachers.

White-Water Rides

Mount Mayday is the setting for three white-water rafting adventures—Keelhaul Falls, Mayday Falls, and Gangplank Falls—all of them offering steep drops, coursing through caves, and passing lush scenery. Keelhaul Falls has the most winding spiral route, Mayday Falls the steepest drops and fastest water, and the slightly tamer Gangplank Falls uses large tubes so the whole family can ride together.

BLIZZARD BEACH

Blizzard Beach is Disney's newest water park—a 66-acre "ski resort" in the midst of a tropical lagoon. The park centers on a 90-foot snowcapped mountain (Mount Gushmore), which swimmers ascend via chairlifts, and the on-premises restaurant resembles a ski lodge. At the base of Mount Gushmore is a sandy beach with several other attractions, including a wave pool and a scaled-down version of Mount Gushmore for younger children. The park is located on World Drive, just north of the All-Star Sports and Music resorts.

ESSENTIALS

HOURS   The park is open from 10am to 5pm most of the year (with extended hours during some holiday periods), 9am to 8pm in the summer.

ENTRANCE FEES   A 1-day ticket to Blizzard Beach is $26.95 for adults, $21.50 for children.

HELPFUL HINTS   Arrive at or before park opening to avoid long lines and to be sure you get in. Beach towels and lockers are available for a small charge, and you can buy beach accessories at the Beach Haus.

MAJOR ATTRACTIONS IN THE PARK

Cross Country Creek

Inner-tubers can float lazily along this meandering 2,900-foot creek, which circles the entire park, but beware: It will take you inside a mysterious cave.

Runoff Rapids

Another inner-tube run, where guests can careen down four different twisting, turning flumes—sometimes in total darkness.

Ski-Patrol Training Camp

Designed for preteens, it features a rope swing, a T-bar drop over water, slides (including the wet and slippery Mogul Mania), and a challenging ice-floe walk along slippery floating icebergs.

Slush Gusher

Another Mount Gushmore–speed slide (a bit tamer than Mogul Mania) that travels along a snowbanked mountain gully.

Snow Stormers

Three flumes descend from the top of Mount Gushmore and follow a switchback course through ski-type slalom gates.

Steamboat Springs

On the world's longest white-water raft ride, your six-passenger raft twists down a 1,200-foot series of rushing waterfalls.

Summit Plummet

Starting 120 feet up, this is a speed slide/thrill ride that makes a 55-mile-per-hour plunge straight down to a splash landing at the base of the mountain.

Toboggan Racers

An eight-lane water slide that sends guests racing head first over exhilarating dips as they descend a snowy slope.

RIVER COUNTRY

One of the many recreational facilities at the Fort Wilderness Resort campground, this mini–water park is themed after Tom Sawyer's swimming hole. Kids can scramble over boulders that double as diving platforms for a 330,000-gallon pool. Two 16-foot water slides also provide access to the pool. Attractions on the adjacent **Bay Lake,** which is equipped with ropes and ships' booms for climbing, include a pair of flumes—one 260 feet long, the other 100 feet—that corkscrew through Whoop-N-Holler Hollow; **White Water Rapids,** which carries inner-tubers along a winding, 230-foot creek with a series of chutes and pools; and **The Ol' Wading Pool,** a smaller version of the swimming hole designed for young children.

There are pool and beachside areas for sunning and picnicking, plus a 350-yard boardwalk nature trail through a cypress swamp. Beach towels and lockers can be obtained for a minimal fee. Light fare is available at **Pop's Place.** To get here without a car, take a launch from the dock near the entrance to the Magic Kingdom or a bus from its Transportation and Ticket Center. River Country is generally open from 10am to 5pm most of the year (with extended hours during holidays), 10am to 7pm during the summer. A 1-day admission to River Country is $15.95 for adults, $12.50 for children.

FANTASIA GARDENS & WINTER SUMMERLAND

Fantasia Gardens Miniature Golf, located across the street from the Swan Hotel, off Epcot Resorts Boulevard, offers two 18-hole miniature courses drawing inspiration from the Walt Disney classic cartoon of the same name. On the **Fantasia Gardens** course, hippos, ostriches, and gators dot the course, and the Sorcerer's Apprentice himself presides over the final hole. It's a good bet for beginners and kids. Seasoned mini-golfers will probably prefer **Fantasia Fairways,** which is a scaled-down golf course complete with sand traps, water hazards, and tricky putting greens.

Santa Claus and his elves provide the theme for **Winter Summerland,** a miniature golf course that opened in 1999, featuring two 18-hole courses. St. Nick can be found in familiar snow scenes along one course while the Jolly Old elf cavorts in the sand along the other 18 holes.

Ticket prices for both run $9.50 for adults and $7.50 for children aged 3 to 9. For information about Fantasia Gardens call ☎ **407/560-8760.** For information on Winter Summerland call ☎ **407/939-7639.**

What to See & Do Beyond Disney: Universal Studios Escape, Sea World & Other Orlando Attractions

Locals call it the theme-park wars, the ongoing "anything-you-can-do-I-can-do-better" tussle between the Walt Disney properties and the many other Orlando-area attractions. Universal Studios Escape is the biggest challenger to Disney. In addition to its popular Universal Studios Florida park, it is opening its own nighttime entertainment complex, CityWalk, a second theme park, Islands of Adventure, and its first on-property resort, Portofino Bay, a 750-room Loews hotel. Sea World is planning a second theme park. Aside from offering greater variety, these changes will mean more multiday packages and special deals for visitors. Sea World and Universal Studios began offering more multiday pass options a few years ago to compete with Disney. Those two parks, plus several other area attractions, have joined together to offer the **Flex Pass,** which offers discounted tickets.

And while the wars rage on in the traditional tourist areas, it has dawned—finally—on the rest of Orlando that central Florida is one of the world's favorite vacation destinations.

Downtown Orlando has in the last decade undergone a major resurgence, with thousands regularly crowding its streets, nightclubs, and restaurants. Recent multimillion-dollar expansions at the Orlando Museum of Art and the Orlando Science Center show that the city is stepping up to compete. A multimillion-dollar performing arts center, to be built in downtown Orlando, is in the works by the city of Orlando. This expansion means that visitors can enjoy the spoils: more variety, greater opportunities, and a world beyond Disney.

THE FLEX PASS The most economical way to see the various "other than Disney" parks is with a Flex Pass. Universal Studios Florida, Islands of Adventure, Sea World, and Wet 'n' Wild, have joined together to fight Disney's multipark pass system. Here's how it works. You pay one price to visit any of the participating parks during either a 7- or 10-day period. A 7-day, four-park pass to Universal Studios Florida, Islands of Adventure, Wet 'n' Wild, and Sea World is $169.95 for ages 10 to adult or $135.65 for children under 10. A 10-day, five-park pass, which also includes Busch Gardens in Tampa, sells for $209.05 for adults and $167.65 for children 3–9.

(Children under 2 are free.) The Flex Pass can be ordered through Universal at ☎ 407/363-8000, Sea World at ☎ 407/351-3600, or Wet 'n' Wild at ☎ 800/992-WILD or 407/351-WILD.

1 Universal Studios Florida

With shorter lines and more thrill rides Universal Studios Florida is actually my favorite park. Even with the fast-paced, grown-up rides such as Twister, Terminator, and Back to the Future, there is still plenty for the kids. As a plus, it is a working motion-picture and television production studio, so occasionally there is some filming done in the park or, more often, at the Nickelodeon soundstages. Remember cable's *The Swamp Thing, Clarissa Explains It All,* or the short-lived *SeaQuest?* Those television series were shot on the property. Whether or not there is a film in production, every day you will amble amid reel history displayed in the form of some 40 actual sets exhibited along "Hollywood Boulevard" and "Rodeo Drive." On hand to greet visitors are **Hanna-Barbera characters** (Yogi Bear, Scooby Doo, Fred Flintstone, and others) and a talented group of actors representing Universal stars from Harpo Marx to the Blues Brothers. The long-running Ghostbusters attraction has been closed. (Now who we gonna call?) Blowing into its place is **Twister . . . Ride it Out,** an attraction based on the 1996 blockbuster movie *Twister,* which brought Universal more than $245 million at the box office.

The real news at Universal Studios Escape is the opening of the second theme park, Islands of Adventure and the first of five on-property resorts, a 750-room Loews hotel called Portofino Bay. Islands of Adventure, with areas dedicated to Dr. Seuss and Marvel comic characters, may give Disney real competition with not only roller coaster loving thrill seekers, but also with the kiddie crowd, especially those dragging along their baby boomer parents.

ESSENTIALS

GETTING TO UNIVERSAL BY CAR   Universal is about half a mile north of I-4, Exit 30B, Kirkman Road or Route 435. There may be construction in the area so keep an eye out for the road signs directing you to Universal Studios.

PARKING   If you park in the multilevel garage, remember the theme and music on your floor to help you later identify your car. Or, do it the old-fashioned way: Write it down. Parking costs $6 for cars, $7 for RVs and trailers. Valet parking is available for $12.

TICKET PRICES   A **1-day ticket** costs $46.65 for ages 10 and over, $37.10 for children 3–9; a 2-day pass is $84.75 for adults, $68.85 for children 3–9; a 3-day pass is $105.95 for adults, $84.75 for children 3–9.

An annual pass is $190.75 for adults, $164.25 for children 3–9. All multi-day passes allow you to move between Universal Studios Florida and Islands of Adventure during the course of a single day. Since the parks are within walking distance

The grand opening of Twister . . . Ride It Out was postponed in April 1998 after a real killer twister roared through central Florida, killing 42 people and destroying hundreds of homes. Universal used the ride's locale to collect donations for storm victims.

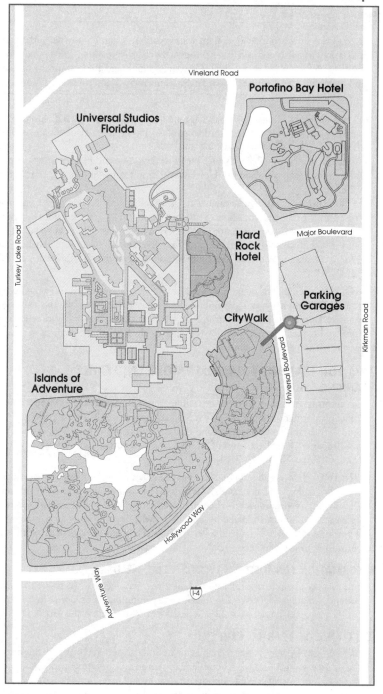

> ### For Families
>
> If you brought a stroller with you on your vacation, bring it with you to the park; it is a long walk from your car—through the massive parking garage and City-Walk—before you get to the park. Carrying a child, and the accompanying bags and bottles, will make it seem even farther. This is especially true after a long day.

of each other, you won't lose too much time in transit. It is a long walk however, so parents with small kids should consider strollers and people with disabilities, wheelchairs.

See the beginning of this chapter for information on the **Flex Pass,** which provides multiple-day admission to Universal Studios Escape, Sea World, and Wet 'n' Wild.

There is also a **VIP tour** available at Universal Studios Florida, which includes line-cutting privileges, for about $120 per person. This pass provides a 5-hour guided tour with quick entrance and preferred seating at seven Universal attractions. A VIP tour is also being developed for Islands of Adventure and may be available by the time of your trip. For more information on the VIP tour call ☎ **407/ 224-7750.**

HOURS   The park is open 365 days a year, generally from 9am to 7pm. Closing hours vary seasonally and depending on special activities within the park. For example, during Halloween Horror Nights the park closes around 5pm, reopens at 7pm, and remains open until at least midnight. The best bet is to call before you go so you are not caught by surprise.

TIPS FOR MAKING YOUR VISIT MORE ENJOYABLE
PLANNING YOUR VISIT

Get information before you leave by calling **Guest Relations** (☎ 407/363-8000). Request information about the new travel packages, as well as theme-park information. Universal often offers a "second-day free" promotion. Ask about details. You can also write Guest Relations at Universal Studios Florida, 1000 Universal Studios Plaza, Orlando, FL 32819-7601.

ONLINE   Information about Universal Studios can be found at **www.usf.com.** Orlando's daily newspaper, the *Orlando Sentinel,* also produces Orlando Sentinel Online at **www.orlandosentinel.com.** Once there, click on "Theme Park Central" for a variety of information and for updates on what is going on at local attractions. If you subscribe to AOL, type the keyword **Go2Orlando** to access a site with a lot of updated information about Universal and other theme parks.

INFORMATION FOR VISITORS WITH SPECIAL NEEDS

Guests with disabilities should go to **Guest Services** located just inside the main entrance for a *Disabled Guest Guidebook,* a Telecommunications Device for the Deaf (TDD), or other special assistance. Wheelchairs are for rent at the park.

BEST TIME OF YEAR TO VISIT

As with Walt Disney World, there is really no "off" season for Universal, but during the winter months, usually from January through April, the park crowds are smallest, the weather coolest, and the air least humid. The summer months, when the masses throng to the park, are not only crowded, but uncomfortably hot, sticky, and humid. During the cooler months, you also don't have to worry about the daily summer storms. Avoid spring-break months.

Universal Has Character(s), Too

Yogi Bear might say that the Universal character breakfast offers up more than just your "ordinary pic-a-nic basket." The kidlets get a chance to have their picture taken with the Universal characters who are, by the way, Woody Woodpecker, Yogi Bear, BooBoo Bear, Scooby Doo, Fred Flintstone, Barney Rubble, Fievel Mouskewitz, George Jetson, and Rocky and Bullwinkle. (A rotating collection comes to each breakfast so don't promise a specific character unless you confirm it through the reservation office.) The menu is your basic breakfast fare of scrambled eggs, Danish, cereal, and, for the adults, coffee and tea. These breakfasts are usually less crowded than the ones at WDW, so the kids get more one-on-one time with each character. *A nice touch:* The children get special cards and crayons so they can get autographs. The character breakfasts are held from 8 to 9am, Tuesday and Thursday. The cost is $13.50 for adults; $8.75 for children ages 3–11. For information call ☎ **407/224-6339.** You can make reservations up to 60 days in advance.

If you are planning a trip during late February or March, keep in mind that a raucous Mardi Gras celebration is going on in the evenings. Also note that Halloween Horror Nights, which usually runs weekend nights throughout October, is a very grown-up event—with lots of alcohol flowing—and really not suitable for younger children. The park is, however, still open during the day.

Many of the park's best rides are action-based thrill rides, which means your options will be limited if you are pregnant or have heart, neck, or back problems. Review the rides and restrictions when you enter the park so you don't stand in line for something you won't be able to appreciate. There are, however, stationary areas available at some moving rides. Check your park guide under "expectant mothers," then ask the attendants for assistance as you enter the ride.

THE BEST DAYS TO VISIT

Go near the end of the week, on a Thursday or Friday. The pace is somewhat faster between Monday and Wednesday, with the heaviest crowds on weekends.

CREATE AN ITINERARY

Pick three or four things that you must see or do and plan your day, along a rough geographical guide. Universal is relatively small, so walking from one end of the park to the other is not that daunting.

CHOOSE AGE-APPROPRIATE RIDES/SHOWS

Here, as in Disney, height and age restrictions are not bent to accommodate a screaming child. Some of the Universal shows contain loud music and pyrotechnics that can frighten children. Check the attraction descriptions that follow to make sure your child won't be unduly disappointed or frightened.

A Suggested Itinerary

A single day is usually sufficient to see the park if you arrive early. Skip the city sidewalks of the main gate and Terminator 2: 3-D Battle Across Time, and veer to the left (clockwise) toward **Hercules & Xena, Alfred Hitchcock's 3-D Theatre,** or the **Funtastic World of Hanna-Barbera,** but we don't recommend that you stop at these. Instead, continue around the park in this direction, beating the crowd to the blockbuster rides such as **Twister, Kongfrontation, Jaws,** and **Earthquake.** Take a break for lunch, watch the **Wild West Stunt Show,** and move on to **Back to the Future** and **ET Adventure.** Let the kids burn off some energy in **Fievel's Playland** and then go to **Terminator 2.** You may have some time before the stunt show to visit a few other attractions. If speed boats and explosions don't excite you, skip the show and revisit your favorite attractions, or beat the crowd to the parking lot.

A second day will allow you to revisit some of the blockbuster rides. Most of them, especially Back to the Future, are worth a second trip. With the pressure to hit all the major rides lessened, tour **Nickelodeon Studios.** This is a must if you have kids, who no doubt will be able to tell you a thing or two about this kids' network. Visitors sometimes have a chance to participate in the taping of some of Nick's often sloppy game shows. You can also visit the **Gory, Gruesome & Grotesque Horror-Makeup Show,** and take a break at **Mel's Diner,** and shows such as the **Beetlejuice Graveyard Revue.**

SERVICES & FACILITIES IN UNIVERSAL STUDIOS FLORIDA

ATMs   Machines accepting cards from banks using the Cirrus, Honor, and Plus systems are located outside of the main entrance and just inside the main entrance.

Baby Care   Changing tables are in both men's and women's rest rooms; there are nursing facilities at Guest Relations at **Family Services,** just inside the main entrance and to the right. No diapers are sold on the premises, but complimentary diapers are available to guests in need at the Animal House, Doc's Candy Store, and the Universal Studios Store.

Cameras & Film   Camcorders are for rent, and film and disposable cameras are available at the Lights, Camera, Action shop in the Front Lot, just inside the main entrance. One-hour photo developing is available in the Darkroom.

Car Assistance   Battery jumps are provided. If you need assistance with your car, raise the hood and tell any parking attendant your location. Use the call boxes located throughout the garage to call for security.

First Aid   The First Aid Center is located between New York and San Francisco, next to Louie's Italian Restaurant.

Lockers   Lockers are across from Guest Relations near the main entrance and cost $3 a day plus a $2 refundable deposit.

Lost Children   If you lose a child, go to Guest Relations near the main entrance or to Security (behind Louie's, between New York and San Francisco). Children under 7 should wear name tags.

Pet Care   An indoor/outdoor kennel is available for $5 a day near the newest parking lot. Ask the attendant for directions upon entering the toll plaza.

Stroller Rental   Strollers can be rented in Amity and at Guest Relations just inside the entrance to the right. The cost is $6 for a single, $12 for a double.

Wheelchair Rental   Regular wheelchairs can be rented for $7 in Amity and at Guest Relations just inside the main gate. Electric wheelchairs are $30, with a $25 deposit.

MAJOR ATTRACTIONS AT UNIVERSAL STUDIOS FLORIDA

Rides and attractions utilize cutting-edge technology—such as OMNIMAX 70mm film projected on seven-story screens—to create terrific special effects. While

Money Saver

You can save 10% off your purchase at any Universal Escape gift shop or meal by showing your AAA (American Automobile Association) card. This discount is not available at food or merchandise carts, and tobacco, candy, film, collectibles, and sundry items are not included.

waiting in line, you'll be entertained by excellent preshows, better even than those at that other theme park. Universal, as a whole, takes itself less seriously than the Mouse That Roared, and the atmosphere is peppered by subtle reminders that in the competitive theme-park industry it is not a small world after all.

Back to the Future: The Ride
Frommer's Rating: A+
Recommended Ages: 8–adult
Visitors blast through the space-time continuum, plummeting into volcanic tunnels ablaze with molten lava, colliding with Ice Age glaciers, thundering through caves and canyons, and briefly being swallowed by a dinosaur in a spectacular multisensory adventure. You twist, you turn, you dip and dive, and feel like you are really flying. Stick to seats in the back of the car—designed to resemble the movie's famous DeLorean—to avoid ruining the illusion by glimpsing your neighbors careening hydraulically in the next bay. This is a very bumpy ride and might not be appropriate for those with certain health problems. *Note:* Pay heed to the posted warnings displayed at the ride, and remember that children must be 40 inches tall.

The Beetlejuice Graveyard Revue
Frommer's Rating: A
Recommended Ages: 6–adult
Dracula, Wolfman, the Phantom of the Opera, Frankenstein and his bride, and Beetlejuice put on a funky—and very funny—rock musical with pyrotechnic special effects and MTV-style choreography. Loud and lively enough to scare some small children.

A Day in the Park with Barney
Frommer's Rating: A+ for kids and their parents, D for singles
Recommended Ages: all ages
Set in a parklike theater-in-the-round, this musical show—starring the popular Purple One, Baby Bop, and BJ—uses song, dance, and interactive play to deliver an environmental message. For young children, this could be the highlight of the day. The playground adjacent to the theater is a lot of fun with chimes to ring, tree houses to explore, and lots to intrigue little visitors. Since it is air-conditioned, it is also a good place to wait before the show.

Earthquake—The Big One
Frommer's Rating: B
Recommended Ages: 6–adult
You board a BART train in San Francisco for a peaceful subway ride, but just as you pull into the Embarcadero Station there's an earthquake—the big one, 8.3 on the Richter scale! As you sit helplessly trapped, vast slabs of concrete collapse around you, a propane truck bursts into flames, a runaway train comes hurtling at you, and the station floods (60,000 gallons of water cascade down the steps). *Note:* Children must be 40 inches tall and must ride with an adult.

Universal Studios Florida

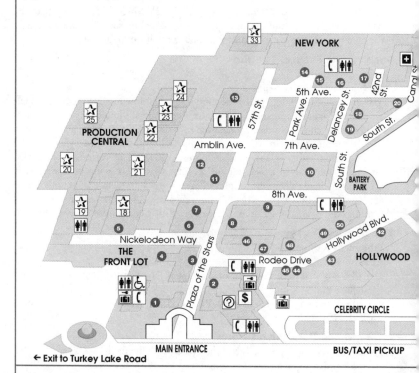

← Exit to Turkey Lake Road

MAIN ENTRANCE

BUS/TAXI PICKUP

The Front Lot:
Nickelodeon Kiosk ④
On Location ②
Studio Gifts ①
Universal Studios Store ③

Production Central:
Alfred Hitchcock: The
  Making of Movies ⑧
The Bates Motel Gift Shop ⑨
The Bone Yard ⑫
The Futuristic World of
  Hanna-Barbera ⑥
Hanna-Barbera Store ⑦

Hercules & Xena: Wizards
  of the Screen ⑩
Jurassic Park Kiosk ⑪
Nickelodeon Studios ⑤

New York:
Arcade ⑯⑳
Bull's Gym ⑲
Doc's Candy ⑱
Kongfrontation ⑭
Safari Outfitters Ltd. ⑮
Second Hand Rose ⑰
Twister ⑬

San Francisco/Amity:
Beetlejuice's Graveyard Revue
Dynamite Night Stuntacular ㉘
Earthquake-The Big One ㉒
Jaws! ㉖
Quint's Nautical Treasures ㉕
Salty's Sketches ㉔
Shaiken's Souvenirs ㉓
Wild West Stunt Show ㉗

Expo Center:
Animal Actors Stage ㊲
Back to the Future Gifts ㉚

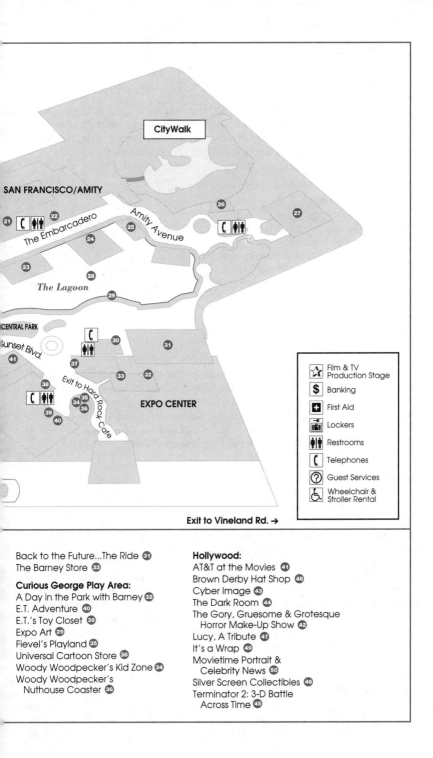

CityWalk

SAN FRANCISCO/AMITY

The Embarcadero

Amity Avenue

The Lagoon

CENTRAL PARK

Sunset Blvd.

Exit to Hard Rock Cafe

EXPO CENTER

Exit to Vineland Rd. →

☆	Film & TV Production Stage
$	Banking
✚	First Aid
🛅	Lockers
🚻	Restrooms
ℂ	Telephones
?	Guest Services
♿	Wheelchair & Stroller Rental

Back to the Future...The Ride ③①
The Barney Store ③③

Curious George Play Area:
A Day in the Park with Barney ③②
E.T. Adventure ④⓪
E.T.'s Toy Closet ③⑨
Expo Art ②⑨
Fievel's Playland ③⑤
Universal Cartoon Store ③⑧
Woody Woodpecker's Kid Zone ③④
Woody Woodpecker's
    Nuthouse Coaster ③⑥

Hollywood:
AT&T at the Movies ④①
Brown Derby Hat Shop ④⑧
Cyber Image ④③
The Dark Room ④④
The Gory, Gruesome & Grotesque
    Horror Make-Up Show ④②
Lucy, A Tribute ④⑦
It's a Wrap ④⑨
Movietime Portrait &
    Celebrity News ⑤⓪
Silver Screen Collectibles ④⑥
Terminator 2: 3-D Battle
    Across Time ④⑤

E.T. Adventure
Frommer's Rating: A
Recommended Ages: all ages

Visitors are given a passport to E.T.'s planet, which needs his healing powers to rejuvenate it. You'll soar with E.T. on a mission to save his ailing planet, through the forest and into space, aboard a star-bound bicycle—all to the accompaniment of that familiar movie theme music. A cool, wooded forest serves to create one of the most pleasant waits for any ride in central Florida. This is a wait worth the ride, a pleasure for kids of all ages.

The Funtastic World of Hanna-Barbera
Frommer's Rating: B+
Recommended Ages: 5–adult

This motion-simulator ride takes guests careening through the universe in a spaceship piloted by Yogi Bear to rescue Elroy Jetson. Prior to this wild ride, you'll learn how cartoons are created. After it, in an interactive area, you can experiment with animation sound effects—*boing! plop! splash!*—and color in your own cartoons. This is a great place for kids of all ages to take some time and play. Although it doesn't make a lot of sense (since this is the park's most blatant kiddie ride), children must be 40 inches tall.

Jaws
Frommer's Rating: A
Recommended Ages: 8–adult

Did you really think it was safe to go back into the water? As your boat heads out to the open seas, an ominous dorsal fin appears on the horizon. What follows is a series of terrifying attacks from a 3-ton, 32-foot-long great white shark that tries to sink its teeth into passengers. And there's more trouble ahead. A 30-foot wall of flame caused by burning fuel surrounds the boat, and you will truly feel the heat. I won't tell you how it ends, but let's just say, blackened shark, anyone? (The effects are more startling after dark.)

Kongfrontation
Frommer's Rating: B
Recommended Ages: 6–adult

It's the last thing the Big Apple needed: King Kong is back! As you stand in line in a replica of a grungy, graffiti-scarred New York subway station, CBS newsman Roland Smith reports on Kong's terrifying rampage. Everyone must evacuate to Roosevelt Island, so it's all aboard the tram. Cars collide and hydrants explode below, police helicopters hover overhead putting you directly in the line of fire, the tram malfunctions, and, of course, you encounter Kong—32 feet tall and 13,000 pounds. He emits banana breath in your face and menaces passengers, dangling the tram over the East River. A great thrill—or just another day in New York. *Note:* Children must be 40 inches tall to ride alone. Younger children may be frightened by the dark waiting area.

Fun Fact

Want to have a little fun and take home a souvenir? Check out the arcade games along the boardwalk near Jaws. Some have a three-player minimum, so if your family stacks the deck someone is bound to win a pretty nifty, if small, stuffed animal.

Nickelodeon Studios Tour
Frommer's Rating: B
Recommended Ages: all ages
You'll tour the soundstages where Nick shows are produced, view concept pilots, visit the kitchen where Gak and green slime are made, play typical show games, and try out new Sega video games. There's lots of audience participation, and a volunteer will get slimed.

Terminator 2: 3-D Battle Across Time
Frommer's Rating: A+
Recommended Ages: 8–adult
He's back . . . at least in Orlando. This is billed as "the quintessential sight and sound experience for the 21st century!" The same director who made the movie, Jim Cameron, has overseen this production. After a little bit of a slow start, this attraction builds to an impressive experience featuring the Big Man himself, along with other original cast members, and combines 70mm 3-D film (utilizing three 23- by 50-foot screens) with live stage action and thrilling technical effects. This ride would probably be rated PG for violence and loud noise, but the crisp 3-D effects are among the best in any Orlando park. Small children may find all the crashing and flying 3-D effects too intense.

Twister...Ride it Out
Frommer's Rating: A
Recommended Ages: 5–adult
Visitors from the twister-prone Midwest may find this re-creation a little too close to the real thing. An ominous funnel cloud, five-stories tall, is created by 2 million cubic feet of air per minute. And the sound of a freight train fills the theater, as cars, signs, and trucks fly about while the audience watches just 20 feet away. It's the windy version of *Earthquake* and packs quite a wallop. Crowds have been known to applaud when it is all over.

Wild, Wild, Wild West Show
Frommer's Rating: A+
Recommended Ages: all ages
Stunt people demonstrate falls from three-story balconies, gun and whip fights, dynamite explosions, and other wild west staples. This is a well-performed, lively show that is especially popular with foreign visitors who have celluloid visions of the American West. Kids, do not try this at home. *Warning:* Heed the splash zone or you will get very wet.

ADDITIONAL ATTRACTIONS
Hercules & Xena: Wizards of the Screen puts you on the set with scantily-clad gladiators, as the audience battles to make the sound effects match the videos. **Alfred Hitchcock's 3-D Theatre** is a tribute to the "master of suspense," in which Tony Perkins narrates a reenactment of the famous shower scene from *Psycho,* and where *The Birds*—as if the movie weren't scary enough—becomes an in-your-face 3-D movie.

Other park attractions include the **Gory, Gruesome & Grotesque Horror-Makeup Show** for a behind-the-scenes look at the transformation scenes from movies like *The Fly* and *The Exorcist. I Love Lucy,* **A Tribute,** is a remembrance of America's queen of comedy; and **Fievel's Playland,** is an innovative western-themed playground based on the Spielberg movie *An American Tail.* You can also catch the **Blues Brothers show** or take a look at old movie props in the **Bone Yard.**

Descendants of Lassie, Benji, Mr. Ed, and other animal superstars perform their famous pet tricks in the **Animal Actors Show.** And **Dynamite Nights Stuntacular,** a nightly show, combines death-defying stunts with a breathtaking display of fireworks.

At press time, Universal had just opened another children's play area, **Woody Woodpecker's Kidzone,** in the summer of 1999. The star attraction there is **Woody Woodpecker's Nuthouse Coaster,** a kid-sized roller coaster that features a slightly scary 30-foot drop.

SHOPPING AT UNIVERSAL

Every major attraction here (thoughtfully) has a theme store attached. Although the prices are relatively high when you consider you are just buying a T-shirt, the **Hard Rock Cafe** shop is extremely popular and has a small but diverse selection of Hard Rock everything. If you've often longed for a pair of Fred Flintstone boxer shorts or, perhaps, some plastic Scooby snacks, visit the **Hanna-Barbera Shop.**

More than 25 other shops in the park sell everything from Lucy collectibles to Bates Motel towels, and restaurants run the gamut from **Mel's Drive-In** (of *American Graffiti* fame) to the **Hard Rock Cafe,** to **Schwab's.** Be warned that, unlike WDW where Mickey is everywhere, these shops are specific to the individual attractions. If you see something you like, buy it. You probably won't find it in another store.

GREAT BUYS AT UNIVERSAL STUDIOS

Here is a sampling of some of the more unusual gifts available at some of the Universal stores. Of course in addition to these options, you can find the standard tourist fare with a staggering array of coffee mugs, key chains, and the like. I tried to include things you probably couldn't find anywhere else that were of good quality for the price.

Back to the Future Gifts: Real fans of the movie series will find lots of intriguing stuff here, but one of the more interesting, and affordable items, is a miniature version of the Back to the Future DeLorean ($24.95).

The Bates Motel Gift Shop: When house guests have stayed just a bit too long you can send a not-so-subtle message by putting out these Bates Motel guest towels ($6.95) or begin lounging around the house in your white, plush terry cloth bathrobe with the Bates Motel logo ($49.95).

E.T.'s Toy Closet: This is the place for plush, stuffed animals, but the thing that caught my eye was the pink, Babe backpack ($12.95). The plush replica of the store's alien namesake ($49.95) is also an interesting find.

Hanna-Barbera Store: Inexpensive and great for kids of all ages are the plush Scooby Doo Slippers ($12) or the Fred Flintstone T-shirt ($16) that allows you to dress just like Bedrock's favorite son.

Kongfrontation: A video copy of the original RKO movie that started it all is available ($19.95), as well as the cuddliest stuffed gorilla you will find anywhere. Pint-sized versions of the big ape start at $5.95.

Quint's Nautical Treasures: This is the place to go for a different kind of T-shirt. Tropical colors, with subtle Universal logos, are the thing here. T-shirts are $19.95; sweatshirts, $39.95.

Second Hand Rose: This is something you will never see at Disney: discounted merchandise. This store sells last season's hot T-shirts, stuffed animals, and a wide variety of souvenirs at the lowest prices you will find in the park.

Universal Cuisine

There are more than a dozen places to eat at Universal Studios Florida, offering everything from fresh lobster to corn dogs. Here are a few of my favorites:

Best sit-down meal: Lombard's Landing's clam basket, lightly fried and plentiful, is ideal for a sit-down meal and reasonably priced at $13.95. Lombard's is located across from Earthquake.

Best counter service: Universal Studios' Classic Monsters Cafe is one of the newest eateries in the park and offers pizza, pasta, and desserts. I recommend the Linguini Primavera at $6.95, although the pizza is also pretty tasty. It is located off 7th Avenue near the Boneyard.

Best place for hungry families: Similar to a mall food court, the **International Food Bazaar** offers a variety of ethnic food in one location. With options ranging from Chinese stir-fry to fajitas, here a family can split up and still eat under one roof. There are kid's meals, under $4, offered at most locations. The food here is far from gourmet, but a cut above regular fast food. It is located near the backside of the Animal Actor's Studio, near the lagoon and the entrance to Back to the Future.

Best Snack: The Frozen Lemon Slush ($2.35) at **Brody's Ice Cream Shop** is just the thing to refresh you on a hot summer afternoon. Brody's is located near the Wild, Wild West Stunt Show arena. There are also carts in Amityville selling the luscious lemon treat.

Silver Screen Collectibles: Fans of *I Love Lucy* will adore the small variety of collectible dolls that begin at $95. For an interesting, practical, and inexpensive, little something to take home check out the Woody Woodpecker back scratcher ($2.95.).

Universal Studios Store: This store, near the entrance, sells just about everything, but for a quality, practical souvenir look for the leather backpack with the Universal logo ($89.95).

2 Islands of Adventure

Universal's second park opened in 1999 with a vibrantly colored, cleverly themed collection of fast, fun rides for kids of all ages. At 110-acres, it is the same size as the original park, but clever planning makes it seem packed with even more to do. Roller coasters roar above pedestrian walkways, water rides careen through the center of the park, and themed eateries are camouflaged to match their surroundings, adding to your overall immersion in the various "islands."

From the wobbly angles and day-glo colors in **Seuss Island** to the lush foliage of **Jurassic Park,** Universal has also done a good job at differentiating various sections of the park—making it easier to navigate. (This is unlike Universal Studios, where it's sometimes hard to tell if you are in San Francisco or New York.)

Islands of Adventure is divided into six areas: the **Port of Entry,** where you will find a collection of shops and eateries, and the themed sections—**Seuss Landing, Toon Lagoon, Jurassic Park, Marvel Super Hero Island** and **The Lost Continent.** This park offers the biggest concentration of thrill rides and coasters of any park in the area, plus it has generous play areas for the kids. The trade-off is fewer shows and stage productions.

Some Practical Advice for Island Adventurers

1. **The Shorter They Are . . .** Ten of the 12 major rides at Islands of Adventure have height restrictions. Some deny access to those under 54 inches. While there is a baby swap at all of the major attractions, allowing one parent to ride while the other watches the tikes, sitting in a waiting room isn't much fun for the little ones. Take your child's height into consideration before coming to the park.

2. **Cruising the Islands** If you hauled your stroller with you on your vacation, then bring it with you to the park. It is a very long walk from your car—through the massive parking garage and the nighttime entertainment district CityWalk—before you get to the park (unlike Disney where you simply get on a tram). Carrying a young child, and the accompanying paraphernalia, can make the long trek seem even longer. Especially at the end of the day.

3. **The Faint of Heart** Even if you don't have children, make sure you consider all the ride restrictions. Expectant mothers, and those with heart, neck, or back trouble, will be prohibited from most of the biggest attractions. There is still plenty to see and do, but without the roller coasters, the thrill of Islands of Adventure is gone.

4. **Beat the Heat** Several rides require that you wait outside without any cover to protect you from the sizzling Florida sun, so bring some bottled water along for the long waits or take a sip or two from the fountains placed in the waiting areas. Also, alcohol is more readily available at this park than at the Disney parks, and liquor, roller coasters, and sweltering heat can make for a messy mix.

5. **Cash in on your Card** You can save 10% on your purchases at any gift shop, or on a meal, in Islands of Adventure by showing your AAA (American Automobile Association) card. This discount is not available at food or merchandise carts, and tobacco, candy, film, collectibles, and sundry items are not included.

PARKING If you park in the multilevel garage, remember the theme and music on your floor to help you later identify your car. Or, do it the old-fashioned way: Write it down. Parking costs $6 for cars, $7 for RVs and trailers. Valet parking is available for $12.

TICKET PRICES A **1-day ticket** costs $46.65 for ages 10 and over, $37.10 for children 3–9; a **2-day pass** is $84.75 for adults, $68.85 for children 3–9; a **3-day pass** is $105.95 for adults, $84.75 for children 3–9.

An annual pass is $190.75 for adults, $164.25 for children 3–9. Multiday passes allow guests to visit both Islands of Adventure and Universal Studios Florida during the course of a single day.

See the beginning of this chapter for information on the **Flex Pass,** which provides multiple-day admission to Universal Studios Escape, Sea World, and Wet 'n' Wild.

A **VIP TOUR,** similar to the one offered at Universal Studios was being considered at press time. The Universal Escape Tour is a 5-hour guided tour providing line-cutting privileges, for about $120 per person. Call the main number (☎ **407/363-8000**) for information.

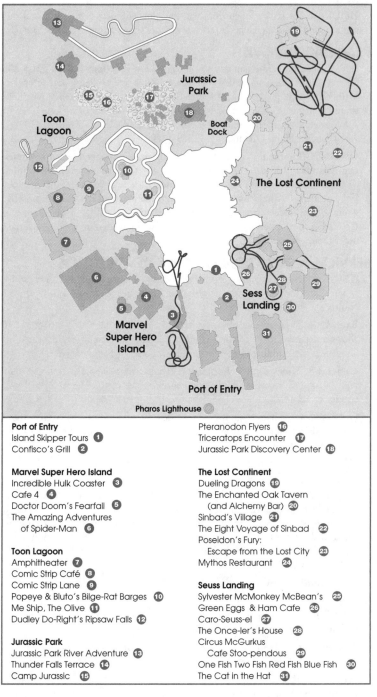

Islands of Adventure

Port of Entry
Island Skipper Tours **①**
Confisco's Grill **②**

Marvel Super Hero Island
Incredible Hulk Coaster **③**
Cafe 4 **④**
Doctor Doom's Fearfall **⑤**
The Amazing Adventures
   of Spider-Man **⑥**

Toon Lagoon
Amphitheater **⑦**
Comic Strip Café **⑧**
Comic Strip Lane **⑨**
Popeye & Bluto's Bilge-Rat Barges **⑩**
Me Ship, The Olive **⑪**
Dudley Do-Right's Ripsaw Falls **⑫**

Jurassic Park
Jurassic Park River Adventure **⑬**
Thunder Falls Terrace **⑭**
Camp Jurassic **⑮**

Pteranodon Flyers **⑯**
Triceratops Encounter **⑰**
Jurassic Park Discovery Center **⑱**

The Lost Continent
Dueling Dragons **⑲**
The Enchanted Oak Tavern
   (and Alchemy Bar) **⑳**
Sinbad's Village **㉑**
The Eight Voyage of Sinbad **㉒**
Poseidon's Fury:
   Escape from the Lost City **㉓**
Mythos Restaurant **㉔**

Seuss Landing
Sylvester McMonkey McBean's **㉕**
Green Eggs & Ham Cafe **㉖**
Caro-Seuss-el **㉗**
The Once-ler's House **㉘**
Circus McGurkus
   Cafe Stoo-pendous **㉙**
One Fish Two Fish Red Fish Blue Fish **㉚**
The Cat in the Hat **㉛**

HOURS   The park is open from 9am to 7pm, 365 days a year, and later during summer and holidays when there are additional shows at night. Call before you go.

PLANNING YOUR VISIT

Get information before you leave by calling **Guest Relations** (☎ **407/363-8000**). Request information about new travel packages, as well as theme-park information. With the opening of Islands of Adventure and the Portofino Bay resort, there should continue to be good deals, especially for packages that include hotel stays. Ask for details on special offers. You can also write Islands of Adventure, 1000 Universal Studios Plaza, Orlando, FL 32819-7610.

ONLINE   Information about Islands of Adventure can be found at **www.uescape. com/islands.** Orlando's daily newspaper, the *Orlando Sentinel,* also produces *Orlando Sentinel Online* at **www.orlandosentinel.com.** Once there, click on "Theme Park Central" for a variety of information, and for updates on what is going on at local attractions. If you subscribe to AOL, type the keyword **Go2Orlando** to access a site with a lot of updated information about Universal and other theme parks.

SERVICES & FACILITIES IN ISLANDS OF ADVENTURE

ATMs   Machines accepting cards from banks using the Cirrus, Honor, and Plus systems are located outside of the main entrance and just inside the main entrance.

Baby Care   There are baby-swap stations at all of the major attractions. This allows one parent to wait while the other rides. Nursing facilities are located in the Guest Services building in the Port of Entry. Look for Family Services.

Cameras & Film   Film and disposable cameras are available at DeSoto's Photography, to the right just inside the main entrance. Most stores have disposable cameras for around $25.

Car Assistance   Battery jumps are provided. If you need assistance with your car, raise the hood and tell any parking attendant your location. Use the call boxes located throughout the garage to call for security.

First Aid   Located in the Lost Continent, across from Oasis Coolers.

Lockers   Lockers are across from Guest Relations near the main entrance and cost $3 a day plus a $2 refundable deposit. There are also lockers located near the Incredible Hulk Coaster in Marvel Super Hero Island, the Jurassic Park River Adventure in Jurassic Park, and the Dueling Dragons in The Lost Continent. These lockers are free for 1 hour, and $1 for each additional 30 minutes. You cannot take loose items on these three rides, so you must put them in a locker or give them to a nonrider.

Lost Children   If you lose a child, go to Guest Relations near the main entrance. Children under 7 should wear name tags.

Pet Care   An indoor/outdoor kennel is available for $5 a day near the newest parking lot. Ask the attendant for directions upon entering the toll plaza.

Stroller Rental   Look to the left as you enter through the turnstiles. The cost is $6 for a single, $12 for a double.

Wheelchair Rental   Regular wheelchairs can be rented for $7 in the center concourse of the parking garage, near the giant hourglass or, to your left as you enter the turnstiles of the main entrance. Electric wheelchairs are $30, with a $25 deposit.

A Suggested Itinerary

If you have children under 10, enter and go to the right to **Seuss Island** where everything is geared to the young and young at heart. You'll easily spend the morning exploring real-life interpretations of the wacky, colorful world of Dr. Seuss. (The wild colors make for some good photographs.) Be sure to ride **The Cat in the Hat; One Fish, Two Fish, Red Fish, Blue Fish;** and **Caro-Seuss-El.** After all that waiting in line, let the little ones burn off some energy playing in **If I Ran the Zoo.** Enjoy a little lunch at the **Green Eggs and Ham Cafe.** Next, head to **The Lost Continent** and enjoy the sit-down show at **Poseidon's Fury: Escape from the Lost City,** and **The 8th Voyage of Sinbad.** If your child meets the height restrictions, head for **Dueling Dragons.** After a snack at **Oasis Coolers,** amble over to Jurassic Park, get a bird's eye view of the place from the **Pteranodon Flyers.** If you have older children visit the thrilling **Jurassic Park River Adventure** or, if you have young children, spend some time at the **Camp Jurassic** play area. If you could use a break from the heat, explore the Jurassic Park Discovery Center. (If you think you are running short on time, skip the **Pteranodon Flyers.**)

Finish up your day in **Toon Lagoon,** spinning down the river in **Popeye & Bluto's Bilge Rat Barges,** or taking the plunge down **Dudley Do-Right's Ripsaw Falls.** Enjoy walking under the giant images of super heroes in **Marvel Super Hero Island** and do a little shopping before ending your day with a show at **Theater of the Islands** and dinner at **Captain America Diner.** (Most rides at **Marvel Super Hero Island** are too intense for children 10 and under.)

If you don't have children, or your children are old enough to be daredevils, go right to **Marvel Super Hero Island,** head straight for the **Hulk Coaster,** hit **Dr. Doom's FearFall,** and then **The Spider-Man Adventure.** In **Toon Lagoon,** don't miss **Popeye & Bluto's Bilge Rat Barges** and **Dudley Do-Right's Ripsaw Falls.** Get a Dagwood sandwich at **Blondie's** before getting an overview of Jurassic Park while dangling from a **Pteranodon Flyer.** That should give lunch enough time to settle so you'll enjoy the wild ride on **Jurassic Park River Adventure.** In **The Lost Continent,** continue your thrill seeking on **Dueling Dragons** and at **Poseidon's Fury.**

After all the speed and thrills, end your day with a leisurely tour of **Seuss Landing.** Don't worry, you won't be the only adult on the **Caro-Seuss-El** or **The Cat in the Hat.** Enjoy dinner or a snack at **Green Eggs and Ham Cafe,** or have a sit down dinner at **Circus McGurkas Cafe Stoopendous.** If you have the energy, do a little shopping before heading home, or take advantage of the evening lull in the lines to take another spin on your favorite thrill ride. If one of your party isn't much of a shopper they can listen to some music, and have a drink, at the **Back-water Bar,** to the left as you go into **Port of Entry.**

PORT OF ENTRY

Here you'll find six shops, four restaurants and the **Island Skipper Tours,** which ferry passengers between the front of the park and **Jurassic Park.** If you plan to save shopping for the end of the day, go to **Universal Studios Islands of Adventure**

Fun Fact

With numerous water attractions it would be a good idea to purchase inexpensive ponchos for the whole family before coming to Islands of Adventure, or bring some dry clothing to keep in a locker for a mid-afternoon change.

Trading Company, which offers a variety of merchandise linked to attractions throughout the park, everything from Jurassic T-shirts to stuffed Cat in the Hat dolls.

The following descriptions offer a rundown of the information that was available at press time for all the major rides and attractions. It is likely that some of this information will change before the park actually opens. *Note:* Since some of these attractions were not yet open and we weren't able to actually try them, there is no Frommer's Rating.

SEUSS LANDING

Here those wonderful Dr. Seuss characters come to life. Needless to say, the main attractions here are aimed at the younger set, though anyone who loved the good Doctor as a child will enjoy some nostalgic fun on these rides.

The Cat in the Hat
Recommended Ages: All ages

Any Seuss fan will recognize the giant candy-striped hat looming over the entrance to this ride. Comparable to It's A Small World at WDW, The Cat in the Hat will surely become one of the signature experiences of Islands of Adventure. Love it or hate it, you'll just have to do it. Six-passenger couches travel through 18 show scenes retelling the Cat and the Hat tale of a day without Mom gone awry and including such characters as Thing 1 and Thing 2. The highlight is a revolving 24-foot tunnel that alters your perceptions and leaves your head spinning.

One Fish, Two Fish, Red Fish, Blue Fish
Frommer's Rating: A+ for kids, B for adults.
Recommended Ages: all ages, but small children will probably love it best

A control allows you to move your funky fish up or down as you spin around. Watch out for the "squirt posts," which spray unsuspecting riders who don't follow along with a special rhyme—so pay attention. Actually, even the most careful driver is likely to get wet. You can begin your up/down movements as soon as the ride begins to turn, so go ahead and get the most out of this ride, an evolved version of the Dumbo ride at Disney's Magic Kingdom.

Caro-Seuss-El
Frommer's Rating: A+ for kids, C for adults.
Recommended Ages: all ages

Not your average carousel, the whimsical characters of Dr. Seuss, including the elephant birds from *Horton Hatches an Egg,* move not only up and down, but in and out. Pull the reins to make eyes blink or heads bob as you twirl through the riot of color surrounding the ride.

A special wheelchair-loading system will make it accessible to guests with disabilities.

If I Ran the Zoo
Frommer's Rating: A+ for kids
Recommended Ages: all ages

Fun Fact

There are kiddie menus for $4.99 at several restaurants, but at Circus McGurkas Cafe Stoopendous and Green Eggs and Ham Cafe children are charged the same price as adults, but also get a souvenir cup with their meal.

An interactive playland for kids of all ages, this attraction includes everything from flying water snakes to a chance to tickle the toes of a Seussian animal. These 19 play stations are a nice place to let the kids burn off some excited energy.

MARVEL SUPER HERO ISLAND

Thrill junkies will love the twisting, turning, and stomach-churning rides, based on characters from Marvel comics, in this land filled with building-high murals of your favorite super heroes lining the street.

The Spider-Man Adventure
Frommer's Rating: A+
Recommended Ages: 8–adult
The original Web Master stars in this mobile ride with 3-D action and special effects. The story line is that guests are on a tour of the Daily Bugle when—yikes—something goes horribly wrong. Peter Parker suddenly encounters evil villains and becomes Spider-Man. This high-tech ride is similar to Back to the Future but is not stationary; cars twist and spin, plunge and soar through this comic book universe. Passengers wearing 3-D glasses squeal as real and computer generated objects alternately fly towards them. There is a simulated 400-foot drop that feels an awful lot like the real thing. *Note:* Expectant mothers or those with heart, neck, or back problems should not ride. Children must be at least 40 inches tall.

Incredible Hulk Coaster
Frommer's Rating: A+
Recommended Ages: 8–adult
Bruce Banner is working in his lab when—oh no—a disaster occurs. But this rocking rocket of a ride makes everything oh so right. From a dark tunnel you burst into the sunlight, while accelerating from zero to 40 miles per hour in 2 seconds. From there you spin upside down 100 feet from the ground, feel weightless, and careen through the center of the park over the heads of other visitors. Coaster-lovers will be pleased to know that this ride, which lasts 2 minutes and 15 seconds, includes seven rollovers and two deep drops. As a nice touch, the metal coaster glows green at night, but it is a blazing success day or night. *Note:* Expectant mothers or those with heart, neck, or back problems should not ride this ride. Children must be at least 54 inches tall.

Dr. Doom's Fearfall
Recommended Ages: 8–adult
The ominous-looking metal skeleton—not to mention the screams that can be heard at the entrance—adds to the anticipation of this straight plunge. The plot line is that you are touring a lab when—are you detecting a theme here—something goes horribly wrong. You'll get a serious rush as you drop, with feet dangling, down one of two 200-foot steel towers. The drop will remind you of the Tower of Terror at Disney–MGM Studios, but with the added thrill of feeling as if you are hanging free. Check the height restrictions carefully.

Note: Expectant mothers or those with heart, neck, or back problems should not ride this ride. Children must be at least 40 inches tall.

Fun Fact

Music at Universal's Islands of Adventure was composed specifically for the theme park, much like a score for a movie. It is the first time such a large-scale musical effort has been mounted for a theme park.

TOON LAGOON

More than 150 life-sized sculpted cartoon images let visitors know they have entered this section dedicated to your favorites from the Sunday funnies.

Dudley Do-Right's Ripsaw Falls
Recommended Ages: 6–adult
Underneath the staid red hat of the heroic Dudley is a splashy water ride, touted as the farthest, fastest drop in the history of flume rides. The boats take you around a 400,000-gallon lagoon and plunge you down a 75-foot drop at 50 miles per hour. At one point you are actually 15 feet below the water's surface. *Note:* You will get wet. Very wet. Expectant mothers or people with heart, neck, or back problems should not ride. Children must be at least 44 inches tall.

Popeye & Bluto's Bilge Rat Barges
Recommended Ages: 6–adult
The ramshackle huts of an old-time riverfront indicate you've come upon the barge ride. Twelve-person rafts bump and churn their way through a white-water ride encountering some scary creatures along the way, including a twirling octopus boat wash. *Note:* Here's another chance to get completely soaked. Expectant mothers or people with heart, neck, or back problems should not ride. Children must be at least 42 inches tall.

Me Ship, The Olive
Recommended Ages: all ages
This three-story boat is a family-friendly playland with dozens of activities from bow to stern. Kids can toot whistles, clang bells, or play the organ.

Comic Strip Lane
Recommended Ages: all ages
Beetle Baily, Hagar the Horrible, and Dagwood & Blondie are highlighted among some 80 characters in this lively jaunt through some of the best-loved comic strips of all times.

JURASSIC PARK

Okay, stay with me here. This is the theme-park creation based on a movie featuring a theme-park creation that might become a movie. Yes, all the basics from Stephen Spielberg's wildly successful films—and some of the high-tech wizardry—are incorporated in the lushly landscaped tropical locale that includes a replica of the familiar visitor's center from the movie. Expect hordes—and long lines—at the River Adventure.

Jurassic Park River Adventure
Recommended Ages: 6–up
After a leisurely tour down the faux river, you guessed it, something goes horribly wrong. Actually, the dreaded raptors have escaped and could hop aboard your boat at any minute.

This is an improved version of Kongfrontation at Universal Studios that allows you to come face to face—literally—with the living, breathing inhabitants of Jurassic Park. Five-story dinosaurs come within inches of the ride; Tyrannosaurus Rex decides you look like a tasty morsel. To escape, you take a breathtaking 85-foot plunge. Did I mention you'll get wet? *Note:* Expectant mothers or those with heart, neck, or back problems should not ride this ride. Children must be at least 42 inches tall.

Fun Fact

Park maps are available at Guest Services in the Port of Entry in French, German, Japanese, Portuguese, and Spanish.

Triceratops Encounter
Frommer's Rating: B-
Recommended Ages: all ages
Meet a "living" dinosaur and learn from the trainers about the care and feeding of the 24-foot-long, 10-foot-high Triceratops. The creature's responses to touch include realistic blinks and muscle flinches and are explained by on-site "trainers" who help you understand everything there is to know about the spiny dino.

Discovery Center
Recommended Ages: all ages
With life-sized dino replicas, and a few interactive games, this is a good place to take an air conditioned break. You can scan a wall for fossils, create a human/dino hybrid, and try to guess what is to be born from dino eggs. You can even play a game show, Paleo Puzzlers. On the down side, each interactive element takes a few minutes and there aren't enough stations to accommodate large crowds.

Pteranodon Flyers
Frommer's Rating: B-
Recommended Ages: All ages
The 10-foot metal spans and simple seats look deceptively flimsy, but this quick spin around Jurassic Park allows a great bird's-eye view. Although the landing is rather bumpy, this is a gentle ride through the sky, but unlike the usual gondolas, your feet hang free and there is little but a restraining belt between you and the ground. (Let's hope something doesn't go horribly wrong.) If you want to take a little tour of Camp Jurassic, go to the right after you get off the ride. Follow the red "Exit" signs. *Note:* Expectant mothers or those with heart, neck, or back problems should not ride this ride. Children must be at least 36 inches tall.

Camp Jurassic
Frommer's Rating: A
Recommended Ages: All ages
A play area with everything from lava pits with dinosaur bones to a rain forest. Watch out for the spitters that lurk in dark caves and mines. This multilevel play area has plenty of places for kids to crawl and explore. Young children will need close supervision because it is easy to get turned around within the caverns.

THE LOST CONTINENT
Although they have kind of mixed their millennia—ancient Greece and medieval forest—Universal seems to have done a good job creating a foreboding mood in this section of the park, where the entrance is marked by menacing stone griffins.

Poseidon's Fury: Escape from the Lost City
Recommended Ages: 6–adult
Similar to the Earthquake attraction in the other Universal park, this ride exposes you to torrents of water and blasts of heat and fire. The idea is that you are trapped in the midst of a battle between Poseidon, the god of the sea, and Zeus, the king of the gods, who hurls fire. It's more interesting than frightening, at least for adults, but still offers a thrill. Young children may find the flaming fireballs a little too intense.

Fun Fact

One Dueling Dragon coaster seems to have an obvious advantage over the other. The Fire Dragon can reach speeds of up to 60 mph, while the Ice Dragon only makes it up to 55 mph.

Dueling Dragons
Frommer's Rating: A
Recommended Ages: 10–adult
This ride is not for the faint of heart. It is scary, as well as surreal, to see another coaster heading right toward you as you zip through the air at 60 mph. True coaster fans will love this intertwined set of souped-up racers that sometimes come within 12 inches of each other. For the best ride try to get one of the two outside seats in each row. Also, pay attention, because the lines of both coasters split near the loading dock so daredevils can claim the very first car. *Note:* Expectant mothers or those with heart, neck, or back problems should not ride this ride. Children must be at least 54 inches tall.

The 8th Voyage of Sinbad
Recommended Ages: 6–adult
The mythical sailor is showcased in this stunt demonstration that takes place in a 1,700-seat theater decorated with blue stalagmites and eerie, gloomy wrecked ships. Relying heavily on pyrotechnics for special effects, this stunt extravaganza is a hot show, especially if you are in the first few rows. It might be too intense for young children.

SHOPPING AT ISLANDS OF ADVENTURE

There are more than 20 shops within the park, offering a variety of unusual, theme merchandise. You may want to check out **Cats, Hats & Things** and **Dr. Seuss' All The Books You Can Read** for special Seussian material. The **Jurassic Outfitters Dinostore** offers an array of stuffed and plastic dinos, plus safari-themed clothing. Super hero fans should check out the **Marvel Alterniverse Store.**

DINING AT ISLANDS OF ADVENTURE

There are a number of stands where you can get a quick bite to eat and a handful of full-service restaurants. The park's creators have taken some extra care to tie in restaurant offerings with the theme. The **Green Eggs and Ham Cafe** may be one of the few places on earth where you'd be willing to eat tinted huevos. (They sell as a sandwich for $5.95.) There are dozens of sit-down restaurants, eateries, and snack carts. To save money look for the kiddie menus, offering a children's meal and a small beverage for $4.99. Also consider the combo meals, which usually offer a slight price break. If you are looking for a relatively light lunch, the combo meals at the sit-down restaurants are big enough to share. Here are some of my favorites:

Best Sit-Down Restaurant   At **Mythos,** choose from gourmet selections such as pepper-painted salmon with lemon coucous or pan-fried crab cakes with lobster sauce and basil. This is a grown-up dining affair, best suited for older children and adults.

Fun Fact

Those green eggs get their color not from food dye but from a variety of spices.

Great Things to Buy at Islands of Adventure

Here is a sampling of some of the more unusual wares available at Islands of Adventure. It represents a cross section of prices and tastes. Prices may change slightly by the time of your visit, but those listed below, which do not include tax, will provide a general range.

Jurassic Outfitters   There are plenty of T-shirts with slogans like "I Survived," but at $16 the cotton boxers are a steal.

WossaMottaU   It's probably a good bet that no one at the office will have a Rocky or Bullwinkle ceramic mug like the one available for $13.50 at this store in Toon Lagoon.

Spider-Man Shop   This shop specializes in—you guessed it—Spider-Man paraphernalia. Here you can buy a $10 red Spidey cap covered with a black web and a $70 denim jacket with the Spider-Man logo.

Comics Shop   Comics junkies will enjoy browsing through the stacks of magazines on display. Where else could you find The Essential Silver Surfer for $14.95?

Toon Extra   Here you'll find a miniature stuffed Mr. Peanut bean bag for $7, an Olive Oyle and Popeye frame for $15, or a stuffed Beetle Baily for $12.

Treasures of Poseidon   This shop in The Lost Continent carries an array of blue glassware—tumblers, shot glasses, and oversized coffee mugs—for $9.

The Mulberry Street Store   Okay, it is a little bit of a splurge to spend $20 on a bib, but when it says "I'm a Little Yerkle," or "Baby Horton," how can you resist? A great place for kid stuff with a Seuss theme.

Best Atmosphere for Adults   The Enchanted Oak Tavern (and Alchemy Bar) has a cavelike interior, which from the outside looks like a mammoth tree, and is brightened by an azure blue skylight with a celestial theme. The tables and chairs are hewed from thick planks, and the servers clad in wench ware add to the fun. Try the chicken/rib combo with waffle fries for $11.95, topped off with Black Forest Shortcake, $2.29. You can also choose from 45 types of beer at the bar.

Best Atmosphere for Kids   The fun never stops under the big top at **Circus McGurkas Cafe Stoopendous** in Seuss Landing, where animated trapeze artists swing from the ceiling and train car tables ring the walls. Kids' meals, including a souvenir cub, are $4.99. The adult fare features fried chicken, lasagna, spaghetti, and pizza. Try the fried chicken platter for $7.50 or the lasagna for $6.79.

Best Vegetarian Fare   **Fire Eater's Grill,** located in The Lost Continent, is a fast food stand that offers a tasty veggie falafel for $4.59. You can also get a tossed salad for $2.79.

Note: There are also many restaurants and clubs that are just a short walk from Islands of Adventure at Universal Studio Escape's new entertainment complex, City-Walk. For more information on the eating spots there, see "CityWalk" in Chapter 10.

3 Sea World

This popular, 200-plus–acre marine-life park explores the mysteries of the deep in a format that combines entertainment with wildlife-conservation awareness. While this is exactly what Disney is attempting with its latest park, Animal Kingdom, the message here is more subtle and is a more inherent part of the experience.

Bell-bottoms and Marcia Brady prints may be all the rage in fashion, but Sea World of Florida has updated its 1970s look. A 55-foot lighthouse topped with a rotating white light in the middle of a harbor decorated with a painting of Shamu anchors the nautically themed renovation. To get to the park visitors walk underneath a sea of blue and aquamarine "metal waves" and cross wooden bridges nestled amid a rocky shore complete with lapping water and splashing waves.

A new gift shop and upgrades of the ticket booths, turnstiles, guest-relations windows, and tram stops make this a new world to explore.

Sea World's beautifully landscaped grounds, centering on a 17-acre lagoon, include flamingo and pelican ponds and a lush tropical rain forest. Shamu, a killer whale, is the star of the park along with his expanding family, which includes several baby whales. The pace is much more laid-back than either Universal or Disney, and it's a good way to end a long week of trudging through other parks. Be sure to budget some extra money to buy smelt to feed the animals. The close encounters offered at many wading and feeding pools are the real attraction here, and more than half the fun. Sea World can't compete with the high-tech wonders abounding elsewhere, but where else can you discover that a stingray feels like crushed velvet or learn the song of a seal?

During 1998, Sea World opened its first major thrill ride, **Journey to Atlantis,** a theme roller coaster with record-breaking twists and turns. If you wonder what Shamu's keepers know about thrill rides remember that Sea World, owned by Anheuser-Busch, is put together by the same folks who operate Busch Gardens where there are wonderful, gut-wrenching thrill rides such as Kumba and Montu.

Sea World will open a second park, Discovery Island, in summer 2000. Although details have been kept under wraps, the 30-acre park promises "experiences and attractions never before offered in a theme park," and a limited guest capacity. Even with just one park, Sea World is definitely worth a visit, especially if you haven't been here in several years. An unofficial poll of friends shows this is a favorite among Floridians—a place you can visit again and again for a lifetime of leisurely afternoons.

ESSENTIALS

GETTING TO SEA WORLD BY CAR   Take I-4 to the Bee Line Expressway (Fla. 528) and follow the signs. It may look like you are going the wrong way, but don't despair, as long as you see the signs.

PARKING   Parking costs $6 per car, $7 for RVs and trailers. The lots are not huge, and you can walk into the park. Trams also run. Note the location of your car. Sections are marked by Sea World characters like Wally Walrus, but it is easy to forget where you parked.

TICKET PRICES   A **1-day ticket** costs $46.45 for ages 10 and over, $37.10 for children 3 to 9; children 2 and under enter free.

See the beginning of this chapter for information on the **Flex Pass,** a multiday admission ticket for Sea World, Universal Studios Escape, and Wet 'n' Wild.

HOURS   The park is open from 9am to 7pm, 365 days a year, and later during summer and holidays when there are additional shows at night. Call ☎ 800/ 351-3600 before you go.

TIPS FOR MAKING YOUR VISIT MORE ENJOYABLE
PLAN YOUR VISIT

Get information before you leave by writing to **Sea World Guest Services** at 7007 Sea World Dr., Orlando, FL 32801, or call ☎ **407/351-3600.**

Orlando Area Attractions

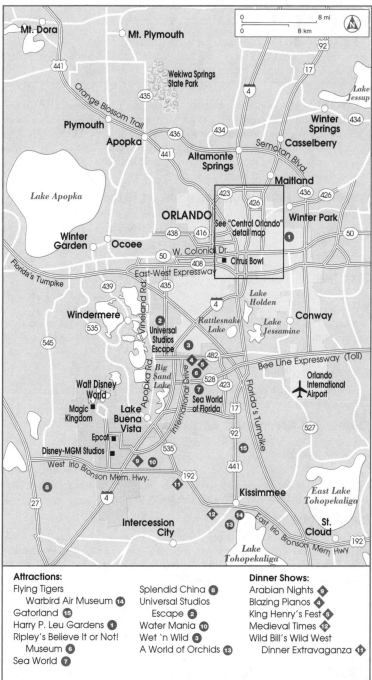

0 ——— 8 mi
0 ——— 8 km

Mt. Dora

Mt. Plymouth

Wekiwa Springs State Park

Lake Jessup

441

92

17

435

Orange Blossom Trail

Plymouth

Apopka

436

434

441

4

Winter Springs

434

Casselberry

Semoran Blvd.

Altamonte Springs

Maitland

436

426

Lake Apopka

423

426

ORLANDO

See "Central Orlando" detail map **1**

Winter Park

50

Winter Garden

Ocoee

438

416

W. Colonial Dr.

50

408

■ Citrus Bowl

East-West Expressway

Florida's Tumpike

439

435

4

Lake Holden

Lake Jessamine

Conway

Windermere

535

545

Vineland Rd.

2 Universal Studios Escape

Rattlesnake Lake

3

4 **5**

6 528

7 Sea World of Florida

482

Big Sand Lake

Apopka Rd.

Bee Line Expressway (Toll)

Orlando International Airport

423

17

Walt Disney World

Magic Kingdom ■

Lake Buena Vista

International Drive

Florida's Tumpike

Epcot ■

Disney-MGM Studios ■

535

92

15

527

9 **10**

West Irlo Bronson Mem. Hwy.

192

441

8

27

4

11

Kissimmee

East Lake Tohopekaliga

Intercession City

12

13 **14**

East Irlo Bronson Mem Hwy

St. Cloud

192

Lake Tohopekaliga

NA-0173

Attractions:
Flying Tigers
    Warbird Air Museum **14**
Gatorland **15**
Harry P. Leu Gardens **1**
Ripley's Believe It or Not!
    Museum **6**
Sea World **7**

Splendid China **8**
Universal Studios
    Escape **2**
Water Mania **10**
Wet 'n Wild **3**
A World of Orchids **13**

Dinner Shows:
Arabian Nights **9**
Blazing Pianos **4**
King Henry's Fest **5**
Medieval Times **12**
Wild Bill's Wild West
    Dinner Extravaganza **11**

215

Millenium Alert!

Sea World will throw a weeklong party to celebrate the Millennium called "Dancing through the Decades." This evening fiesta will include family-friendly activities and bands. A special fireworks extravaganza will ring in the year 2000.

ONLINE Sea World information is available at **www.seaworld.com.** The Orlando daily newspaper, the *Orlando Sentinel,* also produces *Orlando Sentinel Online* at **www.orlandosentinel.com.** Once there, click on "Theme Park Central" for a variety of information, and for updates on what is going on at local attractions. If you subscribe to AOL, type the keyword **Go2Orlando** to access a site with a lot of updated information about Sea World and other theme parks.

INFORMATION FOR VISITORS WITH SPECIAL NEEDS

The park publishes a guide for guests with disabilities, although most of its attractions are easily accessible to those in wheelchairs. Sea World also provides a Braille guide for the visually impaired. For the hearing impaired, there is a very brief synopsis of shows. For information call ☎ 407/351-3600.

BEST TIME OF YEAR TO VISIT

Since this is a mostly outdoor, water-related park, you may want to keep in mind that even in Florida it can get a tad nippy during February and March. Like the other parks, Sea World has smaller crowds during the winter months; usually from January through April the park crowds are smallest, the weather coolest, and the air least humid.

BEST DAYS TO VISIT

Monday and Wednesday are busy days at this park. Thursday and Sunday are the best days to visit if you want to avoid crowds.

CHOOSE AGE-APPROPRIATE ACTIVITIES

Since it has few thrill rides, Sea World has few restrictions, but you may want to check out the special tour programs offered through the education department.

Sea World lives up to its reputation for making education fun with a variety of tours. One of the newest, and most interesting, is the **Polar Expedition Guided Tour.** For information call ☎ 407/351-3600.

BUDGET YOUR TIME

Sea World has a naturally leisurely pace, since the major attraction here is taking time to enjoy up-close encounters with the animals. Don't be in a rush. Sea World's many attractions can easily be enjoyed in a single day. The layout of the park amplifies a feeling of space, and the many outdoor exhibits give it an open feel. Because of the large capacity and walk-through nature of many of the attractions, crowds are generally not a concern. Although you do need to be in Shamu stadium in plenty of time for the show, and Wild Arctic also draws a sizable crowd, lines seldom reach Disney proportions. So, relax. Isn't that what a vacation is supposed to be about?

SERVICES & FACILITIES IN SEA WORLD

ATMs An ATM machine is located at the front of the park. It accepts Cirrus, Honor, and Plus.

A New Addition

From swimming with the dolphins to mingling with the manta rays, **Discovery Cove,** Sea World's new 30-acre park, will be a unique experience.

Only 1,000 people per day will be allowed to make reservations for the park, which is scheduled to open in the summer of 2000. A ticket price of $150 will cover everything a visitor will need for the day, including food, swimming gear, and beach supplies.

Visitors will be able to snorkel and swim in fresh or salt water and will also be allowed, three people at a time, to interact with dolphins. They will also get an up-close view of sharks, barracudas, and other tropical fish through an underwater glass wall.

Baby Care   Changing tables are in or near most women's rest rooms and at the men's rest room at the front entrance near Shamu's Emporium. You can buy diapers in machines located near all changing areas, and at Shamu's Emporium. There is a special area for nursing mothers near the women's rest room at Friends of the Wild gift shop, near the center of the park.

Cameras & Film   Film and disposable cameras are available at stores throughout the park.

First Aid   First Aid Centers staffed with registered nurses are behind Stingray Lagoon and near Shamu's Happy Harbour.

Lockers   Lockers are located next to Shamu's Emporium, just inside the park entrance. The cost is $1 a day.

Lost Children   Lost children are taken to the Information Center. A parkwide paging system helps reunite guests. Children under 7 should wear name tags.

Pet Care   A kennel is available between the parking lot and the main gate. The cost is $4 a day.

Strollers   Strollers, in the shape of dolphins, can be rented at the Information Center near the entrance. The cost is $5 for a single, $10 for a double.

Wheelchair Rental   Regular wheelchairs are available at the Information Center. Regular chairs cost $5, electric $25 with a $25 deposit and a driver's license.

MAJOR ATTRACTIONS

Journey to Atlantis
Frommer's Rating: A
Recommended Ages: 8 and up
This is the park's only true thrill ride. Taking a cue from Disney Imagineers, Sea World has created a storyline to go with a loopy water coaster, something about a Greek fisherman and ancient Sirens in a battle over good and evil. (A "media horde" is somehow involved.) But what really matters is the promise of "two of the steepest, wettest, fastest drops to be found in any theme park." The bottom line is that it's a wild ride down with 60-foot drops and "luge-like curves." Journey to Atlantis breaks from Sea World's edu-tainment formula that stresses equal measures of learning and fun. You'll find no hidden lesson here, just a splashy thrill.

Key West at Sea World
Frommer's Rating: B
Recommended Ages: all ages
It's not quite the way Ernest Hemingway saw it, but this 5-acre paved paradise dotted with palms, hibiscus, and bougainvillea is set in a Caribbean village offering island cuisine, street vendors, and entertainers. The attraction comprises three naturalistic animal habitats: Stingray Lagoon, where visitors enjoy hands-on encounters with harmless southern diamond and cownose rays; Dolphin Cove, a massive habitat for bottlenose dolphins set up for visitor interaction; and Sea Turtle Point, home to threatened and endangered species such as green, loggerhead, and hawksbill sea turtles. Shortly after opening, dolphins showed their intelligence by realizing how easy humans are to tease; they'd routinely swim just out of arm's reach. But they soon discovered that there are advantages to coming in a little closer, namely smelt.

Key West Dolphin Fest
Frommer's Rating: C+
Recommended Ages: all ages
At the Whale and Dolphin Stadium—a big, partially covered open-air stadium—whales and Atlantic bottlenose dolphins perform flips and high jumps, swim at high speeds, twirl, swim on their backs, and give rides to trainers—all to the accompaniment of calypso music. The tricks are impressive, but go before the show-stopping behemoth, Shamu, puts these little mammals to shame.

Manatees: The Last Generation
Frommer's Rating: B+
Recommended Ages: all ages
Today the Florida manatee is in danger of extinction, with as few as 2,000 remaining. Underwater viewing stations, innovative cinema techniques, and interactive displays combine to create an exciting format for teaching visitors about the manatee and its fragile ecosystem. Also on display here are hundreds of other native fish, as well as alligators, turtles, and shore birds. It's amazing to watch the huge beasts move effortlessly through the water. There is something about this mammoth, slow-moving vegetarian that really appeals to children.

Shamu's Happy Harbor
Frommer's Rating: A+ (for kids)
Recommended Ages: children of all ages
This 3-acre play area has a four-story net tower with a 35-foot crow's-nest lookout, water cannons, remote-controlled vehicles, and a water maze. It's one of the most extensive play areas at any park and a great place for kids to burn off some energy between shows. Bring extra clothes for the tots (or for yourself) because this place isn't designed to keep you dry.

Shamu: World Focus
Frommer's Rating: A+
Recommended Ages: all ages
Sea World trainers develop close relationships with killer whales, and in this partly covered open-air stadium, they direct performances that are extensions of natural cetacean behaviors—twirling, waving tails and fins, rotating while swimming, and splashing the audience. Splash zones are clearly marked. Sit in the upper tiers if you don't want to get soaked. The evening show here, called "Shamu: Night Magic," utilizes rock music and special lighting effects. There is no reason to attend both shows unless you really like whales. The tricks are much the same. I'd opt for the

evening show, taking advantage of shorter lines, as others flock to the stadium in the afternoon. If you do decide on the afternoon show, arrive at least 30 minutes early. The stadium does fill up.

Shamu: Close Up!, an adjoining exhibit, lets you get close up to killer whales and talk to trainers; don't miss the underwater viewing area here and a chance to see a mother whale with her offspring. Talk about a big baby.

Swim with the Dolphins
Frommer's Rating: A+
Recommended Ages: adults
Since late 1996, a few lucky visitors have been able to don wet suits and join some of Flipper's cousins for an up-close encounter. This effort is modeled after a similar program started in Sea World San Diego in 1995. Animal-rights activists have voiced some concerns, but Sea World argues that the health and well-being of the dolphins is of the utmost importance and is maintained. Guests pay about $125 for a chance to interact with the dolphins under the watchful eyes of their trainers. (Annual-pass holders pay less.) Call ahead for information since this experience must be arranged in advance.

Take Pirate Island
Frommer's Rating: A+
Recommended Ages: all ages
Two sea lions, along with a cast of otters and walruses, appear in this fishy comedy with a conservation theme. Arrive early to catch the mime doing the preshow.

Terrors of the Deep
Frommer's Rating: B
Recommended Ages: 3–adult
This exhibit houses 220 specimens of venomous and otherwise scary sea creatures in a tropical-reef habitat. Immense acrylic tunnels provide close encounters with slithery eels, three dozen sharks, barracudas, lionfish, and poisonous puffer fish. A theatrical presentation focusing on sharks puts across the message that pollution and uncontrolled commercial fishing make humankind the ultimate "terror of the deep." This is not a ride for the claustrophobic, since you walk under a Plexiglas tube beneath hundreds of millions of gallons of water. Also, small children may find the glowing eels and swimming sharks a little too much to handle.

Wild Arctic
Frommer's Rating: B
Recommended Ages: exhibit, all ages; ride, 6–adult
Enveloping guests in the beauty, exhilaration, and danger of a polar expedition, Wild Arctic combines a high-definition adventure film with flight-simulator technology to evoke breathtaking Arctic panoramas. After a hazardous flight over the frozen north, visitors emerge at a remote research base—home to four polar bears (including star residents and polar twins Klondike and Snow), seals, walruses, and white beluga whales. Kids may find the bumpy ride a little much. There is a separate line for those who want to skip the thrill-ride section.

Fun Fact

Not just anyone can be a Sea World trainer. The qualifying exam includes completing a 220-foot free-style swim, a 110-foot underwater swim, a 240-foot surface dive to retrieve a 5-pound weight, and doing at least 20 military-style pushups.

Window to the Sea
Frommer's Rating: C
Recommended Ages: all ages
A multimedia presentation takes visitors behind the scenes at Sea World and explores a variety of marine subjects. These include an ocean dive in search of the rare six-gilled shark, a killer whale giving birth, babies born at Sea World (dolphins, penguins, walruses), dolphin anatomy, and underwater geology.

ADDITIONAL ATTRACTIONS

The park's other attractions include: **Pacific Point Preserve,** a 2½-acre naturalistic setting that duplicates the rocky northern Pacific Coast home of California sea lions, and harbor and fur seals; and **Tropical Reef,** a tide pool of touchables, such as sea anemones, starfish, sea cucumbers, and sea urchins, plus a 160,000-gallon man-made coral-reef aquarium, home to 1,000 brightly hued tropical fish displayed in 17 vignettes of undersea life.

A **Hawaiian dance troupe** entertains in an outdoor facility at Hawaiian Village; if you care to join in, grass skirts and leis are available. You can ascend 400 feet to the top of the **Sea World Sky Tower** for a revolving 360° panorama of the park and beyond (there's an extra charge of $3 per person for this activity). And at the 5½-acre **Anheuser-Busch Hospitality Center** you can try free samples of Anheuser-Busch beers and snacks, and stroll through the stables to watch the famous Budweiser Clydesdale horses being groomed. (Remember, the Bud-men of Anheuser-Busch own Sea World.)

The **Aloha! Polynesian Luau Dinner and Show,** a full-scale dinner show featuring South Seas food, song, and fire dancing, takes place nightly at 6:30pm. Park admission is not required. The cost is $35.95 for adults, $25.95 for children 8–12, $15.95 for children 3–7, and free for children 2 and under. Reservations are required (☎ **800/227-8048** or 407/363-2559).

Visitors can take 90-minute **behind-the-scenes tours** of the park's breeding, research, and training facilities and/or attend a 45-minute presentation about Sea World's animal behavior and training techniques. The cost for either tour is $5 for ages 10 and over, $4 for children 3–9, and free for children 2 and under. While there are several tours throughout the day, you should make a reservation when you enter the park.

SHOPPING AT SEA WORLD

This is one area where Sea World really knows better than to compete with Universal and the WDW parks. There aren't nearly as many shops, but there are lots of surprisingly cuddly aquatic-based sea creatures. Where else can you get a stuffed manatee but **Manatee Cove?** The **Friends of the Wild** gift shop near Penguin Encounters is also nice, as is the shop attached to **Wild Arctic.** And, because of the Anheuser-Busch connection, the gift shop outside the entrance to the park offers a staggering array of Budweiser-related items.

4 Other Area Attractions

IN KISSIMMEE

Kissimmee sights are close to the Walt Disney World area—about a 10- to 15-minute drive. Kissimmee has a sign system in place to better help tourists navigate U.S. 192. The large roadside signs say "Marker" along with a number. That information is included where appropriate in the following descriptions.

China Town & Florida Splendid China. Formosa Gardens Blvd., off W. Irlo Bronson Memorial Hwy. (U.S. 192, between Entry Point Blvd./Sherbeth Rd. and Black Lake Rd.). ☎ **407/396-7111.** Admission $26.99 adults, $16.99 children 5–12, free for children 4 and under. Daily from 9:30am; closing hours vary seasonally (call ahead). Free parking. From I-4 take Exit 25A, stay left and follow U.S. 192 west; turn left at the Florida Splendid China dragons.

This 76-acre outdoor attraction features more than 60 miniaturized replicas of China's most noted man-made and natural wonders, spanning 5,000 years of history and culture. Park highlights include a half-mile-long copy of the 4,200-mile Great Wall, the Forbidden City's 9,999-room Imperial Palace, Tibet's sacred Potala Palace, the massive Leshan Buddha—which was originally carved out of a mountainside between 713 and A.D. 803, the Stone Forest of Yunan, and the Mongolian mausoleum of Genghis Khan. Live shows (acrobats, martial-arts demonstrations, storytelling, dance, puppetry, and more) take place throughout the day; check your entertainment schedule. There's recorded commentary at each attraction.

Free trams circle the park, stopping at major attractions for pickup and drop-off. This attraction can be explored in several hours.

Gatorland. 14501 S. Orange Blossom Trail (U.S. 441; between Osceola Pkwy. and Hunter's Creek Blvd.). ☎ **800/393-JAWS** or 407/855-5496. Admission $17.95 adults, $10.95 children 10–12, $7.95, children 3–9. Free for 1 child 3–9 with each paying adult. Daily 9am–6pm. Free parking. From I-4 take Exit 26A to 417 north. Take Exit 11 to 441 south. Gatorland is 1 mile farther on the left.

Founded in 1949 with a handful of alligators living in huts and pens, Gatorland today features thousands of alligators and crocodiles on a 70-acre spread. Breeding pens, nurseries, and rearing ponds are situated throughout the park, which also displays monkeys, snakes, deer, goats, birds, sheep, Florida lake turtles, a Galápagos tortoise, and a bear. A 2,000-foot boardwalk winds through a cypress swamp and a 10-acre breeding marsh with an observation tower. Or you can take the free Gatorland Express Train around the park.

There are three shows scheduled throughout the day—Gator Wrestlin', the Gator Jumparoo, and Snakes of Florida. Facilities include an open-air restaurant (where you can try smoked gator ribs and nuggets), a shop (Gatorland also functions as an alligator-breeding farm for meat and hides; you'll find a wide array of alligator leather products here, not to mention canned gator chowder), and a picnic area.

Water Mania. 6073 W. Irlo Bronson Memorial Hwy. (U.S. 192), just east of I-4. ☎ **407/396-2626.** Admission $23.95 adults, $17.95 children 3–9, under 2 free. Nov–Feb admission is half-price after 3pm. Nov–Feb daily 11am–5pm; other times daily 9:30am–7pm with extended hours on some weekends and during spring break. Parking $4. From I-4, take Exit 25A, 1/2 mile. Across from the old-fashioned water tower that marks the entrance to Celebration.

This conveniently located 36-acre water park offers a variety of aquatic thrill rides and attractions. You can boogie-board or bodysurf in continuous-wave pools, float lazily along an 850-foot river, enjoy a white-water tubing adventure, or plummet down spiraling water slides and steep flumes. Or dare to ride the Abyss, an enclosed tube slide that corkscrews through 300 feet of darkness, exiting into a splash pool. There's a rain forest–themed water playground for children. A miniature golf course and wooded picnic area—with arcade games, a beach, and volleyball—adjoin. Water Mania, smaller than many similar parks, lives up to its billing as being family-friendly. There are lots of opportunities for smaller children, and there tend to be fewer rowdy teenagers and young adults than at parks such as Wet 'n' Wild. You can take in coolers, but glass bottles and alcoholic beverages are not allowed.

A World of Orchids. 2501 Old Lake Wilson Rd. (C.R. 545), off U.S. 192. ☎ **407/396-1887.** Admission $8.95 adults, $7.95 seniors, 15 and under free with paid adult. Daily 9:30am–5:30pm. Closed New Year's Day, July 4, Thanksgiving, and Christmas. From I-4 take Exit 25B, head west on U.S. 192; after 2 miles turn left on Old Lake Wilson Rd., or CR 545. (There is a tall blue sign here saying "West Gate Towers.") The conservatory is 1 mile ahead on the left.

Lovers of horticulture will enjoy touring this conservatory filled with tropical trees (including 64 varieties of palms and 21 of bamboo), ferns, lush tropical foliage, and, most notably, thousands of orchids—many of them rare—magnificently abloom at all times. Streams, waterfalls, koi ponds, and birds enhance this little enchanted garden. Also on the premises: a nature walk through a wooded area, aquariums of exotic fish, and a small aviary. Free guided tours are given by resident horticulturists at 11am and 3pm weekdays; 11am, 1pm, and 3pm on weekends.

Note: If this is the kind of attraction you enjoy, be sure to also visit Harry P. Leu Gardens in Orlando (see "Elsewhere in Orlando," later in this chapter).

ON INTERNATIONAL DRIVE

Like Kissimmee attractions, these are about a 10- to 15-minute drive from the Disney area.

Ripley's Believe It or Not! Museum. 8201 International Dr. (1½ blocks south of Sand Lake Rd.). ☎ **407/345-0501.** Admission $10.95 adults, $7.95 children 4–12, free for children 3 and under. Daily 9am–midnight. From I-4 west, take Exit 29, Sand Lake Rd. Turn right on International Dr.

It's always fun to peruse a Ripley collection of oddities, curiosities, and fascinating artifacts from faraway places. Among the hundreds of items and mannequins on display here are a 1,069-pound man, a two-headed kitten, a five-legged cow, a three-quarter–scale model of a 1907 Rolls-Royce made from a million matchsticks, a mosaic of the *Mona Lisa* created from 1,426 pieces of toast, torture devices from the Spanish Inquisition, a Tibetan flute made from human bones, an Ecuadorian shrunken head, a painting on a grain of rice, a "disappearing" nude bather (they do it with mirrors), Ubangi women with wooden plates in their lips, and Burmese Padaung women who stretch their necks up to 15 inches long by wearing heavy brass rings around them. There are exhibits on Houdini and Florida sinkholes, and a film documents people swallowing unusual items . . . coat hangers, a light bulb, and, most notably, a padlock, ring, and keys (when the latter three items were—*ahem!*—evacuated, the ring was locked into the padlock!). Museum visitors are greeted by a hologram of Robert Ripley. *Warning:* A few years back there was a mini–baby boom among employees that was attributed to the statue of a fertility god on display.

Wet 'n' Wild. 6200 International Dr. (at Republic Dr.). ☎ **800/992-WILD** or 407/351-WILD (9453). Admission $26.95 adults, $21.95 children 3–9, free for children 2 and under. Ages 55 and older, $13.48. Open daily; hours vary seasonally (call before you go). Parking: cars, $5; RVs, $7. Take I-4 east to Exit 30A and follow the signs.

Who knew people came in such a variety of shapes and sizes? Stacked or stubby, tan or terribly white, all kinds of people come to Wet 'n' Wild. According to industry polls, Wet 'n' Wild is one of the hottest tourist attractions in the country. When temperatures soar, head for this 25-acre water park and cool off by jumping waves, careening down steep flumes, and running rapids. When temps aren't soaring, you'll be pleased to know that all the pools are heated. Among the highlights: Fuji Flyer, a six-story, four-passenger toboggan ride through 450 feet of banked curves; The Surge, one of the longest, fastest multipassenger tube rides anywhere in the Southeast, with 580 feet of exciting banked curves; Bomb Bay

(enter a bomblike casing 76 feet in the air for a speedy vertical flight straight down to a target pool); Black Hole (step into a spaceship and board a two-person raft for a 30-second, 500-foot, twisting, turning, space-themed reentry through total darkness propelled by a 1,000-gallon-a-minute blast of water!); Raging Rapids, a simulated white-water tubing adventure with a waterfall plunge; and Lazy River, a leisurely float trip. This is the park that really started it all. Disney built its own water parks to compete with Wet 'n' Wild, and the originator still has plenty to offer. Bomb Bay ranks among one of the best thrill rides in central Florida.

There are additional flumes, a vast wave pool, a large, innovative children's water playground where the preceding rides are re-created in miniature, a sunbathing area, and a picnic area. Food concessions are located throughout the park, lockers and towels can be rented, and you can purchase beach accessories at the gift shop. Bring or buy sunscreen.

You can now purchase a multiday **Flex Pass** that allows admission to Universal Studios Escape, Sea World, and Wet 'n' Wild. See the beginning of this chapter for more information.

ELSEWHERE IN ORLANDO

The rest of Orlando's sights and attractions are spread out around the city. Loch Haven Park—the location of the Orange County Historical Museum, Orlando Museum of Art, and Orlando Science Center—is about 35 minutes by car from the Disney area. You may also wish to incorporate a trip to Winter Park in the same day.

✪ **Harry P. Leu Gardens.** 1920 N. Forest Ave. (between Nebraska St. and Corrine Dr.). ☎ **407/246-2620.** Fax 407/246-2849. Admission $4 adults, $1 children grades K–12. Daily 9am–5pm. Leu House tours daily 10am–3:30pm. Closed Christmas. Take I-4 east to Exit 43 (Princeton St.), follow Princeton St. east, making a right on Mills Ave. and a left on Virginia Dr. Look for the gardens on your left, just after you go around the curve in the road.

This delightful, 50-acre botanical garden on the shores of Lake Rowena offers a serene respite from theme-park razzle-dazzle. Meandering paths lead through forests of giant camphors, moss-draped oaks, palms, cicadas, and camellias. (The latter is one of the world's largest collections, comprising some 2,000 plants in 50 species; they bloom October through March.) Exquisite formal rose gardens (the largest in Florida, displaying 75 varieties) are enhanced by Italian fountains, a gazebo, and statuary. Other highlights include orchids, azaleas, desert plants, beds of colorful annuals and perennials, and a 50-foot floral clock. The gardens were created by Orlando businessman Harry P. Leu, who donated his 49-acre estate to the city in the 1960s.

Free 20-minute tours of the Leu House, built in 1888 and restored to reflect the period between 1910 and 1930, take place on the hour and half hour. The house is a decorative arts museum filled with Victorian, Chippendale, and Empire pieces and other furnishings and objets d'art. It takes about 2 hours to see the house and gardens. Inquire about lectures and workshops, including some for children. A new visitor center was added a few years ago, expanding the gift shop and adding a little luster to this laid-back attraction.

Orange County Historical Museum. 812 E. Rollins St. (between Orange and Mills aves.), in Loch Haven Pk. ☎ **407/897-6350.** Fax 407/897-6409. Admission $2 adults, $1.50 seniors 65 and over, $1 children 6–12, under 6 free. Monday admission is by donation. Sun noon–5pm; Mon–Sat 9am–5pm. Closed New Year's Day, Martin Luther King, Jr., Day, Memorial Day, July 4, Labor Day, Thanksgiving, and Christmas. Take I-4 east to Exit 43 (Princeton St.) and follow the signs to Loch Haven Pk.

The museum focuses mainly on central Florida history, beginning with prehistoric projectile points, a Timucuan canoe, and tooled animal bones from hunting cultures that existed here 12,000 years ago.

Other exhibits include displays of Seminole pottery and clothing; items from a pioneer kitchen; artifacts from an 1892 courthouse; a chronicle of the citrus industry and the role it played in the development of central Florida; and re-creations of a turn-of-the-century country store, a Victorian parlor, and the old *Orlando Sentinel* composing room. Also on the premises is Fire Station No. 3, a restored 1926 firehouse containing historic fire trucks, equipment, and memorabilia. The permanent collection is supplemented by changing exhibits of local, national, and international significance. It's best enjoyed by true history buffs. (*Note:* The museum is scheduled for a $24-million renovation in 1999–2000. Specifics were unavailable at press time; call before you go to verify that it is open.)

✪ **Orlando Museum of Art.** 2416 N. Mills Ave. (in Loch Haven Pk. off Hwy. 17/92). ☎ **407/896-4231.** Admission $4 adults, $2 children 4–11, under 4 free. Sun noon–5pm; Tues–Sat 9am–5pm. Art Encounter hours are Sun and Tues–Fri noon–5pm; Sat 10am–5pm. Closed New Year's Day, Memorial Day, July 4, Labor Day, Thanksgiving, and Christmas. Free parking. Take I-4 east to Exit 43 (Princeton St.) and follow the signs to Loch Haven Pk.

After closing for a 4-month, multimillion-dollar makeover, the Orlando Museum of Art reopened in 1997, ready to handle some of the most prestigious exhibits traveling the nation. The improved and expanded museum is worth a look, especially if it is hosting a traveling exhibit, such as the "Imperial Tombs of China," which had an extended stay in the 31,000-square-foot expansion during 1997.

Founded in 1924, the Orlando Museum of Art displays on a rotating basis its permanent collection of 19th- and 20th-century American art, pre-Colombian art dating from 1200 B.C. to A.D. 1500, and African art. These holdings are augmented by long-term loans focusing on Mayan archaeology and art of the African sub-Saharan region. Art Encounter is an interactive hands-on area for young children, where they might weave on a giant loom, piece together a pre-Colombian pot, or play African instruments. Temporary exhibits here range from Hudson River School landscapes to works of Andy Warhol. Inquire about guided tours, workshops for adults and children, gallery talks, and other activities.

From Diego Rivera refrigerator magnets to Georgia O'Keeffe cards, and original jewelry and pottery by local artists, the gift shop's selection alone merits a visit to the museum. Where else could you find Mark Harding birth announcements?

○ **Orlando Science Center.** 777 E. Princeton St. (between Orange and Mills aves.), in Loch Haven Pk. ☎ **407/514-2000** or 888/672-4386. Admission for all exhibits: Basic admission $9.50 adults, $6.75 children 3–11, free for children 2 and under. Additional prices for CineDome film or a planetarium show. Open Sun noon–5pm; Mon–Thurs 9am–5pm; Fri and Sat 9am–9pm. Closed Thanksgiving and Christmas. Parking is available in a garage across the street from the new building and costs $3.50. Take I-4 east to Exit 43 (Princeton St.), and cross Orange Ave.

Dan Rather and the CBS evening news gave America a peek at the newly renovated Orlando Science Center when it was unveiled in February 1997 after a $44-million renovation. It drew Dan's attention because the facility is the largest of its kind in the Southeast. (It probably didn't hurt that the show meant a trip to Florida in February.) Those familiar with the Orlando Science Center's previous incarnation as a stepsister sharing a building with the Orange County Historical Society will be amazed at how Cinderella has evolved. The new center provides 10 exhibit halls that allow visitors to spend the whole day exploring everything from the swamplands of Florida to the arid plains of Mars.

One of the major additions is actually just beneath that Trojan helmet–shaped silver dome that has loomed over Orlando for months. The Dr. Phillips CineDome, a 310-seat theater, uses the latest technology to present large-format films, planetarium shows, and laser light shows

In KidsTown, little folks wander around in exhibits representing a miniature version of the big world around them. In one section is a pint-sized community that includes a construction site, park, and wellness center. Science City, located nearby, includes a power plant, suspension bridge, and the Inventor's Workshop, a garage-like station for creative play. Children stopping by at 123 Math Avenue work on puzzles and play with math-based toys that teach while entertaining.

Both the Virtual Reality Theater and the New Media Living Room show the real advances that will soon become as commonplace as the once-exotic VCR.

5 Staying Active

Recreational facilities of every description abound in Walt Disney World and the surrounding area. These are especially accessible to guests at Disney-owned resorts, official hotels, and the Fort Wilderness Resort and Campground, though many other large resort hotels also offer comprehensive facilities (see details in chapter 5). The Disney facilities described here are all open to the public, no matter where

you're staying. For further information about WDW recreational facilities, call
☎ **407/939-7529.**

Guests at Disney properties can inquire when making hotel reservations or at
guest-services/concierge desks.

BICYCLING

Bike rentals (single and multispeed bikes for adults, tandems, and children's bikes)
are available from the **Bike Barn** (☎ **407/824-2742**) at Fort Wilderness Resort
and Campground. Rates are $5 per hour, $12 per day; overnight rentals are $15.
Both Fort Wilderness and Disney's Village Resort offer good bike trails. There are
even bicycles with training wheels and baby seats. Helmets are available at no additional charge. You must be 12 years old to rent.

Most of the best biking, though, is done in Lake County, north of the Disney
Area. *Florida Backroads* by Robert Howard (under $20 in the bookstore) offers
detailed descriptions of favorite biking paths throughout Florida.

BOATING

Walt Disney World, with its many man-made lakes and lagoons, owns the nation's
largest fleet of pleasure boats. At the **Walt Disney World Village Marina,** you can
rent Water Sprites, canopy boats, and 20-foot pontoon boats. For information call
☎ **407/828-2204.**

The **Bike Barn** at Fort Wilderness (☎ **407/824-2742**) rents canoes ($6 per
hour, $10 per day) and paddleboats ($6 per half hour, $10 per hour). You must be
12 years old to rent a boat.

See hotel facilities listings in chapter 5 for additional boating options.

FISHING

WDW offers a variety of fishing excursions on the various Disney lakes, including
Bay Lake and Seven Seas Lagoon. These lakes are stocked, so you may actually catch
something, but true fishers will probably not find it a great challenge. The excursions can be arranged 2 to 14 days in advance by calling the **Walt Disney World
Village Marina** (☎ **407/824-2621**). No license is required. The fee is $148.40 for
up to 5 people for 2 hours; those rates include refreshments, gear, guide, and tax.
Bait must be purchased.

The **Dixie Landings** and **Port Orleans** resorts offer early morning and evening
sunset fishing trips for $50 per person. The price includes refreshments, guide,
equipment, and artificial bait. These trips are available to non-Disney guests. To get
information, call ☎ **407/939-7529.** Press "0" to avoid a lengthy menu and speak
directly to an operator.

A less-expensive alternative: Rent fishing poles at the **Bike Barn** (☎ **407/824-
2742**) to fish in Fort Wilderness canals. No license is required.

FLYING

The **Flying Tigers Warbird Air Museum** offers rides in a 1934 open-cockpit barnstormer, and hands-on dual-instruction adventures in a historic World War II
fighter trainer. Call ☎ **407/933-1942** for details.

A slightly more offbeat experience is offered by **Fighter Pilots USA.** Ever
dreamed of suiting up, jumping into a fighter plane, and engaging in high-speed
one-on-one dog fighting? This is your chance to experience the excitement of aerial
combat. Actual F-16 pilots are your instructors. To schedule a "mission," call
☎ **800/56-TOPGUN** or 407/931-4333. No license is required, only a very thick
wallet. The cost is $795 per person.

Hot Links: Orlando's Top Golf Courses

Like most of Florida, Orlando is a golfer's paradise, with 123 courses within a 45-minute drive of downtown . . . courses designed by Arnold Palmer, Jack Nicklaus, Tom Fazio, Pete Dye, Robert Trent Jones, and other major players. Its most famous courses include the following:

- The legendary Arnold Palmer's **Bay Hill Club,** 9000 Bay Hill Blvd. ☎ **800/ 523-5999** or 407/876-2429. Its 18th hole, nicknamed the Devil's Bathtub, is supposed to be the toughest par-4 on the tour. Site of the Bay Hill Invitational.

- **Falcon's Fire Golf Club,** 3200 Seralago Blvd., in Kissimmee. ☎ **407/239-5445.** A challenging Ree Jones course with 136 bunkers and water on 10 holes.

- **Walt Disney Resorts** facilities (see chapter 5 for details) comprise 99 holes. Their most famous hazard is a sand trap on the Magnolia Course's 6th hole in the shape of Mickey Mouse. For information call ☎**407/939-4653.**

Also notable are two beautifully landscaped facilities: the award-winning 45-hole/par-72 Jack Nicklaus–designed course at the **Villas of Grand Cypress** (☎ **800/835-7377** or 407/239-4700) and the 18-hole/par-71 Joe Lee–designed championship course at **Marriott's Orlando World Center** (☎ **800/621-0638** or 407/239-4200). See details on both properties in chapter 5.

See Orlando from a different perspective. Hover over tourist hot spots on a ride with **Falcon Helicopter Service.** Located at 8990 International Dr., the service offers nine different aerial tour packages ranging from $15 to $395. (You get 4 minutes for $15.) For information call ☎ **407/396-7222.**

GOLF

Walt Disney World operates five championship 18-hole, par-72 golf courses and one 9-hole, par-36 walking course. All are open to the general public and offer pro shops, equipment rentals, and instruction. For tee times and information, call ☎ **407/824-2270** up to 7 days in advance (up to 30 days for Disney-resort and official-property guests). Call ☎ **407/W-DISNEY** (934-7639) for information about golf packages.

Also consider calling **Golfpac** (☎ **800/327-0878** or 407/260-2288), an organization that packages golf vacations (with accommodations and other features) and prearranges tee times at over 40 Orlando-area courses. The further in advance you call (I'm talking months here), the better your options.

Nick Faldo, three-time winner of the British Open, shares his skills with the average duffer at the new **Faldo Golf Institute by Marriott.** The "institute," as those involved like to call it, features a 9-hole course, a 27-hole putting course, and one of the largest learning centers in the country. Prices begin at $40 for 30-minute private instruction to $195 for a half day and $950 for a 5-day swing-a-thon. You will mostly be dealing with pros trained in the Faldo method, although you may occasionally glimpse the Master himself. The school is located at **Marriott's Grande Vista Resort,** 11301 International Dr., Orlando, FL 32821 (☎ 407/238-6800).

Golf magazine recognized the 45-holes designed by Jack Nicklaus at the **Grand Cypress Resort** as among the best in the nation. Tee times begin at 8am daily. Special rates available for children under 18. For information call ☎ 407/239-1909. The course is generally restricted to guests or guests of guests, but there is limited play available to those not staying at the resort. Those fees begin at $200.

HAYRIDES

The hay wagon departs from **Pioneer Hall** at Fort Wilderness nightly at 7 and 9:15pm for hour-long, old-fashioned hayrides with singing, jokes, and games. Cost is $6 for adults, $4 for children ages 3 to 10, free for children under 3. Children under 12 must be accompanied by an adult. No reservations; it's first-come, first-served.

HORSEBACK RIDING

Disney's Fort Wilderness Resort and Campground offers 45-minute scenic guided-tour trail rides daily, with four to six rides per day. Cost is $23 per person. Children must be at least 9 years old. Maximum weight limit is 250 pounds. For information and reservations up to 30 days in advance, call ☎ **407/824-2832.**

The **Grand Cypress Resort** opens its equestrian center to outsiders. Trail rides, about 50 minutes, are $30. A 30-minute private lesson is $45. For information call ☎ **407/239-4700.** Ask for the equestrian center.

ICE-SKATING

Rock on Ice! Skating Arena, in the Dowdy Pavilion, 7500 Canada Ave., between Sand Lake Road and Carrier Drive (☎ **407/352-9878**), is a gorgeous, Olympic-size indoor rink with high-tech lighting and sound systems. A DJ spins Top 40 tunes. There are ice-skating games with prizes throughout the day. Facilities include video games, a snack bar, and a complete skate shop offering a large selection of figure-skating and hockey equipment. Rental skates are $2. Admission is $4.50 to $6, depending on the season. Hours vary seasonally; call ahead.

To get here from the Disney World area, take International Drive north, turn right at Sand Lake Road and left on Canada Avenue. It's about a 10-minute drive.

JOGGING

Many of the Disney resorts have scenic jogging trails. For instance, the **Yacht** and **Beach Club** resorts share a 2-mile trail; the **Disney Institute** has a 3.4-mile course with 32 exercise stations; the **Caribbean Beach Resort's** 1.4-mile promenade circles a lake; **Dixie Landings** has a 1.7-mile riverfront trail, and **Fort Wilderness's** tree-shaded 2.3-mile jogging path has exercise stations about every quarter mile. Pick up a jogging trail map at any Disney property's guest-services desk.

SWIMMING

The **YMCA Aquatic Center,** 8422 International Dr. Take I-4 to Exit 29. Turn right at the end of the ramp. Turn right on International Drive. Turn right at second light. This YMCA has a full-fitness center, racquetball courts and an indoor Olympic-sized pool. Admission is $10 for both children and adults; $15 for families. For information call ☎ **407/363-1911.**

SWIMMING WITH THE MANATEES

An organization called **Oceanic Society Expeditions** (☎ **800/326-7491** or 415/441-1106) offers a "Swim with the Manatees" program in the Crystal River area, 2 hours east of Orlando. A manatee biologist leads 5-day Monday-to-Friday trips aboard a 12-person skiff. The program includes swimming with manatees, bird watching, snorkeling, slide presentations, and an excursion to a facility for the care of injured and orphaned wildlife. Cost is $985, including accommodations, excursions, and most meals. Reserve as far in advance as possible.

TENNIS

Seventeen lighted tennis courts are located throughout the Disney properties. Most are free and available on a first-come, first-served basis. If you're willing to pay, courts can be reserved up to several months in advance at two Disney resorts: the **Contemporary** (☎ 407/824-3578) and the **Grand Floridian** (☎ 407/824-2435). Both charge $12 per hour; you can also reserve lesson times with resident pros. The Contemporary offers a large pro shop, a ball machine, rebound walls, and equipment rentals.

WATERSKIING

Water-skiing trips (including boats, drivers, equipment, and instruction) can be arranged at **Walt Disney World** by calling ☎ 407/824-2621. Make reservations up to 14 days in advance. Cost is $82 per hour for up to 5 people.

You can get some time behind a boat at **Ski World** near downtown Orlando. Lessons are $25 for 20 minutes. For information call ☎ 407/894-5012. To get there, take I-4 to downtown, then Exit 43, Princeton Street. Turn right at the bottom of the ramp. Turn right at the first light. It's about a mile on your left. The lake will be on your right.

6 Spectator Sports

Disney doesn't want to give the competition a sporting chance. In May 1997, it branched out with a multimillion-dollar **Disney's Wide World of Sports Complex,** a 200-acre facility. The Mouse hopes to hit a home run with a 7,500-seat baseball stadium that is the spring training home to the perpetual almost–World Champs, the Atlanta Braves. The Braves began a 3-year stay in 1998. In addition, there is a 5,000-seat field house featuring six basketball courts, a fitness center, and training rooms; major-league practice fields and pitcher mounds; four softball fields; 12 tennis courts, including a 2,000-seat stadium center court; a track-and-field complex; a golf driving range; and much more. A variety of sporting events from tennis tournaments to band competitions have been held here since the center opened. For information about events taking place during your stay, call ☎ 407/939-1500.

There are three major sporting arenas in downtown Orlando: the **Florida Citrus Bowl,** the **Orlando Arena,** and **Tinker Field,** which together host six major sporting teams.

ARENA FOOTBALL

Orlando is home to the **Orlando Predators,** who play from April until August. For the uninitiated, arena football is an indoor cross between rugby and football played by eight-man teams on a much-abbreviated field. You don't necessarily need to know the rules to enjoy the up-close crunching and beer-fest atmosphere. The Predators are the Buffalo Bills of arena football, coming close, but never quite winning a championship. They have a loyal and rowdy following. Sold-out games are common, but single tickets are often available the day of the game at the Orlando Arena box office. For information call ☎ 407/648-4444.

BASEBALL

From April to September, the **Orlando Rays**—the Tampa Devil Rays' Class AA Southern league affiliate—play at Walt Disney World Wide World of Sports. Call ☎ 407/939-1500 for information. You can get tickets through **TicketMaster** (☎ 407/839-3900), or they can be purchased at the Wide World of Sports Complex in person. Tickets are $3 to $7.

The NFL Experience

Even if your days of gridiron glory have long faded, or never actually material-
ized, you can practice like the big, really big, guys of the NFL at this attraction
located at Disney's Wide World of Sports.

There are 10 drills here that test your running, punting, passing, and receiving
skills. Among other activities, you can dodge cardboard defensemen to run a pass
pattern while a machine shoots you a pass. (A much safer way than actually
risking life and limb.) Depending on your stamina, interest, and the size of the
crowds, the NFL Experience can last anywhere from 45 minutes to several hours.

Football fans know that a similar traveling exhibit is usually set up in Super
Bowl cities during the Big Game. This is the first time a permanent exhibit has
been put into place. Kids, and weekend warriors, will love this chance to grapple
with the pigskin. Plus, at $8 for adults and $6.75 for children 10 and under, the
price is right. For information call ☎ **407/939-1500.** No reservations are
needed.

If you're a true sports fan, you would be well advised to write and get a package
of information about the facilities, and a calendar of events, at **Disney's Wide
World of Sports.** Write to Disney's Wide World of Sports, P.O. Box 10,000,
Lake Buena Vista, FL 32830-1000, or call ☎ **407/939-1500.**

The **Atlanta Braves** began spring training at Disney's Wide World of Sports
Complex in 1998. A 3-year contract ensures play through 2001. There are about 18
games during the 1-month season. Tickets are $10.50 and $13.50. For information
call ☎ **407/939-1500.** You can get tickets through **TicketMaster** (☎ **407/
839-3900**), or they can be purchased at the Wide World of Sports Complex in
person.

BASKETBALL

The 17,500-seat Orlando Arena (the "O-rena"), 600 W. Amelia St., between I-4
and Parramore Avenue (☎ **407/896-2442** for information, 407/839-3900 to
charge tickets), is home to the **Orlando Magic** during their October-to-April
season. Some of the Magic dimmed when the team was left by star center (and marketing phenomenon) Shaquille O'Neal, but it's still the NBA and, unless he's
jumped ship for a better deal, we still have Penny Hardaway. Tickets to games
(about $13 to $50) have to be acquired far in advance; they usually sell out by September before the season starts. Fallout from the 1998–1999 NBA lockout may also
make tickets easier to get in the short term. Several hundred individual seats, sometimes in the nosebleed sections, can often be obtained before games against the
league's less-popular teams, like the Timberwolves.

To get there, take I-4 east to Amelia Avenue, turn left at the traffic light at the
bottom of the off-ramp, and follow signs. For up-to-the-minute parking information, turn your car radio to 1620 AM.

FOOTBALL

The Florida Citrus Bowl, 1 Citrus Bowl Place, at West Church and Tampa streets
(☎ **407/473-2476** for information, 407/839-3900 to charge tickets), hosts the
annual **CompUSA Florida Citrus Bowl** game, college football games, and NFL
preseason games. Tickets to all football events are hard to come by, but you may

have some luck if you try far enough in advance. To get there, take I-4 east to the East-West Expressway and head west to Highway 441. Make a left on Church Street, and follow the signs. Parking is $5.

HOCKEY

Ice Hockey? Orlando? Well, sure, why not? There is an ice rink under the floor at the downtown Orlando Arena; the regular floor is replaced for Orlando Magic games. An International Hockey League team, the **Orlando Solar Bears,** plays from October through April, longer if they do well in the playoffs. Ticket prices are a professional sports bargain, beginning at $6 and topping out at $26 for prime lower-bowl seats. For information call ☎ **407/872-7825.**

JAI ALAI

Orlando Jai Alai, 6405 S. U.S. 17/92, at S.R. 436 in Fern Park (☎ **407/339-6221**), offers the action-packed Basque sport of jai alai (it's the world's fastest game). On a 180-foot court with three walls, the ball is hurled at speeds of up to 150 miles an hour from baskets strapped to the players' wrists, and the object of the game is to throw the ball with such force, spin, and/or placement that the opponent is unable to return it before it bounces twice. A score of 7 points wins. There are two opposing singles, or doubles, teams on the court at all times.

Your program offers extensive information about how the game is played and how to wager, and the public-address announcer explains what is happening on the court.

Your best bet is to watch the action from the moderately priced, and very attractive, open-air Terrace Restaurant, with some tables as close as 20 feet from the court. There's a color TV monitor at every table. Fare is American/continental; there's a full bar; reservations are suggested. Children 39 inches and taller are admitted into the fronton with parents, but are not allowed in the betting area.

Note: The fronton also features intertrack wagering; you can place bets here on thoroughbred and harness races as well as Miami jai alai.

Admission is $1, reserved seats are $2, restaurant seating is $3, and box seats are $3 to $5. Seniors 55 and older get free admission to matinees. Parking is free; valet parking is $1.50. Open year-round Wednesday to Sunday. Evening games are held at 7:30pm, Wednesday to Saturday; matinees at noon Thursday and Saturday, and at 1pm Sunday. From the Walt Disney World area, take I-4 east, make a right at Exit 47A (Maitland Exchange), a right at U.S. 17/92, and look for the fronton 2 miles along on your right. It's about a 40-minute drive.

7 Two Side Trips

Just outside of Orlando, you'll find two more great places to visit—Cypress Gardens, central Florida's first major tourist draw, and Winter Park, a lovely town with some great attractions.

CYPRESS GARDENS

Founded in 1936, ✪ **Cypress Gardens** came into being as a 16-acre public garden along the banks of Lake Eloise, with cypress-wood-block pathways and thousands of tropical and subtropical plants.

The park is located on Fla. 540 at Cypress Gardens Boulevard (40 miles southwest of Walt Disney World), in Winter Haven (☎ **800/282-2123** or 941/324-2111; www.cypressgardens.com). To get there, take I-4 West to U.S. 27 south, and proceed west to S.R. 540; parking is free.

Today, Cypress Gardens has grown to more than 200 acres, with ponds, lagoons, waterfalls, classic Italian fountains, topiary, bronze sculptures, manicured lawns, and ancient cypress trees shrouded in Spanish moss. All this forms a backdrop to ever-changing floral displays of 8,000 varieties of plants from more than 90 countries. Southern belles in Scarlett O'Hara costumes stroll the grounds or sit on benches under parasols in idyllic tree-shaded nooks.

In the late winter and early spring, more than 20 varieties of bougainvillea, 40 of azalea, and hundreds of kinds of roses burst into bloom. Crape myrtles, magnolias, and gardenias perfume the late-spring air, while brilliant birds of paradise, hibiscus, and jasmine brighten the summer landscape. And in winter, the golden rain trees, floss silk trees, and camellias of autumn give way to millions of colorful chrysanthemums and red, white, and pink poinsettias.

Admission is $31.95 for ages 10 and over, $14.95 for children 6 to 17, free for children 6 and under, $26.50 for seniors. You can purchase discounted tickets online at **www.cypressgardens.com.**

It's open daily from 9:30am to 5:30pm, with extended hours during peak seasons. You'll find both restaurants and a picnic area on the premises.

EXPLORING THE GARDENS

Strolling the grounds is, of course, the main attraction (there are more than 2 miles of winding botanical paths, and half the park's acreage is devoted to floral displays), but this being Central Florida, it's not the only one.

Several shows are scheduled throughout the day (check the schedule upon entering the park). The world-famous **Greatest American Ski Team** performs on Lake Eloise in a show augmented by an awesome hang-gliding display. The breathtaking **ice-skating show** is the Russian answer to America's Ice Capades. **Variètè Internationale** features specialty acts from all over the world.

An enchanting exhibit called **Wings of Wonder** surrounds visitors with more than 1,000 brightly colored free-flying butterflies in a 5,500-square-foot Victorian-style glass conservatory. **Electric boats** navigate a maze of lushly landscaped canals in the original botanical gardens area. You can ascend 153 feet to the **Island in the Sky** for a panoramic vista of the gardens and a beautiful chain of Central Florida lakes.

Carousel Cove, with eight kiddie rides and arcade games, centers on an ornate turn-of-the-century–style carousel. It adjoins another kid pleaser, **Cypress Junction,** an elaborately landscaped model railroad that travels over 1,100 feet of track with up to 20 trains moving at one time.

Cypress Roots, a museum of park memorabilia, displays photographs of famous visitors (Elvis on water skis, Tiny Tim tiptoeing through the roses) and airs ongoing showings of *Easy to Love* starring Esther Williams (it was filmed here).

WINTER PARK

This lakeside town is a lovely place to spend an afternoon. Visit the Morse Museum, cruise the lakes, and browse in the posh boutiques that line Park Avenue.

To get to Winter Park from Orlando (about a 5-mile drive), continue east on I-4 to Fairbanks Avenue (Exit 45), turn right, and proceed about a mile, making a left on Park Avenue.

✪ **Charles Hosmer Morse Museum of American Art.** 445 Park Ave. (between Canton and Cole Aves.). ☎ **407/645-5311.** Admission $3 adults, $1 students of any age. Tues–Sat

9:30am–4pm, Sun 1–4pm. Closed New Year's Day, Memorial Day, Labor Day, Thanksgiving, and Christmas.

This gem of a museum was founded by Hugh and Jeannette McKean in 1942 to display their art collection, which includes 40 magnificent, vibrant colored windows and 21 paintings by Louis Comfort Tiffany. In addition, there are non-Tiffany windows ranging from creations by Frank Lloyd Wright to 15th- and 16th-century German masters; leaded lamps by Tiffany and Emile Gallè; paintings by John Singer Sargent, Maxfield Parrish, and others; jewelry designed by Tiffany, Lalique, and Fabergé; photographic works by Tiffany and other 19th-century artists; and art nouveau furnishings.

Scenic Boat Tour. On the lake at the eastern end of Morse Blvd. ☎ **407/644-4056.** Admission $6 adults, $3 children 2–11, free for children under 2. Weather permitting, tours depart daily, every hour on the hour 10am–4pm. Closed Christmas.

For over half a century, tourists have been boarding pontoons at this location for leisurely hour-long cruises on Winter Park's beautiful chain of natural lakes. The ride traverses area lakes, winding through canals built by loggers at the turn of the century and tree-shaded fern gullies lined with bamboo and lush tropical foliage. You'll view magnificent lakeside mansions, pristine beaches, cypress swamps, and dozens of marsh birds—possibly even an American bald eagle. The captain regales passengers with local lore. It's a delightful, laid-back trip.

9 Shopping

What is a vacation without a little shopping . . . okay, without a lot of shopping? Not only do you really need a few extra (bags of) souvenirs, who knows what native Florida treasures you may find?

Of course, the theme parks carry just about everything you can imagine embossed with their name. (Even quite a few things you'd never imagine.) And, we all know you are really paying more than you should. When searching for deals at home, do you hightail it to the tourist areas? I didn't think so. Although I'm not knocking the staggering number of ways Mickey Mouse can be merchandised, there are plenty of other places to shop, and plenty of things to purchase, in Orlando that don't carry the initials M.M. (although as **Mary Meehan**, it works to *my* advantage). The shopping opportunities at the theme parks are outlined in chapters 7 and 8.

Get out and explore some of the local shopping favorites, like Park Avenue in Winter Park, Church Street Station and Church Street Market, or Antique Row in downtown. These side trips are especially worth the effort if you're making a repeat visit to the theme parks or if it's your first trip to the United States.

1 The Shopping Scene

The tourist areas, such as International Drive and Kissimmee, are packed with plenty of 3-for-$10 T-shirt shops and a staggering array of things made of seashells, but try not to limit yourself to only the tourist kitsch.

Because Orlando is naturally geared to tourists, many retailers offer shipping packages. If you are pondering a big purchase, ask about the options for sending it home. If the retailer doesn't offer such a service, check with your hotel. If you really don't want to haul that 6-foot Goofy on the plane, Federal Express, United Parcel Service, and, of course, the good old U.S. Postal Service, all have locations in the tourist areas.

A few words of advice: If you are traveling during the Christmas holiday season, from the end of November to December 25, it is best to avoid local shopping malls on the weekends. They are just as crowded here as they are back home. Also, don't leave your good judgment at the door of the outlet malls. Although there are some good bargains, the prices on many items, such as athletic shoes, are not much lower than you could get anywhere else. The selection,

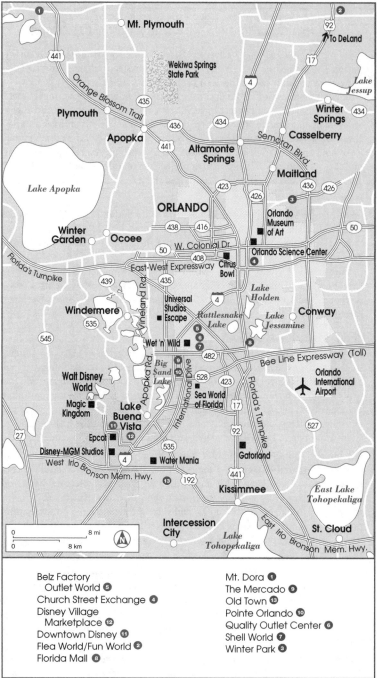

Belz Factory
  Outlet World ⑤
Church Street Exchange ④
Disney Village
  Marketplace ⑫
Downtown Disney ⑪
Flea World/Fun World ②
Florida Mall ⑧

Mt. Dora ①
The Mercado ⑨
Old Town ⑬
Pointe Orlando ⑩
Quality Outlet Center ⑥
Shell World ⑦
Winter Park ③

A Disney Bargain? The World's Best Kept Secret

From pink Cadillacs to 4-foot beer steins, a host of wacky treasures are regularly put up for auction at Walt Disney World. The president of the National Auctioneers Association calls it the "best kept secret at Disney."

In addition to cast-offs from the theme parks and the many Disney hotels, there are more mundane items available, such as lawn maintenance equipment. If you are looking for a unique piece of Disney, the auctions are held four times a year—always on a Thursday when Disney workers get paid. Some of the more unusual items sold in the past include furniture from Miss Piggy's dressing room and motorized surfboards. For information on the auction call ☎ **407/824-6878.**

---

however, may be much larger than what you could find in other places—especially outside of urban areas or the United States.

Most stores are open from 9 or 10am until 9 or 10pm Monday through Saturday and from 10am to 6pm on Sunday.

Sales tax in Osceola County, which includes Kissimmee, is 7%. In Orange County, which includes the International Drive area, and most of the attractions, it is 6%. In Seminole County, about 40 miles north of the Walt Disney World area, the rate is 7%.

GREAT SHOPPING AREAS

Celebration   This is not the place for power shopping, but rather a pleasant diversion—a trip back to how Disney imagines things once were. Think Pleasantville with a Disney touch. Celebration is a Disney created and controlled town that will eventually be home to about 20,000 people. Its downtown includes a dozen or so shops, a couple of art galleries, and four restaurants. The shops—especially the galleries and gift shops—offer some interesting buys. The real plus here is the leisurely, and very clean, atmosphere. Think Pleasantville with folks dressed in up-to-date clothes.

Kissimmee   South of the Disney parks, Kissimmee centers on U.S. 192/Irlo Bronson Memorial Highway—a somewhat tacky strip, as archetypal of American cities as Main Street. U.S. 192 is lined with budget motels, lesser attractions—like Gatorland—and every fast-food restaurant you can name. Kissimmee is still, in many ways, true to its cowboy roots, and there are a couple of cowboys shops to prove it. The shopping here is notable for the quantity, not necessarily quality, but it's a good place to pick up some knickknacks for the folks back home.

International Drive Area (Fla. 536)   Can you say tourist Mecca? This area extends 7 to 10 miles north of the Disney parks between Fla. 535 and the Florida Turnpike. (*Note:* Locally, this road is always referred to as **I-Drive**.) From bungee jumping to ice-skating to dozens of theme restaurants and T-shirt shops, this is the tourist strip in central Florida. The two major shopping draws here are Pointe Orlando, a collection of specialty shops including FAO Schwartz and The Mercado, and the smaller batch of specialty shops.

Downtown Orlando   No, not Downtown Disney, which is not *really* Downtown. To get to the real thing you have to travel on I-4 east, until you reach a burgeoning Sunbelt metropolis 17 miles northeast of Walt Disney World. It includes the entertainment/shopping complex Church Street Station, hundreds of clubs, shops, and restaurants. Dozens of antique shops line "Antique Row" on Orange Avenue near

Lake Ivanhoe, about 3 miles from downtown. Here, as the name implies, you'll find antique shops, vintage clothing stores, and a few funky boutiques.

Winter Park   Just north of downtown Orlando, Winter Park is the place many of central Florida's old-money families call home. As the name implies, it began as a haven for Yankees traveling away from the cold. Today, it's home to Park Avenue, a collection of upscale shops and restaurants along an original cobblestone street that is frequented by local ladies who lunch. Amid the dozens of specialty shops are some upscale chains such as Ann Taylor and Banana Republic. It is also home to a handful of art galleries.

FACTORY OUTLETS

Belz Factory Outlet World. 5401 W. Oak Ridge Rd. (at the north end of International Dr.). ☎ **407/354-0126** or 407/352-9600.

This is the largest of the factory outlet centers in town, with 180 stores in two huge, enclosed malls and four shopping annexes. It offers an immense range of merchandise at savings up to 75% off retail prices. There's even an old-fashioned carousel for the kids (and adults).

At its emporia: 18 shoe stores (including Bass, Bally, and Capezio); 14 housewares shops (including Fieldcrest/Cannon, Corning, Oneida, and Mikasa); and more than 60 clothing shops for men, women, and children (including London Fog, Van Heusen, Jonathan Logan, Guess Jeans, Aileen, Danskin, Jordache, Leslie Fay, Carole Little, Harvé Benard, Calvin Klein, and Anne Klein). You can also shop for books and records, electronics, sporting goods, health and beauty aids, jewelry, toys, gifts, accessories, lingerie, and hosiery here.

Tip: There is a lot of great shopping here, but don't kill yourself trying to get to every building. Many of the manufacturers have more than one location, with much of the same selections, within the complex. Also, unless you are from out of the country, most of the brand sportswear stores, such as Nike and Reebok, don't offer much of a deal, especially on shoes.

Quality Outlet Center. 5527 International Dr. (1 block east of Kirkman Rd.). ☎ **407/423-5885.**

About 20 outlets, including Arrow, American Tourister, Corning-Revere (glassware and cookware), Florsheim shoes, Magnavox, Laura Ashley, Adidas, Great Western Boots, Totes, Le Creuset (cookware), Linens 'n' Things, Mikasa, Royal Doulton, and Villeroy & Boch. Once again, big savings.

Continuing a quarter of a mile north on International Drive, you'll come to the International Drive Value Center, under the same auspices as the Quality Outlet Center (same phone, same hours). Its 15 stores include T.J. Maxx; other women's clothing stores; Old Navy Clothing Company (a lower-priced Gap concept); Lane Bryant; Linea Garbo (Italian shoes); Converse; Perfumania; Books A Million; and Bed, Bath & Beyond.

Manufacturer's Outlet Mall. U.S. 192 (a mile east of Fla. 535 in Kissimmee). ☎ **407/396-8900.**

You'll find about 35 stores here, including Van Heusen, Bugle Boy, Fieldcrest/Cannon, Bass Apparel, Westport (women's fashions), and Acme Boot.

Crossroads of Lake Buena Vista. Exit 27 off I-4. ☎ **407/827-7300.**

Anchored by a 24-hour Goodings supermarket with a full-service pharmacy, this shopping center also features sportswear, electronics, books, cards, gifts, shoes, and Disney merchandise. There's also a post office. Restaurants/fast-food outlets

Going Upscale

Orlando, dubbed by city founders as "The City Beautiful," is beginning to attract more upscale retailers catering to the beautiful people.

Saks Fifth Avenue, Versace, and **FAO Schwarz** aren't exactly names usually associated with the cow-town Orlando once was, but all three have opened here in the last few years. Saks Fifth Avenue, one of the nation's premier retailers, carries a variety of exclusive designer labels. It opened in the Florida Mall in late 1996 and, although there were plenty of people predicting it would fail, expanded in early 1998. With only 4,200 square feet of space, Saks is much smaller than the mall's main department store, which is 105,000 square feet, but there's still plenty of shopping and gawking.

FAO Schwarz, which some call the Saks Fifth Avenue of the toy business, opened its 35,600-square-foot flagship store in 1997. With a huge three-story Raggedy Ann and Teddy Bear adorning the outside, this store on International Drive is hard to miss. Inside, toys are stacked to the ceiling, and there's even a copy of those 3-foot piano keys that Tom Hanks danced upon in the movie *Big.* Just so you don't have to worry about explaining that awkwardly shaped carry-on package, you can arrange to mail your purchases home for an additional fee.

FAO Schwartz is part of a development called **Pointe Orlando,** located at the corner of International and Republic drives along the I-Drive tourist corridor, across from the Orlando/Orange County Convention Center. After much negotiation, Pointe Orlando also landed a Versace boutique that will showcase the line produced by the late Italian fashion designer's company. It is one of the first boutiques opened outside of New York.

include, among others, T.G.I. Friday's, Johnny Rockets, Pebbles (see chapter 6), Pizzeria Uno, and Red Lobster. It's just like a shopping center in the real world.

Orlando Fashion Square Mall. 3201 E. Colonial Dr. ☎ **407/896-1131.** Take I-4 east to Exit 41, the Colonial Dr./Hwy. 50 exit. Take Colonial about 3 miles east; the main entrance is just past Maquire Blvd.

This mall underwent a major renovation in the mid-1990s, and with marblelike walkways, indoor palm trees, and high ceilings, it's a comfortable place to shop. Major stores include Burdines, Gayfers, JC Penney, and Sears. There are 165 stores, plus an extensive food court. You'll also find several arcades for the kiddies, and there are two multiplex theaters nearby. Easily accessible, the mall is about 5 miles from downtown Orlando.

Altamonte Mall. 451 E. Altamonte Dr. (about 15 miles north of downtown Orlando). ☎ **407/830-4400.**

Disney brought new life to Orlando, and this mall brought new life to the little one-stoplight town of Altamonte Springs. The mall, built in the early 1970s, underwent a major renovation in 1989, and added a food court in 1990. It is the area's second largest mall, just behind the newly expanded Florida Mall. It includes major department stores such as Gayfers, Burdines, and JC Penney, as well as 175 specialty shops. This multilevel mall has a light, airy feel, and benches and indoor palm trees make for a relaxing atmosphere (except during the Christmas holiday shopping rush).

2 Other Shopping in Orlando

IN DOWNTOWN ORLANDO

If you can think of nothing better than a relaxing afternoon of bargain hunting, or scouring thrift and antiques shops, check out **Antique Row** in downtown Orlando. This collection of two dozen shops, and a couple of restaurants, is about as far away as you can get from the manufactured fun of Disney. The shops are an interesting assortment of the old, the new, and the unusual.

Stores such as **Fee Fi Faux** offer colorful, hand-painted furniture or other funky, original works of art. **Flo's Attic, Inc.** and **Pieces of Eight Emporium** sell more-traditional antiques.

Down the road is a handful of shops selling upscale clothing, cigars, and traditional works of art such as wildlife sculptures. **Art's Cigars** is a two-story leather-and-tweed kind of place where patrons are encouraged to light up and enjoy the view of Lake Ivanhoe across the street. **Wildlife Gallery** sells pricey, original works of wildlife art, including sculpture.

The Fly Fisherman sells—guess what?—fly-fishing equipment. You can sometimes see people taking lessons in the park across the street.

All these stores are spread out for about 3 miles along Orange Avenue. The heaviest concentration is along Orange Avenue between Princeton Street and New Hampshire Avenue, although Fee Fi Faux and a few others are scattered between New Hampshire and Virginia avenues. The more upscale shops extend a few blocks beyond Virginia. To get there from the theme parks, take I-4 east to Princeton Street (Exit 43). Turn right on Orange Avenue. Parking is limited, so stop wherever you find a space along the street.

These downtown shops are usually open from about 8am to 6pm, Monday to Saturday. (The owners usually run these shops, so hours can vary. A small number of stores are open on Sunday, but it is probably not worth the trip from the resort areas just to shop.)

Built in an ornate Victorian style with hardwood oak floors and hand-painted tin ceilings, **The Exchange Shopping Emporium** is part of Church Street Station. The Exchange offers 50 specialty shops spread over several floors. Although there are some American mall standards such as **Victoria's Secret,** most stores offer more unusual wares. Places to visit include **Black Market Minerals,** which sells an infinite variety of things made from stone—polished semiprecious gems and beads, and even big slabs of quartz in a variety of colors. **The Gothic Shop** sells everything plaster, concentrating on angel figures, gargoyles, and Greek and Roman images.

Just across the tracks is **Church Street Market,** a collection of 30 shops and restaurants. The Market includes **Behr's Chocolates,** which sells a variety of homemade confections, along with retailers like **Hit or Miss,** a woman's clothing store, and **Brookstone,** an upscale shop specializing in electronic equipment like massage chairs and computerized toys of all sorts. All of the merchandise is on display for you to play with, um, try out. Restaurants include **The Olive Garden, Pizzeria Uno,** and **Hooter's,** a restaurant known for scantily clad, shapely waitresses serving up hot wings, curly fries, and suds. (The name, company officials claim with a straight face, in no way refers to a slang term for a certain part of the female anatomy.)

To get to the shopping complexes from the attractions, take I-4 east to downtown Orlando. Get off at Anderson Street (Exit 38). Turn left on Boone Avenue, then left on South Street. Turn right on Garland Avenue. Parking is available in a city-owned lot between South Street and Garland Avenue. Note your parking space and pay at the machines located at the end of the lot.

A Flea Market

Flea World. U.S. 17/92 in Sanford. ☎ **407/321-1792.** Take I-4 to Exit 50, Lake Mary Blvd. Go about 3 miles to U.S. 17/92 and turn left. Continue for about 1 mile. Flea World will be on your right.

The largest flea market in the world; that's what you'll find in Sanford, about 40 minutes north of the attractions. Flea World is pretty much exactly what the name implies, a huge flea market with everything from dentists' and lawyers' offices to lingerie and lamps. Although some folks have affectionately called the place the "white-trash mall," the politically correct term would be "economically challenged shopping emporium." Car tires, plants, ginsu knives, gourmet coffee, fresh produce, leather chaps . . . the array of merchandise is impressive, even if the surroundings aren't. Unlike flea markets in some regions, this one sells mostly new merchandise in its nearly 2,000 booths. (A couple of folks set up booths to sell old auto parts or garage-style finds.) Among this babble of bargains are many shops selling Florida T-shirts and souvenir-worthy knickknacks. Entertainment as diverse as live demonstrations by lions and tigers to Elvis impersonators and bingo games is regularly featured on the Flea World stage.

Nearby **Fun World** offers miniature golf courses, a miniature race track with gas-powered cars for the kiddies, a video arcade, and a small collection of carnival rides.

Although it is about 40 minutes from the theme parks, Flea World is more American than apple pie and a good place for bargains. *Be warned:* Some of the barnlike buildings are not air-conditioned, so this is not the best place to shop in the hot summer months.

A More Homespun Alternative

Mount Dora is a haven for artists and retirees, and is a wonderful day trip, not to mention a wonderful alternative to Disney. (Parents: Put the kids in one of the day-long camp programs—see chapter 2—and take a day to yourselves.) Mount Dora, established in 1874, has the genuine feel of an old Florida town with an authentic Main Street—like the one Disney tries to re-create. The 19th-century buildings still lining the streets are picture-perfect, leading up to the calm dark-green waters of Lake Dora. Unlike most of Florida, this town actually has rolling hills, adding to the charm.

Stroll through the dozens of shops featuring crafts, art, antiques, and collectibles, and then take a break with lunch at the Beauclair Dining Room at the historic Lakeside Inn. Enjoy lemonade and cookies while rocking on the front porch overlooking the lake.

For information call the Mount Dora Area Chamber of Commerce ☎ **352/383-2165.**

To get there, take I-4 to U.S. 441 and go west. Take Old U.S. 441 or Route 44B into town. Look for signs directing you to the "business district."

Sports Stores

Magic FanAttic. 301 W. Colonial Dr. ☎ **407/649-2222.** Take I-4 east to Exit 41 (Amelia St.). Stay to the right as the road goes around the bend. At the next light, turn left. Go under the freeway overpass.

Sports fans aching to add to their collection can tackle their shopping obsession at several stores specializing in merchandise for the Orlando Magic, the University of Florida Gators, and the Florida State University Seminoles.

This location of the FanAttic, sells every conceivable item embossed with the logo of the NBA's Orlando Magic. From lamps to alarm clocks to jerseys from the Magic's most popular player, "Penny" Hardaway, the FanAttic delivers. There are even talking "Lil Penny" dolls, made famous in Nike television commercials. (The store also carries merchandise featuring the cool images of the shades-wearing polar-bear mascot of Orlando's ice-hockey team, the Solar Bears. (Yes, I said ice hockey.)

The large silver building is on the right. The store is open daily from 10am to 6pm.

Gatorstuff. 1021 E. Colonial Dr., Orlando. ☎ **407/898-2129.**

The name gives you a strong hint as to what is sold here.

University Store. 1406 N. Mills Ave. ☎ **407/896-9391.** Take I-4 to Princeton St. (Exit 43). Turn right on Orange Ave. Turn left at Virginia Ave. The store is on the left at the corner of Mills and Virginia aves. There is a Seminole Indian rasslin' a gator painted on the wall.

It's a wonder they can keep the peace among the rabid University of Florida and Florida State University fans at this location. But there is a selection of merchandise from both schools, in addition to some stuff from the up-and-coming University of Central Florida Golden Knights. (They lost a coach because of a scandal, so they've officially made the big time.) Open Monday through Friday from 10am to 6pm and Saturday from 10am to 4pm.

10 Walt Disney World & Orlando After Dark

My hat's off to those of you who, after a long day traipsing around amusement parks, still have the energy to venture out at night in search of entertainment. You'll find plenty to do. This is primarily a kid's world, so many of the theme-park evening shows are geared to families. There is, however, plenty of adults-only entertainment both at the parks, and in downtown Orlando. The opening of Universal's nighttime entertainment complex, **CityWalk,** shows that the powers that be seem to feel visitors need more places to go after a long day of schlepping around the theme parks.

CityWalk's arrival follows the expansion of Disney's nighttime options through a set of restaurants and clubs called **Disney's West Side.** Those venues, along with Pleasure Island and the Disney Village Marketplace, are promoted as Downtown Disney. But don't be fooled, this is not Orlando's downtown. It is 25 miles or so up the road, and has its own collection of bars, clubs, and restaurants.

Check the "Calendar" section of Friday's **Orlando Sentinel** for up-to-the-minute details on local clubs, visiting performers, concerts, and events. It has hundreds of listings. The **Orlando Weekly** is a free magazine circulated in red boxes throughout central Florida that highlights more offbeat and often more of-the-minute performers and performances. It is online at **orlandoweekly.com.** Another option is **go2orlando,** a service of the Orlando Sentinel Online. On AOL, press the keyword button and type go2orlando for a menu of options. For a listing of cultural events go to **bizport. com/ua/culcal.**

Tickets to many Orlando performances are handled by **Ticket-Master** (☎ 407/839-3900 to charge tickets; there is a handling fee).

1 What's New in 2000 (& What's in the Works)

Lately, every year figures to be a big year for nightlife in Orlando. In 1999, Disney and Universal began going head-to-head for the after-dark dollars with Universal's CityWalk competing against Pleasure Island and its sister entertainment complex, Disney's West Side. Plus, the once-stagnant nightlife of downtown Orlando continues to flourish, offering locals and tourists something to do in addition to Church Street Station.

Not Your Ordinary Circus

A vision in white flies through the air on a billowing stream of orange as four women wind themselves in sheets of color, rising to the ceiling, only to fall unexpectedly back to mid-air. This is a typical scene in the **Cirque du Soleil**—if you can call anything about this unusual show, which wraps traditional circus performers in the colorful garb of the avant-garde, typical. Called *La Nouba,* it is presented by the Montreal-based troupe that has impressed audiences with its traveling shows since 1984. The Orlando location is the first permanent show outside of Las Vegas, and only the third worldwide. There are no animals in this circus, so dozens of acrobats, culled from the world's best, make up the intriguing cast of characters. The performers use a mixture of high-tech effects and old-fashioned showmanship in a 1,671-seat arena. Shows are at 5:30pm and 8:30pm, Wednesday through Saturday and 2:30pm and 5:30pm on Sunday. Ticket prices are $56.50 for adults, and $45.20 for children 3 to 9. For information call ☎ 407/939-7600. Although the cost of the Cirque is more than theme-park admission, try to make room in your budget for this truly unique, and invigorating experience. Adults traveling without children will definitely want to figure this into their budget.

In the spring of 1999, Universal Studios Escape opened a multibillion-dollar expansion including a dynamic, high-energy 12-acre entertainment complex called **CityWalk.** Occupying a two-tiered promenade with authentic streetscapes, a 4-acre lagoon, waterfalls, and lush landscaping, CityWalk could easily be renamed theme-restaurant heaven. Not only is it home to the world's largest **Hard Rock Cafe**—the grande dame of all theme restaurants—but also the **NASCAR Café** and the **Motown Cafe,** among others.

The other big unveiling of the past year was Cirque du Soleil. Since the beginning of 1999, the avant-garde circus troupe has established one of three permanent shows in the United States in a state-of-art facility located in Downtown Disney.

2 The Performing Arts

While Disney occasionally hosts classical musical acts—notably at the Disney Institute—to get a taste of traditional performing arts, you will have to go into Orlando.

CONCERT HALLS & AUDITORIUMS

The city is currently in the midst of securing the financing for a multimillion-dollar, world-class performing arts center in downtown. For now, however, there are three large entertainment facilities, administered by the Orlando Centroplex, which host the majority of big-name performers and cultural troupes playing the Orlando area.

The **Florida Citrus Bowl,** 1610 W. Church St., at Tampa Street (☎ 407/849-2020 for information, 407/839-3900 to charge tickets), with 70,000 seats, is the largest setting for major rock concerts and headliners such as Elton John and the Rolling Stones. To reach the Citrus Bowl, take I-4 east to the East-West Expressway and head west to Highway 441; make a left on Church Street and follow the signs. Parking is $5.

The 17,500-seat **Orlando Arena** at 600 W. Amelia St., between I-4 and Parramore Avenue (☎ 407/849-2020 for information, 407/839-3900 to charge tickets), also hosts major performers (Garth Brooks, Elton John, Bruce Springsteen), in addition to an array of family-oriented entertainment: Ringling Bros. Barnum & Bailey Circus every January, Discover Card Stars on Ice in February, the Tour of World Figure-Skating Champions in April or May, and Walt Disney's World on Ice in September. To reach the arena, take I-4 east to Amelia Avenue, turn left at the traffic light at the bottom of the off-ramp, and follow the signs. Parking is $5.

The area's major cultural venue is the 2,500 seat **Bob Carr Performing Arts Centre,** 401 W. Livingston St., between I-4 and Parramore Avenue (☎ **407/ 849-2020** for information, 407/839-3900 to charge tickets). Concert prices vary with performers. To get here, take I-4 east to Amelia Avenue, turn left at the traffic light at the bottom of the off-ramp, and follow the signs. Parking is $5.

THEATER

The **Orlando-UCF Shakespeare Festival,** offers both a fall and spring schedule. The spring shows feature Shakespeare in the park at downtown's Lake Eola. The company is known for placing traditional plays in contemporary settings and offers special programs throughout the year, such as Shakespeare Unplugged, a free reading series. Tickets do sell out, so it's best to call ahead for reservations. Ask about tickets for dress rehearsals, which go for about $7. For information online, go to **pegasus.cc.ucf.edu/~shaksper** or call ☎ **407/317-7800.**

The **Civic Theatre of Central Florida** offers traditional fare on the main stage, and more avant-garde offerings on the Second Stage. (Although things never get too wild in Orlando.) There is also a children's theater program. Tickets are usually available for main stage productions, but it's best to call ahead to reserve seats for the smaller Second Stage or children's performances. For information, call ☎ **407/ 896-7365.**

OPERA

The **Orlando Opera Company** is a professional troupe with a repertoire of traditional fare featuring guest artists from around the country. Shows held during the October to May season are rarely sold out. For ticket information, call ☎ **407/ 426-1700.**

DANCE

The **Southern Ballet Theatre** presents traditional shows with guest artists from around the county augmenting local talent. Although there has been a recent resurgence of interest in the ballet, performances rarely sell out. The exception is the Nutcracker performed annually during December. The season runs from October to May. For information, call ☎ **407/426-1733.**

CLASSICAL MUSIC

The **Festival of Orchestras,** brings orchestras from around the world to perform several times a year. Call ☎ **407/896-2451.**

The **Orlando Philharmonic Orchestra,** a professional orchestra, performs a varied schedule of classics and pop-influenced concerts throughout the year. Call ☎ **407/896-6700.**

3 Walt Disney World Dinner Shows

Two distinctly different dinner shows are offered at Walt Disney World: Hoop-Dee-Doo Musical Revue and Polynesian Luau Dinner Show. However, there are other nighttime shows in the parks if a dinner show isn't in your evening itinerary. These include the Main Street Electrical Parade, fireworks, and IllumiNations (details in chapter 7).

Hoop-Dee-Doo Musical Revue. 3520 N. Fort Wilderness Trail (at Disney's Fort Wilderness Resort and Campground). ☎ **407/WDW-DINE** (939-3463). Reservations required. Adults $38, children 3–11 $19.50. Taxes and gratuities extra. Show times at 5, 7:15, and 9:30pm nightly. Free self-parking.

Fort Wilderness's rustic log-beamed Pioneer Hall is the setting for this 2-hour foot-stompin', hand-clappin', down-home musical revue. It's a high-energy show, with 1890s costumes, corny vaudeville jokes, rousing songs, and lots of good-natured audience participation.

During the show, the audience chows down on an all-you-can-eat barbecue dinner, including chips and salsa, salad, smoked ribs, country-fried chicken, corn on the cob, baked beans, loaves of fresh-baked bread with honey butter, and a big slab of strawberry shortcake for dessert. Beverages (coffee, tea, beer, sangria, and soda) are included.

If you catch an early show, stick around for the Electrical Water Pageant at 9:45pm, which can be viewed from the Fort Wilderness Beach.

Polynesian Luau Dinner Show. 1600 Seven Seas Dr. (at Disney's Polynesian Resort). ☎ **407/WDW-DINE** (939-3463). Reservations required. Adults $38, children 3–11 $19.50. Taxes and gratuities are extra. Show times 6:45 and 9:30pm nightly. Free self- and valet parking.

This delightful 2-hour dinner show is a big favorite with kids, all of whom are invited up on the stage. It features a colorfully costumed cast of entertainers from New Zealand, Tahiti, Hawaii, and Samoa performing authentic hula, warrior, ceremonial, love, and fire dances on a flower-bedecked stage. The show also includes a Hawaiian/Polynesian fashion show.

It all takes place in an open-air theater (dress for nighttime weather) with candlelit tables, red-flame lanterns suggesting torches, and tapa-bark paintings adorning the walls. Arrive early; there's a preshow highlighting Polynesian crafts and culture (lei making, hula lessons, and more).

The all-you-can-eat meal includes a big platter of fresh island fruits, barbecued chicken, corn on the cob, other vegetables, roasted red potatoes and sweet potatoes, pull-apart cinnamon bread, beverages, and a tropical ice-cream sundae.

There's also a 4:30pm version daily called **Mickey's Tropical Luau** (see character-meal listings in chapter 6).

4 More Dinner Shows

Arabian Nights. 6225 W. Irlo Bronson Memorial Hwy. (or U.S. Hwy. 192, just east of I-4 at Exit 25A), Kissimmee. ☎**800/553-6116** or 407/239-9223. Reservations recommended. Admission $36.05 adults, $23.05 children 3–11. Shows nightly. Free parking.

Arabian Nights offers a little bit of everything, from prancing Lipizzaner Stallions to chariot races. The 2-hour show claims to have more characters, costumes, and lights than any show on Broadway. You certainly won't find the "land of the mythical unicorn" on the Great White Way. The menu includes salad, prime rib, vegetables, new potatoes, dinner rolls, dessert, soft drinks, and wine. The price of admission covers dinner and the show.

Medieval Times. 4510 W. Irlo Bronson Memorial Hwy. (or U.S. Hwy. 192, 11 miles east of the main Disney entrance, next to Super Wal-Mart) in Kissimmee. ☎ **800/229-8300** or 407/239-0214. Reservations recommended. Admission $36.95 adults, $22.95 children 3–12. Daily at 8pm. Free parking.

Jim Carrey fans know that the Cable Guy went to a California branch of Medieval Times to duel with his hapless friend. A longtime favorite of Orlando visitors, the Kissimmee-based show is billed as "dinner and tournament." Living up to its name, it includes jousting contests, armored clashes, and 80 Andalusian stallions performing with military precision. It's all put on for you and 1,000 of the "special" guests of the castle, who eat off heavy metal plates while watching the tournament contestants tumble about before them. Dark and cavernous, Medieval Times has an ambience all its own. The menu includes a wine cocktail, fresh-vegetable soup, a whole roasted chicken, spare ribs, herb-basted potatoes, and dessert. The price includes dinner, beverages, and the show. The castle is air-conditioned, and accessible to guests with disabilities. Medieval Times is very popular, so reservations are suggested.

Wild Bill's Wild West Dinner Extravaganza. 5260 U.S. 192 (just east of I-4). ☎ **800/883-8181** or 407/351-5151. Reservations recommended. Admission $36.95 adults, $22.95 children 3–11, under 3 free. Nightly at 7pm, with 9:30pm shows on selected nights. Free parking.

Located at Fort Liberty, a 22-acre western-themed shopping/dining/entertainment complex, this rambunctious dinner show takes place in a big, barnlike wooden building. You'll be given a cardboard cowboy hat when you sit down, which identifies you as a shepherd or a cowherd for audience-participation activities (there are a lot of these). The show includes rousing song-and-dance numbers ("Annie Get Your Gun," "Oklahoma," "Back in the Saddle Again"); rodeo roping, knife-throwing, and archery demonstrations; sing-alongs; a cancan; and Comanche ceremonial and war dances. All the children in the audience get to go up on the stage.

Dinner—served on pewterware—is a hearty four-course meal consisting of salad, soup, beef stew, fried chicken, barbecued pork ribs, biscuits with honey butter, corn, beans, a baked potato, and hot apple pie. Beer, wine, and Coca-Cola are included.

5 At Walt Disney World

The places described in this section can be located on the map "Downtown Disney" in this section.

A PAY-ONE-PRICE ENTERTAINMENT COMPLEX

Pleasure Island. In Downtown Disney, adjacent to Walt Disney World Village Marketplace. ☎ **407/934-7781.** Free admission before 7pm, $18.95 after 7pm. Admission included in the All-In-One-Hopper Pass. Clubs open daily 7pm–2am; shops 11am–2am. Free self-parking; valet parking $5.

This Walt Disney World theme park is a rollicking 6-acre complex of nightclubs, restaurants, shops, and movie theaters where, for a single admission price, you can enjoy a night of club-hopping until the wee hours.

Pleasure Island is patterned after an abandoned waterfront industrial district, with clubs in "converted" ramshackle lofts, factories, and warehouses, but the streets are decorated with brightly colored lights and balloons. Dozens of searchlights play overhead, and rock music emanates from the bushes. You'll be given a map and show schedule when you enter the park; take a look at it, and plan your evening around the shows that interest you.

The mood here is always festive. For one thing, every night at Pleasure Island is New Year's Eve, celebrated on the stroke of midnight with a high-energy street party, live entertainment, a barrage of fireworks, and showers of confetti.

Although this is Disney, it is essentially a bar district where liquor is served, so when sending out your older children, use the same rules that you use at home.

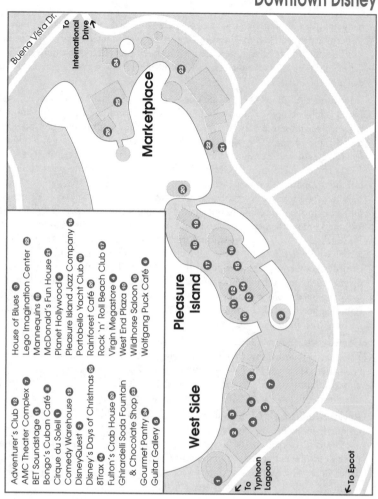

(This is the place where the singer Bobby Brown got arrested for fighting.) They must be 18 to get in unless accompanied by a parent or legal guardian.

Pleasure Island has six clubs. The Wildhorse Saloon, on nights there is not a major concert, and the BET Soundstage, are also part of the Pleasure Island ticket.

Pleasure Island Jazz Company   This big, barnlike club—purported to be an abandoned waterfront carousel factory—features contemporary and traditional live jazz. Performers are mostly locals, but about once a month there are big names such as Kenny Rankin, Lionel Hampton, Maynard Ferguson, the Rippingtons, and Billy Taylor. Light fare, international coffees, and a variety of foreign and domestic wines are available.

Mannequins Dance Palace   Housed in a vast dance hall with a small-town movie-house facade, Mannequins is supposed to be a converted theatrical mannequin warehouse (remember, you're still in Disney World). It's a high-energy club with a large rotating dance floor and is a local favorite. Three levels of bars and hangout space are festooned with elaborately costumed mannequins and moving scenery suspended from overhead rigging. A DJ plays contemporary tunes at ear-splitting decibel levels, and there are high-tech lighting effects. You must be 21 to get in, and they're very serious about it. Have your ID ready, even if you learned to dance to the Platters.

Adventurers Club The most unique—and my personal favorite—of Pleasure Island's clubs occupies a multistory building that, according to Disney legend, was designed to house the vast library and archaeological trophy collection of island founder and compulsive explorer, Merriweather Adam Pleasure. It's also headquarters for the Adventures Club, which Pleasure headed up until he vanished at sea in 1941. The plushly furnished club is chock-full of artifacts—early aviation photos, hunting trophies, shrunken heads, Buddhas, Indian goddesses, spears, and a mounted "yakoose" (half yak, half moose), who occasionally speaks. He's not the only one. In the eerie Mask Room, strange sounds are often heard, and more than 100 masks move their eyes, jeer, and make odd pronouncements. Also on hand are Pleasure's zany band of globe-trotting friends and club servants, played by skilled actors who interact with guests and always stay in character. Improvisational comedy shows take place throughout the evening in the main salon, and there are diverse 20-minute cabaret shows/events in the library (during which "volunteers" are dragooned from the audience). You could easily hang out here all night imbibing potent tropical drinks in the library and at the bar—where elephant-foot barstools rise and sink mysteriously.

Comedy Warehouse Housed in the island's former power plant, the Comedy Warehouse—another favorite of mine—has a rustic interior with tiered seating. A very talented troupe—the Who, What and Warehouse Players—perform 45-minute improvisational comedy shows based on audience suggestions. There are five shows a night, and bar drinks are available. Arrive early.

Rock & Roll Beach Club Once the laboratory in which Pleasure developed a unique flying machine, this three-story structure today houses a dance club where live bands play "classic rock from the 60s through the 90s." There are bars on all three floors, including one serving international beers. The first level contains the dance floor. The second and third levels offer air hockey, pool tables, basketball machines, pinball, video games, darts, and a pizza and beer stand.

8 Trax This 1970s-style club, with about 50 TV monitors airing diverse shows and videos over the dance floor, occupies three levels, all with bars. Period movie posters (*Bananas, Star Wars*) adorn the walls, and the top-floor lounge is vaguely psychedelic in decor. A DJ plays disco music, and guests engage in games of Twister.

You can star in your own music video at **SuperStar Studios.** And there are carnival games, a video-game arcade, virtual-reality games, a Velcro wall (don a jumpsuit over your clothes, bounce on a trampoline, and stick yourself on), and an Orbitron (a "21st-century workout machine," originally developed for NASA, that lets you experience weightlessness). Shops and eateries (with outdoor umbrella tables) are found throughout the park. **Planet Hollywood** (see chapter 6 for details) is adjacent and does not require an admission charge.

DISNEY'S WEST SIDE

In Downtown Disney, this area of clubs and restaurants is located next to Pleasure Island. The following could be considered "night spots," though they also serve food.

Bongo's Cuban Cafe. In Disney's West Side. ☎ **407/828-0999.** No reservations. AE, DC, DISC, MC, V. Wed–Sun after 10am.

DisneyQuest

"It's like a miracle," said one awestruck, dark-haired tot, craning his neck to take in the wave-shaped blue building with the swirling lavender decorations. The little tourist could only imagine that the impressive architecture at DisneyQuest was just the beginning. From the Cybrolator—an elevator to the uninitiated—with an introductory video featuring Robin Williams as Genie, to the human pinball machine to the virtual coaster CyberSpace Mountain, the 100,000 square foot facility is unlike anything you've experienced.

Inside you can create and ride your own virtual roller coaster, shoot the rapids without getting wet, or ride Aladdin's Magic Carpet. There is also a variety of less high-tech arcade games, such as skee ball, where you accumulate tickets to win prizes, and almost an entire floor, the Underground Arcade, filled with the kind of shoot 'em up games that boys of all ages love. Older children may enjoy Sports Arena Arcade's computerized games, where you ski, drive a race car, or drive a motorcycle. Parents may indulge in a bit of nostalgia with "ancient" video games like Centipede and Space Invaders.

Although DisneyQuest is open from 10:30am until midnight, it's most crowded after dark as theme park crowds drift to Downtown Disney. Also inside is FoodQuest, on the fifth floor, and the Wonderland Cafe, on the fourth; both offer excellent food at traditional theme park prices. A meal and drink will run about $10 at FoodQuest; a piece of cheesecake and coffee at Wonderland Cafe, about $7. There is no specific children's menu, but the servings are plentiful and can easily be enough for two. Admission to DisneyQuest is $25 for adults, $20 for children 3 to 11. Children 10 and under are not admitted without an adult.

Created by Cuban-American songstress Gloria Estefan and her husband, Emilio, the cafe is Disney's version of old Havana. There are leopard spotted chairs and mosaic bar stools shaped like bongo drums. A Desi Arnaz look-alike might even show up to sing a few tunes. There is no dance floor to speak of, although you could cha-cha on the patio. This upstairs patio, which overlooks the rest of the West Side, is a great place to sit back and enjoy a good (faux) Cuban cigar while basking in the Latin rhythms.

House of Blues. In Disney's West Side, under the old-fashioned water tower. ☎ **407/934-2583.** AE, DISC, MC, V. Valet parking, $6.

Cover charges vary here in proportion to the stature of the artist. A variety of top names popped up during the first year. The barnlike building, with three tiers, may be a little difficult for those with disabilities to maneuver, but there is not a bad seat in the house. The atmosphere is dark and boozy, perfect for the bluesy sounds. The sound system rocks to the rafters, and the dance floor is big enough to boogie without doing the bump with a stranger. You can eat in the adjoining restaurant, which is described in chapter 6.

BET Soundstage. In Disney's West Side. ☎ **407/934-2583.** Cover charge included in Pleasure Island Pass. AE, DISC, MC, V. Valet parking, $6.

This club grooves with the smooth moves of traditional R&B and the rhyme of the time—hip-hop. Basically, if you like the BET Cable Network, you'll like this club. Boogie on an expansive dance floor, or chill while relaxing on an outdoor terrace. The club also serves a Caribbean-style finger food menu.

Wildhorse Saloon. In Disney's West Side. ☎ **407/934-2583.** Cover charge included in Pleasure Island Pass, except on nights of big concerts. On those nights there is a separate charge. AE, DISC, MC, V. Valet parking, $6.

Yeehaaww! The Wildhorse Saloon is country music at its boot-stompin' finest, with the best in contemporary country 7 days a week. The Wildfires Dancers can show you some down-home moves before you go boot-scootin' across the 1,500-square-foot dance floor. After working up an appetite, feast on barbecued ribs and chicken, steaks, chops, entree salads, and home-baked desserts. You can even buy some fancy, fringed duds at Wildhorse Western Wear.

6 CityWalk

Located between Islands of Adventure and Universal Studios Florida, CityWalk (☎ **407/363-8000**) is a collection of nighttime entertainment spots, organized along the same lines as Pleasure Island and Church Street Station. Centered around a man-made lagoon that helps stir a cooling breeze, the complex is open daily from 11am to 2am with most of the action starting after 6pm. Operating hours of the clubs, bars, and restaurants, however, vary and are listed below. These hours are subject to change so call ahead before you visit.

There is no admission charge to walk through the two-levels of clubs, restaurants, and shops. A CityWalk Party Pass, which allows entry into any club with a cover charge, is **$17.97.** Unlike Disney's Pleasure Island, you can also opt to pay the individual cover charges, usually under $6. The cover charges are listed below. Again, they are subject to change. Parking, $6 in the Universal Studios Escape parking garages.

This expansive 30-acre complex—compared to the 6-acre Pleasure Island—has a laid-back, open-air feel that adds to its atmosphere. Alcohol is more prominently featured here than at the Disney properties, so an adult should accompany all teenagers and young children. The party can get pretty wild when the special Mardi Gras celebration at Universal spills over to the clubs and bars. Mardi Gras runs mid-February through late March.

Bob Marley: A Tribute to Freedom. ☎ **407/224-2262.** Cover, $4.25 after 7pm.

This is a hybrid bar/restaurant with the partying mood overwhelming the food as the night wears on. The white, clapboard building is said to be an exact replica of Bob Marley's island home. Jamaican food, such as meat patties and roti, is served here under patio umbrellas amid colorful portraits of the original rastamon. Reggae bands, some local some national, perform on a small stage. Hours are Monday to Friday from 5pm to 2am, and Saturday to Sunday from 11am to 2am.

CityJazz. ☎ **407/224-2189.** Cover charge $5.25 after 8:30pm.

The cover charge includes the **Downbeat Jazz Hall of Fame,** a museum, and the **Thelonious Monk Institute of Jazz,** a performance venue that is also the site of jazz workshops. The octagonal, two-story 10,500 square-foot building houses more

Fun Fact

You can grab a margarita to go and "chill" in the brightly colored wooden chairs near Jimmy Buffet's Margaritaville. It is a perfect spot to look over the man-made lagoon and watch the crowds go by.

than 500 pieces of memorabilia representing Dixieland, swing, bebop, and modern jazz, and a state-of-the-art sound system and stage. The mood is set by graphic murals and oversized black-and-white photographs. Acts of national renown perform frequently. A real treat for true jazz fans. Open daily from 7:30pm to 2am.

Emeril's. ☎ **407/224-2424**. No cover. Seatings Sun–Thurs 5:30–10pm; Fri–Sat 5:30pm–11pm.

The spunky chef from cable television brings his—BAM!—unique culinary stylings to this upscale restaurant. Large abstract paintings cover the walls of this two-story restaurant, where the waiters are smartly dressed in white shirts and dark ties. Dinner entrees range from a barbecue for $18.50 to grilled veal chops for $27. If you want the experience on the cheap side, you can make a meal of the milky Louisiana Oyster Stew ($10), usually served as an appetizer. The menu also features cigars and a fair selection of cognac and wine by the glass. There is no dress code, but you will probably feel a little underdressed in shorts and a T-shirt, so plan accordingly. With the relatively costly menu and reserved atmosphere, this is not the best place for family dining.

The groove. ☎ **407/363-8000.** Cover charge $5.25. Must be 21 to be admitted.

This is Universal's answer to Mannequin's at Pleasure Island. There is a high-tech sound system that makes your hair blow back, and a spacious dance floor in a room gleaming with chrome. Featuring the latest in house, hip-hop, jazz fusion, techno, and alternative music, a live DJ spins tunes on the nights when national and local recording artists aren't booked. In addition to the main club room, there are three smaller alcoves, each possessing its own unique design, a bar, and a specialty drink to fit their particular ambience. The blue room is icy and cool, with nightly martini specialties. The red room is hot and spicy, featuring fruity drinks with umbrellas, and the green room features classic architecture and classic Scotch apéritifs. Open daily from 9pm to 2am.

Hard Rock Live. ☎ **407/351-5483.** Cover charges vary depending on the act in concert; range from $6 to $150.

The largest Hard Rock Cafe in the world, and the first concert hall with the Hard Rock name, this building, crafted to look like an ancient coliseum, combines the theme restaurant that pays homage to great rock 'n' rollers, and a 2,000-seat hall. Call ahead to find out what acts will be featured during your visit. Tickets for big-name national and international acts sell out quickly. You can always linger among the memorabilia, which for some reason is heavy on kitsch from KISS, but also highlights other hard-rocking artists. Restaurant is open daily from 11am to 2am. Concerts generally begin about 8pm.

Jimmy Buffet's Margaritaville. ☎ **407/224-2155.** Cover charge, $3.25 after 10 pm.

More laid back than Emeril's, flip flops and flowered shirts are the correct apparel here. Music from the master is piped throughout the building with live music performed on a small stage inside later in the evening, and a Jimmy sound-alike strumming on the spacious back porch. If you opt for dinner among the palm trees, go for the true Key West experience by starting with conch chowder as an appetizer ($3.75), followed by the golden brown Coconut Tempura Fried Shrimp ($13.95); finish it off with some Key lime pie. If you just want to soak up the atmosphere—along with a few margaritas—go sit under the thatched roof at the bar in the back. (There is also a margarita's-to-go stand you can access from the main CityWalk avenue.) Open daily from 11am to 2am.

Latin Quarter. ☎ 407/363-5922. Cover charge $3.25 after 10pm.

This two-level restaurant/nightclub offers you the chance to Salsa—if you don't know how, don't worry, there's a dance studio to help you learn the steps—while sampling the cuisine and the cocktails of 21 Latin nations. The club features acts ranging from Merengue and Mariachi bands to Latin rock groups to costumed dance troupes. The Aztec- and Mayan-influenced decor, including a gallery of Latin American art, adds spice to the South American atmosphere. Be aware, however, that the sound system is so loud, it's intrusive. If you want to Tango the night away, you'll feel right at home, but this is not the place for casual conversation. Open daily from 11:00am to 1:30am.

Motown Cafe Orlando. ☎ 407/224-2500. Cover charge $3.25.

You can chow down here on good ol' American cuisine to the tunes of Motown artists such as the Supremes and Smokey Robinson. Walk up the Stairway of Success—literally paved with gold records—to get a good look at the world's largest record—a 28-foot version of the Jackson 5's hit single, "ABC"—and other Motown memorabilia. The Motown Cafe Moments, performers who cover the label's classic hits, entertain daily on the club's first two floors. The Big Chill Lounge on the third level offers a great view, retro decor, and specialty drinks such as the "My Girl." The food here is classic American, from a MotownPhilly Cheesesteak ($9.95) to Berry's BBQ Chicken ($11.95). Hours are Sunday to Thursday 5:00pm to midnight, and Friday to Saturday 5:00pm to 2:00am.

NASCAR Café. ☎ 407/224-7223. No cover charge.

Equal parts restaurant, NASCAR museum, arcade, and shop, this is a must-see for anybody who can spot Jeff Gordon's rainbow stripes amid the pack on the far turn, or knows drafting isn't something you do on a table. There is a small, but interesting, collection of photographs and NASCAR memorabilia, plus at least two authentic cars parked nearby for inspection. The arcade features interactive rides that allow you to hop on a Harley, or downshift at the Daytona 500. Upstairs is the restaurant offering serviceable, if not exactly fancy food, with the most expensive dinner entree going for $17. Because of the arcade and the lack of a cover charge, this place is one of the best options for families. Open daily from 10am to 10pm.

Pat O'Brien's. ☎ 407/224-2122. Cover charge $3.25 from 6pm–2am.

It doesn't take a genius to figure out the focus of a place that has a one-page menu of appetizers—and a small booklet filled with drinks. Just like the French Quarter, which is home to the original Patty Os, drinking, drinking and drinking some more, is the highlight here. Enjoy dueling pianos in a medium-sized, wood-paneled bar, or bask in the balmy Orlando night on a patio decorated with the kind of iron work you might find in New Orleans. You can also sit on the upstairs balcony and watch the crowds while you down the drink of the Big Easy, a Hurricane. Although you can order a soft drink, Pat O'Brien's certainly promotes the hard stuff, and no one under 21 is permitted after 7pm. Open daily from 11am to 2am.

CityWalk broke ground for an NBA-themed restaurant in the spring of 1999. Eventually, a 20-screen Cineplex will also open at the entertainment complex.

7 Hot Spots in Downtown Orlando

Dozens of clubs and restaurants line Orange Avenue, the main street in downtown Orlando. A free public transportation system called **Lymmo** runs in a designated lane that connects many of these clubs, but since Lymmo stops running about

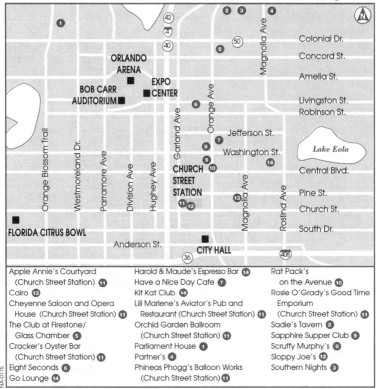

Apple Annie's Courtyard
(Church Street Station) **11**
Cairo **13**
Cheyenne Saloon and Opera
House (Church Street Station) **11**
The Club at Firestone/
Glass Chamber **5**
Cracker's Oyster Bar
(Church Street Station) **11**
Eight Seconds **6**
Go Lounge **14**

Harold & Maude's Espresso Bar **14**
Have a Nice Day Cafe **7**
Kit Kat Club **14**
Lili Marlene's Aviator's Pub and
Restaurant (Church Street Station) **11**
Orchid Garden Ballroom
(Church Street Station) **11**
Parliament House **1**
Partner's **4**
Phineas Phogg's Balloon Works
(Church Street Station) **11**

Rat Pack's
on the Avenue **10**
Rosie O'Grady's Good Time
Emporium
(Church Street Station) **11**
Sadie's Tavern **2**
Sapphire Supper Club **9**
Scruffy Murphy's **8**
Sloppy Joe's **12**
Southern Nights **3**

NA-0175

11pm, it may stop moving before you do. Keep enough money for a taxi. These places can be located on the map "Downtown Orlando Nightlife" in this section.

Church Street Station. 129 W. Church St. (off I-4, between Garland and Orange aves. in downtown Orlando). ☎ **407/422-2434.** Free admission prior to 5pm, after which you have to pay $17.95. Clubs open nightly 7:15pm–2am; shops 11am–11pm. AE, DC, DISC, MC, V. There are several metered lots nearby (call for specifics). Metered parking runs about $1 an hour. Take I-4 east to Exit 38 (Anderson St.), stay in the left lane, and follow the signs.

Though not part of Walt Disney World, Church Street Station in downtown Orlando operates on a similar principle to Pleasure Island (in fact, it started the concept). Occupying a cobblestone city block lined with turn-of-the-century buildings (real ones), it, too, is a shopping/dining/nightclub complex offering a diverse evening of entertainment for a single admission price. There are 20 live shows nightly (consult your show schedule upon entering), plus an array of street performers. Major blow-out celebrations are held for special events such as St. Patrick's Day and the Super Bowl.

Stunning interiors are the rule here. It's worth coming by just to check out the magnificent woodwork, stained glass, and thousands of authentic antiques. And capitalizing on the traffic that Church Street generates, many other clubs have opened in the immediate area, further enlarging your bar-hopping potential.

Entry to restaurants, the Exchange Shopping Emporium, and the Midway game area is free. Check out the following highlights.

Rosie O'Grady's Good Time Emporium: This 1890s-style gambling hall–cum-saloon, with beveled- and leaded-glass panels, etched mirrors, and vast globe chandeliers suspended from a high pressed-tin ceiling, is filled with interesting antiques. The band here, a collection of seasoned professionals, really jams, and their collaborative efforts reflect the long time they've played together. The train benches came from an old Florida rail station, back-bar mirrors from a Glasgow pub, and bank tellers' cages from a 19th-century Pittsburgh bank. Dixieland bands, banjo players, singing waiters, and cancan dancers entertain nightly. Light fare (deli sandwiches, chili dogs) is available. The house specialty drink is a rum and fruit concoction called the Flaming Hurricane (served in a souvenir glass). The "Good Time Piano Man" plays at 1:30, 2:30, 3:30, and 4:30pm; visitors are encouraged to sing along.

Apple Annie's Courtyard: Adjoining Rosie's, this brick-floored establishment, domed by arched trusses from an early 19th-century New Orleans church, evokes a Victorian tropical garden. The room is further embellished by 12-foot, hand-carved filigree mirrors created in Vienna circa 1740 and magnificent 1,000-pound chandeliers suspended from an ornate, vaulted cherry-wood ceiling. An 18th-century French communion rail serves as the front bar. Seating is in wicker peacock chairs at English pub tables. Patrons sip potent tropical fresh fruit and ice-cream drinks while listening to folk and bluegrass music.

Lili Marlene's Aviator's Pub & Restaurant: Its plush, oak-paneled interior is embellished with World War I memorabilia, stained-glass transoms, and accoutrements from an 1850 Rothschild town house in Paris, the latter including a walnut fireplace and wine cabinets. Eclectic seating ranges from hand-carved oak pews that came from a French church to a place at a large drop-leaf mahogany table where Al Capone once dined. Model airplanes and marvelous Victorian chandeliers are suspended from a beamed pine ceiling with a stained-glass skylight. The menu features premium aged steaks, prime rib, and fresh seafood.

Phineas Phogg's Balloon Works: This whimsical bar, with hot-air balloons and airplanes over the dance floor, is a high-energy club playing loud, pulsating music. (This is where the NBA's Charles Barkley threw a fellow patron through a plate glass window.) It doubles as a virtual ballooning museum, housing photographs and artifacts from historic flights, including Orlando native Joe Kittinger—the first man to cross the Atlantic in a gas balloon. Every Wednesday from 6:30 to 7:30pm, beers cost just 5¢ here. No one under 21 is admitted.

Cheyenne Saloon and Opera House: This stunning trilevel, balconied saloon, crowned by a lofty stained-glass skylight, is constructed of golden oak lumber from a century-old Ohio barn. Quality western art is displayed throughout, including many oil paintings and 11 Remington sculptures. This place offers the best show of the bunch, with a tight country band that really knows how to kick. Well-known artists do occasionally drop by to join in. If you know how to line dance or do the two-step, you'll love this place. If not, you can always take advantage of those slow songs. Balcony seating, in restored church pews, overlooks the stage—the setting for entertainment ranging from country bands (some big names) to clogging exhibitions—and the dance floor. There are free country-dance lessons in the saloon on Friday, Saturday, and Sunday from 2 to 5:30pm. The menu features steaks, barbecued chicken and ribs, and hickory-smoked brisket.

Orchid Garden Ballroom: This stunning space, with ornate white wrought-iron arches and Victorian lighting fixtures suspended from an elaborate oak-paneled ceiling, is the setting for an oldies dance club. A DJ plays rock 'n' roll classics like "Great Balls of Fire" and "Let's Go to the Hop," interspersed with live bands. As the evening progresses, so do the musical decades.

Blazing Pianos: A Perfect Hell for the Shy

A rambunctious crowd of all ages hangs out at this popular sing-along club, where talented singers and musicians—on fire-red grand pianos—perform classic rock tunes, do a bit of comedy, and try to embarrass audience members. Most of the songs they select are on the lively side—"Great Balls of Fire," "The Twist," "Jailhouse Rock," and the like, as well as TV theme songs.

Audience members occasionally get up on the stage—or are dragooned there—to dance. And probably once a night, everybody stands up to perform "Hand Jive." Blazing Pianos promotes audience participation to the max; it's an exhibitionist's paradise, and perhaps unbearable for the sensitive. (You might be spotlighted if they see you're not singing!) The ambiance is slick and upscale; special effects include smoke, mirror balls, and strobe lights. A fairly extensive bar menu has items such as fried calamari and buffalo wings, plus gourmet desserts.

Blazing Pianos is located in the **Mercado** at 8445 International Blvd., just south of Sand Lake Road (☎ **407/363-5104**). Admission is $5. Though it opens earlier, the action begins about 9:30pm and continues until 2am nightly. No one under 21 is admitted weekend nights. Sunday through Thursday, children are admitted, and it makes for a fun family outing.

Crackers Oyster Bar: Brick columns, oak paneling, and a gorgeous antique oak and mahogany bar, characterize this cozy, late 1800s–style dining room. Fresh Florida seafood is featured, along with more than 50 imported beers. You can nibble on appetizers such as oysters Rockefeller, smoked fish dip, and steamed mussels; or, opt for more serious entrees ranging from crab cakes rémoulade to paella.

In addition, the 87,000-square-foot Exchange houses the carnival-like **Commander Ragtime's Midway of Fun, Food, and Games** (including an enormous video-game arcade), a food court, and more than 50 specialty shops. You can rent a horse-drawn carriage out front for a drive around the downtown area and Lake Eola. And hot-air balloon flights can be arranged (☎ **407/841-8787**).

Note: Most hotels offer transportation to and from Church Street, and, since you'll probably be drinking, I advise it. As long as I'm giving advice, if you are disabled or are in a wheelchair, prepare to arrive early for each show so you can get a floor seat. Although my husband's Nana, who is in her late 70s, tromped right to the top, the steps in the multitiered theaters are steep and can be difficult to navigate for those with physical limitations. Also, it's difficult to get around inside the theaters with a baby stroller.

.08 Seconds. 100 W. Livingston Ave., Orlando. ☎ **407/839-4800.** 8-seconds.com. Cover charge is $4 for 21 and older; $6, under 20. AE, MC, V. Open Wed, Fri, and Sat. Parking in city lot, $3. Valet Parking, $6.

What used to be the hottest concert spot in downtown has been transformed into a honky-tonk. There's not a whole lot to distinguish the dark cavernous interior, except a huge dance floor. (Ask about free line-dancing lessons early in the evenings.) Outside is what really sets this place apart. Just next to the parking lot is a rodeo pen where there are "Buckin' Bull Nights," with live bulls. There are also monster-truck pulls in the back lot. This place has really gone country; the managers even carry walkie-talkies painted white and black like cowhides. Just say, "Yeeehaaaawww" and hang on. (In order to score, a cowboy or cowgirl needs to stay atop his or her steer for 8 seconds.) Country stars rising up the charts occasionally hold concerts here. Recent performers include Mark Chestnut.

Rat Pack's On the Avenue. 25 S. Orange Ave. (corner of Orange and Pine), Orlando. ☎ **407/649-4803.** unishopper.com/ratpacks.htm. Cover charge varies but is usually between $5 and $10. AE, DISC, MC, V.

It's Money, Baby. Formerly a hard-rocking bar for those who favored big hair and heavy metal, this has become one of the swingiest joints in town. Free swing lessons several times a week, along with live bands. There is live comedy on Friday and Saturday nights, before the music starts around 10pm.

Have a Nice Day Cafe. 120 N. Orange Ave., Orlando. ☎ **407/839-1939.** Cover on Fri and Sat, $5. AE, MC, V.

If you had a Brady Bunch lunch box or a crush on Keith (or Laurie) Partridge, this place will send you skipping down memory lane in wide-legged bell bottoms. Although some folks here will be over 30, there are a lot of younger regulars who view all the seventies memorabilia as strictly retro. A large lighted disco floor in the back will give you Saturday night fever.

Kit Kat Club/Go Lounge/Harold & Maude's. 25 Wall St. Plaza (off Orange Ave.), Orlando. ☎ **407/422-6990.** No cover for the Kit Kat or Harold & Maude's. Cover for Go Lounge is usually under $5. AE, DISC, MC, V.

Possessing lush red-velvet couches, pool tables, and the atmosphere of a swinging joint of a different era—complete with a cigarette girl—the Kit Cat Club is a magnet for Generation-X types who dig the Tony Bennett on the jukebox. The club is attached to the coffeehouse Harold & Maude's, which features delicious javas—mostly of the spiked Irish variety—and a variety of sandwiches, and the Go Lounge, a small alternative dance club.

Cairo. 22 S. Magnolia Ave. (1 block off Orange Ave.), Orlando. ☎ **407/422-3595.** Cover charge $5. AE, MC, V. Street parking available.

One of the newer arrivals to downtown, this large, popular dance club has bars on three levels. You'll find lots of seventies retro-clothes, and kids trying to look older than their age. Reggae is played on an open-air rooftop on the weekends. There are also special weekly events such as ladies' or Latin night.

Sapphire Supper Club. 54 N. Orange Ave., Orlando. ☎ **407/246-1419.** sapphiresupper club.com. Cover charge varies. AE, DC, DISC, MC, V.

Local and national acts perform at this laid-back club with vintage brick walls. Jazz legend and transplanted Orlando resident Sam Rivers is a regular. This place is as cool and jazzy as the music it often features, and offers specials like "Martini and Cigar" nights. It's popular with young professionals and music lovers of all ages, and called by one local newspaper, "The Best Place to See Beautiful People."

Scruffy Murphy's. 9 W. Washington St. (off Orange Ave.). ☎ **407/648-8233.** No cover.

Here you'll find Irish beers, special events like the "Celtic Throw Down," and bartenders with authentic Irish brogues saying there is "no, never" a cover charge. A good place to hang out and enjoy some unusual—for Florida at least—entertainment. But it's more watering hole than wild dance palace.

Zuma Beach. 46 N. Orange Ave. ☎ **407/648-8363.** zumabeach.com. Open to those 18 and over. Under 21, generally a $5 cover. Over 21, $7 cover charge. AE, DISC, MC, V. Free street parking; valet parking, $6.

The bouncers are well muscled, and servers wear G-strings. One local newspaper dubbed Zuma Beach the "Best Pickup Place"; that is, if you are hot, hot, hot like the pumping dance music. Located in the former Becham Theater, this is still the site of occasional special live performances.

8 Gay & Lesbian Nightspots

Same-sex dancing is not expressly forbidden anywhere in Orlando—even in WDW—but we are still in Dixieland. Travelers interested in sampling some of the gay and lesbian hot spots can check out the following places.

The Club at Firestone. 578 N. Orange Ave. (at Concord St., in a converted garage still bearing the Firestone sign). ☎ **407/426-0005** for information and a weekly schedule. clubatfirestone.com. Cover varies from $6 to $10. AE, MC, V. Limited lot parking available for $5.

Go-go boys dance on lifts converted into raised platforms, and a diverse group boogies on the large concrete dance floor. This is a serious dance club with dark lighting and cavernous rooms and a high-energy sound. World-renowned DJs are sometimes featured.

The upper floors have been recently transformed, via a $500,000 renovation, into a separate, more low-key martini bar—The Glass Chamber. Completely enclosed in glass, you can get a good look at the dance floor below while sipping your drink shaken, not stirred.

Parliament House. 410 N. Orange Blossom Trail (just west of downtown Orlando). ☎ **407/425-7571.** Cover $5 Fri–Sat; $2 Sun. Drag shows, Fri–Sun 10 and 12pm.

Attached, conveniently, to a hotel, this is one of Orlando's wilder, and most popular, gay spots. Not a fancy place, the Parliament House shows the wear and tear of years of hard partying. This is a place to drink, dance, and watch as the infamous "Miss P" holds bawdy court in the packed drag shows. (There is also a weekly amateur night on Tuesdays.) The dance floor is relatively good sized, but it gets small quickly as the crowd swells. There is also a small piano lounge. The show is a big draw and seats go fast.

Sadie's Tavern. 415 S. Orlando Ave. (in Winter Park). ☎ **407/628-4562.** Cover varies, but most entry is free on most nights. AE, MC, V. Free parking.

This is your local, neighborhood lesbian bar. There is a laid-back crowd in this small club. Weekend entertainment is usually a local artist playing an acoustic guitar. Voted Best Lesbian Bar in Orlando by the local newspaper.

Southern Nights. 375 S. Bumby Ave. (between Anderson St. and Colonial Dr.). ☎ **407/ 898-0424.** No cover.

Voted "Best Gay Bar" by the readers of a local alternative weekly paper, theme nights pack in women on Saturdays and men on Sundays. On Friday night there are three female-impersonator shows.

9 More Entertainment

SPORTS BARS

All-Star Cafe. At Walt Disney World's Wide World of Sports Complex. ☎ **407/WDW-DINE** (939-3463). No cover.

Well, not a sports bar per se, this ninth entry in the theme restaurant chain opened at Disney in late 1998. Just a line-drive away from the entrance to the main stadium, the interior is packed with sports memorabilia and television monitors. One of the major investors, Tiger Woods, actually lives in the area. Who knows, you might catch a glimpse of him away from the links.

Champions. In Marriott's Orlando World Center, 8701 World Center Dr. ☎ **407/ 239-4200.** No cover. Free self-parking; valet parking, $7.

Champions is a sports-bar chain—one so appealing, it's easy to see why the concept has succeeded. Its interior is chock-a-block with $25,000 worth of signed sports photos, posters, and artifacts such as Lou Gehrig's baseball bat, a golf bag autographed by former Dallas Cowboys coach Jimmy Johnson, and (of local interest) a wet suit belonging to Cypress Gardens' famed barefoot water-skiing star, Banana George. Some nights a DJ plays music (mostly Motown and oldies) for dancing. Otherwise, entertainment includes three pool tables, video games, Foosball, darts, coin-op football and basketball, and blackjack tables. In addition, sporting events are aired on large-screen TVs and on smaller monitors around the room (a calendar at the entrance lists all game times). Champions offers a fairly extensive bar-food menu. Open nightly until 2am.

Note to single women: Men outnumber women about five to one, so this is a good place to meet guys—if you can distract them from the sports action on the screen.

ESPN Sports. In Walt Disney World at Disney's Boardwalk. ☎ **407/WDW-DINE** (939-3463). No cover.

Seventy-one monitors. Need I say more? If you are jonesing for a sports fix, this is the place. There is a full-service bar, but there is also a restaurant and a small arcade, so you have an excuse to drag your family along.

AN ALCOHOL-FREE ALTERNATIVE

Club Soda. 6341 N. Orange Blossom Trail (about 35 miles from the heart of tourist central, near the intersection of Clarcona–Ocoee Rd. and Orange Blossom Trail), Orlando. ☎ **407/ 523-1556.**

Those looking to party away from the (at times) alcohol-drenched tourist areas can have an alcohol-free night at Club Soda. Sunday and Tuesday are karaoke nights. There's live music with a house band on Wednesdays and a DJ and dancing on the weekends. Various local 12-step groups sometimes sponsor weekend dances. This place is very laid-back, very low-key. Crowds are small.

MOVIE THEATERS

Downtown Disney AMC Theater. In Walt Disney World adjacent to the Pleasure Island nightclub complex. ☎ **407/827-1300.** Matinees $4.75 adults, seniors, and children 2–13, under 2 free; twilight shows (4:30–6pm) $3.75 for all seats; evening shows $6.75 adults, $4.75 students, $4.75 Disney resort guests, $3.75 seniors (over 55) and children 2–13, under 2 free. AE, MC V. Free parking.

This 24-screen AMC theater complex—equipped with state-of-the-art Dolby-digital sound systems and 70mm projection capability—extends the variety of nighttime entertainment available to Disney World guests, and will soon extend it further. It's adding 14 new screens to become Florida's largest multiplex! A bridge connects the theater complex with Pleasure Island clubs. New Disney films premiere here, and first-run films are shown; check the *Orlando Sentinel* for show times.

Beach Vacations in Central Florida

by Bill Goodwin

Bill Goodwin began his career as an award-winning newspaper reporter before becoming legal counsel and speech writer for two U.S. senators. Now based in Virginia, he is also the author of *Frommer's Florida, Frommer's USA, Frommer's South Pacific,* and *Frommer's Virginia.*

1 Daytona Beach

54 miles NE of Orlando, 251 miles N of Miami, 78 miles S of Jacksonville.

Daytona Beach is a town with many personalities. It is at once the "World's Most Famous Beach," the "World Center of Racing," and a mecca for spring break. It has been a destination for racing enthusiasts since the days when "horseless carriages" raced on the hard-packed sandy beach. One thing is for sure: Daytonans still love their cars. Recent debate over the environmental impact of unrestricted driving on the beach caused an uproar from citizens who couldn't imagine it any other way. As it turned out, they can still drive on the sand, but not in areas where sea turtles are nesting.

Today, hundreds of thousands of race enthusiasts come to the home of the National Association for Stock Car Auto Racing (NASCAR) for the Daytona 500, the Pepsi 400, and other races throughout the year. The Speedway is home to Daytona USA, a state-of-the-art motor-sports entertainment attraction worth a visit even by nonracing fans.

Daytona Beach Shores even provides a drive-in church where a dedicated following flocks to hear Sunday morning sermons from speakers hooked to their car windows.

But you don't have to be a car aficionado to enjoy Daytona. It has 23 miles of sandy beach, surprisingly good museums, and an active nightlife. Be sure to check the "Orlando Calendar of Events" in chapter 2 to know when the town belongs to college students during spring break, hundreds of thousands of leather-clad motorcycle buffs during Bike Week, or racing enthusiasts for big competitions. Don't bother trying to find a hotel room, drive the highways, or enjoy a peaceful vacation at those times. You won't be able to.

ESSENTIALS

GETTING THERE   If you're driving from north or south, take I-95 and head east on International Speedway Boulevard (U.S. 92). From Tampa or Orlando, take I-4 east and follow the Daytona Beach signs to I-95 north to U.S. 92. From northwestern Florida, take I-10 east to I-95 south to U.S. 92.

VISITOR INFORMATION   The **Daytona Beach Area Convention & Visitors Bureau,** 126 E. Orange Ave. (P.O. Box 910), Daytona Beach, FL 32115 (☎ **800/ 854-1234** or 904/255-0415; fax 904/255-5478; www.daytonabeach.com), can help you with information on attractions, accommodations, dining, and events. The office is on the mainland just west of the Memorial Bridge. The information area of the lobby is open daily from 9am to 7pm; office hours are Monday to Friday from 9am to 5pm. The bureau also maintains a branch at Daytona USA, 1801 W. International Speedway Blvd.

GETTING AROUND   Although it's primarily a driver's town, VOTRAN, Volusia County's public transit system (☎ **904/761-7700**), runs a **trolley** along Atlantic Avenue on the beach, Monday to Saturday from noon to midnight during summer. Fares are 75¢ for adults, 35¢ for seniors and children 6 to 17, free for kids under 6 riding with an adult. VOTRAN also runs **buses** throughout downtown and the beaches.

For a taxi call **Yellow Cab** (☎ **904/255-5555**) or **Komfort Cab** (☎ **904/ 252-2222**).

Over at the beach, **Scooters Cycles,** 2020 S. Atlantic Ave. (Fla. A1A; ☎ **904/ 253-4131**), rents both.

A VISIT TO THE WORLD CENTER OF RACING

Opened in 1959 with the first Daytona 500, the 480-acre ✪ **Daytona International Speedway complex,** at 1801 W. International Speedway Blvd. (U.S. 92 at Bill France Boulevard; P.O. Box 2801), Daytona Beach, FL 32120-2801 (☎ **904/ 253-RACE** for tickets, or 904/254-2700 for information), is certainly the keynote of the city's fame. It presents about nine weekends of major racing events annually, featuring stock cars, sports cars, motorcycles, and go-carts, and is also used for automobile and motorbike testing. Its grandstands and infield can accommodate more than 120,000 fans.

Big events sell out months in advance (tickets to the Daytona 500 in February are gone as early as a year ahead of time), so get your tickets and reserve your accommodations well before leaving home.

You don't have to be a racing fan to enjoy the World Center of Racing Visitors Center, in the NASCAR office complex at the east end of the speedway. Admission to the center is free, and you can walk out to the track during nonrace days (there's a small admission to the track during qualifying races leading up to the main events). The center is also the departure site for entertaining 25-minute guided tram tours of the facility. The tram rides cost $6, free for children 6 and under. The center and track are open daily from 9am to 5pm (until 6pm during summer). The trams depart every 30 minutes between 9:30am and 4pm (until 6pm in summer), except during races and special events.

The visitors center houses a large souvenir shop, a snack bar, and the phenomenally popular ✪ **Daytona USA** (☎ **904/947-6800**), a 50,000-square-foot, state-of-the-art interactive motor-sports entertainment attraction. Here you can learn about the history, color, and excitement of stock car, go-cart, and motorcycle racing in Daytona. You can participate in a pit stop on a NASCAR Winston Cup stock car, see the actual winning Daytona 500 car still covered in track dust, talk via video with favorite competitors, and play radio or television announcer by calling the finish of a race. An action-packed IMAX film will put you in the winner's seat of a Daytona 500 race. Allow at least 3½ hours and bring your video camera: There are lots of colorful photo-ops here. Daytona USA is open daily except Christmas from 9am to 7pm (later during race events). Admission is $12 for adults, $10 seniors,

Daytona Beach

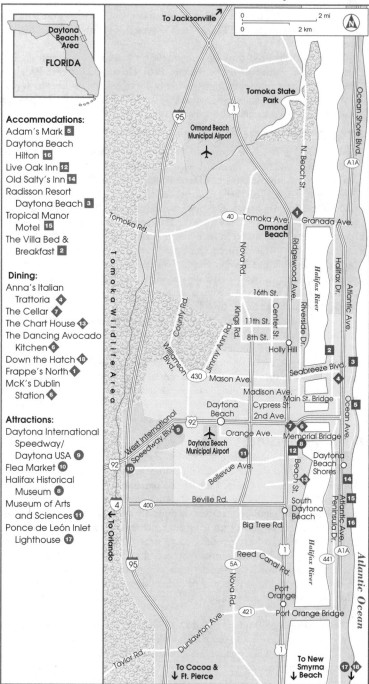

Accommodations:
Adam's Mark **5**
Daytona Beach Hilton **16**
Live Oak Inn **12**
Old Salty's Inn **14**
Radisson Resort Daytona Beach **3**
Tropical Manor Motel **15**
The Villa Bed & Breakfast **2**

Dining:
Anna's Italian Trattoria **4**
The Cellar **7**
The Chart House **13**
The Dancing Avocado Kitchen **6**
Down the Hatch **18**
Frappe's North **1**
McK's Dublin Station **5**

Attractions:
Daytona International Speedway/Daytona USA **9**
Flea Market **10**
Halifax Historical Museum **8**
Museum of Arts and Sciences **11**
Ponce de León Inlet Lighthouse **17**

$6 children 6 to 12, free for children 5 and under. Combination tickets including the speedway tram tour cost $16 adults, $14 seniors, $11 for children 6 to 12, free for kids under 6.

You can actually make three laps around the track in a real stock car from May to October if you participate in the **Richard Petty Driving Experience Ride-Along Program.** Neither you nor racing legend Petty does the driving—other professionals will be at the wheel—but you'll see just how fast an average 115 m.p.h. speed really is. Rides cost $105. Contact the speedway for schedules and reservations.

HITTING THE BEACH

The hard-packed beach here runs for 24 miles along a skinny peninsula separated from the mainland by the Halifax River. The bustling hub of activity is at the end of Main Street, near the Adam's Mark Daytona Beach Resort. Here you'll find the **Main Street Pier,** at 1,006 feet the longest wooden pier on the east coast. Out here you'll find a restaurant, bar, bait shop, beach-toy concessions, a chair lift running its entire length ($3 per ride), and views from the 180-foot-tall Space Needle ($2 round trip on the elevator). Admission as far out as the restaurant and bar is free (at about a third of the way, this is far enough for a good view down the beach), but you'll have to pay $1 to walk out beyond there, more if you fish (see "Outdoor Pursuits," below). Beginning at the pier, the city's famous oceanside **Boardwalk** is lined with restaurants, bars, and T-shirt shops, as are the four blocks of Main Street nearest the beach. Adventure Landing is two blocks away (see "Amusement Parks," below).

There's another busy beach area at the end of **Seabreeze Boulevard,** which has a multitude of restaurants, bars, and shops.

Couples seeking greater privacy usually prefer the northern or southern extremities of the beach. Especially peaceful is **Ponce Inlet** at the very southern tip of the peninsula, where there is precious little commerce or traffic to disturb the silence.

You can drive and park directly on the sand along most of the beach, but watch for signs warning of sea turtles nesting. There's a $5 access fee, although in some areas like Ponce Inlet, the fee is waived in winter.

OUTDOOR PURSUITS

CRUISES   Take a leisurely cruise on the Halifax River aboard the 14-passenger, 25-foot *Fancy,* a replica of the old fantail launches used at the turn of the century. It's operated by **A tiny Cruise Line River Excursions,** 425 S. Beach St., at Halifax Harbor Marina (☎ **904/226-2343**). Captain Jim regales passengers with river lore and points out dolphins, manatees, herons, diving cormorants, pelicans, egrets, osprey, oyster beds, and other natural phenomena during the morning cruise. Cruises are $8.75 to $14 for adults, $5.50 to $7.50 for children 4 to 12, free for children 3 and under. Weather permitting, cruises depart year-round (with a brief hiatus during the holidays), Monday through Saturday at 11:30am. A 1-hour tour of riverfront homes is at 2pm and of historic downtown at 3:30pm; there are no Monday cruises in winter months. Call for reservations. Romantic sunset cruises are also available.

Water Wheels of Daytona (☎ **407/255-2400**) uses one vehicle for combined land-and-river tours: It's an amphibious "duck" that crawls into the river at the Riverfront Parking Lot, International Speedway Boulevard and Beach Street. Call for schedule and prices.

FISHING   The easiest and least expensive way to fish offshore for marlin, sailfish, king mackerel, grouper, red snapper, and more is with the **Critter Fleet,** 4950 S. Peninsula Dr., just past the lighthouse in Ponce Inlet (☎ **800/338-0850** or

904/767-7676), which operates two party boats. One goes on all-day trips ($50 adults, $30 kids under 12), while the other makes morning and afternoon voyages ($30 adults, $20 kids under 12). The fares include rod, reel, and bait.

Deep-sea charter fishing boats are available from the Critter Fleet and from **Sea Love Marina,** 4884 Front St., Ponce Inlet (☎ **904/767-3406**).

Save the cost of a boat and fish with the locals from the **Main Street Pier,** at the ocean end of Main Street near the Adam's Mark (☎ **904/253-1212**). Admission for fishers is $3.50 for adults, $1.50 for kids under 12. Bait and fishing gear are available, and no license is required.

GOLF   There are more than 25 courses within 30 minutes of the beach, and most hotels can arrange starting times for you. **Golf Daytona Beach,** 126 E. Orange Ave., Daytona Beach, FL 32114 (☎ **800/881-7065** or 904/239-7065; fax 904/239-0064; www.golf-daytona.com), publishes an annual brochure describing the major courses. It's available at the tourist information offices (see "Essentials," above).

Two of the nation's top-rated links for women golfers are at the ✪ **LPGA International, 300 Championship Dr.** (☎ **904/274-5742**): the Champions course designed by Rees Jones, and the Legends at LPGA course designed by Arthur Hills. Both boast 18 outstanding holes. LPGA International is a center for professional and amateur women golfers (workshops and teaching programs), and the pro shop carries a great selection of ladies' equipment and clothing. Greens fees with a cart are usually about $75, less in summer.

A Lloyd Clifton–designed course, the centrally located 18-hole, par-72 **Indigo Lakes Golf Course,** 2620 W. International Speedway Blvd. (☎ **904/254-3607**), has flat fairways and large bunkered Bermuda greens. Fees here are about $55 in winter, including a cart, less in summer.

The semiprivate **South Course at Pelican Bay Country Club,** 550 Sea Duck Dr. (☎ **904/788-6494**), is one of the area's favorites, with fast greens to test your putting skills. With-cart fees are $40 in winter, less in summer (no walking allowed). The North Course here is for members only.

The city's prime municipal course is the **Daytona Beach Country Club,** 600 Wilder Blvd. (☎ **904/258-3119**), which has 36 holes. Winter fees here are $18 to walk, $26.50 to share a cart. They drop $3 in summer.

HORSEBACK RIDING   **Shenandoah Stables,** 1759 Tomoka Farms Rd., off U.S. 92 (☎ **904/257-1444**), offers daily trail rides and lessons. Call for prices and schedules.

WATER SPORTS   Water-sports equipment, as well as bicycles, beach buggies, and mopeds, can be rented along the Boardwalk, at the ocean end of Main Street (see "Hitting the Beach," above), and in front of major beachfront hotels. For jet-ski rentals, contact **Daytona High Performance—MBI,** 925 Sickler Dr., at the Seabreeze Bridge (☎ **904/257-5276**).

AMUSEMENT PARKS

The first stage of Ocean Walk Village, a development which will include shops, entertainment, and resort facilities, **Adventure Landing,** 601 Earl St., west of Atlantic Avenue (☎ **904/258-0071**), offers an assortment of indoor and outdoor activities to keep you and especially the kids entertained—and thoroughly wet. You enter into a cacophony of deafening noise and music in a huge electronic games arcade. Doors at the back lead outside to the water park, with pools, slides, and waterfalls, plus go-kart rides and a 27-hole mini-golf course. It costs nothing to enter the noisy arcade (vending machines dispense tokens for the games). Admission to the water park is $19.95 for anyone over 48 inches tall, $14.95 for anyone shorter, free for kids under 4. There's an $11.95 "night splasher" pass from 4 to 8pm. The facility is open during summer daily from 10am to midnight, with the water activities closing at 8pm. The water activities are closed off-season, but the arcade, go-kart, and mini-golf are open Monday to Thursday 11am to 10pm, Friday 11am to midnight, Saturday 10am to midnight, Sunday 10am to 10pm.

MUSEUMS

Halifax Historical Museum. 252 S. Beach St. (just north of Orange Ave.). ☎ **904/ 255-6976.** Admission $3 adults, $1 children 11 and under; free for adults Thurs after noon; free for children Sat. Open Tues–Sat 10am–4pm.

Located on Beach Street, Daytona's original riverfront commercial district on the mainland side of the Halifax River (see "Shopping," below), this local history museum is worth seeing just for the 1912 neoclassical architectural details of its home, a former bank. A mural of Old Florida wildlife graces one wall, the stained-glass ceiling reflects the sunlight, and across the room, an old gold metal teller's window still stands. Its eclectic collection includes Native American artifacts, more than 10,000 historic photographs, possessions of past residents (such as a ball gown worn at Lincoln's inauguration), and, of course, model cars.

Klassix Auto Attraction. 2909 W. International Speedway Blvd., at Tomoka Farms Rd., just west of I-95. ☎ **904/252-3800.** Admission $8.50 adults, $4.25 children 7–12, free for children under 7. Open daily 9am–6pm.

True aficionados of the car will enjoy a visit to this attraction, which showcases Corvettes—a model from every year since 1953—and historic vehicles from every motor sport. The rest of us will head to the original "Batmobile" from the 1960s *Batman* TV series, the car from *The Flintstones* series, the "Dragula" owned by the Munsters, and the "Greased Lightening" from the movie *Grease*. A 1950s-style soda shop and gift shop are on the premises.

✪ **Museum of Arts and Sciences.** 1040 Museum Blvd. (off Nova Rd./Fla. 5A between International Speedway Blvd. and Bellevue Ave.). ☎ **904/255-0285.** Museum $5 adults, $1 children and students with ID, free for children 5 and under; planetarium shows $3. Tues–Fri 9am–4pm, Sat–Sun noon–5pm. Take International Speedway Blvd. west, make a left on Nova Rd. (Fla. 5A), and look for a sign on your right.

An exceptional institution for a town Daytona's size, this museum is best known for its Cuban Museum, with paintings acquired in 1956, when Cuban dictator Fulgencio Batista donated his private collection to the city. Among them is a portrait of Eva ("Evita") Perón, said to be the only existing painting completed while she was alive (it hangs in the lobby, not in the Cuban Museum). The Dow Gallery displays Smithsonian-quality examples of American decorative arts, and the Bouchelle Study Center for the Decorative Arts contains both American and European masterpieces. Other rooms worth visiting include the Schulte Gallery of Chinese Art; Africa: Life and Ritual, with the largest collection of Ashante gold ornaments in the United States; and the Prehistory of Florida gallery, with the skeleton of a 13-foot-tall, 130,000-year-old giant ground sloth. Except for the skeleton, children are apt to be bored here.

Ponce de León Inlet Lighthouse & Museum. 4931 S. Peninsula Dr., Ponce Inlet. ☎ **904/ 761-1821.** Admission $4 adults, $1 children 11 and under. May–Aug daily 10am–8pm; Sept–Apr daily 10am–4pm. Follow Atlantic Ave. south, make a right on Beach St., and follow the signs.

If you are in the area, this 175-foot lighthouse—the second tallest in the United States—is worth a quick stop. Built in the 1880s, and restored in the 1970s, this brick-and-granite sentinel's beacon is visible for 16 nautical miles. The head lighthouse keeper's cottage now houses a museum of exhibits of maritime artifacts. The first-assistant keeper's house is furnished to reflect turn-of-the-century occupancy. A concise 12-minute video details the structure's history. Outside, you can walk around the tugboat *F.D. Russell,* now sitting high-and-dry in the sand. The museum shop here carries fascinating lighthouse-theme gifts.

SHOPPING

Daytona Beach's main riverside drag, Beach Street, is one of the few areas in town where people actually stroll. The street is wide and inviting, with palms down its median and decorative wrought-iron archways and fancy brickwork overlooking the Halifax River. Today, between Bay Street and Orange Avenue, Beach Street offers antique shops, art galleries, clothiers, a magic shop, an excellent historical museum (see "Museums," above), and several good cafes.

"Hog" riders will find several shops to their liking along Beach Street north of International Speedway Boulevard, including the **Harley Davidson Store,** 290 Beach St., at Dr. Mary McLeod Bethune Boulevard (☎ **904/253-2453**), a 20,000 square-foot retail outlet and diner serving breakfast and lunch. It's one of the nation's largest dealerships. In addition to hundreds of gleaming new and used Hogs, you'll find as much fringy leather as you've ever seen in one place.

The **Daytona Flea Market,** on Tomoka Farms Road at the junction of I-95 and U.S. 92, a mile west of the Speedway (☎ **904/252-1999**), is huge, with 1,000 covered outdoor booths plus 100 antique vendors in an air-conditioned building. It's open year-round Friday through Sunday from 8am to 5pm. Admission and parking are free.

WHERE TO STAY

Room rates here are highest from the day after Christmas all the way to Labor Day, and they skyrocket during major events at the Speedway, during bikers' gatherings, and whenever college students are on break. Daytona Beach hotels fill to the bursting point during these periods, and even if you can find a room, there's often a minimum-stay requirement.

In addition to the listings below, there are dozens of hotels and motels along Atlantic Avenue, many of them family owned and operated. The Daytona Beach Area Convention & Visitors Bureau (see "Essentials," above), distributes a list of Superior Small Lodgings. None of these properties has more than 75 rooms, and all have been inspected for cleanliness, quality, comfort, privacy, and safety.

Among the other chain motels here, one of the better options is the **Days Inn,** 1909 S. Atlantic Ave., at Flamingo Ave. (☎ **800/224-5056** or 904/255-4492), a nine-story beachfront hotel with a swimming pool/kiddie pool and a sundeck overlooking the beach. There are three oceanfront **Howard Johnsons** to choose from (☎ **800/446-4656**).

Note: In addition to the 6% state sales tax, Daytona levies a 4% tax on hotel bills.

AT THE BEACHES

Adam's Mark Daytona Beach Resort. 100 N. Atlantic Ave. (between Earl St. and Auditorium Blvd.), Daytona Beach, FL 32118. ☎ **800/872-9269** or 904/254-8200. Fax 904/253-0275. 413 units. A/C MINIBAR TV TEL. $99–$189 double; $159–$249 suite. AE, DC, DISC, MC, V. Valet parking $8.50; free self-parking in lot across the street.

Already Daytona's largest beachfront hotel, the Adams Mark at press time was planning to add another 350 units, bringing it to almost 800 rooms. With extensive on-site meeting facilities and the city's convention center virtually across the street, that means lots of big groups staying here. One of Daytona's most luxurious properties, it's designed so that every room has an ocean view. Although the lobby and common areas are more elegantly detailed, the existing guest rooms are not as spacious or well laid out as the less-expensive and quieter Hilton farther south (see below). It's centrally located right at the band shell, on the city's boardwalk, and a block north of the Main Street pier (see "Hitting the Beach," above). Plenty of beach activities are out front: parasailing, bicycle rentals, motorized four-wheelers, surfboards, boogie boards, cabanas, and umbrellas.

Clock Towers Restaurant, with picture windows overlooking the beach and umbrella tables outside, serves all meals, and an adjacent lounge provides live music most evenings. Splash Bar and Grill has light fare, libation, and indoor-outdoor seating. There's also a small food court at the beach level.

Amenities: Concierge, room service, dry cleaning and laundry, self-service Laundromat, free newspapers in executive-level rooms, baby-sitting, secretarial services, express checkout, massage, indoor/outdoor heated swimming pool and kiddie pool, health club, two whirlpools, steam and sauna, bicycle rental, children's center, games arcade, business center, conference rooms, sundeck, water-sports equipment, sand volleyball court, playground, and gift shops.

Daytona Beach Hilton Oceanfront Resort. 2637 S. Atlantic Ave. (between Florida Shores Blvd. and Richard's Lane), Daytona Beach, FL 32118. ☎ **800/525-7350** or 904/767-7350. Fax 904/760-3651. 214 units. A/C TV TEL. $89–$198 double; from $250 suite. AE, DC, DISC, MC, V.

Far from the maddening crowds of Main Street, the Hilton is among the best choices here. It welcomes you in an elegant terra-cotta–tiled lobby with comfortable seating areas, a fountain, and potted palms. The large guest rooms are grouped in pairs and can be joined to form a suite; one of each pair has a balcony, the other does not. All have ocean and/or river views and safes, coffeemakers, irons, full-size ironing boards, hair dryers, and small refrigerators. The hotel also has a small fitness room, unisex hair salon, and gift shop. Daily newspapers are complimentary. Kids appreciate the video-game room with pool table and the kiddie pool on the beautiful oceanfront sundeck where you can often see seagulls drinking from the large heated pool. A surprisingly good lobby restaurant, one of Daytona's most beautiful, serves all meals; patio dining is an option. A comfy bar/lounge with game tables adjoins; it's the setting for nightly entertainment.

Old Salty's Inn. 1921 S. Atlantic Ave. (at Flamingo Ave.), Daytona Beach Shores, FL 32118. ☎ **800/417-1466** or 904/252-8090. Fax 904/441-5977. www.visitdaytona.com/oldsaltys. 19 units. A/C TV TEL. $45–$101. AE, DISC, MC, V.

The most unusual beachside property here, Old Salty's began life in 1954 as a simple Mom-and-Pop motel (there are scores of them still standing along this beach). Today it's a lush tropical enclave carrying out a *Gilligan's Island* theme, with old motors, rotting boats, life-savers, and a Jeep lying about, and the TV series' main characters depicted in big murals painted on the buildings. The two-story wings flank a courtyard festooned with palms and banana trees (you can pick one for breakfast). Facing this vista, the bright rooms have microwaves, refrigerators, and front-and-back windows to let in good ventilation. Efficiencies also have reclining chairs, dining tables, kitchens with coffeemakers, and ceiling fans over their beds. The choice units have picture windows overlooking the beach. There are gas grills and white rocking chairs under a gazebo out by a heated beachside swimming pool.

Radisson Resort Daytona Beach. 640 N. Atlantic Ave. (between Seabreeze and Glenview blvds.), Daytona Beach, FL 32118. ☎ **800/333-3333** or 904/239-9800. Fax 904/239-0735. 206 units. A/C TV TEL. $59–$169 double. AE, DC, DISC, MC, V. Free self-parking; valet parking $8 (weekends only).

An older hotel on this site, ½ mile north of the Main Street Pier and around the corner from restaurants and bars on Seabreeze Boulevard, was gutted in 1998 and transformed into this 11-story, all-modern Radisson. The spacious rooms here are among the best on the beach, with bright furniture including easy chairs or sofas, writing desks or tables, two phones (one with data port), ample lighting, coffeemakers, irons and boards, and angled balconies facing the beach. About a third have small additional rooms with wet bars with microwaves. Other than groups prowling around between meetings, the only drawback here is that your neighbor's air conditioner exhausts onto your balcony, which can create a bit of noise and heat when you're sitting out there. A sundeck surrounds an outdoor swimming pool with a kiddie pond. Off the lobby, Atlantic Jacks' provides all meals and limited room service; the adjacent bar here looks out to the beach through huge windows. Other amenities include laundry service, coin laundry, gift and snack shop, and exercise and games rooms.

Tropical Manor Motel. 2237 S. Atlantic Ave. (at Bonner Ave.), Daytona Beach, FL. ☎ **800/253-4920** or 904/252-4920. 71 units. A/C TV TEL. Winter $33–$43 double; $34–$100 efficiency/suite; $95–$135 3-bedroom suite. High-season $52–$63 double; $54–$127 efficiency/suite; $165–$237 3-bedroom suite. AE, DC, DISC, MC, V.

This Caribbean-tinted beachfront motel wins points for its unique and colorful murals, pleasant staff/owners, and meticulous upkeep. Located square in the middle of Daytona's nicest beach, these funky accommodations also offer sundecks, umbrella-covered tables, lounge areas, a large heated pool, water slide, shuffleboard court, cookout area, heated kiddie pool, and two gazebos—all surrounded by lush tropical foliage. The rooms are not large or particularly fancy, but many come with cable TV, kitchens, and ocean views. Especially good for families are the two- and three-bedroom suites.

The Villa Bed & Breakfast. 801 N. Peninsula Dr. (at Riverview Blvd.), Daytona Beach, FL 32118. ☎ **904/248-2020.** Fax same as phone. 4 units (all with bathroom). A/C TV. $85–$190 double. Rates include continental breakfast. AE, MC, V.

You'll think you're in Iberia upon entering this Spanish mansion's great room with its fireplace, baby grand piano, terra-cotta floors, and walls hung with Mediterranean paintings. Also downstairs are a sunroom equipped with a TV and VCR, a formal dining room, and a breakfast nook where guests gather at their leisure to start the day. The lush backyard surrounds a swimming pool and covered, four-person Jacuzzi. Upstairs, the nautically-themed Christopher Columbus room has a vaulted ceiling and a small balcony overlooking the pool. The largest quarters here is the King Carlos suite, the original master bedroom with a four-poster bed, entertainment system, refrigerator, a rooftop deck, a dressing area, and bathroom equipped with a four-head shower. The Queen Isabella room has a portrait of the queen over a queen-size bed, and the Marco Polo room has Chinese black lacquer furniture and Oriental rugs evoking the great explorer's adventures. Owner Jim Camp's friendly black lab Andy keeps an eye on things, but he accepts neither your pets nor your children. The beach is 4 blocks away; the river, 1 block.

ON THE MAINLAND

Live Oak Inn. 444-448 S. Beach St. (at Loomis Ave.), Daytona Beach, FL 32114. ☎ **888/ 881-4667** or 904/252-4667. Fax 904/239-0068. 12 units (all with bathroom). A/C TV TEL. Spring and summer $100–$200 double. Off-season $75–$150 double. Rates include full breakfast. AE, MC, V. Free parking. No children 9 and under accepted.

Facing the river and occupying two adjoining Victorian-era houses with a front lawn enclosed by a white picket fence, this B&B in the city's historic district is surrounded by centuries-old live oaks. An inviting front porch with white wicker rocking chairs faces the street and a marina beyond. The guest rooms—seven with private sun porches or balconies—are delightfully decorated, with area rugs strewn on polished oak floors and wood-bladed fans whirring slowly overhead. Yours might be furnished with an Eastlake bed, or perhaps you'll get a Victorian sleigh bed with a patchwork quilt and a private plant-filled sun porch furnished with Adirondack chairs. The rooms look out on the Halifax Harbor Marina or a garden, and all are equipped with remote-control cable TVs, VCRs, and Victorian soaking tubs or Jacuzzis. Breakfast is served on an enclosed porch with lace-curtained windows. An independently operated restaurant in one of the houses is open Tuesday to Saturday for good, moderately priced lunches and dinners. No smoking is permitted in the house.

WHERE TO DINE

Don't come to Daytona Beach specifically for fine dining. The town has some interesting venues, but none is likely to leave an indelible memory. A profusion of fast-food joints line the major thoroughfares, especially along Atlantic Avenue on the beach and along International Speedway Boulevard near the racetrack. Restaurants come and go in the Beach Street district on the mainland, and along Main Street and Seabreeze Boulevard on the beach. A casual restaurant serves burgers and chicken wings and lots of suds out on the Main Street Pier.

The local **Shells** seafood restaurant is on the beach at 200 S. Atlantic Ave. (☎ **904/258-0007**), a block north of International Raceway Boulevard. See "Where to Dine" in section 3 below for details about this inexpensive chain.

AT THE BEACHES

✪ **Anna's Italian Trattoria.** 304 Seabreeze Blvd. (at Peninsula Dr.). ☎ **904/239-9624.** Reservations recommended. Main courses $9–$17. AE, DISC, MC, V. Daily 5–10pm. ITALIAN.

Originally from Sicily, the Triani family lends a warm, friendly air to this simple yet comfortable trattoria. Many of the pastas are homemade, but a star here is risotto alla Anna, an Italian version of Spanish paella. Portions are hearty; main courses come with soup or salad and a side dish of angel-hair pasta or a vegetable, and a bit of between-course sorbet will cleanse the palate. There's a good selection of Italian wines to complement your meal. Everything is cooked to order, so allow plenty of time. Free parking is available in a lot on Seabreeze Boulevard across Peninsula Drive.

Down the Hatch. 4894 Front St., Ponce Inlet. ☎ **904/761-4831.** Reservations not accepted; call ahead for priority seating. Breakfast $2–$5; main courses $8–$15; early-bird menu (served 11am–5pm) $5–$7. Kids' menu. AE, MC, V. Daily 7am–10pm. Take Atlantic Ave. south, make a right on Beach St., and follow the signs. SEAFOOD.

Occupying a half-century-old fish camp on the Halifax River, Down the Hatch serves up fresh fish and seafood (note its shrimp boat docked outside). You can start your day here with a bagel or a country-style breakfast while taking in the scenic views of boats and shorebirds through the big picture windows—you might even see dolphins frolicking. At night, arrive early to catch the sunset over the river, and also to beat the crowd at this very popular place. In summer, light fare is served outside on an awninged wooden deck. Portions are large.

ON THE MAINLAND

The Cellar. 220 Magnolia Ave. (between Palmetto and Ridgewood aves.). ☎ **904/ 258-0011.** Reservations accepted only for large parties. Soups, salads, sandwiches $6–$7. AE, DC, DISC, MC, V. Mon–Fri 11am–3pm. AMERICAN.

Another excellent place for lunch, this tea room occupies the basement of a Victorian home built in 1907 for Pres. Warren G. Harding and now listed in the National Register of Historic Places. It couldn't be more charming, with low ceilings and fresh flowers on every table. In the warm months there's outdoor seating at umbrella tables on a covered garden patio. A small but varied menu includes soups, salads, sandwiches, fresh seafood, chicken, and pastas.

✪ **The Chart House.** 1100 Marina Point Dr. (off Beach St. south of business district). ☎ **904/255-9022.** Reservations recommended. Main courses $15–$36. AE, DC, DISC, MC, V. Sun–Thurs 5–9:30pm, Fri–Sat 5–10:30pm. SEAFOOD/STEAKS/PRIME RIB.

This member of the upscale chain offers some of the area's finest dining. The setting is stunning—under a soaring teepee roof and with big windows looking out to water views on three sides. The menu is led by gargantuan cuts of tender prime rib, but the daily fresh-catch dishes and perfectly grilled steaks also draw the locals for special-occasion dinners. Caviar stars on the bountiful salad bar.

The Dancing Avocado Kitchen. 110 S. Beach St. (between Magnolia St. and International Raceway Blvd.). ☎ **904/947-2022.** Reservations not accepted. Breakfast $2–$4.50; sandwiches, salads, pizzas $4–$5.50. MC, V. Mon–Sat 7:30am–3pm. DELI/VEGETARIAN.

A good place to start your day, or have lunch while touring downtown, this storefront establishment purveys a number of vegetarian omelets, burritos, salads, personal-size pizzas, and hot and cold sandwiches such as an avocado Reuben. A few chicken and turkey items are on the menu, but the only red meat selection is a hamburger. You can dine outside or inside the store with vegetable drawings on its brick walls and ceiling fans suspended from black rafters. Order at the counter and wait for your number to be called. When finished, take your waste to the recycling bins at the front door. No smoking.

✪ **Frappe's North.** 123 W. Granada Blvd. (between Ridgeview Ave. and Washington St.), Ormand Beach. ☎ **904/615-4888.** Reservations recommended. Main courses $14–$24; ($4–$8 at lunch). AE, MC, V. Mon–Thurs 11:30am–2:30pm and 5–9pm, Fri 11:30am–2:30pm and 5–10pm, Sat 5pm–10pm. CREATIVE AMERICAN/FUSION/VEGETARIAN.

It's worth the 6-mile drive north from downtown Daytona to Ormand Beach and this sophisticated, hip establishment providing this area's best and most entertaining cuisine. It's in a storefront on the mainland stretch of Granada Boulevard, the town's main drag. Several chic dining rooms—one has beams extending like spokes from a central pole—set the stage for an inventive, ever-changing "Menu of the Moment" fusing a multitude of styles. Outstandingly presented with wonton strips and a multihued rice cake, my Southeast Asian–style pompano in a piquant peanut sauce was a dish to long remember. Frappe's always has at least two vegetarian main courses, plus a vegetable-broth soup. Lunch is a steal here, with dinner-size main courses at a fraction of the nighttime price.

McK's Dublin Station. 218 S. Beach St. (between Magnolia St. and Ivy Lane). ☎ **904/ 238-3321.** Reservations not accepted. Main courses $8–$14; salads and sandwiches $4–$7. AE, MC, V. Mon–Sat 11am–3am, Sun 11am–midnight. IRISH/AMERICAN.

Especially worth knowing about because it serves food until three in the morning, this upscale Irish tavern has a highly eclectic menu. The pub fare includes vegetarian burritos and a few main courses of steaks, chicken, and "Mumzy's" meat loaf. Club sandwiches and burgers round out the large and reasonably priced selection. The food is not exceptional, but it's perfectly acceptable, especially once you've had a few Bass ales. The service is sometimes rushed, but usually pleasant.

DAYTONA BEACH AFTER DARK

THE PERFORMING ARTS Check the Friday edition of the Daytona Beach *News-Journal* for weekly listings of upcoming events, or call the **Peabody Auditorium,** 600 Auditorium Blvd., between Noble Street and Wild Olive Avenue (☎ **904/255-1314**), the city's major venue for high-brow performances.

Under the city auspices, the **Oceanfront Bandshell** (☎ **904/258-3169**), on the boardwalk next to the Adam's Mark Hotel, hosts a series of free big-band concerts at the band shell every Sunday night from early June to Labor Day. It's also the scene of raucous spring-break concerts.

You can sample Polynesian food and dancing at **Teauila's Hawaiian Luau Feast,** atop the Daytona Beach Resort and Conference Center, 2700 N. Atlantic Ave. (☎ **800/654-6216** or 904/672-3770). Seating usually is at 6:30pm Wednesday through Sunday, with the show at 8pm. The schedule can vary, so call for reservations. Cost is $19.95 adults, $9.95 children 5 to 10, free for kids under 5.

THE CLUB & BAR SCENE In addition to the following, the sophisticated **Clocktower Lounge** at the Adam's Mark (see "Where to Stay," above) is worth a visit.

Main Street and **Seabreeze Boulevard** on the beach are happening areas where dozens of bars (and a few topless shows) cater to the black-leather set.

A popular beachfront bar for more than 40 years, **Ocean Deck,** 127 S. Ocean Ave., next to the Mayan Inn (☎ **904/253-5224**), is packed with a mix of locals and tourists, young and old, who come for live music and cheap drinks. Often reggae or ska bands will play after 9:30pm. Park across Ocean Avenue at the beach and surf shop, Reggae Republic (under the same ownership).

2 Cocoa Beach, Cape Canaveral & the Kennedy Space Center

46 miles SE of Orlando, 186 miles N of Miami, 65 miles S of Daytona.

The area around Cape Canaveral was once a sleepy place where city dwellers escaped the crowds from the exploding urban centers of Miami and Jacksonville. But then came the NASA space program. Today the region accommodates its own crowds, especially hordes of tourists who come to visit the Kennedy Space Center and enjoy 72 miles of beaches, plus fishing, surfing, golfing, and tennis.

I Dream of Jeannie fans will recognize this as the home of television's most famous astronaut, Maj. Anthony Nelson, who lived with his bottle-dwelling Jeannie in Cocoa Beach. Many of the nation's first real astronauts did, too.

Thanks to NASA, this also is a prime destination for nature lovers. The space agency originally took over much more land that it has needed to launch rockets. Rather than sell off the unused portions, it turned them over to the Cape Canaveral National Seashore and the Merritt Island National Wildlife Refuge, which have preserved them in their pristine natural states.

A handful of the major Caribbean-bound cruise ships depart from the man-made Port Canaveral. The south side of the port is lined with seafood restaurants and marinas, which serve as home base for gambling ships and the area's deep-sea charter- and group fishing boats.

ESSENTIALS

GETTING THERE   Most people who visit the Space Center stay in nearby Cocoa Beach; dozens of beachfront hotels and restaurants make it a convenient home base. If you're driving from north or south, take I-95 to Fla. 520 east (the Merritt Island Causeway). You'll cross the Indian River and Banana River before hitting Fla. A1A, the north-south artery running along the Atlantic Ocean and connecting the beach towns from Sebastian Inlet to Port Canaveral.

VISITOR INFORMATION   For information about the area, contact the **Florida Space Coast Office of Tourism,** 8810 Astronaut Blvd., Suite 102, Cape Canaveral, FL 32920 (☎ **800/872-1969** or 407/868-1126; fax 407/868-1193; www.spacecoast.com). The office is on Fla. A1A at Central Boulevard and is open Monday to Friday from 8am to 5pm. The office also operates an information booth at the Kennedy Space Center Visitor Center (see below).

You can also get specific information from the **Cocoa Beach Chamber of Commerce,** 400 Fortenberry Rd., Merritt Island, FL 32952 (☎ **407/459-2200;** fax 407/459-2232). The chamber is between Plumosa Street and Merritt Square Mall. Open Monday to Friday from 9am to 5pm.

GETTING AROUND   A car is essential in this area. The **Space Coast Area Transit** (☎ **407/633-1878**) operates buses, but routes tend to be circuitous and therefore extremely time-consuming.

TOURING THE KENNEDY SPACE CENTER

Whether you're a space buff or not, you're sure to appreciate the sheer grandeur of the facilities and the achievement of technology displayed at NASA's ✪ **John F. Kennedy Space Center.** Astronauts departed Earth at this site in 1969 en route to the most famous "small step" in history—man's first voyage to the moon—and today space shuttles regularly lift off on their missions in orbit.

All visitors must stop at the privately operated **Kennedy Space Center Visitor Center,** on NASA Parkway (Fla. 405), 6 miles east of Titusville and ½ mile west of Fla. 3 (☎ **407/452-2121;** www.kscvisitor.com). Other than Fla. 405 and Fla. 3, all roads in the space center are closed to the public.

The visitor center is open daily from 9am to dusk, except Christmas and some launch days. Admission and parking are free, but you'll have to pay for bus tours and IMAX movies (see below). Arrive early and pick up a schedule of events, which change frequently, and a map to help plan your visit. You'll need at least a full day to see and do everything.

The visitor center has exhibits, rockets, IMAX movies, and several dining venues, but you will need to take the **Kennedy Space Center Tour** to see the facilities actually in use.

The tour's shuttle buses go to the massive Vehicle Assembly Building where shuttles are prepared for launch; the Complex launch pads where space shuttles blast off; the International Space Station Center where scientists and engineers prepare additions to the space station now in orbit; and the impressive Apollo/Saturn V Center, which includes artifacts, photos, interactive exhibits, and the 363-foot-tall *Saturn V,* the most powerful rocket ever launched by the United States. Buses depart the

---

Fun Fact

You could fit New York's Empire State Building into the Vehicle Assembly Building at the Kennedy Space Center 3¾ times.

---

visitor center every 10 minutes starting at 9:45am, with the last tour leaving at 3pm, later in summer. Don't start your tour after 3pm, since it will take at least 2 hours to see the highlights, up to 5 hours if you linger at the stops along the way. Buses run continuously, and you can reboard as you wish.

If you have time at the end of your day, the **Historic Cape Canaveral Tour** visits the Cape Canaveral Air Station, where America's first satellites and astronauts were launched into space. It passes the launch pads currently used for unmanned launches, the original site of Mission Control, and the Air Force Space Museum. The history tour runs only at 3:30pm daily, and is subject to frequent cancellations.

Back at the visitor center, **IMAX movies** will both inform you and keep you entertained. Not to be missed, the 3-D IMAX *Movie L-5: First City in Space* depicts future life among the stars. Two other IMAX films are also shown on the 5½-story-high screens every day: the 37-minute *Dream Is Alive*, giving an insider's view of the Space Shuttle program with in-flight footage shot by astronauts on various missions; and *Mission to Mir*, a tour of the aging Russian space station.

Tickets for the **bus tours** cost $14 for adults, $10 for children 3 to 11, free for children under 3. The **IMAX films** cost $7.50 for adults, $5.50 for children 3 to 11, free for children under 3. If you have a full day here, a **Mission Pass** is a good deal, offering a bus tour and any two IMAX movies at $26 for adults, $20 for children 3 to 11, free for children under 3. Or a **Crew Pass** includes a bus tour and one IMAX movie for $19 adults, $15 for kids 3 to 11, free for children under 3. American Express, Discover, MasterCard and Visa cards are accepted throughout the visitor center.

If you'd like to **see a launch,** call ☎ **407/867-4636** for a schedule of upcoming take-offs and ☎ **407/452-2121** for ticket information. Launch tickets cost $10 per person, and you must buy them in person at the visitors center up to 5 days before a launch. They are sold on a first-come, first-served basis.

OTHER ASTRONAUT ATTRACTIONS

Children will enjoy a playful visit to the **Astronaut Hall of Fame,** 6225 Vectorspace Blvd., Titusville (☎ **407/269-6100**), at the mainland end of NASA Causeway (Fla. 405). In addition to honoring our space voyagers, the hall has artifacts from the space program and several interactive exhibits. A flight simulator and a G-Force Trainer will subject the kids (and you, too) to four times the pull of gravity. A moon walk uses swings to let them experience a degree of weightlessness. And a Mars mission ride will take them on a simulated trip to the red planet. That full-size replica of a space shuttle you see by the highway actually holds a theater with a multimedia presentation. Admission is $13.95 for adults, $9.95 for children 6 to 12, free for kids under 6. Or you can buy a family pass for $39.95. Open daily from 9am to 5pm.

The **Astronaut Memorial Planetarium and Observatory,** 1519 Clearlake Rd., Cocoa Beach (☎ **407/634-3732**), south of Fla. 528, has its own International Hall of Space Explorers, but its big attractions are sound and light shows in the planetarium. Call for a schedule of events. Shows cost $4 for adults, $3 for seniors and students, and $2 for kids 12 and under.

Fun Fact

During launch, it takes just 8 minutes for the space shuttle to reach its orbiting speed of 17,500 miles per hour.

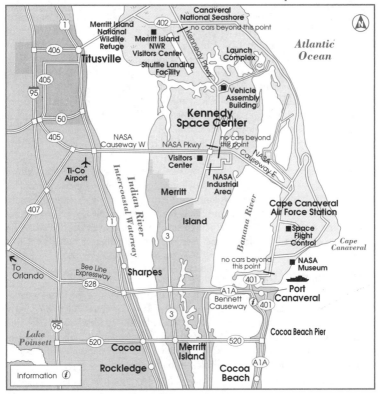

BEACHES & WILDLIFE REFUGES

To the north of the Kennedy Space Center, ✪ **Canaveral National Seashore** is a protected 13-mile stretch of barrier island beach backed by cabbage palms, sea grapes, palmettos, marshes, and Mosquito Lagoon. This is a great area for watching herons, egrets, ibis, willets, sanderlings, turnstones, terns, and other birds, and giant sea turtles nest here from May to August. You might also glimpse dolphins and manatees in Mosquito Lagoon. Canoeists can paddle along a marked trail through the marshes of Shipyard Island, and you can go backcountry camping here from November through April (permits required).

The southern access gate and ranger station are 8 miles east of Titusville on Fla. 402, just east of Fla. 3. A paved road leads from there to undeveloped ✪ **Playalinda Beach,** one of Florida's most beautiful. It's now officially illegal, but nude sunbathing has long been a tradition here (at least for those willing to walk a few miles to the more deserted areas). The main visitor center is at **Apollo Beach,** at the north end of the island, via Fla. A1A south from New Smyrna Beach. The seashore is open daily from 6am to 8pm during daylight savings time, daily 6am to 6pm during standard time. Admission fees are $5 per motor vehicle, $1 for pedestrians or bicyclists. For more information, contact the seashore at 308 Julia St., Titusville, FL 32796 (☎ **407/267-1110**).

Its neighbor to the south and west is the 140,000-acre **Merritt Island National Wildlife Refuge,** home to hundreds of species of shorebirds, waterfowl, reptiles, alligators, and mammals, many of them endangered. Stop and pick up a map and other information at the visitors center, on Fla. 402 about 4 miles east of Titusville (it's on the way to Playalinda Beach). You can see some of nature's creatures from the 6-mile-long **Black Point Wildlife Drive,** or you can hike one of three nature trails through the hammocks and marshes. The visitors center is open Monday to Friday from 8:30am to 4:30pm, Saturday and Sunday from 9am to 5pm (closed Sunday from April through October). Admission is free. For more information, contact the refuge at P.O. Box 6504, Titusville, FL 32782 (☎ **407/861-0667**).

The beach at ✪ **Cocoa Beach Pier,** on Meade Avenue east of Fla. A1A (☎ **407/ 783-7549**), is also a popular spot, especially for surfers. Appearing rustic and slapped-together, the pier was built in 1962 and shortly thereafter became the East Coast's surfing capital. It has 842 feet of fishing, shopping, and food and drinks overlooking a wide, sandy beach (see "Where to Dine," below).

Other beach areas here include Jetty Park, on Jetty Drive at the south entry to Port Canaveral. From here you can watch the big cruise ships as they enter and leave the port's narrow passage. It has lifeguards, a fishing pier with bait shop, children's playground, volleyball court, horseshoe pitch, picnic tables, snack bar, grocery store, and a campground (see "Where to Stay," below). The park is open daily from 7am to 10pm, 24 hours for fishing. Admission is $1 per car, $5 for RVs. No pets are allowed.

OUTDOOR PURSUITS

CRUISES   You can go on day trips under sail on the 45-foot cutter *San John* with **Tradewinds Sail Charters,** on the south side of Port Canaveral (☎ **888/635-1898** or 407/635-1898; fax 407/456-5770; www.yourlink.net/tradewinds). Many cruises are offered, including a 2-hour port excursion ($70 per person), full-day excursions on the ocean or Intercoastal Waterway ($200 per person), and dinner cruises ($140 per person). The boat also is available for longer charters.

ECOTOURS   Funday Discovery Tours (☎ **407/725-0796**) offers 16 day trips, including backcountry kayaking, airboat rides, horseback tours, and bird-watching expeditions. Prices range from $39 to $69 for adults, $19 to $49 for children 6 to 12. Call or pick up a copy of their list of trips from the visitors center (see "Essentials," above).

FISHING   Whether you choose freshwater, shore, or deep-sea fishing, the Space Coast has endless opportunities to cast a line. **Mosquito Lagoon** and **Eddy Creek** to the north are where you'll find trout and redfish. The **Indian River** and **Banana River** also yield trout and redfish as well as snook, ladyfish, and black drum. Bass fishers enjoy a region in the west called **Farm 13/Stick Marsh** with more than 20,000 acres of freshwater angling. For private outings, call **Dominics Guide Service** (☎ **800/BASS-909** or 407/242-892), one of the oldest licensed guides in the area.

Head to Port Canaveral for catches like snapper and grouper. **Jetty Park,** at the south entry to the port, has a fishing pier equipped with a bait shop (see "Beaches & Wildlife Refuges," above). The south bank of the port is lined with charter boats, and you can go deep-sea fishing on two party vessels based here. The *Orlando Princess* (☎ **800/481-FISH** or 407/784-FISH) runs 6-hour trips, departing daily at 10:30am. These cost $38 for adults, $33 children 11 to 17, and $28 for kids 6 to 10, including lunch, soft drinks, gear, and bait. The *Miss Cape Canaveral* (☎ **407/783-5274** or 407/648-2211 in Orlando) has 9-hour voyages departing daily at 8am, for $60 per person, including breakfast, lunch, soft drinks, gear, bait, and license.

GOLF   You can read about Northeast Florida's best courses in the free *Golfer's Guide,* available at the tourist information offices and in many hotel lobbies.

In Cocoa Beach, the municipal **Cocoa Beach Country Club,** 500 Tom Warringer Blvd. (☎ **407/868-3351**), has 27 holes of championship golf and 10 lighted tennis courts set on acres of natural woodland, rivers, and lakes. Greens fees are about $38 in winter, dropping to about $32 in summer, including cart.

On Merritt Island south of the Kennedy Space Center, **The Savannahs at Sykes Creek,** 3915 Savannahs Trial (☎ **407/455-1377**), has 18 holes over 6,636 yards bordered by hardwood forests, lakes, and savannahs inhabited by a host of wildlife. You'll have to hit over a lake to reach the seventh hole. Fees with cart are $35 in winter, less in summer.

The best nearby course is the Gary Player–designed **Baytree National Golf Club,** 8010 N. Wickham Rd., ½ mile east of I-95 in Melbourne (☎ **407/ 259-9060**). Challenging marshy holes are flanked by towering palms. This par-72 course has 7,043 yards with a unique red-shale waste area. Fees are $85 in winter, dropping to about $50 in summer, including cart.

In Melbourne Beach, the expanded executive course at **Spessard Holland Golf Club,** 2374 Oak St. (☎ **407/952-4530**), lies between the Atlantic and the bays, making it one of the area's most scenic. The par-67 course covers 5,130 yards, with six holes of no more than 191 yards presenting opportunities for holes-in-one. Winter fees here are $32 with cart, less in summer.

KAYAKING   One way to venture into Mosquito Lagoon and other backwaters in Canaveral National Seashore and Merritt Island National Wildlife Refuge (see "Beaches & Wildlife Refuges," above) is on a guided kayak trip with **Osprey Outfitters,** 132 S. Dixie Ave., Titusville (☎ **407/267-3535;** www.nbbd.com/osprey). Half-day trips cost $35 for one person, $20 for children under 13 or the second person in a kayak. Full-day trips cost $60 and $30, respectively. Kayaks, safety equipment, water, and snacks are included (plus lunch on the full-day trips). Reservations are required.

SPECTATOR SPORTS   The Boys of Spring here take the form of Miami's **Florida Marlins,** who play their spring-training baseball games from mid-February through March at the Space Coast Stadium, 5800 Stadium Pkwy., off I-95 Exit 73 in Melbourne (☎ **407/633-9200**). Tickets range from $5 to $12.

SURFING   Rip through some totally awesome waves at the **Cocoa Beach Pier** area or down south at **Sebastian Inlet.** Get outfitted at Ron Jon Surf Shop (see "Shopping," below). Or, call **Cocoa Beach Surfing School,** 301 N. Atlantic Ave., at Desperados Restaurant (☎ **407/452-0854**). They offer equipment and lessons for beginners or pros at area beaches. Be sure to bring along a towel, flip-flops, sunscreen, and a lot of nerve.

SHOPPING

Hundreds of billboards will lure you to the **Ron Jon Surf Shop,** at 4151 N. Atlantic Ave. (☎ **407/799-8888**), a block from the beach. It's a Hollywood version of art deco gone wild with tropical colors, lights, and towering sand sculptures of famous sports heroes. The stock doesn't live up to the hype: mainly souvenirs of every description and equipment and clothing to make you look like a surfer—most at relatively high prices. The shop also rents beach bikes, boogie boards, surfboards, scuba diving gear, and in-line skates by the hour, day, or week, and they teach scuba lessons. They even have a cafe (more like a fast-food burger joint).

The **Merritt Square Mall,** at 777 E. Merritt Island Causeway, has more than 100 stores, including Florida's own department store, Burdine's, and many specialty shops as well as a 12-screen movie theater.

Bargain hunters can dig through the wares of hundreds of merchants at **Frontenac Flea Market,** open Friday through Sunday from 8am until 4pm. It's located at 5605 U.S. 1 midway between Cocoa and Titusville.

WHERE TO STAY

The area has a plethora of rental condominiums and cottages. **King Rentals Inc.,** 320 N. Atlantic Ave., Cocoa Beach, FL 32930 (☎ **888/295-0934** or 407/784-5046; www.kingrentals.com), has a wide selection in its inventory.

For camping, **Jetty Park,** 400 E. Jetty Rd., Cape Canaveral, FL 32910 (☎ **407/783-1111;** fax 407/783-5005), on the south side of Port Canaveral, has 82 sites, some of them shady, all with hook-ups. They cost from $14.85 to $20.35 a night. See "Beaches & Wildlife Refuges," above, for more information about Jetty Park.

Given the proximity of Orlando, the generally warm weather all year, and business travelers visiting the space complex, there is little if any seasonal fluctuation in room rates here. They are highest weekends, holidays, and during special events, such as space shuttle launches.

You'll pay a 4% hotel tax on top of the Florida sales tax here.

Cocoa Beach Hilton. 1550 N. Atlantic Ave., Cocoa Beach, FL 32931. ☎ **800/526-2609** or 407/799-0003. Fax 407/799-0344. 298 units. A/C TV TEL. $129–$179 double. AE, DC, DISC, MC, V. Free parking.

Instead of balconies or patios from which you can enjoy the fresh air and the view down the shore, the rooms at this seven-story Hilton have smallish, sealed-shut windows. That and other architectural features make it seem more like a downtown commercial hotel transplanted to a beachside location. Nevertheless, it's one of the few upscale properties here. No doubt you will run into a crew of name-tagged conventioneers, since it's especially popular with groups. Rooms are a decent size and all have coffeemakers, irons and boards, and hair dryers. Club rooms also have a concierge and get complimentary breakfast and evening cocktails. A short boardwalk leads across the dunes from a modestly sized outdoor pool to the beach, where you can rent water and sports equipment. Other diversions include games and weight rooms. A restaurant-bar facing the ocean serves food and drinks, and limited room service is available. Laundry, dry cleaning, and complimentary weekday newspaper delivery are convenient features.

DoubleTree Oceanfront Hotel. 2080 N. Atlantic Ave., Cocoa Beach, FL 32931. ☎ **800/552-3224** or 407/783-9222. Fax 407/799-3234. 148 units. A/C TV TEL. $105–$150 double; $175–$275 suite. AE, DC, DISC, MC, V.

Formerly the Howard Johnson Plaza, this six-story hotel was extensively remodeled and upgraded in 1998 and is now the pick of the beachside properties here. All rooms have balconies with ocean views, and all sport bright writing desks and other furniture, coffeemakers, irons and boards, hair dryers, and at least one phone with data port. Oceanfront units also have easy chairs, and 10 suites have living rooms with sleeper sofas, separate bedrooms with TVs and phones, and wet bars with microwaves. Plaza Club rooms on the top floor have their own concierge and complimentary continental breakfast and evening cocktails. Facing the beach, the charming Three Wishes restaurant serves Mediterranean fare and opens to a bilevel brick patio with water cascading between two heated swimming pools. Doubling as a gift shop, the Deli & Marketplace offers snacks. Amenities here include limited room service, exercise and games rooms, laundry service, and coin laundry. Conference facilities draw groups.

Econo Lodge of Cocoa Beach. 1275 N. Atlantic Ave. (Fla. A1A, at Holiday Lane), Cocoa Beach, FL 32931. ☎ **800/553-2666** or 407/783-2252. Fax 407/783-4485. 128 units. A/C TV TEL. $45–$125 double. AE, DC, DISC, MC, V. Pets accepted.

About half of the spacious rooms at this Econo Lodge—more charming than most members of this budget-priced chain—face a tropical courtyard with an L-shaped swimming pool whose bottom displays the names of the seven original astronauts, who once owned this establishment. A variety of comfortable and clean units here include standard motel rooms and suites with living rooms and kitchenettes. A poolside tiki hut and a sports bar serve libation and other refreshments, and there's a Chinese restaurant on the premises. The complex sits directly across the avenue from the Holiday Inn Cocoa Beach (see below).

Holiday Inn Cocoa Beach. 1300 N. Atlantic Ave. (Fla. A1A, at Holiday Lane), Cocoa Beach, FL 32931. ☎ **800/226-6587** or 407/783-2271. Fax 407/783-8878. 515 units. A/C TV TEL. $69–$199 double. AE, DC, DISC, MC, V.

Set on 30 beachside acres, this sprawling family-oriented complex offers a wide variety of spacious hotel rooms, efficiencies, and apartments. A few suites even come equipped with bunk beds and Nintendo games for the kids. Most are in 1960s-style motel buildings flanking a long central courtyard with tropical foliage and eight tennis courts. Only those rooms directly facing the beach or pool have patios or balconies; the rest are entered from exterior corridors. A large heated pool with adjacent bar sits to one side, and guests can use sports equipment at the beach. Dining outlets include Willard's Restaurant, specializing in buffets, and the Ocean-side Cafe by the beach. There's a volleyball court, whirlpool, concierge desk, beauty salon, coin-op laundry, and gift shop. A convention center draws groups here.

WHERE TO DINE

On the **Cocoa Beach Pier,** at the beach end of Meade Avenue, you'll get a fine view down the coast to accompany the seafood offerings at **Atlantic Ocean Grill** (☎ 407/783-7549) and inexpensive pub fare at adjacent **Marlins Good Times Bar & Grill** (same phone). Even if you don't dine on the pier, the outdoor, tin-roofed **Boardwalk Bar** is a fine place to have a drink while watching the surfers or a sunset.

Cocoa Beach has fast-food outlets along Fla. A1A and Fla. 520, a profusion of bars serving bar snacks, Chinese restaurants, and barbecue joints. The best dining choices here, however, are on Fla. A1A about 3 miles south of the Fla. 520 causeway, to wit:

Bernard's Surf/Fischer's Seafood Bar & Grill. 2 South Atlantic Ave. (at Minuteman Causeway Rd.), Cocoa Beach. ☎ **407/783-2401.** Reservations recommended in Bernard's, not accepted in Fischer's. Bernard's main courses $13–$25; early-bird specials (4–6:30pm) $8–$11. Fischer's main courses $8–$13; sandwiches and salads $5–$9. AE, DC, DISC, MC, V. Bernard's Mon–Sat 11am–11pm, Sun 10am–2pm (brunch) and 5–10pm. Fischer's daily 11am–11pm (bar to 2am). Closed Christmas. SEAFOOD/STEAKS.

Photos on the walls testify that many astronauts—and Russian cosmonauts, too—come to these adjoining establishments to celebrate their landings. It all started as Bernard's Surf, which has been serving standard steak and seafood fare in a large and elegant setting since 1948. Bernard's offers house specials such as filet mignon served with sautéed mushrooms and béarnaise sauce, but your best bets are char-grilled fish supplied by the Fischer family's own boats. The fresh seafood also finds its way into Fischer's Seafood Bar & Grill, a friendly, Cheers-like lounge popular with the locals. Fischer's menu features fried combo platters, shrimp and crab claw meat sautéed in herb butter, and mussels with a wine sauce over pasta, to mention a few worthy selections. Fischer's also provides sandwiches, burgers, and other pub fare, and it has the same 25¢ happy-hour oysters and spicy wings as Rusty's Seafood & Oyster Bar (see below), also part of this complex.

✪ **The Mango Tree.** 118 N. Atlantic Ave. (Fla. A1A, between N. 1st and N. 2nd sts.), Cocoa Beach. ☎ **407/799-0513.** Reservations recommended. Main courses $13–$29. AE, MC, V. Tues–Sun 6–9pm. CONTINENTAL.

Gourmet seafood, pastas, and chicken are served in a plantation-home atmosphere with elegant furnishings in this stucco house, the finest dining venue here. Goldfish ponds inside and a waterfall splashing into a Japanese koi pond out in the lush tropical gardens provide pleasing backdrops. Start with finely seasoned Indian River crab cakes, then go on the chef's expert spin on fresh tuna fillets, roast Long Island duckling, tournedos with peppercorn mushroom sauce, and other excellent dishes drawing their inspiration from the continent.

Rusty's Seafood & Oyster Bar. 2 S. Atlantic Ave. (Fla. A1A, at Minuteman Causeway Rd.), Cocoa Beach. ☎ **407/783-2401.** Reservations not accepted. Sandwiches and salads $3–$8; main courses $7–$17.50. AE, DC, DISC, MC, V. Daily 11am–1am (bar to 2am). SEAFOOD/PUB FARE.

Part of the Bernard's Surf family (see above), this lively sports bar offers inexpensive chow ranging from very spicy seafood gumbo to a pot of seafood that will give two normal persons their fill of steamed oysters, clams, shrimp, crab legs, potatoes, and corn on the cob. There's indoor and outdoor seating. Daily happy hours from 3 to 6pm see tons of oysters (raw or steamed) and spicy Buffalo wings go for 25¢ each.

There's a waterfront Rusty's at 628 Glen Cheek Dr. in Port Canaveral (☎ **407/783-2033**), on the south side of the harbor. Like the original, it's a noisy sports bar, but the clientele tends to be somewhat older if not more reserved. Both have the same menu and hours.

THE SPACE COAST AFTER DARK

For a rundown of current performances and exhibits, call the **Brevard Cultural Alliance's Arts Line** (☎ 407/690-6819). For live music, walk out on the **Cocoa Beach Pier,** on Meade Avenue at the beach, where **Shuck's Seafood Bar & Grill** (☎ 407/783-7549) and **Marlins Good Times Bar & Grill** (☎ 407/783-7549) have bands on weekends, more often during the winter season, and the al fresco **Boardwalk Bar** is a great place to hang out over a cold beer.

3 The Tampa Bay Area

Tampa: 74 miles southwest of Orlando. St. Petersburg: 84 miles southwest of Orlando. Clearwater: 94 miles southwest of Orlando.

Many families visiting Orlando's theme parks eventually drive an hour west on I-4 to another major kiddie attraction, Busch Gardens Tampa Bay. But this area shouldn't be a mere side trip from Disney World, for Florida's central west coast is an exciting destination unto itself.

At the head of the bay, the city of Tampa is the commercial center of Florida's west coast—the country's eleventh busiest seaport and a center of banking, high-tech manufacturing, and cigar making (half a billion drugstore stogies a year). Downtown Tampa may roll up its sidewalks after dark, but you can come here during the day to see the sea life at the Florida Aquarium and stroll through the Henry B. Plant Museum, housed in an ornate, Moorish-style hotel built a century ago to lure tourists to Tampa. A trolley will take you on a short ride to Ybor City, the historic Cuban enclave that is now an exciting entertainment and dining venue.

And out in the suburbs, Busch Gardens may be best known for its scintillating rides, but it's also one of the world's largest zoos.

Two bridges and a causeway will whisk you westward across the bay to the Pinellas Peninsula, one of Florida's most densely packed urban areas. Over here on the bay front, lovely downtown St. Petersburg is famous for wintering seniors, a shopping and dining complex built way out on a pier, and the world's largest collection of Salvador Dalí's surrealist paintings.

Keep driving west and you'll come to a line of barrier islands where St. Pete Beach, Treasure Island, Clearwater Beach, and other gulf-side communities boast 28 miles of sunshine, surf, and white sand. Yes, they're lined with resorts and condos of every description and price, but parks on each end preserve two of the nation's finest beaches.

Drive north up the coast, and you'll go back in time at the old Greek sponge enclave of Tarpon Springs, one of Florida's most attractive small towns, and at Weeki Wachee Springs, a tourist attraction where "mermaids" have been entertaining under water for half a century.

Heading south, the Sunshine Skyway will take you soaring 175 feet above the bay to Bradenton, Sarasota, and another chain of barrier islands. One of Florida's cultural centers, affluent Sarasota is the gateway to St. Armands and Longboat keys, two playgrounds of the rich and famous, and to Lido and Siesta keys, attractive to families of more modest means. Even more reasonably priced is Anna Maria Island, off the riverfront town of Bradenton. You might say the bridge from Longboat to Anna Maria goes from one price range to another.

TAMPA

Even if you stay at the beaches 20 miles to the west, you should consider driving into Tampa to see its sights. If you have children in tow, they will *demand* that you go into the city so they can ride the rides and see the animals at Busch Gardens. While here, you can educate them at the Florida Aquarium and the city's fine museums. And if you don't have kids, historic Ybor City has the bay area's liveliest nightlife.

Tampa was a sleepy little port when Cuban immigrants founded Ybor City's cigar industry in the 1880s. A few years later Henry B. Plant put Tampa on the tourist map by building a railroad to town and the bulbous minarets over his garish Tampa Bay Hotel, now a museum named in his honor. During the Spanish American War, Teddy Roosevelt trained his Rough Riders here and walked the Ybor City streets with Cuban revolutionary José Marti. A land boom in the 1920s gave the city its charming, Victorian-style Hyde Park suburb, just across the Hillsborough River from downtown, now a gentrified redoubt of the baby boomers.

Today's downtown skyline is the product of the 1980s and early 1990s boom, when banks built skyscrapers and the city put up an expansive convention center, a performing arts center, and the Ice Palace, a 20,000-seat bay-front arena that is home to professional hockey's Tampa Bay Lightning. Alongside the new Florida Aquarium, the Garrison Seaport Center is a major home port for cruise ships bound for Mexico and the Caribbean. Baseball's New York Yankees helped things along by building their spring-training complex here, including a scaled-down replica of Yankee Stadium. And the sparkling Raymond James Stadium became the home to pro football's Tampa Bay Buccaneers in 1998.

All this adds up to a fast-paced, modern city on the go.

Tampa & St. Petersburg

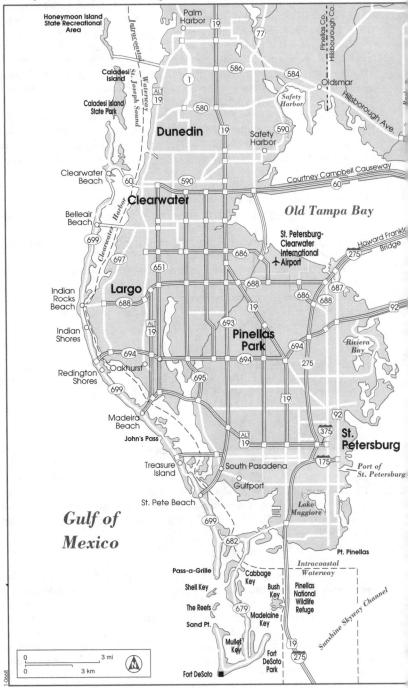

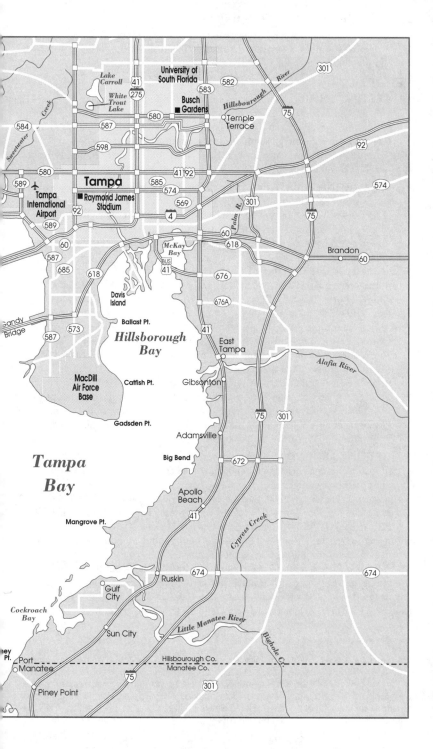

Tampa isn't a beach vacation destination, but there's plenty here to keep both adults and kids happy for a few days.

ESSENTIALS

GETTING THERE Tampa is accessible via I-275, I-75, I-4, U.S. 19, U.S. 41, U.S. 92, and U.S. 301. The Busch Gardens area lies between I-75 and I-275 north of downtown; exit at Busch Boulevard and follow the signs. Downtown is south of I-275; take Exit 26 and go south on Ashley Street.

Amtrak trains arrive downtown at the **Tampa Amtrak Station,** 601 Nebraska Ave. N. (☎ **800/USA-RAIL**).

VISITOR INFORMATION Contact the **Tampa/Hillsborough Convention and Visitors Association (THCVA),** 400 N. Tampa St., Tampa, FL 33602-4706 (☎ **800/44-TAMPA** or 813/223-2752; fax 813/229-6616; www.thcva.com) for advance information. Once you're downtown, head to the THCVA's visitors information center at the corner of Ashley and Madison streets. It's open Monday to Saturday from 9am to 5pm.

The **Ybor City Chamber of Commerce** has a visitors' center in an old cigar-roller's cottage at 1800 E. 9th Ave. (at 18th Street), Tampa, FL 33605 (☎ **877/934-3782** or 941/248-3712; fax 941/247-1764; www.ybor.org). Open Monday to Friday from 9am to 5pm.

Near Busch Gardens, the privately-owned **Tampa Bay Visitor Information Center,** 3601 E. Busch Blvd., at N. Ednam Place (☎ **813/985-3601;** fax 813/985-7642), offers free brochures about attractions in Tampa and sells discounted tickets to many attractions. You may be able to save $2 a head and avoid waiting in long ticket lines at Busch Gardens by buying here, and owner Jim Boggs worked for the park for many years and gives expert advice about how to get the most out of your visit. Open Monday to Saturday from 9am to 5:30pm, Sunday from 9am to 2pm. Operating as Swiss Chalet Tours, this same company also has organized excursions of the area (see "Organized Tours," below).

GETTING AROUND Like most other Florida destinations, it's virtually impossible to see Tampa's major sights and enjoy the best restaurants without a car.

At press time, a streetcar on rails was to begin hauling passengers between downtown and Ybor City in 2000, traveling by the Florida Aquarium; check with the visitor center (see above), or call the **Hillsborough Area Regional Transit/HARTline** (☎ 813/254-HART). If you're on a budget, HARTline also provides regularly scheduled bus service between downtown Tampa and the suburbs. Pick up a route map at the visitor information center (see above).

Taxis in Tampa don't normally cruise the streets for fares, but they do line up at public loading places, such as hotels, the performing arts center, and bus and train depots. If you need a taxi, call **Tampa Bay Cab** (☎ 813/251-5555), **Yellow Cab** (☎ 813/253-0121), or **United Cab** (☎ 813/253-2424). Fares are 95¢ at flag fall plus $1.50 for each mile.

WHAT TO SEE & DO

Adventure Island. 10001 McKinley Dr. (between Busch Blvd. and Bougainvillea Ave.). ☎ **813/987-5600.** Admission $22.95 adults, $20.95 children 3–9, plus tax. Free for children 2 and under. *Note:* Prices keep increasing, so expect to pay slightly more. Seasonal passes available. Mid-Feb to Labor Day daily 10am–5pm; Sept–Oct Fri–Sun 10am–5pm (extended hours in summer and on holidays). Closed Nov to mid-Feb. Take Exit 33 off I-275, go east on Busch Blvd. for 2 miles, turn left onto McKinley Dr. (N. 40th St.), and entry is on right.

If the summer heat gets to you before one of Tampa's famous thunderstorms brings late-afternoon relief, you can take a water-logged break at this 25-acre outdoor water theme park near Busch Gardens Tampa Bay (see below). In fact, you can frolic here even during the cooler days of spring and fall, when the water is heated. The Key West Rapids, Tampa Typhoon, Gulf Scream, and other exciting water rides will drench the teens, while other calmer rides are geared for kids. There are places to picnic and sunbathe, a games arcade, a volleyball complex, and an outdoor cafe. If you forget to bring your own, a surf shop sells bathing suits, towels, and suntan lotion.

✪ **Busch Gardens Tampa Bay.** 3000 E. Busch Blvd. (at McKinley Dr./N. 40th St.). ☎ **813/ 987-5283.** Admission $38.95 adults, $32.95 children 3 to 9, plus tax. Free for children 2 and under. *Note:* Prices keep increasing, so expect to pay slightly more. Seasonal passes available. Daily 9am–6pm (extended hours to 7 and 8pm in summer and holidays). Parking $6 cars, campers, and trailers; $5 motorbikes. Take I-275 north of downtown to Busch Blvd. (Exit 33), and go east 2 miles. From I-75, take Fowler Ave. (Exit 54) and follow the signs west.

Although its thrill rides, live entertainment, shops, restaurants, and games get most of the ink, this venerable theme park (it predates Disney World) ranks among the top zoos in the country. This is a great place for the kids to see in person all those wild beasts they've watched on the Discovery Channel. The animals—several thousand of them—live in naturalistic environments and help carry out an overall African and Egyptian theme.

The park is divided into eight areas, each with its own theme, animals, live entertainment, thrill rides, kiddie attractions, dining, and shopping. A monorail train will take you from one to another. A Skyride cable car soars over the park, offering a bird's-eye view of the park.

Allow at least a day here, and arrive early—but try not to come when it's raining, since some rides may not operate and you won't get a rain check for admission on another day (but do ask if your tickets can be stamped for admission the following day, which sometimes occurs during slow periods). Bring comfortable shoes, and remember, you can get wet on some of the rides, so wear appropriate clothing.

You can avoid waiting in long lines, and save a few dollars, by buying your tickets in advance at the **Tampa Bay Visitor Information Center** near the main entrance (see "Essentials," above). You can exchange foreign currency in the park, and interpreters are available.

As soon as you're through the turnstiles, pick up a copy of a park map and the day's activity schedule, which tells what's showing and when at the park's 14 entertainment venues. Then take a few minutes to carefully plan your time—it's a big park with lots to see and do. Busch Gardens continues to grow—a set of dueling roller coasters known as Gwazi was scheduled to crank up in 1999—so be on the lookout for new attractions.

Just past the main gate you'll come to **Morocco,** a walled city with exotic architecture, craft demonstrations, a sultan's tent with snake charmers, and an exhibit featuring alligators and turtles. The Moroccan Palace Theater features "Hollywood Live on Ice," which many families consider to be the park's best entertainment. Here you can also attend "American Jukebox," a song and dance show, in the Marrakesh Theater.

After watching the snake charmers in Morocco, walk eastward to **Egypt,** where you can see Anheuser-Busch's fable Clydesdale horses, visit King Tut's tomb, and listen to comedian Martin Short narrate "Akbar's Adventure Tours," a wacky simulator that "transports" one and all across Egypt via camel, biplane, and mine car. Adults and older kids can ride Montu, the tallest and longest inverted roller coaster in the world with seven upside-down loops, one of them barely missing a crocodile pit. Youngsters can dig for their own ancient treasures in a sand area.

Tampa Attractions

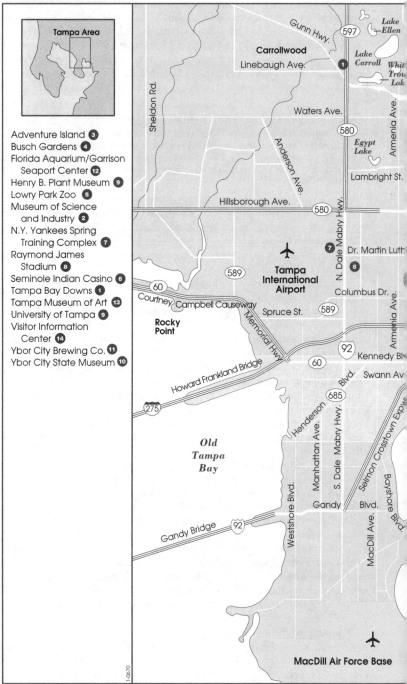

Tampa Area

Adventure Island **3**
Busch Gardens **4**
Florida Aquarium/Garrison
  Seaport Center **12**
Henry B. Plant Museum **9**
Lowry Park Zoo **5**
Museum of Science
  and Industry **2**
N.Y. Yankees Spring
  Training Complex **7**
Raymond James
  Stadium **8**
Seminole Indian Casino **6**
Tampa Bay Downs **1**
Tampa Museum of Art **13**
University of Tampa **9**
Visitor Information
  Center **14**
Ybor City Brewing Co. **11**
Ybor City State Museum **10**

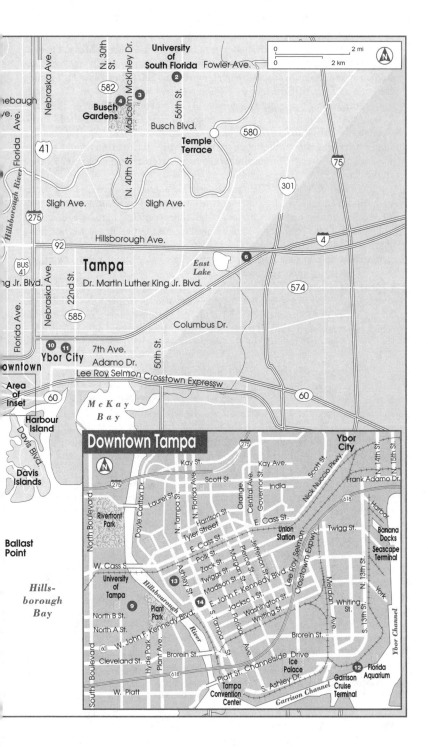

From Egypt, walk under the monorail and out onto the **Edge of Africa,** the most unique part of the park. Here glass walls separate you from lions, hippos, crocodiles, hyenas, meerkats, and vultures—among more than 500 African animals roaming freely on an 80-acre natural grassy veldt known here as the Serengeti Plain. After you've seen them close-up, the monorail will take you on "safari" out on the plain.

Next stop is **Nairobi,** where you can see gorillas and chimpanzees in the Myombe Reserve, replicating their natural tropical habitat. Nairobi also has a baby animal nursery, a petting zoo, turtle and reptile displays, an elephant exhibit, and Curiosity Caverns, a simulated environment that allows you to observe animals that are active in the dark.

From Nairobi, walk into **Timbuktu,** evoking an ancient desert trading center with African craftspeople at work. Here you'll find several rides, including the Sandstorm, the Phoenix, and the Scorpion, a 360° roller coaster. Plan to have lunch here at Das Festhaus, a 1,200-seat, air-conditioned German festival hall featuring a lively musical show "The International Celebration" (be sure to arrive at least 15 minutes before show time to get a seat). The kids will enjoy the Dolphin Theater, with performing porpoises, otters, and sea lions.

After lunch, head to **The Congo,** highlighted by rare white Bengal tigers living on Claw Island. The Congo also is home to two roller coasters: the Kumba, the largest and fastest roller coaster in the southeastern United States; and the Python, which twists and turns for 1,200 feet. You will get drenched (and refreshed on a hot day) by riding the Congo River Rapids. There are bumper cars and kiddie rides here, too.

From The Congo, walk south into **Stanleyville,** a prototype African village, with a shopping bazaar, orangutans living on an island, and the Stanleyville Theater, featuring "Stars of the Future," a show about children. Two more water rides are here: the Tanganyika Tidal Wave and Stanley Falls. Serving ribs and chicken, the Stanleyville Smokehouse has some of the best chow here. This also is a good place to board the trans-veldt railway for a sightseeing ride all the way around the park and back, since you'll avoid the crowds waiting to board elsewhere (the air-conditioned train also is a good way to cool off on a hot summer's day).

From Stanleyville, the next stop is **Land of the Dragons,** where the younger set can easily spend an entire day enjoying a variety of play elements in a fairy-tale setting, plus just-for-kids rides. The area is dominated by Dumphrey, a whimsical dragon who interacts with visitors and guides children around a three-story tree house with winding stairways, tall towers, stepping stones, illuminated water geysers, and an echo chamber.

The last stop is **Bird Gardens,** the park's original core, offering rich foliage, lagoons, and a free-flight aviary for hundreds of exotic birds, including golden and American bald eagles. Catch the Bird Show here, and be sure to see the Florida flamingos and Australian koala bears.

You can finish your visit back at the **Hospitality House,** which offers piano entertainment and free samples of Anheuser-Busch's famous beers (you must be 21 to imbibe, and there's a limit of two free mugs per seating).

✪ **Florida Aquarium.** 701 Channelside Dr. ☎ **813/273-4000.** Admission $11.95 adults, $10.95 seniors, $6.95 children 3–12, free for children under 3. Daily 9:30am–5pm. Closed Thanksgiving and Christmas. Parking $3.

Visitors here are introduced to more than 5,300 aquatic animals and plants that call Florida home. Various exhibits allow you to follow the pristine springs of the Florida Wetlands Gallery, go through a mangrove forest in the Bays and Beaches

Gallery, and stand amazed at the Coral Reefs. The most impressive display is a 43-foot-wide, 14-foot-tall panoramic window with schools of fish and lots of sharks and stingrays. You can watch a diver twice a day. There's a half-million-dollar "Explore a Shore" playground to educate the kids, a deep-water exhibit, and a tank housing moray eels. The Cafe Ray serves snacks and light meals.

Henry B. Plant Museum. 401 W. Kennedy Blvd. (between Hyde Park and Magnolia aves.). ☎ **813/254-1891.** Free admission; suggested donation $5 adults, $1 children 12 and under. Tues–Sat 10am–4pm, Sun noon–4pm. Take Fla. 60 west of downtown.

You can't miss the 13 silver minarets and distinctive Moorish architecture, modeled after the Alhambra in Spain, that make this National Historic Landmark a focal point of the Tampa skyline. Originally built in 1891 as the 511-room Tampa Bay Hotel by railroad tycoon Henry B. Plant, it's filled with art and furnishings from Europe and Asia. Other exhibits focus on the history of the original railroad resort, Florida's early tourist industry, and the hotel's role as a staging point for Teddy Roosevelt's Rough Riders during the Spanish American War.

Lowry Park Zoo. 7530 North Blvd. ☎ **813/932-0245.** Admission $8.50 adults, $7.50 seniors, $4.95 children 3–11, free for children under 3. Daily 9:30am–4:45pm. Closed Thanksgiving and Christmas. Take I-275 to Sligh Ave. (Exit 31) and follow the signs.

Watching the 2,000-pound manatees, the komodo dragons, and the rare red pandas makes this a worthwhile excursion after the kids have seen the plains of Africa at Busch Gardens. With lots of greenery, bubbling brooks, and cascading waterfalls, this 24-acre zoo displays animals in settings similar to their natural habitats. Other major exhibits include a Florida wildlife display, an Asian Domain, a Primate World, an Aquatic Center, a free-flight aviary with a birds of prey show, a children's petting zoo and hands-on Discovery Center, and an endangered species carousel ride. There are plenty of food outlets here, including an on-site McDonald's.

✪ **Museum of Science and Industry (MOSI).** 4801 E. Fowler Ave. (at N. 50th St.). ☎ **813/987-6300.** www.tampatrib.com/mosi. Admission $12 adults; $10 seniors, college students with identification, and children 13–18; $8 children 2–12; free for children under 2. IMAX tickets $6 adults; $5 seniors, college students, and children 13–18; $4 kids 2–12. Combination tickets available. Daily 9am–5pm or later. Free parking. From downtown, take I-275 north, then Fowler Ave. east 2 miles to museum on right.

A great place to take the kids on a rainy day, MOSI is the largest science center in the Southeast and has more than 450 interactive exhibits. Guests can step into the Gulf Hurricane and experience gale-force winds, defy the laws of gravity in the unique *Challenger* space experience, or cruise the mysterious world of microbes in LifeLab. "The Amazing You" allows visitors to explore the body, "Our Florida" focuses on environmental factors, and "Our Place in the Universe" introduces them to space, flight, and beyond. You can also watch stunning movies in Florida's first IMAX dome theater.

Tampa Museum of Art. 600 N. Ashley Dr. (at Twiggs St.), downtown. ☎ **813/274-8130.** Admission $5 adults, $4 seniors and students with identification, $3 children 6–18, free for children 5 and under, by donation for everyone Wed 5–9pm and Sat 10am–noon. Mon–Tues and Thurs–Sat 10am–5pm, Wed 10am–9pm, Sun 1–5pm. Take I-275 to Exit 25 (Ashley Dr.).

Located on the east bank of the Hillsborough River next to the round NationsBank building (locals facetiously call it the "Beer Can") and just south of the Tampa Bay Performing Arts Center, this fine-arts complex offers eight galleries with changing exhibits ranging from classical antiquities to contemporary Florida art. There's also a 7-acre riverfront park and sculpture garden. Museum tours are offered on Wednesday and Saturday at 1pm and on Sunday at 2pm.

YBOR CITY

Northeast of downtown, the city's historic Latin Quarter takes its present name from Don Vicente Martinez Ybor (*Ee*-bore), a Spanish cigar maker who arrived here in 1886 via Cuba and Key West. Soon his and other Tampa factories were producing more than 300,000 hand-rolled stogies a day.

It may not be the cigar capital of the world anymore, but Ybor is the happening part of Tampa, a cross between New Orleans's Bourbon Street, Washington's Georgetown, and New York's SoHo. By day, you can stroll past the art galleries, boutiques, and trendy new restaurants and cafes that line 7th Avenue East. At night, when good food and great music dominate the scene, streets will be bustling until 4am. Unique shops offer a wide assortment of goodies, from silk boxer shorts to unique tattoos. Dozens of outstanding nightclubs and dance clubs have waiting lines out the door. Live-music offerings run the gamut from jazz and blues to indie rock.

The area is becoming even more active with the planned opening of **Centro Ybor,** a dining-shopping-entertainment complex at 7th Avenue and 19th Street, in 2000.

Cigar smokers will enjoy a stroll through the **Ybor City State Museum,** 1818 9th Ave., between 18th and 19th streets (☎ **813/247-6323**), housed in the former Ferlita Bakery (1896–1973). You can take a self-guided tour around the museum to see a collection of cigar labels, cigar memorabilia, and works by local artisans. Admission is $2 per person, including a 30-minute guided tour of **La Casita,** a renovated cigar worker's cottage adjacent to the museum; it's furnished as it was at the turn of the century. The museum is open daily from 9am to noon and 1 to 5pm (La Casita, from 10am to noon and 1 to 2:30pm).

Check with the museum about **walking tours** of the historic district. **Ybor City Ghost Walks** (☎ **813/242-9255**) will take you to the spookier parts of the area at night. Call for reservations, schedules, and prices.

Another interesting stop here is the **Ybor City Brewing Company,** 2205 N. 20th St., facing Palm Avenue (☎ **813/242-9222**). Housed in a 100-year-old, three-story former cigar factory, this microbrewery produces Ybor Gold and other brews, none with preservatives. Admission of $2 per person includes a tour of the brewery and taste of the end result. Open Tuesday to Saturday from 11am to 3pm.

ORGANIZED TOURS

Swiss Chalet Tours, 3601 E. Busch Blvd. (☎ **813/985-3601**), opposite Busch Gardens in the privately run Tampa Bay Visitor Information Center (see "Essentials," above), operates guided bus tours of Tampa, Ybor City, and environs. The 4-hour tours of Tampa are given from 10am to 2pm daily, with a stop for lunch at the Columbia Restaurant in Ybor City. They cost $40 for adults and $35 for children. The 7-hour full-day tours of both Tampa and St. Petersburg cost $70 for adults and $65 for children. Reservations are required at least 24 hours in advance; passengers are picked up at major hotels and various other points in the Tampa/St. Petersburg area. Tours can also be booked to Orlando, Sarasota, Bradenton, and other regional destinations.

OUTDOOR ACTIVITIES & SPECTATOR SPORTS

Tampa Outdoor Adventures (☎ **800/44-TAMPA,** ext. 6, or 813/223-2752) is a one-stop source of information and reservations for a variety of recreational activities in the Tampa area, from ballooning to yachting.

BIKING, IN-LINE SKATING & JOGGING Bayshore Boulevard, a 7-mile promenade, is famous for its sidewalk right on the shores of Hillsborough Bay. Reputed to be the world's longest continuous sidewalk, it's a favorite for runners, joggers, walkers, and in-line skaters. The route goes from the western edge of downtown in a southward direction, passing stately old homes of Hyde Park, a few high-rise condos, retirement communities, and houses of worship, ending at Ballast Point Park. The view from the promenade across the bay to the downtown skyline is unmatched here (Bayshore Boulevard also is great for a drive).

Rent bicycles and in-line skates at **Blades & Bikes,** in a pink-and-blue shop at 201-A W. Platt St., at South Parker Street (☎ 813/251-0780), a block west of the northern end of Bayshore Boulevard. Prices for both bikes and blades range from $8 for 1 hour to $20 for all day. Hours are Monday to Friday from 10am to 7pm, Saturday from 9am to 7pm, and Sunday from 10am to 5pm.

CANOEING   You can paddle downstream along a 20-mile stretch of the Hillsborough River amid 16,000 acres of rural lands in Wilderness Park, the largest regional park in Hillsborough County. **Canoe Escape,** 9335 E. Fowler Ave. (☎ 813/986-2067), rents canoes for $14 per person. The company also has 2- to 6-hour guided trips. Open Monday to Friday from 9am to 5pm and Saturday and Sunday from 8am to 6pm.

FISHING   Pier fishing on **Hillsborough Bay** is available from **Ballast Point Park,** 5300 Interbay Blvd. (☎ 813/831-9585). Ballast Point Park is at the southern end of Bayshore Boulevard and has a terrific view back across the bay to downtown.

Light Tackle Fishing Expeditions (☎ 813/963-1930) offers sport-fishing trips for tarpon, redfish, cobia, trout, and snook. Call for schedule, prices, and required reservations.

GOLF   Tampa has three municipal golf courses where you can play for $26 to $34, a relative pittance when compared to the privately owned courses here and elsewhere in Florida. The **Babe Zaharias Municipal Golf Course,** 11412 Forest Hills Dr., north of Lowry Park (☎ 813/631-4374), is an 18-hole, par-70 course with a pro shop, putting greens, and a driving range. It's the shortest of the municipal courses, but small greens and narrow fairways present ample challenges. Water presents obstacles on 12 of the 18 holes at **Rocky Point Municipal Golf Course,** 4151 Dana Shores Dr. (☎ 813/673-4316), located between the airport and the bay. It's a par-71 course with a pro shop, practice range, and putting greens. On the Hillsborough River in north Tampa, the **Rogers Park Municipal Golf Course,** 7910 N. 30th St. (☎ 813/673-4396), is an 18-hole, par-72 championship course with a lighted driving and practice range. They all are open daily from 7am to dusk, and lessons and club rentals are available.

Another inexpensive place to play is the **University of South Florida Golf Course,** Fletcher Avenue and 46th Street (☎ 813/632-6893), just north of the USF campus. This 18-hole, par-71 course is nicknamed "The Claw" because of its challenging layout. It offers lessons and club rentals. Greens fees range from about $19 to $25, or $25 to $35 with a cart, depending on the season and time of day. It's open daily from 7am to dusk.

Other public courses include the **Hall of Fame Golf Club,** just south of the airport at 2222 N. Westshore Blvd. (☎ 813/876-4913), an 18-hole, par-72 affair with a driving range; **Persimmon Hill Golf Club,** 5109 Hamey Rd. (☎ 813/623-6962); **Silver Dollar Trap & Golf Club,** 17000 Patterson Rd., Odessa (☎ 813/920-3884); and **Westchase Golf Club,** 1307 Radcliff Dr. (☎ 813/854-2331).

You can book starting times and get information about these and the area's other courses by calling **Tee Times USA** (☎ 800/374-8633).

If you want to do some serious work on your game, the **Arnold Palmer Golf Academy World Headquarters** is at Saddlebrook Resort, 5700 Saddlebrook Way, Wesley Chapel, 12 miles north of Tampa (☎ **800/729-8383** or 813/973-1111). Half-day and hourly instruction is available, and there are 2-, 3-, and 5-day programs available for adults and juniors starting at $248 per night, double occupancy, including accommodations, breakfast, daily instruction, 18 holes of golf daily, cart and greens fees, and nightly club storage and cleaning. You have to stay at the resort or enroll in the golf program to play at Saddlebrook. See "Where to Stay," below, for more information about the resort.

SPECTATOR SPORTS National Football League fans can catch the improving **Tampa Bay Buccaneers** at the modern, 66,321-seat Raymond James Stadium, 4201 N. Dale Mabry Hwy., at Dr. Martin Luther King, Jr., Boulevard (☎ **813/879-2827**). The Bucs' season runs from September through December.

The National Hockey League's **Tampa Bay Lightning** play in the Ice Palace, beginning in October (☎ **813/229-8800**).

New York Yankees fans can watch the Boys in Blue during baseball spring training from mid-February through March at Legends Field (☎ **813/879-2244**), opposite Raymond James Stadium. A scaled-down replica of Yankee Stadium, it's the largest spring-training facility in Florida, with a 10,000-seat capacity. Tickets range from $6 to $10. The club's minor league team, the **Tampa Yankees** (same phone), plays at Legends Field from April to September. Tickets are $3 for adults, $2 for kids.

The only oval thoroughbred race course on Florida's west coast, ♦ **Tampa Bay Downs,** 11225 Racetrack Rd., Oldsmar (☎ **800/200-4434** in Florida, or 813/855-4401), is the home of the Tampa Bay Derby. Races are held from December to May, and the track presents simulcasts year-round. Call for post times.

TENNIS Beginners to highly skilled players can sharpen their games at the **Hopman Tennis Program,** at the Saddlebrook Resort, 5700 Saddlebrook Way, Wesley Chapel (☎ **800/729-8383** or 813/973-1111). Packages start at $372 person for 2 days, double occupancy, including tennis instruction, unlimited playing time, video analysis, agility exercises, fitness center, and accommodations at the Saddlebrook Resort for 5 days and 6 nights. You must be a member or a guest to play here (see "Where to Stay," below).

SHOPPING

Hyde Park and Ybor City are two areas of Tampa worth some window shopping, perhaps sandwiched around lunch at one of their fine restaurants (see "Where to Dine," below).

CIGARS Ybor City is no longer a major producer of hand-rolled cigars, but you can watch artisans making stogies at the **Gonzales y Martinez Cigar Factory,** 2025 7th Ave., in the Columbia Restaurant building (☎ 813/247-2469). Gonzales and Martinez are recent arrivals from Cuba and don't speak English, but the staff does at the adjoining **Columbia Cigar Store** (it's best to enter here). Rollers are on duty Monday to Saturday from 10am to 6pm.

A single roller puffs away while he makes them at **Tampa Rico Cigar Co.,** one of the stores in **Ybor Square,** 1901 13th St., at 8th Avenue (☎ 813/247-4497), a shopping complex listed on the National Register of Historic Places. The three brick buildings date from 1886 and once comprised the largest cigar factory in the world. Today it's primarily notable for several small shops selling an amazing variety of collectibles. Shops here are open Monday to Saturday from 10am to 6pm, and Sunday from noon to 5:30pm.

You can stock up on fine domestic and imported cigars at **El Sol,** 1728 E. 7th Ave. (☎ **813/247-5554**), the city's oldest cigar store; **King Corona Cigar Factory,** 1523 E. 7th Ave. (☎ **813/241-9109**); and at **Metropolitan Cigars & Wine,** 2014 E. 7th Ave. (☎ **813/248-3304**).

SHOPPING CENTERS   Old Hyde Park Village, 1507 W. Swann Ave., at South Dakota Avenue (☎ **813/251-3500**), is a terrific alternative to cookie-cutter suburban malls. Walk around little shops in the sunshine and check out Hyde Park, one of the city's oldest and most historic neighborhoods at the same time. The cluster of 50 upscale shops and boutiques is set in a village layout. The selection includes Williams-Sonoma, Pottery Barn, Banana Republic, Brooks Brothers, Crabtree & Evelyn, Godiva Chocolatier, Laura Ashley, Polo Ralph Lauren, and Talbots, to name a few. There's a free parking garage on South Oregon Avenue behind Jacobson's department store. The shops are open Monday to Wednesday and Saturday from 10am to 6pm, Thursday and Friday from 10am to 9pm, and Sunday from noon to 5pm.

The main mall in the city is **West Shore Plaza,** on Kennedy Boulevard where it turns into Memorial Highway (Fla. 60). **University Mall** is nearest Busch Gardens, on Fowler Avenue just east of I-275. The area's largest complex is **Brandon Town-Center,** at I-4 and Fla. 60 in the eastern suburb of Brandon, where most stores have unusually large amounts of floor space and, hence, more merchandise from which to choose.

WHERE TO STAY

If you're going to Busch Gardens, Adventure Island, Lowry Park Zoo, and the Museum of Science and Industry (MOSI), the motels near Busch Gardens are much more convenient than those downtown, about 7 miles to the south. The downtown hotels are geared to business travelers, but staying there will put you near the Florida Aquarium, the Museum of African-American Art, the Tampa Museum of Art, the Henry B. Plant Museum, the Tampa Bay Performing Arts Center, scenic Bayshore Boulevard, the dining and shopping opportunities in the Hyde Park historic district, and Ybor City's restaurants and nightlife.

The Westshore area, near the bay west of downtown and south of Tampa International Airport, is another commercial center, with a wide range of national chain hotels catering to business travelers and conventioneers. It's convenient to Raymond James Stadium and the New York Yankees' spring-training complex. Here you'll find the Spanish-style **Doubletree Guest Suites,** 4400 W. Cypress St., at Manhattan Avenue (☎ **800/222-TREE** or 813/873-8675); **Courtyard by Marriott,** 3805 W. Cypress St., at Dale Mabry Highway (☎ **800/321-2211** or 813/874-0555); the **Hyatt Regency Westshore,** 6200 Courtney Campbell Causeway (☎ **800/233-1234** or 813/874-1234), nestled on a 35-acre bay-side nature preserve; the **Sheraton Grand Hotel,** 4860 W. Kennedy Blvd., at Shore Boulevard (☎ **800/325-3535** or 813/286-4400), across the street from West Shore Plaza mall and home to one of former Miami Dolphins Coach Don Shula's steak houses; and the **Tampa Marriott Westshore,** 1001 N. Westshore Blvd. (☎ **800/228-9290** or 813/287-2555).

The high season in Tampa generally runs from January to April, but you won't find as large an increase here as at the beach resorts. Most hotels offer discounted package rates in the summer and weekend specials all year, dropping their rates by as much as 50%. Hotels often combine tickets to major attractions like Busch Gardens in their packages, so always ask about special deals.

If you want to stay outdoors, **Hillsborough River State Park,** 15402 U.S. 301 North, Thonotosassa, FL 33592 (☎ **813/986-1020**), offers 118 campsites year-round, plus fishing, canoeing, and boating.

Hillsborough County adds 12% tax to your hotel room bill.

Tampa Accommodations & Dining

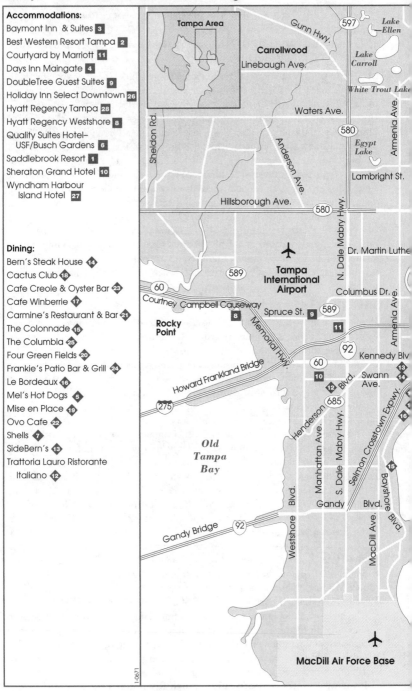

Accommodations:

Baymont Inn & Suites **3**
Best Western Resort Tampa **2**
Courtyard by Marriott **11**
Days Inn Maingate **4**
DoubleTree Guest Suites **9**
Holiday Inn Select Downtown **26**
Hyatt Regency Tampa **28**
Hyatt Regency Westshore **8**
Quality Suites Hotel–
   USF/Busch Gardens **6**
Saddlebrook Resort **1**
Sheraton Grand Hotel **10**
Wyndham Harbour
   Island Hotel **27**

Dining:

Bern's Steak House **14**
Cactus Club **18**
Cafe Creole & Oyster Bar **23**
Cafe Winberrie **17**
Carmine's Restaurant & Bar **21**
The Colonnade **15**
The Columbia **25**
Four Green Fields **20**
Frankie's Patio Bar & Grill **24**
Le Bordeaux **16**
Mel's Hot Dogs **5**
Mise en Place **19**
Ovo Cafe **22**
Shells **7**
SideBern's **13**
Trattoria Lauro Ristorante
   Italiano **12**

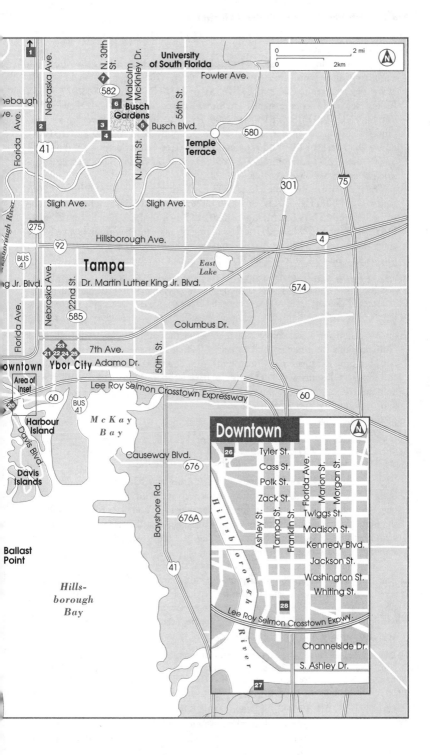

Near Busch Gardens

The plushest and most expensive establishment near the park is the 500-room **Embassy Suites Hotel and Conference Center,** 3705 Spectrum Blvd., actually facing Fowler Avenue (☎ **800/EMBASSY** or 813/977-7066; fax 813/977-7933). Almost across the avenue stands **LaQuinta Inn & Suites,** 3701 E. Fowler Ave. (☎ **800/NU-ROOMS** or 813/910-7500; fax 813/910-7600). There also are new, modern editions of **AmeriSuites,** 11408 N. 30th St. (☎ **800/833-1516** or 813/979-1922; fax 813/979-1926), and **DoubleTree Guest Suites,** 11310 N. 30th St. (☎ **800/222-TREE** or 813/971-7690; fax 813/972-5525). They stand side-by-side just south of Fowler Avenue.

The inexpensive **Red Roof Inn,** 2307 E. Busch Blvd., between 22nd and 26th streets (☎ **800/THE-ROOF** or 813/932-0073), is a pleasant property on land-scaped grounds. **Days Inn Maingate,** 2901 E. Busch Blvd., at 30th Street (☎ **800/ DAYS-INN** or 813/933-6471), is less appealing than the Baymont Inn & Suites across the street (see below), but it's convenient for families on a budget since you can walk to Busch Gardens from here. Both motels have outdoor pools.

Baymont Inn & Suites. 9202 N. 30th St. (at Busch Blvd.), Tampa, FL 33612. ☎ **800/ 428-3438** or 813/930-6900. Fax 813/930-0563. 146 units. A/C TV TEL. Winter $80 double. Off-season $57 double. Rates include continental breakfast. AE, DC, DISC, MC, V.

Fake banana trees and a parrot cage welcome guests to the terra-cotta–floored lobby of this comfortable and convenient member of the former Budgetel Inn chain of cost-conscious but amenity-rich motels. All rooms are spacious and have ceiling fans, bright wood furniture with tropical trim, desks, phones with long cords, and coffeemakers. Rooms with king beds also have recliners. Outside, a courtyard with an unheated swimming pool has plenty of space for sunning. There's a game room and coin laundry, and local telephone calls are free. There's no restaurant on the premises, but plenty are nearby.

Best Western Resort Tampa at Busch Gardens. 820 E. Busch Blvd. (at I-275), Tampa, FL 33612. ☎ **800/288-4011** or 813/933-4011. Fax 813/932-1784. 255 units. A/C TV TEL. Winter $119 double. Off-season $70–90 double. AE, DC, DISC, MC, V.

Right at the Busch Boulevard exit off I-275, this motel is fine for families on a budget. An enclosed skylit atrium-style courtyard with fountains, streetlights, benches, and pool is a fine place for the kids when it's too hot or too cool to enjoy the outdoors. Guest rooms in the main wing open to walkways facing the indoor atrium or the parking lots. Newer units are in a four-story annex. They all have standard furnishings and coffeemakers.

The Palm Grill Restaurant off the lobby features a variety of dishes, while the Bull Pen Sports Bar offers pub fare and libation. Services include a concierge desk, secretarial services, valet laundry, limited room service, and courtesy transport to Busch Gardens. There are indoor and outdoor heated swimming pools, two whirlpools, a sauna, four lighted tennis courts, exercise and game rooms, a coin-operated laundry, and a gift shop.

✪ Quality Suites Hotel—USF Near Busch Gardens. 3001 University Center Dr., Tampa, FL 33612. ☎ **800/786-7446** or 813/971-8930. Fax 813/971-8935. 150 units. A/C TV TEL. Winter $99–$159 suite for 2. Off-season $89–$139 suite for 2. Rates include full breakfast buffet and evening beer-and-wine reception. AE, DC, DISC, MC, V.

Actually on North 30th Street between Busch Boulevard and Flower Avenue, this hacienda-style, all-suite hotel sits about a mile from the Busch Gardens entrance. The three-story building encloses a lush tropical courtyard with heated pool, hot tub, covered games area, sundeck (with data ports in the surrounding railing), and a lively tiki bar known as Ruzic's Roost (in honor of hands-on owner John Ruzic), making this the most beachlike vacation venue as you'll find close to the park. The bar can get noisy before closing at 9pm, and bare-footed, wet-bathing-suited guests can leave some of the ground-level units musty, so ask for an upstairs suite away from the action. The suites' living rooms have sofa beds, recliners, dining tables, wet bars, coffeemakers, microwaves, phones, TVs, VCRs, and stereo units. Their separate bedrooms are equipped with TVs, phones, built-in armoire and mirrored vanity areas, and narrow screened patios or balconies. About 10 "family suites" have over-and-under bunk beds for kids. Guests can graze a full breakfast buffet, and the bar serves inexpensive barbecued steak, fish, and chicken for lunch and dinner. Facilities here also include a 24-hour gift shop/food store, VCR rentals, whirlpool, meeting rooms, and coin-operated laundry. Sports teams visiting the nearby University of South Florida like to stay here.

Downtown Tampa

✪ **Hyatt Regency Tampa.** 2 Tampa City Center (corner of E. Jackson St.), Tampa, FL 33602. ☎ **800/233-1234** or 813/225-1234. Fax 813/273-0234. 519 units. A/C TV TEL. Winter $129–$200. Off-season $99–$200 double. Weekend packages available off-season. AE, DC, DISC, MC, V. Valet parking $7.

In the center of the downtown business district, it's not surprising that this Hyatt—renovated in 1998 to the tune of $10 million—caters primarily to the corporate crowd. It's just off the Franklin Street pedestrian mall and a short walk from the Harbour Island People Mover. The Hyatt signature eight-story atrium lobby has a cascading waterfall and lots of foliage. Many units on the upper floors have bay or river views. Creative American cuisine is featured at City Center Cafe, while the deli offers light lunches. For libations with piano music, try Saltwaters Lounge (there's not much else going on downtown after dark). Amenities include concierge, 24-hour room service, newspaper delivery, baby-sitting, business center, valet laundry, guest laundry, airport courtesy shuttle, outdoor heated swimming pool, whirlpool, and health club.

Radisson Riverwalk Hotel. 200 N. Ashley Dr., Tampa, FL 33602. ☎ **800/333-3333** or 813/233-2222. Fax 813/221-5929. 284 units. A/C TV TEL. Winter $159 double. Off-season $99-$119. AE DC, DISC, MC, V. Valet parking $5.

Sitting on the east bank of the Hillsborough River, this six-story former Quality Inn was completely remodeled and reborn as a better-equipped Radisson in 1998. Half the rooms face west and have views from their balconies of the Arabesque minarets atop the Henry B. Plant Museum across the river—quite a scene at sunset. They cost the same as units on the east, which face downtown's skyscrapers, so be sure to request a riverside room. Sporting quality Drexel Heritage furniture, the spacious rooms have coffeemakers, hair dryers, phones with data ports, and either two full beds or a king bed and writing desk. Beside the river, the Ashley Street Grill serves indoor-outdoor breakfasts and lunches, then turns to fine dinner in the evenings. Open 24 hours, Boulanger baker and deli purveys fresh pastries, soups, sandwiches, and snacks. A brick deck surrounds the outdoor riverside pool with its own bar. The Tampa Town Ferry stops at the dock, where you can rent Jets. Amenities include concierge and valet laundry service.

✪ **Wyndham Harbour Island Hotel.** 725 S. Harbour Island Blvd., Harbour Island, Tampa, FL 33602. ☎ **800/WYNDHAM** or 813/229-5000. Fax 813/229-5322. 299 units. A/C MINIBAR TV TEL. Winter $139–$219 double. Off-season $99–$169 double. AE, DC, DISC, MC, V. Valet parking $6.

With the shops closed, there's not much action on Harbour Island, but you'll enjoy quiet elegance at this 12-story luxury property. It has great views of the surrounding channels that link the Hillsborough River and the bay. The bedrooms, all with views of the water, are furnished in dark woods and floral fabrics, and each has a well-lit marble-trimmed bathroom, executive desk, and work area, plus in-room conveniences such as a coffeemaker, iron, and ironing board. Watch the yachts drift by as you dine at the Harbourview Room, or enjoy your favorite drink in the Bar, a clubby room with equally good views. Snacks and drinks are available during the day at the Pool Bar. Amenities here include concierge, limited room service, secretarial services, notary public, evening turndown, valet laundry, courtesy airport shuttle, outdoor heated swimming pool and deck, newsstand/gift shop, and guest privileges at a nearby health club.

A NEARBY RESORT

✪ **Saddlebrook Resort.** 5700 Saddlebrook Way, Wesley Chapel, FL 33543. ☎ **800/ 729-8383** or 813/973-1111. Fax 813/973-4504. 800 units. A/C TV TEL. Winter $165–$242 per person. Off-season $107–$147 per person. Rates include breakfast and dinner. AE, DC, DISC, MC, V. Free self-parking; valet parking $3. Take I-75 north to Fla. 54 (Exit 58), go 1 mile east to resort.

Set on 480 acres of natural countryside, this internationally renowned golf and tennis resort is off the beaten path (30 minutes north of Tampa International Airport) but worth the trip. Join pros such as Pete Sampras at the Hopman Tennis Program, or perfect your swing at the Arnold Palmer Golf Academy (see "Outdoor Activities & Spectator Sports," above).

Dining/Diversions: The casual but elegant Cypress Restaurant consistently wins accolades. It's famous for grand holiday buffets and popular Friday-night seafood buffets. Enjoy indoor or outdoor dining at Terrace on the Green, overlooking the Cypress Lagoon and the 18th green. The Little Club offers an American menu and the popular TD's sports bar/tavern. The Poolside Cafe is great for dining in your bathing suit alfresco.

Amenities: Concierge, limited room service, newspaper delivery, in-room massage, baby-sitting, children's activities program, airport courtesy shuttle. Two 18-hole championship golf courses, 45 tennis courts, 270-foot-long half-million-gallon superpool, whirlpool, 7,000-square-foot luxury spa, fitness center, basketball and volleyball courts, and softball field.

WHERE TO DINE

As with the hotels, I have organized the restaurants below by geographic area: near Busch Gardens, in or near Hyde Park (just across the Hillsborough River from downtown), and in Ybor City (on the northeastern edge of downtown).

Near Busch Gardens

You'll find the national fast-food and family restaurants east of I-275 on Busch Boulevard and along Fowler Avenue near University Mall.

✪ **Mel's Hot Dogs.** 4136 E. Busch Blvd., at 42nd St. ☎ **813/985-8000.** Main courses $3–$6.50. No credit cards. Daily 11am–9pm. AMERICAN.

Catering to everyone from businesspeople on a lunch break to hungry families craving inexpensive all-beef hot dogs, this red-and-white cottage offers everything from "bagel-dogs" and corn dogs to a bacon/cheddar Reuben. All choices are served on a poppy seed bun and most come with French fries, and a choice of cole slaw or baked beans. Even the decor is dedicated to wieners: The walls and windows are lined with hot-dog memorabilia. And just in case hot-dog mania hasn't won you over, there are a few alternative choices (sausages, chicken breast, and beef and veggie burgers).

Shells. 11010 N. 30th St. (between Busch Blvd. and Fowler Ave.). ☎ **813/977-8456.** Reservations not accepted. Main courses $6–$17. AE, DISC, MC, V. Mon–Thurs 11:30am–10pm, Fri–Sat 11:30am–11pm, Sun noon–10pm. SEAFOOD.

You'll see Shells restaurants in many parts of Florida, and with good reason, for this casual, award-winning chain consistently provides excellent value, especially if you have a family to feed. They all have the same menu and prices and are particularly known for their spicy Jack Daniel's buffalo shrimp and scallop appetizers. Main courses range from the usual fried seafood platters to pastas and charcoal-grilled shrimp, fish, steaks, and chicken. I counted 21 tender, bite-size shrimp in a light, garlic-tinged cream sauce served over linguine—a bargain for $9.50. Another 30 of them were perfectly charcoal-grilled on a skewer and served with saffron rice and steamed vegetables for $11. There's also a children's menu.

Hyde Park

Bern's Steak House. 1208 S. Howard Ave. (at Marjory Ave.). ☎ **813/251-2421.** Reservations required. Main courses $19–$35. AE, DC, DISC, MC, V. Daily 5–11pm. Closed Christmas. AMERICAN.

The exterior of this famous steak house looks like a factory built almost under the Lee Roy Selmon Crosstown Expressway. Inside, however, you'll find eight ornate dining rooms with themes like Rhône, Burgundy, and Irish Rebellion. They set an appropriately dark atmosphere for meat lovers, for here you order and pay for charcoal-grilled steaks (beef or buffalo) according to the thickness and weight. They come with onion soup, salad, baked potato, garlic toast, onion rings, and vegetables grown in Bern's own organic garden. The phone book–size wine list offers more than 7,000 selections.

The big surprise here is the dessert quarters upstairs, where 50 romantic booths paneled in aged California redwood can privately seat from 2 to 12 guests. Each of these little chambers is equipped with a phone for placing your order and a closed-circuit TV for watching and listening to a resident pianist. The dessert menu offers almost 100 delicious selections, plus some 1,400 after-dinner drinks. It's possible to reserve a booth for dessert only, but preference is given to those who dine. You can get some of the same sweet things nearby at SideBern's (see below).

Cactus Club. In Old Hyde Park shopping complex, 1601 Snow Ave. (south of Swan St.). ☎ 813/251-4089. Reservations not accepted. Burgers and sandwiches $6.50–$7.50; main courses $6.50–14. AE, DC, MC, V. Mon–Thurs 11am–11pm, Fri–Sat 11am–midnight, Sun 11am–10:30pm. AMERICAN SOUTHWEST.

Watch all the shoppers go by at Old Hyde Park from this fun and casual cafe with a Southwestern accent. Dine inside or outside on tacos, enchiladas, chili, sizzling fajitas, hickory-smoked baby back ribs, Jamaican jerk chicken, burgers, fajitas, quesadillas, enchiladas (including vegetarian versions), sandwiches, smoked chicken salad, and more. It's always packed at lunchtime—get here early.

The Colonnade. 3401 Bayshore Blvd. (at W. Julia St.). ☎ 813/839-7558. Reservations accepted only for large parties. Main courses $8–$20. AE, DC, DISC, MC, V. Sun–Thurs 11am–10pm, Fri–Sat 11am–11pm. AMERICAN/SEAFOOD.

Locals have been flocking to this rough-hewn place since 1935, primarily for the great view of Hillsborough Bay across Bayshore Boulevard. The food is a bit on the Red Lobsterish side, but get here early or wait for a window table; the vista is worth it. Fresh seafood is the specialty: grouper prepared seven ways, crab-stuffed flounder, Maryland-style crab cakes, even wild Florida alligator as an appetizer. Prime rib, steaks, and chicken are also available.

Four Green Fields. 205 W. Platt St. (between Parker St. and Plant Ave.). ☎ **813/254-4444.** Reservations accepted. Sandwiches $6; main courses $8.50–$14. AE, MC, V. Mon–Sat 11am–2am, Sun 1pm–2am. IRISH/AMERICAN.

Just across the bridge from the downtown convention center, America's only thatched-roof Irish pub may be surrounded by palm trees instead of potato fields, but it still offers the ambiance and tastes of Ireland. Staffed by genuine Irish immigrants, the large room with a square bar in the center smells of Irish ale. The Gaelic stew is predictably bland, but the salads and sandwiches are passable. The crowd usually is young, especially for live Irish music on Thursday, Friday, and Saturday nights.

Le Bordeaux. 1502 S. Howard Ave. (2 blocks north of Bayshore Blvd.). ☎ **813/254-4387.** Reservations recommended. Main courses $15–$28. AE, DC, MC, V. Mon–Thurs 5:30–10pm, Fri–Sat 5:30–11pm, Sun 5:30–9:30pm. CLASSICAL FRENCH.

This bistro's authentic French fare is some of the region's best, but keep a reign on your credit card—everything's sold a la carte, so you can ring up a hefty bill quickly. French-born chef/owner Gordon Davis offers seating in a living room–style main dining room of this converted house expanded to include a plant-filled conservatory. His classical French menu changes daily, but you can count on homemade pâtés and pastries and specials often the likes of *filet de snook a la pistache* (local snook encrusted with pistachio nuts). Part of the establishment is the lounge-style Left Bank Jazz Bistro, with live entertainment Thursday to Saturday from 9pm.

✪ Mise en Place. In Grand Central Pl., 442 W. Kennedy Blvd. (at S. Magnolia Ave., opposite the University of Tampa). ☎ **813/254-5373.** Reservations accepted only for parties of 6 or more. Main courses $13–$21. AE, DC, DISC, MC, V. Mon–Fri 11am–3pm, Tues–Thurs 5:30–10pm, Fri–Sat and 5:30–11pm. INTERNATIONAL.

Look around at all those happy, stylish people soaking up the trendy ambiance, and you'll know why chef Marty Blitz and his wife, Marianne, are the culinary darlings of Tampa. They continue to present the freshest of ingredients, with a creative international menu that changes daily. Main courses often include such choices as roast duck with Jamaica wild-strawberry sauce, grilled swordfish with three-melon mint salsa, or Ethiopian lentil stew served with steamed *injera* bread. There's valet parking at the rear of the building on Grand Central Place.

After dinner you can wander next door into **442,** an upscale bar with live jazz and blues.

SideBern's. 2208 W. Morrison Ave. (at S. Howard St.). ☎ **813/258-2233.** Reservations not accepted. Sandwiches and salads $4–$7.50; desserts $4–$5.50. AE, DC, DISC, MC, V. Sun and Tues–Thurs 6–11pm, Fri–Sat 6pm–1am. SANDWICHES/SALADS/DESSERTS.

The owners of Bern's Steak House (see above) opened this informal outlet to accommodate everyone who wanted to partake of their gourmet goodies but couldn't fit into the dessert rooms at the main restaurant. Their most popular desserts are offered at this sophisticated bistro, whose cathedral ceiling covers an open kitchen (wonderful aromas) and cherry-wood tables and chairs. Banana cheesecake is a consistent winner, as is the chocolate pâté served with Curaçao, raspberry, or rum sauce. Sandwiches are served on a choice of regular wheat, focaccia, or roasted garlic potato bread. Tops among these features a tender, perfectly charcoal-grilled tenderloin steak accompanied by baked-potato salad, lettuce, tomato, a huge slice of onion, and shaved cucumber salad—a meal in itself. Top-notch coffees are roasted on the premises.

✪ **Trattoria Lauro Ristorante Italiano.** 3915 Henderson Blvd. (2 blocks west of Dale Mabry Hwy., between Watrous and Neptune aves.). ☎ **813/281-2100.** Reservations recommended. Main courses $9.50–$19. AE, DC, DISC, MC, V. Mon–Fri 11:30am–2pm and 5:30–10pm, Sat 5:30–11pm, Sun 5:30–10pm. ITALIAN.

Known for extraordinary sauces and pastas, chef/owner Lauro Medeglia is a native Italian who cooks his home fare with love. Though his restaurant is off the beaten track, it's worth the detour. Classical decor and soft music have made it one of Tampa's favorite places to "pop the question," and smartly attired waiters render efficient yet friendly and unobtrusive service. Try the caprese, puttanesca, gnocchi, or agnolotti.

Ybor City

✪ **Cafe Creole and Oyster Bar.** 1330 9th Ave. (at Avenida de Republica de Cuba/14th St.). ☎ **813/247-6283.** Reservations not accepted but call for preferred seating. Main courses $9–$18. AE, DC, DISC, MC, V. Mon–Thurs 11:30am–10pm, Fri 11:30am–11:30pm, Sat 5–11:30pm. CREOLE/CAJUN.

Resembling a turn-of-the-century railway station, this brick building dates from 1896 and was originally known as El Pasaje, the home of the Cherokee Club, a gentlemen's hotel and private club with a casino and a decor rich in stained-glass windows, wrought-iron balconies, Spanish murals, and marble bathrooms. Specialties include exceptionally prepared Louisiana crab cakes, oysters, blackened grouper, and jambalaya. If you're new to cuisine of the bayou, try the Creole sampler. Dine inside or out.

Carmine's Restaurant & Bar. 1802 E. 7th Ave. East (at 18th St.). ☎ **813/248-3834.** Reservations not accepted. Sandwiches $4–$7; main courses $5–$15 (most $6–$9). No credit cards. Mon–Tues 11am–10pm, Wed–Thurs 11am–midnight, Fri–Sat 11am–3am, Sun 11am–6pm. CUBAN/ITALIAN/AMERICAN.

Bright blue poles hold up an ancient pressed-tin ceiling above this noisy corner cafe, one of Ybor's most popular hangouts. A great variety of loyal local patrons gather here for genuine Cuban sandwiches—smoked ham, roast pork, Genoa salami, Swiss cheese, pickles, salad dressing, mustard, lettuce, and tomato on a crispy, submarine roll. There's a vegetarian version, too, and the combination half sandwich and bowl of Spanish soup made with sausages, potatoes, and garbanzo beans makes a hearty meal for just $4. Main courses are led by Cuban-style roast pork, thin-cut pork chops with mushroom sauce, spaghetti with a blue crab tomato sauce, and a few seafood and chicken platters.

✪ **Columbia.** 2117 E. 7th Ave. (between 21st and 22nd sts.). ☎ **813/248-4961.** Reservations recommended. Main courses $12–$23. AE, DC, DISC, MC, V. Mon–Thurs 11am–10pm, Fri–Sat 11am–11pm, Sun noon–9pm. SPANISH.

Dating from 1905, this hand-painted tile building occupies an entire city block in the heart of Ybor City. Tourists flock here to soak up the ambiance and so do the locals because it's so much fun to clap along during fire-belching floor shows in the main dining room. You can't help coming back time after time for the famous Spanish bean soup and original "1905" salad. The paella à la valenciana is outstanding, with more than a dozen ingredients from gulf grouper and gulf pink shrimp to calamari, mussels, clams, chicken, and pork. The decor throughout is graced with hand-painted tiles, wrought-iron chandeliers, dark woods, rich red fabrics, and stained-glass windows. You can breathe your own fumes in the Cigar Bar.

Frankie's Patio Bar & Grill. 1905 E. 7th Ave. (between 19th and 20th sts.). ☎ **813/249-3337.** Reservations accepted only for large parties. Main courses $10–$15; sandwiches $5–$9. AE, DISC, MC, V. Mon–Tues 11am–3pm, Wed 11am–midnight, Thurs–Fri 11am–3am, Sat 5pm–3am. INTERNATIONAL.

This Ybor City attraction is known mostly as a venue for outstanding musical acts—live jazz, blues, reggae, and rock Wednesday to Saturday. With exposed industrial pipes, the large three-story restaurant stands out from the usual Spanish-themed, 19th-century architecture of Ybor City. There's seating indoors, on a large outdoor patio, or on an open-air balcony overlooking the action on the street. It's a fun atmosphere, and the food blends Cuban, American, Creole, and Italian influences. Build-your-own sandwiches are available during all hours.

✪ **Ovo Cafe.** 1901 E. 7th Ave. (at 19th St.). ☎ **813/248-6979.** Reservations not accepted. Main courses $6.50–$13.50. AE, DC, DISC, MC, V. Mon–Tues 11am–3pm, Wed–Thurs 11am–10pm, Fri–Sat 11am–1am, Sun 11am–9pm. INTERNATIONAL.

This cafe, popular with the business set by day and the club crowd on weekend nights, is Tampa's answer to SoHo. The menu features a melange of sophisticated offerings. Pierogies and pasta pillows come with taste-tempting sauces and fillings. The likes of tangy jerk sauce over chicken, bananas, mozzarella cheese, and roasted sweet peppers top the individual-size pizzas. Strawberries or blackberries and a splash of liqueur cover the thick waffles. And there are several creative salads. Portions are substantial, but be careful with your credit card here: Pricing is strictly a la carte. The big black bar dispenses a wide variety of martinis, plus some unusual liqueur drinks.

TAMPA AFTER DARK

The Tampa/Hillsborough Arts Council maintains an **Artsline** (☎ 813/229-ARTS), a 24-hour information service providing the latest on current and upcoming cultural events. Racks in many restaurants and bars have copies of *Weekly Planet, Focus,* and *Accent on Tampa Bay,* three free publications detailing what's going on in the entire bay area. And you can check the "Baylife" and "Friday Extra" sections of the *Tampa Tribune* and the Friday "Weekend" section of the *St. Petersburg Times.* The visitor center usually has copies of the week's newspaper sections (see "Essentials," above). And be on the lookout for the slick bimonthly magazine *Event Guide Tampa Bay,* which gives a rundown on what's going on.

THE CLUB & MUSIC SCENE   Ybor City is Tampa's favorite nighttime venue by far. All you have to do is stroll along 7th Avenue East between 15th and 20th streets to find a club or bar to your liking. The avenue is packed with people of every possible age and description on Friday and Saturday from 9pm to 3am, but you'll also find something going on from Tuesday to Thursday and even on Sunday. You don't need addresses or phone numbers; your ears will guide you along 7th Avenue East.

Starting at 15th Street and heading east, you'll come first to **The Masquerade,** with retro and old-wave bands on Friday to Sunday. The body-pierced 20-something crowd gets primed at **Club Hedo, Atomic Age Cafe & Lounge,** and **Cherry's** before dancing at **The Rubb** across the avenue.

At 16th Street you should come to **Centro Ybor,** a dining, shopping, and entertainment complex that was under construction at press time.

Between 17th and 18th streets, you'll smell the cigar smoke coming from the sidewalk tables of the **Green Iguana Bar & Grill,** a refined establishment frequented by young professionals. The **Irish Pub** is just that, while **Fat Tuesday** has a large dance floor and long bar. Between 18th and 19th streets, you'll see **Harpo's,** which doesn't extract a cover charge. Keep going across 19th Street to one of Ybor's best clubs, **Blues Ship Café on Top,** which features live blues, jazz, and reggae. And last but not least is the warehouselike **Frankie's Patio Bar & Grill,** known for its reasonably priced food, as well as its outstanding musical acts (see "Where to Dine," above). Across the avenue, country meets city at **Spurs in Ybor,** a country-and-western joint.

Although not in the heart of Ybor's bar scene, the ✪ **Jazz Cellar,** on 9th Avenue East between 13th Street and Avenida de Republica de Cuba (14th Street), features contemporary jazz, rhythm and blues, and just plain blues from 8pm to 2am Friday and Saturday. This basement establishment is on the north side of Ybor Square. Call ☎ **813/248-1862** for reservations.

Elsewhere in town, you can lose your life savings playing bingo, poker, and the video slot machines at the **Seminole Indian Casino,** 5223 N. Orient Rd., at Hillsborough Road east of the city (☎ **800/282-7016** or 813/621-1302). It's open 24 hours every day of the year.

THE PERFORMING ARTS   With a prime downtown location on 9 acres along the east bank of the Hillsborough River, the huge ✪ **Tampa Bay Performing Arts Center,** 1010 N. MacInnes Pl. (☎ **800/955-1045** or 813/229-STAR), is the largest performing-arts venue south of the Kennedy Center in Washington, D.C. Accordingly, this four-theater complex is the focal point of Tampa's performing arts scene, presenting a wide range of Broadway plays, classical and pop concerts, operas, cabarets, improv, and special events.

A sightseeing attraction in its own right, the restored ✪ **Tampa Theatre,** 711 Franklin St. (☎ **813/223-8981**), dates from 1926 and is on the National Register of Historic Places. It presents a varied program of classic, foreign, and alternative films, as well as concerts and special events.

The 66,321-seat **Raymond James Stadium,** 4201 N. Dale Mabry Hwy. (☎ **813/ 673-4300**), is frequently the site of headliner concerts. The **USF Sun Dome,** 4202 E. Fowler Ave. (☎ **813/974-3111**), on the University of South Florida campus, hosts major concerts by touring pop stars, rock bands, jazz groups, and other contemporary artists.

4 St. Petersburg

On the western shore of the bay, St. Petersburg stands in contrast to Tampa, much like San Francisco compares to Oakland in California. While Tampa is the area's business, industrial, and shipping center, St. Petersburg was conceived and built almost a century ago primarily for tourists and wintering snowbirds. Here you'll find one of the most picturesque and pleasant downtowns of any city in Florida, with a waterfront promenade and the famous, pyramid-shaped Pier offering great views across the bay, plus quality museums, interesting shops, and fine restaurants.

Away from downtown, the city pretty much consists of strip malls dividing residential neighborhoods, but plan at least to have a look around the charming bayfront area. If you don't do anything else, go out on The Pier and take a pleasant stroll along Bayshore Drive.

All is not completely happy in this urban paradise, however, for St. Petersburg was rocked by riots after a white police officer shot and killed a black motorist in late 1996. Although all was calm at press time, you should avoid the area south of I-175 and east of I-275.

ESSENTIALS

GETTING THERE   To reach downtown St. Petersburg from Tampa, take I-275 or the Gandy Causeway (U.S. 92) across the bay, and then I-275 south to I-375 east to the waterfront. From Sarasota and Bradenton, take I-275 north across the towering Sunshine Skyway ($2 toll) to I-175 or I-375 east. From points north, take congested U.S. 19 straight to downtown.

VISITOR INFORMATION   For advance information about both St. Petersburg and the beaches, contact the **St. Petersburg/Clearwater Area Convention & Visitors Bureau,** 14450 46th St. N., Clearwater, FL 34622 (☎ **800/345-6710,** or 727/464-7200 for advance hotel reservations; fax 727/464-7222; www.stpete-clearwater.com). The office is south of Roosevelt Boulevard (Fla. 686) opposite St. Petersburg–Clearwater International Airport.

A wealth of information is also available from the **St. Petersburg Area Chamber of Commerce,** 100 2nd Ave. N. (at 1st Street), St. Petersburg, FL 33701 (☎ **727/821-4069;** fax 727/895-6326; www.stpete.com). This downtown main office and visitor center is open Monday to Friday from 8am to 5pm, Saturday from 9am to 4pm, Sunday from noon to 3pm. Ask for a copy of the chamber's visitor guide, which lists hotels, motels, condominiums, and other accommodations.

Also downtown, there are **walk-in information centers** on the first level of The Pier and in the lobby of the Florida International Museum (see "Seeing the Top Attractions," below).

The chamber also operates the **Suncoast Welcome Center** (☎ 727/573-1449), on Ulmerton Road at Exit 18 southbound off I-275 (there's no exit here for northbound traffic). Open daily from 9am to 5pm except New Year's Day, Easter, Thanksgiving, and Christmas.

GETTING AROUND   You can see everything on the **Looper: the Downtown Trolley** (☎ 727/571-3440), which runs out to the end of The Pier and past all of the downtown attractions every 30 minutes from 11am to 5pm daily except Thanksgiving and Christmas. Rides cost 50¢ per person.

The **Pinellas Suncoast Transit Authority/PSTA** (☎ 727/530-9911) operates regular bus service throughout Pinellas County.

If you need a cab, call **Yellow Cab** (☎ 727/821-7777) or **Independent Cab** (☎ 727/327-3444).

Pierside Rentals, on The Pier (☎ 727/822-8697), rents bicycles and in-line skates for $5 an hour, $25 a day.

SEEING THE TOP ATTRACTIONS

Florida International Museum. 100 2nd St. N. (between 1st and 2nd aves. N.). ☎ **800/777-9882** or 727/822-3693. www.floridamuseum.org. Admission $13.95 adults, $12.95 seniors, $5.95 children 6–18, free for children under 6. Sun–Fri 9am–6pm, Sat 9am–8pm (or later depending on special exhibits).

This facility attracted 600,000 visitors from around the world when it opened its first exhibition in 1995, and the success has continued (its recent exhibits on the *Titanic* and on the Incas were smash hits). Call to see what's scheduled during your visit. The museum is housed in the former Maas Brothers Department Store, long an area landmark. Tickets should be reserved and purchased in advance to be sure of a specific time. Each visitor is equipped with an audio guide as part of the admission price; allow at least 2 hours to tour a major exhibition. There's an excellent museum store here.

Museum of Fine Arts. 255 Beach Dr. NE (at 3rd Ave. N.). ☎ **727/896-2667.** Admission Mon–Sat $6 adults, $5 seniors, $2 students. Admission free on Sun (donation suggested). Tues–Sat 10am–5pm, Sun 1–5pm; winter, third Thurs of each month 10am–9pm. Closed New Year's Day, Thanksgiving, and Christmas.

Resembling a Mediterranean villa on the waterfront, this museum houses a permanent collection of European, American, pre-Colombian, and Far Eastern art, with works by such artists as Fragonard, Monet, Renoir, Cézanne, and Gauguin. Other highlights include period rooms with antiques and historical furnishings, plus a

Downtown St. Petersburg

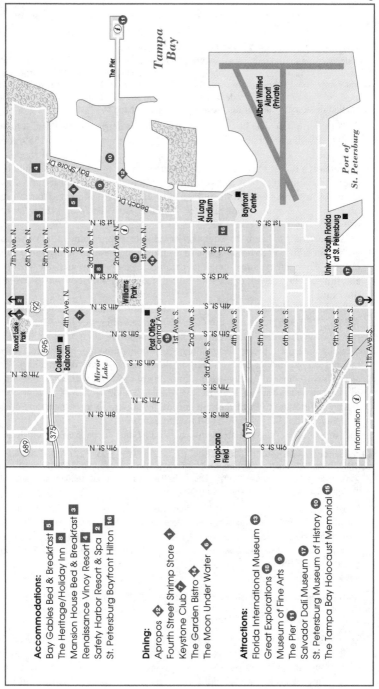

Accommodations:
Bay Gables Bed & Breakfast 5
The Heritage/Holiday Inn 8
Mansion House Bed & Breakfast 3
Renaissance Vinoy Resort 4
Safety Harbor Resort & Spa 2
St. Petersburg Bayfront Hilton 16

Dining:
Apropos 12
Fourth Street Shrimp Store 1
Keystone Club 7
The Garden Bistro 14
The Moon Under Water 6

Attractions:
Florida International Museum 13
Great Explorations 18
Museum of Fine Arts 9
The Pier 11
Salvador Dali Museum 17
St. Petersburg Museum of History 10
The Tampa Bay Holocaust Memorial 15

gallery of Steuben crystal, a new decorative-arts gallery, and world-class rotating exhibits.

The Pier. 800 2nd Ave. NE. ☎ **727/821-6164.** www.stpete-pier.com. Free admission to all the public areas and decks; donations welcome at the aquarium. Russian Submarine $8 adults, $6 seniors, $5 children. Great Explorations $5, free for children under 3. Pier Mon–Thurs 10am–9pm, Fri–Sat 10am–10pm, Sun 11am–7pm. Aquarium Mon–Sat 10am–8pm, Sun noon–6pm. Russian Submarine daily 10am–7pm. Great Explorations Mon–Fri 9am–5pm. Shops and restaurant hours vary. Self-parking $3, valet parking $5.

Walk or ride out on The Pier and enjoy this festive waterfront dining and shopping complex overlooking Tampa Bay. Originally built as a railroad pier in 1889, today it's capped by a spaceshiplike inverted pyramid offering five levels of shops and restaurants, a tourist information desk, observation deck, catwalks for fishing, boat docks, miniature golf, boat and water-sports rentals, sightseeing boats, and a food court. There's also an aquarium and a hands-on, children's museum. You can rent boats and go on cruises from here (see "Outdoor Activities & Spectators Sports," below).

With a variety of hands-on exhibits, **Great Explorations Hands-On Museum** is great for a rainy day or for kids who've overdosed on the sun and need to cool off indoors. They can explore a long, dark tunnel; measure their strength, flexibility, and fitness; paint a work of art with sunlight; and play a melody with a sweep of the hand.

You can also buy tickets here to visit the 300-foot-long **Russian Submarine** (☎ 727/897-9151), actually the *U-484,* which served in the Soviet/Russian navy from the 1960s until 1994. Its retirement home was to be alongside The Pier; however, the water here wasn't deep enough, so pending a dredging operation, it was moored at press time at Bayboro Harbor. Buses shuttle visitors to the ship.

From November to April you can climb aboard the *H.M.S. Bounty,* a replica of the famous vessel built in 1960 for the Marlon Brando version of *Mutiny on the Bounty* (30-minute tours of the ship cost $6 for adults, $5 for seniors, and $4 for kids 5 to 17; call ☎ **727/896-5668** for more information).

A free trolley service operates between The Pier and the parking lots on shore.

✪ **Salvador Dalí Museum.** 1000 3rd St. S. (near 11th Ave. S.). ☎ **727/823-3767.** Admission $8 adults, $7 seniors, $4 students, free for children 9 and under. 50% discount Thurs 5–8pm. Mon–Wed 9:30am–5:30pm, Thurs 9:30am–8pm, Fri–Sat 9:30am–5:30pm, Sun noon–5pm. Closed Thanksgiving and Christmas.

Located on Tampa Bay south of The Pier, this starkly modern museum houses the world's largest collection of works by the renowned Spanish surrealist. Valued at over $150 million, it includes 94 oil paintings, more than 100 watercolors and drawings, and 1,300 graphics, plus posters, photos, sculptures, objets d'art, and a 5,000-volume library on Dalí and surrealism. There also are special exhibits of works by other famous artists.

St. Petersburg Museum of History. 335 2nd Ave. NE. ☎ **727/894-1052.** Admission $5 adults, $4 seniors, $2 children 7–17, free for children 6 and under. Mon–Sat 10am–5pm, Sun 1–5pm.

Located at the foot of The Pier, this museum chronicles St. Petersburg's history with artifacts, documents, clothing, photographs, and computer stations where you can "flip through the past." Walk-through exhibits include a replica of the Benoist airboat, which made the world's first scheduled commercial flight from St. Petersburg in 1914.

The Tampa Bay Holocaust Memorial. 55 5th St. S. (between Central Ave. and 1st St. S.). ☎ **727/820-0100.** Admission $6 adults, $5 seniors. Mon–Fri 10am–4pm, Sat–Sun noon–4pm. Closed Rosh Hashanah, Yom Kippur, and Christmas.

This thought-provoking museum has exhibits about the Holocaust, including a boxcar used to transport human cargo to the Auschwitz death camp in Poland. Its main focus, however, is to promote tolerance and understanding in the present. It was founded by Walter P. Loebenberg, a local businessman who escaped Nazi Germany in 1939, and fought with the U.S. Army in World War II.

OUTDOOR ACTIVITIES & SPECTATOR SPORTS

You can get up-to-the-minute recorded information about the city's sports and recreational activities by calling the **Leisure Line** (☎ 727/893-7500).

BIKING   With miles of flat terrain, the St. Petersburg area is ideal for bikers, in-line skaters, and hikers. The **Pinellas Trail** is especially good, since it follows an abandoned railroad bed 47 miles from St. Petersburg north to Tarpon Springs. The St. Pete trailhead is on 34th Street South (U.S. 19) between 8th and Fairfield avenues south. It's packed on the weekends. Free strip maps of the trail are available at the St. Petersburg Area Chamber of Commerce (see "Visitor Information," above).

It's a long way from the trailhead, but you can rent bikes from **Pierside Rentals** on The Pier (see "Getting Around," above, and "Boat Rentals," below).

BOAT RENTALS   On The Pier, **Pierside Rentals** (☎ 727/363-0000) rents WaveRunners and jet boats. Prices for WaveRunners begin at $45 for an hour; for jet boats, from $55 per 30 minutes. Open daily from 10am to 9pm.

CRUISES   The *Caribbean Queen* (☎ 727/895-BOAT) departs from The Pier and offers 1-hour sightseeing and dolphin-watching cruises around Tampa Bay. Sailings are daily at 1, 3, and 5pm; they cost $10 for adults, $8 for seniors and juniors 12 to 17, $5 for children 3 to 11, and free for children 2 and under.

GOLF   One of the nation's top 50 municipal courses, the **Mangrove Bay Golf Course,** 875 62nd Ave. NE (☎ 727/893-7797), hugs the inlets of Old Tampa Bay and offers 18-hole, par-72 play. Facilities include a driving range; lessons and golf-club rental are also available. Fees are about $22, $32 including a cart in winter, slightly lower off-season. Open daily from 6:30am to 6pm.

The city also operates the challenging, par-3 **Twin Brooks Golf Course,** 3800 22nd Ave. S. (☎ 727/893-7445).

In Largo, the **Bardmoor Golf Club,** 7919 Bardmoor Blvd. (☎ 727/397-0483), is often the venue for major tournaments. Lakes punctuate 17 of the 18 holes on this par-72 championship course. Lessons and rental clubs are available, as is a Tom Fazio–designed practice range. Call the clubhouse for seasonal greens fees. Open daily from 7am to dusk.

Adjacent to the St. Petersburg–Clearwater airport, the **Airco Flite Golf Course,** 3650 Roosevelt Blvd., Clearwater (☎ 727/573-4653), is a championship 18-hole, par-72 course with a driving range. Golf-club rentals are also available. Greens fees including cart range from $25 to $35 in winter, about $20 off-season. Open daily from 7am to 6pm.

Call **Tee Times USA** (☎ 800/374-8633) to reserve times at these and other area courses.

If you want to take up golf or sharpen your game, TV "Golf Doctor" Joe Quinzi hosts his **Quinzi Golf Academy** (☎ 727/725-1999) at the Safety Harbor Resort and Spa (see "Where to Stay," below). His school offers personalized instructions and clinics for up to six players.

SAILING   The **Annapolis Sailing School,** 6800 Sunshine Skyway Lane S. (☎ 800/638-9192 or 727/867-8102), almost at the foot of the Sunshine Skyway bridge, can teach you to sail, or perfect your sailing skills. Various courses are offered at this branch of the famous Maryland-based school, lasting 2, 5, or 8 days. Call for prices and schedules.

The school is based at the **Holiday Inn SunSpree Resort,** 6800 Sunshine Skyway Lane S., St. Petersburg, FL 33711 (☎ **800/227-8045** or 727/867-1151), a recently renovated motel with an expansive bayside pool area.

SPECTATOR SPORTS   St. Petersburg has always been a baseball town, and **Tropicana Field,** a 45,000-seat domed stadium alongside I-175 between 9th and 16th streets south, is the home of the **Tampa Bay Devil Rays,** the area's expansion team that began American League play in 1998. The season runs from April through September. Call ☎ **727/898-RAYS** for schedule and ticket information. The Devil Rays move outdoors to Al Lang Stadium, on 2nd Avenue South at 1st Street South (☎ **727/825-3137**), for their spring-training games from mid-February through March. Tickets to the spring games range from $3 to $12.

The **Philadelphia Phillies** play their spring-training season at Jack Russell Stadium, 800 Phillies Dr., in nearby Clearwater (☎ **727/442-8496**). Admission is $8 to $9. Their minor league **Clearwater Phillies** play in the stadium from April to September. The **Toronto Blue Jays** do their spring thing at Grant Field, 373 Douglas Ave., in nearby Dunedin (☎ **727/733-0429**).

SHOPPING

The Pier, at the end of 2nd Avenue NE (☎ **727/821-6164**), houses more than a dozen boutiques and craft shops, but nearby Beach Drive, running along the waterfront, is one of the most fashionable downtown strolling and shopping venues. Here you'll find the **Glass Canvas Gallery,** at 4th Avenue NE (☎ **727/821-6767**), featuring a dazzling array of glass sculpture, tableware, art, and craft items by 250 local, national, and international artists. Also at 4th Avenue NE, **P. Buckley Moss** (☎ **727/894-2899**), a museum-grade store carrying the works of this artist best known for her portrayal of the Amish and the Mennonites. The works include paintings, graphics, figurines, and collector dolls. **Red Cloud,** between 1st and 2nd avenues (☎ **727/821-5824**), is an oasis for Native American crafts, from jewelry and headdresses to sculpture and art.

Central Avenue is another shopping area, featuring the **Gas Plant Antique Arcade,** between 12th and 13th streets (☎ **727/895-0368**), the largest antique mall on Florida's west coast, with over 100 dealers displaying their wares. The **Florida Craftsmen Gallery,** at 5th Street (☎ **727/821-7391**), is a showcase for the works of more than 150 Florida artisans and craftspeople: jewelry, ceramics, woodwork, fiber works, glassware, paper creations, and metalwork.

In the suburbs, outlet shoppers can browse Corning Revere, Linens 'N Things, BonWorth, Dress Barn, Van Heusen, Bugle Boy, L'eggs, Bass Shoes, T.J. Maxx, and more at the air-conditioned **Bay Area Outlet Mall,** at the intersection of U.S. 19 and East Bay Drive (☎ **727/535-2337**), west of St. Petersburg–Clearwater International Airport.

WHERE TO STAY

Ask the **St. Petersburg Area Chamber of Commerce** (see "Essentials," above) for a copy of its visitors guide, which lists a wide range of hotels, motels, condominiums, and other accommodations.

The **St. Petersburg/Clearwater Area Convention & Visitors Bureau** (see "Essentials," above) publishes a brochure listing members of its Superior Small Lodging program; all with less than 50 rooms, they have been inspected and certified for cleanliness and value. In addition, the Bureau has a free **reservations service** (☎ **800/345-6710**).

You'll find plenty of chain motels along U.S. 19.

With regard to prices, the high season is from January to April. The hotel tax rate in Pinellas County is 11%.

Bay Gables Bed & Breakfast. 136 4th Ave. NE (between Beach Dr. and 1st St. N), St. Petersburg, FL 33701. ☎ **800/822-8803** or 727/822-8855. Fax 727/824-7223. 9 units. A/C TV TEL. Winter $85–$135 double. Off-season $65-$105 double. Rates include continental breakfast. AE, MC, V.

You can walk to The Pier from this charming B&B with wrap-around porches on all three of its stories. Built in the 1930s, it overlooks a flower-filled garden with a gazebo. The guest quarters have been furnished with ceiling fans and Victorian pieces, including a canopy bed in one room. The honeymoon suite is equipped with a large double shower, Jacuzzi, and bidet; the rest have both claw-foot tubs and modern showers in their bathrooms. Half of the rooms open to the porches, while the rest have a separate sitting room and kitchenette. Continental breakfast is served in a restaurant next door. This is a professionally managed operation; the owners don't live on the premises.

✪ **Heritage/Holiday Inn.** 234 3rd Ave. N. (between 2nd and 3rd sts.), St. Petersburg, FL 33701. ☎ **800/283-7829** or 727/822-4814. Fax 727/823-1644. 71 units. A/C TV TEL. $97–$139 double. AE, DC, DISC, MC, V.

No ordinary Holiday Inn, the Heritage dates from the early 1920s and is the closest thing to a Southern mansion you'll find in the heart of downtown. With a sweeping verandah, French doors, and tropical courtyard, it attracts an eclectic clientele, from young families to seniors. The furnishings include period antiques. There's a heated swimming pool and a whirlpool in a small tropical courtyard between the main building and the Heritage Grill restaurant next door. Amenities include limited room service and valet laundry.

Mansion House Bed & Breakfast. 105 5th Ave. NE (at 1st St. N.), St. Petersburg, FL 33701. ☎ **800/274-7520** or 727/821-9391. Fax same as phone. www.mansionbandb.com. 10 units (all with bathroom). A/C TV TEL. Winter $110–$165 double. Off-season $95–$150 double. Rates include full breakfast. AE, MC, V.

Mirror images of each other, these two arts-and-crafts-style houses separated by a landscaped courtyard were built in 1904 and 1912 by a local doctor (one house served as his office). The comfortable living room in the main house, which has 6 of the 10 units here, opens to a sunroom, off which a small screened porch provides mosquito-free lounging and the only place where guests can smoke. Both houses have upstairs front parlors with TVs, VCRs, and libraries. Tall, old-fashioned windows let lots of light into the attractive guest rooms, in which some furniture has been decorated by a local artist. The "Pembrooke" room actually is upstairs over the carriage house; it has its own refrigerator, phone, TV, and four-poster bed with mosquito net. In an unusual architectural twist, the "Harlech" room has a toilet and hand basin in one converted closet, a shower in another. Proprietors Rob and Rosie Ray serve a full breakfast in two formal dining rooms and keep fruit bowls and snacks available at all hours in both houses. There's a whirlpool bath in its own screened hut in the backyard.

✪ **Renaissance Vinoy Resort.** 501 5th Ave. NE (at Beach Dr.), St. Petersburg, FL 33701. ☎ **800/HOTELS-1** or 727/894-1000. Fax 727/822-2785. 360 units. A/C MINIBAR TV TEL. Winter $269–$299 double. Off-season $149–$269 double. AE, DC, DISC, MC, V. Self-parking $5; valet parking $12.

Built as the Vinoy Park in 1925, during Florida's heyday of grand hotels, this elegant Spanish-style establishment reopened in 1992 after a total and meticulous $93 million restoration that has made it more luxurious than ever. Dominating the northern part of downtown, it overlooks Tampa Bay and is within walking distance of The Pier, Central Avenue, museums, and other attractions. All the guest rooms, many of which enjoy lovely views of the bay front, are designed to offer the utmost in comfort and include three phones, an additional TV in the bathroom, hair dryer, bath scales, and more; some units in the new wing also have whirlpools and private patios/balconies.

Dining/Diversions: Marchand's Grille, an elegant, Mediterranean-style room overlooking the bay, serves the best steaks, seafood, and chops in town. The Terrace Room is the main dining room for breakfast, lunch, and dinner. Casual lunches and dinners are available at the indoor-outdoor Alfresco, near the pool deck, and at the Clubhouse at the golf course on Snell Isle. There are also two bar/lounges.

Amenities: Concierge, 24-hour room service, laundry service, tour desk, child care, complimentary coffee and newspaper with wake-up call. Two swimming pools (connected by a roaring waterfall), 14-court tennis complex (11 lighted), 18-hole private championship golf course on nearby Snell Isle, private 74-slip marina, two croquet courts, fitness center (with sauna, steam room, spa, massage, and exercise equipment), access to two bay-side beaches, shuttle service to gulf beaches, hair salon, gift shop.

St. Petersburg Bayfront Hilton. 333 1st St. S. (between 3rd and 4th aves. S., opposite Al Lang Field), St. Petersburg, FL 33701. ☎ **800/HILTONS** or 727/894-5000. Fax 727/823-4797. 333 units. A/C TV TEL. Winter $159 double. Off-season $119 double. Packages available. AE, DC, MC, V.

This 15-story convention hotel has a spacious lobby with a rich decor of marble, tile, and potted trees and plants. The bedrooms are furnished with traditional dark woods, floral fabrics, a king-size bed or two double beds, and an executive desk; many have views of the bay. Cafe 333 is a full-service restaurant specializing in continental cuisine, while the First Street Deli provides light fare and Pizza Hut pies. Brandi's Lobby Bar has piano entertainment. Facilities include an outdoor heated swimming pool, whirlpool, health club with a sauna, and gift shop.

A NEARBY SPA

✪ **Safety Harbor Resort and Spa.** 105 N. Bayshore Dr., Safety Harbor, FL 34695. ☎ **888/BEST-SPA** or 727/726-1161. Fax 727/726-4268. www.southseas.com. 193 units. Winter $169–189 double. Off-season $99–$169 double. Packages available. AE, DC, DISC, MC, V. Free self-parking; valet parking $4. Pets up to 30 pounds accepted with nonrefundable deposit.

Hernando de Soto thought he had found Ponce de Léon's fabled Fountain of Youth when he happened upon five mineral springs here on the shores of Old Tampa Bay in 1539. You won't get your youth back at this venerable spa, which has been in operation since 1926, and got a face-lift in 1998, but you are in for some serious pampering, from massages to hydrotherapy and a full menu of fitness classes from boxing to yoga. The springs enable the spa to offer acclaimed water-fitness programs. This is also a good place to work on your games at the Quinzi Golf Academy (see "Outdoor Activities & Spectator Sports," above) and the Phil Green Tennis Academy. The sprawling complex of beige stucco buildings with Spanish tile roofs sits on 22 waterfront acres in the sleepy town of Safety Harbor, north of St. Petersburg. Moss-draped Safety Harbor has a charming, small-town ambiance, with a number of shops and restaurants just outside the spa's entrance.

Dining: Nutritious menus emphasizing American fusion cuisine use lots of Florida ingredients in both the Spa Dining Room and the resort's cafe, which is open to the public for lunch and dinner.

Amenities: Concierge, limited room service, valet laundry, guest laundry, valet parking, Clarins Skin Institute, 50,000-square-foot spa and fitness center, 3 heated pools, 9 lighted tennis courts, bike rentals, business center, beauty salon, boutiques.

WHERE TO DINE

Don't overlook the food court at **The Pier,** where the inexpensive chow is accompanied by a very rich, but quite free, view of the bay. Among The Pier's restaurants is a branch of Tampa's famous Columbia (☎ **727/822-8000;** see "Where to Dine" in section 3, above).

Apropos. 300 2nd Ave. NE (at Bayshore Dr.). ☎ **727/823-8934.** Reservations accepted only for dinner. Breakfast $3.50–$6; lunch $5–$9; dinner main courses $14–$21. AE, DC, MC, V. Tues–Sat 7:30–10:30am and 11am–2pm, Thurs–Sun 6–10:30pm (Sun brunch 8:30am–2pm). AMERICAN.

Sitting at the foot of The Pier, Apropros is a fine place to breakfast before your tour of downtown, perhaps with a brie and bacon omelet, or a seasonal fruit plate, or just plain eggs. At lunch, the view through the masts in the adjacent marina sets the scene for the likes of shrimp and artichoke salad with a sherry mayonnaise dressing. At night, the scene changes to linen tablecloths, bow-tied waiters, and a menu of fine nouvelle American cuisine. You'll find as many locals here as tourists.

✪ Fourth Street Shrimp Store. 1006 4th St. N. (at 10th Ave. N.). ☎ **727/822-0325.** Reservations not accepted. Sandwiches $2.50–$6; main courses $4–$12. MC, V. Sun–Thurs 11am–9pm, Fri–Sat 11am–10pm. SEAFOOD.

If you're anywhere in the area, you should at least drive by to see the colorful, cartoonlike mural on the outside of this eclectic establishment just north of downtown. On first impression it looks like graffiti, but it's actually a gigantic drawing of people eating. Inside, it gets even better, with paraphernalia and murals on two walls making the dining room seem like a warehouse with windows looking out on an early-19th-century seaport (one painted sailor permanently peers in to see what you're eating). You'll pass a seafood market counter when you enter, from which comes the fresh namesake shrimp, the star here. You can also pick from grouper, clam strips, catfish, or oysters fried, broiled, or steamed, all served in heaping portions. This is the best and certainly the most interesting bargain in town.

Garden Bistro. 217 Central Ave. (between 2nd and 3rd sts.). ☎ **727/896-3800.** Reservations recommended for dinner. Main courses $11–$17. AE, DISC, MC, V. Daily noon–2am. MEDITERRANEAN.

This lively restaurant combines European ambiance with Moroccan cuisine. Choice seats are under huge shade trees in the garden, screened from the street by a trellis fence. Inside, the decor blends the American Southwest with the Mediterranean, with arches, a 19th-century tiled floor, modern local art, and lots of flowers and plants. The creative menu features couscous, a daily tajin (a traditional Moroccan stew), pastas such as wild mushrooms with strips of roast duck, and smoked salmon in a light cream sauce. On Friday and Saturday, live jazz adds to the ambiance from 9pm to 1am.

Keystone Club. 320 4th St. N. (between 3rd and 4th aves. N.). ☎ **727/822-6600.** Reservations recommended. Main courses $11–$23; early bird specials $7.50–$12. AE, DC, DISC, MC, V. Mon–Fri 11am–2:30pm and 5–10pm, Sat 4–10pm, Sun 4–9pm. Early bird specials winter only, Mon–Fri 4:30–5:30pm, Sat–Sun 4–5:30pm. STEAKS/PRIME RIB.

Resembling an exclusive men's club, this cozy restaurant's forest-green walls accented by dark wood and etched glass create an atmosphere that's reminiscent of a Manhattan-style chophouse. But women are also welcome to partake of the beef, which is king here. Specialties include roast prime rib, New York strip steak, and filet mignon. Seafood also makes an appearance, with fresh lobster and grouper at market price. During winter, "sunset" early bird specials include lunch-size portions, a beverage, and dessert.

The Moon Under Water. 332 Beach Dr. (between 3rd and 4th sts.). ☎ **727/896-6160.** Reservations not accepted. Sandwiches and salads $6–$8; main courses $8–$16. AE, DC, DISC, MC, V. Sun–Thurs 11:30am–9:30pm, Fri–Sat 11:30am–10pm. AMERICAN/INDIAN.

The British raj rules supreme at this pub facing the bayfront park. You can choose a table on the verandah out front, or inside the darkly paneled dining room with a host of slowly twirling fans hung from the ceiling and a plethora of colonial artifacts along the walls, including obligatory pith helmets. The menu covers a number of former British outposts, including America (grilled steak and pork chops), but the emphasis here is on mild, medium, or blazing hot Indian curries—with a recommended wine or cold Irish, British, or Australian beer to cool the tastebuds. For lighter fare, consider specialty salads served in a tortilla basket, or perhaps mid-eastern taboule. Served until 5pm, lunch includes burgers, sandwiches, beef pastry turnovers, and spicy, pizzalike *bombayli*, made with Indian *nan* bread. There's entertainment Friday and Saturday evenings.

ST. PETERSBURG AFTER DARK

Good sources of nightlife information are in the Friday "Weekend" section of the *St. Petersburg Times*, the "Baylife" and "Friday Extra" sections of the *Tampa Tribune*, and the *Weekly Planet*, a tabloid available at the visitor information offices and in many hotel and restaurant lobbies. The bimonthly magazine *Event Guide Tampa Bay* gives a rundown on what's going on.

PERFORMING ARTS VENUES   Tropicana Field, 1 Stadium Dr. (☎ 727/ 825-3100), has a capacity of 50,000 for major concerts, but also hosts a variety of smaller events when the Devil Rays aren't playing baseball.

The **Bayfront Center,** 400 1st St. S. (☎ 727/892-5767, or 727/892-5700 for recorded information), houses the 8,100-seat Bayfront Arena, and the 2,000-seat Mahaffey Theater. The schedule includes a variety of concerts, Broadway shows, big bands, ice shows, and circus performances.

THE CLUB & MUSIC SCENE   A historic attraction as well as an entertainment venue, the Moorish-style **Coliseum Ballroom,** 535 4th Ave. N. (☎ 727/ 892-5202), has been hosting dancing, big bands, boxing, and other events since 1924 (it even made an appearance in the 1985 movie *Cocoon*). An acquaintance of mine said it's fun to watch the town's many seniors doing the jitterbug just like it was 1945 again! Call for the schedule and prices.

A much younger set heads to the casual, downtown **Big Catch,** 9 1st St. NE (☎ 727/821-6444), featuring live and danceable rock and Top 40 hits, as well as darts, pool, and hoops. North of downtown, the **Ringside Cafe,** 2742 4th St. N. (☎ 727/894-8465), in a renovated boxing gymnasium, is an informal neighborhood cafe with a decided sports motif. The music focuses on jazz and blues (and sometimes reggae).

THE ST. PETE & CLEARWATER BEACHES

If you're looking for sun and sand, you'll find plenty of both on the 28 miles of slim barrier islands that skirt the gulf shore of the Pinellas Peninsula. With some

Accommodations:
Beach Haven 16
Belleview Biltmore
  Resort & Spa 1
Best Western Sea
  Stone Resort 27
Captain's Quarters Inn 8
Clearwater Beach Hotel 21
Days Inn Island
  Beach Resort 11
Don CeSar Beach
  Resort and Spa 17
Great Heron Inn 4
Island's End Resort 19
Palm Pavilion Inn 20
Pelican—East & West 2
Radisson Suite Resort
  on Sand Key 29
Sheraton Sand Key
  Resort 28
Sun West Beach Motel 26
TradeWinds Resort 15
TradeWinds Sandpiper
  Beach Resort 13
Travelodge St. Pete
  Beach 9

Dining:
Bob Heilman's
  Beachcomber 23
Bobby's Bistro
  & Wine Bar 24
Crabby Bill's 14
Frenchy's Cafe 22
Guppy's 3
Hurricane 18
Internet Outpost 10
Lobster Pot 6
Seafood & Sunsets
  at Julie's 25
Scandia 5
Skidder's 12
The Wine Cellar 7

1 million visitors coming here every year, don't be surprised if you have lots of company. But you'll also discover quieter neighborhoods geared to families, and this area has some of the nation's finest beaches, which are protected from development by parks and nature preserves.

At the southern end of the strip, St. Pete Beach is the granddaddy of the area's resorts. In fact, visitors started coming here nearly a century ago, and they haven't quit. Today St. Pete Beach is heavily developed and often overcrowded during the winter season. If you like high-rises and mile-a-minute action, St. Pete Beach is for you. But even here, Pass-a-Grille, on the island's southern end, is a quiet residential enclave with eclectic shops and a fine public beach.

A more genteel lifestyle begins just to the north on 3½-mile-long Treasure Island. From there, you cross famous John's Pass to Sand Key, a 12-mile island occupied by primarily residential Madeira Beach, Redington Beach, North Redington Beach, Redington Shores, Indian Shores, Indian Rocks Beach, and Belleair Beach. Finally the road crosses a soaring bridge to Clearwater Beach, whose silky sands attract active families and couples.

If you like your great outdoors unfettered by development, the jewels here are Fort Desoto Park, down below St. Pete Beach at the mouth of Tampa Bay, and Caladesi Island State Park, north of Clearwater Beach. They are consistently rated among America's top beaches. And Sand Key Park, looking at Clearwater Beach from the southern shores of Little Pass, is one of Florida's finest local beach parks.

ESSENTIALS

GETTING THERE   To reach St. Pete and Treasure Island from I-275, take Exit 4 and follow the Pinellas Bayway (Fla. 682) west (50¢ toll). For Indian Rocks Beach, take Exit 18 and follow Ulmerton Road due west to the gulf. For the Redington beaches, take Exit 15 and follow Gandy and Park boulevards (Fla. 694) due west (Park Boulevard is also known as 74th Avenue North). For Clearwater Beach, take the Courteney Campbell Causeway (Fla. 60) west from Tampa; the causeway becomes Gulf-to-Bay Boulevard (also Fla. 60), which leads straight west into Clearwater.

VISITOR INFORMATION   See "Visitor Information" in section 4 for the St. Petersburg/Clearwater Area Convention & Visitors Bureau and the St. Petersburg Area Chamber of Commerce. You can get information specific to the beaches from the **Gulf Beaches of Tampa Bay Chamber of Commerce,** 6990 Gulf Blvd. (at 70th Avenue), St. Pete Beach, FL 33706 (☎ **800/944-1847** or 727/360-6957; fax 727/360-2233). The main office is open Monday to Friday from 9am to 5pm. The chamber also has welcome centers at 501 150th Ave. in Madeira Beach (☎ 727/391-7373); on Walsingham Road just east of Gulf Boulevard in Indian Rocks Beach (☎ 727/595-4575); and at 152 108th Ave. in Treasure Island (☎ 727/367-4529).

For advance information about Clearwater Beach, contact the **Greater Clearwater Chamber of Commerce,** 128 N. Osceola Ave. (P.O. Box 2457), Clearwater, FL 34615 (☎ **727/461-0011**). You can also walk into the beaches' branch of the city-operated **Clearwater Tourist Information Center,** on Causeway Boulevard in the Clearwater Beach Marina Building lobby (☎ **727/462-6531**). It's open daily in winter from 9am to 5pm, off-season Monday to Saturday from 9am to 5pm, Sunday from 1 to 5pm.

GETTING AROUND   **BATS City Transit** (☎ **727/367-3086**) offers bus service along the St. Pete Beach strip. The fare is $1.

Treasure Island Transit System (☎ 727/547-4575) runs buses along the Treasure Island strip. The fare is $1.

The **Jolley Trolley** (☎ 727/445-1200), operated in conjunction with the City of Clearwater, provides service in the Clearwater Beach area, from downtown to the beaches as far south as Sand Key. The ride costs 50¢ per person, 25¢ for seniors.

Along the beach, the major cab company is **BATS Taxi** (☎ 727/367-3702).

HITTING THE BEACH

This entire stretch of coast is one long beach, but since hotels, condominiums, and private homes occupy much of it, you may want to sun and swim at one of the area's public parks. The very best are described below, but there's also the fine **Pass-a-Grille Public Beach,** on the southern end of St. Pete Beach, where you can watch the boats going in and out of Pass-a-Grille Channel. This and all other Pinellas County public beaches have metered parking lots, so bring a supply of quarters.

Clearwater Public Beach (also known as Pier 60) has beach volleyball, watersports rentals, lifeguards, rest rooms, showers, and concessions. The swimming is excellent, and there's a children's playground and a pier for fishing. Gated municipal parking lots here cost $1 per hour or $7 a day. The lots are right across the street from Clearwater Beach Marina, a prime base for boating, cruises, and other waterborne activities (see "Outdoor Activities," below).

✪ **CALADESI ISLAND STATE PARK**   Occupying a 3½ -mile island north of Clearwater Beach, Caladesi Island State Park boasts one of Florida's top beaches, a lovely, relatively secluded stretch with fine soft sand edged in sea grass and palmettos. Dolphins cavort in the waters offshore. In the park itself, there's a nature trail, and you might see one of the rattlesnakes, black racers, raccoons, armadillos, or rabbits that live here. A concession stand, ranger station, and bathhouses (with rest rooms and showers) are available. Caladesi Island is accessible only by ferry from Honeymoon Island State Recreation Area, which is connected by Causeway Boulevard (Fla. 586) to Dunedin, north of Clearwater. You'll first have to pay the admission to Honeymoon Island: $4 per vehicle with two to eight occupants, $2 per single-occupant vehicle, $1 for pedestrians and bicyclists. Beginning daily at 10am, the ferry departs Honeymoon Island every hour on winter weekdays, every 30 minutes on summer weekdays, and every 30 minutes on weekends year-round. Rides cost $6 for adults and $3.50 for kids. The two parks are open daily from 8am to sunset. The two islands are administered by Gulf Islands Geopark, no. 1 Causeway Blvd., Dunedin, FL 34698 (☎ 727/469-5942).

Dolphin Encounter, the concessionaire that operates the Honeymoon-Caladesi ferry (☎ 737/442-7433), also has cruises to Caladesi Island from Clearwater Beach, usually on Wednesday and Fridays from 10:30am to 5:30pm. These cost $24.30 for adults, $20.55 for children, including lunch. Call for reservations.

✪ **FORT DESOTO PARK**   South of St. Pete Beach at the very mouth of Tampa Bay, this group of five connected barrier islands has been set aside by Pinellas County as a 900-acre bird, animal, and plant sanctuary. Besides the stunning white-sugar sand beach (where you can watch the manatees and dolphins play offshore), there's a Spanish American War–era fort, great fishing from piers, large playgrounds for kids, and 4 miles of trails winding through the park for in-line skaters, bicyclists, and joggers.

Sitting on an island by themselves, the park's 230 campsites all have water and electricity hookups, but they are usually sold out, especially on weekends. Sites cost $18.76 a night. To make reservations, you must appear in person and pay for your site no more than 30 days in advance at the campground office, at 631 Chestnut St. in Clearwater, or at 150 5th St. North in downtown St. Petersburg. You must camp here at least 2 nights, but you can stay no more than 14 nights. The park is open from 8am to dusk, although campers and persons fishing from the piers can stay later. Admission is free. To get here, take the Pinellas Bayway (50¢ toll) east from St. Pete Beach and follow Fla. 679 (35¢ toll) and the signs south to the park. For more information, contact the park at 3500 Pinellas Bayway, Tierra Verde, FL 33715 (☎ **727/582-2267**).

SAND KEY PARK   This fine county park on the northern tip of Sand Key facing Clearwater Beach sports a wide beach and gentle surf and is relatively off the beaten path in this commercial area. It's great to get out of the hotel for a morning walk or jog here. Open 8am to dark. Admission is free, but the parking lot has meters. For more information, call ☎ **727/464-3347**.

OUTDOOR ACTIVITIES

BICYCLING & IN-LINE SKATING   With miles of flat terrain and paved roads, the beach area is ideal for bikers and in-line skaters, and the 47-mile-long Pinellas Trail runs close by on the mainland (see "Outdoor Activities & Spectator Sports," under St. Petersburg, above). In St. Pete Beach, you can rent bicycles, skates, and scooters from **Beach Cyclist Sports Center,** 7517 Blind Pass Rd. (☎ **727/ 367-5001**). In Clearwater Beach, contact **Transportation Station,** 652 Gulfview Blvd. (☎ **727/443-3188**). Bikes at all three range from about $5 per hour to $20 a day; scooters, about $13 an hour to $40 per day.

BOATING, FISHING & OTHER WATER SPORTS   You can indulge in para-sailing, boating, deep-sea fishing, wave running, sightseeing, dolphin watching, waterskiing, and just about any other waterborne diversion your heart could desire here. All you have to do is head to one of two beach locations: **Hubbard's Marina,** at John's Pass Village and Boardwalk (☎ **727/393-1947**), in Madeira Beach on the southern tip of Sand Key; or **Clearwater Beach Marina,** at Coronado Drive and Causeway Boulevard (☎ **800/772-4479** or 727/461-3133), which is at the beach end of the causeway leading to downtown Clearwater. Agents in booths there will give you the schedules and prices, answer any questions you have, and make reservations if necessary. Go in the early morning to set up today's activities, or in the afternoon to book tomorrow's.

CRUISES   Several boats cruise from John's Pass Village and Clearwater Beach Marina to undeveloped barrier islands, with dolphin viewing on the way out and back.

The largest operator is **Hubbard's Sea Adventures,** based at John's Pass Village and Boardwalk in Madeira Beach (☎ **727/398-6577**). It offers a 2-hour dolphin-watching excursion, Monday to Saturday from 10am to noon, 1 to 3pm, and 4 to 6pm (1 to 3pm on Sunday), at $15 for adults, $7.50 for kids under 12. A 6-hour trip goes to lovely **Shell Key,** one of Florida's last completely undeveloped barrier islands. Shell Key is great for bird-watchers; there are a remarkable 88 different species, including some of North America's rarest shorebirds. These trips usually depart at 10:30am Monday, Tuesday, and Saturday, for $25 adults, $13 kids. You can rent beach chairs, umbrellas, snorkeling gear, and other equipment once you get there. A third cruise goes to **Egmont Key State Park,** on historic Egmont Key at the mouth of Tampa Bay. This uninhabited island is the site of a lighthouse, the now-crumbling Fort Dade (built in 1900 during the Spanish American War but abandoned long ago), and some threatened gopher tortoises. Sea turtles come ashore here to nest. You can go snorkeling and shelling here, so bring your swimsuit (snorkeling gear is available for $5 per person). This cruise leaves at 10:30am Tuesday, Friday, and Sunday and costs $30 for adults, $20 for children. A barbecue lunch on either Shell or Egmont keys costs $7 for adults, $5 for kids. Call to confirm the schedule and make reservations, which are recommended.

The **Shell Key Shuttle,** Merry Pier, on Pass-a-Grille Way at the eastern end of 8th Avenue in southern St. Pete Beach (☎ **727/360-1348**), uses a 57-passenger catamaran to shuttle out to Shell Island. Boats leave daily at 10am, noon, and 2pm. Prices are $12 for adults, $6 for children 12 and under. The ride takes 15 minutes, and you can return on any shuttle you wish.

The most unusual outings here are with **Captain Memo's Pirate Cruise,** at Clearwater Beach Marina (☎ **727/446-2587**), which sails the *Pirate's Ransom,* a reproduction of a pirate ship, on 2-hour daytime "pirate cruises" as well as sunset and evening champagne cruises. Cruises operate year-round, daily at 10am and 2, 4:30, and 7pm. For adults, daytime or sunset cruises cost $27; evening cruises, $30; both daytime and evening cruises cost $20 for seniors and juniors 13 to 17, $17 for children 2 to 12, free for children under 2.

Two paddle-wheel riverboats operate here: The *Show Queen* has lunch, sunset dinner, and Sunday brunch cruises from Clearwater Beach Marina (☎ **727/461-3113**). The *Starlite Princess* does likewise from 3400 Pasadena Ave. S. (☎ **727/462-2628**), at the eastern side of the Corey Causeway linking St. Pete Beach to the mainland. Call for schedules and prices.

ATTRACTIONS ON LAND

Clearwater Marine Aquarium. 249 Windward Passage, Clearwater. ☎ **888/239-9414** or 727/447-0980. Admission $6.75 adults, $4.25 children 3–11, free for children 2 and under. Mon–Fri 9am–5pm, Sat 9am–4pm, Sun 11am–4pm. The aquarium is off the causeway between Clearwater and Clearwater Beach; follow the signs.

This little jewel of an aquarium on Clearwater Harbor is very low-key and friendly; it's dedicated to the rescue and rehabilitation of marine mammals and sea turtles. Exhibits include dolphins, otters, sea turtles, sharks, stingrays, mangroves, and sea grass.

✪ **John's Pass Village and Boardwalk.** 12901 Gulf Blvd. (at John's Pass), Madeira Beach. ☎ **800/944-1847** or 727/397-1511. Free admission. Shops and activities daily 9am–6pm or later.

Casual and charming, this Old Florida fishing village on John's Pass consists of a string of simple wooden structures topped by tin roofs and connected by a 1,000-foot boardwalk. Most of the buildings have been converted into shops, art galleries, restaurants, and saloons. The focal point is the boardwalk and marina, where many water sports are available for visitors (see "Outdoor Activities," above).

✪ **Suncoast Seabird Sanctuary.** 18328 Gulf Blvd., Indian Shores. ☎ **727/391-6211.** Free admission, donations welcome. Daily 9am–dusk. Free tours Wed and Sun 2pm.

At any one time there are usually more than 500 sea and land birds living at the sanctuary, from cormorants, white herons, and birds of prey to the ubiquitous brown pelican. The nation's largest wild-bird hospital, dedicated to the rescue, repair, recuperation, and release of sick and injured wild birds, is also here.

SHOPPING

In addition to being a sightseeing attraction here, **John's Pass Village and Boardwalk,** on John's Pass in Madeira Beach, just north of Treasure Island (☎ **727/391-7373**), is the key shopping venue on the beaches. The houses of this old, fishermen's village have been converted into more than 60 shops selling everything from antiques and beachwear to every souvenir you can imagine. There are also several art galleries, including the **Bronze Lady** (☎ **727/398-5994**), featuring the world's collection of works by the late comedian-artist Red Skelton, best known for his numerous clown paintings. The shops here are open daily from 9am to 6pm or later.

If you're in the market for some one-of-a-kind hand-hammered jewelry, try **Evander Preston Contemporary Jewelry,** 106 8th Ave., Pass-a-Grille (☎ **727/ 367-7894**), a unique gallery/workshop housed in a 75-year-old building in Pass-a-Grille's 1-block-long 8th Avenue business district. Check out the golden miniature train with diamond headlight (it's not for sale). Open Monday to Saturday from 10am to 5:30pm.

Among the shops in St. Pete Beach's Corey Landings Area, the town's original business strip along 75th Street east of Gulf Boulevard, **The Shell Store** (☎ **727/ 360-0586**) specializes in corals and shells, with an on-premises mini-museum illustrating how they live and grow. There's a good selection of shell home decorations, shell hobbyist supplies, shell art, planters, and jewelry. Open Monday to Saturday from 9:30am to 5pm.

On the mainland in Clearwater, the **Senior Citizen Craft Center Gift Shop,** 940 Court St. (☎ **727/442-4266**), is one of the area's most unique gift shops—an outlet for the work of some 400 local senior citizens. You'll find knitwear, crochet work, woodwork, stained glass, clocks, scrimshaw, jewelry, pottery, tile work, ceramics, and hand-painted clothing. It's off-the-beaten tourist track but well worth a visit. It's open Monday to Friday from 10am to 4pm, but it's staffed by volunteers, so call ahead.

WHERE TO STAY

St. Pete Beach and Clearwater Beach have national chain hotels and motels of every name and description. For even more choices, the **St. Petersburg Area Chamber of Commerce** lists a wide range of hotels, motels, condominiums, and other accommodations in its annual visitor guide, and it publishes a brochure listing all members of its Superior Small Lodgings Program (see "Essentials" in section 4). You can also use the St. Petersburg/Clearwater Convention & Visitors Bureau's free **reservations service** (☎ **800/345-6710**).

As is the case throughout Florida, there are at least as many rental condominiums here as there are hotel rooms. Many of them are in high-rise buildings right on the beach. Among several local rental agents: **Excell Vacation Condos,** 14955 Gulf Blvd., Madeira Beach, FL 33708 (☎ **800/733-4004** or 727/391-5512; fax 727/393-8885; www.islandtime.com/vacation) and **JC Resort Management,** 17200 Gulf Blvd., North Redington Beach, FL 33708 (☎ **800/535-7776** or 727/397-0441; fax 727/397-8894; www.jcresort.com) have many from which to choose. **Resort Rentals,** 9524 Blind Pass Rd., St. Pete Beach, FL 33707 (☎ **800/ 293-3979** or 727/363-3336; fax 727/360-5086; www.resort-realty.com), specializes in luxury rental homes.

With regard to prices, high season runs from January to April. Ask about special discounted packages in the summer. Any time of year, though, it's wise to make reservations early. The hotel tax in Pinellas County is 11%.

St. Pete Beach Area

✪ **Beach Haven.** 4980 Gulf Blvd. (at 50th Ave.), St. Pete Beach, FL 33706. ☎ **727/ 367-8642.** Fax 727/360-8202. E-mail: jzpag@aol.com. 18 units. A/C TV TEL. Winter $75–$125 double. Off-season $50–$108 double. MC, V.

Nestled on the beach between two high-rise condos, these low-slung, pink-with-white-trim structures look from the outside like the early 1950s motel they once were. But Jone and Millard Gamble (they also own the charming Island's End Resort, see below) have replaced the innards and installed bright tile floors, vertical blinds, pastel tropical furniture, and many modern amenities, including TVs, VCRs, refrigerators, and coffeemakers. Five of the original quarters remain as motel rooms (with shower-only bathrooms), but the Gambles linked the others to make 12 one-bedroom and one two-bedroom units. The top choice is the one-bedroom unit with sliding glass doors opening to a deck shaded by a sprawling Brazilian pepper tree. There's an outdoor heated pool surrounded by a white picket fence, plus a sunning deck with lounge furniture by the beach. You don't get maid service on Sunday or holidays, and the rooms and baths are 1950s smallish, but every unit here is bright, airy, and comfortable. Complimentary coffee and tea are served to all guests 2 days a week, and guests can use barbecue grills and a coin laundry. This is the heart of the hotel district, so lots of restaurants are just steps away.

Captain's Quarters Inn. 10035 Gulf Blvd. (between 100th and 101st aves.), Treasure Island, FL 33706. ☎ **800/526-9547** or 727/360-1659. Fax 727/363-3074. 8 units, 1 cottage. A/C TV TEL. Winter $70–$100 double. Off-season $55–$75 double. Weekly rates available. MC, V. Pets accepted at extra charge.

Purchased in 1998 by Britishers Nick and Deborah Russell, this nautically themed property offers well-kept accommodations on the gulf at inland rates. All but one of the units are huddled along 100 yards of beach, an ideal vantage point for sunset-watching. Six units are efficiencies (two of them on the beach) with minikitchens including microwave oven, coffeemaker, and wet bar or sink. There's also a bay-side cottage with separate bedroom and a full kitchen. Facilities include an outdoor solar-heated freshwater swimming pool, a sundeck, guest barbecues, and a library.

Days Inn Island Beach Resort. 6200 Gulf Blvd. (at 62nd Ave.), St. Pete Beach, FL 33706. ☎ **800/544-4222** or 727/367-1902. Fax 727/367-4422. 102 units. A/C TV TEL. Winter $118–$148 double. Off-season $78–$108 double. AE, DC, DISC, MC, V.

Two long, gray buildings flank a courtyard with heated swimming pool at this beachside property popular with young families. Furnished in dark woods and rich tones, most of the guest rooms have picture-window views of the courtyard. All units have refrigerators and coffeemakers, and about half have kitchenettes. Inside the building, Players Bar & Grille has sports TVs, pizzas, pub fare, and free hot snacks from noon to 7pm daily. Outside, Jimmy B.'s beach bar is a fine place for a sunset cocktail (happy hour runs from noon to 7:30pm) and evening entertainment, including beachside bonfires on Saturdays in winter. Facilities include two outdoor heated swimming pools, volleyball, horseshoes, shuffleboard, and a game room.

✪ Don CeSar Beach Resort and Spa. 3400 Gulf Blvd. (at 34th Ave./Pinellas Bayway), St. Pete Beach, FL 33706. ☎ **800/282-1116,** 800/637-7200, or 727/360-1881. Fax 727/367-6952. www.media.don-cesar.com. 345 units. A/C MINIBAR TV TEL. Winter $289–$369 double; $359–$784 suite. Off-season $184–$314 double; $244–$709 suite. Packages available. AE, DC, MC, V. Parking $10.

Dating from 1928, and listed on the National Register of Historic Places, this Moorish-style "Pink Palace" tropical getaway is so romantic you may bump into six or seven honeymooning couples in one weekend. Sitting majestically on 7½ acres of beachfront, the landmark sports a lobby of classic high windows and archways, crystal chandeliers, marble floors, and original artworks. Most rooms have high ceilings and offer views of the gulf or Boca Ciega Bay. In addition to the 275 rooms under the minarets of the original building (some of these may seem rather small by today's standards), the resort has 70 spacious luxury condos in The Don CeSar Beach House, a midrise building ¾ mile to the north (there's complimentary transportation between the two). The service is good, although the front desk can get a bit overwhelmed when groups are checking in.

Dining/Diversions: The pricey but intimate Maritana Grille can't be beat for fresh gourmet seafood and caviar, if your budget can afford a serious splurge. Other outlets include the King Charles Restaurant (offering a sumptuous Sunday brunch), the Sea Porch Cafe for indoor or outdoor dining by the pool and beach, the Lobby Bar, two beachside bars, and an ice-cream parlor.

Amenities: Concierge, 24-hour room service, valet parking, laundry, newspaper delivery, in-room massage, business services, complimentary coffee in lobby, baby-sitting, children's program. Beach, two outdoor heated swimming pools, whirlpool, exercise room, sauna, steam room, volleyball, gift shops, rentals for water-sports equipment, hairdresser, shopping arcade with upscale jewelers and men's and women's resort wear.

✪ **Island's End Resort.** 1 Pass-a-Grille Way (at 1st Ave.), St. Pete Beach, FL 33706. ☎ **727/360-5023.** Fax 727/367-7890. www.stpetebeach.com/islandsend. E-mail: jzgpag@aol.com. 6 units. A/C TV TEL. Dec 15 to June 1 $82–$175 cottage. Off-season $61–$175 cottage. Weekly rates available. MC, V.

A wonderful respite from the maddening crowd, and a great bargain to boot, this little all-cottage hideaway sits right on the southern tip of St. Pete Beach, smackdab on Pass-a-Grille, where the Gulf of Mexico meets Tampa Bay. You can step from the six contemporary cottages right onto the beach. And since the island curves sharply here, nothing blocks your view of the emerald bay. Strong currents run through the pass, however, but you can safely swim in the gulf or grab a brilliant sunset at the Pass-a-Grille public beach, just one door removed. Linked to each other by boardwalks, the comfortable one- or three-bedroom cottages have dining areas, living rooms, VCRs, and kitchens; the one three-bedroom unit also has its own private beachside pool. You can meet your fellow guests at complimentary continental breakfasts served under a gazebo Tuesday, Thursday, and Saturday mornings (you can squeeze your own oranges). Facilities include a fishing dock, patios, decks, barbecues, and hammocks. Owners Jone and Millard Gamble are no fools: They live at this shady, idyllic setting.

TradeWinds Sandpiper Beach Resort. 6000 Gulf Blvd. (at 60th Ave.), St. Pete Beach, FL 33706. ☎ **800/237-0707** or 727/562-1212. Fax 727/562-1222. 159 units. A/C TV TEL. Winter $155–$207 double; $235–$299 suite. Off-season $115–$147 double; $157–$199 suite. Packages available. AE, DC, DISC, MC, V.

Right on the beach, this employee-owned sister of the TradeWinds Resort (see below) has two six-story chevron-shaped wings, both set back from the main road. The beach wing is more expensive but much more desirable. Decorated with light woods, pastel tones, and touches of rattan, most units here have coffeemakers, toasters, small refrigerators, dishwashers, and wet bars. Suites also have a living area with sofa bed. *But note:* None of the units here has a patio or balcony.

Dining: Piper's Patio is a casual poolside cafe with indoor/outdoor seating, and the Sand Bar offers frozen drinks, snacks, and fine sunsets by the pool.

Amenities: Concierge, room service, valet laundry, newspaper delivery, in-room massage, children's activities program, baby-sitting, beachfront heated swimming pool, another heated swimming pool in its own greenhouse, fitness center, volleyball, shuffleboard, game room, gift shop/general store.

✪ **TradeWinds Resort.** 5500 Gulf Blvd. (at 55th Ave.), St. Pete Beach, FL 33706. ☎ **800/237-0707** or 727/562-1212. Fax 727/562-1222. 577 units. A/C TV TEL. Winter $199–$309 double; $295–$569 suite. Off-season $140–$221 double; $185–$399 suite. Packages available. AE, DC, DISC, MC, V. Free self-parking; valet parking $3–$6.

Don't be dismayed by the outward appearance of this six- and seven-story, concrete-and-steel monstrosity, for underneath and beside it runs a maze of brick walkways, patios, and lily ponds connected by a quarter mile of streams. It all gives surprising charm to this employee-owned hotel. The guest units, which look out on the gulf or the 18 acres of grounds, have up-to-date kitchens or kitchenettes, contemporary furnishings, and private balconies. The children's program and summer packages are a big hit with families from around the world, attracting lots of Europeans.

Dining/Diversions: The top spot for lunch or dinner is the Palm Court, with an Italian-bistro atmosphere; for dinner, there's also Bermudas, a casual family spot. Other food outlets include the Fountain Square Deli, Pizza Hut, and Tropic Treats. Bars include Reflections piano lounge; B. R. Cuda's, with live entertainment and dancing; and the Flying Bridge, a Florida cracker-house-style beachside bar floating on one of the lily ponds.

Amenities: With the employees having a stake in the profits as well as the tips, you should get good service here. Room service, valet parking, laundry, baby-sitting, children's program. Four heated swimming pools, whirlpools, sauna, fitness center, four tennis courts, racquetball, croquet, water-sports rentals, gas grills, guest laundry, gift shops, full-service hair salon with massage and tanning.

Travelodge St. Pete Beach. 6300 Gulf Blvd. (at 63rd Ave.), St. Pete Beach, FL 33706. ☎ **800/237-8918** or 727/367-2711. Fax 727/367-7068. 200 units. A/C TV TEL. Winter $99–$131 double. Off-season $75–$119 double. Efficiencies $10 more. AE, DC, DISC, MC, V.

Formerly the Colonial Gateway Inn, this U-shaped beachfront complex of one- and two-story units is a favorite with families. The rooms, most of which face the pool and a central landscaped courtyard, are contemporary, with light woods and beach tones. About half the units are efficiencies with kitchenettes.

On the premises is a branch of the very good Shells seafood restaurant (see "Where to Dine," in section 3). An indoor lounge and a beach bar offer light refreshments. Facilities include an outdoor heated swimming pool with an expansive concrete deck, a kiddie pool, shuffleboard, and a game room. The water-sports shack here offers parasailing equipment rentals and also services the Days Inn Island Beach Resort next door (see above).

Indian Rocks Beach Area

Great Heron Inn. 68 Gulf Blvd. (south of 1st Ave.), Indian Rocks Beach, FL 33785. ☎ **727/595-2589.** Fax 727/596-7309. www.llc.net/~heroninn. E-mail: heroninn@llc.net. 16 units. A/C TV TEL. Winter $85–$88 double. Off-season $59–$63 double. Weekly and monthly rates available. DISC, MC, V. Hotel is 4 blocks south of Fla. 688.

A real heron named Harry patrols the beach at this family-oriented motel owned and operated by transplanted Michiganders Ralph and Teena Hickerson. It sits at the narrowest section of Indian Rocks Beach, facing the gulf on one side and its own Intracoastal Waterway dock on the other. The buildings flank a central courtyard, with a heated pool, which opens to the beach. The rooms offer modern furnishings and Berber carpets, and each unit has a full kitchen and dining area. Facilities include coin-operated laundry and picnic tables. There's a boat dock across the boulevard.

✪ **Pelican—East & West.** 108 21st Ave. (at Gulf Blvd.), Indian Rocks Beach, FL 33785. ☎ **727/595-9741.** Fax 727/596-4170. 8 units. A/C TV. Winter $50–$75 double. Off-season $45–$65 double. Weekly rates available. MC, V.

"PDIP" (Perfect Day in Paradise) is the motto at Mike and Carol McGlaughlin's motel complex, which offers a choice of two settings. Their lowest rates are at

Pelican East, in a residential setting 500 feet from the beach, where four suites each have a bedroom and a separate kitchen. You'll pay more at Pelican West, but it's directly on the beachfront. The four beachside apartments each have a living room, bedroom, kitchen, patio, and unbeatable views of the gulf. You don't get phones in your rooms here or a swimming pool to splash around in, but it's clean and modern in all other respects. There's no restaurant on the premises, either, but Guppy's is 4 blocks away (see "Where to Dine," below).

Clearwater Beach

Best Western Sea Stone Resort. 445 Hamden Dr. (at Coronado Dr.), Clearwater Beach, FL 33767. ☎ **800/444-1919,** 800/528-1234, or 727/441-1722. Fax 727/449-1580. 106 units. A/C TV TEL. Winter $103–$201 double. Off-season $72–$140 double. AE, DC, DISC, MC, V.

Located just across the street from the beach in Clearwater's busy south end, the Sea Stone Suites is a six-story building of classic Key West–style architecture containing 43 one-bedroom suites, each with a kitchenette and a living room. Their living room windows look across external walkways to the harbor. A few steps away, the older five-story Gulfview Wing offers 65 bedrooms. The furnishings are bright and airy, with pastel tones, light woods, and sea scenes on the walls. The on-site Marker 5 Restaurant serves breakfast only. There's valet laundry service, newspaper delivery, and complimentary coffee in the lobby. Facilities include a heated outdoor swimming pool, whirlpool, boat dock, coin-operated laundry, and meeting rooms.

✪ **Clearwater Beach Hotel.** 500 Mandalay Ave. (at Baymont St.), Clearwater Beach, FL 33767. ☎ **800/292-2295** or 727/441-2425. Fax 727/449-2083. 157 units. A/C TV TEL. Winter $109–$249 double. Off-season $98–$118 double. AE, DC, MC, V.

Besides the great beach location, you'll enjoy easy access to many nearby shops and restaurants from this Old Florida–style hotel. It's been owned and operated by the same family for more than 40 years and attracts an older clientele. Directly on the gulf, the complex consists of a six-story main building and two- and three-story wings. Rooms and rates vary according to location—bay view or gulf view, poolside or beachfront. Some rooms have balconies. The dining room is romantic at sunset and offers great views of the gulf, while the nautically themed lounge has entertainment nightly. A bar provides snacks and libations beside an outdoor heated swimming pool. There's limited room service, valet laundry and parking, newspaper delivery, and in-room massage.

Palm Pavilion Inn. 18 Bay Esplanade (at Mandalay Ave.), Clearwater Beach, FL 33767. ☎ **800/433-PALM** or 727/446-6777. 28 units. A/C TV TEL. Winter $82–$117 double. Off-season $56–$81 double. AE, DISC, MC, V.

Just north of the tourist area, this three-story walk-up beachfront spot is removed from the bustle yet within easy walking distance of all the action. The three-story art deco building is artfully trimmed in peach and teal. The lobby area and guest rooms, also art deco in design, feature rounded light-wood and rattan furnishings, bright sea-toned fabrics, photographs from the 1920s to 1950s era, and vertical blinds. Entered from internal corridors (no balconies or patios here), rooms in the west side of the house face the gulf, while those in the east face the bay. Four efficiencies have kitchenettes. Facilities include a rooftop sundeck, beach access, heated swimming pool, complimentary coffee, and beach chair and umbrella rentals. By the beach, the Palm Pavilion Grill & Bar is a fine place to catch the sunset and some live entertainment Tuesday to Sunday nights during winter, and on weekends off-season. Lighted tennis courts and an athletic center are across the street.

✪ **Radisson Suite Resort on Sand Key.** 1201 Gulf Blvd., Clearwater Beach, FL 33767. ☎ **800/333-3333** or 727/596-1100. Fax 727/595-4292. 220 units. A/C MINIBAR TV TEL. $239–$289 suite. AE, DC, DISC, MC, V.

You'll see the beauty of Sand Key from the suites in this boomerang-shaped, 10-story hotel overlooking Clearwater Bay. The gulf is just beyond a row of high-rise condos across the street, and beautiful Sand Key Park is a few steps away. The whole family will enjoy exploring the adjacent boardwalk with 25 shops and restaurants. Each suite has a bedroom with a balcony offering water views, as well as a complete living room with a sofa bed, wet bar, entertainment unit, coffeemaker, and microwave oven. Like the Sheraton Sand Key across the boulevard (see below), this Radisson gets many European guests during the summer months, so there's negligible fluctuation in room rates during the year.

Dining/Diversions: The Harbor Grille offers fresh seafood, steaks, and grand bay views. The Harbor Lounge has live entertainment. In a clapboard, shingle-roof building out by the pool, Kokomo's serves light fare and tropical drinks.

Amenities: Room service, laundry, free trolley to the beach, year-round children's activities program at "Lisa's Klubhouse," free valet parking, masseuse. Bay-side outdoor heated swimming pool with rock waterfall and bar, sundeck, sauna, exercise room, guest laundry, and waterfront boardwalk with a variety of shops and restaurants.

Sheraton Sand Key Resort. 1160 Gulf Blvd., Clearwater Beach, FL 33767. ☎ **800/325-3535** or 727/595-1611. Fax 727/596-8488. 390 units. A/C TV TEL. Winter $170–$220 double. Off-season $109 –$170 double. AE, DC, DISC, MC, V.

Away from the honky-tonk of Clearwater, this nine-story hotel on 10 acres next to Sand Key Park is a big favorite with water-sports enthusiasts and groups. It also gets lots of European guests year-round. The guest rooms here all have dark-wood furniture, coffeemakers, hair dryers, and a balcony or patio with views of the gulf or the bay.

Rusty's Restaurant serves breakfast and dinner; for lighter fare, try the Island Café, the Sundeck, or Fast Johnny's Poolside Snack Bar. The Snack Store is open 24 hours.

Amenities include limited room service, newspaper delivery, in-room massage, valet parking, laundry, baby-sitting, children's program (summer only), beachside outdoor heated swimming pool, fitness center, whirlpool, three lighted tennis courts, beach volleyball, newsstand, game room, children's pool, playground, water-sports rentals, 24-hour general store.

✪ **Sun West Beach Motel.** 409 Hamden Dr. (at Bayside Dr.), Clearwater Beach, FL 33767. ☎ **727/442-5008.** Fax 727/461-1395. www.clearwaterbeach.com/SUNWEST/sunwest. E-mail: sunwest@gte.net. 14 units. A/C TV TEL. $40–$61 double; $48–$79 efficiency. MC, V.

Sitting among several small motels a 2-block walk from the beach, John and Pat Joniec's one-story establishment dates from 1954, but it's well-maintained, overlooks the bay, and has a fishing/boating dock, a heated bayside pool and sundeck, a shuffleboard court, and guest laundry. All units, which face either the bay, the pool, or the sundeck, have contemporary resort-style furnishings. The four motel rooms have small refrigerators, the 10 efficiencies have kitchens, and a few units have separate bedrooms.

Two Nearby Golf Resorts

Belleview Biltmore Resort & Spa. 25 Belleview Blvd. (P.O. Box 2317), Clearwater, FL 33757. ☎ **800/237-8947** or 727/442-6171. Fax 727/441-4173 or 727/443-6361. 240 units. A/C MINIBAR TV TEL. Winter $190–$210 double; $260–$450 suite. Off-season $150–$190 double; $220–$430 suite. AE, DC, DISC, MC, V. Resort is 1 mile south of downtown on Belleview Rd., off Alt. U.S. 19.

The Gulf Coast's oldest operating luxury tourist hotel, this gabled clapboard structure was built in 1896 by Henry B. Plant as the Hotel Belleview to attract customers to his Orange Belt Railroad. On a bluff overlooking the bay, it's the largest occupied wooden structure in the world. Today it attracts mostly groups and serious golfers (guests can play at the adjoining Belleview Country Club, an 18-hole par-72 championship course), but there's no denying its Victorian charm and old-fashioned ambiance—once you get past the out-of-place, glass-and-steel foyer added by more recent owners. Historic tours are given daily at 11am ($5 for adults, $3 for children 13 to 17, free for kids under 13). The creaky hallways lead to several shops and a museum explaining the hotel's history. Large, high-ceilinged guest rooms are decorated in Queen Anne style, with dark-wood period furniture.

Dining/Diversions: The informal indoor/outdoor Terrace Café provides breakfast, lunch, or dinner. There's also a pub in the basement, a lounge, and a poolside bar.

Amenities: Room service, dry cleaning and valet laundry, nightly turndown on request, currency exchange, baby-sitting. Four red-clay tennis courts; indoor and outdoor heated swimming pools (one with a waterfall); whirlpool; spa with sauna, Swiss showers, workout gym; jogging and walking trails; bicycle rentals; yacht charters; gift shops; newsstand; golf privileges at the country club.

✪ **The Westin Innisbrook Resort.** 36750 U.S. 19 (P.O. Box 1088), Tarpon Springs, FL 34688. ☎ **800/456-2000** or 727/942-2000. Fax 727/942-5577. 900 units. Winter $260–$585 double. Off-season $190–$340 double. Golf packages available. AE, DC, DISC, MC, V.

Golf Digest, Golf magazine, and others pick this as one of the country's best places to play (provided you stay here, of course). Situated off U.S. 19 between Palm Harbor and Tarpon Springs, this 1,000-acre resort has 90 holes on championship courses that are more like the rolling links of the Carolinas than the usually flat courses found in Florida. The most famous course, the Copperhead, hosts the JC Penney Classic, a major stop on the PGA circuit, the first weekend in December. Innisbrook has the largest resort-owned and -operated golf school in North America. The resort also boasts 11 clay and 4 Laykold tennis courts. There's even a children's program to take care of the kids. The spacious quarters actually are privately owned homes, and apartments, spread all over the premises, so there are no focal points here except the building where you check in, and the golf and tennis clubhouses.

WHERE TO DINE

St. Pete Beach and Clearwater Beach both have a wide selection of national chain fast-food and family restaurants along their main drags.

St. Pete Beach Area

✪ **Crabby Bill's.** 5100 Gulf Blvd. (at 51st Ave.), St. Pete Beach. ☎ **727/360-8858.** Reservations not accepted. Sandwiches $4–$6; main courses $6–$18. AE, MC, V. Mon–Thurs 11:30am–10pm, Fri–Sat 11:30am–11pm, Sun noon–10pm. SEAFOOD.

Offering the least expensive gulf-side dining here, this member of a small local chain sits right on the beach in the heart of the hotel district. It's a great place to bring the kids, especially after 5:30pm Tuesday, when they eat free and are entertained by games and contests. There's a rooftop tiki bar and a small alfresco area off one of the two bars here, but big glass windows enclose the large dining room. They offer fine water views from picnic tables equipped with rolls of paper towels and buckets of saltine crackers, the better to eat the Alaskan, snow, golden, and stone crabs that are the big draws here. The crustaceans fall into the moderate price category, but most other main courses, such as fried clam strips or a combo broiled fish platter, are inexpensive. The creamy smoked fish spread is a delicious appetizer, and you'll get enough to whet the appetites of at least two persons for just $4.

Hurricane. 807 Gulf Way (at 9th Ave.), Pass-a-Grille. ☎ **727/360-9558.** Reservations not accepted. Salads and sandwiches $2.50–$9; main courses $8–$16. AE, MC, V. Daily 8am–1am (breakfast Mon–Fri 8–11am, Sat–Sun 8am–noon). SEAFOOD.

A longtime institution across the street from Pass-a-Grille Public Beach, this three-level gray Victorian building with white gingerbread trim is a great place to toast the sunset, especially on the rooftop. It's more beach bar than fine restaurant, but the grouper sandwiches are a big hit, and there's always fresh fish to be broiled or fried and shrimp and crab to be steamed. Downstairs you can dine inside the knotty-pine paneled dining room or on the sidewalk terrace, where bathers from across Gulf Way are welcome (there's a walk-up bar for beach libation). The second floor dining area also has seating on a wrap-around verandah, and up on the roof, the Hurricane Watch adds great sunset views. The joint jumps at night when the second level turns into a virtual dance hall.

Internet Outpost Cafe. 7400 Gulf Blvd. (at Corey Ave./75th Ave.), St. Pete Beach. ☎ **727/360-7806.** Reservations not accepted. Coffee and pastries $1–$3; sandwiches $3.50–$5.50. AE, MC, V. Mon–Thurs 10am–10pm, Fri–Sat 10am–midnight. PASTRIES/SANDWICHES.

If you left your laptop at home and can't stand not getting your e-mail or surfing the Net any longer, head for this cozy coffee emporium with nine computer termi-nals, all with fast connections to the Internet ($2 for 15 minutes access time). You can also lounge on the sofas and wing chairs while sipping your caffeine, kill a rainy afternoon playing chess, or listen to live music on Friday and Saturday evenings. In addition to coffees, teas, and pastries available all hours, the lunch fare (11am to 2pm) includes freshly made chicken salad, as well as Cuban, spicy turkey, and other sandwiches.

Skidder's Restaurant. 5799 Gulf Blvd. (at 60th Ave.), St. Pete Beach. ☎ **727/360-1029.** Reservations not accepted. Breakfast $3–$6; sandwiches and burgers $3.50–$8; pizza $5.50–$16; main courses $7.50–$15. AE, DC, DISC, MC, V. Daily 7am–11pm. ITALIAN/GREEK/AMERICAN.

A local favorite, this inexpensive family restaurant in the hotel district offers a full range of breakfast fare plus pizzas (available to eat here or carry out), burgers and sandwiches, big salads, gyro and souvlaki platters, and Italian-style veal and chicken dishes (sautéed in wine with artichokes is a house specialty). Divided by cut-glass panels, the dining room has ceiling fans rotating over gray tables and booths. A chil-dren's menu features burgers and spaghetti.

Indian Rocks Beach Area

You'll find a bay-front edition of **Shells,** the fine and inexpensive local seafood chain, opposite the Lobster Pot on Gulf Boulevard at 178th Avenue in Redington Shores (☎ **813/393-8990**). See "Where to Dine," in section 3, for more informa-tion about Shells' menu and prices, which are the same at all branches.

✪ **Guppy's.** 1701 Gulf Blvd. (at 17th Ave.), Indian Rocks Beach. ☎ **813/593-2032.** Reser-vations not accepted. Sandwiches $5–$7; main courses $9–$20. AE, DC, DISC, MC, V. Sun–Thurs 11:30am–10:30pm; Fri–Sat 11:30am–11pm. SEAFOOD.

Locals love this small bar and grill across from Indian Rocks Public Beach because they know they'll always get terrific chow (it's associated with the excellent Lobster Pot, mentioned below). You won't soon forget the salmon coated with potatoes and lightly fried to brown, then baked with a creamy leek and garlic sauce; it's fattening, yes, but also a bargain at $9. Another good choice is lightly cooked tuna (only slightly more done than sushi) finished with a peppercorn sauce. The atmosphere is casual beach friendly, with a fun bar in the rear. The famous upside-down apple-walnut pie topped with ice cream will require a little extra work on the weights tomorrow. You can dine outside on a patio beside the main road.

✪ **Lobster Pot.** 17814 Gulf Blvd. (at 178th Ave.), Redington Shores. ☎ 727/391-8592. www.beachdirectory.com. Reservations recommended. Main courses $14.50–$29.50. AE, DC, MC, V. Mon–Thurs 4:30–10pm, Fri–Sat 4:30–11pm, Sun 4–10pm. SEAFOOD.

Step into this weathered-looking restaurant near the beach and owner Eugen Fuhrmann will tell you to get ready to experience the finest seafood in the area. The prices are high, but the variety of lobster dishes is amazing. The lobster américaine is flambéed in brandy with garlic, and the bouillabaisse is as authentic as any you'd find in the south of France. In addition to lobster, there's a wide selection of grouper, snapper, salmon, swordfish, shrimp, scallops, crab, and Dover sole, pre-pared simply or with elaborate sauces. There's no ordinary children's menu here: It features half a main lobster and a petite filet mignon.

Scandia. 19829 Gulf Blvd. (between 198th and 199th aves.), Indian Shores. ☎ 727/595-5525. Reservations accepted. Main courses $6–$20. Early-bird specials $6–$8. DISC, MC, V. Tues–Sat 11:30am–9pm, Sun noon–8pm. Early-bird specials Mon–Fri 4–6pm. Closed Sept. SCANDINAVIAN.

Unique in decor and menu in these parts, this chalet-style restaurant in the northern fringes of Indian Shores brings a touch of Hans Christian Andersen to the beach strip. The menu offers Scandinavian favorites, from smoked salmon and pickled herring to roast pork, sausages, schnitzels, and Danish lobster tails. There are also a few international dishes such as curried chicken, North Sea flounder, Canadian scallops, Boston scrod, and shrimp and grouper from gulf waters.

✪ **Wine Cellar.** 17307 Gulf Blvd. (at 173rd Ave.), North Redington Beach. ☎ 727/393-3491. Reservations recommended. Main courses $15–$26. Five-course sampler $35. AE, DC, MC, V. Tues–Sat 4:30–11pm, Sun 4–11pm. CONTINENTAL.

Every evening during the high season and on weekends all year, the cars pack the parking lot at this restaurant, which is highly popular with locals and visitors alike. You'll find an assortment of divided dining rooms with lots of wine racks and casks. The cuisine offers the best of Europe and the States. Start off with garlicky peppered shrimp in dry vermouth, move on to a fresh North Carolina rainbow trout in butter and pecans, and top it all off with chocolate velvet torte. There's music and dancing in the lounge on Thursday, Friday, and Saturday evenings and jazz on Sunday.

Clearwater Beach

✪ **Bob Heilman's Beachcomber.** 447 Mandalay Ave. (at Papaya St.). ☎ 727/442-4144. Reservations recommended. Main courses $12–$27. AE, DC, DISC, MC, V. Mon–Sat 11:30am–11pm, Sun noon–10pm. AMERICAN.

In a row of restaurants, bars, and T-shirt shops, Bob and Sherri Heilman's estab-lishment has been popular with the locals since 1948. Each dining room here has its own special theme: large model sailing crafts making one seem nautical, a pianist making music in a second, works of art creating a gallery in a third, and booths and a fireplace making for a cozy fourth. The menu presents a variety of fresh seafood, beef, veal, and lamb selections. If you tire of fruits-of-the-sea, the "back-to-the-farm" fried chicken—from an original 1910 Heilman family recipe—is incredible. The Beachcomber shares an extensive wine collection with Bobby's Bistro & Wine Bar (see below).

Bobby's Bistro & Wine Bar. 447 Mandalay Ave. (at Papaya St., behind Bob Heilman's Beachcomber). ☎ **727/446-9463.** Reservations not accepted. Sandwiches and pizzas $6–$10; main courses $10–$16. AE, DC, DISC, MC, V. Daily 5pm–midnight. AMERICAN.

Bob and Sherri Heilman opened this dark, very urban bistro behind their popular restaurant in 1993, and it's been a local hit ever since. The wine-cellar theme is amply justified by the real thing: a walk-in closet with several thousand bottles kept at a constant 55°F. Walk through and pick your vintage, then listen to jazz while you dine inside at tall bar-height tables or outside on a covered patio. The chef specializes in gourmet pizzas on homemade focaccia crust (as a tasty appetizer), plus charcoal-grilled veal chops, filet mignon, fresh fish, and monstrous pork chops with caramelized Granny Smith apples and a Mount Vernon mustard sauce. Everything's served a la carte here, so watch your credit card. On the other hand, there's an affordable sandwich menu featuring the likes of bronzed grouper and chicken with a spicy Jack cheese.

Frenchy's Cafe. 41 Baymont St. ☎ **727/446-3607.** Reservations not accepted. Sandwiches and burgers $4–$7. AE, MC, V. Mon–Thurs 11:30am–11pm, Fri–Sat 11:30am–midnight, Sun noon–11pm. SEAFOOD.

Always popular with locals and visitors in the know, this casual pub makes the best grouper sandwiches in the area and has all the awards to prove it. They're fresh, thick, juicy, and delicious. The atmosphere is pure Florida casual style, and there's usually a wait during winter, on weekends all year.

For more casual fare directly on the beach, **Frenchy's Rockaway Grill,** at 7 Rockaway St. (☎ **727/446-4844**), has a wonderful outdoor setting.

✪ **Seafood & Sunsets at Julie's.** 351 S. Gulfview Blvd. (at 5th St.), Clearwater Beach. ☎ **727/441-2548.** Reservations not accepted. Salads and sandwiches $5–$8; main courses $8–$22. AE, MC, V. Daily 11am–10pm. SEAFOOD.

A Key West–style tradition takes over Julie Nichols' place at dusk as both locals and visitors gather at sidewalk tables or in the tiny, rustic upstairs bar to toast the sunset over the beach across the street. The predominately seafood menu features fine renditions of charcoal-broiled mahimahi with sour cream, Parmesan and herb sauce; bacon-wrapped barbecued shrimp on a skewer; broiled, fried, or blackened fresh Florida grouper; and flounder stuffed with crabmeat. Everything is cooked to order here, so come prepared to linger over a cold drink.

THE BEACHES AFTER DARK

If you haven't already found it during your sightseeing and shopping excursions, the restored fishing community of **John's Pass Village and Boardwalk,** on Gulf Boulevard at John's Pass in Madeira Beach, has plenty of restaurants, bars, and shops to keep you occupied after the sun sets. Elsewhere, the nightlife scene at the beach revolves around rocking bars that pump out the music until 2am.

Down south in Pass-a-Grille, there's the popular, always lively lounge in **Hurricane,** on Gulf Way at 9th Avenue opposite the public beach (see "Where to Dine," above).

On Treasure Island, **Beach Nutts,** on West Gulf Boulevard at 96th Ave. (☎ 727/367-7427), is perched atop a stilt foundation like a wooden beach cottage on the Gulf of Mexico. The music ranges from Top 40 to reggae and rock. **Manhattans,** Gulf Boulevard at 116th Avenue (☎ 727/363-1500), offers a variety of live music, from country to contemporary and classic rock. Up on the northern tip of Treasure Island, **Gators on the Pass** (☎ 727/367-8951) claims to have the world's longest waterfront bar, with a huge deck overlooking the waters of John's

Pass. The complex also includes a nonsmoking sports bar and a three-story tower with a top-level observation deck for panoramic views of the Gulf of Mexico. There's live music, from acoustic and blues to rock, most nights.

In Clearwater Beach, the **Palm Pavilion Grill & Bar,** on the beach at 18 Bay Esplanade (☎ **727/446-6777**), has live music Tuesday through Sunday nights during winter, on weekends off-season. Nearby, **Frenchy's Rockaway Grill,** at 7 Rockaway St. (☎ **727/446-4844**), is another popular hangout.

If you're into laughs, **Coconuts Comedy Club,** at the Howard Johnson motel, Gulf Boulevard at 61st Avenue in St. Pete Beach (☎ **727/360-5653**), has an ever-changing program of live stand-up funny men and women. Call for the schedule, performers, and prices.

For a more highbrow evening, go to the Clearwater mainland and the 2,200-seat **Ruth Eckerd Hall,** 1111 McMullen-Booth Rd. (☎ **727/791-7400**), which hosts a varied program of Broadway shows, ballet, drama, symphonic works, popular music, jazz, and country music.

Appendix A:
Orlando in Depth

1 History 101, or How a Sleepy Southern Town Met a Mighty Mouse

Outsiders, weaned on orange juice commercials and mouse tales, might think the history of the region could be condensed into three terse sentences: (1) There were orange groves. (2) Walt Disney came. (3) You can buy three T-shirts for $10. There is, however, considerably more juice to be squeezed from the story. The modern metropolis of Orlando began as a rough-and-tumble Florida frontier town, where early voters were lured to the polling booths by the promise of a good barbecue dinner.

SETTLERS VS. SEMINOLES: THE ROAD TO STATEHOOD

Florida history dates back to 1513—more than a century before the Pilgrims landed at Plymouth Rock—when Ponce de León, in search of the fabled "fountain of youth," spied the beaches and lush greenery of Florida's Atlantic coast. He named it La Florida—"the Flowery Land." After years of alternating Spanish, French, and British rule, the territory was ceded (by Spain) to the United States in 1821. Lost in the international shuffle were the Seminole Indians, who after migrating from Georgia and the Carolinas in the late 18th century to some of Florida's richest farmlands, were viewed by the Americans as an obstacle to white settlement. A series of compromise treaties and violent

Dateline

- **1843** Mosquito County in central Florida is renamed Orange County.
- **1856** Orlando becomes the official seat of Orange County.
- **1875** Orlando is officially incorporated as a municipality under state law.
- **1880** The South Florida Railroad facilitates the expansion of Orlando's agricultural markets.
- **1884** Fire rages out of control, destroying much of Orlando's fledgling business district.
- **1894–95** Freezing temperatures destroy 2 years of citrus crops and wreck orchards. Many growers lose everything.
- **1910–25** A land boom hits Florida. Fortunes are made overnight.
- **1926** The land boom goes bust. Fortunes are lost overnight.
- **1929** An invasion of Mediterranean fruit flies devastates Orlando's citrus industry. Its ruined economy is capped by the stock market crash.
- **1939–45** World War II revives Orlando's ailing economy. The city becomes "Florida's Air Capital."

continues

- **1964** Walt Disney begins surreptitiously buying up central Florida farmland, purchasing more than 28,000 acres at a cost of nearly $5.5 million.
- **1965** Disney announces his plan to build the world's most spectacular theme park in Orlando.
- **1971** The Magic Kingdom opens its gates.
- **1972** A new 1-day attendance mark is set on December 27, when 72,328 people visit the Magic Kingdom. It will be broken almost every year thereafter.
- **1973** Shamu ventures into Orlando waters. Sea World opens.
- **1979** Mickey Mouse welcomes the Magic Kingdom's 100-millionth visitor, 8-year-old Kurt Miller from Kingsville, Maryland.
- **1982** Epcot opens to the public with vast hoopla. Participating celebrities include everyone from Richard Nixon to George Steinbrenner.
- **1989** WDW launches Disney–MGM Studios Theme Park (offering a behind-the-scenes look at Tinseltown), Typhoon Lagoon (a 56-acre water theme park), and Pleasure Island (an adult-nightclub theme park).
- **1990** Universal Studios opens, offering visitors thrilling encounters with E.T. and King Kong.
- **1993** Sea World continues a major expansion. Universal Studios unleashes the fearsome *Jaws*.
- **1998** Disney starts its own cruise line, and opens most of Animal Kingdom. Universal Studios Escape opens CityWalk, a vast new entertainment complex. Disney's West Side, the West

continues

clashes between settlers and the Seminoles continued through 1832, when a young warrior named Osceola strode up to the bargaining table, slammed his knife into the papers on it, and, pointing to the quivering blade, proclaimed, "The only treaty I will ever make is this!"

But, even with such a dramatic agreement, the struggle continued. Guerrilla warfare thwarted the U.S. army's attempt to remove the Seminoles for almost 8 years, during which time many of the resisters drifted south into the interior of central Florida. In what is today the Orlando area—on a small, triangular parcel of land formed by Lake Gatlin, Lake Gem Mary, and Lake Jennie Jewell near what is now downtown Orlando—the white settlers built Fort Gatlin in 1838 to offer protection to pioneer homesteaders. The Seminoles kept up a fierce rebellion until 1842, when, undefeated, they accepted a treaty whereby their remaining numbers (about 300) were given land and left in peace. The same year, the Armed Occupation Act offered 160 acres to any pioneer willing to settle here for a minimum of 5 years. The land was fertile: Wild turkeys and deer abounded in the woods, grazing land for cattle was equally plentiful, and dozens of lakes provided fish for settlers and water for livestock. In 1843, what had been Mosquito County was more invitingly renamed Orange County. And with the Seminoles more or less out of the way (though sporadic cattle rustling and bloody uprisings still occurred), the Territorial General Legislature petitioned Congress for statehood. On March 3, 1845, President John Tyler signed a bill making Florida the 27th state in the Union.

Settlements and statehood notwithstanding, at the middle of the 19th century, the Orlando area (then named Jernigan for one of its first settler families) consisted largely of pristine lakes and pine-forested wilderness. There were no roads, and you could ride all day (if you could find a trail) without meeting a soul. The Jernigans successfully raised cattle, and their home and stockade, which was granted a post office in 1850, became a way stop for travelers and the seat of future development. In 1856, the boundaries of Orange County were revised, and, thanks to the manipulations of resident James Gamble Speer, a member of the Indian Removal Commission, Fort Gatlin (Jernigan) became its official seat.

How the fledgling town came to be named Orlando is a matter of some speculation. Some say Speer renamed the town after a dearly loved friend, whereas other sources say he named it after his favorite Shakespearean character in *As You Like It*. But the most accepted version is that the town was named for plantation owner Orlando Reeves (or Rees), whose homestead had been burned out in a skirmish. For years, it was thought a marker discovered near the shores of Lake Eola, in what is now downtown, marked his grave. But Reeves died later, in South Carolina. It's assumed the name carved in the tree was a marker for others who were on the Indians' trail. Whatever the origin, Orlando was officially recognized by the U.S. Postmaster in 1857.

Side combined with Pleasure Island and Disney Village Marketplace, becomes known as Downtown Disney.

- **1999** Islands of Adventure, Universal Studios' second theme park, opens, featuring stomach-churning thrill rides tied to baby boomer faves such as Dr. Seuss and Spiderman. The final section of Animal Kingdom, Asia, opens.

THE 1860s: CIVIL WAR/CATTLE WARS Throughout the early 1860s, cotton plantations and cattle ranches became the hallmarks of central Florida. Orlando was ringed by a vast cotton empire. Log cabins went up along the lakes, and the pioneers eked out a somewhat lonely existence, separated from each other by miles of farmland. But there were troubles brewing in the 31-state nation that would soon devastate Orlando's planters. By 1859, it was obvious that only a war would resolve the slavery issue. In 1861, Florida became the third state to secede from the Union, and the modest progress it had achieved came to a standstill. The Stars and Bars flew from every flagpole, and local men enlisted in the Confederate army, leaving the fledgling town in poverty. A federal blockade made it difficult to obtain necessities, and many slaves fled. In 1866, the Confederate troops of Florida surrendered, the remaining slaves were freed, and a ragtag group of defeated soldiers returned to Orlando. They found a dying cotton industry, unable to function without slave labor or transport to markets. In 1868, Florida was readmitted to the Union.

Its untended cotton fields having gone to seed, Orlando now concentrated on cattle ranching, a business heavily taxed by the occupation government, and one that ushered in an era of lawlessness and violence. A famous battle involving two families, the Barbers and the Mizells, left at least nine men dead in 2 months, in a Florida version of the Hatfields and the McCoys.

Like frontier cattle towns out West, post–Civil War Orlando was short on civilized behavior. Gunfights, brawls, and murders were commonplace. But as the 1860s drew to a close, large-herd owners from other parts of the state moved into the area and began organizing the industry in a less chaotic fashion. Branding and penning greatly reduced rustling, though they never totally eliminated the problem. Even a century later—as recently as 1973— soaring beef prices caused a rash of cattle thievery. Some traditions die hard. Even today, an Orange County Sheriff's unit still investigates a number of cattle rustling incidents each year.

Fun Fact

Legend has it that Florida's citrus industry has its roots in seeds spit onto the ground by Ponce de León and his followers as they traversed the state searching for the Fountain of Youth. The seeds supposedly germinated in the wild amidst the rich Florida soil.

AN ORANGE TREE GROWS IN ORLANDO   In the 1870s, articles in national magazines began luring large numbers of Americans to central Florida with promises of arable land and a warm climate. In Orlando, public roads, schools, and churches sprang up to serve the newcomers, many of whom replanted defunct cotton fields with citrus groves. Orlando was officially incorporated under state law in 1875, and definitive boundaries, and a city government, were set up.

New settlers poured in from all over the country, businesses flourished, and by the end of the year the town had its first newspaper, the *Orange County Reporter.* The first locomotive of the South Florida Railroad chugged into town in 1880, sparking a building and land boom—the first of many. Orlando got sidewalks and its first bank in 1883—the same year the town voted itself "dry" in hopes of averting the fistfights and brawls that ensued when cowboys crowded into local saloons every Saturday night for some rowdy R&R. For many years the city continued to vote itself alternately wet and dry, but in actuality it made very little difference. Legal or not, liquor was always readily available.

FIRE & ICE   In January 1884, a grocery fire that started at 4am wiped out blocks of businesses, including the offices of the *Orange County Reporter.* But 19th-century Orlando was a bit like a Frank Capra movie. The town rallied 'round, providing a new location for the paper and presenting its publisher, Mahlon Gore, with $1,200 in cash to help defray losses, and $300 in new subscriptions. The paper not only survived, but flourished. And the city, realizing the need, created its first fire brigade. By August 1884, a census revealed that the population had grown to 1,666. That same year, 600,000 boxes of oranges were shipped from Florida to points north— most of those boxes originating in Orlando. By 1885, Orlando was a viable town, boasting as many as 50 businesses. This is not to say it was New York. Razorback hogs roamed the streets, and alligator wrestling was a major form of entertainment.

Disaster struck a week after Christmas in 1894, when the temperature plummeted to an unseasonable 24°F. Water pipes burst, and orange blossoms froze, blackened, and died. The freeze continued for 3 days, wrecking the citrus crop for the entire year.

Many grove owners went bust, and those who remained were hit with a second devastating freeze the following year. Tens of thousands of trees died in the killing frost. Small growers were wiped out, but large conglomerates that could afford to buy up the small growers' properties at bargain prices, and to wait for new groves to mature, assured the survival of the industry.

SPECULATION FEVER: GOOD DEALS, BAD DEALS . . .   As Orlando entered the 20th century, citrus and agriculture had surpassed cattle ranching as the mainstay of the local economy. Stray cows no longer had to be shooed from the railway tracks. Streets were being paved, and electricity and telephone service installed. The population at the turn of the century was 2,481. In 1902, the city passed its first automobile laws, which

---

Fun Fact

The "Wet/Dry" battle in Orlando continued even into 1998, when the city removed "Blue Laws" that restricted the sale of liquor on Sundays within the city limits.

included an in-town speed limit of 5 miles per hour. In 1904, the city flooded. And in 1905 it suffered a drought that ended—miraculously or coincidentally—on a day when all faiths united at the local First Baptist Church to pray for rain. By 1910, prosperity had returned, and Orlando, with a population of nearly 4,000, was, in a small way, becoming a tourism and convention center. World War I brought further industrial growth, and a real-estate boom, not just to Orlando, but to all of Florida. Millions of immigrants, speculators, and builders descended on the state in search of a quick buck. As land speculation reached a fever pitch, and property was bought and resold almost overnight, many citrus groves gave way to urbanization. Preeminent Orlando builder and promoter Carl Dann described the action: "It finally became nothing more than a gambling machine, each man buying on a shoestring, betting dollars a bigger fool would come along and buy his option."

Quite suddenly, the bubble burst. A July 1926 issue of the *Nation* provided the obituary for the Florida land boom: "The world's greatest poker game, played with lots instead of chips, is over. And the players are now . . . paying up." Construction slowed to a trickle, and many newcomers who had arrived in Florida to jump on the bandwagon returned to their homes in the north. Though Orlando was not quite as hard hit as Miami—scene of the greediest land grabs—some belt-tightening was in order. Nevertheless, the city managed to build a municipal airport in 1928. Then came a Mediterranean fruit-fly infestation that crippled the citrus industry. Hundreds of thousands of acres of land in quarantined areas had to be cleared of fruit, and vast quantities of boxed fruit were destroyed. The 1929 stock market crash that precipitated the Great Depression seemed almost an afterthought to Florida's ruined economy.

. . . AND NEW DEALS　President Franklin D. Roosevelt's New Deal helped the state climb back on its feet. The Works Progress Administration (WPA) put 40,000 unemployed Floridians back to work—work that included hundreds of public projects in Orlando. Of these, the most important was the expansion and resurfacing of the city's airport. By 1936, the tourist trade had revived somewhat; construction was up once again, and the state began attracting a broader range of visitors than ever before. But the event that finally lifted Florida—and the nation—out of the depression was World War II.

Orlando had weathered the Great Depression. Now it prepared for war with the construction of army bases, housing for servicemen, and training facilities. Enlisted men poured into the city, and the airport was again enlarged, and equipped with barracks, a military hospital, administration buildings, and mess halls. By 1944, Orlando had a second airport and was known as "Florida's Air Capital"—home to major aircraft and aviation-parts manufacturers. Thousands of U.S. servicemen did part of their hitch in Orlando, and when the war ended, many returned to settle there.

POSTWAR PROSPERITY　By 1950, Orlando, with a population of 51,826, was the financial and transportation hub of central Florida. The city shared the bullish economy of the 1950s with the rest of the nation. In the face of the Cold War, the Orlando air force base remained and grew, funneling millions of dollars into the local economy. Florida's population increased by a whopping 78.7% during the decade—making it America's 10th most populous state—and tourists came in droves, nearly 4.5 million in 1950 alone.

In the Words of Walt Disney

Why be a governor or a senator when you can be king of Disneyland?

You can dream, create, design, and build the most wonderful place in the world . . . but it requires people to make the dream a reality.

One reason for the influx was the advent of the air conditioner, which made life in Florida infinitely more pleasant. Also fueling Orlando's economy was a brand-new industry arriving in nearby Cape Canaveral in 1955—the government-run space program. Cape Canaveral became NASA's headquarters for the Apollo rocket program that eventually blasted Neil Armstrong heavenward toward his famous "giant leap." During the same decade, the Glenn L. Martin Company (later Martin Marietta), builder of the Matador Missile, purchased 10 square miles for a plant site 4 miles south of Orlando. Its advent sparked further industrial growth, and property values soared. More than 60 new industries moved to the area in 1959 alone. But even the most optimistic Orlando boosters could not foresee the glorious future that was the city's ultimate destiny.

THE DISNEY DECADES   In 1964, Walt Disney began secretly buying up millions of dollars worth of central Florida farmland. As vast areas of land were purchased in lots of 5,000 acres here, 20,000 there—at remarkably high prices—rumors flew as to who needed so much land, and had the money to acquire it. Some thought it was Howard Hughes; others, the space program. Speculation was rife almost to the very day, November 15, 1965 ("D" Day for Orlando), when Disney himself arrived in town and announced his plans to build the world's most spectacular theme park ("bigger and better than Disneyland"). In a 2-year construction effort, Disney employed 9,000 people. Land speculation reached unprecedented heights, as hotel chains and restaurateurs grabbed up property near the proposed park. Mere swampland sold for millions. The total cost of the project by its October 1971 opening was $400 million. Mickey Mouse personally led the first visitor into the Magic Kingdom, and numerous celebrities, from Bob Hope to Julie Andrews, took part in the opening ceremonies. In Walt Disney World's first 2 years, the attraction drew 20 million visitors and employed 13,000 people. The sleepy citrus-growing town of Orlando had become the "Action Center of Florida," and the fastest-growing city in the state. A 1972 referendum revitalized downtown Orlando, which continues to grow, adding an increasing number of restaurants, bars, and attractions of its own.

Additional attractions multiplied faster than fruit flies, and hundreds of firms relocated their businesses to the area. Sea World, a major theme park, came to town in 1973. All the while, Walt Disney World continued to grow and expand, adding Epcot in 1982 and Disney–MGM Studios in 1989, along with water parks, over a dozen "official" resorts, a shopping/restaurant village, campgrounds, a vast array of recreational facilities, and several other adjuncts that are thoroughly described in this book. In 1998, Disney opened yet another theme park, this one dedicated to zoological entertainment and aptly called Animal Kingdom.

As if that weren't enough, Disney has built its own version of a small-town utopia, Celebration, where tourists slowly drive by houses where real people actually live. (You'll sometimes see signs in the front yards that say THIS HOUSE IS OCCUPIED so people will know it is not the movie set for *Stepford, The Sequel.*)

Since Celebration opened in 1997 a rogue resident has staged a protest against all the strict rules and regulations by regularly planting plastic pink flamingos in public spaces throughout the community.

Universal Studios Escape, whose Universal Studios Florida opened in 1990, continues to expand and keep the stakes high. In late 1998, it unveiled a new entertainment district, CityWalk, and in 1999, it opened Islands of Adventure, a second theme park including, among other things, attractions dedicated to Dr. Seuss, Marvel Comics, and Jurassic Park. Also scheduled to open in 1999 is the Portofino Bay Resort at Universal City Florida, a 750-room Loews hotel. Universal will open three more hotels by 2005.

Stoked by tourism dollars, the Orlando area is looking increasingly to the future. Many national firms, including the American Automobile Association and Tupperware, have relocated their headquarters to this thriving Sun-belt region. By the year 2004, the metro Orlando area is expected to lead the nation in the growth of office employment, adding some 65,900 jobs.

2 Orlando Today (& Tomorrow)

All of those tourist dollars flowing into the city, helps Orlando to enjoy the best overall business climate in the state of Florida. In addition to tourism, its dynamic economy thrives on diverse industry, thousands of technology-related companies, and agriculture. The only remnant of Orlando's slow-paced, pre-Disney Southern image is its down-home friendliness (but don't look for it during rush-hour traffic on the freeway).

For the observant visitor, this part of Florida is very different from the rest of the state. Indeed, the parts of town most tourists see are unlike any others on the planet. Locals become somewhat immune, after a time, to the endless miles of perfectly manicured landscapes courtesy of Disney and the other major players here. Aside from the theme parks, the "attractions area" is filled with strip malls, theme restaurants, and resort hotels. This can create a kind of sterile *Twilight Zone* quality. Unfortunately, this plastic presence is only going to increase as Walt Disney World and other parks continue to expand. Disneyesque street signs have even begun to appear downtown within the last few years, and a whole Disney town—Celebration—has opened. Just 20 or so miles in any direction from the tourist mecca, you'll find real towns like those found anywhere else, where people live, work, play, and send their children to school. But most attraction builders recognize that people coming to Orlando aren't looking for reality.

Recent major developments include:

- **The Millennium.** Ringing in the year 2000 at a WDW hotel will be next to impossible—word is that rooms at WDW for New Years have been long booked—but that doesn't mean you can't be part of the celebration. Look for special events, discount tickets, and new attractions to be unveiled, at all the major theme parks throughout the year to celebrate the new millennium.

- **CityWalk** and **Islands of Adventure.** Universal Studios Escape opened its new nighttime entertainment complex in late 1998, and its second theme park, Islands of Adventure, in 1999. Built with the help of creative consultant Steven Spielberg, the new park is billed as the most technologically advanced theme park ever constructed. You'll find the Dinosaurs of Jurassic Park, and a slew of other attractions based on cartoon heroes and villains as diverse as Spider Man, Popeye, and Dr. Doom. In typical Orlando fashion, press kits called the landlocked Islands of Adventure a "21st-century theme park set among the exotic coastlines of the oceans."

- **New Resorts.** Universal has opened Portofino Bay, the first hotel in a multibillion-dollar expansion plan to help parkgoers spend their vacation dollars on Universal property (just like the Mouse up the road). Utilizing 600 previously undeveloped acres, the company will ultimately offer more than 5,000 rooms; a golf-villa community centered on an 18-hole championship course; a top-of-the-line tennis complex; and a series of lakes, winding rivers, canals, and other waterways that will be traversed by water taxis and ferries. The 750-room Portofino Bay opened in 1999. The second hotel in the plan, a Hard Rock Hotel based on the theme restaurant, will open in 2000 with 650 rooms.

- **Disney's Animal Kingdom.** An exotic "live-animal adventure park," Animal Kingdom is, at 500 acres, five times the size of the Magic Kingdom. "The next best thing to Africa" says head cheese Michael Eisner. Centering on the 14-story "Tree of Life," it combines thrill rides, exotic landscapes divided into five "regions" (the last, Asia, opened in 1999), and close encounters with great herds of wild animals. Disney has outdone itself on the artistic aspect of this endeavor, even bringing tribal experts from Africa to build the thatched roofs, and hiring a team of 12 sculptors who worked for a year to create the "Tree of Life."

- **Disney Cruises.** Disney Cruise Lines offers park vacations in conjunction with Caribbean cruises on two vessels. The ships, reminiscent of classic luxury liners, offer theme restaurants, nightclubs, family entertainment, supervised children's activities, a day at the beach on Disney's own private island, and much more. Extremely popular in the first year, now may be the time to find a slightly better deal, but it will continue to be important to book far in advance.

- **DisneyQuest.** This attraction lives up to its reputation as a virtual, high-tech theme park. You can create and ride a virtual roller coaster, be a human pinball, or fight aliens in an interactive spaceship within this blue-hued 100,000-square-foot, wave-shaped building in Downtown Disney. To keep the games on the cutting edge, 20% to 30% of the content is changed each year. Disney will also open DisneyQuest-like centers in select markets throughout the country.

- **Safari Lodge.** Although no details have been released at press time, a jungle-themed hotel adjacent to the Animal Kingdom's 100-acre savannah is still in the works.

- **All-Star Movie Resort.** The newest Disney resort, which opened in 1999, is one of three, family-friendly, low-priced properties with rooms starting at around $74. Decorated with a theater-inspired food court and a hockey-rink themed pool—a la the Mighty Ducks—the decor benefits from the Disney connection with whimsical touches culled from celluloid classics as varied as *The Love Bug* and *Toy Story.*

- **Sea World's Second Park.** Details at press time are sketchy, but Discovery Cove, a second park offering visitors the opportunity for special 2-day rates, along with a host of new attractions and entertainment, is expected to open sometime after the year 2000.

- **Cirque du Soleil.** Renowned worldwide for its blend of acrobatics and state-of-art special effects, the troupe opened a permanent, 1,671-seat theater home in Downtown Disney in early 1999.

Appendix B:
Useful Toll-Free Numbers
& Web Sites

AIRLINES

Air Canada
☎ 800/776-3000
www.aircanada.ca

Alaska Airlines
☎ 800/426-0333
www.alaskaair.com

American Airlines
☎ 800/433-7300
www.americanair.com

America West Airlines
☎ 800/235-9292
www.americawest.com

British Airways
☎ 800/247-9297
☎ 0345/222-111 in Britain
www.british-airways.com

**Canadian Airlines
International**
☎ 800/426-7000
www.cdnair.ca

Continental Airlines
☎ 800/525-0280
www.flycontinental.com

Delta Air Lines
☎ 800/221-1212
www.delta-air.com

Hawaiian Airlines
☎ 800/367-5320
www.hawaiianair.com

Kiwi International Air Lines
☎ 800/538-5494
www.jetkiwi.com

Midway Airlines
☎ 800/446-4392

Northwest Airlines
☎ 800/225-2525
www.nwa.com

Southwest Airlines
☎ 800/435-9792
www.iflyswa.com

Tower Air
☎ 800/34-TOWER
(800/348-6937)
www.towerair.com

Trans World Airlines (TWA)
☎ 800/221-2000
www.twa.com

United Airlines
☎ 800/241-6522
www.ual.com

US Airways
☎ 800/428-4322
www.usair.com

Virgin Atlantic Airways
☎ 800/862-8621 in
Continental U.S.
☎ 0293/747-747 in Britain
www.fly.virgin.com

CAR-RENTAL AGENCIES

Advantage
☎ 800/777-5500
www.arac.com

Alamo
☎ 800/327-9633
www.goalamo.com

Auto Europe
☎ 800/223-5555
www.autoeurope.com

Avis
☎ 800/331-1212 in
   Continental U.S.
☎ 800/TRY-AVIS in Canada
www.avis.com

Budget
☎ 800/527-0700
www.budgetrentacar.com

Dollar
☎ 800/800-4000
www.dollarcar.com

Enterprise
☎ 800/325-8007
www.pickenterprise.com

Hertz
☎ 800/654-3131
www.hertz.com

Kemwel Holiday Auto (KHA)
☎ 800/678-0678
www.kemwel.com

National
☎ 800/CAR-RENT
www.nationalcar.com

Payless
☎ 800/PAYLESS
www.paylesscar.com

Rent-A-Wreck
☎ 800/535-1391
www.rent-a-wreck.com

Thrifty
☎ 800/367-2277
www.thrifty.com

Value
☎ 800/327-2501
www.go-value.com

MAJOR HOTEL & MOTEL CHAINS

Best Western International
☎ 800/528-1234
www.bestwestern.com

Clarion Hotels
☎ 800/CLARION
www.hotelchoice.com/
   cgi-bin/res/webres?clarion.html

Comfort Inns
☎ 800/228-5150
www.hotelchoice.com/
   cgi-bin/res/webres?comfort.html

Courtyard by Marriott
☎ 800/321-2211
www.courtyard.com

Days Inn
☎ 800/325-2525
www.daysinn.com

Doubletree Hotels
☎ 800/222-TREE
www.doubletreehotels.com

Econo Lodges
☎ 800/55-ECONO
www.hotelchoice.com/
   cgi-bin/res/webres?econo.html

Fairfield Inn by Marriott
☎ 800/228-2800
www.fairfieldinn.com

Hampton Inn
☎ 800/HAMPTON
www.hampton-inn.com

Hilton Hotels
☎ 800/HILTONS
www.hilton.com

Holiday Inn
☎ 800/HOLIDAY
www.holiday-inn.com

Howard Johnson
☎ 800/654-2000
www.hojo.com/hojo.html

Hyatt Hotels & Resorts
☎ 800/228-9000
www.hyatt.com

ITT Sheraton
☎ 800/325-3535
www.sheraton.com

La Quinta Motor Inns
☎ 800/531-5900
www.laquinta.com

Marriott Hotels
☎ 800/228-9290
www.marriott.com

Motel 6
☎ 800/4-MOTEL6
   (800/466-8536)

Quality Inns
☎ 800/228-5151
www.hotelchoice.com/
   cgi-bin/res/webres?quality.html

Radisson Hotels International
☎ 800/333-3333
www.radisson.com

Ramada Inns
☎ 800/2-RAMADA
www.ramada.com

Red Carpet Inns
☎ 800/251-1962

Red Lion Hotels & Inns
☎ 800/547-8010
www.travelweb.com

Red Roof Inns
☎ 800/843-7663
www.redroof.com

Residence Inn by Marriott
☎ 800/331-3131
www.residenceinn.com

Rodeway Inns
☎ 800/228-2000
www.hotelchoice.com/
   cgi-bin/res/webres?rodeway.html

Super 8 Motels
☎ 800/800-8000
www.super8motels.com

Travelodge
☎ 800/255-3050

Vagabond Inns
☎ 800/522-1555
www.vagabondinns.com

Wyndham Hotels and Resorts
☎ 800/822-4200 in Continental
   U.S. and Canada
www.wyndham.com

Toll-Free Numbers & Web Sites

Frommer's Online Directory

By *Michael Shapiro*

Michael Shapiro is the author of *Internet Travel Planning* (Globe Pequot Press).

Frommer's Online Directory is a new feature designed to help you take advantage of the Internet to better plan your trip. Part I lists some general Internet resources that can make any trip easier, such as sites for booking airline tickets. It's not meant to be a comprehensive list—it's a discriminating selection of useful sites to get you started. In Part II you'll find some top online guides specifically for Walt Disney World, including local lodging, specific attractions, and getting around.

1 Top Travel-Planning Web Sites

Among the most popular sites are online travel agencies. The top agencies, including Expedia, Preview Travel, and Travelocity, offer an array of tools that are valuable even if you don't book online. You can check flight schedules, hotel availability, car-rental prices, or even get paged if your flight is delayed.

While online agencies have come a long way over the past few years, they don't always yield the best price. Unlike a travel agent, for example, they're unlikely to tell you that you can save money by flying a day earlier or a day later. On the other hand, if you're looking for a bargain fare, you might find something online that an agent wouldn't take the time to dig up. Because airline commissions have been cut, a travel agent may not find it worthwhile spending half an hour trying to find you the best deal. On the Net you can be your own agent and take all the time you want.

Online booking sites aren't the only places to book airline tickets—all major airlines have their own Web sites and often offer incentives, such as bonus frequent flyer miles or Net-only discounts, for buying online. These incentives have helped airlines capture the majority of the online booking market. According to Jupiter Communications, online agencies such as Travelocity booked about 80 percent of tickets purchased online in 1996, but by 1999 airline sites (such as www.ual.com) were projected to own about 60 percent of the online market, with online agencies' share of the pie dwindling each year.

Below are the Web sites for major airlines serving the Orlando airport. These sites offer schedules, flight booking and most have pages where you can sign up for e-mail alerts on weekend deals.

Fun Fact

Far more people look online than book online, partly due to fear of putting their credit cards through on the Net. Though secure encryption has made this fear less justified, there's no reason why you can't find a flight online and then book it by calling a toll-free number or contacting your local travel agent. To be sure you're in secure mode when you book online, look for a little icon of a key (in Netscape) or a padlock (Internet Explorer) at the bottom of your Web browser.

American Airlines   www.aa.com
Continental Airlines   www.flycontinental.com
Delta Airlines   www.delta-air.com
Northwest Airlines   www.nwa.com
United Airlines   www.ual.com
U.S. Airways   www.usair.com

WHEN SHOULD YOU BOOK ONLINE?

Online booking is not for everyone. If you prefer to let others handle your travel arrangements, one call to an experienced travel agent should suffice. But if you want to know as much as possible about your options, the Net is a good place to start, especially for bargain hunters.

The most compelling reason to use online booking is to take advantage of last-minute specials, such as American Airlines' weekend deals or other Internet-only fares that must be purchased online. Another advantage is that you can cash in on incentives for booking online, such as rebates or bonus frequent flyer miles.

Online booking works best for trips within North America—for international tickets, it's usually cheaper and easier to use a travel agent or consolidator.

Online booking is certainly not for those with a complex itinerary. If you require follow-up services, such as itinerary changes, use a travel agent. Though Expedia and some other online agencies employ travel agents available by phone, these sites are geared primarily for self-service.

LEADING BOOKING SITES

Below are listings for the top travel booking sites. The starred selections are the most useful and best designed sites.

Cheap Tickets. www.cheaptickets.com
Essentials: Discounted rates on domestic and international airline tickets and hotel rooms.

Sometimes discounters such as Cheap Tickets have exclusive deals that aren't available through more mainstream channels. Registration at Cheap Tickets requires inputting a credit card number before getting started, which is one reason many people elect to call the company's toll-free number rather than booking online. Cheap Tickets actually regards this policy as a selling point, arguing that "lookers" who don't intend to buy will be scared off by its "credit card first" approach and won't bog down the site with their queries. Despite its misguided credit card policy, Cheap Tickets is worth the effort because its fares can be substantially lower than those offered by its competitors.

✪ Expedia. expedia.com
Essentials: Domestic and international flight hotel and rental car booking; late-breaking travel news, destination features and commentary from travel experts; deals on cruises and vacation packages. Free registration is required for booking.

Take a Look at a Frommer's Site

We highly recommend Arthur Frommer's Budget Travel Online (**www.from-mers.com**) as an excellent travel planning resource. Of course, we're a little biased, but you will find indispensable travel tips, reviews, monthly vacation giveaways, and online booking.

Subscribe to Arthur Frommer's Daily Newsletter (**www.frommers.com/ newsletters**) to receive the latest travel bargains and inside travel secrets in your mailbox every day. You'll read daily headlines and articles from the dean of travel himself, highlighting last-minute deals on airfares, accommodations, cruises, and package vacations. You'll also find great travel advice by checking our Tip of the Day or Hot Spot of the Month.

Search our Destinations archive (**www.frommers.com/destinations**) of more than 200 domestic and international destinations for great places to stay, tips for traveling there, and what to do while you're there. Once you've researched your trip, you might try our online reservation system (**www.frommers.com/ book-travelnow**) to book your dream vacation at affordable prices.

Expedia makes it easy to handle flight, hotel, and car booking on one itinerary, so it's a good place for one-stop shopping. Expedia's hotel search offers crisp, zoomable maps to pinpoint most properties; click on the camera icon to see images of the rooms and facilities. But like many online databases, Expedia focuses on the major chains, such as Hilton and Hyatt, so don't expect to find too many one-of-a-kind resorts or B&Bs here.

Once you're registered (it's only necessary to do this once from each computer you use), you can start booking with the Roundtrip Fare Finder box on the home page, which expedites the process. After selecting a flight, you can hold it until midnight the following day or purchase online. If you think you might do better through a travel agent, you'll have time to try to get a lower price. And you may do better with a travel agent because Expedia's computer reservation system does not include all airlines.

Expedia's World Guide, offering destination information, is a glaring weakness—it takes a lot of page views to get very little information. However, Expedia compensates by linking to other Microsoft Network services, such as its Sidewalk city guides, which offer entertainment and dining advice for many of the cities it covers.

Preview Travel. www.previewtravel.com
Essentials: Domestic and international flight, hotel, and rental car booking; Travel Newswire lists fare sales; deals on cruises and vacation packages. Free (one-time) registration is required for booking. Preview offers express booking for members, but at press time this feature was buried below the fold on Preview's reservation page.

Preview features the most inviting interface for booking trips, though the wealth of graphics involved can make the site somewhat slow to load. Use Farefinder to quickly find the lowest current fares on flights to dozens of major cities. Carfinder offers a similar service for rental cars, but you can only search airport locations, not city pick-up sites. To see the lowest fare for your itinerary, input the dates and times for your route and see what Preview comes up with.

Preview has a great feature called the Best Fare Finder; after it searches for the best deal on your itinerary, it will check flights that are a bit later or earlier to see if it might be cheaper to fly at a different time. While these searches have become quite sophisticated, they still occasionally overlook deals that might be uncovered by a top-notch travel agent. If you have the time, see what you can find online and then call an agent to see if you can get a better price.

With Preview's Fare Alert feature, you can set fares for up to three routes and you'll receive e-mail notices when the fare drops below your target amount. For example, you could tell Preview to alert you when the fare from New York to Walt Disney World drops below $250. If it does, you'll get an e-mail telling you the current fare.

Minor quibbles: When you search for a fare, hotel, or car—at least when we went to press—Preview launched an annoying little "Please Wait" window that gets in the way of the main browser window, even when your results begin to appear. The hotel search feature is intuitive, but the images and maps aren't as crisp as those at Expedia. Also: all sorts of other extraneous information that's irrelevant to most travelers is listed on maps.

Note to AOL Users: You can book flights, hotels, rental cars, and cruises on AOL at keyword: Travel. The booking software is provided by Preview Travel and is similar to Preview on the Web. Use the AOL "Travelers Advantage" program to earn a 5% rebate on flights, hotel rooms, and car rentals.

Priceline.com. www.priceline.com

Launched in 1998 with a $10 million ad campaign, Priceline lets you "name your price" for domestic and international airline tickets. In other words, you select a route and dates, guarantee with a credit card, and make a bid for what you're willing to pay. If one of the airlines in Priceline's database has a fare that's lower than your bid, your credit card will automatically be charged for a ticket.

But you can't say when you want to fly—you have to accept any flight leaving between 6am and 10pm, and you may have to make a stopover. No frequent flyer miles are awarded, and tickets are nonrefundable and can't be exchanged for another flight. So if your plans change, you're out of luck. Priceline can be good for travelers who have to take off on short notice (and who are thus unable to qualify for advance purchase discounts). But be sure to shop around first—if you overbid, you'll be required to purchase the ticket and Priceline will pocket the difference.

Travelocity. www.travelocity.com

Essentials: Domestic and international flight, hotel, and rental-car booking; deals on cruises and vacation packages. Travel Headlines spotlights latest bargain airfares. Free (one-time) registration is required for booking.

Travelocity almost got it right. Its Express Booking feature enables travelers to complete the booking process more quickly than they could at Expedia or Preview, but Travelocity gums up the works with a page called "Featured Airlines." Big placards of several featured airlines compete for your attention—if you want to see the fares for all available airlines, click the much smaller box at the bottom of the page labeled "Book a Flight."

Some have worried that Travelocity, which is owned by American Airlines' parent company AMR, directs bookings to American. This doesn't seem to be the case; I've booked there dozens of times and have always been directed to the cheapest listed flight, for example on Tower or ATA. But this "Featured Airlines" page seems to be Travelocity's way of trying to cash in with ads and incentives for booking certain airlines. (*Note:* It's hard to blame these booking services for trying to generate some revenue; many airlines have slashed commissions to $10 per domestic booking for online transactions so these virtual agencies are groping for revenue streams.) There are rewards for choosing one of the featured airlines. You'll get 1,500 bonus frequent flyer miles if you book through United's site, for example, but the site doesn't tell you about other airlines that might be cheaper. If the United flight costs $150 more than the best deal on another airline, it's not worth spending the extra money for a relatively small number of bonus miles.

On the plus side, Travelocity has some leading-edge techie tools for modern travelers. Exhibit A is Fare Watcher E-mail, an "intelligent agent" that keeps you informed of the best fares offered for the city pairs (round-trips) of your choice. Whenever the fare changes by $25 or more, Fare Watcher will alert you by e-mail. Exhibit B is Flight Paging: If you own an alphanumeric pager with national access that can receive e-mail, Travelocity's paging system can alert you if your flight is delayed. Finally, though Travelocity doesn't include every budget airline, it does include Southwest, the leading U.S. budget carrier.

FINDING LODGINGS ONLINE

While the services above offer hotel booking, it can be best to use a site devoted primarily to lodging because you may find properties that aren't listed on more general online travel agencies. Some lodging sites specialize in a particular type of accommodation, such as bed-and-breakfast inns, which you won't find on the more mainstream booking services. Other services, such as TravelWeb, offer weekend deals on major chain properties, which cater to business travelers and have more empty rooms on weekends.

All Hotels on the Web. www.all-hotels.com
Well, this site *doesn't* include all the hotels on the Web, but it does have tens of thousands of listings throughout the world. Bear in mind that each hotel listed has paid a small fee ($25 and up) for placement, so it's not an objective list; it's more like a book of online brochures.

Hotel Reservations Network. www.180096hotel.com
You'll find bargain room rates at hotels in more than two dozen U.S. cities here. The cool thing is that HRN prebooks blocks of rooms in advance, so sometimes it has rooms—at discount rates—at hotels that are "sold out." Select a city, input your dates and you'll get a list of the best prices at a selection of hotels. Descriptions include an image of the property and a locator map. HRN is notable for some deep discounts, even in cities where hotel rooms are expensive. The toll-free number is printed all over this site; call it if you want more options than are listed online.

InnSite. www.innsite.com
InnSite has B&B listings for inns in all 50 states. To find an inn at your destination, have a look at images of the rooms, check prices and availability, and then send e-mail to the innkeeper if you have further questions. While the directory is extensive, it only includes a listing if the proprietor submitted one (*Note:* it's free to get an inn listed). The descriptions are written by the innkeepers, and many listings offer links to an inn's own Web site, where you can find more information.

Places to Stay. www.placestostay.com
Mostly one-of-a-kind places in the U.S. and abroad that you might not find in other directories, with a focus on resort accommodations. Again, listing is selective—this isn't a comprehensive directory, but can give you a sense of what's available at different destinations.

✪ TravelWeb. www.travelweb.com
TravelWeb lists more than 16,000 hotels worldwide, focusing on chains such as Hyatt and Hilton, and you can book almost 90 percent of these online. TravelWeb's Click-It Weekends, updated each Monday, offers weekend deals at many leading

hotel chains. TravelWeb is the online home for Pegasus Systems, which provides transaction processing systems for the hotel industry.

LAST-MINUTE DEALS AND OTHER ONLINE BARGAINS

There's nothing airlines hate more than flying with lots of empty seats. The Net has enabled airlines to offer last-minute bargains to entice travelers to fill those seats. Most of these are announced on Tuesday or Wednesday and are valid for travel the following weekend, but some can be booked weeks or months in advance. You can sign up for weekly e-mail alerts at airlines' sites (For airline's Web site addresses, see above) or check sites such as WebFlyer (see below) that compile lists of these bargains. To make it easier, visit a site (see below) that will round up all the deals and send them in one convenient weekly e-mail. But last-minute deals aren't the only online bargains—other sites can help you find value even if you can't wait until the eleventh hour.

✪ **1travel.com. www.1travel.com**

Deals on domestic and international flights, cruises, hotels, and all-inclusive resorts such as Club Med. 1travel.com's Saving Alert compiles last-minute air deals so you don't have to scroll through multiple e-mail alerts. A feature called "Drive a little using low-fare airlines" helps map out strategies for using alternate airports to find lower fares. And Farebeater searches a database that includes published fares, consolidator bargains, and special deals exclusive to 1travel.com. *Note:* The travel agencies listed by 1travel.com have paid for placement.

BestFares. www.bestfares.com

Budget seeker Tom Parsons lists some great bargains on airfares, hotels, rental cars, and cruises, but the site is poorly organized. News Desk is a long list of hundreds of bargains, but they're not broken down into cities or even countries, so it's not easy trying to find what you're looking for. If you have time to wade through it, you might find a good deal. Some material is available only to paid subscribers.

Go4less.com. www.go4less.com

Specializing in last-minute cruise and package deals, Go4less has some eye-popping offers, such as off-peak Caribbean cruises for under $100 per day. The site has a clean design, but the bargains aren't organized by destination. However, you avoid sifting through all this material by using the Search box and entering vacation type, destination, month, and price.

Moment's Notice. www.moments-notice.com

As the name suggests, Moment's Notice specializes in last-minute vacation and cruise deals. You can browse for free, but if you want to purchase a trip you have to join Moment's Notice, which costs $25.

Handy Tip

While most people learn about last-minute weekend deals from e-mail dispatches, it can be best to find out precisely *when* these deals become available and check airlines' Web sites at this time. To find out when deals become available, check the pages devoted to these deals on airlines' Web pages. Because these deals are limited, they can vanish within hours, sometimes even minutes, so it pays to log on as soon as they're available. An example: Southwest's specials are posted at 12:01am Tuesdays (Central time). So if you're looking for a cheap flight, stay up late and check Southwest's site at that time to grab the best new deals.

Smarter Living. www.smarterliving.com

Best known for its e-mail dispatch of weekend deals on 20 airlines, Smarter Living also keeps you posted about last-minute bargains on everything from Windjammer Cruises to flights to Iceland.

✪ **WebFlyer. www.webflyer.com**

WebFlyer is the ultimate online resource for frequent flyers and also has an excellent listing of last-minute air deals. Click on "Deal Watch" for a round-up of weekend deals on flights, hotels, and rental cars from domestic and international suppliers.

TRAVELER'S TOOLKIT

Seasoned travelers always carry some essential items to make their trips easier. Following is a selection of online tools to smooth your journey.

ATM LOCATORS

Visa (www.visa.com/pd/atm/)

MasterCard (www.mastercard.com/atm)

Find ATMs in hundreds of cities in the U.S. and around the world. Both include maps for some locations and both list airport ATM locations, some with maps.

✪ **CultureFinder. www.culturefinder.com**

Up-to-date listings for plays, opera, classical music, dance, film, and other cultural events in more than 1,300 U.S. cities. Enter the dates you'll be in a city and get a list of events happening then—you can also purchase tickets online. Also see FestivalFinder (**www.festivalfinder.com**) for the latest on more than 1,500 rock, folk, reggae, blues, and bluegrass festivals throughout North America.

Intellicast. www.intellicast.com

Weather forecasts for all 50 states and cities around the world. Note that temperatures are in Celsius for many international destinations, so don't think you'll need that winter coat for your next trip to Athens.

✪ **MapQuest. www.mapquest.com**

Specializing in U.S. maps, MapQuest enables you to zoom in on a destination, calculate step-by-step driving directions between any two U.S. points, and locate restaurants, hotels, and other attractions on maps.

✪ **Net Café Guide. www.netcafeguide.com**

Locate Internet cafés at hundreds of locations around the globe. Catch up on your e-mail, log onto the Web, and stay in touch with the home front, usually for just a few dollars per hour.

Trip.com: Airport Maps and Flight Status. www.trip.com

A business travel site where you can find out when an airborne flight is scheduled to arrive. Click on "Guides and Tools" to peruse airport maps for more than 40 domestic cities.

2 The Top Sites for Walt Disney World and Nearby Attractions

WALT DISNEY WORLD'S OFFICIAL SITE INFORMATION

✪ **Walt Disney World—Official Site. disney.go.com/disneyworld**

Essentials: Disney World's site on the Web is a vast virtual wonderland designed to help you take care of the real-world tasks necessary to make your Disney fantasy

Check Your E-Mail at Internet Cafés While Traveling

Until a few years ago, most travelers who checked their e-mail while traveling carried a laptop, but this posed some problems. Not only are laptops expensive, but they can be difficult to configure, incur expensive connection charges, and are attractive to thieves. Thankfully, Web-based free e-mail programs have made it much easier to check your mail.

Just open an account at a freemail provider, such as Hotmail (hotmail.com) or Yahoo! Mail (mail.yahoo.com), and all you'll need to check your mail is a Web connection, easily available at Net cafés and copy shops around the world. After logging on, just point the browser to www.hotmail.com, enter your username and password, and you'll have access to your mail.

Internet cafés have become ubiquitous, so for a few dollars an hour you'll be able to check your mail and send messages back to colleagues, friends, and family. If you already have a primary e-mail account, you can set it to forward mail to your freemail account while you're away. Freemail programs have become enormously popular (Hotmail claims more than 10 million members), because they enable everyone, even those who don't own a computer, to have an e-mail address they can check wherever they log onto the Web.

come true. In the left-hand column of the home page, you'll find tools for planning and booking your vacation, as well as links to advice about the theme parks, resorts, entertainment, and dining options. Each of these areas will be covered in the sections below. The rest of the home page includes features on what's new at Disney World, such as the latest Cirque du Soleil extravaganza, or the newest addition to Disney's Animal Kingdom. Don't miss the calendar link near the bottom of the home page to get a month-by-month update of what's going on.

Note: Web addresses for the following sections are not listed because each is just one click from Disney World's home page (**disney.go.com/disneyworld**).

WDW: Vacation Planning

Start by getting oriented with maps of Walt Disney World, and then peruse the hotel and restaurant options. Use the Theme Park Attraction Search to locate attractions suited to any age group at Epcot, Magic Kingdom, or any of the other Disney theme parks. For example, find attractions for 6- to 13-year-olds, or simply view all the attractions at the Magic Kingdom. You can use the hotel search feature to find resorts by price, amenities, or location; the restaurant finder can help you select some dining choices by location, cuisine type, and price.

WDW: Tickets Online

Learn about the myriad selection of theme park passes, as well as packages that include park admissions and lodging. You can then order online. You can also make hotel reservations and order park admission passes by clicking on the Resort Reservations link.

WDW: Theme Parks

This is where to find all the latest nitty-gritty details on Epcot, Magic Kingdom Park, Disney–MGM Studios, and Disney's Animal Kingdom. Information includes operating hours, ticket information, parade descriptions, maps, special services for disabled visitors, and even cameras where you can see, through the wonder of the Web, live images from Disney World. (*Note:* These images are only live during the day; if you click here at night, you'll see the last daytime image from around the sunset hour.)

WDW: Entertainment, Shopping and Dining

Disney World has become so much more than a bunch of rides—the fun can continue well into the evening in places like Downtown Disney and Pleasure Island. This page is a jumping-off point to each of the major entertainment areas, such as Disney's BoardWalk. From here you can explore dining, shopping, and entertainment options to get a better sense of where you want to go before your trip. There are also links to kids' programs, baby-sitting services, and Camp Disney, so that you'll know your children will be taken care of while you enjoy a night on the town.

WDW: Water Parks, Recreation & Sports

The mind-boggling array of activities continues on this page, which has links to several water parks; detailed information on golf courses (and mini-golf for the kids), tennis courts, and fishing holes; health clubs and spas; and Disney's Wide World of Sports Complex.

WDW: More Vacations and Special Events

Here's where you can learn more about Disney cruises, "Fairy Tale" weddings and honeymoons, and the Disney Institute, a sort of new-age camp for adults.

IN AND AROUND ORLANDO

Though you could easily spend a couple of weeks at Disney World without running out of things to do, the Orlando area has other worthy attractions. SeaWorld and Universal Studios Escape are not to be missed, and the city of Orlando offers metropolitan pleasures. The guides below can help you make good use of your time.

FLA USA. www.flausa.com/Orlando

Check out this site only for its camping and state parks listings. The dining listings are ridiculously thin, and the events calendar was out of date when I checked.

☻ Go2Orlando. www.go2orlando.com

Essentials: Detailed practical information on attractions, dining, lodging, shopping, beaches, and recreation. Produced in conjunction with the *Orlando Sentinel,* Go2Orlando is a clean, well-organized place to browse. Planning tools include restaurant and hotel searches by area and price. The shopping guide lists malls, specialty shops, factory outlets, antique shops, and flea markets. The Beach Guide includes maps and tips for enjoying the coast, as well as safety information, fishing advice, and lodging options in Daytona and Cocoa Beach. Clicking on Recreation leads to golfing, cruises, fishing, even auto-racing schools. And there's extensive transportation information to help you get around if you don't rent a car. All in all, Go2Orlando is a great one-stop shop to get your bearings.

InsideCentralFlorida. www.insidecentralflorida.com

This is clearly a site for locals, but it's also useful for visitors who want to check the weather, see what's on TV, or know where to find the best Key lime pie. Click on Things to Do for upcoming music festivals, outdoor activities, and the latest additions to the big theme parks. The dining guide's listings are very limited.

Orlando.com Vacation Guide. www.orlando.com/vacation

A well-organized round-up of attractions, events, and tips for planning your Orlando vacation. You'll also find dining, shopping, and lodging guides, and can book a room through the site. Other sections cover nightlife, kid's activities, and outdoor recreation.

Orlando Magic (pro basketball team). www.nba.com/magic

If the games were held in Disney World, Orlando would win every time, but they're held in the real world, at the Orlando Arena. The site has ticket information, schedules, and player profiles.

Orlando Travel.com. www.orlandotravel.com
Essentials: Information on lodging, theme parks, and other attractions. Perhaps the biggest draw at the site is that you can sign up—online—for two free tickets to Disney World, Sea World, or Universal Studios if you're willing to sit through a 90-minute presentation on a condominium resort. You'll also get a free buffet breakfast. Click on Central Florida Guide for attraction information, a guide to dinner shows, and transportation tips. The lodging guide offers prices, amenities, and pictures, but appears to only list hotels that pay for pages on the site. This doesn't mean it's useless, just keep in mind that there are other options beyond those listed here.

Sea World. www.seaworld.com
Essentials: Information on attractions, ticket prices, vacation packages, and special programs. At Sea World's site you can meet Shamu the killer whale and learn about attractions including Journey to Atlantis and Manatees: The Last Generation?. Click on Tickets for current prices, multi-day passes and online ordering; some passes include admission to Sea World, Universal Studios, Busch Gardens and Wet 'n' Wild. The Park Information link includes hours (which vary by month) and directions to Sea World. Finally, don't forget to click on Special Programs for information on birthday parties, shark encounters, dolphin interaction, and even weddings, where couples give new meaning to the term "taking the plunge."

✪ **Universal Studios Escape. www.universalstudiosescape.com**
Essentials: Links to all of Universal's theme parks, including Universal Studios Florida, Islands of Adventure, and CityWalk. You'll find information on tickets, vacation packages, attractions, and what's shooting. This Web site is more than just a way to get the facts; it has up-to-date schedules on what's going on at the parks, as well as mini-movies that give you a taste of the rides and attractions. (*Note:* You'll need QuickTime to see and hear the movies, if you don't have it you can download it for free at **www.apple.com/quicktime.**) There are also links to general information, directions, a park map, family services, and much more.

NEWSPAPERS AND MAGAZINES

See what's going on before you arrive, or, if you have a laptop, while you're there.

Orlando Sentinel. **www.orlandosentinel.com**
Everything you'd expect from a big-city newspaper—the online calendar, which includes listings for the arts, dining, attractions, and sports is especially useful for visitors.

Orlando Weekly. **www.orlandoweekly.com**
Cutting-edge reviews and recommendations for arts, movies, music, and much more, from Orlando's alternative weekly.

GETTING AROUND

The following sites will help you get out of the airport and navigate around Orlando.

I-Ride Trolley. www.iridetrolley.com
Route map and fares for this trolley that provides service to the International Drive resort area.

Orlando Airport. fcn.state.fl.us/goaa/index.html
The Web site was under construction at press time so it's impossible to fully evaluate, but you'll find airport maps and ground transportation services to help you get from the airport to your hotel.

Lynx. www.golynx.com
Fares and schedules for central Florida's public transit agency.

Index

See also separate Accommodations and Restaurant indexes below.
Page numbers in italics refer to maps.

ACCOMMODATIONS

RESTAURANTS

WHEREVER YOU TRAVEL, *H*ELP IS NEVER FAR AWAY.

From planning your trip to providing travel assistance along the way, American Express® Travel Service Offices are always there to help you do more.

Orlando

American Express Travel Service
2 West Church St.
Sun Trust Bldg.
407/843-0004

A Time to Travel (R)
7512 Dr. Phillips Blvd.
407/345-1181

Cruise & Tour Travel (R)
2447 S. Hiawassee
407/578-5587

do more AMERICAN EXPRESS

Travel

www.americanexpress.com/travel

American Express Travel Service Offices
are located throughout the United States.
For the office nearest you, call 1-800-AXP-3429.